D1828535

CSWE EPAS 2015 Core Competencies and Behaviors in this Text

Competency	Chapter
Competency 1: Demonstrate Ethical and Professional Behavior	1, 2 , 4, 5, 6, 7, 8, 9, 10, 13
Behaviors:	
Make ethical decisions by applying the standards of the NASW Code of Ethics, relevant laws and regulations, models for ethical decision-making, ethical conduct of research, and additional codes of ethics as appropriate to context	2, 4, 5
Use reflection and self-regulation to manage personal values and maintain professionalism in practice situations	1, 2, 4, 5, 6, 7, 8, 9, 10, 13
Demonstrate professional demeanor in behavior; appearance; and oral, written, and electronic communication	2, 4, 5, 6, 7, 8, 9, 10
Use technology ethically and appropriately to facilitate practice outcomes	
Use supervision and consultation to guide professional judgment and behavior	
Competency 2: Engage Diversity and Difference in Practice	1, 2, 3, 4, 5, 6, 7, 8, 9, 10, 11
Behaviors:	
Apply and communicate understanding of the importance of diversity and difference in shaping life experiences in practice at the micro, mezzo, and macro levels	2, 3, 4, 5, 6, 7, 8, 9, 10, 11
Present themselves as learners and engage clients and constituencies as experts of their own experiences	4, 8, 9, 11
Apply self-awareness and self-regulation to manage the influence of personal biases and values in working with diverse clients and constituencies	1, 2, 3, 4, 5, 6, 7, 8, 9, 10, 11
Competency 3: Advance Human Rights and Social, Economic, and Environmental Justice	1, 2, 3, 4
Behaviors:	
Apply their understanding of social, economic, and environmental justice to advocate for human rights at the individual and system levels	2, 3, 4
Engage in practices that advance social, economic, and environmental justice	1, 2, 3, 4
Competency 4: Engage In Practice-informed Research and Research-informed Practice	3, 4, 5, 6, 7, 8, 9, 10, 11, 12
Behaviors:	
Use practice experience and theory to inform scientific inquiry and research	3, 4, 11, 12
Apply critical thinking to engage in analysis of quantitative and qualitative research methods and research findings	12
Use and translate research evidence to inform and improve practice, policy, and service delivery	12
Competency 5: Engage in Policy Practice	1, 2, 3
Behaviors:	
Identify social policy at the local, state, and federal level that impacts well-being, service delivery, and access to social services	2, 3
Assess how social welfare and economic policies impact the delivery of and access to social services	2, 3
Apply critical thinking to analyze, formulate, and advocate for policies that advance human rights and social, economic, and environmental justice	1

CSWE EPAS 2015 Core Competencies and Behaviors in this Text

Competency	Chapter
Competency 6: Engage with Individuals, Families, Groups, Organizations, and Communities	2, 3, 4, 5, 6, 7, 8, 9, 10, 11
Behaviors:	
Apply knowledge of human behavior and the social environment, person-in-environment, and other multidisciplinary theoretical frameworks to engage with clients and constituencies	2, 3, 4, 9, 10, 11
Use empathy, reflection, and interpersonal skills to effectively engage diverse clients and constituencies	1, 2, 3, 4, 5, 6, 7, 8, 9, 10, 11
Competency 7: Assess Individuals, Families, Groups, Organizations, and Communities	1, 3, 4, 11, 12
Behaviors:	
Collect and organize data, and apply critical thinking to interpret information from clients and constituencies	1, 5, 6, 7, 8, 9, 10, 11, 12, 13
Apply knowledge of human behavior and the social environment, person-in-environment, and other multidisciplinary theoretical frameworks in the analysis of assessment data from clients and constituencies	3, 4, 8, 9, 11
Develop mutually agreed-on intervention goals and objectives based on the critical assessment of strengths, needs, and challenges within clients and constituencies	8, 9, 10, 11
Select appropriate intervention strategies based on the assessment, research knowledge, and values and preferences of clients and constituencies	4, 8, 9, 10, 11
Competency 8: Intervene with Individuals, Families, Groups, Organizations, and Communities	1, 3, 4, 11, 12
Behaviors:	
Critically choose and implement interventions to achieve practice goals and enhance capacities of clients and constituencies	1, 4, 9, 10, 11
Apply knowledge of human behavior and the social environment, person-in-environment, and other multidisciplinary theoretical frameworks in interventions with clients and constituencies	3, 4, 8, 9, 10, 11
Use inter-professional collaboration as appropriate to achieve beneficial practice outcomes	12
Negotiate, mediate, and advocate with and on behalf of diverse clients and constituencies	4
Facilitate effective transitions and endings that advance mutually agreed-on goals	1, 11, 13
Competency 9: Evaluate Practice with Individuals, Families, Groups, Organizations, and Communities	1, 3, 4, 11, 12
Behaviors:	
Select and use appropriate methods for evaluation of outcomes	1, 12
Apply knowledge of human behavior and the social environment, person-in-environment, and other multidisciplinary theoretical frameworks in the evaluation of outcomes	3, 4, 11, 12
Critically analyze, monitor, and evaluate intervention and program processes and outcomes	11, 12
Apply evaluation findings to improve practice effectiveness at the micro, mezzo, and macro levels	12

FOURTH EDITION

Social Work Skills for Beginning Direct Practice

Text, Workbook and Multimedia Interactive Case Studies

Linda K. Cummins
Northcentral University

Judith A. Sevel
Illinois State University

PEARSON

Boston Columbus Indianapolis New York San Francisco Hoboken
Amsterdam Cape Town Dubai London Madrid Milan Munich Paris Montreal Toronto
Delhi Mexico City São Paulo Sydney Hong Kong Seoul Singapore Taipei Tokyo

Editor in Chief: Kevin Davis
Executive Editor: Julie Peters
Editorial Assistant: Pamela DiBerardino
Program Manager: Megan Moffo
Executive Field Marketing Manager: Krista Clark
Executive Product Marketing Manager: Christopher Barry
Cover Designer: Carie Keller, Cenveo
Cover Art: Lyndsie Schlink
Digital Media Project Manager: Michael Goncalves
Full-Service Project Management: Revathi Viswanathan / Lumina Datamatics, Inc.
Composition: Lumina Datamatics, Inc.
Printer/Binder: LSC Communications
Cover Printer: LSC Communications

Credits and acknowledgments borrowed from other sources and reproduced, with permission, in this textbook appear on appropriate page within text.

Cataloging-in-Publication Data is available on file at the Library of Congress.

46 2025

ISBN 10: 0-13-489466-9
ISBN 13: 978-0-13-489466-9

PEARSON

Brief Contents

Contents

Preface

Writing any textbook is a labor of love and a commitment to sharing knowledge and skills with students and fellow professionals. As we began our writing journey on this fourth edition, we reflected on our first slim edition that was primarily a supplemental text with CD-ROM featuring teaching video clips—to where we have come in this fourth edition. The book has evolved into a full-fledged primary text in digital format for learning direct practice skills in the context of theory, practice settings, treatment strategies, and culture. This edition's enhancements have been directly informed by generous feedback from our loyal users.

As technologies have evolved so, too, have our opportunities to enhance the teaching videos and quizzes and to develop new video case studies. In this edition, you will meet Kim, a United States military veteran who has returned from service in Afghanistan and is struggling with homelessness, addiction, and mental health problems. With the help of her social worker Louis, and collaborative supports from other community resources, Kim finds her footing and creates new opportunities for a stable and productive life.

This fourth edition offers a highly interactive digital tool in REVEL™—which replaces the eText and MySocialWorkLab—that meets millennial tech-savvy students where they are. Teaching and learning never have to stop. Students and faculty now have access to interactive content with embedded videos, assessments, and practice examples on their desktop, laptop, tablet, and smartphones.

Digital Content in REVEL

REVEL™ is Pearson's newest way of delivering our content. Fully digital and highly engaging, REVEL offers an immersive learning experience designed for the way today's students read, think, and learn. Enlivening course content with media interactives and assessments, REVEL empowers educators to increase engagement with the course and to better connect with students. REVEL offers:

Dynamic Content Matched to the Way Today's Students Read, Think, and Learn

- Integrated Videos and Interactive Content

Integrated within the narrative, brief video clips of social workers demonstrating social work skills, instructional video clips by one of the authors, longer video case study clips and other interactive content empower students to engage with concepts and modeled skills and take an active role in learning. REVEL's unique presentation of media as an intrinsic part of course content brings the features of this popular title to life. Multiple video examples of each practice skill are embedded throughout, especially in the practice skills Chapters 5, 6, and 7, providing students instant viewing of each skill (and pitfall) as it is presented and applied.

- Quizzing

Located throughout REVEL, multiple-choice section quizzes, with feedback, afford students opportunities to check their understanding at regular intervals before moving on. In Chapters 5, 6, and the Workbook, *Video Assessment* quizzes are multiple choice in format, prompting students to select the best item based on video content.

- Short-Answer Response Exercises

Application items, called "Try It" and "Pitfalls", in the Workbook (essentially the last chapter, *not* a separate product) provide question prompts that encourage students to reflect on and apply their knowledge with feedback provided to scaffold student learning.

New to This Edition

Striving to meet the requests of users and reviewers while retaining the basic readability and accessibility to beginning practice knowledge that our book has become known for, we worked to condense some of the old material where it was somewhat redundant while expanding in other areas to augment student learning. The new material included in this edition should provide social work students with a greater understanding of how to use social work skills in the context of each of the stages of the helping process. Below is a summary of the changes you will encounter in this fourth edition of *Social Work Skills for Beginning Direct Practice: Text, Workbook, and Multimedia Interactive Case Studies*:

- *Cultural Competence* boxes are found throughout the chapters and the Workbook (the last chapter in the book) to better infuse cultural knowledge into all stages of the helping process.
- *Policy to Practice* boxes are new feature boxes written to help students strengthen their understanding of the connection between agency, state, and federal social welfare and public policies and direct practice with clients.
- A new video case study of a homeless female United States military veteran with addiction and mental health challenges was filmed and integrated in REVEL to help students relate to clients currently being served by social workers in variety of practice settings. This brings the number of video case studies in REVEL to six.
- Embedded assessments throughout each chapter help students assess their mastery of the material, section by section. Feedback is provided.
- Learning Outcomes have been included to help guide and orient students as they acquire new knowledge and skills.
- The section on confidentiality discussed in Chapter 8 on engagement in the third edition has been moved to Chapter 2 in the fourth edition, where the concept of confidentiality is first introduced.
- Chapter 4 on cultural competence has been expanded and reorganized to provide a more comprehensive discussion and application of cultural competence to

social work practice with diverse clients. To meet this goal, the information on "special populations" included in Chapter 9 on assessment in the third edition has been incorporated into Chapter 4 in the fourth edition.

- Chapter 12 on evaluation has been expanded with a section on the use of single-subject design in evaluating client progress in a more scientific manner that supports the development of evidence-based practice.
- Chapter 13 in the third edition has been eliminated, as much of the material included in that chapter is discussed in other locations in the book or in other courses in the social work curriculum.
- A new Chapter 13 has been added and more fully discusses client termination in the helping process. Material on termination previously located in Chapter 12 of the third edition has been moved to Chapter 13 of the fourth edition. A richer treatment of the importance of termination is offered to help students understand the fundamental process of preparing clients for termination early in the helping process.
- Part B of the Workbook now includes questions that focus on aspects of client diversity. These questions can be responded to individually or discussed in small groups.
- References were updated and increased by 30 percent throughout the book to reflect the latest developments in the social work knowledge base on beginning direct practice.
- A new Appendix E provides six video case summaries, links to the full cases, links to embedded concept maps as a graphic organizer for each video case, embedded Case Notes, and an embedded Sample Treatment Plan.

As always, we are grateful to our loyal users and hope that the new materials will further support you in preparing your social work students for face-to-face practice with diverse clients in diverse practice settings. We sincerely hope that this fourth edition of *Social Work Skills for Beginning Direct Practice* will help in transitioning well-prepared students into the real world of direct social work practice.

In service to social work education, we are truly yours,

Linda K. Cummins, PhD

Judith A. Sevel, MSW, LCSW, ACSW

1

An Introduction to Social Work and the Helping Process

WDSTOCK/E+/GETTY IMAGES

There are few things that get social work students more enthused than learning how to work with clients in direct practice and mastering the necessary skills for becoming an effective practitioner. This chapter reviews the mission of the social work profession and introduces the six stages of the helping process. Using case studies to demonstrate the roles of social workers in the helping process, students can experience the complexity of the human condition and come to understand the breadth of knowledge needed to competently enter into direct social work practice. The scenarios demonstrate the variety of roles that social workers can play in improving the lives of clients, families, and communities. This chapter sets the stage for a more in-depth look at the many dimensions of direct practice and the application of basic and advanced interviewing skills covered in subsequent chapters of this book.

LEARNING OUTCOMES

- Compare the two founding mothers of social work and their contributions to the profession.
- Define social work in terms of mission, educational requirements, and fundamental principles.
- Illustrate each stage of the helping process.
- Describe at least two roles that social workers fill at each level of practice (micro, mezzo and macro).

CHAPTER OUTLINE

HISTORY OF SOCIAL WORK

Since its inception, social work has developed along two parallel practice philosophies; one focused on working with individuals and families, while the other centered on social reform and community and policy practice. The two founding members of the profession, Mary Richmond and Jane Addams, spearheaded these two areas of practice, respectively. Mary Richmond, in alignment with the charity organizations, developed theories of interpersonal intervention (now called micro, or direct practice), while Jane Addams, in her work with Hull House and the settlement house movement, focused on helping poor immigrants and was involved in social reform and political activism (now called community practice and policy practice, or macro practice) (Dinerman, 1984; Ehrenreich, 1985; Richmond, 1930; Stern & Axinn, 2012; Trattner, 1999).

During the late nineteenth century, volunteer "friendly visitors" from charitable organizations visited the poor and determined their eligibility for services (Ehrenreich, 1985). In their work with the poor, early social workers began to develop skills and techniques to enhance the quality of life for the poor. By 1897, pioneer Mary Richmond was advocating a university-based training program in "applied philanthropy," and by 1904, three schools had been opened (Dinerman, 1984). Mary Richmond's 500-page book *Social Diagnosis*, originally published in 1917, was the first effort to document the theory and practice of social work. "Almost overnight, social diagnosis or casework became the method of social work and the badge of professionalism" (Trattner, 1999, p. 258). Since these humble beginnings, social work has evolved into a knowledge-based profession, drawing on empirical research, theoretical frameworks, and practical wisdom to advance practice. A growing body of expert knowledge of helping professionals has proven vital in leading effective helping initiatives, in creating and maintaining social service agencies, and in supporting the well-being of the most vulnerable in society (Cummins, Byers, & Pedrick, 2011).

Assess your understanding of the history of social work by taking this brief quiz.

DEFINING SOCIAL WORK

Fundamentally, **social work** is the art and science of helping others. The field has a long tradition of helping the disadvantaged and disenfranchised and influencing social policy to meet the dynamic continuum of human needs. Social workers are represented in an array of professional settings and positions; the clinical social worker, case manager, school social worker, community educator, agency administrator, program planner, and legislator are just a few career choices available to social workers. Professional social workers hold an earned degree from an accredited school of social work. With a minimum of a bachelor's degree in social work (BSW), social workers can work under supervision to perform tasks that assist in evaluating client psychological needs or providing services that help people meet their physical, emotional, and environmental needs. Common positions for BSW social workers include intake worker at a substance abuse center, group home counselor, case manager for the chronically mentally ill, and caseworker for foster care, adoption, and child protective services. Jobs in management, supervision, and clinical social work require a master's degree in social work (MSW). In most states, social workers must pass a state licensing exam in order to practice and call themselves social workers. Beyond the MSW level, the **National Association of Social Workers** (NASW), the oldest and most prestigious professional organization for social workers, provides credentialing for specialization in social work practice. These specializations include leadership, military, clinical, hospice and palliative care, gerontology, youth and family, health care, addiction, case management, and school social work. With additional credentials beyond the MSW, social work practitioners gain access to increased autonomy in their practice. For more information on credentialing, see the NASW credentialing center on the NASW website (NASW, 2015a).

Regardless of the level of social work preparation, the profession is bound by common values and ethics that are grounded in client self-determination, respect for the individual, and helping individuals reach their potential by helping them function within the context of their environment. Whether it is a homeless person looking for shelter, an HIV/AIDS patient needing government assistance, a married couple addressing their differences, a group advocating for the legalization of same-sex marriage, or a community in need of after-school care, social workers fulfill a variety of functions that meet the needs of individuals, families, organizations, communities, and society at large.

The National Association of Social Workers has put forward this defining statement:

> The primary mission of the social work profession is to enhance human well-being and help meet the basic human needs of all people, with particular attention to the needs and empowerment of people who are vulnerable, oppressed, and living in poverty. (NASW, 2015b, preamble, para 1)

Social workers bring the mission of the profession to life through the art of social work practice that requires the professional application of social work values, principles, knowledge, skills, and techniques to individuals, families, groups, organizations, and communities. For example, social workers help people obtain a wide variety of tangible services, such as counseling, housing, employment and training, child care, health care, and so on. Social workers help communities or groups provide or improve social and health services, assess community needs, run community agencies, and advocate for those in need through advocacy and legislative processes. The practice of social work requires knowledge of human development and behavior; emotional, psychological, and spiritual functioning; social, economic, and political systems (local, state, and national); and diverse cultural norms. Social workers understand the interactions among life and societal factors and the impact they can have on client groups and communities. Social workers are highly trained professionals who care about people, who see what is possible in people, and who want to make a difference. There are over 650,000 professional social workers in the United States who are working to make a difference in the lives of people, in communities, and in the world (NASW, 2015b). Of these, over 250,000 are licensed social workers, and the profession continues to grow. The Bureau of Labor Statistics (2014) projects that the need for social workers will increase by 19 percent between 2012 and 2022, with the greatest growth in child, family, and school social work.

Fundamental social work principles are based on the assumption that people aspire to reach their full potential. The aim of social work is to create enriched environments that support individuals' optimal personal development, allowing them to hone their innate abilities within their social setting. When people are confronted with problems in life, their levels of coping and ability to adapt to current circumstances can change

Box 1.1 Case Study: Elisa

Elisa is a 30-year-old Latina. She and her two sons moved from Mexico to New York City two years ago. She and her children are now living with her sister and her three children in a small apartment. Last week, Elisa's 14-year-old son, Antonio, was arrested for drug possession. This incident with Antonio has caused Elisa to question whether she wants to remain in New York. In addition to Antonio's involvement with the legal system, Elisa has just been laid off from her position as a housekeeper at a Manhattan hotel. She anticipates going back to work but in the meantime has been receiving a very small unemployment check. She is now feeling hopeless and overwhelmed and is unable to figure out what she needs to do next. She made a comment to the court services social worker that she has thought about running away and never coming back.

Points for reflection

When considering the level of strength and perseverance Elisa had to amass when she moved her family to the United States (leaving behind her community, country, and family; learning a new language; navigating in a completely unknown environment; getting a job; and enrolling her children in school), the current "small" series of life events do not appear to be insurmountable from a social worker's perspective. However, to effectively engage Elisa, the social worker must be able to understand how Elisa is experiencing these events. From Elisa's perspective, what do you believe makes the current situation seem overwhelming to the point of wanting to run away?

their perceptions of reality. How individuals interpret reality is influenced by the level of stress they experience in any given situation. For example, consider Elisa in the case study provided in Box 1.1.

Assessment

Behavior: Apply knowledge of human behavior and the social environment, person-in-environment, and other multidisciplinary theoretical frameworks to engage with clients and constituencies.

Critical Thinking Question: In the case study of Elisa (Box 1.1), what environmental factors have contributed to her state of "overwhelm" and consequently feeling like she wants to "run away"?

Evaluate your understanding of defining social work by taking this brief quiz.

THE HELPING PROCESS

Skovholt (2005) described the work of counselors in the helping process as a "**cycle of caring**" that involved three distinct phases: 1) empathetic attachment, 2) active involvement, and 3) felt separation. Social workers experience this cycle of caring over and over again with each new client. This is the work that is at the core of the **helping process**. Social workers create optimal professional attachments to their clients, actively engage the client throughout the helping process, and then end in separation when the professional relationship is terminated, hopefully having achieved client goals. Central to the helping process is the ability to form professional attachments that are grounded in the fundamental ability to care.

When doing direct practice, the social worker helps clients distinguish between healthy and maladaptive behaviors and ways of being. This can be a complex process since many client problems and behaviors are long term and have developed through the individual's interactions with multiple subsystems. For example, consider Trevor, a 12-year-old boy with attention-deficit/hyperactivity disorder (ADHD). He presents with coping deficits at home (yelling and tantrums) and in school (inability to complete work and follow directions, fights with other children), demonstrating impaired academic performance, social isolation, and low self-esteem. At the individual level, there are biological influences that affect Trevor's coping challenges that may need to be treated with medication. At home and at school, the consequences of his undiagnosed and untreated ADHD, over time, has caused him to be isolated from peers and to feel high levels of frustration in the family unit at home. In addition, Trevor has been labeled as a "difficult child and student." At school, his ADHD has interfered with his learning process, and consequently he is lagging behind his peers academically. All of these limiting outcomes collectively, over time, have led Trevor to conclude that he is in some way inadequate, which has contributed to his low self-esteem. Sorting out the multiple influences in his life and deciding on appropriate interventions require a significant amount of knowledge and skill on the part of the social worker.

Multiple interventions are often required to sufficiently alleviate the presenting and interconnected problems of clients. Social workers use the helping process (a problem-solving process) to guide them in structuring a plan of action aimed at improving the quality of life for clients. Many common factors of social workers (such as empathy, genuineness, and acceptance) and common factors of clients (such as social networks, hope, and active engagement) have been shown to improve client outcomes in the therapeutic process (Drisko, 2013; Mark & Keenan, 2010). Fundamental to creating a successful helping relationship is the social worker's ability to establish a partnership with the client that is grounded in mutual respect and trust. Together, the client and social worker mutually identify goals to be attained. The social worker facilitates the helping process through the application of social work theory, skills, techniques, and strategies and guides the client through the six stages of the problem-solving or helping process: 1) **engagement**, 2) **assessment**, 3) **planning** and **contracting**, 4) **treatment/intervention**, 5) **evaluation**, and 6) **termination**.

Intake and Engagement

The first stage of the helping process is intake and engagement. During this stage, the social worker makes initial contact with the client and begins to establish the framework for the helping relationship. The kind of information gathered during the intake process is then used as the foundation for the next phase of the helping process: assessment. Part of the intake process requires understanding how the client came to be in your care (i.e., voluntary or mandated), some general history of the problem, and previous circumstances that led to the problem.

One of the primary tasks for the social worker in the helping relationship is to develop rapport and trust in order for the social worker to then gather information from the client and other important people in the client's life. Engagement is a critical stage in the helping process because clients who leave the initial session feeling understood and having gained some information and clarity about their problem are more likely to return for a second session. Clients who feel engaged and return for a second session are much more likely to stay in treatment and complete the full cycle of the helping process (Tryon, 1986, 1989, 2003; Tryon & Winograd, 2011). Using the case study in Box 1.1, practice an engaging introduction to the client, Elisa (see Box 1.A).

Box 1.A Now You Try It . . . Engagement

Read the case study of Elisa in Box 1.1. Imagine that you are the social worker meeting with Elisa for the first time. What would you say to her?

A. Your response:

____

Assessment

During the intake and assessment phase of the helping process, the social worker gathers information from the client and sometimes from other people close to the client (known as collateral contacts). The social worker must first request and receive written consent from the client before contacting and interviewing collateral contacts about the client. Most social service agencies use standardized consent and release-of-information forms. During the information gathering process, it is critical that the social worker identify and clarify not only the client's problem(s) but also the client's strengths. Client strengths will become central to helping clients resolve their problems and gain control over their lives (Germain & Gitterman, 2008). During the engagement and assessment phases, the social worker and client are involved in forming a partnership for future work together. This work may include the following:

- Identifying client challenges
- Taking an inventory of the client's resources and strengths
- Encouraging the client to identify and name feelings
- Envisioning broad goals together as a working team
- Defining directions for action
- Clarifying respective roles within the helping relationship
- Identifying any cultural concerns that either party might have (Johnson & Yanca, 2001; Miley, O'Melia, & DuBois, 2013; Sheafor & Horejsi, 2015)

When the social worker has gathered sufficient information from the client about the current situation and concerns, the social worker sorts through the information and analyzes the interacting dynamics of the actors and elements in the client's life that have contributed to the presenting problem(s). The social worker also takes stock of the resources and strengths the client possesses that can be used in resolving his or her problems. These strengths and resources are not limited to the client alone but should be assessed of anyone in the client's environment (family, friends, community, and organizations) that may be available and willing to contribute to the client's recovery process and well-being. Keeping the client involved during the assessment phase is important. It is equally important to clarify with the client what he or she sees as his or her "problem," needs, and goals. This alignment between social worker and client is called the "therapeutic alliance" and significantly affects client outcomes. The greater the alliance and the earlier the therapeutic alliance is established in the helping relationship, the greater the positive effects on client outcomes (Arnow et al., 2013; Bedics, Atkins, Harned, & Linehan, 2015). Finally, the social worker and client prioritize the challenges and obstacles facing the client. Assessment is a discovery process that is ongoing throughout the

Cultural Competency

You are the social worker seeing Elisa, the Latina single mother from the case study in Box 1.1, for the first time. As you strive to gain insight into Elisa's situation, what Mexican cultural values as they relate to family, gender, and responsibility would assist you in stepping into Elisa's world and understanding the sources of her stress and the most culturally relevant interventions to help her manage her stress and her family?

helping relationship (Johnson & Yanca, 2011; Miley et al., 2013; Sheafor & Horejsi, 2015). Through assessment and analysis, the social worker and client together mutually agree on the problems to be addressed and move on to the next phase of the helping process: *planning* and *contracting*.

Problem Identification, Planning, and Contracting

Early therapeutic alliance helps to facilitate the planning and contracting stages of the helping process.

Mrs. Kita is overwhelmed by all of her responsibilities and unsure how to move forward. Listen to session #1, where the social worker and Mrs. Kita discuss problems that Mrs. Kita faces. Can you identify some problems that they may mutually agree to work on together?

Clients and social workers secure their relationships through the development of a contract that may be formal or informal. The contract clarifies the types and terms of service that the client and social worker agree to and provides a basis for implementing the agreed-on plan of action. The best contracts provide much clarity and flexibility to the helping process (Miley et al., 2013).

During the planning stage, the social worker and client do the following:

- Set goals
- Frame solutions to the client's challenges within cultural contexts
- Explore strategies for successfully meeting client challenges
- Develop a plan of action that moves the client forward
- Create a contract or agreement that outlines the above and that both agree to focus on during the helping process.

Setting goals provides focus and direction to the helping process (Hepworth, Rooney, Rooney, Strom-Gottfried, & Larsen, 2012), helps in identifying obstacles that need to be overcome by the client, and establishes a clearer vision of life's possibilities for the client. Together, the social worker and client develop specific strategies for attaining the mutually agreed-on goals of the helping relationship. During this stage, the social worker and client develop a detailed treatment plan and contract defining the long-term and short-term goals and the specific tasks to be completed within a designated time period. The social worker–client contract can be written or verbal. The treatment plan and contract function to provide a means of accountability for monitoring client progress and determining when termination of the helping relationship is appropriate (Hepworth et al., 2012). For examples of treatment plans and contracts that reflect client goals and plans of action, see appendix E. Study the plans and contracts for the Web-based clients (Anna, Anthony, Mike, Mrs. Anderson, Maria, Mrs. Kita and Kim).

Treatment and Intervention

Engagement well done motivates clients to stay in the helping process, and a thorough assessment informs the social worker about the most appropriate treatment and intervention for improving the client's life. After the social worker and client have agreed on a plan of action, fulfilling the contract agreement occurs during the treatment and intervention stage. Successful implementation of the action plan requires a goal-oriented interaction between the social worker and client. Both parties are accountable for completing specific tasks agreed to within the contract. Tasks may be directed toward the client's individual issues or may be related to other resource systems within the client's environment (Hepworth et al., 2012). As with all parts of the helping process, resources, treatment, and/or interventions must be initiated and sustained with a sense of connectedness and caring toward the client. Research indicates that the quality of the helping relationship is one of the most important factors in obtaining positive client outcomes regardless of the treatment (Skovholt, 2005; Wampold, 2001). This indicates that effective social workers must be able to bond with clients who may not have the skills to form positive attachments (Skovholt, 2005).

Another consideration for social workers to keep in mind is the client's ability to be actively involved in completing the treatment phase of the relationship. Clients should help in determining the pace of the evolution of the helping process and the implementation and completion of the action or intervention plan. Essential to successful implementation of the action plan is the development and mobilization of resources. This may include the following:

- Tapping into client resources and strengths identified in the assessment phase
- Activating resources identified and committed by the client's family or friends
- Creating alliances with community agencies who may possess important resources for the client
- Using existing and future alliances to expand opportunities for the client (Johnson & Yanca, 2009; Miley et al., 2013; Sheafor & Horejsi, 2015).

Together, the social worker and client carry out the mutually agreed-on plan of action. In this process, the client and social worker take on specific roles. Roles are defined as the particular obligations and expectations that both have accepted as an outcome of the social worker–client contract (Zastrow & Kirst-Ashman, 2013). (For a more complete discussion of social work roles, see the "Social Worker Roles" section later in this chapter.) For example, a client presenting with the problem of unemployment due to a work-related injury requires the social worker to be a broker of services. Expectations of this role may include the social worker seeking out training programs for reemployment, workers' compensation benefits, and transportation and child care for the client if needed. Additionally, the social worker would take on the role of counselor and would provide emotional support as the client works through his or her issues of loss related to injury and job displacement. In the role of an advocate, the social worker might assist the client in campaigning for better safety measures being put in place at the work site in order to protect other workers from possible future injuries. Client roles would include following up on employment leads, completing necessary paperwork for workers' compensation benefits, seeking out child care from friends and relatives, and exploring education and training opportunities. Successful implementation occurs in the context of a social worker–client relationship that is imbued with trust, a belief that change is possible, and a commitment to fulfilling the role expectations as defined by the action plan and contract (Hepworth et al., 2012).

Evaluation

Completing the plan of action or intervention phase is followed by an evaluation of how successful the intervention has been at alleviating the client's problem. Evaluation seeks answers to practical questions about how practice or intervention was implemented, how the intervention and the process of treatment helped mitigate the client problem, and how the evaluation outcomes of practice can inform future practice (Julkunen, 2011). During the evaluation and termination phases, the social worker assesses client successes and barriers to change and the extent to which the goals set by the client and social worker at the outset of the helping relationship have actually been attained. Ultimately, evaluation asks, how effective has the intervention been in resolving the client's presenting problem (Sheafor & Horejsi, 2015)? Does the problem still exist, or has it been mitigated or completely resolved? In order to answer these evaluation questions, the social worker may assess some of the following factors that were identified as contributing to the client's presenting problem(s):

- Change in client-specific attitudes, beliefs, and behaviors
- Change in the ability and manner in which the client interacts with various members of his or her environment and success in completing transactions in various settings (home, school, work, community, etc.)
- Essential changes to the client's environment (e.g., extracting oneself from an unhealthy relationship)
- Changes in client roles within his or her family and peer structures, workplace, and community
- Changes that have occurred outside of the client as a result of the intervention (e.g., more autonomy in the workplace, greater respect from others in the client's environment, improved school performance by client's child as a result of better parent/teacher relationships) (Johnson & Yanca, 2001; Miley et al., 2013; Sheafor & Horejsi, 2015)

Like assessment, evaluation is an ongoing process that occurs throughout the helping relationship to give direction to intervention strategies. When one intervention does not appear to be effective, the social worker and client may agree on an alternative approach. This process may continue until the presenting problems and subsequent issues are resolved.

It is through the evaluation process that the social worker and client come to a conclusion about the effectiveness of the helping relationship. Based on this conclusion, the social worker and client may mutually decide if the therapeutic relationship should continue, be renegotiated, or be terminated. If the goals set forth at the beginning of the helping process remain relevant to the client's progress, the relationship will most likely continue. If the client's circumstances have changed and the goals are no longer relevant, the contract may be renegotiated, new goals set, and a new action plan developed. If the goals have been attained and the presenting problem has been resolved, the relationship will most likely be terminated. Over time, the social work practitioner will acquire a repertoire of successful treatment strategies that can be valuable for treating a wide range of client problems.

Termination

Termination, the final stage of the helping relationship, is the process where the client and the social worker mutually determine when and how the helping relationship will end. Optimally, termination is a planned process that begins at the outset of the helping relationship and occurs when the client has reached treatment goals. Social workers introduce the idea of termination early in the relationship to underscore the temporary nature of the helping relationship, to place professional boundaries on the relationship, and to instill the belief that problems are solvable, answers will be discovered, and the client will achieve some relief from the problem that brought him or her into treatment. When the problem is resolved, the client moves with new skills and resources, able to navigate his or her world without the help of the social worker. In reality, the helping relationship may also be terminated for reasons other than successful treatment of the presenting problem or situation. The helping relationship may also end because, as a professional social worker, you determine that the client can be better served by another agency or worker and you refer the client to that agency or because the client disengages (or was never fully engaged in the relationship) from the helping process. One of the cornerstones of social work is client self-determination and empowerment. The client and social worker come to a decision about termination by examining the client's willingness and ability to make healthy life decisions for himself or herself and follow through and act on those decisions. If the client is unable or unwilling to engage in the helping process (this can occur for many reasons, such as an involuntary treatment situation [e.g., court-ordered counseling], a poor fit between the worker and client, or the client's unwillingness to address underlying issues that keep him or her stuck in dysfunctional patterns or relationships), then the helping relationship is terminated. A client who is beginning to disengage from the relationship may signal this by the following:

- Showing up late for appointments
- Canceling appointments or simply not showing up
- Neglecting or "forgetting" to carry out planned activities
- Being inattentive at meetings
- Becoming nontalkative and passive at appointments
- Displaying hostility and anger toward the worker

When the client is giving signs of disengagement, the social worker should clarify with the client the intent to withdraw and validate the client's right to withdraw if the client so chooses. In this clarifying process, the social worker may come to realize that the client has attained a level of success with which he or she is satisfied even though it may fall short of the goals set at the outset of the helping process. This is a good time to help refocus the client on the original goal(s) as a means of motivating the client to continue in the helping relationship. If the client sees the level of success as sufficient, then the social worker can use this opportunity to evaluate the client's progress today, which may also help to motivate the client to stay in the helping relationship. It is in the looking back that clients often gain a greater appreciation for how far they have come in the healing and growing process. Still, some clients will chose to leave care before all of the treatment goals have been attained. When this occurs, the social worker is obliged to end the relationship but will leave the door open for the client to return in the future.

In the termination process, it is important to discuss with the client the possible consequences if the client prematurely terminates the relationship. For example, a resistant client may have been seeing the social worker because he was mandated by a parent and given the ultimatum of being thrown out of the house if he did not comply. In this situation, these consequences will need to be reviewed with the client so that he understands the possible outcomes of the decision to end the relationship. As a social worker, pointing out and discussing the possible consequences of terminating the client–social worker relationship with the client is a part of information giving that helps inform the client's decisions while in care and can be essential in helping the client avoid prematurely terminating the relationship. It is helpful to come to some agreement for the mutual resolution of issues and to review any client progress that has occurred thus far. Finally, the social worker should invite the client back for future work when the client feels ready and motivated to work on issues (Miley et al., 2013).

Watch the video of Mike, who was mandated into alcohol treatment. How did Mike's choices threaten an early termination to his relationship with his social worker?

For those clients involved in meeting treatment goals, the social worker should periodically monitor and review the client's progress in moving toward established goals. During review periods, evaluation data are critical to making objective assessments about the client's progress. In the review process, the social worker considers the following:

- The client's ability to problem solve independently
- The client's willingness to access available resources when problems arise in the future
- The client's commitment to maintaining the progress made throughout the helping process

As the social worker and client engage in problem solving throughout the helping relationship, they are, in fact, preparing for termination. The helping relationship provides the client with the steps for problem solving and a repertoire of skills for successfully navigating life's problems beyond the helping relationship. As the social worker approaches successful termination with a client, it is important to frame the termination for the client in three ways and respond to them appropriately. First, recognize that termination can be understood as a loss for the client. The involved and present social worker will also feel a sense of separation (Skovholt, 2005) as a result of being a witness and mentor to the client's life for a considerable amount of time. In recognition of the ending of a positive relationship, it is often helpful to incorporate some ending ritual into your work with the client that recognizes the loss and provides the client the space to express his or her grief. Ending rituals can also provide the social worker with the opportunity to process, with the client, feelings of loss. Second, termination can be viewed as a period of new beginnings for the client. This moves the client beyond the grief of loss and into embracing the future armed with the new skills he or she has acquired during the helping process. Finally, social workers can use termination as an opportunity to affirm and integrate client gains (Johnson & Yanca, 2011; Miley et al., 2013; Sheafor & Horejsi, 2015). Watch the video clip of the final session of Mrs. Kita and the social worker Diane.

In final meeting of Mrs. Kita and her social worker Diane, note their exchange of small gifts as tokens of their appreciation for each other and in keeping with the practice of Mrs. Kita's Japanese culture.

Evaluation

Behavior: Critically analyze, monitor, and evaluate intervention and program processes and outcomes.

Critical Thinking Question: In the case study of Sarah (Box 1.2), how effective was the social worker in helping the client achieve her treatment goals? How would you account for unmet client goals?

The helping process is a fluid and dynamic sequence of social worker–client interactions directed toward problem resolution and growth. The stages of the helping process are not discrete but rather build on one another as the helping relationship evolves. Neither are they strictly linear, as the social worker assesses the client situation, evaluates the client's progress, and introduces new interventions as the helping relationship unfolds. Box 1.2 demonstrates the dynamic and complex nature of the helping relationship.

Using the case study of Sarah in Box 1.2, consider how you might prepare her for terminating the helping relationship. Complete the exercise in Box 1.B.

Box 1.2 Case Study: Sarah

You are a social worker at a not-for-profit social service agency that provides support services and training to help young single mothers achieve self-sufficiency. Sarah, a 17-year-old single pregnant female, was referred to your agency by her school counselor. At intake, the social worker tries to put Sarah at ease by providing her with a comfortable chair to sit in, asking about her general well-being, and letting Sarah guide the pace of the interview. A few questions on the intake form may include an inquiry about her current life situation, identifying and contact information, current support systems in place, level of education, and so on. Using these techniques, the social worker reaches out to *engage* Sarah in the helping process and to build a rapport that communicates care and concern. In such an atmosphere, Sarah is able to begin to tell the story of what has led her to seek services on this day. By taking the time to make Sarah feel comfortable and cared for, the social worker has learned that Sarah's *presenting problem* is that of impending homelessness. She is four months pregnant and has been kicked out of her parents' home. When Sarah informed her boyfriend of two years, Joseph, about her pregnancy, he broke up with her, saying he had plans for college and could not take on raising a family at this point in his life. Sarah is confused and depressed and uncertain about how to handle her situation. During the *assessment* process, you discover that Sarah is without family support, has dropped out of school, has isolated herself from her peers, and has no money and no place to live. For the past week, Sarah has been spending the night at various classmates' homes, sometimes without the knowledge of their parents. She has worn out her welcome with her friends' families, and last night she slept under a bridge about a mile from her parents' home. Although fearful, confused, and uncertain, prior to her current crisis, Sarah presented herself as a responsible student and daughter. Consequently, she is motivated to establish some stability in her life and is seeking help in improving her situation. Together, you and Sarah identify problem areas that need to be addressed and accentuate her strengths in constructing a *plan of action* and a *contract*.

The following treatment goals are mutually agreed on between you and Sarah:

1. Gain access to prenatal care
2. Apply for Medicaid and TANF
3. Explore temporary housing and apply for subsidized housing benefits
4. Enroll in a support group for single teen parents
5. Engage in ongoing individual counseling for dealing with issues of family disruption, self-esteem, and depression
6. Enroll in GED classes
7. Sign up for vocational training for job placement
8. Begin parenting and family planning classes
9. Pursue child support payments

Together, you and Sarah prioritized the treatment goals and placed them within a specific time frame. During the *treatment and intervention stage*, Sarah was able to find temporary housing with a family friend until the birth of her child. Meanwhile, as her social worker, you linked her to a local public health clinic where she received prenatal care and referred her to the public aid office, where she applied for and received Medicaid and TANF benefits. Sarah attended her GED classes twice a week and planned on completing her diploma by the

Box 1.2 Case Study: Sarah *(Continued)*

time her child is born. You also referred her to the local housing authority, where Sarah applied for subsidized housing. At the time, she was facing a waiting list of six months. Sarah continued her weekly counseling session and was able to consider mending her broken relationships with her parents. Sarah enrolled in an early childhood development training program in preparation for employment after the birth of her child. Classes will begin when she completes her GED program. After six months of working with Sarah as her primary social worker, you *evaluated* her progress and assessed the extent to which Sarah had been able to attain her treatment goals. Over the five-month period, Sarah made the following progress on her treatment goals:

1. Consistently kept her prenatal care appointments, followed her physician's instructions, and gave birth to a full-term, healthy son
2. Received Medicaid and TANF benefits and maintained her eligibility
3. Moved into a one-bedroom public housing unit in a safe neighborhood
4. Attended only two sessions of her support group for single teen parents
5. Attended 90 percent of her weekly counseling sessions and was feeling more focused and less depressed
6. Reestablished communication with her family
7. Completed her GED
8. Was scheduled to begin child care development classes in six weeks
9. Had information on the local family planning clinic
10. Received in-home parenting instruction from a home interventionist working with new mothers
11. Spoke to a legal aid attorney about pursuing child support

Together, you and Sarah conclude that she has acquired a sufficient level of empowerment and determine that it is time to *evaluate and terminate* the helping relationship. You and Sarah have created an environmental structure that will support and nurture her and her son, and as her social worker, you leave the door open for future contact.

Box 1.B Now You Try It . . . Termination

Read the case study of Sarah in Box 1.2. Imagine that you have been Sarah's social worker throughout the helping relationship described above. You know that soon you and Sarah will part ways as she completes more and more of her treatment goals. What steps would you take to begin to prepare her for the termination? What type of ritual might you use on the final meeting with Sarah that would help her move forward on her own?

Your response:

1. Write in the steps you would take to prepare Sarah for termination.

2. Describe a ritual you might plan for Sarah's last session.

Assess your understanding of the helping process by taking this brief quiz.

SOCIAL WORKER ROLES

As in any helping relationship, the case study of Sarah presented in Box 1.2 demonstrated the wide variety of roles that social workers need to fill in order to engage clients in the helping process, negotiate a plan of action, intervene on behalf of clients, and evaluate and terminate the relationship. Figure 1.1 graphically displays common social worker roles in the helping process. What roles can you identify that the social worker filled in her work with Sarah in the case study represented in Box 1.2?

Figure 1.1
Concept Map of Social Work Practice Roles

Social work role is defined as expected professional behaviors and functions accepted by the social work profession and frequently employed in social work practice (Zastrow & Kirst-Ashman, 2013). Over the course of a career, a social worker may fulfill many social worker roles and over time will develop competency in most of these roles. Several factors influence which roles a social worker will fulfill, such as the goals of the agency where one is employed, the latitude of the social worker's responsibilities in a given work setting, the needs of the client, and one's level of practice (see Box 1.3). The social worker's roles may be restricted to one level of practice or may encompass all three levels (micro, mezzo, and macro). Roles will shift when the responsibilities of the social worker move across levels of practice (see Box 1.4). For example, Sarah's social worker in the scenario presented in Box 1.2 was required to practice at the micro and mezzo levels in order to serve the best interests of the client. At the **micro level**, the social worker took on the roles of *enabler* and *counselor*. At the **mezzo level**, the social worker acted as a *broker* where she connected Sarah to community resources (prenatal care, single-parent support group, GED classes, vocational training, parenting classes, Medicaid and TANF benefits, housing assistance, and family planning). The social worker also served in the role of *mediator* (mezzo) in resolving the conflict between Sarah and her parents. If there had been no parenting classes available in Sarah's community, the social worker could have taken on the role of *planner* (**macro level**) and developed a parenting class for Sarah and other expectant teen mothers in the community. For definitions of common social worker roles, see Box 1.3.

On any given day, the social worker may find oneself in the role of advocate, educator, clinician, facilitator, mediator, and broker and executing these roles on many different levels of practice. For example, as a micro practitioner, you may find yourself advocating on behalf of an individual client (case advocate), a group of similar clients with the same problem (class advocate), or agencies or organizations trying to address the unmet needs of this group of clients (organizational advocate) or the community as a whole (community advocate) when it is discovered that the problem goes beyond your clients and agency to encompass the majority of similar people across the community. For example, as a case advocate, the social worker with a client who recently became disabled and was subsequently fired from his job (though still able to do the work) may advocate for the client by pursuing legal recourse on his behalf. A class advocate advocating for low-income disabled clients living in substandard housing may file a complaint with the local housing authority in an effort to improve the quality of housing for this group. On an organizational level, the social worker may advocate for more resources to meet the training and housing needs of disabled clients using the agency. As a community advocate, the social worker may lobby with other social workers for a more equitable application of the Americans with Disabilities Act to improve the plight of disabled people everywhere.

Ethical and Professional Behavior

Behavior: Demonstrate professional demeanor in behavior; appearance; and oral, written, and electronic communication.

Critical Thinking Question: In the case study of Sarah (Box 1.2), how many roles can you identify that the social worker filled in her work with Sarah? Are there other roles that she could have filled that would have helped her client?

Box 1.3 Social Worker Roles

Activist: The social worker initiates and sustains change through social action. For example, in response to rising teen crime rates, the social worker may pull together a coalition of concerned citizens to push for change in the police department, schools, religious community, and local agencies to address the growing gang problem in the community.

Advocate: The social worker champions the rights of others through empowerment or direct intervention. The social worker may advocate for a client, group, organization, or community.

Agency Administrator: The social worker is an agency director or assistant director and has responsibility for the functioning of an agency.

Broker: The social worker provides linkages between the client and other agencies or sources of needed resources. For a client recently diagnosed as HIV positive, for example, the social worker investigates various medical and supportive services and assesses them in light of the client's insurance coverage and available financial resources.

Case Manager: The social worker creates and coordinates a network of formal and informal resources for the purpose of optimizing the functioning of clients with multiple needs. For example, as a case manager with a treatment program for severely mentally ill, polyaddicted drug addicts who are homeless, you will link clients with public supports and treatment services and pull together formal and informal supports, such as self-help groups, family members, and friends, for the purpose of keeping the client's mental illness well managed, limiting drug use

(Continued)

Box 1.3 Social Worker Roles *(Continued)*

relapses, stabilizing housing, providing job training and employment skills, and emotional supports to draw on during difficult periods.

Clinician/Counselor: The social worker helps improve client functioning through a variety of clinical intervention approaches and by providing ongoing support. The social worker may help the client gain insights into feelings, change unhealthy behaviors, and acquire problem-solving skills.

Coordinator: The social worker helps a variety of systems to work together at fulfilling goals. For example, the social worker may coordinate community efforts to develop a drug awareness program by working with the police department, local schools, public health department, and parents.

Educator/Teacher: The social worker instructs or imparts knowledge to others at the individual, group, organizational, or community level. For example, the social worker may teach a client job search skills, teach a group of expectant mothers prenatal classes, train agency personnel on new intervention methods, or provide community education on transracial adoption. New knowledge can be empowering to clients, groups, organizations, and communities.

Enabler: Empowers clients in finding solutions to the challenges they face. The social worker offers support and encouragement to clients so that they can more easily accomplish tasks and solve problems. For example, the social worker may help a mental health patient adjust to day treatment.

Facilitator: The social worker leads a group, such as a rape survivors' recovery group, a community group investigating gang crime, or a professional peer group implementing organizational change.

Mediator: The social worker takes a neutral stance between two systems in order to help resolve conflict and to help establish a better communication flow, such as divorce mediation or business mediation between quarreling business partners.

Planner: The social worker may work in an agency as a program planner creating new services for clients or in the community as a community planner enhancing social services and resources for the community.

Outreach Worker: The social worker works within the clients' environments to identify individuals with unmet needs and to engage them in the helping process and social service system. For example, as an outreach worker for the local homeless shelter, you may work with a team of workers who cruise or walk the neighborhoods looking for homeless individuals, engage them in conversation to assess their needs, and link them to needed services.

Researcher/Program Evaluator: The social worker evaluates program effectiveness by gathering and analyzing data and interpreting the findings. For example, the social worker may be asked to assess how well the local health clinic is meeting the needs of uninsured community members.

Source: Sheafor & Horejsi (2015); Zastrow & Kirst-Ashman (2013).

Engagement

Behavior: Apply knowledge of human behavior and the social environment, person-in-environment, and other multidisciplinary theoretical frameworks to engage with clients and constituencies.

Critical Thinking Question: Study the roles of the social worker in Boxes 1.3 and 1.4. Which role would you find the most challenging and why? How can you begin to prepare for these roles in your future social work practice?

Given the complexity of the social service system and the unpredictability of the human experience, social workers often have ethical and moral obligations to serve in multiple roles across multiple levels of practice in order to meet client needs. The multidimensional nature of social work makes it unlikely that a direct-practice social worker could restrict the social worker roles to one or two roles or limit his or her practice to only one level. All social worker roles serve to move us in the direction of social justice by improving quality of life and structuring supportive environments at the family, community, organizational, and institutional levels. Box 1.4 provides a summary of common social worker roles across three levels of practice.

Box 1.4 Social Work Roles and Levels of Practice

Level of Practice	Role
Micro	Case advocate; case manager; client educator; clinician/counselor; enabler; group facilitator; outreach worker
Mezzo	Agency administrator; agency staff trainer; broker; class advocate; mediator; organizational facilitator; program planner; researcher/program evaluator
Macro	Activist; broker; community advocate; community educator; community facilitator; community planner; coordinator

Assess your understanding of social work roles by taking this brief quiz.

Policy to Practice Medicaid

Since its passage in 1965, Medicaid policy was passed to provide health coverage for low-income people and is now the nation's primary public health insurance program. Medicaid is an essential policy for ensuring child and maternal health in the country, financing 40% of all births. This important policy provides pregnant women prenatal care, labor and delivery services, and continued care to the mother for 60 days after the birth of the child. Medicaid ensures a healthy start for all babies born to Medicaid eligible women, providing them care until the child's first birthday. How did the social worker's knowledge of Medicaid support her client Sarah in the case study in Box 1.2? In what ways was the social worker able to turn policy into essential tangible resources in her social work practice with Sarah? What role(s) did the social worker fill in translating policy to practice for her client?

Sources: CMS.gov: Centers for Medicare and Medicaid Services: *History*

SUMMARY

- Social work developed along two parallel paths to helping people. Following the visions and philosophies of founders Jane Addams and Mary Richmond, social work has focused on working with individuals and families while simultaneously seeking social reform and policy change. To that end, the field has a long tradition of helping the disadvantaged and disenfranchised and influencing social policy.
- Social workers are professionally educated in degree programs and credentialed as specialists to meet the contemporary needs of families and communities and are bound by common values self-determination, respect for the individual, and helping individuals reach their potential.
- Social workers engage the "caring cycle" in each stage of the helping process—1) engagement, 2) intake and assessment, 3) planning and contracting, 4) treatment and intervention, and 5) evaluation and 6) termination—often requiring them to take on many roles across multiple levels of practice.

- The roles a social worker fulfills can be influenced by the goals of the agency where one is employed, the latitude of the social worker's responsibilities in a given work setting, the needs of the client, and one's level of practice. Roles may be restricted to one level of practice, or may encompass the micro, mezzo, and macro levels of practice simultaneously. Regardless of the roles that social workers fill as direct practitioners, interviewing skills are a requisite skill for meeting the needs of clients.

APPLY IT

1. Review session one of **Interactive Case Study #3** Mike and social worker Karen; and session one of **Interactive Case Study #2** Anthony and social worker James. Compare the engagement process in both of these case studies. How effective were the two social workers? How did their engagement styles differ? What techniques did the social workers use to lead the clients? In what ways did the clients direct the social workers' selected approach to engagement?
2. Review all three sessions of **Interactive Case Study #2** Anthony and social worker, James. Identify when James begins preparing the client for termination. What techniques did he use to lead the client into the termination process? How did this preparation affect the client when termination actually occurred?

Assess Your Competence

Use the scale below to rate your current level of achievement on the following concepts or skills associated with each competency presented in the chapter:

1	2	3
I can accurately describe the concept or skill	I can consistently identify the concept or skill when observing and analyzing practice activities	I can competently implement the concept or skill in my own practice

_______ Understands and can demonstrate basic understanding of the history of social work.

_______ Understands and can describe the six helping stages/problem-solving process.

_______ Understands the three levels of social work practice.

_______ Can identify social worker roles at each level of practice.

2

Values and Ethics in Social Work

STUART MILES/FOTOLIA

Social work is a practice-oriented profession grounded in the core values of **service**, **social justice**, the inherent **dignity and worth of the person**, the fundamental **importance of human relationships**, **integrity**, and **competence**. These values can be seen in the value directed practice behaviors that dominate social work practice: 1) **self-determination**, 2) **empowerment**, and 3) **confidentiality**. As practitioners, social workers are involved in the lives of people facing difficult and trying problems and circumstances. The actions of social workers can have a direct impact on the quality of life of their clients. When working with troubled individuals, we can just as easily add to the hardships of clients' lives if our professional actions are not grounded in the values and practice theory of the profession and guided by the mission of social work. It is therefore essential that social workers be self-aware about the possible outcomes of their interactions with clients.

LEARNING OUTCOMES

- Name the crucial elements of the mission of social work.
- Identify the core social work values and describe how they are reflected in social work practice.
- Discuss the relationship between the social work mission, social work values, and social work practice behaviors.
- Describe the ethical decision-making process and its application to resolving ethical dilemmas in practice.

CHAPTER OUTLINE

Social work values are idealistic and can be difficult to sustain in our human condition. To be a social worker requires that you aspire to the values and mission of the profession, that you strive to derive your actions from them in your professional life, and that you recommit to them every day. Social work values guide the profession toward the fulfillment of its mission of social justice, whose goal is that all members of society have equal access to resources sufficient for a healthy and supportive environment. It is important that individual social workers understand the nature of social work values and incorporate them into their daily practice with clients.

Social work practice can take many forms. At the micro level, social workers work with clients as individuals, in families or in groups, and in public, not-for-profit, or private agencies. At the mezzo level of practice, social workers may find themselves involved in program and policy development or research evaluation within community agencies or private corporations. On the macro level, social workers may be involved with community organizing and development or working in the political arena as a state or federal employee, elected official, policy analyst, or lobbyist. Regardless of the setting of social work practice, consideration must be given to how we personify the values of the profession. Social work values are expressed in how social workers relate to clients, how service delivery systems are structured, and how social workers serve as a political voice for disadvantaged and marginalized people in society.

Introductory social work skills courses most often focus of practice with individual clients. Keep in mind, however, that social work values infuse every level of practice, whether you are involved with individual, group, or community practice, or at the macro-level practice of policymaking.

SOCIAL WORK MISSION

Ultimately, the **social work mission** is to advance the quality of life for all people through the enhancement of mutually beneficial interactions between individuals and society (Minahan, 1981). Social work stands for the social welfare of all people and is committed to social justice through social change at the individual, family, community, agency, and structural levels. As such, social work has historically been and continues to be in alliance with those members of society who live under difficult or oppressive conditions that keep them disadvantaged and marginalized. The profession of social work envisions a more decent and humane society (Ehrenreich, 1985).

Unique to social work as a helping profession is the *person-in-environment perspective,* which is based on the idea that one cannot understand the problems of individuals without understanding the context in which they occur. The context, or environment, encompasses the individual's perceptions of self, family roles and conditions, community supports, agency functioning in meeting the individual's needs, and the interactions between the individual and societal institutions, such as economic, political, educational, religious, family, and social welfare systems. Social work, then, has a dual focus of enhancing individuals' functioning in society by empowering them to achieve life goals and pursuing social changes that are likely to provide a supportive environment for all members of society (Reamer, 2014). Supportive environments give individuals access to opportunities and resources within all the institutions in society without regard to attributes such as age, race, gender, religious or political affiliation, or sexual orientation. In doing so, disadvantaged individuals and groups have equal access to mainstream institutions that provide education, employment, wages, housing, nutrition, social supports, health care, and other essential services and opportunities. Equal access to these basic resources can alleviate distress and suffering for many people.

Opportunities to contribute to society are vital to one's well-being. Ultimately, human beings are created for the purpose of expressing the innate talents that we possess. Without opportunities for self-expression, human beings become withdrawn, fearful, and weighted down by a sense of having little worth. The social work profession supports the notion that people should be treated humanely and that transactions between individuals and the environment should enhance one's dignity, feelings of self-worth, and full self-expression. The mission of social work rests on professional values that ennoble men and women and call forth their greatest being (Ehrenreich, 1985).

Assess your understanding of the social work mission by taking this brief quiz.

CORE SOCIAL WORK VALUES

Social work values support the mission of social work and guide the profession in creating a humane vision of the world. The social work vision calls for individuals, regardless of their beliefs, practices, or backgrounds, to be treated with dignity; given equal access to societal institutions, opportunities, and resources; and supported in contributing their unique talents to their families, communities, and country. At a fundamental level, social work values are congruent with and supportive of the values and beliefs reflected in the Declaration of Independence—that all are created equal and endowed with certain inalienable rights, such as life, liberty, and the pursuit of happiness. And much like the visionaries who crafted the Declaration of Independence, social workers belong to a profession of action and passion in advocating for the downtrodden. They stand for social justice and human decency (Ehrenreich, 1985). However, values are just words until put into action. For the passion of the profession's values to come alive, they must be incorporated into one's way of being when fulfilling our role as social worker. Helen Harris Perlman (1976) captured this concept best when she wrote, "A value has small worth except as it is moved, or is moveable, from believing into doing, from verbal affirmation into action" (p. 381). Social work practitioners are called to relate to clients in ways that preserve and enhance their dignity and self-worth. Social workers structure services in a manner that gives equal access to resources and support policies that reflect the belief in a just society and the belief that change is possible in individuals, communities, and organizations. Only when we have moved social work values from the abstract ideal into empowering action in our professional lives can we claim them as our own (Reamer, 2014). Social work practice is the application of social work values to helping relationships with clients, groups, communities, organizations, and other professionals (Zastrow, 2013) in the context of evidence-based social work theories, models, and interventions.

Service

Supported by the ethical principle of helping people with their social problems, service, as a value, is expressed in how services are structured, accessible, and relevant to the needs of those being served. This then infers that the client's needs are paramount, and social workers, in the service to others, draw on their knowledge and skills to expedite favorable outcomes while setting aside self-interest of profits and self-promotion. Organizing volunteer efforts, offering pro bono services, and supporting service-oriented community groups are some ways in which social workers bring the value of service to life (National Association of Social Workers [NASW], 2008a).

Social Justice

Challenging social injustices has historically been a mission of social work. Social justice as a value has driven social change for over a century on the behalf of vulnerable and oppressed groups. Historically, this can be seen in campaigns to extend rights to all citizens, such as the right to vote, the right to public education, and the right to safe workplace practices. Today, it is apparent in the Affordable Care Act, passed in 2010, giving health care access to millions of uninsured individuals, in the June 26, 2015 Supreme Court decision that legalized gay marriage, and in the continued push for equal pay across gender, race, and beliefs (Obergefell et al. v. Hodges, 2015; U.S. Department of Health and Human Services, 2014). Social justice comes through social change that promotes equality of opportunity to all (NASW, 2008a).

Dignity and Worth of the Person

A core value of the social work profession is respect for every human being's innate greatness and that all are inherently worthy. Social workers are trained to regard clients as having worth and to treat them with dignity regardless of their outward appearances and behaviors. Social workers provide supportive environments for clients to find the full expression of their innate greatness. In doing so, a process of affirmation is created that, over time, generates a growing sense of self-worth (NASW, 2008a).

To put into action the value of inherent worth and dignity, the social worker needs to be able to view people as unique individuals and not impose preconceived notions, or stereotypes, that we may unconsciously carry with us (see Box 2.1). This is the process of **individualization** (Zastrow, 2013), of knowing people for themselves, instead of "knowing" people through the distortions of our own biases.

Box 2.1 Stereotyping versus Individualization

Consider your initial impressions and assumptions about the following types of clients whom you may encounter in your practice. Write them down and then identify what is true for everyone with a particular characteristic; identify your beliefs that are based on stereotypes you've learned in your experiences and socialization.

1. A single African American mother on welfare
2. A homeless teenage prostitute of Mexican descent alone on the streets
3. A 24-year-old white male recently diagnosed with AIDS
4. A 52-year-old female executive working for a large corporation
5. A 75-year-old male diagnosed with dementia

The only indisputable things we can say about the potential clients described in this list are that you would be working with a poor African American mother, a Mexican teenager who has no home, a young white male infected with AIDS, a very successful career woman, and an elderly person. What other assumptions did you make about your potential clients? Consider where your impressions came from and the types of values reflected in your assumptions. Through honest self-reflection, one can begin to let go of stereotypes and move toward individualization and the possibility of knowing our clients as unique human beings.

Box 2.2 Separating Client Behaviors from the Client

Consider your reactions to the following clients. How difficult would it be for you to view these clients with respect? Identify the values and emotions that limit your ability to relate to these clients with unconditional regard.

1. A 35-year-old father who has sexually abused his six-year-old daughter
2. A 15-year-old girl who shot and killed her mother while she slept
3. A 45-year-old man arrested for selling drugs to grade-school children
4. A 30-year-old single mother who left her three-year-old daughter locked in her room for a weekend while she went away with her boyfriend

Respecting people for their inherent worth and dignity also requires social workers to be willing and able to separate clients' behaviors from who they are inherently as human beings. When our clients adhere to values, lifestyles, and behavior patterns that are similar to our own, relating to our clients with unconditional regard is easy to do. However, when a client's behaviors are at odds with our personal value system, engaging the client with unconditional regard can be very difficult (see Box 2.2).

Zastrow (2013) offers two guidelines for working with clients whose behaviors appall and disgust us. First, accept that the individual and their behaviors can be separated. In doing so, you create an opening for treating clients with respect and viewing them as capable of change. By separating the behavior from the person, you can give yourself permission to despise the behavior without disrespecting the person. Second, recognize that with some clients, it will be difficult for you to get past the heinousness of their behavior and treat them with the respect that is needed in a helping relationship. When this occurs—and it happens for almost all social workers at some point in their practice careers—it may be in the best interest of the client to transfer the case to another social worker. Talk to your supervisor or a trusted colleague about your feelings. Then assess your own values to determine what might be getting in your way. However, we don't always have the option of transferring a case. Consider putting a plan in place with your supervisor for working through your biases. Begin with the question, "What buttons does this client push with me, and why?"

All people are inherently great; it's just that some have forgotten. When we forget who we are innately, we become disconnected from ourselves and, through destructive behaviors, express who we are *not*. When we can stand in the possibility of our clients' greatness, we have transcended our own biases and made an empathic connection with them. Only then can we effectively enter into our clients' world and their lived experiences. The role of the social worker is to help individuals remember who they are innately and support them in expressing their greatness. Often this is unfamiliar territory, and clients will need considerable support, encouragement, and affirmation to engage in ways of being that have, to this point in their lives, been foreign to them. To stay in this process with the client requires the social worker to acknowledge and draw on his or her own innate gifts and to have compassion for clients when they fail and for ourselves when we fail to stay in our commitment to our client's ability to change. Social work practice requires an ongoing recommitment to the values and mission of the profession and to our clients.

Importance of Human Relationships

Social workers appreciate the central place that human relationships hold in the helping process and that relationships between and among people are the core mechanism through which change occurs. Therefore, the balancing of power between the social worker and the client is essential to engaging clients as partners in the therapeutic process. Recognizing the importance and power of relationships, social workers work to strengthen relationships among people, organizations, and communities toward established purposes of individual and group well-being (NASW, 2008a). To that end, social workers enter into relationships with acceptance, respect, integrity, and purpose. Whether those relationships are with clients in resolving life issues, program planning with fellow social workers to address unmet needs in the community, engaging agency leaders to conduct a community-wide needs assessment, working with established community groups to build a coalition, or educating political leaders on the need to expand state human services budgets to meet the health care needs of state residents, relationships are built and sustained in pursuit of services and social justice for and with those in need.

Integrity

Integrity in behaviors and relationships is inherent in the values of social work and thus needs to be reflected in how social workers negotiate their relationships with clients, colleagues, and leaders in the community and how they arrive at practice decisions. Trustworthiness is a quality that social workers strive to emanate in all areas of practice and personal arenas. At times, it can be difficult to know what the most ethical and trustworthy path may be, but discussions with supervisors and colleagues and consulting the social work **code of ethics** can help social workers through difficult decisions facing them in the practice world. When in doubt, ask and then process circumstances and situations with other professional social workers whom you trust and hold in high regard (NASW, 2008a).

Competence

Clients and the public at large have a right to expect that social workers are competent to engage practice in their assigned or chosen areas. Graduating from an accredited school of social work and passing your state licensure exams are beginning levels of competence. Beyond that, social workers can seek out credentialing in specialized areas and aspire to graduate degrees in social work. In pursuing continuing education and training, social workers develop expertise in their areas of practice and provide the best care possible to those they serve in their daily practice. When social workers have reached an area of expertise in practice, it is expected that they will also aspire to contribute to the knowledge base of the profession (NASW, 2008a).

? Assess your understanding of core social work values by taking this brief quiz.

VALUE-DRIVEN PRACTICE BEHAVIORS

When working to meet the professional ethical responsibilities to clients and while reflecting the values of the profession, social workers need to develop three core areas of practice behaviors. These include granting self-determination to the client, engaging and intervening in ways that empower clients, and establishing and maintaining confidentiality within the helping relationship (NASW, 2008a).

Self-Determination

Self-determination is the act of giving clients the freedom to make choices in their lives and to move toward established goals in a manner that they see as most fitting for themselves as long as clients' choices don't infringe on the rights of others (Zastrow, 2013). Grounded in self-determination theory, which posits that client changes are more apt to be long lasting and more effective if they are autonomously motivated to change (Deci & Ryan, 2012), research findings have supported this theory. In a meta-analysis of medical patients Ng et al. (2012) found that autonomous motivation among patients was associated with improved health outcomes. As social workers, we may not agree with our clients' choices, but supporting self-determination requires that we respect our clients in their life choices, knowing that their informed choices are more likely to last and be most fitting for them. The job of the social worker is not to tell clients what to do or what not to do but rather to explore options with the client and the possible outcomes of life choices. A social worker can restrict a client's right to self-determination if the client's actions or potential actions could be harmful or pose a serious danger to self or others (Boyle, Hull, Mather, Smith, & Farley, 2009). Often, we may experience conflicts between our personal or professional value base and that of clients (see Box 2.3).

As social workers dedicated to enhancing the quality of clients' lives, we are obliged to allow the clients' values to dominate their own lives. This is much easier said than done when confronted with client values and behaviors that are counter to our own. Social workers often struggle with the desire to impose personal values on clients in practice situations. All people are strongly attached to their personal value system. It is the base from which all our opinions and behaviors emanate. Professional social workers are required by practice standards to give up the notion that our personal value system is the model that our clients should follow. We may prefer our personal value system to that of our clients, but ours may not

Box 2.3 Self-Determination and Personal Value Conflicts

You are a drug and alcohol counselor employed at an outpatient treatment center. Tina is a new client of yours who was referred by her employer for alcohol treatment after having repeated "hangover" mornings at work. Recently, she appeared at work fully intoxicated. Tina is an architect at a local firm, married, and the mother of two daughters, ages 12 and 14 years. During your third session with Tina, she mentions that she is having an affair. By the sixth session, you learn that Tina has had a series of affairs throughout her 16-year marriage and that it is a common practice of Tina's to introduce her daughters to her lovers. Tina does not seem troubled by her extramarital affairs and does not ask you for any help in this area of her life.

You are also married with children but adhere to the middle-class traditional family values of monogamy and honest and open communications in your marital relationship. You find Tina's behavior quite disturbing.

Points for reflection

1. Are the value conflicts inherent in your relationship with Tina personal or professional?
2. How relevant are Tina's extramarital affairs to her alcohol problem and recovery program?
3. As a social worker committed to client self-determination, how would you proceed in your professional relationship with Tina?

Source: Reamer (2014).

Diversity and Difference in Practice

Behavior: Apply and communicate understanding of the importance of diversity and difference in shaping life experiences in practice at the micro, mezzo, and macro levels.

Critical Thinking Question: Identify some of the challenges that social workers might encounter when supporting client self-determination when working across cultures.

necessarily be a better value system, only different. For clients to be self-determining, it is essential that they be permitted to live within their own value system and make their own decisions. Self-determination enhances clients' abilities to help themselves and fosters self-reliance and self-sufficiency. As we offer clients the opportunity to take on the power of decision making in their lives, we also invite them to accept the responsibility that goes with the outcomes of those decisions. When social workers support clients through self-determination, they help create an avenue for clients' expression of their inherent worth and dignity (Zastrow, 2013). Clients often know what is best for them and what is realistic and possible. Our job is to help them sort through their options, identify barriers, and develop problem-solving strategies to achieve their goals (NASW, 2008a).

Empowerment

Empowerment lays the groundwork for informed self-determination. Although social workers provide opportunities for empowerment, only clients can empower themselves (the desire to change must originate within the client for it to be genuine). Through the decision-making process and under the skillful guidance of the social worker, clients are able to move themselves toward their life goals. Social workers assist in this process by providing information, assisting the client in building support systems, and exploring possible outcomes of various life choices. Social workers guide clients to a position where they can make informed choices about their lives. On the surface, empowerment sounds like a fairly simple yet ideal process. In reality, creating empowering options for clients whose behaviors violate our personal sense of what is right and wrong can be challenging. Knowledge is a fundamental ingredient of empowerment. As social workers, we impart new information and knowledge to clients, teach problem-solving skills, and allow the power of their own decisions to dominate clients' lives. In the end, we hope clients learn to seek out knowledge, problem solve, and advocate for themselves and reap all the benefits and responsibilities that come with such self-actions. When clients are able and willing to take these steps, they have empowered themselves. Box 2.4 provides an example of how social workers can create empowering options for clients.

Confidentiality

Confidentiality refers to the safeguarding of the information that passes between the social worker and the client. This aspect of the social worker–client relationship facilitates the evolution of a trusting relationship that is essential for client change. Trusting that what transpires during the interview session will remain private, clients can begin to express their concerns and aspirations within a safe environment. Once that occurs, the social worker can obtain the necessary information to create empowering options with clients and support them in their life choices. This requires that conversations between the social worker and the client take place in a private location with closed doors where others cannot overhear what is being said.

Watch the video clip from case #6. Notice how Louis directs Kim to a private conference room to continue their conversation after bumping into her in the hallway.

Box 2.4 Creating Empowering Options

As a case manager at the local Housing Authority office, you are responsible for helping low-income families gain access to safe, affordable, and, when eligible, subsidized housing. Judy is a 30-year-old single mother of two who has been on welfare assistance for three years. For two years, Judy and her family drifted in and out of homelessness when her unstable housing arrangements fell apart. You have been working with Judy in finding her housing for 18 months. After Judy was on the waiting list for public housing for a full year, you were able to help her secure a two-bedroom apartment in a public housing unit designated for young families that is located in a safe neighborhood. Judy and her family have been in their new apartment for six months, and for the first time in their young lives, her children are experiencing what it means to have a stable home. This afternoon, you received a call from the local police informing you that Judy has been arrested for drug trafficking in her apartment. The Housing Authority's policy forbids the use or selling of drugs in public housing units and requires that residents who violate this rule be evicted immediately.

Points for reflection

1. As a case manager with the local Housing Authority, what empowering options can you create for your client, Judy?
2. Do you see any value conflicts between the agency's drug policy and social work values? If so, what are they?
3. When you go to the jail to visit Judy, what will you say to her?
4. How would you feel about this case if Judy's children were not involved?

It is also important to note that there are two types of confidentiality, one absolute, the other relative. According to the NASW *Social Work Dictionary* (Barker, 2014), absolute confidentiality means the professional never shares information in any form with anyone. Although social workers may strive for absolute confidentiality, it is impossible to guarantee a client that information will never be shared. There would be no written record of any interaction and no oral transmission of data. The principle of relative confidentiality allows for the sharing of information within the agency (such as in supervision or team meetings) but not with outside agencies or collateral contacts unless the client has given consent in writing.

State laws, the NASW *Code of Ethics* (NASW, 2008a), and certain agency policies impose limitations on confidentiality within the social worker–client relationship, requiring social workers to report to the appropriate authorities clients' intentions to harm another individual or themselves. All states require that social workers report known or suspected cases of child abuse or neglect and elder abuse and neglect. Social service agencies that use a team treatment approach may require that all team members have access to pertinent information about the client. It is the ethical responsibility of the social worker to inform clients of the limits of confidentiality at the outset of the helping relationship (Mizrahi & Davis, 2009; NASW General Counsel & NASW Legal Defense Fund, 2014). However, even when we are knowledgeable about the legal and ethical limits of confidentiality, in the real practice world, it is often difficult to identify when we have reached these limits within the helping relationship. Box 2.5 provides an example of this dilemma.

The NASW *Code of Ethics*, Ethical Standard 1.07 (NASW, 2008a), requires that social workers respect clients' right to privacy. Information should be solicited only when it is essential to providing services that address clients' problems and possible resolutions. To maintain confidentiality, social workers must refrain from disclosing information about a client to others. It is because of this expectation that trust can be developed between the client and the social worker over time (Miley, O'Melia, & DuBois, 2013).

Box 2.5 A Confidentiality Issue

You are a caseworker at a Family Service Center where you have worked for one month since receiving your BSW. Richard is a 48-year-old construction worker whom you have been seeing weekly since your first week at the agency. Richard came to your agency seeking assistance after unexpectedly losing his job following a back injury that left him permanently limited in his abilities to lift or carry more than 20 pounds, to climb, or to do twisting motions. Richard is a devoted husband and father and is feeling that he has let his family down because he has not been able to provide for them financially in recent months. With your help, Richard has been able to enter an eight-week reemployment-training program where he is being trained as a tax preparer for a local firm. He has done well in his classes but has become depressed and frustrated in the past two weeks as his family's financial situation has worsened. Today, you notice that Richard seems more agitated and restless. When you asked him what is on his mind, he explains that the previous night he had been out at the local tavern having a few beers and on the way home was stopped for speeding and was given a DUI when he failed to pass the breathalyzer test. The ordeal resulted in Richard being held in jail overnight, causing him to miss his tax preparer's class the following morning. He is feeling unjustly persecuted by the police and fears that he will not be permitted to complete the class. As Richard is telling you of the events of the previous evening, he becomes enraged at the unfortunate hand that fate has dealt him and blurts out, "I feel like walking into the police station and shooting those bastards!"

Points for reflection

1. How will you handle the issue of confidentiality in your relationship with Richard?
2. How do you determine whether Richard is serious about his threat or just venting his anger?
3. What actions would you take?
4. How would you address this with Richard given confidentiality and issues of trust?
5. What safety issues do you need to consider for yourself, for Richard, and for the staff in your agency?

Minors (typically 12 years and younger) are generally incapable of giving consent to health treatment, and a parent or guardian will need to consent on the minor's behalf. Exceptions to the general rule vary from state to state. Commonly, a full explanation (or informed consent) is given to the child, parent, or guardian. If the child does not object or the social worker doesn't identify any compelling reason to deny access to information, he or she may do so. When the social worker provides a full explanation of confidentiality and its limits, the possibility of being caught between a parent and a child is reduced. As always, when you are unsure about how to proceed, consult your supervisor. In some cases, legal counsel may be required.

There are some exceptions to confidentiality, such as evidence of child and/or elder abuse or neglect, threats by a client to harm self or others, the need for emergency services, guardianship hearings, lawsuits filed against a social worker, consultation with colleagues and attorneys, and for purposes of internal quality assurance reviews (Miley et al., 2013). Be careful not to discuss your clients with family and friends (even if you do not give any identifying information) or talk about clients in public spaces where others may be within earshot. Also, always follow the agency's procedures concerning the safeguarding of client records. Social service agencies are firmly entrenched in the digital age, and client records are now computerized. It is extremely important that these records be password protected or otherwise secured to protect the confidentiality of the client. Confidentiality is a core social work value. To assess your knowledge of confidentiality, answer the questions in Box 2.A.

Clients can give the social worker permission to share information about their case with others. This is often necessary when a client is using multiple service providers and client services are coordinated across agencies. For the client to give "informed consent

Box 2.A Now You Try It . . . Confidentiality

1. What are the most important aspects of confidentiality to you?
2. Where do you see the potential conflicts arising in adhering to the NASW *Code of Ethics* and the reality of everyday practice?

for releasing information," the worker must share with the client the conditions, risks, and alternatives to sharing this information. Should the need for sharing information occur, be sure to have the client (or, in the case of a child, the parent or guardian) sign a consent form that includes the information that will be shared with whom, for what purpose, and within what time frames.

Watch the video clip as Diane, the social worker, obtains consent from her client, Mrs. Kita, and establishes the limits of confidentiality.

Some communities are now using software that allows multiple agencies serving the same client to share client information online (with the client's permission). This provides an easy way to coordinate client services along a continuum of care. For clients, this often means that they have to tell their story only once to the primary service agency rather than repeating it for social service workers they see at each separate service agency. For such software to be used safely and ethically, it must contain multiple layers of security to ensure that client information remains secure and confidential. It is important that when talking with a client about parameters of confidentiality, you discuss the details up front and acquire the consents for information sharing as soon as possible. This will reduce the likelihood of misunderstanding should the client situation require the social worker to limit the boundaries of confidentiality. (See Appendix A for more information about professional documentation.)

Finally, the Privacy of **Health Information/Health Insurance Portability and Accountability Act of 1996 (HIPAA)** provides clear privacy guidelines for health care providers. Social workers have a strong tradition of safeguarding information. However, in today's world, the old system of paper records in locked filing cabinets is not enough. With information now broadly held and transmitted electronically, HIPAA provides clear standards for the protection of personal health information. To learn more about HIPAA, check out the U.S. Department of Health and Human Services website.

Privileged communication. There is a distinction between adhering to client confidentiality and privileged communication. Privileged communication provides the legal grounds for confidentiality, meaning that clients can claim legal privilege and ethical social workers maintain confidentiality. Legal privilege protects the client's private communication with a social worker by prohibiting the social worker from revealing information in court (Miley et al., 2013). According to Miley et al. (2013), establishing privilege involves the following: 1) the client can invoke privilege to prevent the social worker's testimony or records from being used as evidence in court, 2) the social worker can assert privilege at the client's request, and 3) the judge considers relevant laws and the client waiver and entitlement to determine whether privilege applies. By invoking privilege, clients can restrict the social worker from revealing confidential information in a court of law. Without the client invoking privilege, the social worker can be compelled to testify and provide documentation to the court. Rules of privilege vary from jurisdiction to jurisdiction; therefore, a social worker should determine whether privilege is available in the state in which they practice (Hackney & Cormier, 2013). It is important to determine whether privilege is available in your state and to determine what information is protected and in what situations privilege applies (NASW, 2008b).

Assess your understanding of value-driven practice behaviors by taking this brief quiz.

SOCIAL WORK ETHICS

Social work ethics provide social work practitioners with a set of guidelines for practice. These guidelines are established by the NASW, the major professional social work organization, and reflect the values of the profession. Social work ethics translate the abstract values of the profession into action statements and give social workers concrete guidelines for ethical ways of being in the practice setting.

The first *Code of Ethics* was adopted in 1960 and was later revised in 1979, 1996, 1999, and, most recently, 2008 to reflect the changing emphasis and direction of social work practice and changing social and political times (Reamer, 2014). Box 2.6 summarizes the six ethical principles of the NASW *Code of Ethics*.

The *Code of Ethics* provides guidance on how to deal with issues in contemporary social work practice. Some of the major societal changes affecting practice today include the following:

- Reductions in human services at the federal and state levels, fundamental changes in the welfare system and immigration laws, and tighter eligibility standards for accessing publicly funded social welfare benefits
- Evidence of community disintegration emerging in social problems, such as homelessness, domestic violence, increased incidents of police brutality, poverty, substance abuse, job instability, unemployment, multiple jobs, and increased family stress
- Population shift with growing numbers of people of color and the elderly
- New health and information technologies and major changes in health policy favoring managed care
- The development of a culture of consumerism reflected in "me first" attitudes and "for profitism" in the human services (Brill, 2001)

Box 2.6 Ethical Principles of the Social Work Profession

1. Social workers' primary goal is to help people in need and to address social problems.
2. Social workers challenge social injustice.
3. Social workers respect the inherent dignity and worth of the person.
4. Social workers recognize the central importance of human relationships.
5. Social workers behave in a trustworthy manner.
6. Social workers practice within their areas of competence and develop and enhance their professional expertise.

Source: Excerpt from NASW (2008a) *Code of Ethics*, Ethical Principles section. Used with permission.

All of these changes call into question the ethics and commitment to public services by the public at large, the government, and professionals in the human services. Social workers are facing more complex issues in practice and are expected to work effectively and efficiently with fewer resources. The changes in the social, economic, and political landscape of America have created a context of social work practice that has more ethical challenges. In response to these societal changes, the 1996 revised NASW *Code of Ethics* covered more areas of practice and provided more specificity in professional behaviors. In all, the code now consists of 155 ethical standards. In 2008, the code was revised again, adding more inclusive language concerning the need to avoid discrimination and to respect individuals' gender identity/expression and immigration status.

Fourteen practice standards complement the *Code of Ethics*. Covering social work practice in areas such as cultural competence, palliative care, technology, substance abuse, and genetics, the practice standards provide detailed guidance on social work in these areas, including ethical considerations. Box 2.7 excerpts the ethics section of the practice standards for working with family caregivers of older adults.

Box 2.7 Standards for Social Work Practice with Family Caregivers of Older Adults: Standard 1: Ethics and Values

Social workers practicing with family caregivers of older adults shall adhere to the ethics and values of the social work profession, using the NASW *Code of Ethics* (2008a) as a guide to ethical decision making.

Interpretation

The primary mission of the social work profession is to enhance human well-being and to help meet the basic needs of all people, with particular attention to the needs of people who are vulnerable and oppressed. This mission is rooted in a set of core values that constitutes the foundation of social work and relates closely to social work with family caregivers of older adults:

- **Service.** Social workers apply their knowledge and skills to support the well-being of family caregivers of older adults and to address challenges faced by family caregivers.
- **Social justice.** Social workers act on individual and systemic levels to ensure access to needed information, services, and resources for family caregivers of older adults and to facilitate family caregivers' meaningful and comfortable participation in decision making.
- **Human dignity and worth.** Social workers treat family caregivers of older adults in a respectful and caring manner. They promote family caregivers' self-determination, with sensitivity and respect for the self-determination of older adults when confronted with conflicting values and goals.
- **Importance of human relationships.** Social workers engage family caregivers, to the extent possible, as partners in goal identification, progress, and achievement. They strive to strengthen relationships between family caregivers and older adults so as to maintain and enhance the well-being of the family system.
- **Integrity.** Social workers use the power inherent in their professional role responsibly, exercising judicious use of self and avoiding conflicts of interest. Their practice with, and on behalf of, family caregivers of older adults is consistent with the profession's mission and ethics.
- **Competence.** Social workers practice within their areas of competence and continually strive to enhance their knowledge and skills related to family caregiving and aging. Competence also requires that social workers recognize the importance of, and attend to, their own self-care.

The very term *family* is, in fact, rooted in ethical values. For the purposes of these standards, *family* refers to family of origin, extended family, domestic partners, friends, or other individuals who support an older adult and whose primary relationship with the older adult is not based on a financial or professional agreement. Social work practice with family caregivers of older adults begins with honoring the uniqueness of each family system.

Effective practice with family caregivers of older adults requires social workers to identify their own values and perspectives regarding aging and family caregiving, including

(Continued)

Box 2.7 Standards for Social Work Practice with Family Caregivers of Older Adults: Standard 1: Ethics and Values *(Continued)*

their personal experiences as family caregivers or with aging family members. Social workers have an ethical responsibility to assess how their own experiences influence their practice with family caregivers of older adults, to ensure they are not imposing their own values on family caregivers of older adults.

Differences in the wishes, perceptions, and capacity of older adults and family caregivers can present complex ethical and legal challenges to social workers. Social workers must know and comply with federal, state, local, and tribal laws, regulations, and policies related to older adults, such as reporting requirements for elder abuse and neglect, guardianship, and advance directives. Obtaining informed consent, maintaining confidentiality, and protecting privacy are critical. Careful application of ethical principles is especially important when older adults or family caregivers have limited decision-making capacity or are experiencing or perpetuating mistreatment. Collaboration with colleagues can also help resolve ethical dilemmas.

Points for reflection

1. How are social work values embedded in the practice standards for working with family caregivers?
2. How do the standards protect the vulnerable?
3. What do social workers need to know to serve this population ethically?

Source: Excerpt from *NASW (2008a)*, NASW Standards for Social Work Practice with Family Caregivers of Older Adults. Used with permission.

Charles Levy notes that the NASW *Code of Ethics* serves three functions for the profession: "It guides professional conduct, it is a set of principles that social workers can apply in the performance of the social work function, and it is a set of criteria by which social work practice can be evaluated" (Levy, 1976, p. 108). By understanding the established ethics of social work practice, social workers can make the difficult moral and value-laden decisions that are an inescapable part of working with people from diverse walks of life. Social workers who find themselves within practice settings that may not adhere to the values of the social work profession have a supportive and clear set of guidelines. Box 2.8 outlines the areas of social workers' ethical responsibilities that are addressed in the NASW *Code of Ethics*. For a full reading of the code, visit the NASW website.

The Ethic of Care

Developed by feminist theorists Nel Noddings and Joan C. Tronto, the **ethic of care** is a comprehensive theoretical framework that offers insight into how people can best live together in a more just society. Tronto defines care as "a species activity that includes

Box 2.8 Social Workers' Ethical Responsibilities

1. Social workers have ethical responsibilities to clients.
2. Social workers have ethical responsibilities to colleagues.
3. Social workers have ethical responsibilities in the practice setting.
4. Social workers have ethical responsibilities as professionals.
5. Social workers have ethical responsibilities to the social work profession.
6. Social workers have ethical responsibilities to the broader society.

Source: NASW (2008a).

everything we do to maintain, continue, and repair our 'world' so that we can live in it as well as possible. That world includes our bodies, our selves, and our environment, all of which we seek to interweave in a complex, life-sustaining web" (Fisher & Tronto, 1990, p. 40). The ethic of care focuses on the life span and our interdependence as members of society (e.g., "I may be an independent adult right now, but I depended on care as a child so that I could reach adulthood, and I may need additional care as I age"). At some level, we all are, have been, or will be vulnerable. Other themes in the ethic of care include the following:

- Equality (all people have equal moral worth, and thus the distribution of care in a society should be equitable)
- The inadvisability of making sweeping generalizations about "human nature" that hold true in all circumstances (in providing care, we should think about the person receiving care as being unique and irreplaceable)
- Responsiveness—whose needs must be met; is the care that is being offered meeting the needs?

In the ethic-of-care perspective, care is seen as a reflection of the power dynamics within the society: Who receives quality care? How is care distributed across gender, racial, and socioeconomic lines? What is the status of caregivers in the society? By asking whose needs are unmet and why, the ethic-of-care perspective bridges the micro level of practice and the social worker's ethical obligations to the broader society (Cummins, Byers, & Pedrick, 2011). Box 2.I shows how reflection on the ethic of care could inform social work practice.

Engagement

Behavior: Apply knowledge of human behavior and the social environment, person-in-environment, and other multidisciplinary theoretical frameworks to engage with clients and constituencies.

Critical Thinking Question: What aspects of modern society make it challenging to adopt the long-term perspective called for in the ethic- of- care framework?

Box 2.I Theory into Practice—the Ethic of Care—Case Study

Elena is a youth worker in a shelter for adolescents who have a history of running away from home and living on the streets. One of her clients in the shelter, Angel, is a 17-year-old who will "age out" of the shelter in eight months. Elena needs to develop a transition plan for Angel to help her in the adjustment to adulthood. Nine years ago, when Elena first began her social work practice, she would have approached this task with the goal of maximizing Angel's autonomy, focusing on how Angel could obtain additional schooling or a job and a safe place to live in. After reading an article on the ethic of care in a social work journal as part of her MSW course work, Elena is now more aware of Angel as part of an interconnected web of relationships that can either nurture or impede Angel's positive development as a human being. The web consists of formal supports, such as Elena, the other youth workers in the shelter, and the teachers who conduct GED classes at the shelter, but it also consists of informal supports, such as the friends Angel has made at the shelter, the cousins who sometimes visit her, and the members of the partying crowd Angel hangs out with when she is on the streets. Considering Angel in light of the ethic of care, Elena attends to Angel's interconnected relationships, seeing the need for positive supports and the continuity of healthy friendships with current shelter residents as a priority, along with the need for Angel to receive an education and have a job and a place to live in.

Source: To read the article that influenced Elena, see S. Holland, "Looked After Children and the Ethic of Care," *British Journal of Social Work*, *40*(6, 2010), 1664–1680.

Ethical Decision Making

Resolving **ethical dilemmas** in social work practice is not a simple task. It requires knowledge of the *Code of Ethics* and Practice Standards, a close analysis of all the relationships involved in the situation, the imagination to visualize the probable consequences of different courses of action, and a commitment to take the time needed to think through all of the above (Cummins et al., 2011).

The Ethical Principles Hierarchy ranks ethical principles that can be a resource in weighing different courses of action. Figure 2.1 presents the ranked principles, showing protection of life at the top of the hierarchy as the most important ethical consideration and truthfulness and full disclosure at the lower end of the hierarchy. Note that the figure does not mean that truthfulness is unimportant as an ethical practice—it simply means that in a situation involving competing ethical considerations, the preservation of life would be the most important consideration. In the Ethical Principles Hierarchy, a quality-of-life issue, such as access to decent housing, while important, would not be as crucial as preserving life in the face of an immediate threat (Dolgoff, Harrington, & Loewenbere, 2012).

Figure 2.2 outlines a process you can use to work your way through the ethically questionable "gray areas" of the helping relationship. In some cases, you will need to broaden ethical reflection, drawing on the collective wisdom of colleagues and other professionals, as noted in the *Code of Ethics*:

Ethical and Professional Behavior

Behavior: Use reflection and self-regulation to manage personal values and maintain professionalism in practice situations.

Critical Thinking Question: You have been working at a small local agency for a year and have just received Melissa as a new case. She is a 16-year-old who has been in and out of the judicial system since she was 12. She is currently seeing you as part of a court-remanded decision as part of her sentence for the attempted murder of her three-year-old brother. Would you take this client? Why or why not? If you took Melissa as a client, explain some tools you would use in order to be able to treat Melissa with respect and see her inherent potential.

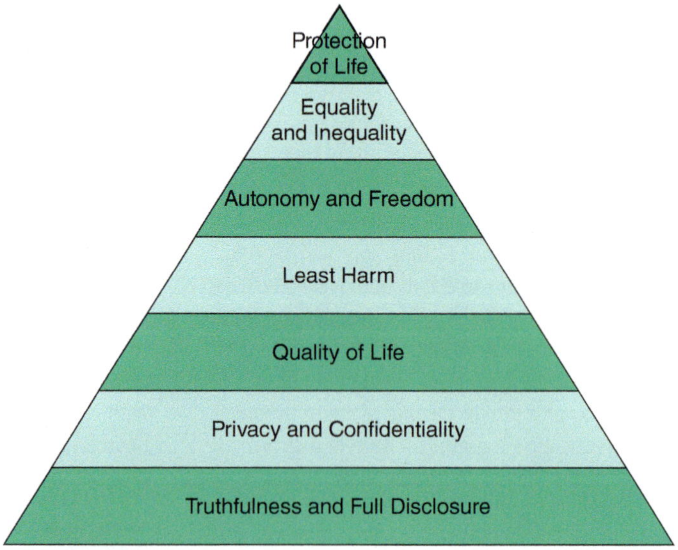

Figure 2.1
Ethical Principles Hierarchy

Source: Boyle et al. (2009); Loewenberg, Dolgoff and Harrington (2000).

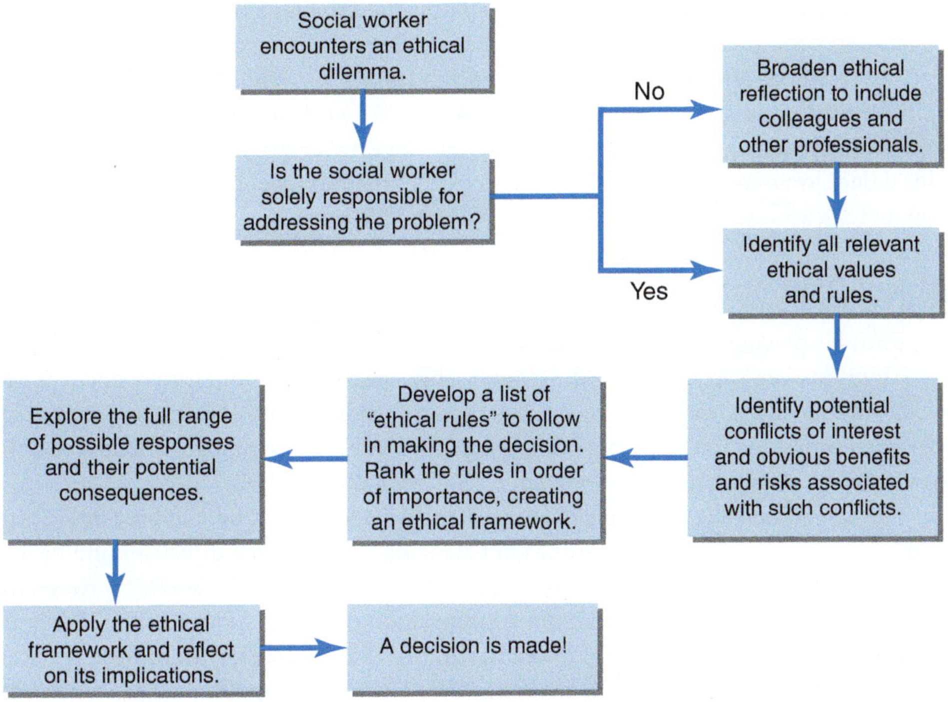

Figure 2.2
Steps for Resolving Ethical Dilemmas

Source: Adapted from D. Hardina, "Guidelines for Ethical Practice in Community Operation," *Social Work, 49* (4, 2004), 595–604, and M. Reisch and J. I. Lowe, "'Of Means and Ends' Revisited": Teaching Ethical Community Organizing in an Unethical Society," *Journal of Community Practice*, *7*(1, 2000), 19–38.

> *[Social workers] should be aware of any conflicts between personal and professional values and deal with them responsibly. For additional guidance, social workers should consult the relevant literature on professional ethics and ethical decision-making and seek appropriate consultation when faced with ethical dilemmas. This may involve consultation with an agency-based or social work organization's ethics committee, a regulatory body, knowledgeable colleagues, supervisors, or legal counsel. (NASW, 2008a, "Purpose of the NASW Code of Ethics" section)*

The next step in this model for ethical decision making is to identify the applicable ethical values and rules (including the NASW *Code of Ethics* but also other frameworks, such as the ethic of care, agency-specific mission and guiding principles, and state and federal laws). The model takes potential conflicts of interest into consideration (e.g., is there a financial incentive to meet managed care financial targets that could lead to a course of action contrary to the client's best interests?).

The model then calls for the explicit definition of ethical rules, ranked in order of importance. See Figure 2.1 for an example of such a ranking.

After any needed consultation, a review of applicable ethical values and rules, the determination of whether any conflicts of interest exist, and the identification of ethical rules and their ranking, the social worker explores the full range of possible responses to the situation and their potential consequences. After reflecting on the best choice that emerges from this analysis, a decision is made and acted on. While this model may seem complex on first introduction, its purpose is to make ethical deliberation a conscious thought process for the beginning practitioner. Experienced social workers internalize ethical decision making, and thus the process becomes less mechanical as practice wisdom increases.

Ethical Dilemmas

The most perplexing ethical issues involve cases that do not have an immediately apparent "right answer." As Frederic G. Reamer observes, "Ethical dilemmas occur when social workers must choose among conflicting professional values, duties, and rights that arise sometimes due to their competing obligations to clients, employers, colleagues, the social work profession, and society at large" (Reamer, 2008, p. 144).

The case in Box 2.B highlights differences in micro-level treatment approaches. Social workers can also face ethical dilemmas in balancing public policy directives and professional social work values. The social work profession is sanctioned by society through the passage of public laws and through the appropriation of public funds to fulfill the mandates of public law. Social work therefore has an obligation to society to provide services, counseling, and interventions for those in need. In this sense, the public at large shows support for the values and mission of social work. Public laws and regulations also direct social work practice insofar as social workers are mandated by law to provide certain services and to structure those services in predetermined ways. Often, the values inherent in the public

Box 2.B Now You Try It . . . Resolving Ethical Dilemmas

You are a social worker in a residential treatment program for children ages 8 through 12. These are children who have been diagnosed with severe behavioral issues, such as physical aggressiveness, verbal impulsivity, and self-harm. For Joey, age nine, to be placed in such a restrictive environment, many other treatment options were considered before his placement into your 24-hour facility. Joey has been in and out of 12 foster homes since age two. There has been no contact with any biological family members since the Department of Children and Family Services became involved seven years ago. Joey's mother left him on the steps of a local hospital. Now seven years later, he finally seems to be adjusting to the structure and close supervision on the unit. You have seen Joey initiate a few conversations with the staff, and on one occasion he offered to help Mike, another resident, work on a puzzle. His sessions with a special education teacher are going fairly well, and Joey is making progress. However, he remains disruptive around mealtimes and has been removed from the dining area for throwing utensils and plates at other children. He is a light sleeper and wanders on the unit after bedtime. In your assessment, Joey is deeply troubled but has the potential to benefit further from the highly structured environment in your facility. Yesterday, you learned that Joey's court-appointed special advocate (CASA) is going to seek to have Joey placed in a group home facility that is located near an elementary school that has a well-resourced special education department. The CASA advocate is seeking greater access to educational resources for Joey and a smaller group living arrangement that will be less institutional.

Using the Steps in Resolving Ethical Dilemmas model and the Ethical Principles Screen, explore the full range of possible responses to the situation and their potential consequences. Consider the situation from the perspectives of a residential treatment social worker and a CASA advocate, both of whom are seeking what is best for Joey. How can the model help reduce interagency differences concerning Joey's care? What are your recommendations in this case?

Box 2.9 Conflicting Values: Social Work and Social Policy

Let's return to the case of Sarah. Recall that you are a social worker at a not-for-profit social service agency that provides support services and training to help young single mothers achieve self-sufficiency. Over the past two years, you have seen Sarah intermittently. She has become one of your favorite clients, in part because of her perseverance and her willingness to follow through on her commitments. Sarah is now 19-years-old; her son, Seth, is two. Since you began working with Sarah, she has attended parenting classes and proven herself to be a loving and skilled mother. She has also completed her GED. With the help of housing assistance, she has been able to secure a two-bedroom apartment after being on the waiting list for six months. Eight months ago, Sarah got her first real job as an assistant teacher in a day care center, working 20 hours per week. Sarah likes her job very much, and she excels at her work. The job pays only minimum wage and provides no health care or paid time-off benefits. However, as an employee of the day care center, Sarah receives free day care for her son Seth. With her TANF (Temporary Aid to Needy Families) income, food stamps, Medicaid, subsidized housing, part-time job, and free day care, Sarah has managed to create a stable life for her son.

In the state where you practice, clients can receive TANF benefits for only two years. As you review Sarah's case file, you see that her welfare benefits will expire in one month. Sarah needs the welfare check to meet basic survival needs for herself and her son. If she budgets carefully, her welfare check and work income together just cover her rent, secondhand clothing for Seth, bus fare to work, the phone bill, and essential items, like toothpaste and soap, that are not covered by food stamps. Without her welfare check, Sarah is likely to find herself in the same situation she was in two years earlier, homeless with her young son.

Points for reflection

1. What social work value does the state TANF policy contradict?
2. As a social worker, how do you comply with state law without violating social work values?
3. What options can you present to Sarah that will be empowering to her and her son?

laws directing social work practice are in conflict with the values inherent in the social work profession. At times, this may put the social work practitioner in an ethical dilemma when trying to satisfy the demands of two competing value systems (see Box 2.9).

As discussed earlier, changes in the complexity of society and social problems have created new ethical challenges to the contemporary social worker. Consider, for example, that cuts in human services funding have resulted in fewer salaried social workers and thus higher caseloads for those social workers who have retained their jobs. How do you as a social worker provide adequate levels of care to 25 child welfare cases on your workload? The move toward contract/fee-for-service positions among social workers shifts the focus of the work from an internal altruistic motivation to one that is money driven. How will this affect the quality of service delivery? In the privatization of human services, service delivery has become competitive and funding driven rather than need driven, raising the question of who is getting served and who is not. Another ethical challenge is the increase in unionization among social workers. Does this violate the professional code? The use of technologies that computerize client records and allow for sharing of client information across agencies raises questions about our ability to ensure client confidentiality (Brill, 2001). Consider the three cases in Box 2.10. Identify the ethical dilemma present in each case and then discuss how you would respond if you were the social worker in each case.

Ethical and Professional Behavior

Behavior: Make ethical decisions by applying the standards of the NASW *Code of Ethics*, relevant laws and regulations, models for ethical decision making, ethical conduct of research, and additional codes of ethics as appropriate to context.

Critical Thinking Question: For each of the ethical dilemmas outlined in Box 2.10, consider whether you would consult with colleagues. If so, what questions would you ask?

Assess your understanding of social work ethics by taking this brief quiz.

Box 2.10 Ethical Dilemmas: Case Examples

Case #1. A social worker employed in a county social services department as an eligibility worker has learned that local welfare reforms direct that she report any new children born to current welfare recipients. She fears that the new reporting requirement could prevent children born into welfare families from receiving income supports later in their lives. The worker is aware of the requirement that social workers should comply with the law. However, she is convinced that reporting newborns might preclude future essential services. The social worker also believes that the new regulations will create a new class of citizens (children born to welfare mothers) that might be discriminated against in various ways. She feels caught between complying with the law and ignoring the law to prevent what she views as likely injustice.

A. What is/are the ethical dilemma(s) facing the social worker?
B. Are these legitimate concerns? Why or why not?
C. As the social worker in this county agency, how would you respond in this situation? What are your possible courses of action?

Case #2. A clinical social worker in a remote community trains paraprofessionals to do mental health counseling with members of their Asian, Pacific Islander, and Central American communities. She believes that well-trained paraprofessionals familiar with community members' cultures and languages could broaden mental health services by bringing cultural depth in service to those communities. Months after those she trained began providing services, the state department that licenses her agency adopted new policies prohibiting unlicensed social workers from providing mental health counseling services. A regional department representative reports that he is considering filing a complaint against the social worker for facilitating the unauthorized practice of social work.

A. What do you see as the ethical dilemma here for the social worker? For the state department representative?
B. Which action would provide the best services to the clients? Why do you think so?
C. As the social worker at the agency, what would you do to protect your paraprofessionals and the services they provide to your clients?
D. As a state department representative (which may well be social worker too), on what ethical grounds can you feel justified in enforcing the law?
E. Is there a win-win solution to this dilemma? What do you think it might be?

Case #3. When a nonprofit hospital downsized, all social work positions were eliminated. The social workers were transferred to an affiliated home health care agency. The hospital then offered to contract with the home health social workers for the same work they had done previously for the hospital. At times, the social workers who do both hospital and home-based work experience conflicts of interest when faced with the need to refer hospital patients to home-based services. The social workers understand that they should not exclusively refer to the hospital's home health care agency and that self-determination requires that patients have information about a range of available, appropriate services. But from the patient's perspective, they also see that it would often be more desirable to be able to continue to work with the social worker who had been assigned during the hospitalization period. The hospital's risk management officer has argued, however, that when patients choose their home health care agency, the same social worker should not continue to work with the patient because of the appearance of conflict of interest—that is, the social worker would receive compensation for services because of a referral he or she made.

A. If a patient chooses to continue with her hospital social worker as her home health social worker, is there really a conflict of interest for the social worker? If so, what do you believe the conflict to be?
B. What underlying social work values may be jeopardized in the above working arrangement?
C. Are there any standards of practice being violated in this working arrangement as set forth by the NASW *Code of Ethics*? Which one(s)?

Source: Case studies reprinted with permission from NASW (1998a).

SUMMARY

- Social work as a profession is dedicated to social justice and the empowerment of all people through the creation of a just society where men and women and all diverse populations are given equal access to resources and opportunities. These ideals often attract to the profession people who are committed to helping people.

- Putting social work values into practice is an ongoing challenge, especially in today's complex world. Ethical dilemmas are common to social work practice, and social workers need to be familiar with the profession's code of ethics to guide them through the challenges of practice with people facing multiple problems in a rapidly changing world.
- Staying focused on creating a society where all people enjoy a safe and supportive environment helps us through the difficult cases. Witnessing our clients' successes as they reconnect with their own innate worth and create stable and fulfilling lives is the priceless reward that social workers reap in direct social work practice.

APPLY IT

1. Watch **Interactive Case Study #4** of Maria, Mrs. Anderson, and social worker Nicole. Identify two ways that Nicole could have provided Maria with some reassurance about the confidential nature of their conversation. Take into consideration that Maria is a minor.
2. Watch **Interactive Case Study #5** of Mrs. Kita and social worker Diane. Consider the network of relationships that support Mrs. Kita, including formal social service supports and informal family and friend supports. Identify and consider Mrs. Kita's different caregiver roles and how her family's need for care would be met.

Assess Your Competence

Use the scale below to rate your current level of achievement on the following concepts or skills associated with each competency presented in the chapter:

1	2	3
I can accurately describe the concept or skill	I can consistently identify the concept or skill when observing and analyzing practice activities	I can competently implement the concept or skill in my own practice

_______ Understands and can articulate core social work mission and values.

_______ Can identify and describe components of the NASW *Code of Ethics*.

_______ Can identify ethical dilemmas and tools or actions to help resolve them.

_______ Understands the value of ethical reflection.

LEARNING OUTCOMES

- Articulate the relationship between the five categories of theory and social work practice, providing examples of applications.
- Distinguish between a practice theory and a meta-framework as applied to selected client scenarios.

CHAPTER OUTLINE

Categories of Practice Theory
Psychodynamic Theories
Cognitive-Behavioral Theories
Humanistic Theories
Postmodern Theories

Meta-Frameworks for Practicing Social Work
Systems Theory
Ecological Perspective
Life Model of Social Work Practice
Strengths Perspective
Empowerment-Based Practice Model

Summary

3

Theory-Directed Social Work Practice

ADRIAN_ILIE825/FOTOLIA

Social workers are prepared through their BSW education and in their first year of MSW education to practice as generalist social workers. As generalist social workers, social workers draw on a broad knowledge base in practice with diverse clients, situated in a wide range of contexts, and involved in many interlocking systems, such as family, work, community, and institutional, political, and judicial systems. To be an effective generalist, a social worker must be grounded in a broad range of practice theory. To be a generalist social worker means one is able to draw on many theories, perspectives, and models and weave them together to create a reasoned and comprehensive approach to practice for specific clients in specific contexts. Client problems, values, culture, and belief systems influence the practitioner's selection of theoretical frameworks when constructing practice interventions.

From its beginning, social work has been concerned with providing care that is grounded in tested knowledge. Early in the profession's development, pioneers such as Jane Addams and Mary Richmond worked to provide theoretical bases for social work practice. The publication of Mary Richmond's *Social Diagnosis* in 1917 was one of the first efforts to link theory to practice. Likewise at the family, agency/community (mezzo), and national (macro) levels of practice, Jane Addams's knowledge of and work within and across these multiple system levels made her an effective advocate for bringing needed resources and social justice to those in need (Addams, 1893; Dinerman, 1984; Trattner, 1999). While the profession of social work has been active in developing theories of social work practice since its inception, it has always borrowed relevant theories from other disciplines such as psychology, medicine, nursing, anthropology, biology, and sociology. While many of these theories continue to inform social work practice, with maturity, the profession developed empirically tested theories of its own. Today, there are more than 400 practice theories, perspectives, frameworks, and models that direct and inform social work practice (Boyle, Hull, Mather, Smith, & Farley, 2009; Wedding & Corcini, 2014). See Box 3.1 for a list of commonly used theories, frameworks, perspectives, and models across four broad categories of practice theories: psychodynamic, cognitive-behavioral, humanistic, and postmodern theories.

Fundamentally, practice theory is a body of knowledge that has been empirically tested and shown to be effective. Theory then guides the action of practice, and its evidence of effectiveness becomes the standard of accountability for practitioners (Turner, 2011). Without the application of tested knowledge, social workers cannot claim to be practicing professionals. If we did not use theory to guide us in our practice decisions, social workers would not be distinguishable from kind, warmhearted people wanting to be of help and doing what they felt was the "right thing to do." Theory becomes the basis of our assessments and interventions with clients. We use it to give meaning to situations, to assess the strengths and challenges (or barriers) in presenting situations, and to understand our clients' lives and the environments in which they live and function. Usually, practice requires that we employ multiple theories when working with a client (which may be an individual, family, group, organization, or community) (Turner, 2011). For example, we may use the person-in-environment perspective to understand the complexity of our client's life, psychodynamic theory to understand her low self-esteem, crisis theory to counsel her after a rape, and grief theory to help her through the recovery process.

CATEGORIES OF PRACTICE THEORY

Direct practice theories and models have been categorized into four broad groups. These include psychodynamic theories, cognitive-behavioral theories, humanistic theories, and postmodern theories. In this section, you will be introduced to each of these categories of theory and provided some examples of some of those theories and an explanation of their application in direct social work practice.

Psychodynamic Theories

Psychodynamic theories can be traced to Sigmund Freud and attempt to link current problems clients may be having to past traumas, usually occurring during childhood. Treatment is focused on gaining insights that then can be translated into personality changes within the client. Common psychodynamic theories include psychoanalysis

Box 3.1 Theorists and Their Works

Theory	Original Theorists	Sample Publications
Psychodynamic Theories	Sigmund Freud (1856–1939)	Freud, S. (1900/1999). *Interpretation of dreams*. Cambridge, UK: Oxford University Press. Freud, S. (1920). *General introduction to psychoanalysis*. New York: Horace Liveright.
	Melanie Klein (1882–1960)	Klein, M. (1930). The importance of symbol-formation in the development of the ego. *International Journal of Psychoanalysis, 11,* 24–39. Klein, M. (1948). *Contributions to psychoanalysis. 1921–1945*. London: Hogarth Press. Klein, M. (1957). *Envy and gratitude. A study of unconscious sources*. New York: Basic Books.
	Karen Horney (1885–1952)	Horney, K. (1942). *Self-analysis*. New York: W. W. Norton. Horney, K. (1942). *The collected works of Karen Horney* (Vol. 2). New York: W. W. Norton. Horney, K. (1967). *Feminine psychology*. New York: W. W. Norton.
	Ronald Fairbairn (1889–1964)	Fairbairn, R. (1952). *Psychoanalytic studies of the personality*. London: Tavistock Publications. [This is a collection of papers previously published in different reviews.]
	Harry Stack Sullivan (1892–1949)	Sullivan, H. S. (1925). The oral complex. *Psychoanalytic Review, 12,* 30–38. Sullivan, H. S. (1926). Erogenous maturation. *Psychoanalytic Review, 13,* 1–15. Sullivan, H. S. (1926). The importance of a study of symbols in psychiatry. *Psyche, 7,* 81–93.
	David Winnicott (1896–1971)	Winnicott, D. W. (1965). *Maturational processes and the facilitating environment: Studies in the theory of emotional development*. Madison, CT: International Universities Press. Winnicott, D. W. (1965). *The family and individual development*. London: Tavistock. Winnicott, D. W. (1971). *Playing and reality*. New York: Penguin.
	Margaret Mahler (1897–1985)	Mahler, M. S. (1972). On the first three phases of the separation-individuation process. *International Journal of Psychoanalysis, 53,* 333–338.
	Erich Fromm (1900–1980)	Fromm, E. (1941). *Escape from freedom*. New York: Henry Holt and Company. Fromm, E. (1955). *The sane society*. New York: Henry Holt. Fromm, E. (1970). *The crisis of psychoanalysis: Essays on Freud, Marx, and social psychology*. New York: Fawcett Publications.
	Erik Erikson (1902–1994)	Erikson, E. (1946). Ego development and historical change. *Psychoanalytic Study of the Child, 2,* 359–396. Erikson, E. (1963). *Childhood and society*. New York: W. W. Norton.
	Heinz Kohut (1913–1981)	Kohut, H. (1959). Introspection, empathy, and psychoanalysis: An examination of the relationship between modes of observation and theory. *Journal of American Psychoanalytic Association, 7,* 459–483. Kohut, H. (1982). Introspection, empathy, and the semi-circle of mental health. *International Journal of Psychoanalysis, 63,* 395–407.
Cognitive-Behavioral Theories	Albert Ellis (1913–2007)	Ellis, A. (1991). The revised ABC's or rational-emotive therapy (RET). *Journal of Rational-Emotive and Cognitive-Behavior Therapy, 9*(3), 139–172. Ellis, A. (1994). Post-traumatic stress disorder (PTSD): A rational emotive behavioral theory. *Journal of Rational-Emotive and Cognitive-Behavior Therapy, 12*(1), 3–25.
	Aaron Beck (1921–)	Beck, A. (1970). Cognitive therapy: Nature and relation to behavior therapy. *Behavior Therapy, 1,* 184–200. Beck, A. (1979). *Cognitive therapies and emotional disorders*. New York: Plume. Beck, A. (2000). *Prisoners of hate: The cognitive basis of anger, hostility and violence*. New York: Harper Books.

Box 3.1 Theorists and Their Works *(Continued)*

Theory	Original Theorists	Sample Publications
Humanistic Theories	Carl Rogers (1902–1987)	Rogers, C. R. (1940). The process of therapy. *Journal of Consulting Psychology*, *4*(5), 161–164. Rogers, C. R. (1951). *Client-centered therapy: Its current practice, implications, and theory*. Boston: Houghton Mifflin. Rogers, C. R. (1957). The necessary and sufficient conditions of therapeutic personality change. *Journal of Consulting Psychology*, *21*(2), 95–103.
	Abraham Maslow (1908–1969)	Maslow, A. (1954). *Motivation and personality*. New York: Harper. Maslow, A. (1962). *Toward a psychology of being*. New York: Van Nostrand.
	Rollo May (1909–1994)	May, R. (1967). *Psychology and the human dilemma*. New York: W. W. Norton. May, R. (1983). *The discovery of being: Writings in existential psychology*. New York: W. W. Norton.
Postmodern Theories	Steve de Shazer (1940–2005)	de Shazer, S. (1982). *Patterns of brief family therapy: An ecosystemic approach*. New York: Guilford Press. de Shazer, S. (2005). *More than miracles: The state of the art of solution-focused therapy*. Binghamton, NY: Haworth Press.
	Michael White (1948–2008)	White, M., & Epston, D. (1990). *Narrative means to therapeutic ends*. New York: W. W. Norton. White, M., & Morgan, A. (2006). *Narrative therapy with children and their families*. Adelaide, South Australia: Dulwich Centre Publications.
	David Epston (1944–)	White, M. & Epston, D. (1992). *Experience, contradiction, narrative, and imagination: Selected papers of David Epston & Micael White, 1989–1991*. Adelaide, South Australia: Dulwich Centre Publications. Epston, D., & Bowen, B. (2008). *Down under and up over: Travels with narrative therapy. London: Karnac Books.* Epston, D. (2013). *Ethnography, co-research and insider knowledges. International Journal of Narrative Therapy and Community Work, 2014(1),* 65–68.

(originated by Sigmund Freud), ego psychology (developed out of the psychosocial development model of Erik Erikson), object relations theory (from the work of Ronald Fairbairn, Melanie Klein, Margaret Mahler, and Donald Winnicott), psychodynamic therapy (neo-Freudian) (from the work of Karen Horney, Harry Stack Sullivan, and Erich Fromm), and self psychology (from Heinz Kohut) (Boyle et al., 2009; Singer, 2009; Walsh, 2013).

Cognitive-Behavioral Theories

Cognitive-behavioral theories represent an integration of cognitive theories and behavioral theories. While behavioral therapy is grounded in learning theory and classical conditioning, the role of cognitive processes and their influence on behaviors cannot be ignored. How one thinks and experiences the world informs behaviors. Cognitive theorist Aaron Beck observed that "an individual's belief systems, expectancies, and assumptions exert a strong influence on his state of well-being, as well as his directly observed behavior" (Beck, 1970, p. 184). Similarly, Albert Ellis, who developed rational emotive behavior therapy (a form of cognitive-behavioral therapy), worked under the assumption that "cognition, emotion, and behavior are not disparate human functions but are, instead, intrinsically integrated and holistic" (Ellis & MacLaren, 1998, p. 3). Cognitive-behavioral theories focus on present conditions in a client's life and identify cognitive distortions, conflicts in belief systems, and misconceptions that may contribute to problematic behaviors and symptoms in the client. Through restructuring how clients perceive their world and themselves in relation to it, symptoms can be reduced or eliminated and future behaviors changed. This process of change is referred to as cognitive restructuring. While cognitive-behavioral therapies (CBT) tend to focus on the present with a hope for an improved future, they also acknowledge that current behavioral and thinking problems often have their origins in the past. Both behavioral and cognitive therapies assume that a client's maladaptive behaviors and associated thinking patterns can be unlearned (Beck, 1970; Singer, 2009; Walsh, 2013).

Humanistic Theories

Humanistic theories emerged from the work of Carl Rogers, who posited that people have within them everything that they need to achieve their full potential. Humanistic psychology seeks to understand what it means to be fully human and to use the highest forms of humanity to illuminate lower forms so that we may more fully be. This supposes there is greatness in each of us to achieve and is at odds with the work of reductionists who look to abnormal psychology to explain human behavior. Rather than limiting our views to understanding illness and maladaptive behaviors, we might come to know what lifts people up toward the expression of their highest potential (Moss, 2015). Central to humanistic approaches is the therapeutic relationship, with a primary focus on the therapists being authentic and genuine and having unconditional positive regard for their clients. Humanistic therapeutic approaches are concerned with the here and now and place little emphasis on the past or future. Widely used humanistic therapies include person-centered counseling, Gestalt therapy, humanistic psychology, transactional analysis, and transpersonal psychology (Moss, 2015; Rogers, 1957; Singer, 2009; Walsh, 2013).

Postmodern Theories

The fourth category of practice theories is postmodern theories. Postmodern practice theories are grounded in the belief that reality is subjective in nature and therefore open to multiple interpretations, which themselves are influenced by personal experiences and values and the social and political norms and language in a given historical context. For example, in the context of twelfth-century religious influence, self-starvation was interpreted as a saintly act of women who had learned to detach from the world and to miraculously sustain themselves on spiritual sustenance alone. This starkly contrasts with the current scientific context of the twenty-first century, when self-starvation is considered one of the most resistant and difficult-to-treat psychological disorders and has been given the label of anorexia nervosa (Lock, Epston, & Maisel, 2004).

Postmodern theories reject therapeutic approaches that privilege the interpretation of a client's reality at the expense of others (e.g., the application of the

Diagnostic and Statistical Manual of Mental Disorders over the meaning given by the client). Postmodernists believe that since reality is a social construction, the therapeutic relationship is central to positive change in clients' lives by reconstructing the meaning attached to the contexts in which they live and experience life. Postmodern approaches argue that the very labeling of a group of client symptoms with a diagnosis serves to elevate the social worker to a "healthier" and therefore preferred status. The fundamental power differential that exists between the client and social worker within the traditional human service and medical models denigrates the client to a position of "other" or "less than" from the outset of the therapeutic relationship. Within the postmodern perspective, therapeutic interventions, then, are the means of those in power to gain and maintain control over others (Carpetto, 2008; Singer, 2009; Sommers-Flanagan & Sommers-Flanagan, 2004; Walsh, 2013).

Two popular and effective therapeutic approaches that grew out of postmodernism are narrative therapy (originated by David Epston and Michael White) and solution-focused therapy (developed by Steve de Shazer). The narrative therapy approach focuses on helping clients resolve their problems through restorying their lives. The narrative social worker sees the problems that the client presents with as socially constructed stories influenced by family and cultural norms and the dominant social, economic, and political interpretations of who they are. For example, in today's social, economic, and political context, there are dominant ideas about the poor, who they are, and why they are poor. Many of these interpretations of the poor place the problem within poor persons, making them problematic. Thus, to be poor is a problem with which comes many negative assumptions about individuals who are poor (i.e., they are lazy, unmotivated, uneducated, or trapped in a culture of poverty). The role of the narrative therapist is to help clients to restory their lives, or to find a more positive alternative story that frees them from their problem situation (Lock et al., 2004).

Solution-focused therapy seeks to help clients construct a preferred future state through the application of the miracle question strategy developed by de Shazer (1988):

> Suppose you were to go home tonight, and while you were asleep, a miracle happened and this problem was solved. How will you know the miracle happened? What will be different? (p. 5)

The miracle question becomes the core from which the client is guided by the therapist into the construction of change in his or her life (Carpetto, 2008).

It is unlikely that you will know *all* practice theories well, but it is important to read and know theories and therapies that are relevant to your particular area of social work practice in order to achieve competent application and to move with ease from one theoretical framework and practice model to another as needed. It is helpful to read the original theorists to gain a clear understanding of the foundation of theories, frameworks, perspectives, and therapies that you will be using in the practice setting.

Research-Informed Practice

Behavior: Use practice experience and theory to inform scientific inquiry and research

Critical Thinking Question: Select one category of practice theory, then explain its benefits to social work practice. What are the shortcomings of this body of theories?

Assess your understanding of categories of practice theory by taking this brief quiz.

META-FRAMEWORKS FOR PRACTICING SOCIAL WORK

Our earliest concern in social work practice was to understand the person in the context of his or her environment. However, initially this understanding of person in relation to his or her environment was limited to including important members of the client's family in the initial assessment. For example, it was common to gather information from family members, employers, and even neighbors, but the full understanding of the physical, economic, religious, social, and cultural impacts of the environment on clients' lives had not yet evolved. The importance of the role these factors had on influencing clients' lives emerged in the 1970s as new concepts were borrowed from general systems theory and ecology that would eventually lead the profession into the development of ecological systems theory or ecosystems theory (Beckett & Johnson, 1997; Bronfenbrenner, 1977; Germain, 1973; Germain & Gitterman, 2011; Miller, 1978).

Ecological perspective provides a broad theory base to social work practice and is used as a context for applying more practice-specific theories. Other overarching frameworks common to social work practice today include the life model (drawn from ecological perspective), the strengths perspective, and empowerment-based practice theory. This chapter provides an overview of these meta-frameworks or general theories for social work practice.

Systems Theory

People's environments extend beyond their immediate families and encompass the entirety of their lived experiences, including interactions with extended families, friends, neighborhoods, schools, religious centers, public laws, cultural norms, and the economic system. To understand the complex interactions among individuals and all the components of their environment, social work draws on general **systems theory** as a framework for understanding people's problems and for intervening in the lives of their clients. General systems theory was developed in the physical sciences and later expanded for application to the applied professions as a conceptual framework within which diverse theories could be organized. It was also seen as a framework that could bring a common language to practitioners, thus facilitating communications and cooperation (Beckett & Johnson, 1997).

A system is defined as a whole made up of many interacting parts or subsystems. For example, a person represents an individual subsystem within a larger family system, a family is seen as a subsystem within a larger community system, and a community is a subsystem within a larger societal system. Systems and subsystems have a structural relationship to each other and are separated by boundaries. Boundaries can be either impermeable, creating closed systems that are self-contained and allow few influences from the outside, or permeable, creating open systems that actively exchange with other subsystems and as such are constantly changing. The interactions or exchanges among subsystems are dynamic processes that keep open systems constantly in flux. As long as systems can readily adapt to change, the system will remain in balance or maintain a state of equilibrium. When major changes occur to a system where adaptation will occur over time, systems may be in a state of disequilibrium until the system can adapt and compensate for the change that has affected the system. For example, when 9/11 occurred in New York City, the change to the city system was so immense that it could not adapt to the massive destruction that occurred. With the response of many subsystems (communities, organizations, and individuals) and suprasystems (state, federal, and international responses), New York was slowly able to come back into balance or equilibrium and function again. However, this took a long period of time, and many businesses, families, and aspects of the economy were long in recovering. These enormous shocks to the subsystem of New York occurred in the context of a nation (suprasystem) that was struggling with the shattering of a long-held belief that in America individuals can count on feeling a sense of safety and security.

Assessment

Behavior: Apply knowledge of human behavior and the social environment, person-in-environment, and other multidisciplinary theoretical frameworks in the analysis of assessment data from clients and constituencies

Critical Thinking Question: Take a moment and explore your own life—what systems can you identify as immediately affecting your life? What are the positive/supporting features of these systems? Do you see any problems in any of the systems in your life?

In response to insults and disruption to systems, whether they be families, communities, or nations, social workers direct their attention to the interactions among individuals and the sum of all social forces or systems (Miley, O'Melia, & DuBois, 2013) so that they may "promote or restore a mutually beneficial interaction between individuals and society in order to improve the quality of life for everyone" (Minahan, 1981, p. 6). In the case of 9/11, this was an ongoing effort for many years on all levels of practice for the profession, as families continued to grieve their losses and cities confronted their vulnerability to threats of terrorist attacks. Professional systems of care can also be disrupted in trying to respond to massive needs that occur following man-made and natural disasters, such as 9/11 and Hurricane Katrina. For example, social work practitioners in New York City endured secondary traumatic stress and compassion fatigue as a result of witnessing the 9/11 disaster and then caring for so many traumatized individuals, families, and communities (Boscarino, Figley, & Adams, 2004), indicating a need for the New York City social work system of care to also restore equilibrium to itself.

Optimal functioning of an individual in the environment, whether it is the client or the professional social worker, requires subsystems that are functioning at an optimal level and that promote individual development toward self-actualization. System dysfunction is understood as functioning that limits or deters individuals from reaching innate potentials. System dysfunctions can occur at the individual, family, community, organizational, or societal level. Regardless of where the dysfunction originates within a system, it can create chaos that can be perpetuated throughout the associated subsystems. Our client Sarah disrupted many systems in her crisis around her pregnancy and interacted with many subsystems in an effort to bring balance back into her life. See Box 3.2 for a description of interactions between Sarah and the multiple subsystems in her environment. Justin, the young homeless client depicted in Box 3.A, is another example of how systems can dramatically impact an individual's life. See if you can identify the systems that are at work in shaping Justin's reality and future possibilities.

The primary goal of direct practice is to assess and improve the interaction of subsystems (the individual, family, group, community, and organization) within the context of a larger societal system. The social work profession recognizes the importance of addressing systems at three levels. The micro system is the individual and encompasses the individual's past history, experiences, unique personality, and accessibility to

Box 3.2 Sarah

When Sarah first came to the agency, she was a 17-year-old girl who was pregnant; as such, Sarah affected not only her life but also the lives of those around her. Sarah's family became quite distressed, reacted angrily, and expelled her from their home, leaving her to fend for herself. Confused and alone, Sarah dropped out of school in order to pursue employment to financially support herself and her forthcoming child. Sarah's limited education seriously impaired her ability to become self-sufficient and to support her child in the future. The employment and wage system is geared toward promoting people with education and skills and has few supports for young single parents without an adequate education. Sarah's baby will also face many challenges, such as poverty and undernutrition, which in turn will have a direct impact on the baby's physical, mental, and psychological growth and development. Cultural norms that support a traditional family structure may negatively affect the psychological well-being of both Sarah and her child, as they understand themselves to be outside the norms of their family and community. The social worker at the level of direct practice worked with Sarah across a variety of subsystems in order to restore stability to Sarah's life. The social worker worked on the individual system through assessment and counseling with Sarah, on the family system by reestablishing relationships with her family, on organizational systems by linking her to a prenatal care clinic and parenting classes and connecting her to an educational program where she completed her GED, on the economic system by assisting her in an employment search, and on the federal benefits system by helping her apply and receive Temporary Assistance to Needy Families, (TANF) housing assistance, and Medicaid welfare services.

Box 3.A Now You Try It . . . Identifying Systems, Needs, and Interventions

Justin recently exited foster care when he turned 21 and aged out of the system. He had been in foster care on and off since the age of eight years. He finds himself in a homeless shelter with only three weeks of guaranteed residency before having to move out of this temporary "home" as well. Justin has few marketable skills, as he dropped out of high school at 16 and has never been on his own before. His daily living skills are limited, but he has learned to do his laundry, locate the local soup kitchens for food, and find enough day jobs to keep his basic daily needs met. He also sells his blood and plasma. However, he does not earn enough to manage rent or transportation when he leaves the shelter. He has little knowledge of how to prepare for permanent employment and few job skills to market. In addition, Justin was diagnosed with attention-deficit/hyperactivity disorder (ADHD) when he was 12 and has been maintained on medication since that time. With the loss of his Medicaid benefits when he left foster care, Justin also lost his ability to purchase his medication. He has one week's supply of pills remaining.

As the social worker attending to clients in the homeless shelter where Justin temporarily resides, identify the systems and subsystems that are active in Justin's life. Then identify the types of needs and interventions needed within each system in order for Justin to begin to build some stability in his life.

System Involved	System Needs	System Interventions

resources. The mezzo system is the small group, such as the family, which has its own complexities and dynamics. Such small groups strongly influence and are influenced by their individual members. Community organizations and agencies also fall under the mezzo system classification. The macro system is the large group, such as the societal institutions of work, schools, and the religious community (Bronfenbrenner, 1977; Zastrow, 2013). To this aim, Zastrow (2013) put forward four goals of social work practice that address all levels of system intervention:

1. To support the development of people's problem-solving, coping, and developmental abilities
2. To connect people with systems that offer them opportunities, resources, and services
3. To ensure the humane operation of systems that respond to people's needs
4. To advance social policy

Individual, community, and national systems interact along a continuum with the aim of enhancing system performance so that healthy functioning dominates and dysfunction is minimized. This environment or ecology of systems plays an important part in the development of individuals, families, and communities. Social work is at its best when the transactions of these systems promote growth and development, and creates an environment that is amenable to positive growth (Ashford & Lecroy, 2013). In Box 3.3, the social worker intervenes at the micro level when involved in individual assessment and counseling with Sarah, at the mezzo level when working with Sarah's family and linking Sarah to the prenatal clinic and parenting class, and at the macro level when intervening with the educational, employment, and social welfare systems. Practice interventions at all three system levels were necessary to bringing stability to Sarah's world and to support her growth and progress over the two years that followed.

Ecological Perspective

Ecological perspective, or the person-in-environment perspective of social work practice, expanded and benefited from the transfer of general systems theory in the physical sciences to the living systems of the human family. The work of Germain (1973, 1979) and Germain and Gitterman (2011) further deepened our understanding of the complexities of the human condition in the context of various subsystems in their groundbreaking ecological perspective. Borrowing concepts from ecology (the study of organisms and their relationship with their environment), the ecological perspective provided more concrete ways for understanding the person in environment than systems theory had been able to do. For example, the notion of "goodness of fit" between a person and the environment sprang from the ecological framework and provides a lens through which to assess the extent to which a person's adaptive behaviors promote growth and health (a good fit) or support a decline of physical, social, or psychological functioning (bad fit). Other important concepts that are part of understanding a person in the environment are the role of stress and coping measures that individuals bring to their environment and their ability to relate or build attachments, friendships, and positive family relationships, all of which serve as resources when meeting life's challenges (Germain & Gitterman, 2011).

The ecological perspective also challenges social workers to think in much more complex patterns that capture the mutually shaping back-and-forth interactions among individuals, groups, organizations, and institutions (Germain & Gitterman, 2011). Logical thinking tends to be linear, where we assume a cause-and-effect relationship between two events, whereas "ecological thinking" requires that we understand the back-and-forth interactions of a person in the environment. In logical thinking, A causes B, and that's the end of the story. In ecological thinking, A has an impact on B, which changes B, which in turn has an impact on A, which changes A, which in turn changes B, and so on. For example, a mother who views the challenges of toilet training her two-year-old as a normal developmental stage and major developmental accomplishment for her child will approach the task with greater ease and excitement than a mother who interprets her child's inconsistency in toileting as defiant behavior. The latter mother sees her child as a problem, while the first mother does not. Clearly, the mother who views toilet training as a normal part of her child's growth and development will be able to create a more supportive environment for the child (good fit) to complete this critical task than the mother who sees the lack of toileting mastery in her two-year-old as a discipline problem (bad fit). Each mother's responses shape the child's sense of self and feelings of competence. To the extent to which we experience success in shaping our environments, we grow in self-esteem and feelings of competence (Bronfenbrenner & Ceci, 1994; Zastrow, 2013).

This mother–child scenario reflects Bronfenbrenner's ecological systems theory and how the relationships among systems and system components impact a child's development. A new component recently added to this model is the awareness of the child's biology, which interacts with his or her environmental systems and affects the child's development. Renaming the theory *bioecological systems theory* has brought new attention to the study of a child's development and the need to consider the child in his or her immediate environment as well as the interaction with the larger environment (Bronfenbrenner, 1977; Bronfenbrenner & Ceci, 1994; Guhn & Goelman, 2011; Paquette & Ryan, 2001).

From a social work perspective, mothers are part of the environment that either enhances or deters their child's developmental potential. The reciprocal nature of the relationship between individuals and their environments means that as individuals we move and shape our surroundings and that our surroundings have a profound effect on us as well. For example, the mother who acknowledges and praises her child's mastery of toilet training affects the child's sense of competence and self-worth. As the child responds with pride in his or her accomplishment, the mother feels competent in her role as a mother. Both the mother and the child mutually shape their sense of well-being. Conversely, the mother who sees toilet training as a discipline problem and responds with anger and punishment equally influences her child's sense of self-worth. The child may respond with fear, confusion, and a feeling of inadequacy in meeting his or her mother's demands. The child's failure at toilet training may affirm the mother's suspicions of her own inadequacies as a parent. In both cases, the child and the mother mutually contribute to the stress or satisfaction they individually experience around the task of toilet training and the role of mothering. Box 3.3 provides a summary of important concepts central to understanding the ecological perspective in assessing the goodness of fit between a person and his or her environment. The case study in Box 3.I demonstrates how the theory of ecological perspective can inform practice with a grieving client.

Box 3.3 Ecological Perspective Concepts

Person–Environment Fit: The relationship between an individual or group and his or her physical and social environment within a historical and cultural context. When the environment supports growth and health, then a good fit between the person and the environment is said to exist.

Adaptations: Internal or external changes to self or one's environment that maintain or enhance the goodness of fit between an individual and the environment.

Life Stressors: Critical life events or issues that disrupt the goodness of fit between an individual and the environment. Common issues include traumatic events, such as the loss of a loved one, one's job, or one's health; major life transitions, such as marriage, divorce, or retirement; or larger issues that impair the goodness of fit and often bring on other life stressors, such as poverty and oppression.

Stress: An internal response to life stressors that produces negative emotions, such as guilt, anxiety, depression, despair, or fear, and result in a person feeling less competent, producing a lower level of relatedness, self-esteem, and self-direction.

Coping Measures: Behaviors that individuals initiate to respond to life stressors in ways that restore or heighten the goodness of fit between an individual and the environment.

Relatedness: One's ability to form attachments to friends, family, coworkers, and neighbors and attain a sense of belonging in the world.

Competence: When individuals are provided with opportunities to shape their environment from infancy on, they have the opportunity to develop a sense of efficacy. Ongoing experiences of efficacy accumulate to provide a feeling of competence at shaping and managing one's environment.

Self-Esteem: Represents an assessment of oneself as worthy of love and respect. People with high self-esteem feel competent, valued, and respected. Those with low self-esteem perceive themselves as inadequate, unlovable, inferior, and unworthy and often experience depression. How we feel about ourselves deeply influences our thinking and behaviors.

Self-Direction: The capacity to make decisions, take control of one's life, and direct it in desired paths while taking responsibility for one's decisions and navigating one's life with respect to others' rights and needs. The ability to self-direct is strongly related to feelings of power and powerlessness. If individuals are not provided with opportunities to make decisions and direct their own lives, they will likely feel powerless and lack self-direction. Living in oppressive conditions often robs people of their power and can profoundly influence their ability to self-direct.

Habitat: Refers to the nature and location of the person's "home" territory or where he or she feels most at home. Some terms often applied to habitat are "nesting places," "home range," or "territory." For humans, it may include home community, school, workplace, or local hangout and people's behaviors within these spaces.

Niche: Social position or ranking within one's community or the status one holds within the family, with coworkers, or in the community. For example, a man may be a patriarch at home, the boss at work, and a buddy at the local pub, all indicating high levels of status across his habitat. Conversely, a man might be a drifter to his family, undependable at work, and homeless in the community, all of which signify low status across the habitat.

Source: Germain and Gitterman (2011).

Life Model of Social Work Practice

In response to changing practice needs in the 1970s, Germain and Gitterman (1997, 2008) developed a life model practice method that implemented the concepts of the ecological perspective into a practice approach. It differed from popular practice approaches in that it did not focus on the deficits of a person but rather modeled interactions in the practice relationship around life processes and focused on client strengths. The goals of the life model are not to provide remedial treatment but rather to do the following:

- Promote health, growth, and the expression of one's potential
- Make changes to the environment that will promote and sustain growth and well-being
- Improve the person–environment fit (Germain & Gitterman, 1997, 2008)

Box 3.1 Theory into Practice—Ecological Perspective and Grief Therapy: Case Study

Grief Therapy: Erich Lindemann (1944) first introduced the idea that grief was a unique syndrome that required specific clinical techniques to address it appropriately and effectively. Worden (2009) distinguishes grief counseling from grief therapy, noting that counseling guides clients through acute grief, while grief therapy focuses on helping people resolve disabling or prolonged complicated grief through the use of clinical tools, skills, and family and community resources appropriate to the client's needs and environment.

Janine is a 45-year-old recently widowed professional photographer and mother of three teenage girls, ages 13, 16, and 19. Janine has always counted herself lucky to have been born into a well-established family of successful business entrepreneurs, which gave her opportunities for exploring the world and her passions throughout her developmental years and into her chosen career of photography. She and her husband of 20 years, Roger, an environmental attorney, lived a well-established, stable, upper-middle-class life throughout their married life until his sudden and unexpected death six months ago. They have resided in the same historic neighborhood in the suburbs of Chicago for the past 15 years and have been involved in community life with neighborhood friends, volunteered at their daughters' schools, and served on several boards of directors for nonprofit agencies that promote the arts, especially among underprivileged children. Since the death of her husband, Janine has found it increasingly difficult to meet her professional and community obligations and to be attentive to her daughters' needs. She is prone to depression and bouts of uncontrollable sobbing and feels empty and alone and unprepared for navigating this new territory of loss in her life. Family members have been supportive but have returned to their own lives and routines, adjusting to the loss of Roger.

Over the past two weeks, Janine's oldest daughter, Christina, has been increasingly concerned about her mother. After contacting the 24-hour crisis line and talking with a volunteer, Christina is even more convinced that her mother needs help.

Christina finally convinced her mother to reach out for help. Although not willingly, Janine has agreed to give therapy a chance. Now you are sitting with her, and she can barely catch her breath, as she cannot stop crying. You sit with her and do not say much other than to give her the space to "let go." After about 30 minutes, Janine is finally able to talk in very general terms about how hard her life is now and how much she misses Roger. She tells you that she had the perfect life and the perfect husband. They were best friends, and she can barely make it through the day, as she aches so much for him. Losing Roger has changed her world completely, and she no longer feels the rhythm and balance that life once offered.

She apologizes for spending the entire time crying and gets up to leave. You ask her to stay, as you are concerned about her leaving in such a highly emotional state. She sits back down and states, "I am so sad and so miserable. Will this ever get better?" As a social worker, you know that things will eventually get better for her, but it will be a different life, and Janine will eventually find new things, interests, and people to bring the rhythm and balance back into her life. You say, "You were fortunate to have Roger in your life and feel unsure about how to carry on without him. Grieving takes time, and we all deal with death in very different ways. I can support you as you start the process of grieving, but you must be kind to yourself. You have children who love you and count on you too. I believe that you will feel better and will find peace, but it takes time. Please consider coming back next week."

Janine agrees to meet with you next week. After the session ends, she tells Christina that you, the social worker, were hopeful, and therefore she felt a tinge of hope too.

The life model application in practice guides the practitioner in assessing life stressors, stress levels, and coping mechanisms in the client and seeks to use interventions that restore or enhance relatedness, self-esteem, and self-direction. Specific goals toward these aims are outlined and established with the client. The life model is grounded in the principle of empowerment and as such is particularly sensitive to cultural, physical, and social contexts. Aspects of empowerment that are central to the life model include the following:

- Client and social worker as partners in change
- Recognizing clients as expert on their lives
- Sensitivity to the power differential in the client–social worker relationship (Germain & Gitterman, 1997, 2008)

Box 3.B Now You Try It . . . Applying the Life Model

Review the case study of Janine in the Theory into Practice Box 3.I.

1. What strengths can you identify in Janine?
2. What resources can you identify in Janine's environment?
3. Suggest one change that Janine might make to her environment that may help her create a better person in environment fit.

The evolving working relationship between the client and social worker within the empowerment practice principles is geared to enhancing clients' access to personal power and in turn promoting a sense of self-worth. When clients have the ability to experience efficacy in their relationship to their environment, they grow in feelings of competence, promoting decision making that gives direction to clients' lives (Germain & Gitterman, 1997, 2008). Using the guidance provided in Box 3.B, try to apply some of the life model concepts to the case study of Janine presented in Box 3.I.

Human Rights and Justice

Behavior: Apply their understanding of social, economic, and environmental justice to advocate for human rights at the individual and system levels

Critical Thinking Question: How is the life model of social work practice similar to the ecological perspective? How is it different?

Strengths Perspective

The **strengths perspective** of social work practice springs from the values that permeate the profession—inherent worth, human dignity, and self-determination. Putting these values into action requires that we believe in the unleashed power that resides in all human beings and the possibility of change. Client strengths become the resources for change that move them forward to growth, mastery, and self-actualization (Miley et al., 2013). Box 3.4 summarizes the assumptions that underlie the strengths perspective.

An important aspect of the strengths perspective is that it provides social work practitioners with an alternative framework for practice that is counter to the deficit model that has dominated human services perspectives (Saleebey, 2013). Often, social workers find themselves in practice contexts that subscribe to the medical model of practice that focuses on remedial care and "fixing" what is broken. If social workers are not armed with theoretical frameworks that emphasize the inherent worth of

Box 3.4 Underlying Assumptions of the Strengths Perspective

1. Everyone is imbued with abilities, capacities, talents, and competencies.
2. People have an inherent capacity for growth and change.
3. Life traumas may have a negative impact on people's lives, but they can also serve as a source of growth.
4. The upper limits of people's ability to grow and overcome adversity is unknown and unknowable.
5. Problems do not reside within the person but occur in the transactions within and across systems.
6. People are experts on their own lives.
7. People's friends, families, and communities are reservoirs of resources that are or can be made available.
8. Growth is future focused on what is possible.
9. Mastery and competence are best attained within a supportive process.
10. People generally know what will and will not be helpful in overcoming the challenges they face.

Sources: Miley et al. (2013); Sheafor and Horejsi (2015).

Box 3.5 Comparison of Deficit Model and Strengths Perspective

Deficit Perspective	Strengths Perspective
Cumulative symptoms = diagnosis	Individual uniqueness, abilities, talents, resources = strength
Interventions focus on the diagnosis of "problems"	Interventions focus on possibilities
Practitioner doubts client stories and becomes the "expert" in client's life	Practitioner views the client as the expert in his or her life and comes to know the person from the inside out
Adult problems are rooted in childhood traumas	Childhood traumas are not predictive of later life events
Treatment is directed by a treatment plan devised by the practitioner	Interventions are directed by client's aspirations
Client's possibilities in life are limited by his or her pathology	Life possibilities are open
Resources for therapeutic work reside in the knowledge and skills of the practitioner	Resources for therapeutic work reside in client, family, and community
Therapeutic work is focused on reducing symptoms and their negative impact on client	Therapeutic work is focused on moving the client forward in living into his or her possibilities and vision for his or her life

Source: Adapted from Saleebey's (1996) comparison of pathology and strengths.

individuals, families, and communities, it is all too easy to slip into a deficit model of practice. Box 3.5 provides a contrast of pathology (inherent in the medical model) with a strengths perspective.

When using a strengths perspective in practice, social workers use a wide range of practice principles, ideas, skills, and techniques to promote and draw out the resources of clients and those in their environments to initiate change, energize the change process, and sustain change once it has occurred (Miley et al., 2013).

It is not uncommon to automatically fall into a deficit perspective when in contact with individuals who have obvious physical challenges. Using the cultural competence case study below, identify how you might begin to transcend the "deficits" perspective and reframe challenges into strengths.

Developing Cultural Competence

Michael is a new student in the social work program, having recently transferred from another university in another state. He shows up in your social work practice class at the beginning of your second semester of your junior year. You have been in social work classes with most of your classmates for over a year now, and everyone is familiar and chummy with each other. Michael is new and an outsider. In addition, he has obvious differences with others in the class: he is wheelchair bound, significantly overweight, and of Haitian descent, speaking with a heavy accent and making it difficult to understand him. After one class together, you notice that Michael is eager to participate in class, seems well-read, and sports a big smile much of the time. From a culturally competent strengths perspective, how might you frame Michael's cultural differences around mobility, weight, ethnicity, and speech as strengths and/or resources? Use the strengths perspective demonstrated in Box 3.6 to guide you in your deliberations.

Box 3.6 Personal Power: A Case Study

Sylvia perceives herself to be self-sufficient and holds an expectation that she can and will take care of herself. She does this by accessing resources from 1) her friends, such as support, socializing, and fun, and borrowing items when needed; 2) her family, such as information on the pros and cons of owning a home, a place of comfort to return to for visits, referrals to family contacts when trusted information is needed, or a loan for a down payment on her new condo; and 3) the community, such as locating retail stores to purchase her needs and community agencies that will support her in meeting life and role expectations (i.e., a tax preparation firm or gaining membership into the local YWCA, where she develops an exercise routine to support her health). Sylvia may experience interpersonal power in persuading her father to give her a loan or her knowledge that she is highly regarded by her peers and colleagues at work, which is affirmed by positive feedback and acknowledgments of her contributions to the work community. To the extent that Sylvia can access and gain control over resources in all areas of her life, she possesses political power. For example, Sylvia's ability to negotiate a raise with her boss at work, voice her opinion at a town meeting and influence local policy on how to spend town funds, or sit as a board member on a local social service agency in her community are just a few ways in which she and others can exercise political power. In each of these examples, access to and control over resources are actualized.

To intervene from a strengths perspective effectively, practitioners must first examine their own underlying perspectives and resulting language about problems in society. Do you fundamentally believe that people are powerful and able to direct their own lives in positive ways, or do you believe them to be powerless and in need of repair? Your perspective will be communicated in your language. For example, do you see people as having "problems" or facing "challenges" that, while difficult, can transform their lives? Problems have a way of demoralizing us, making us feel like victims or failures, and generally bringing us down. Challenges are viewed as opportunities for growth and inspire us to pull on our internal and external resources to meet the challenge and attain our goals. Challenges lift us up. For example, an immigrant from Haiti with limited English-speaking skills may struggle with finding her place in a new country and community, but the external resource of strong family connectedness of her culture (even from a distance) can be used to move her forward toward stability and create the life she envisioned when she left her home country. When you see unusual behaviors, do you see pathology or strengths? When social workers focus on pathology as the central point in working with clients, it may block their ability to see the strengths that lie within the client or to use techniques in the helping process that will uncover client strengths. When designing interventions, are you focused on undoing the past or creating a future? A "past" perspective in treatment assumes that something in the past happened that caused the client to be "not okay" today. Overemphasis on the past prevents the use of the present in exploring resources and options and planning for the desired future. Shifting our focus to the present and future can have the power of releasing the past and giving up negative assumptions about ourselves that keep us stuck in positions we would rather not be in (Miley et al., 2013). Yes, problems exist, as do pathologies and past events that stop us in our tracks. We cannot ignore these realities, but we can redirect our thinking in ways that see beyond these negative and deficit interpretations of clients' lives. Dennis Saleebey captured the challenge in transition to a vision of strength in practice:

> We are not asking you to forget the problems and pains that people may bring to your doorstep. Rather, we are asking that you honor and understand those dilemmas, and

> that you also revise, fill out, expand, illuminate your understanding with the realization that the work to be done, in the end, depends on the resources, reserves, and assets in and around the individual, family or community. (Saleebey, 2001, p. 221)

Applying the strengths perspective requires that the social work practitioner reorient from a deficit or pathology framework to a strengths and possibility perspective. In interacting with clients, we ask ourselves, What is he doing right? What life skills does she possess that she can bring to bear on the challenges at hand? What untapped resources does he hold within him? What other resources reside in her family, friends, and community that can lift her up to meet today's challenges and create a preferred vision of her future?

Empowerment-Based Practice Model

Social work has a long tradition in empowerment practice, dating back to the early settlement houses. In more recent years, empowerment-based practice emerged from work with women and people of color and built on the belief that members in groups with limited social and political power suffer personal loss of power and opportunities across systems in mainstream society (Gutiérrez, DeLois, & GlenMaye, 1995; Turner & Maschi, 2015). The concept of power in the context of empowerment practice has been defined by Gutiérrez et al. (1995) in three ways:

1. The ability to get what one wants
2. The ability to influence how others think, feel, act, or, believe
3. The ability to influence the distribution of resources in social systems such as family, organization, community, and society (p. 535)

Power described in this way suggests that practice interventions will need to occur at multiple levels of practice (individual, family, organization, community, and national levels) and that the dimensions of power encompass the personal, interpersonal, and political levels. To have personal power is experienced as a sense of control over one's life and feelings of competence. Individuals who experience internal power feel competent in their ability to take care of themselves, to access resources as needed across systems, and to contribute to community and system resources. When we have interpersonal power, we have the ability to influence others, know ourselves to be effective in interactions with others, and are highly regarded by others (Gutiérrez & Ortega, 1991; Miley et al., 2013; Turner & Maschi, 2015). When people experience political power, their interactions with their environment results in access to and control over resources. Box 3.6 illustrates how the client perceives issues of personal power and how the client uses this to meet her needs.

Human Rights and Justice

Behavior: Engage in practices that advance social, economic, and environmental justice

Critical Thinking Question: Identify the central concept of the empowerment model. How is this concept applied and brought to life in direct social work practice?

Activating clients' internal power requires that social workers understand the context of clients' lives (person-in-environment) and perceive clients as reservoirs of latent power waiting to be awakened (strengths perspective). Helping clients attain personal, interpersonal, and political power requires that social work practitioners collaborate with clients and assist them in structuring interventions at the individual,

Policy to Practice Veterans Affairs Supportive Housing

In cooperation with the U.S. Department of Housing and Urban Development, Veterans Affairs provides assistance to homeless veterans through the Veterans Affairs Supportive Housing (VASH) program. Federal funding is allocated to local public housing authorities, and as of September 2013, more than 58,000 Housing Choice Vouchers were available to assist homeless veterans in acquiring permanent housing. The program also provides clinical and supportive services and intensive case management to homeless veterans (U.S. Department of Veteran Affairs, 2014).

Louis: Kim, there is a shelter program, Safe Harbor, in Indianapolis that offers alcohol treatment, counseling, and medical and vocational services. It is close to the VA clinic too. You work at the shelter and get paid. Plus, they only work with vets.

Kim: Okay, I am willing to see the place, but no promises.

Louis: No promises, understood.

Kim: But I could stay there for six months?

Louis: Once you finish the Safe Harbor program, the VA offers a voucher program called VASH, Veteran's Affairs Supportive Housing. Your apartment is free for the six months. During that time, you are expected to work, but after month 6, you are on your own.

Kim: Then what?

Louis: Once you have a job, you pay for what you can, and the VASH vouchers will cover the rest. You will always have affordable housing.

Watch Case Study #6, in which Louis the social worker offers Kim, a homeless veteran, the opportunity to enroll in VASH (Veteran's Affairs Supportive Housing) program to help turn her life around. Kim completes the Safe Harbor/ VASH program. Watch to the video clip as she checks in with Louis following her program completion. In what ways did the VASH policy empower Kim into a new life?

For more information on the VASH program, visit the U.S. Department of Veteran Affairs website.

family, and community levels. The work of social work practitioners is to recognize, facilitate, and promote clients' connections with their internal power (resources) and to mobilize those connections across systems in ways that increase their mastery in shaping their environments in desirable ways. Social workers must also look for ways to enhance clients' feelings of competency and clients' ability to forge effective relationships. Finally, social workers must assist clients in identifying ways to draw on and contribute to community resource pools. To do this, the focus of practice must be on accentuating client potentials and resiliencies and minimizing client vulnerabilities (Miley et al., 2013). In video Case Study #6, Kim the homeless veteran is empowered through the Veterans Affairs Supportive Housing program. This program also empowers social workers in helping clients access community resources and in turn improve their lives. See the policy to practice box below which provides an example of how policy can empower social workers and clients.

Assess your understanding of meta-frameworks for practicing social work by taking this brief quiz.

SUMMARY

- Effective and accountable social work practitioners ground their practice in evidence-based practice strategies that are supported by a wide range of practice theories, perspectives, and models appropriate to their specific area of practice.
- Whether social workers are working from a meta-theoretical framework of ecological perspective, a strength-based practice, or an empowerment model, they will

need to draw on many narrower "target" theories as well to meet the needs of their diverse clients and the circumstances in which they find themselves.

- Client problems, values, cultures, and belief systems will also influence how social workers select, interpret, and apply theories that will guide their actions of practice.

APPLY IT

1. Watch all three sessions of **Interactive Case Study #2** of Anthony and social worker James. Identify and consider the systems that Anthony is involved with in his life. What systems are problematic? What systems need some intervention by the social worker?
2. Watch all three sessions of **Interactive Case Study #4** of Maria, Mrs. Anderson, and social worker Nicole. Using the strengths perspective, make a list of Maria's strengths and resources (both internal and external) available to her. What possibilities do you envision for Maria?
3. Watch all five sessions of **Interactive Case Study #6** of Kim and social worker Louis. In what ways does Louis use his skills and knowledge of resources to lead Kim to self-empowerment?

Assess Your Competence

Use the scale below to rate your current level of achievement on the following concepts or skills associated with each competency presented in the chapter:

1	2	3
I can accurately describe the concept or skill	I can consistently identify the concept or skill when observing and analyzing practice activities	I can competently implement the concept or skill in my own practice

_______ Can identify and describe the four major categories of direct practice.

_______ Can articulate the correct application, focus, and desired result of direct practice theories presented in this chapter.

_______ Can understand and articulate the concept of meta-frameworks and their application in the social work practice.

_______ Can name and describe the five major meta-framework theories.

4

The Cultural Context of Practice: Using Interviewing Skills Effectively

GINO SANTA MARIA/FOTOLIA

LEARNING OBJECTIVES

- Articulate the language of cultural competence and its relevance to social work practice with diverse client populations.
- Describe how values, beliefs, and attitudes shape one's cultural perspective and can limit one's cultural awareness.
- Self-assess one's level of intercultural sensitivity using the Developmental Model of Intercultural Sensitivity.
- Identify multiple areas of cross-cultural knowledge needed to be considered a cultural competent social worker.
- Differentiate between cross-cultural knowledge base and culturally competent skill set when serving diverse clients.
- Describe special populations encountered in social work practice and verbalize specific approaches to assessing the needs of each group.

CHAPTER OUTLINE

How well we understand our clients and their problems is, to a large extent, dependent on how well we understand the context of their lives. Nothing influences our values, our commitments, our life practices, and our worldviews more than the culture into which we were born, socialized by, and live in. To this end, cultural competence is an indispensable part of the social worker's skill set. In different cultural contexts, the same skill can have very different meanings. For example, touching someone's arm in a gesture of caring can be perceived as either comforting or invasive, depending on the client's cultural traditions. The social worker's interaction with the client should be informed by knowledge of the client's cultural background and value system as well as by the social worker's self-knowledge of any biases or gaps in cultural knowledge he or she may bring to the helping relationship. The dialogue between social worker and client is thus embedded in a cultural context on both sides. The **culturally aware** social worker approaches the client relationship mindfully and with the intent and ability to adjust the interview to best meet the client's needs.

INTRODUCTION TO CULTURAL COMPETENCE

As the U.S. population grows more diverse by nationality, race, age, sexual orientation, and transgender identity, diversity issues move to the fore of social work practice and public policy. With the growing diversity within the population, **cultural competence** is an increasingly critical factor in the success of any social work intervention. The U.S. Census Bureau estimates that 1) one in five Americans will be age 65 by 2030, 2) more than half the population will belong to a minority group by 2044, and, 3) one in five will be foreign born by 2060 (Colby & Ortman, 2015). Social workers understand diversity as a positive resource that clients can draw on when facing challenges in life (Saleebey, 2013). The strengths perspective in social work practice places culture at the center of the helping process as a valuable resource and should guide the design and planning of client interventions. The cultural competent social worker builds on empowering client cultural strengths (Fong & Furuto, 2001). Although general cultural knowledge is useful, it is your interaction with the client that will enable you to assess the client's cultural identity and subsequently work toward a culturally congruent intervention.

Cultures are not static or uniform but rather change in response to new circumstances, such as economic conditions, technological innovations, and demographic shifts. Cultures often contain a wide variety of intragroup variation, defined as cohesive and distinctly different groups that exist within the larger culture. For example, there is a vibrant Latino culture in the United States, and in the broad Latino culture, there are Latinos of Mexican, Puerto Rican, or Central American descent; first- versus second-generation or earlier families; and so on. These within-group differences can be as great as the variation between larger cultures. Each culture is also influenced by other cultures. Some groups, such as the Amish, are relatively isolated from the larger society, while others are more assimilated into the dominant culture. At the individual level, clients may identify with more than one culture. For example, a teenager whose mother is a Japanese American and whose father is of German extraction may be comfortable in both of her parents' cultures of origin. Nearly 9 million Americans identified themselves as being of two or more races in the 2010 census (U.S. Census Bureau, 2011).

Increasingly, an individual is able to draw from a number of cultures in responding to any given situation. The give-and-take of the interview process is what enables the social worker to identify and best utilize the combination of cultural strengths the client brings to the helping relationship. It is important to understand the impact of oppression and racism on clients' lives. While racism affects all members of society, whether they are discriminated against or not, members of historically disadvantaged groups face formidable challenges in many areas of their lives. Social workers need to understand the institutional barriers to services clients may face. These can include poor housing; lack of access to good schools, jobs, and public transportation; greater risk of being arrested; and environmental degradation and loss of community due to the tendency of

Box 4.1 Core Cultural Concepts

Culture is a quality of all communities of people identified by geographic location, common characteristics, or similar interests. This includes values, norms, beliefs, language, and traditions. For example, there is a rural culture, a drug culture, a homeless culture, a teenage culture, an Italian culture, and a white supremacist culture, to name a few.

Cultural diversity refers to human differences as generated by membership in various identifiable human groups. Cultural diversity includes not only race, ethnicity, and gender but also nationality, language, sexual orientation, persons with physical or cognitive impairments, religion, socioeconomic status, political persuasion, and age. This is not an exhaustive list.

Cultural awareness is the state of knowing one's own values and biases and requires an ongoing self-exploration of one's own cultural background and the values and attitudes that go with it. A process of an ongoing self-examination builds cultural awareness regarding individuals and groups that are different from you. Cultural awareness guards against cultural imposition in social work practice (Campinha-Bacote, 2002; Leininger & McFarland, 2002).

Cultural imposition is the tendency to impose one's individual beliefs, values, and assumptions on another culture or individual different from oneself (Leininger, 1978).

Cultural encounter is the willingness to seek out face-to-face experiences with diverse individuals, groups, and communities in order to increase one's cultural knowledge and cultural sensitivity (Campinha-Bacote, 2002).

Cultural desire is a component of caring where social workers really want to build their cultural knowledge, skill, and awareness to better serve their cross-cultural clients.

Social workers possess **cultural sensitivity** when they have an attitude of acceptance, respect, and appreciation for each client's cultural uniqueness and a willingness to learn about each client's uniqueness.

Social workers are said to be **culturally responsive** when they demonstrate the ability to use client perspective–centered practice skills as a method to achieve cultural competence with each client they serve. An example of cultural responsiveness would be knowing which interviewing strategies are most effective in communicating with a client who is a Somali immigrant.

Cultural competence embodies a set of values, behaviors, and practices that enables individuals and organizations to work effectively across cultures and reflects a valuing, honoring, and respect for diverse beliefs, language, and interpersonal styles represented across clients and client groups. Practitioners recognize cross-cultural help-seeking behaviors and provide services and treatment options that match the preferences and cultural needs of clients. Acquiring cultural competence evolves and changes over time as cultural knowledge and skills expand (National Center for Cultural Competence [NCCC], n.d.).

low-income areas to serve as sites for heavy industry and freeway development or neighborhood gentrification. Box 4.1 introduces some core concepts necessary to understand and apply when developing cultural competence.

Cultural competence is achieved by identifying and understanding the needs and help-seeking behaviors of diverse individuals, and recognizing that culturally competent social work practice and service delivery is driven by client-preferred choices that recognize the unique cultural needs of clients being served (NCCC, n.d.). At its foundation, cultural competence requires an attitude of accepting and valuing diversity, cultural knowledge, and skills; an awareness of one's own biases; and a desire to learn more about cultural diversity through cultural encounters and training so that one can achieve culturally sensitive client engagement. Campinha-Bacote (2002) offers a cultural competence model that reflects the core components of cultural competence (see Figure 4.1).

The National Association of Social Workers (NASW, 2001) provides 10 standards for cultural competence in social work practice to guide social workers toward developing a culturally competent practice and can be read

? Assess your understanding of cultural competence by taking this brief quiz.

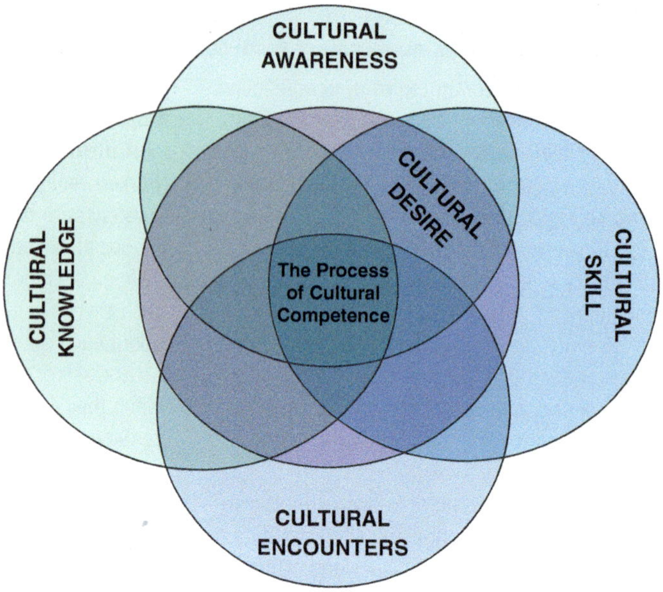

Figure 4.1
The Process of Cultural Competence in the Delivery of Health Care Services

Source: Campinha-Bacote (2002). The process of cultural competence in the delivery of health care services: A model of care. *Journal of Transcultural Nursing, 13*(3), 181–184; Transcultural C.A.R.E. Associates. Reprinted with permission.

in full on the NASW website. Many of these standards will be discuss in detail throughout the remainder of the chapter.

ATTITUDES

Values, beliefs, and attitudes underlie most of our choices and decisions in life. We are often unconscious of them until we are confronted with others different from our own. This often occurs when you move outside your culture of origin. When you are born into a culture, your worldview is conditioned by the values, norms, beliefs, language, and traditions of that culture. You are raised to value the things that the culture values, and it can be difficult to see the ways in which your attitudes, beliefs, and behaviors are not central to how others view the world. When cultural awareness is first experienced, people begin to understand that the attitudes, values, and beliefs they have been raised with and taken for granted are, to a great extent, specific to their culture of origin. People tend to be conditioned into specific roles in their home culture. These roles can be related to gender, age, class status, or some other arbitrary attribute. It is easy to conclude that values and actions arising from a culture other than one's own can somehow be "wrong" or "deviant," especially if people experience others as foreign or the customs of others fall outside mainstream societal values and practices.

It is particularly difficult to develop a broader perspective when a member of a dominant cultural group. In U.S. society, members of historically disadvantaged groups, such as African Americans, Hispanics, and American Indians, can and must function both in their own culture and in the dominant culture—a survival strategy reflected in the phenomenon known as **code switching**, in which a minority cultural members, such as African Americans, switch from Standard English to African American vernacular, depending on the setting in which they find themselves (Cooper, Cooper, Azmitia, Chavira, & Gullatt, 2002; Turner, Wieling, & Allen, 2004). White European Americans, however, have not had to develop such bicultural expertise, and this more limited worldview can lead to the minimization of others' ongoing experience of oppression (Frankenberg, 1997).

Attitudes about Oppression

Despite a history of profound racism in the United States, including slavery, exclusionary immigration policies, internment camps during World War II, and racially discriminatory laws restricting access to housing, jobs and even marriage partners, many whites deny the impact of race on American society (Miller & Garran, 2008; Utsey, Ponterotto, & Porter, 2008). Researchers have found that when whites hold a "color-blind" perspective, believing that "race should not and does not matter" (Neville, Lilly, Duran, Lee, & Browne, 2000, p. 60), they are more likely to hold negative attitudes about people of other races (Awad, Cokley, & Ravitch, 2005; Neville et al., 2000).

The Color Blind Racial Attitudes Scale (CoBras) measures the extent to which individuals deny the impact of racism on contemporary society (Neville et al., 2000). Box 4.2 excerpts several of the statements that make up the scale. As you read the items, consider the extent to which the statements reflect your own view of the world. Consider this activity as a step in building your own cultural awareness about yourself. If you find yourself agreeing with some of the "color-blind" statements, contemplate a cultural encounter that may help to expand your views and diminish any biases you may have.

Holding a color-blind view of the world is a particularly limiting perspective for any student of social work because it can obscure awareness of the potential for the social work profession itself to have an oppressive effect on minority groups.

? Assess your understanding of attitudes by taking this brief quiz.

Box 4.2 CoBras Scale Sample Statements

Racially Aware Statements

- White people in the United States have certain advantages because of the color of their skin.
- Race plays an important role in who gets sent to prison.
- Race plays a major role in the type of social services (such as type of health care or day care) that people receive in the United States.
- Racial and ethnic minorities do not have the same opportunities as white people in the United States.

Color-Blind Statements

- Everyone who works hard, no matter what race they are, has an equal chance to become rich.
- Social policies, such as affirmative action, discriminate unfairly against white people.
- English should be the only official language in the United States.
- Racism may have been a problem in the past; it is not an important problem today.

Source: Neville et al. (2000).

CULTURAL AWARENESS

The NASW's standards for cultural competence in social work practice, standard #2, "Self-Awareness," states, "Social workers shall seek to develop an understanding of their own personal, cultural values and beliefs as one way of appreciating the importance of multicultural identities in the lives of people" (NASW, 2001, p. 16). Such self-awareness creates the opportunity for the social worker to recognize and become comfortable with cultural difference.

Comfort with Cultural Difference

Becoming culturally aware is a quality that evolves over time but only with a commitment to periodically taking a personal cultural-awareness inventory, identifying one's own cross-cultural limitations, and intentionally taking action to become culturally competent. When completing a personal cultural-awareness inventory, we assess where we fall on the continuum of cultural competence. One way to gauge one's level of cultural competence is to apply the **Developmental Model of Intercultural Sensitivity (DMIS)** (see Figure 4.2). The DMIS provides a progression of cross-cultural awareness along a continuum, moving from an ethnocentric worldview to an ethnorelative perspective. In an **ethnocentric worldview**, the individuals' culture dominates their thinking to the exclusion of other cultural perspectives (Bennett, 1986, 1993, 2004). Ethnocentric individuals will often deny or minimize the value of other cultural views. Conversely, individuals who hold an **ethnorelative worldview** experience their culture in the context of, or relative to, other cultures. They have greater awareness of and appreciation for other cultures. At the ethnorelative stages of cross-cultural experience, there is acceptance of other cultures, and individuals are able to function effectively within other cultures. Figure 4.2 illustrates the developmental stages that individuals move through in acquiring intercultural sensitivity.

Stages of Cultural Sensitivity

Each of the six developmental stages on Bennett's DMIS has a unique worldview, or perspective, that influences the attitudes, values, and behavior of individuals holding that worldview. As one moves from the left to the right side of the spectrum, there is increasing intercultural sensitivity, or awareness and appreciation of cultural difference.

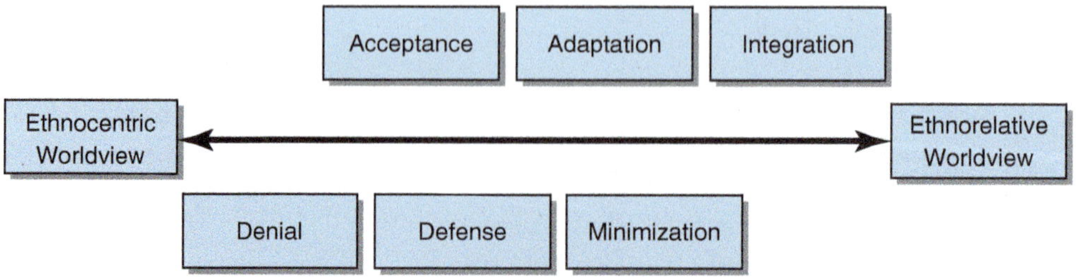

Figure 4.2
Bennett's Developmental Model of Intercultural Sensitivity

The first three DMIS stages fall within the larger spectrum of the ethnocentric worldview, where the individual's culture dominates his or her thinking about other cultures.

Diversity and Difference in Practice

Behavior: Apply and communicate understanding of the importance of diversity and difference in shaping life experiences in practice at the micro, mezzo, and macro levels.

Critical Thinking Question: Reflect on the three ethnocentric worldviews. In your opinion, which view would be the most difficult to change?

Ethnocentric Worldview (Stages 1–3)

Denial. Individuals at this first stage of intercultural sensitivity do not have any meaningful experience of cultures other than their own. Cultural avoidance is the norm and is achieved by strategies of isolation or separation (Bennett, 1986). An example of denial would be a religious group that strongly emphasizes socializing within the group, homeschooling, and avoidance of mainstream culture as expressed on television.

Defense. The second stage of intercultural sensitivity is characterized by a very limited engagement with other cultures. When these limited engagements occur, the ethnocentric individual reacts in a defensive manner, feeling the need to defend his home culture as the only "true" culture, or the "correct" culture, thus reflecting a lack of awareness of the value of all cultures. An individual who can argue about the superiority of her culture by citing the ways in which her own culture is better than another culture is at the defense stage of cultural sensitivity.

Minimization. When individuals relate to cultural difference by minimizing those differences, generally under the umbrella of "we're all the same on the inside," they are at the minimization stage. This seemingly positive worldview is, in reality, rooted in a refusal to explore the implications of cultural differences. A minimizer assumes that what is the "same" is generally in line with the individual's home culture. On one level, it is true to say that "we all have ceremonies to celebrate marriage," but if we stop at that level of generality, we miss underlying differences. In one culture, marriages may be arranged, based on an economic match between two families; in another, it may be an autonomous decision between two adults based on mutual love and respect for each other. These two perspectives can lead to very different behaviors, something that is not accounted for in the minimization stage.

Ethnorelative Worldview (Stages 4–6)

Acceptance. This is the fourth stage of intercultural sensitivity and represents a shift to a more ethnorelative worldview. Individuals at the acceptance stage acknowledge that cultural differences are real and should be respected. Cross-cultural knowledge is understood at this stage. For example, a grade school teacher who realizes that not every culture socializes children the same way and seeks out information to enhance her understanding of her students is at the acceptance stage.

Adaptation. The fifth stage of intercultural sensitivity represents growth in the ethnorelative worldview in the form of adaptation. At this stage, individuals use their cross-cultural knowledge and skills in their interactions with members of other cultural groups. To extend the previous example, a grade school teacher who adapts her teaching strategies based on knowledge of her students' culture is at the adaptation stage of intercultural sensitivity.

Integration. The sixth stage of intercultural sensitivity—and the most evolved stage—is that of integration. This ethnorelative worldview is characterized by a high degree of fluency in more than one culture, to the point that an individual can fully adopt different worldviews, depending on the cultural setting (Bennett & Hammer, 1998). An immigrant who has learned to function in both her own subculture and in mainstream society and who can think in both English and her native language could be said to have reached the integration stage of intercultural sensitivity.

A social worker's self-awareness of his or her cultural identity is a prerequisite to building cross-cultural knowledge and skills. Start by assessing the frame of reference that you bring to the helping process. Take a moment to assess yourself on your cultural self-awareness by completing Part 1 of the Cultural Self-Inventory in Box 4.3. Think about your own worldview, your values and traditions, your cultural experiences, and your understanding of other cultures. After completing the self-awareness inventory, locate yourself on the DMIS continuum. Where do you find yourself? There is no right or wrong placement. Most important is that you become aware of where you fall on the continuum of cultural awareness—then you are in a good position to move forward toward cultural competence. What steps can you begin to take to increase your cultural knowledge, skills, and encounters?

As you reflect on your responses to the self-inventory, step back and try to observe your life from a distance. Acknowledge your own biases, which, depending on your background, may arise from white privilege, ageism, sexism, weight bias, religious affiliation, where you grew up, where you went to college, or your peer group.

Developing self-awareness is the foundation for growing in cultural competence. The case study in Box 4.4 demonstrates how a new social worker's increased self-awareness can lead to a deeper understanding of her clients.

? Assess your understanding of cultural awareness by taking this brief quiz.

Box 4.3 Cultural Self-Inventory Part 1: Self-Awareness

Personal Identity

- What ethnicity(ies) do you identify with?
- What other cultural groups do you consider yourself a member of?
- With which cultural groups do you most strongly identify? How do they influence your personal identity?
- In what ways do your language, style, appearance, and behaviors reflect the influence of these cultural groups?
- What values do you hold that link you to your cultural memberships?
- On a scale of 1 to 10 (with 10 being most positive), rate how you feel about each of your cultural identities or membership groups.
- Describe an episode or an experience of discrimination as a result of a cultural membership.
- Identify the benefits or privileges attached to your cultural memberships.

Spiritual Beliefs

- How would you describe your spiritual beliefs?
- When did you adopt these beliefs, and to where can you trace the influences that led to your adopting these beliefs?
- On a scale of 1 to 10 (with 10 being most important), rate the level of importance of your spiritual beliefs in your day-to-day life.
- When you encounter others with different spiritual beliefs, how do you perceive them in relation to your personal beliefs?

Source: Based on Miley, O'Melia, and DuBois (2013).

Box 4.4 Jennifer

Jennifer is a white 23-year-old female who is just starting out on a career in social work. She grew up in a rural area, attended a state university, and is now a family transition facilitator in a community-based family transition program, working with incarcerated women to help them prepare for their release from prison. Although the prison is located in a small town near where Jennifer grew up, the population she works with is largely from the state's urban center. In her first months on the job, Jennifer found herself getting frustrated with what she perceived as an unrealistic attitude on the part of her clients. In discussing career options, clients sometimes talked of becoming doctors or actresses or of finding a man who would take care of them. She felt that, in many cases, clients either did not understand the extent of preparation and training for some careers or were pinning their hopes on things that were very unlikely to happen. As part of the training for her position, Jennifer took a workshop on cultural competence and did an inventory of her beliefs and values. Here are her results:

Ethnic identity:
German and Swedish.

Cultural group memberships:
"American"—no strong roots in heritage other than traditional Christian holiday traditions, such as Easter and Christmas; part of a farming community; identifies with being an "alum" of her university and with other people who participate in her favorite hobbies—horseback riding and camping.

Behaviors and values derived from these memberships:
Belief in self-reliance—putting herself through school, sense of community and of belonging to something larger; has a network of people she draws on for support and is optimistic; has made concrete plans for the future with the expectation that things will work out for the best.

Feels positive:
About her cultural identity. She has never, to her knowledge, experienced overt discrimination (but wonders why her father did not teach her more about farming given her love of animals and the outdoors—is it because she's female?). Has also encountered stereotypical thinking about being a "hick" but doesn't see it as affecting her life in any way.

Privileges:
Access to support networks, financial stability, good health care, education, and knowledge of possible career paths.

Spiritual beliefs:
Has attended a Protestant church all her life.

Influences on the way she perceives others who hold different beliefs:
While her church does not actively "preach" intolerance, neither does it encourage exploration of other faith traditions.

After thinking about these results, Jennifer realizes that nothing in her upbringing has prepared her to work closely with people from other cultural backgrounds. Although she learned about cross-cultural competence in her social work courses, she did not take the initiative to develop deeper knowledge, arrange for cultural encounters, or practice cultural competence skills. As she compares her personal history with the very different life experiences of her clients, Jennifer is beginning to sense that it is an urgent priority for her to learn more about who her clients are within their many cultural contexts in order to understand the "why" underlying their past actions and future aspirations.

KNOWLEDGE

The NASW *Code of Ethics* articulates "dignity and worth of the person" as a core professional value, supported by the ethical principle that "social workers treat *each person* in a caring and respectful fashion, *mindful of individual differences* and *cultural and ethnic diversity* (NASW, 2008; emphasis added). A culturally competent social worker devotes ongoing time and effort to developing a nuanced knowledge base regarding cultural and ethnic diversity. While there are group-level patterns of thinking and acting that characterize any culture, the value of respect for the dignity and worth of the person requires social workers to consider each client as a unique individual within the context of the various circumstances, settings, and cultural contexts that have shaped their unique personhood. This is how social workers come to understand each client as a culture of one.

Intersectionality

The theory of **intersectionality**, introduced by Crenshaw (1991) and contributed to by other feminist scholars (Collins, 2000; Harding & Norberg, 2005; McCall, 2005), presents a new understanding of the complexity of culture and the many facets of life that position individuals in places of privilege and power or in places of discrimination, exploitation, and marginalization. The theoretical framework of intersectionality expanded the understanding of the multiple interacting dimensions of culture that shape individual identity and one's position in society. Consider for a moment the various factors that define the identity of a middle-class white heterosexual student council president high school male and the privileges he has access to by the nature of this identity. Contrast that with the position of a low-income Mexican immigrant bisexual high school girl uninvolved in school activities because of the need to help her family with migrant work after school. What privileges are denied her because of these arbitrary cultural traits? Can you see the complexity of each identity and how each factor compounds one's position in society and access to power, privilege, resources, and voice?

Lum (2010) described intersectionality as taking into account "those multiple interactions and crossroads in our lives that are replete with multiple social group memberships that are interconnected and interrelated" (p. 42). Diversity encompasses race, ethnicity, socioeconomic status, sexual orientation, the able/differently abled spectrum, gender, religious belief, values, political persuasions, and other qualities of difference that distinguish one group from another and influence their status in society. Intersectionality highlights the complex and shifting nature of cultural belonging, in which each of us has membership in multiple social groups.

Intersectionality also connects personal characteristics, such as skin color, language, gender, and sexual orientation, with macro-level dimensions, such as economic, political, legal, immigration, education, and other social systems and a cultural group's past and present experiences of oppression. It exposes the multiple ways in which race, gender, class, sexual orientation, and other statuses intersect to determine a person's fate; social, political, and economic status; and the privilege or oppression that accompanies each position (Brah & Phoenix, 2004; Malveaux, 2002).

The diagram in Figure 4.3 depicts intersectionality and the many qualities, characteristics, and factors that come into play to influence one's position in society. The image displays the various dimensions the client brings to the social worker in a help-seeking situation. At the center of the diagram are the dimensions that make up the client's cultural uniqueness—the intersection of personal traits with the environment. This figure is hardly exhaustive and you may want to add some other conditions or traits to the diagram to expand the influences of intersectionality in people's lives. While some of the client dimensions can be visible (e.g., skin color, age, and gender), many are invisible. A culturally competent social worker has a heightened awareness of the "invisible" dimensions of the client's lived experience, partnering with the client to better understand *who* the client is and *how* his or her internal and external resources can be brought

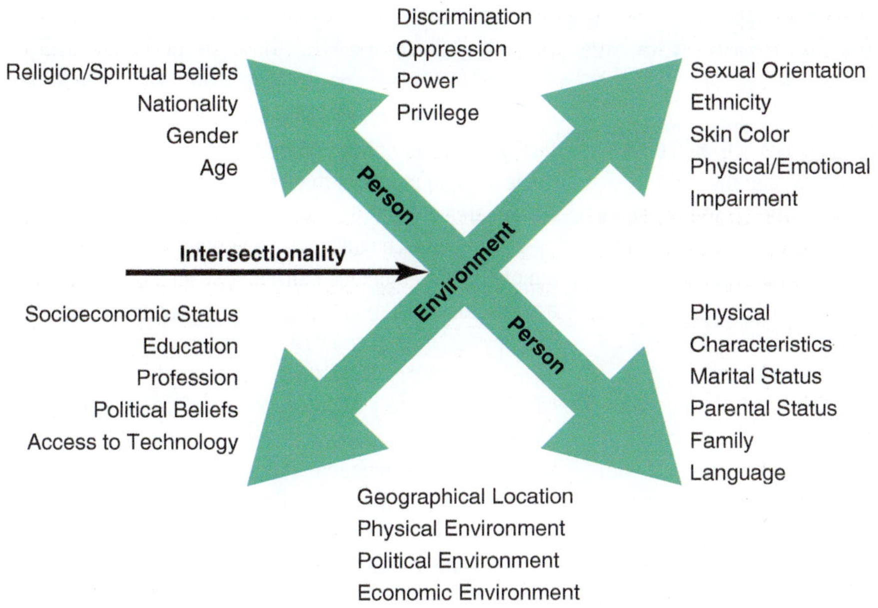

Figure 4.3
Intersectionality

Source: Scott and Singleton (2005). Intersectionality diagram. Prepared for faculty meeting at Barry University School of Social Work, Miami Shores, FL.

to bear on the helping process (Cummins & Gray, 2008; Scott & Singleton, 2005). One way to begin to appreciate the multiple dimension of clients' lives and how they come to bear on the current contexts of their lives is to ask a question describing the client's diversity within a particular context. For example, a question regarding a diverse client with intersecting realities receiving services from a Salvation Army agency might be, "What does it mean to be a black, lesbian, poor woman in the context of a faith-based service organization?" Another example for a school social worker providing services to a diverse student might be, "What does it mean to be an eighth-grade physically disabled Hispanic male in the context of this middle school?" These kinds of questions discussed with clients at the appropriate time can give voice to the client's concerns, experiences, and needs while providing cultural insight to the social worker, who then has a greater potential for structuring culturally appropriate care. Box 4.I applies intersectionality to increase understanding of a particular client and her needs.

Diversity and Difference in Practice

Behavior: Apply self-awareness and self-regulation to manage the influence of personal biases and values in working with diverse clients and constituencies.

Critical Thinking Question: Apply the intersectionality model to yourself and two of your classmates or friends to assess diversity in a small sample of individuals. Across how many dimensions of the human experience do the three of you vary?

Developing Specialized Cultural Knowledge

The NASW's standards for cultural competence in social work practice, standard #3, states that "social workers shall have and continue to develop specialized knowledge and understanding about the history, traditions, values, family systems, and artistic expressions of

Box 4.1 Theory into Practice—The Application of Intersectionality in Culturally Competent Practice—Case Study

Intersectionality recognizes that people are made up of a wide range of diverse identities (Cummins & Gray, 2008). It recognizes the subjective, the structural, and the social position of clients and challenges social workers to look at multiple intersections in the lives of people they serve rather than focusing on one dimension, such as class, gender, or race (Cummins & Gray, 2008).

Eliana is a Latina veteran who served in Iraq. She identifies with Latino culture, Catholicism, military culture, her female gender, and the community of veterans dealing with posttraumatic stress disorder. Depending on the situation, the "presenting" cultural identity shifts as she interacts with different social groups. Among her extended family, she is the beloved daughter of the household. As a female veteran, she has experienced pride of service but also marginalization in securing mental health services given the greater numbers of male combat veterans also in need of support. As a Catholic, she has taken on a leadership role in running a church-sponsored food kitchen. As a Latina, she grew up in an industrial, less desirable part of the community, her family's housing options limited by discriminatory "redlining" home lending practices that restricted minority groups to certain areas.

Using intersectionality, we can gain a deeper understanding of Eliana as a unique individual, shaped by her Latina roots and religious affiliation, her military service, and the mental and physical injuries she sustained in service. Her life choices have been subtly influenced by macro-level forces, such as Latinos' relative lack of power and privilege in relation to whites; by the physical and political environment; and by her family's low socioeconomic status, which led her to enlist as a way to improve her life conditions.

Eliana is a "culture of one," a unique person who is shaped by her group memberships and life characteristics but not determined by them. Her personhood lies at their intersection, and it is the task of the social worker to discern, *with her help*, the components of Eliana's identity that have bearing on the helping process.

major client groups that they serve" (NASW, 2001). Acquiring specialized cultural knowledge is a process that occurs over time, an effort that cannot be achieved by reading a short list of "cultural dos and don'ts." Although this chapter uses examples and case studies, it does not outline comprehensive strategies for interviewing members of specific cultural groups. Instead, we provide markers of cultural competence to help you gauge your progress toward culture competence, and we offer strategies on "learning how to learn" about other cultures. In acquiring cultural knowledge, the following traits can serve as indicators that you are on your way to building an ample cross-cultural knowledge base:

- **Cultural empathy:** "The ability to empathize with the feelings, thoughts, and behaviors of members from different cultural groups" (Van der Zee & Van Oudenhoven, 2000, p. 296). Having empathy means that you can internalize what's happening to a client. For example, a social worker who is working with a Latina girl whose father is in prison would understand the significance of the client's father not being there for the father–daughter waltz at the Quinceanera coming-of-age celebration that many Latina girls experience at age 15. Note that the "feeling" part of empathy rests on a base of knowledge. Cultural empathy is not simply wanting things to be better for the client—it's rooted in knowledge about the client's cultural traditions.
- **Intercultural sensitivity:** A multiculturally competent social worker takes into account the client's norms and values, understanding that the client's value system may be quite different from his or her own. For example, cultures deal with death in different ways. In a situation in which a social worker has the norm of

"moving on" to recover from grief but the client's culture stresses a formal, extended mourning period, an interculturally sensitive social worker will set aside her own cultural norms to work within the client's norms.

- **Open-mindedness:** Defined as an "open and unprejudiced attitude toward different groups and toward different cultural norms and values" (Van der Zee & Van Oudenhoven, 2000, p. 296). Difference can be exciting and fascinating, but it can also be threatening or perceived as inferior. A client whose culture values faith healing, for example, may be viewed by members of a more science-oriented culture as "quaint" or superstitious. To understand the client's needs, the social worker who finds herself across a cultural divide such as this must strive to comprehend a worldview with different foundational assumptions from her own. Clients will sense when they are being patronized—you don't need to adopt the client's cultural practices, but as a social work professional, you should be able to learn about them with an open mind and a nonjudgmental attitude.

Ethical and Professional Behavior

Behavior: Use reflection and self-regulation to manage personal values and maintain professionalism in practice situations.

Critical Thinking Question: What ethical considerations come into play when working with clients whose cultural practices contradict your deeply held beliefs?

Being open-minded is easy to achieve in principle. In actuality, our thinking processes often rely on making snap judgments (Chaiken, 1980). Mental shortcuts, such as making an immediate association between two people or events based on superficial similarities, result in stereotypical thinking. In the context of a social work interview, stereotypical thinking leads to the pitfall of judgmental response. Overcoming the implicit associations we make between people is difficult, but being aware of these tendencies is a first step toward reducing their power. One way to assess our tendencies toward cultural biases is to test ourselves. Greenwald and Banaji (1995) developed an interactive web-based assessment tool to help people understand the extent to which they have conscious and unconscious cultural biases. The assessment tool, called the Implicit Association Test, assesses one's tendencies to associate certain attributes and qualities to different groups (Poehlman, Uhlmann, Greenwald, & Banaji, 2005). Try taking the test, which is available online the Project Implicit website at Harvard University. This is easily found by googling 'Project Implicit.'

Building cross-cultural knowledge occurs more readily in people who are curious, who have a genuine desire to acquire cultural knowledge, and who are open-minded about values and practices different from their own. Assess your cultural knowledge and open-mindedness by completing Part 2 of the Cultural Self-Inventory in Box 4.5.

As you consider your responses, assess the extent of your cultural knowledge. Rate your cultural knowledge on a scale of 1 to 10, with 1 being very little cultural knowledge and 10 being extensive culture knowledge. Where do you fall on the cultural knowledge continuum? If you placed yourself on the low end, chances are you may have had very little exposure to other cultures. One way to begin to expand your cultural knowledge is to begin exploring various cultural groups by setting up cultural encounters, such as attending cultural festivals or visiting a culturally diverse church. If it feels intimidating, think about arranging a cultural encounter with a friend or a group of friends. A less intimidating approach might be to ask a culturally diverse friend or acquaintance to help you with the plans. Other strategies for expanding your cultural knowledge are

Box 4.5 Cultural Self-Inventory Part 2: Cross-Cultural Knowledge

- Name the cultural groups present in your community.
- Select two of the cultural groups present in your community. Then identify beliefs, values, and traditions associated with each group.
- How did you gain cultural knowledge about your community groups?
- Describe your cultural encounters with the cultural groups in your community. What have you learned through these encounters?
- As you think about the cultural groups in your community, identify any stereotypes, prejudices, or assumptions that you hold about them currently or have held in the past.
- How do you account for these biases?
- In what ways can you enhance your knowledge about the cultural groups that live in your community?

Source: Based on Miley et al. (2013).

presented in Box 4.A. If you scored high on the cultural knowledge continuum, explore your cultural knowledge base and determine if it is broad or narrow and shallow or deep. For example, do you know a little about a lot of cultures, a lot about one or two cultures, or somewhere in between these two poles of knowledge? Identify where to start exploring to begin to deepen your cultural knowledge or expand the scope of the cultures you are competent with. Authors and educators in the areas of cultural diversity and practice have suggested a number of activities that you can engage in to help you build your cross-cultural knowledge base. Some of these are listed in Box 4.A. Indicate whether you

Box 4.A Now You Try It . . . Building Cross-Cultural Knowledge

Think about your life experiences with other cultures. Then complete the following inventory of ways to gain cross-cultural knowledge. Which activities have you been involved in, and how have they affected your view of the world?

	Activity	Tried It?	
1	Include diverse perspectives in writing assignments	Yes___	No___
2	Be an active listener in class discussions; attend closely to comments from students who are culturally different from you	Yes___	No___
3	Talk with students of a different race or ethnicity than your own	Yes___	No___
4	Talk with students who differ from you in religious beliefs, political opinions, or personal values	Yes___	No___
5	Make friends outside your group	Yes___	No___
6	Take a service learning class	Yes___	No___
7	Take courses on other cultures	Yes___	No___
8	Study abroad, either for a semester or during a short-course period	Yes___	No___
9	Go on an alternative spring break	Yes___	No___
10	Get involved with the international student office at your university	Yes___	No___
11	Read widely—look for novels set in other cultures	Yes___	No___
12	Use the Internet as a resource to learn about other cultures	Yes___	No___
13	Seek out a mentor who is a member of the culture you want to learn about	Yes___	No___

Box 4.A Now You Try It . . . Building Cross-Cultural Knowledge *(Continued)*

	Activity	Tried It?	
14	Visit a mosque, synagogue, African American church, or Buddhist temple	Yes___	No___
15	Host a dinner; ask guests to provide foods from their culture along with the recipe	Yes___	No___
16	Participate in your campus's Safe Zone program for people who are supportive of gay, lesbian, transgender, and bisexual people	Yes___	No___
17	Learn another language	Yes___	No___
18	Attend workshops and trainings on developing cultural competence	Yes___	No___
19	Attend university and community lectures given by individuals from other countries	Yes___	No___
20	Visit museums (e.g., the Holocaust Museum or the National Museum of the American Indian in Washington, D.C.)	Yes___	No___
21	Visit an independent living center, sheltered workshop group home, or a homeless shelter	Yes___	No___

have engaged in any of these activities or cultural encounters by checking "yes" or "no" at the end of each item. If you find that you have not been very proactive in acquiring cross-cultural knowledge, you can choose to increase your knowledge by implementing some of these actions in your daily life. For those who have had limited exposure to cultures other than their own, some of these suggestions might feel a bit intimidating. Consider trying them with a friend and remember that this is a lifelong learning process. Move at your own pace.

For those experiences for which you checked "yes," consider how these experiences affected the way you see your world and interact with others. What other activities have you tried or can you think of that could facilitate building your cross-cultural knowledge base? As you pursue knowledge of cultures, recognize that there are some key dimensions along which they vary (see Box 4.6).

Using the key areas of cultural differences listed in Box 4.6, how would you describe your own culture? To get you started on how you might use these key areas in describing

Box 4.6 Key Areas of Cultural Difference

- Whether the culture tends toward individualistic or collectivistic values
- Gender roles
- Religion and spirituality
- Orientation to authority/presence or relative absence of hierarchies
- Family structure
- Perceptions of time and space
- Attitudes toward the future and life planning
- Sense of personal control over one's life circumstances
- Humor
- Speech norms (including the use of silence)
- Degree of openness toward members of other cultures
- Preference for direct versus indirect communication
- Level of formality in communication
- The extent to which meetings are focused on completing tasks or building relationships

Source: Fong and Furuto (2001).

Box 4.7 Frederick

Frederick is a hospital social worker in a large metropolitan area. He grew up in San Francisco, California, in a middle-class community that was predominantly Protestant. Many of the patients receiving medical care at the hospital are of Chinese ancestry. Mrs. Wang, a widow, was seen in the emergency room for stroke symptoms. Mrs. Wang has three children, all of whom accompanied her to the emergency room. Mrs. Wang does not speak English, so her children served as the translator. The oldest daughter, Ying, plans to have Mrs. Wang move in (at least temporarily) to her home on her release from the hospital. The other siblings are very supportive, as the thought of a nursing home (or any other out-of-home care) is culturally unacceptable. It would be a dishonor to their mother.

It was through Frederick's college education and internship that he began to develop an interest in other cultures. He has studied a wide variety of cultures and religions and sees himself as fairly open-minded and flexible in his work with clients. Because of his understanding of the Chinese culture and norms, he knows that any effective intervention will have to include all the family, including Mrs. Wang's extended family. He knows that Mrs. Wang is highly regarded and valued by her children. He also knows that she may have some suspicion and fears regarding Western medical practices.

Points for Reflection

If you were Frederick's supervisor, what might you suggest to help him further his cultural competence? What does he need to consider to better understand his client's environment and barriers to services? How might (or how do you anticipate) Frederick respond to this family if he were of Chinese descent as well? Finally, what do you need to learn about Chinese culture in order to be more competent in your work with Chinese clients?

your own culture (or cultures), review the case study of Frederick in Box 4.7 and identify the key areas of cultural difference reflected in the practice scenario. Then, study the examples below that illustrate how some of these factors vary across cultures:

- The extent to which a culture stresses *individualistic* or *collectivistic* values is an important difference between cultures (Guss, 2002). In the United States, for example, the dominant culture has historically valued the individual over the group. This cultural trait is evident in many facets of American culture. For example, in one study, Ohbuchi, Fukushima, and Tedeschi (1999) found that American college students favor assertive tactics in decision making (i.e., the group gets everything "out in the open"), while Japanese students prefer indirect strategies that minimize open conflict, which might disrupt group harmony. In the context of the social work interview, tactics such as confrontation that might seem healthy from an individualistic perspective may be perceived as a threatening disruption from a collectivistic perspective. Watch Interactive Case Study #5 and notice that Mrs. Kita usually refers to herself as "we," indicating her collective perspective.

As you watch this video clip of Mrs. Kita as she talks to the social worker, what words and body language suggest a collectivist perspective?

- *Gender roles* are culturally constructed. In the United States, for example, the experience of gender is different for women in Appalachia than it is for mainstream urban and suburban American women. In some areas of Appalachia, such as rural West Virginia, Georgia, and Kentucky, gender roles tend to be more traditional (Borman, Mueninghoff, & Piazza, 1988; Oberhauser, 1995, 2014). While gender roles are slowly shifting in Appalachia, it is still common for girls to grow up expecting to "put family first," which can mean deferring or not pursuing education and staying close to home, not moving away to pursue different or richer life opportunities. In contrast, national trends in family attitudes and values have moved more toward individual autonomy and equality in marriage (Thornton & Young-DeMarco, 2001).

- *Religion* and *spirituality* influence the way most people conduct their lives and the choices they make and therefore are important parts of the cultural knowledge base for competent direct social work practice. For elderly African Americans, for example, clergy can be an important link to formal support systems and a counseling resource (Frame & Williams, 2011). There is variation not only between religions (one versus many gods, belief in an afterlife, extent of faith community hierarchy) but also within religions. Individuals within a religious group may vary, for example, in the extent to which they believe that God directly controls their lives or in the extent to which their religious practice is motivated by an intrinsic search for meaning or an extrinsic connection to community (Cohen, Hall, Koenig, & Meador, 2005; Schieman, Pudrovska, & Milkie, 2005). For some social work practitioners, this can be an area of practice that can cause uncertainty and discomfort. Sometimes this discomfort can be related to the social work practitioner's own lack of clarity around religion and spiritual beliefs and practices, thus leaving one feeling incompetent to delve into this aspect of clients' lives. Unresolved religious issues in the lives of social work practitioners can create barriers to competent social work practice around religious and spiritual values, beliefs, and practices of their clients (Hodge & McGrew, 2006; McCarthy & Peteet, 2003). Social workers are encouraged to understand the meaning of clients' stories in the contexts of their clients' beliefs, family, and cultural values. Most important, avoid being judgmental when the client's beliefs and values conflict with your own.
- Cultures vary with respect to *attitudes toward the future and life planning*. While there are commonalities across cultures (e.g., adolescents tend to focus on education, career, and family in thinking about the future), there are also culture-specific differences (Kagitchibasi, 1996). In working-class culture, for example, adolescents have a relatively short future-time horizon (defined as how far into the future an individual makes plans). Adolescents from more affluent backgrounds have longer future-time horizons. Limited access to a university education reduces the likelihood that individuals will be inclined to make long-range life plans (Nurmi, 1987). Differences are also seen in long-term care and end-of-life planning across cultures. For example, blacks and Hispanics are less likely than whites to have a durable power of attorney for health care or to have discussed end-of-life preferences. These differences have been linked to varying beliefs about God's control of time and end-of-life events (Carr, 2011).
- Perceptions of time are culture bound. In their influential book *Metaphors We Live By*, George Lakoff and Mark Johnson (2003) analyze how our thinking is

Engagement

Behavior: Use empathy, reflection, and interpersonal skills to effectively engage diverse clients and constituencies.

Critical Thinking Question: Religious experience can be gendered—within a faith tradition, women's experiences can be quite different from men's. As a social worker, how would you approach this dimension of cultural variability?

reflected in and shaped by the use of metaphor. They identify a cluster of metaphors in Western culture around the "time is money" concept:

How do you spend your time these days?

That flat tire cost me an hour.

I've invested a lot of time in her.

You need to budget your time. (p. 8)

Underlying the "time is money" metaphor is an understanding of time as a limited resource and a valuable commodity that is characteristic of the industrialized world. In non-Western cultures, people are more attuned to looser agricultural time cycles. These differences can affect the social worker–client relationship when the social worker and the client have different expectations regarding meeting times and timelines for meeting goals.

The breadth of cultural diversity—and thus the breadth of knowledge that social workers need to be considered culturally competent—is striking. Box 4.7 provides an example of how one social worker uses cultural knowledge in direct practice. As previously defined, cultural diversity includes not only race, ethnicity, and gender but also sexual orientation, physical or cognitive impairments, religion, socioeconomic status, geographic location (urban versus rural), and age. Social work practice takes a "person-in-environment" approach that situates the individual within his or her ecosystem, which is shaped by all of these cultural factors (Bronfenbrenner, 1979). The NASW's standards for cultural competence in social work practice treat the acquisition of cultural knowledge as a lifelong learning commitment on the part of the social worker (NASW, 2008). In a process-oriented model of cultural competence, professionals ideally "see themselves as *becoming* culturally competent rather than already being culturally competent" (Campinha-Bacote, 2002, p. 181). As you work toward cultural competence, expect that you will make mistakes. Whether our errors are culturally grounded or come from some other source, we all experience pitfalls in the interview process from time to time. Use these moments to acquire cultural humility and to learn about your client's culture of one.

The strengths perspective in social work practice regards clients' cultural traits as assets in the helping process. Viewing the client as a cultural teacher can bring more balance to the social worker–client relationship. The social worker does not possess all of the resources needed to address the client's needs—instead, the client's own culturally endowed protective factors are a rich resource for strategies and solutions (Anderson, Anderson, & Gear, 2015). That being said, we also want to caution against using our clients as learning laboratories. Differentiate between a need to know in order to advance the helping process and your client's quality of life versus pure curiosity on your part. The focus of the interview should always be on the client.

? Assess your understanding of knowledge by taking this brief quiz.

SKILLS

The NASW's standards for cultural competence in social work practice, standard #4, states that "social workers shall use appropriate methodological approaches, skills, and techniques that reflect the workers' understanding of the role of culture in the helping process." Meeting this standard will require both direct and indirect practice in acquiring skills to effectively engage your culturally diverse clients. As you develop interviewing skills, both verbal and nonverbal, be conscious that the use of these important skills always occur within the context of clients' cultural realities. Watch Interactive Case Study #5 for an example of the social worker Diane demonstrating cultural competence in working with a client of Japanese ancestry by removing her shoes at the outset of the interview, bringing a gift basket of food to Mrs. Kita, and accepting the offer of tea.

In honoring her client's cultural practices of hospitality, Diane conveys that she understands her client and is open to the client's worldview.

Culture influences the decision to use a particular social work skill. The attending behavior of maintaining eye contact, for example, will be more effective when working with clients for whom direct eye contact is the cultural norm, such as European Americans. For clients who are members of a culture that favors indirect communication, such as many Asian cultures, direct eye contact may be intimidating. Similarly, the use of silence can be comforting in some cultures but cause tension in others. The optimal amount of personal space and acceptability of touch also vary widely across cultures. An interviewing skill may be applied correctly from a technical perspective, but it can turn into a pitfall if cultural appropriateness is lacking. The skill of information giving is also highly influenced by culture, as demonstrated in the LGBT (lesbian, gay, bisexual, and transgender) youth case study profiled in Box 4.8.

Box 4.8 Cultural Competence and LGBT Youth

Matthew is a bright 18-year-old only child from a middle-class conservative Christian family. He attends a local college affiliated with his church denomination, and his father is active in the church council. While his parents are supportive of Matthew, they have grown apart in their marital relationship and are now going through a divorce. After a particularly difficult day of family conflict, Matthew's mother Jenny goes online to pay bills and accidentally views her son's Facebook account (Matthew had forgotten to log out). Jenny is very concerned to read the most recent posting, in which Matthew writes that he is sad all the time and "wants a new life." Jenny turns to the family's divorce mediation social worker, Elaine, for assistance.

After clarifying with Jenny that the counseling session with Matthew would be confidential, Elaine schedules an appointment with him. Elaine anticipates that the meeting will focus on the typical range of issues and relationship difficulties often experienced by adolescents during their parents' divorce. During their meeting, however, when Elaine asks how things are going, Matthew blurts out that he thinks he's gay.

Elaine is not caught off guard by Matthew's statement. She is ready to offer assistance to Matthew because she approaches her practice with an affirming attitude of positive regard for her clients. Elaine draws on her knowledge of the LGBT community, recognizing that coming out is often a difficult process for adolescents. Family, peers, and prevailing religious and cultural biases can send powerfully negative messages to LGBT youth at a critical point in their self-identity formation. In this context, it is important that the culturally competent social worker use the skill of information giving to direct a gay, bisexual, transgendered, or lesbian client toward the most supportive resources.

Matthew has access to a counselor through his college, but Elaine understands that the affiliated church's negative stance on same-sex relationships means that it is unlikely that the counselor would provide the support Matthew needs. Instead, Elaine refers him to a gay-safe youth counseling center so that he can address the dual stresses of his parents' divorce and his exploration of his sexual orientation. After making the referral, Elaine does not inform Matthew's mother Jenny about the reasons for making the referral, only letting her know that she spoke with Matthew and made a referral.

Points for Reflection

1. Why did Elaine prioritize Matthew's privacy over Jenny's parental oversight role?
2. What factors enabled Elaine to effectively support Matthew given that Elaine did not know in advance of their meeting that Matthew was dealing with questions about his sexual orientation?

Offering information about community resources to a client can be counterproductive if the social worker fails to understand the client's culturally formed attitudes about the information. The culturally competent social worker knows about a wide range of community resources that may be of particular use to culturally diverse clients, thus matching resources with clients appropriately. For example, knowing which housing agency has experience placing Syrian refugees will help the social worker make a "best-fit" referral to an agency, increasing the likelihood of success.

A sound cross-cultural knowledge base and skill set is essential for the culturally appropriate application of social work interviewing skills. Within this context, the use of interviewing skills can help you adjust to a variety of cultural contexts. Open-ended questions such as "What do you mean by that?" and the skill of clarification can be used to learn about the client's culture. In addition to social work skills, there are some general characteristics and skills that will increase the likelihood of success in working with members of other cultures. Individuals who are effective in multicultural settings are flexible. They possess the "ability to switch easily from one strategy to another . . . [with] a tendency to feel attracted to new and unknown situations, experiencing them as a challenge rather than as a threat" (Van der Zee & Brinkmann, 2004, p. 289). Flexibility means that you learn from your mistakes and adjust your behavior accordingly.

A quality related to flexibility is tolerance of ambiguity (Van der Zee & Brinkmann, 2004). The cross-cultural encounter is inherently a situation in which engrained expectations are continually overturned. Instead, expect to be surprised and have confidence that any confusion can be resolved. The phenomenon of culture shock is real. When you first immerse yourself in another culture, you may not know why someone is laughing, why someone *isn't* laughing, or why you feel like you're somehow involved in a joke you don't understand. With greater familiarity and cross-cultural knowledge, you will acquire insider knowledge. Until then, though, your best coping strategy is to simply accept that the situation is ambiguous.

Another marker of multicultural competence is the ability to take the social initiative. Defined as "a tendency to actively approach social situations and to take the initiative rather than to wait and see" (Van der Zee & Brinkmann, 2004, p. 289), social initiative enables an individual to reach out to members of other cultures. Developing cultural competence takes effort—having the desire to interact with members of another culture makes the effort seem less like work and more like an opportunity for personal growth. Also, the act of reaching out, of being culturally humble and open to new experiences, sends the positive message that you are interested in the culture.

? Assess your understanding of skills by taking this brief quiz.

SERVING SPECIAL POPULATIONS

As social workers, developing competency in regard to special populations is also an important part of understanding similarities and differences. In this section, we introduce you to assessment considerations with **special populations**; however, it is not intended to provide you with a full presentation of information regarding working with special and unique populations. This is just a snapshot of ways to assess what may be contributing to the difficulties, strengths, and circumstances in the client's life. Is the client mandated by a parent, the school, or court? During intake, examine the circumstances under which the client ended up working with you. Regardless of the route taken, there may be some challenges along the way.

Take the multicultural knowledge and awareness assessment in Box 4.10 to gain self awareness of your cultural knowledge and limitations that could lead to some challenges when working with special populations and diverse clients.

Young Children and Adolescents

Be mindful of the child's level of development by planning activities that are appropriate for that child's level. For instance, a six-year-old child may be able to answer straightforward questions but may need some prompting to fill in the details. An adolescent may simply want you to listen.

Be creative in working with young children, for example, by singing songs, drawing pictures, and playing with dolls, building blocks, paint, toys, and puppets. These creative ways to engage a child can help to lower anxiety and fear and increase communication between the child and the social worker. Watch how the child approaches the activity. Can the child follow your directions? Look for themes in the child's play. For example, does a child repeatedly hit another doll during play? Try parallel play as a way to slowly move toward more interactive communication.

The setting is important. Is the office filled with child friendly artwork, sturdy chairs, and low-level tables? Sit at the child's eye level so as to not be intimidating or threatening in any way. Find the inner child in you, look for a carefree moment, be silly, and smile.

Adolescence is a time in life that is filled with many physical, behavioral, developmental, and emotional changes. Many adolescents are trying to figure out their identity and their place in the world. Peer pressure, popularity, and independence mark these important years. Listening to some favorite music together and then talking about the lyrics, reading magazine articles, and playing an interactive game together are good activities to try with adolescents. Journaling, creating a collage together, working on a model car, walking around the group home grounds, and sharing drawings or notes back and forth can open up communication. Patience is so important when working with adolescents; do not let your frustration show. Providing a structured environment with clear rules and expectations can set the stage for trust and, therefore, movement toward a treatment goal. With adolescents, be yourself, express a genuine interest in your client's well-being, and offer uncompromising care.

Begin with a friendly conversation, discuss a favorite activity, or ask about the client's favorite TV show or character. With a young child, you may want to offer a bit of information about yourself—for example, "When I was your age, I had lost my two front teeth too, and I didn't like to smile, especially because I didn't think I would get new ones." With an adolescent, "My senior year in high school was hard too; I wanted to drop out and almost did. I was lucky that Mr. Green, my history teacher, stood by me."

Be a keen observer. Pay attention to the child's nonverbal communication. Does he or she seem tense and worried? Does he or she seem sad and tearful? If at all possible, observe the child in a variety of settings, such as at school and home and while interacting with other children. If your agency permits taking the child off grounds, sometimes getting an ice cream cone, feeding the ducks (see Interactive Case Study #4 of Maria), or shooting baskets can help the child feel more comfortable with the social worker.

View Interactive Case Study #4 as the social worker engaged the young client, Maria, in feeding the ducks at the park.

Gaining insights and information from collateral contacts (teacher, physician, Girl Scout troop leader, foster parent, or coach) can be helpful in assessing a client situation involving a minor. Of course, you will need the parent's or legal guardian's written consent to talk with other people involved in the child's life.

With a young child, develop a shared story together; drawing a picture of your client's family, ask the child to tell you the story of his or her family. Ask "what-if" questions, such as the following: "If I miss another day of school, what happens then?" "If I end up living with my grandmother, what will happen then?" "If I get good grades in school, what happens then?" "If my daddy gets home late from work, what happens then?, "If my teacher asks me to read out loud in class, what happens then?" Again, you can develop word games as a way to gain important information about the child's life. With an adolescent, writing in a journal about events and feelings can serve the same purpose.

Write a poem or a song about whatever is causing the child stress. Develop sentence-completion questions as a way of assisting the child to talk about the situation, for example, "When I feel sad, I ___________," "When my sister gets home from school, I feel ___________," or "The best part of the day is ___________." Sometimes writing your own sentence-completion statements for an individual client can be very helpful.

Take Angel, an eight-year-old girl now living with her foster family. She is very lonely and worried about her parents. She feels protective of them and doesn't want them (or her) to get into any more trouble. Asking Angel to talk about her imaginary friend Hillary may be a good way to gain insight into how she is feeling and managing. A series of sentence-completion questions about Hillary could include the following: "Sometimes when Hillary is in bed, she ___________," "Hillary is the most popular girl in school because ___________," "Sometimes Hillary gets into trouble at her foster home because ___________," "Hillary loves when her mom comes to visit her because ___________," "Hillary has fun, especially when ___________," "Hillary sometimes feels scared when ___________," or "When Hillary was thinking about being three or four years old, she remembers ___________." The value of these sentence-completion exercises is to gain some insights and understanding into Angel's world without asking her to share it directly. Box 4.9 provides an example of an exchange between an adolescent client and a social worker.

Box 4.9 Adolescent and Social Worker Interaction

Stacey's journal entry: "This whole week SUCKED. You asked me to write about my week and it SUCKED!!! My stepmom came to school today for that stupid parent teacher meeting. My dad was a NO SHOW!! I had no intention of being there, but Ms. Nickels came to my 7th hour class to find me. She made me sit in the room with that BITCH. She had absolutely nothing good to say about me or my sister Dekala, I want to be with my mother, not them."

Social worker response: "Thanks for telling me about your week. It must have been hard sitting in that room with her and without your dad there. Did you talk at all during the meeting? Was there any part of the meeting that went okay? You mentioned Dekala; you sound so protective of her. Am I right? Write back."

Stacey's journal response to social worker: "I am still so mad at my dad. He totally knew that I wanted him there, not her. I refuse to talk to her, the way she strutted into that meeting. I didn't say a word, she did all of the talking, of course. There was nothing good that came from the meeting, other than Ms. Nickels handed me a candy bar. I want to help Dekala too, but she is hardly around. When I saw her in the hallway yesterday she barely said hi. She is hanging out with her 'group,' which doesn't include me."

Box 4.10 Multicultural Counseling Knowledge and Awareness Scale

Low Awareness

- I believe all clients should maintain direct eye contact during counseling.
- I think clients who do not discuss intimate aspects of their lives are being resistant and defensive.
- I think that clients should perceive the nuclear family as the ideal social unit.
- I think that being highly competitive and achievement oriented are traits that all clients should work toward.

High Awareness/Knowledge

- I am aware that being born a white person in this society carries with it certain advantages.
- I am aware that being born a minority in this society brings with it certain challenges that white people do not have to face.
- I am aware of individual differences that exist among members within a particular ethnic group based on values, beliefs, and level of acculturation.
- I am aware of differential interpretations of nonverbal communication (e.g., personal space, eye contact, handshakes) within various racial/ethnic groups.
- I have an understanding of the role culture and racism play in the development of identity and worldviews among minority groups.

Source: Ponterotto et al. (2002).

Assessing People with Intellectual Disability/Developmental and Physical Disabilities

Think about your client with a **disability** in terms of things he or she can do rather than what is not possible. Always think about the client's safety and well-being. Many clients with intellectual disabilities may be unable to be fully independent. It is important to communicate with them on their intellectual level so that they are as informed as possible about what is happening in the helping process. When working with a client with intellectual challenges, family members may be an important part of the team. Depending on the client's cognitive abilities, include him or her in decision-making opportunities. Show support for the client's decisions. As with any client, if you are concerned about his or her choices, do not interfere unless the client is potentially harming himself or herself or others. Empowerment and encouragement are core professional values the social worker needs to uphold.

When assessing a client's intelligence or physical challenges and other disabilities, consider the following:

Problem-Solving Ability: Can the client find practical solutions to a common problem, think through a problem, and arrive at a solution? Kimberly, a person with a mild intellectual disability, may be able to ride the bus independently to and from work. Amanda, a person with a severe intellectual disability, may have to be supervised at all times, including help with independent living skills. Mark is a person who has been deaf since birth. He uses American Sign Language and can read lips. He recently completed his undergraduate degree at Gallaudet University. Notice the range of ability and needs across this group of disabled clients.

Verbal Ability: Is the client able to express emotions and ideas and understand the verbal communication of others? For example, Joe, a person with a mild intellectual disability, is able to drive and lives in a group home. He is able to communicate with the staff and has developed a close relationship with Kay, a coworker, also with a diagnosis of intellectual disability.

Social Intelligence: Is the client able to read social cues, adapting his or her behaviors to fit the situation and having the skills to interact and participate in social groups and activities? At age 22, Barry was in a diving accident that left him with a traumatic brain injury. Highly social before his accident, he is now unable to read nonverbal cues and is easily agitated and confused. His ability to manage his feelings has also been affected by the injury to his brain (Summers, 2003). Melinda is a person who has epilepsy. In the past, her seizures were controlled with medication; however, recently she is experiencing grand mal seizures and has been hospitalized twice. She feels foggy and disoriented, a likely side effect of the new medication.

In considering the environment in which the client lives, determine whether his or her basic needs are being met, such as food, clothing, safety, and health care. Is the client receiving love and affection? Is the person included in community events and being stimulated by planned activities? Does the client have some control over how he or she spends his or her time? Is the environment, such as a group home or apartment, safe and stable? What supports need to be in place for the client to function most independently?

Physical disabilities are often visually apparent, such as a client in a wheelchair or a person with a prosthetic arm. There are other types of disabilities that cannot easily be seen, such as a person who is deaf or a person with a chronic heart condition. When working with a person who is physically challenged, be cognizant of your behaviors and attitudes. Screaming at a person who is deaf or talking loudly to a person who is legally blind is neither helpful nor empowering to the clients. One important aspect of working with people who have any type of disability is to serve as an advocate. Buildings that are accessible, employers who hire the most qualified person, family members who are embracing, and a community that provides transportation services improve the quality of the lives disabled persons tremendously.

Familiarize yourself with the Americans with Disabilities Act, which prohibits discrimination against people with disabilities in employment, transportation, public accommodation, communications, and governmental activities. Visit the government website on the act to gain more knowledge on the resources and legal rights of disabled persons in the United States.

Older Adults

Growing old is a normal part of life but can present challenges, as injuries occur and take longer to heal or chronic health problems develop. We live in a youth-centered society where how our society responds to the elderly can be perceived as a problem. When completing an assessment, it can be helpful to include important people, such as a spouse or child, in the process, especially if there appears to be a change in the client's cognitive abilities. Assessing the needs of the caretaker (most often a family member) can be equally important as the day-to-day responsibility of caring for a loved one can be physically and emotionally exhausting.

Sense of Purpose: Having a sense of purpose in life improves one's mental, emotional, and physical well-being. This is often tied to one's career or employment. When retired, one's life purpose may need to be adjusted. Does the client feel useful? Does the client seem generally content with his or her life? Is there a project the client is looking forward to completing? Is the client involved in the community as a volunteer, such as with the local hospital or as a tutor in an after-school program?

Plans for Aging: Often, a sense of vulnerability can accompany aging. Assessing an aging client's sense of safety, security, and ability to function independently can be important in understanding his or her current concerns. Does the client have plans for retirement and the financial wherewithal to follow through? Has the client thought about specific ways to maintain his or her independence? Consider how the client is physically and emotionally feeling. Can the client still drive? Does he or she wear hearing aids or glasses? Does the client use a walker? Are the client's medical needs being met?

Support System: We all feel better in the context of family and friends who care about us. This feeling of safely and being loved is of growing importance as we age and become more vulnerable both physically and emotionally when alone for long periods of time. Assess the client's connectedness to family and community. Who does the client talk to daily? Is he or she part of a Scrabble club or other social group? Does family spend time with the older person? Is the client involved in a respite care program? Are the client's dietary needs being met; for example, are meals delivered to his or her home daily? Is there a person who can assist with paying bills?

Coping: Understanding how an older client manages his or her day on all fronts—emotionally, physically, and financially—helps one understand the context of the client's life and the coping skills he or she has at his or her disposal to successfully negotiate day-to-day challenges. In your assessment, try to determine the following: How has the older person managed day-to-day living, the loss of a partner or being uprooted from the only home the client has ever known? How does the client manage losing his or her hearing or mobility? Ascertain, for example, if the person's irritability is recent or if this is a long-standing aspect of his or her personality. If you note an extreme change in an older person's disposition, inform his or her medical care provider. Always consider the client's level of depression, as older adults can experience prolonged and acute feelings of loss, hopelessness, and sadness. Older adults are at higher risk for suicide completion.

Faith: Faith can be a central and anchoring aspect of clients lives and a resource as well as a source of strength when contending with life challenges. Is the client a member of a religious community? What are the client's beliefs about an afterlife? Does the client find comfort in solitary prayer or in community prayer?

The Older Americans Act provides specific objectives for maintaining the dignity and welfare of older individuals and created the primary vehicle for organizing, coordinating, and providing community-based services and opportunities for older Americans and their families through community-based Area Agencies on Aging. Visit the government website of the Act for more information on resources available for serving older clients.

People with Mental Illness

Mental illness is common in the United States. The National Institute of Mental Health reported that 43.8 million Americans (or nearly 19 percent of the population) suffered from a mental illness within the past year (2013). Chances are that you will encounter people with mental health challenges in your social work practice. People with mental illness may also have other problems in life. For example, a person with schizophrenia may be arrested for disorderly conduct that leads to time in jail, or a person with depression may self-medicate by drinking alcohol to excess. In interacting with a client who is mentally ill, be patient; do not be overtly critical, challenging, or confronting, as this can cause extreme distress.

There are many symptoms of mental illness. including depression, anxiety, aggression, and many others you will study about in your social work education. For example, a panic attack is a symptom of mental illness. These attacks can mimic a heart attack, an asthma attack, or possibly a drug interaction (Summers, 2003). Phobias, caused by extreme anxiety, can lead to the client avoiding contact with others. Look for responses from clients that indicate that their suffering is so intolerable that they must avoid the stimuli at any cost.

Assess the client's support, such as a family member, a community-based program, or a court-appointed guardian who is involved in the client's life. Does the person with mental illness interact with others on a regular basis? Does the client have meaningful work? Is the client receiving ongoing and appropriate mental health care? Make use of these collateral contacts when planning care for the mentally ill client.

How is the client's general health? Does the client have access to medications and psychiatric services? Is the client participating in a day treatment program, group treatment, community meetings, or individual or family counseling? Is a risk of suicide present? Is the client experiencing side effects of medications, causing discomfort and complaint?

Assess your understanding of serving special populations by taking this brief quiz.

Assess the family's needs regarding practical information, such as treatment options. A family's isolation can be countered by joining a support group. Case management services, such as locating a day treatment program for a child or securing finances for housing, can be very helpful.

SUMMARY

- With the growing changes diversity within the population, cultural competence is an increasingly critical factor in the success of any social work intervention.
- Holding a color-blind view of the world is a particularly limiting perspective for any social worker because it can obscure awareness of the potential for

the social work profession itself to have an oppressive effect on minority groups.

- Self-awareness creates the opportunity for the social worker to recognize and become comfortable with cultural difference. Social workers can grow in self-awareness by applying the Developmental Model of Intersensitivity to themselves.
- A culturally competent social worker devotes ongoing time and effort to developing a nuanced knowledge base regarding cultural and ethnic diversity. Social workers can grow in their understanding and implications of the complexity of culture in clients' lives through the application of the theoretical framework of intersectionality.
- Culture influences the decision to use a particular social work skill when working with diverse clients. These skills can be verbal, such as the use of confrontation; nonverbal, such as eye contact; and environmental, such as the appropriate use of personal space.
- The growing diversity of the U.S. population requires social workers to know culture-specific assessment skills when working with special populations, such as children; those who are intellectually, physically, and mentally disabled; and older adults.

APPLY IT

1. Watch all three sessions of **Interactive Case Study #2** of Anthony and social worker James. Identify and reflect on likely differences between James and Anthony, both African American men. In your judgment, what accounts for the within-group differences between James and Anthony?
2. Watch session one of **Interactive Case Study #5** of Mrs. Kita and social worker Diane. Put yourself in the place of Mrs. Kita and reflect on how you would respond to the life stressors of having a sick child, an incarcerated spouse, and chronic money problems. How would your responses be different from Mrs. Kita's? In what ways would they be similar? Reflect on universal versus culturally specific ways of dealing with problems.

Assess Your Competence

Use the scale below to rate your current level of achievement on the following concepts or skills associated with each competency presented in the chapter:

1	2	3
I can accurately describe the concept or skill	I can consistently identify the concept or skill when observing and analyzing practice activities	I can competently implement the concept or skill in my own practice

_______ Understands and can apply the concept of intersectionality.

_______ Understands and can articulate core cultural concepts and NASW standards for cultural competence.

_______ Can identify and explain components of the attitude–knowledge–skills model of cultural competence.

_______ Can articulate and explain the consequences of the color-blind perspective.

_______ Understands and can describe the Developmental Model of Intercultural Sensitivity and each developmental stage.

_______ Can identify and articulate key areas of cultural difference.

5

Basic Skills for Direct Practice

WESTEND61/GETTY IMAGES

LEARNING OUTCOMES

- Demonstrate attending behaviors.
- Demonstrate interviewing skills.

CHAPTER OUTLINE

For social workers, the key to working effectively with clients is developing expertise in the basic skills of communication. This involves formal academic education, professional training, and supervision. During the interview process, the social worker connects with the client through the use of empathic responses such as **reflection of feelings, paraphrasing,** and **attending behaviors**. Using skills effectively requires knowing when it is appropriate to use the skill by gauging (or anticipating) the client's likely response. This level of expertise takes considerable effort to develop. Social work **interviewing skills** requires both the discipline to practice and the faith that you will develop the skills that enable you to move forward with confidence. This chapter introduces you to foundational interviewing skills and attending behaviors with a focus on understanding the way information is transmitted and received.

ATTENDING BEHAVIORS

As you begin reading this chapter, watch this clip where the instructor introduces you to the concept of attending to the client through the use of the social worker's nonverbal communication. What are the main purposes for both verbal and nonverbal messages?

Nonverbal Messages

Social workers must be verbally and nonverbally responsive to clients. There are many ways that the social worker can communicate concern, caring, and involvement with the client nonverbally. Most importantly, be genuine and not mechanical (or simply going through the motions) in your interactions. Attending behaviors include **tone of voice**, eye contact, **body positioning**, head movements and a warm smile. **Furthering responses**, statements such as "please go on" or "tell me more about what happened," and mirroring the client's emotional/facial responses are also components of this skill (Cormier, Nurius, & Osborn, 2011). It is important for the client to feel listened to and valued. If a client senses a genuine interest on the social worker's part, he or she will be more open. In order to convey sensitivity to cultural variations and communication patterns, the social worker must show openness and respect for each person's uniqueness (Cormier & Cormier, 2011). The social worker's presence, being fully there and available, is instrumental in establishing and developing the helping relationship.

Body Positioning and Spatial Considerations

Body positioning is what we communicate through hand gestures, leaning in, facing our clients, and maintaining a relaxed and approachable stance and are ways of conveying "I'm here with you; you have my undivided attention."

When considering the location of an interview, whether it is in your office, in the client's kitchen, or at the park, minimizing environmental distractions is also a part of attending. Be sure that the space is private enough to ensure client confidentiality. For example, in a client's home, it may be appropriate to sit away from the television (if it is on) or in a room outside the normal traffic flow where you can have some privacy. In your office, having telephone calls diverted to voice messages or the receptionist can provide uninterrupted time with your client. If you share an office, a Do Not Disturb sign can indicate that you are in session. In a public place, find a remote spot for a private conversation, such as a secluded table in a restaurant or a private room in a public library.

When taking notes during a session, be sure to let the client know what you are writing and the reason for taking notes. Offer a statement such as "I want to be sure that I get all this information down correctly" or "Do you mind if I write a few notes?" But put your pen down and listen, especially when the client is very emotional. Use shorthand or symbols that will jog your memory when writing the finalized case note. Knowing how to adjust your need to document with your need to be fully present is a skill that takes time and practice.

Seating arrangements will depend on the setting and type of the interview. If visiting a client's home, wait for the client to indicate where to sit. In an office, it is best to place the chairs about three to four feet apart. This distance appears to be the least anxiety provoking for the client (Cormier & Hackney, 2011). Be aware of the client's need for personal space and respectful by allowing the client to determine the most comfortable distance. Should three to four feet not be enough or too much, allow the client to adjust accordingly. This is of particular concern when working with clients from different cultural backgrounds. When interacting with children, be sure to position yourself at their level by bending down or sitting at their eye level. Find yourself a comfortable sitting position and relax.

When working with mandatory or potentially aggressive clients, sometimes having a desk between you can provide a physical barrier, as the desk can be viewed as protection between you and your client. A less confrontational arrangement is to sit at the corner of your desk or table, which allows for less intimacy than a shoulder-to-shoulder stance. Although most clients pose no physical threat to the social worker, sitting close to an exit is a sensible strategy. A word of caution, however: familiarity with your client can help you determine if this type of protective measure is needed or if it could serve to alienate the client.

There are some nonverbal distractions that can present barriers to communication, such as the social worker fidgeting, yawning, sitting with arms tightly crossed, gazing out the window, staring at the clock or looking at a watch, looking bored or disinterested, checking for text messages on a cell phone (be sure to put your cell phone on airplane mode during the interview), playing with hair or nails, and nervous laughter.

Touch

Touch is also a part of how a social worker uses his or her body to convey interest and to show that you care. However, be aware of the client's cultural background and past experiences; for example, having been sexually abused as a child and gender-related issues such as touch could be interpreted by the client as a sexual overture. Pointing a finger, hand beckoning, or using other hand gestures can be interpreted as being critical, demeaning, judgmental, and otherwise offensive by the client, depending on his or her cultural norms and lived experiences.

Watch this video to learn more about touch through the words of the instructor. What effect can touch have on a relationship with a client?

When used correctly, touch can be a very powerful way of communicating that "I care, I'm listening, and I'm concerned." A nonthreatening way to attend to a client who is crying is to offer a tissue, thus responding to the need without actual touch. You can also ask the client if it is all right to touch him or her (e.g., "This must be so hard for you. Is it okay if I give you a hug?").

Watch Diane touch Mrs. Kita's shoulder as she is crying and stating softly, "It's okay." As you reflect on your own comfort with touch, is this something you would do? If not, how else could you convey that you are fully present?

As you finish reading this section, take time to watch these clips. You will see the attending skills, body positioning, and touch demonstrated. Following each clip, listen to the narration, which provides the context to understand how and why this attending behavior was used as a way to convey interest in each client's situation.

Body Positioning 1

Body Positioning 2

Tone of Voice

Tone of voice is another aspect of attending behavior. It is not just the spoken words but also the way the words are delivered (Cormier & Hackney, 2011; Sheafor & Horejsi, 2015). Strive for a warm and pleasant tone of voice, as this can add richness to the message. By being verbally expressive, the social worker can mirror or match the client's feelings.

In this video the instructor discusses the tone of voice and how to pace the interview. Why are these considerations so important to a social worker?

In Box 5.1, the social worker matches the tone of voice to the words chosen. Through her soft tone and slow pace, Judith has a chance to cry without feeling judged or rushed. The client thus experiences the social worker's concern at many levels. Be sure to speak clearly but not too loudly, which could frighten the client, or too softly, which can leave your message unheard or misunderstood. It is best to vary your volume, tone, and pitch. Pace your speech patterns, questions, and responses in a way that conveys interest, not boredom. Using a "singsong voice" may be appropriate when working with children but not with adults.

Watch this clip of James talking with Anthony. How does James's tone of voice change when asking the question, "What about the risks of being associated with a gang?" Listen to James as he reflects a tone of voice that indicates the repetition of Anthony's life in the future as he says, "So five, ten years from now, you still see yourself in the same gang, doing the same old things." Describe how you would have reacted to his questions if you were Anthony.

Box 5.1 Tone of Voice

In the example below, notice how the intentional use of tone of voice by the social worker affects the meaning and the message of the spoken words.

Social Worker: You sound really sad (Said in a quiet, soft tone).

Judith: I am very sad and depressed; I've never felt worse in my life.

Social Worker: It's understandable; you are still in mourning over your son's death (Said with an intonation of sadness).

Judith: And I can't stop crying. Wherever I go, I see parents with their children, and I just break down (She starts to tear up).

Social Worker: It's okay (Very softly, and hands the client a tissue).

Judith: Thank you. My husband and friends think I should be able to contain all my tears, but they just keep coming.

Social Worker: (Sits silently)

Now that you have finished reading this section, take time to watch this clip. You will see the attending skill of tone of voice demonstrated. Following the clip, listen to the narration, which provides the context to understand how and why this attending behavior was used as a way to convey interest in the client's situation.

Empathetic Tone of Voice

Silence

Using **silence** appropriately can be a very effective way to communicate with clients; however, there may be some anxieties about silence in an interview. For example, as the social worker, you assume that you are not doing an adequate job if there is a lull in the conversation; therefore, you might jump in too quickly and try to fill in the gaps or "rescue" the client. In order to keep the conversation flowing, the social worker continues to ask a series of questions or moves to a topic that might be less threatening to the client. Resist the urge to fill every silence with a question or response. Conversely, if the silence continues and the client is becoming uncomfortable (squirming in his or her seat or looking to you directly for assistance), interrupting the silence can be useful. In this instance, the social worker may comment on the possible meaning of the silence: "You seem to be struggling with this issue. I am sensing you need to slow down the pace"; or you can acknowledge the silence and then ask an appropriate question: "You are so quiet; I wonder if part of your silence relates to all the struggles you feel inside?"

Watch this video and listen to the instructor talk about silence. How is silence an important part of the interviewing process?

According to Shebib (2007), there are six types of silence:

- Thinking—client needs time to process information and respond.
- Confused and unsure about what to say or do—client doesn't know what is expected and therefore may become anxious. Here, the social worker may need to interrupt the silence and clarify the question, expectation, or direction.
- Encountering painful feelings—client needs space to feel and experience pain and anxiety.
- Dealing with issues of trust—client is reluctant and self-protective; may be involuntary.
- Quiet by nature—client is quiet by nature and prefers other ways of communicating, such as through art or journaling.
- Reached closure on a particular point—client has nothing more to say on the topic or idea.

Ethical and Professional Behavior

Behavior: Use empathy, reflection, and interpersonal skills to effectively engage diverse clients and constituencies.

Critical Thinking Question: In determining when to use a particular attending behavior, what considerations must a social worker take into account?

In each of these instances, the social worker will respond differently to the meaning of the client's silence. For example, the involuntary client who is dealing with issues of trust uses silence as a way to control the interview and demonstrate hostility (Shebib, 2007). The client who is quiet by nature and is not used to giving lengthy explanations may be more comfortable sitting with thoughts rather than giving a spontaneous response. If you understand the meaning behind the silence, you can use an empathy statement to convey such a situation (Boyle, Hull, Mather, Smith, & Farley, 2011). Offering a statement such as "I can understand how it may be hard to trust a stranger; take your time and only tell me things that you are ready to talk about" can put the client at ease.

Generally speaking, the best approach to silence is not to be intimidated by it or uncomfortable with it but to understand and embrace the silence as an appropriate attending behavior. Wait with patience, take a deep breath, drink a sip of water, but remain relaxed and attentive. As you develop your ability to use this skill, you will find that silence is an asset to the relationship. Being able to sit quietly, waiting to see what new revelation will emerge, is worth the wait. Sometimes saying absolutely nothing is exactly what is needed. Use silence intentionally as a way of encouraging the client to be reflective and sit with his or her thoughts and feelings. On a final note, for nonnative English speakers, it is important slow the pace of the conversation to give the client the time he or she needs to think in his or her second language (English) and respond to your questions.

As you watch Mrs. Kita and Diane interact, pay close attention to their attending behaviors. You can hear and see the pacing of the interview. Watch for the give-and-take; pay attention to how they lean into each other. Watch as Diane gives Mrs. Kita plenty of time to think about how she wants to respond to questions. Listen to their tone of voice. Close your eyes and simply listen to the conversation. Can you hear the care and concern being conveyed? Watch their facial expressions, eye contact, and body posture. It is through the nonverbal portion of their communication that the essence of the relationship is affirmed.

Watch the exchange between Diane and Mrs. Kita. Pay attention to the pace of Diane's questions and the silence between them. Think about Diane's use of silence; was it too hurried or just right?

Furthering Responses

The use of **furthering responses** offered by the social worker is another way of conveying understanding, and these are used as a way of saying, "Keep talking," "Tell me more," and "I am listening to you." Furthering responses can be used to highlight a particular word (e.g., Client: "I doubt he'll ever forgive me!" Social worker: "Forgive you?"). Hand gestures and nodding of the head are other ways of nonverbally communicating that the social worker is listening and for the client to continue.

Single-word/phrase utterances such as "hmmm," "uh-huh," "okay," "um," and "go on" also convey an interest in the client and serve as inducements for the client to proceed. Furthering responses provide noninvasive support and a way to monitor the flow of the interview (Hill & O'Brien, 2014).

As you listen to the instructor discuss furthering responses, how might you use this skill to convey interest in your client's continuation of their story?

Additionally, using furthering responses such as "And . . . ?" or "hmmmm" or "but" encourage the client to continue talking. The social worker is subtly directing the client to follow the line of conversation by saying very little yet letting the client know where the social worker would like to take the interview.

Watch as James uses the furthering response "um . . .hm" to encourage Anthony to continue with his train of thought. Can you see how this simple strategy keeps Anthony talking?

The example in Box 5.2 illustrates the use of attending behaviors and other basic interviewing skills. Through reflection of feeling statements, paraphrasing, and furthering responses, social workers convey to clients an understanding of their experiences.

Box 5.2 Franny—Attending Behaviors

Franny is in her mid-70s. She is living on a very limited budget. She is concerned about her daughter's financial demands.

Franny: My daughter refuses to discuss her finances with me, but she insists she has no money and needs a loan.

Social Worker: A loan? (Furthering responses, direct eye contact)

Franny: A loan, for something, but she won't tell me what. That leaves me thinking the worst, like she owes money to some criminals.

Social Worker: And . . . (Furthering response)

Franny: It scares me to death. I don't want anyone coming after her or me.

Social Worker: That is unsettling. (Paraphrasing, said slowly and with concern) What do you think is going on with her? (Open-ended question)

Franny: I don't know, but she always ends up in some kind of trouble, with me bailing her out.

Social Worker: hmmmm (Furthering response)

Franny: I know she counts on me to help her, and I usually do, but I won't lend her money unless she tells me what it's for. I can't keep doing this. It's tearing me up inside.

Social Worker: (Silence 10–15 seconds—a furthering response strategy)

Franny: You know, I really feel angry about this whole thing. She uses me and doesn't give it a second thought. She feels justified and entitled to anything I have. . . . many people in my life treat me this way. She is my daughter, so I make excuses for her. But as much as I hate to admit it, it isn't just her.

Social Worker: You end up feeling used. (Reflection of feeling) Can you describe some other situations when you have felt this way? (Open-ended question, leaning in and looking directly at client)

In the next clip, you will see the attending skill called furthering response demonstrated. Listen to the narration, which provides the context to understand how and why this attending behavior was used as a way to convey interest in the both Anthony's and Maria's situation.

Furthering

Facial Expressions, Eye Contact, and Head Movements

Social workers use **facial expressions** to mirror back to the client an awareness of his or her emotional state. If a client is talking about the great time she had at the high school dance and excitedly describes this new experience, it is appropriate for the social worker to smile with pleasure. Conversely, if a client is discussing how lonely and out of place she felt at the school dance, the social worker's face should mirror back a sense of sadness and disappointment. The social worker's facial expressions should reinforce the verbal communication (e.g., by saying, "I'm interested in hearing your story" and looking and truly being interested in the client). This nonverbal display of interest serves as a reinforcement for the client to continue.

In the next video, the instructor addresses the use of facial expressions. What is the importance of mirroring the client's facial expressions, eye contact, and head nodding to convey understanding?

Mirroring, Eye Contact, and Head Movements

In this video, Marie is affirming Anna's feeling through her facial expression and words. How do Marie's facial expressions convey her understanding of Anna's relief now that she is home? Put yourself in Anna's place as you review this session and identify three ways in which Marie and Anna are mirroring each other's feelings as they move toward ending their relationship.

Maintaining intermittent eye contact with the client is a way of saying, "I am here with you." This is not the same as staring or glaring at a client, which can cause extreme discomfort. Mutual eye contact on the part of the client and/or social worker can demonstrate a readiness to delve into the problem situation. However, cultural patterns differ regarding eye checking (looking to a loved one or a person in authority before responding), which can be misinterpreted by the worker. It could be considered disrespectful to maintain eye contact with a person who is

Policy to Practice The Affordable Care Act, March 2010

The Affordable Care Act (ACA) puts Anna in control of her health care. It reduces her insurance premium costs and reduces her out-of-pocket expenses by capping her portion of medical expenses. The ACA stipulates that a patient with a preexisting condition or illness is covered by insurance and can't be penalized by charging the patient more for medical care. In Anna's case, she is receiving treatments for cancer. The ACA will protect Anna's family from losing all of their financial resources as the cost of her treatments continues to rise.

From Case Study #1

Social Worker: Do you know when you're actually leaving for Indianapolis?

Anna: In two weeks. My husband wants to come with me. I want him there, but at the same time we're not going to have any money if he takes off work.

Social Worker: So you're also worried about finances.

Anna: How are we gonna make house payments if he's not working?

Social Worker: But you want him there, which is understandable.

Anna: Uh-huh, I don't want to be alone.

Social Worker: But if he's with you and not working, finances will be tight.

Anna: Exactly.

Social Worker: So, you're really in a bind.

Anna: Plus I always stayed home with my kids, and so I don't think that I can get any type of disability. If he's off work for a long time, we'll have to make the payments to keep our insurance, and I can't do without it.

Social Worker: Not now. There are so many different areas to consider: your finances, your children, making sure that you're okay. There are health care options available to you through the Affordable Care Act. It is a program that offers insurance to you at a cost that you can afford, plus you qualify for coverage even though you will need additional medical care. Here is some information that may be helpful to you. I am happy to answer any questions you have about this program.

To learn more about The Affordable Care Act, visit the U.S. Department of Health and Human Services website.

considered an authority figure (social worker) or of higher status. For example, with Native American culture, averting one's eyes is customary. As a worker, practice looking away intermittently so that the client can observe you too. In addition, it is imperative for the social worker to attend to the incongruence of the client's words and facial expressions (e.g., the client saying "I feel great" as her eyes fill with tears). Using this example, the social worker can respond to the tears versus the words by saying, "Although you say you feel great, your tears tell me something different. Can we talk about the sadness you're experiencing right now?" Being aware of cultural differences is important, as in the case of Mrs. Kita.

In this video clip, watch Mrs. Kita's relatively still face. What emotions does she convey?

The social worker's head movements can also offer nonverbal feedback by encouraging or discouraging the client from further discussion. The head nodding

? Assess your understanding of attending behaviors by taking this brief quiz.

up and down offers a sense that the social worker is listening and agreeing. Because the client feels understood, the communication is likely to continue. Shaking of the head from left to right may convey that the social worker disagrees or disapproves, causing the communication to stop or be severely limited.

Now that you have finished reading this section, watch these clips. You will see the attending skills of eye contact and head nodding demonstrated by Nicole and Karen. Following each clip, listen to the narration, which provides the context to understand how and why this attending behavior was used as a way to convey interest in the client's situation.

Nodding

Eye Contact

INTERVIEWING SKILLS

In this section, students will be introduced to lead-in responses and basic interviewing skills. How to use these skills in a meaningful and productive way will be described and illustrated throughout the remainder of the chapter.

Lead-In Responses

Now that you have some understanding of attending behaviors, let's look at **lead-in responses**, which are the introductory part of a sentence stem or question that begins the social worker's response to the client. Lead-in responses give the social worker an opportunity to match the client's verbal style (Brems, 2001). It is helpful to develop a wide variety of lead-in responses so that you are not repeating the same ones over and over. See Box 5.3 for examples of lead-in responses organized by sensory categories. Experienced interviewers can adjust their responses to match a client's primary sensory orientation—for example, if a client seems most focused on the physical, then kinesthetic responses are indicated (e.g., "I could feel . . ."); for clients who seem to think more visually, visual lead-in responses (e.g., saying "I see") are an effective strategy (Brems, 2001).

When meeting a client for the first time or during subsequent visits, small talk is a good way to "break the ice" or start off on safe topics. Asking about the weather or commenting on traffic or the pictures on the walls in the client's home are examples of small talk. This is a time that is used to put the client at ease as you gently begin to guide the client toward the purpose of the interview. Box 5.4 provides a sample agenda for your review.

Box 5.3 Lead-In Responses

Auditory	Kinesthetic	Visual
What I am hearing you say . . .	Could you feel . . . ?	I am observing . . .
As I hear it . . .	You feel . . .	I detect . . .
You sound . . .	I gather . . .	From where you are watching . . .
Does this ring a bell . . . ?	From where you stand . . .	I noticed . . .
From what I am hearing . . .	Right now, you feel . . .	From your point of view . . .
It echoes the sound of . . .	I sense that . . .	I imagine . . .
You are telling me . . .	I have the feeling . . .	You are focused on . . .
It sounds like . . .	I gather . . .	Am I perceiving this correctly . . . ?
It sounds as if . . .	From where you are . . .	As I see it . . .
Sounds to me . . .	Am I close . . . ?	My sense is that . . .
I hear you saying . . .	I am drawing . . .	It seems like . . .
If I am hearing you correctly . . .	You felt . . .	You are considering . . .
It sounds as though you are saying . . .	**General**	You are describing . . .
	Correct me if I am wrong . . .	It appears as though . . .
	Could it be . . . ?	It looks like . . .
	I wonder what else . . .	Following what you just said . . .
	I am wondering if . . .	I see what you mean . . .
	Go on . . .	You appear . . .
	And . . .	

Box 5.4 A Sample Agenda for Meeting with a Client

1. Welcome and small talk.
2. General open-ended questions about the client.
3. Ask if there are issues the client wants to cover.
4. Review "homework" assignments from previous session and determine level of progress or barriers.
5. Discuss new ideas and strategies toward progress.
6. Offer ideas and suggestions as appropriate, reaffirming the client's strengths and efforts.
7. Provide time to discuss extraneous issues that may be a factor in goal attainment. For example, to an adolescent female, how are her classes going at school? Her babysitting schedule? Her relationships with friends, foster parents, and siblings? Extracurricular activities? How are all of these issues related to her remaining sober?
8. Check to see if there are any other pressing issues.
9. Wrap up what was discussed and plan of what needs to be done prior to the next session.
10. Close the session and document the required aspects of your session. For more about this, read Appendix A at the back of the book on how to document a session.

Paraphrasing

Paraphrasing is a way to check that the client's and the social worker's perceptions are similar and that there is a shared understanding between them. Paraphrasing focuses on the content of the client's message and the thinking/cognition of the client. The social worker restates what the client has said using his or her own words (Boyle et al., 2011; Hepworth, Rooney, & Larsen, 2013). Paraphrasing can elicit feedback from the client, confirming that the social worker understands the meaning of the client's message. A paraphrase conveys that, generally, the client has been heard and now can move on to another aspect of the topic. In the following clips, the instructor defines the skill of paraphrase. How and when is it helpful to use paraphrase in an interview?

Paraphrase

The paraphrase points out what the client has said and his or her view of the situation under discussion. It should not reflect the social worker's viewpoint or opinion. Box 5.5 demonstrates a social worker using the paraphrasing skill and lead-in responses to better comprehend how the client understands her problem.

In the example in Box 5.5, the social worker captures the true meaning of Mary's addictive spending pattern. Hearing this "cycle" repeated back to Mary highlights for her the major counseling issue: developing other ways to reduce stress and conflict in her life. Also, in this example, the social worker uses two types of lead-in responses: auditory ("If I am hearing you correctly . . .") and visual ("You are describing . . .").

In this video clip, watch as Louis paraphrases what Kim just said by stating, "You were always on high alert." Does he capture the true meaning of her words? Does she feel understood?

Paraphrasing should not be used so excessively as to avoid conveying the impression that the social worker is simply mimicking what the client is saying; instead, the social worker should express the important words and ideas back to the client (Miley, O'Melia, & DuBois, 2011). Be true to the essence of what the client has said. Paraphrasing should be used in conjunction with other methods of facilitating the client's responses, such as reflection of feelings and interpretation. Paraphrasing helps the client see clearly what he or she is thinking or experiencing. Hearing the social worker restate ideas gives the client an opportunity to rethink or to see issues from a different perspective (Hepworth et al., 2013). It is always a good idea to check back with the client after delivering a

Box 5.5 Mary—Paraphrasing

Mary is a 47-year-old female who has been struggling with finances. She spends money excessively and is deeply in debt.

Social Worker: What do you experience when you go to the mall? (Open-ended question)

Mary: I go in the evening, especially when I'm feeling stressed. The kids will get me upset, and I'll go straight to the mall after dinner.

Social Worker: If I am hearing you correctly, most of the time you go to the mall because of a difficult situation at home. (Lead-in response and paraphrase)

Mary: Yeah, I'll feel frustrated, and then when I go shopping, I get this intense rush. I mean it really works. I charge up my credit cards on a lot of things I really don't need. It gives me a quick thrill. But by the time I get home, I feel like crap because I realize that I've just dug myself deeper into debt.

Social Worker: Your excessive spending is a way to help you feel better. But you are not sure how else to manage all the feelings you have pent up inside. (Paraphrase)

Mary: Yeah, I feel awful, and then I feel worthless. That's when my husband and I fight—and then I just want to go back to the mall. The whole thing just keeps going round and round.

Social Worker: You are describing this as a pattern or a cycle. You spend money to relieve stress but then regret your actions. And then it starts all over. (Lead-in/paraphrase)

Mary: That's exactly it.

paraphrase by asking, "Is that right?" or "Am I following you correctly?" This is the social worker's chance to modify the response, depending on the client's reaction to what was just stated. Importantly, a paraphrase focuses on the client's thought process and less on his or her emotional experiences. Read the client's response in Box 5.A and then write a paraphrase in the indicated space.

Reflection of Feelings

Reflection of feeling is one of the most important skills in the social worker's repertoire. It requires the social worker to restate and explore the client's affective (feeling) statements. Frequently, the client is experiencing a wide variety of feelings and has difficulty

Box 5.A Now You Try It . . . Paraphrasing

A father is talking to the home interventionist about his children.

"I want to get my life back in order. I know I messed up in the past, but I want my kids back. They have been away from me for too long—it's been almost a year. Imagine, strangers raising my kids. I know the foster care system is supposed to help us. Frankly, I think things are much worse since that social worker got involved."

A. Key points in the client's message:

1. ______________________________

2. ______________________________

B. Your paraphrasing response:

1. ______________________________

Developing Cultural Competence Working with a Japanese Client

Mrs. Kita is the parent of two children. Her family has emigrated from Japan, and both she and her husband Jirou are U.S. citizens. Currently, Jirou is in prison for embezzlement. Diane is the social worker assigned to the case. As a guest in Mrs. Kita's home, there are some cultural considerations to take into account. For example, Mrs. Kita is a very proud person who is uncomfortable asking for help. Diane recognizes her discomfort and tries to put Mrs. Kita at ease. On entering Mrs. Kita's home, Diane takes off her shoes and also offers Mrs. Kita a basket of fruit. This demonstrates an awareness of Mrs. Kita's customs. Mrs. Kita looks down periodically during the interview, consistent with her cultural norms. She wants to "save face," a trait characteristic of Japanese culture. Diane's tone of voice conveys care and concern. The pace of the interview works, as Diane mirrors Mrs. Kita's voice volume, expressions, and nuances.

Social Worker: My name is Diane Jones. I am the social worker with the Family Promise program. (Show her your name tag. Diane looks around and notices shoes lined up by door; she then removes her shoes with no comment.)

Social Worker: Thank you for meeting with me today. (Hands Mrs. Kita a small box with some fruit in it)

Social Worker: I brought this for you. (Mrs. Kita looks down very slightly)

Mrs. Kita: Thank you. (Bow) Please come in. I have been expecting you. (Mrs. Kita shows the social worker where to sit [facing the entrance])

Mrs. Kita: Please have some. (Offers her a drink of water and some already prepared food on a tray. All this is through gestures)

Social Worker: Yes, that would be great. Thank you. (Slight smile)

▶ Watch Mrs. Kita's case here.

Watch the greeting between the social worker and Mrs. Kita.

1. What did you notice about the social worker, Diane, and Mrs. Kita's introduction to each other?
2. What would you do differently?
3. How can you assure Mrs. Kita that you are a social worker who wants to enter into a working relationship with her?

separating them from each other and understanding how these feelings are related to one another. Social workers use reflection of feelings to understand how a client responds emotionally to life (Cormier et al., 2011). However, there are no right or wrong feelings—they just are. In these videos, you'll learn more about the skill reflection of feeling. Listen as the instructor walks you through the definition. When is it helpful to use this skill?

▶ Reflection of Feeling

Sometimes the social worker may have a difficult time fully appreciating the complexity of the client's emotions and misreads them. When this happens, it is important to acknowledge your possible mistake and try again. When a beginning social worker attempts this skill, limited life experiences may be seen as a barrier. For example, it may be hard to express authentic sadness if you have never experienced the death of a close friend, parent, or other close relative. The social worker must also be sensitive to nonverbal language since feelings tend to express themselves nonverbally (e.g., a nervous laugh, rolling of the eyes, nervous twitching, blushing, or looking down). Additionally, if the client has difficulty expressing a feeling, the social worker may want to present several feeling words, all with similar meanings, so that the client can select the one with the best fit (Kadushin & Kadushin, 2013). For example, "I am observing that things are overwhelming and challenging for you right now, but you also get a thrill out of winning the game and finishing first. Am I correct?" This enables the client to confirm the feeling but without experiencing the pressure of identifying feeling states. The social worker can also normalize feelings; for example, "Many people who lose a beloved pet feel the way you do—very empty and alone." Reflection of feeling is a technique that helps the social worker explore the extent of the client's problems and how the client views the situation. Validating the client's feelings can be good modeling, thus showing the client that his or her feelings matter and have a powerful effect on cognition and behavior.

The best way to gauge if you are using this skill appropriately is to listen to the client's response. If you correctly capture the meaning, the client will likely feel understood and continue speaking. Think about how affirmed you feel when someone is listening to you and conveys an accurate reflection of your emotional state.

Social workers must be comfortable in the world of feelings in order to assist clients in the management and understanding of their emotional responses. Clients can express their feelings either explicitly (outward indication of feeling state) or implicitly (the inner emotional response but not necessarily expressed). Clients may correct the social worker's attempt to pinpoint the feeling. With that "correction," the social worker can gain valuable insight into how the client describes the experience versus the social worker's perception of it.

Ethical and Professional Behavior

Behavior: Use empathy, reflection, and interpersonal skills to effectively engage diverse clients and constituencies.

Critical Thinking Question: Explain why conveying an understanding of the client's emotional state is so critical to the helping relationship.

It is important to determine the readiness of the client to explore feelings. For some clients, dealing with emotions is a very unnatural and foreign concept. Testing out feeling choices by offering some alternatives can open the client to deeper exploration of feelings. The social worker can sometimes infer what the client is feeling and reflect that understanding back to the client.

Clients often experience conflicting feelings regarding the same situation—for example, being excited about summer camp and at the same time fearful and scared about being away from home for the first time. Exploring these conflicting feelings can be very helpful in assisting the client in understanding the complexity of life. Resolving conflicting feelings can also lead the client to change. Conversely, strong feelings can interfere with a client's ability to make rational life choices. Once a client is better able to identify and explore feelings that may be at odds with each other, the opportunity for a more open discussion can be followed by problem solving.

Consider a male high school student who just got caught cheating on a test. In talking with the school social worker, he expressed feelings of remorse and shame. These two feelings would be considered very similar. At the same time, he may feel as though the teacher was out to get him. Helping shed light on where some of the conflict between feelings may lie can open up other areas of exploration. For example, what may be contributing to the student's feeling of being targeted by the teacher? Are there similar situations that may have occurred in the student's past? Does he often feel misunderstood and see himself as a victim of circumstance? What personal meaning does the student ascribe to the situation? Discussing his conflicting feelings can assist the social worker in helping the student develop insight into his feelings and in developing a plan of action. Once the student has an understanding of his feelings, even if they are still conflicting, the social worker can practice, in a role play, for example, ways to approach the teacher that are respectful but that also get his point across.

Sometimes clients appear to justify their feelings as a way to protect themselves from unwanted feelings, experiences, or emotional responses. The social worker may see the situation differently and can point out some of the inconsistencies. However, never attempt to *tell* the client how he or she feels; you can only offer your perspective. To force a feeling on a client who is not ready to delve into that arena would be considered a pitfall, such as premature interpretation or confrontation.

Stay with feelings in the moment; for example, "Right now I get the sense that you are uncomfortable talking about your dad. Your tone of voice changed, and you are fidgeting in your chair. Let's talk about what is so painful for you in relation to your dad." This gives the client feedback and allows for on-the-spot, in-the-moment discussion and focus. Box 5.6 demonstrates the social worker utilizing the skill of reflection of feeling.

Box 5.6 Eileen—Reflection of Feeling

Eileen is a 35-year-old female seeing a social worker because of depression. She has recently remembered episodes of childhood sexual abuse by an adult relative. She has managed to avoid the issue for 20 years.

Eileen: I just don't know how to deal with this pain.

Social Worker: It's a lot to digest. Right now you're hurting and feeling very confused. (Reflection of feeling)

Eileen: I just wish I could run away from the world.

Social Worker: I imagine that your memories of the abuse are having an overwhelming effect on you. (Lead-in response/reflection of feeling)

Eileen: I just never really thought about it before. It makes me so crazy. I'm having a difficult time staying focused at work and at home.

Social Worker: That's understandable. You are trying to make sense of what happened to you. It was a frightening and scary time. (Lead-in response/reflection of feeling)

Eileen: Yeah, it was. I know it is important to deal with this. I've hid it from myself for so many years. I never really let myself *feel* anything.

Watch this clip as Maria reflects back to Anna how hard this journey has been. But regardless of her health status there is a sense of hope that Anna feels, too.

The social worker in this case is validating Eileen's ambivalent emotions. Eileen begins to realize how the experience of abuse has had a significant impact on her life. By helping Eileen identify the layers of feelings and thoughts, she will gain more insight into her problem, which will lead to progress in functioning more effectively and alleviating feelings of distress. Eileen recognizes that she has hidden her feelings for a long time. By acknowledging this, she has gained insight into how sexual abuse as a child affects her current relationships ("I never really let myself *feel* anything").

The example in Box 5.6 also illustrates that it is important for the social worker to have a rich vocabulary of feeling words in order to match the affect of the client and to mirror the client's depth and intensity of feeling. For example, a social worker who is working with a depressed client can use words ranging from "down" (mild expression of sadness), "dejected" (moderate expression), or "hopeless" (strong expression) in reflecting feelings back to the client, depending on the intensity of the client's feelings.

Box 5.7 displays a list of feeling words, starting from the most intense or strong to the least intense. There is variation throughout this list, and, of course, the student may interpret these feeling words differently. Use these categories as a guide.

In conclusion, there are a few additional points to consider regarding the reflection of feeling skill:

- Feelings have two dimensions: the *category* of the affect, such as happy, angry, sad, and fearful, and the *intensity* of the affect (Hepworth et al., 2013). To accurately reflect feelings, the social worker must be cognizant of and use both dimensions of this skill. Grasping the intensity of a feeling and matching it with the appropriate overarching feeling (or shades of a feeling) takes skill and time to develop. Always be mindful of your tone of voice, as it can convey intensity, depending on the loudness, softness, tenderness, or harshness of your response.
- Cultures vary in the extent to which emotions are expressed (Cormier et al., 2011). You may have a very expressive client who is Italian American or a very reserved client whose family comes from Japan, as in Interactive Case Study #5. Sue and Sue (2003) observed that Asian Americans value the restraint of strong feelings. Consider the cultural context of your client's life when using a reflection of feeling during the interview process. Keep in mind that in collectivistic cultures (where the client's identity emphasis lies within the family and community), such as Asian and Native American cultures, affective expression is likely to be withheld. It means that the client is experiencing the feeling but is reluctant to express it outright.
- Strong feelings can interfere with your client's ability to think clearly about a situation. Giving the client the opportunity to vent and then restating the affective message (in a calmer voice) can help to deescalate the client and lead to more rational and thoughtful action. For example, your client Joanne is very upset with Manny, her landlord, regarding his lack of response to repeated complaints. The sink has been leaking, and now the flooring is damaged. Your client is threatening to sue Manny and bring this matter to a housing inspection officer. Feeling mistreated and ignored, she threatened to do further damage to the apartment. You do want to determine and assess the seriousness of her plan or if she is venting to "blow off steam." Having someone acknowledge how upset you are can serve as a "safety valve." This can be a releasing and healing experience simultaneously.
- As a social worker, do not convey that you may be afraid or intimidated by your client's strong feelings. Empathy and understanding is your best response. Unfortunately, sometimes the social worker can be the misplaced target of the client's feelings, such as anger, hurt, or jealously. Staying calm and centered is the best way to respond. However, if you sense that the client is threatening you, always follow the safety plan of your agency.

Box 5.7 Feeling Words

STRONG

Happiness	Sadness	Fear	Uncertainty	Anger
Impressive	Devastated	Stunned	Flustered	Unforgivable
Excited	Despairing	Panicked	Bewildered	Outraged
Splendid	Hopeless	Terrified	Disoriented	Hostile
Delighted	Depressed	Afraid	Distrustful	Furious
Overjoyed	Crushed	Frightened	Confused	Angry
Ecstatic	Miserable	Scared	Mystified	Hateful
Elated	Abandoned	Overwhelmed	Baffled	Harsh
Marvelous	Anguished	Tortured	Flustered	Branded
Fantastic	Wretched	Petrified	Disconcerted	Mean
Jubilant	Defeated	Frantic	Confounded	Vindictive
On cloud nine	Desolate	Alarmed	Jittery	Mortified
Superb	Despondent	Paralyzed	Befuddled	Disgraced

Strength/ Potency	Weakness/ Inadequacy	Shame	Surprise
Brave	Demoralized	Exploited	Bewildered
Powerful	Powerless	Mortified	Flabbergasted
Authoritative	Helpless	Disgraced	Shocked
Forceful	Stupid	Scandalized	Astounded
Potent	Inferior	Humiliated	Astonished
Bold	Useless	Degraded	Confounded
Courageous	Impaired	Terror-stricken	Stumped
Invulnerable	Deficient	Humiliated	Stunned
Resolute	Immobilized	Ruined	Terror-stricken
Brave	Incompetent	Ridiculed	
Conviction	Impaired		
Splendid	Insignificant		

MODERATE

Happiness	Sadness	Fear	Uncertainty	Anger
"Up"	Dejected	Worried	Doubtful	Mad
Good	Dismayed	Shaky	Mixed up	Frustrated
Happy	Lonely	Vulnerable	Disturbed	Resentful
Confident	Bad	Anxious	Skeptical	"Sore"
Thrilled	Unhappy	Intimidated	Puzzled	Upset
Optimistic	Pessimistic	Agitated	Perplexed	Impatient
Cheerful	Sad	Threatened	Trapped	Obstinate
Enthusiastic	Hurt	Dread	Stumped	Crummy
Joyful	Lost	Rattled	Adrift	Lousy
"Turned on"	Bleak	Scared	Torn	
Terrific	Downcast		Ambivalent	
Amused	Down in the dumps		In a fog	
Tranquil	Lousy		Conflicted	
Super	Awful		In a bind	

Box 5.7 Feeling Words *(Continued)*

Strength/ Potency	Weakness/ Inadequacy	Shame	Surprise
Tough	Embarrassed	Belittled	Surprised
Important	Useless	Discredited	Amazed
Offended	Worn out	Guilty	Stunned
Fearless	Helpless	Ashamed	Disturbed
Energetic	Inept	Remorseful	Floored
Courageous	Incapable	Demeaned	Perplexed
Daring	Incompetent	Stupid	Conflicted
Assured	Inadequate	Crippled	Perplexed
Satisfied	Shaken	Bashful	Disorganized
Skillful	Cheapened	Devalued	Disoriented
Self-reliant	Washed up	Disappointed	Discombobulated
Self-confident	Worthless	Slammed	Apprehensive
Skillful	Demeaned		
Trust in yourself	Powerless		

MILD

Happiness	Sadness	Fear	Uncertainty	Anger
Pleased	Down	Jittery	Unsure	Annoyed
Glad	Discouraged	Jumpy	Uncertain	Perturbed
Content	Disappointed	Nervous	Bothered	Grouchy
Relaxed	Blue	Edgy	Mistrust	Hassled
Satisfied	Alone	Uptight	Distracted	Bothered
Calm	Left out	Uneasy	Hesitant	Disagreeable
At ease	Doldrums	Defensive	Fidgety	Wrong
Secure	Rotten	Restless	Anxious	Blew it
Good	Weepy	Hesitant	Mixed up	
Calm	Deflated	Uncomfortable	Uneasy	
Fine		Tense	Undecided	
Pleased		Apprehensive	Uncomfortable	
Neat		Timid	In a bind	

Strength/ Potency	Weakness/ Inadequacy	Shame	Surprise
Determined	Frail	Humbled	Startled
Firm	Meek	Discredited	Puzzled
Able	Unable	Exposed	Taken off guard
Strong	Weak	Silly	Taken aback
Stable	Insecure	Embarrassed	Bothered
Adequate	Timid	Wounded	Stumped
Prepared	Uncertain	Mistreated	Feeling pulled apart
Equal to it	Lacking confidence	Cast off	Lost
Ready	Unable	Laughed at	Torn
Effective	Like two cents	Pained	Adrift
In charge	Goofed	Hurt	Uneasy
Contented	Small	Put down	Uncomfortable
In charge	Unimportant	Used	Mixed feelings

Sources: Hepworth et al. (2013); Zangerle (1996).

- Feelings can change over time as circumstances change. Be aware that how a client feels at a particular point in time may be quite different from how he or she feels just moments, hours, or days later. Be patient with your client and with yourself.

Always attend to the nonverbal messages; for example, "I see a smile on your face. You must feel pleased with the way things have turned out." (See the "Attending Behaviors" section.)

The boy's recounting of his parent's fighting in Box 5.B reflects many feelings. Try to identify three feeling words and then write a reflection of feeling response.

Open-Ended Questions

Asking relevant, purposeful, and insightful questions requires skill. In reality, the social worker defines what is important to ask, and the client has the willingness to answer or not. Asking questions comes naturally to the social worker. Sometimes, however, the social worker may be uncomfortable asking very personal and intimate questions. It is important to do so, however, if the question is relevant and can yield new information. The social worker can direct the interview by asking relevant questions, thus exploring the issues and situations that concern the client. In the following segments, listen to the instructor define what an open-ended question is. How can open-ended questions be used to move the interview forward?

Open-Ended Questions

In Interactive Case Study #5, Diane asks Mrs. Kita to tell her more about her husband Jirou. Using an **open-ended** question such as the one Diane used, the social worker can prompt the client to elaborate on a point. Understanding the context of the client situation, such as who was involved and how the parties interacted or what the sequences of events were, allows the social worker to navigate through the issues most salient to

Box 5.B Now You Try It . . . Feeling Words

A 12-year-old male talking to a hotline worker:

"My Mom and Dad always fight. Sometimes they scream so loud that they wake me up at night. I wish they'd stop it. I lie awake waiting for them to stop. They just keep on and on and on. Maybe if they didn't live together they'd stop fighting. Is there any chance things will get better?"

A. Feeling words in the client's message:

1. ______________________

2. ______________________

3. ______________________

B. Your reflection of feeling response:

1. ______________________

the presenting problem. Open-ended questions give the client the opportunity to discuss important aspects of the problem in more depth (Kadushin & Kadushin, 2013). Questions also convey interest in what the client has to say. Often, the social worker will begin with a general question that relates to the client's situation and over the course of the interview ask questions that probe a bit deeper; for example, "How did you react when you found out that your mom had cancer?" and "What is your relationship like with your mom?" And, finally, "Can you talk about how you are coping with the news?" It is important to pace your questions, giving your client time to respond. Also, using a variety of interviewing skills is preferred, as there are many other techniques and skills for gathering data. For example, using a reflection-of-feeling response such as "It seems like you are feeling tired and worn down right now," the social worker can pause and wait for the client to elaborate, as you have pinpointed an important aspect of his or her feeling state. By offering a reflection-of-feeling statement, the client may elaborate about his or her emotions without explicitly being asked to do so.

Questions can be asked in a linear fashion; for example, asking for the sequence of events: "What happened first?" and "And then what happened?" These questions provide insights into the client's thought processes. Asking a hypothetical question may also be useful in getting the client to elaborate. In this instance, the client may share some insight about an "imaginary situation" while at the same time giving the social worker some important information about how the client may think, feel, or behave in a similar circumstance. For example, the social worker might ask, "If you were in your daughter's place and had to choose between good grades or spending time with your friends, but you can't do both, how would you have chosen, knowing what you know today?" or "If you were in her shoes and could make the whole situation better, how would you fix it?"

Asking an open-ended question at the beginning of an interview can be very effective in order to learn about the client and their current situation. This gives the client an opportunity to decide what he or she would like to talk about. Open-ended questions tend to be general (e.g., "How are you feeling today?" or "What has been going on since we last met?"). Once the social worker has an overview of the situation, asking more specific questions will fill in the picture (e.g., "You said that you are very upset about having to talk to me. Please tell me, what aspects of being here troubles you the most?").

When asking an open-ended question, there are several issues to consider: Is the question relevant, and does it help achieve the purpose of the interview? Is there perceived harm that may come to the client if answered truthfully? Are there cultural/societal taboos attached to my question, such as sexual assault or child abuse? Is the client answering in a way to placate the social worker—saying what the client believes the social worker wants to hear. Or is the client considering, if I answer this way, that the probable outcome will be X. Questions should be phrased in a way that invites a response, not in a way that demands a response (e.g., "Please tell me" or "Can you please elaborate?" versus "I must know"). Questions can take the form of who, what, why, where, when, and how (Ivey & Ivey, 2009). See Box 5.8 for some examples of open ended questions.

The best questions are short, focused on the client, and to the point. Typically, the best question is also the least directive question (Hepworth et al., 2013). Ask yourself, what exactly do I need to know in order to fully understand the issue at hand? Also, does my question focus on the client's strengths? You want to ask questions that help the

Box 5.8 Examples of Open-Ended Questions

What—what are the facts/details about a situation?
What happened after _____?
What are some of the issues about _____ that concern you?
What would you like to talk about today?
What was your reaction?
What have you tried thus far?
What if that doesn't work out?
What do you make of all of this?
How—elicits a process or sequence about a situation or elicits emotions
How do you feel about _____?
How does this whole situation change your view of _____?
How were things before _____ happened?
How do you feel about that?
How do you suppose you could find out more about it?
How does this affect you?
How do you suppose this will work out?
How do you explain this to yourself?
How does it look right now?
How do you view the situation?
How did you feel when that happened?
How can I be of help?
Why—reasons or rational
Why are you so angry at _____?
Why do you feel such anger toward _____?
Why is this so important to you?
Why do you think that you feel the way you do?
Where—details about location/place
Where does all of this pain come from?
Where would you like to see your relationship with _____ a year from now?
Where do we go from here?
Where do you plan on being in the future?
When—various time frames
When you think about this whole situation, how do you feel?
When in your life did you realize _____?
When is it most difficult for you to talk to him?
When do you think all this started taking place?
When are you going to be able to move on?
Who—types of details about the people involved
Who else in your life has experienced the kind of pain you have surrounding _____?
Who do you count on for support in your life?
Who else have you talked to about this?
Who are your social supports?
Could—a request for information or clarification
Could you fill me in on the background?
Could you give me an example?
Could you tell me a little more about that?
Could you help me understand?

client begin to explore issues and go deeper into the issue or situation. You have begun to probe for deeper meaning, which can lead to new insights, which in turn can lead to change.

Social workers must be careful in using "why" questions. Frequently, clients don't know why they do something a certain way. Asking them to explain themselves may cause them to become defensive and feel judged, closing down communication (Boyle et al., 2011). The client can feel criticized or blamed. Sometimes clients may not understand their own motives and why they do what they do. Therefore, "why" questions should be asked infrequently and with discretion (Sheafor & Hoerjsi, 2015). If the client becomes angry, use a paraphrase or a reflection-of-feeling response and then ask the question another way (e.g., instead of "Why are you so sure you can't do it on your own?," ask "Please tell me, what makes being on your own so hard?"). Box 5.9 demonstrates the social worker asking open-ended questions.

Box 5.9 Latisha—Open-Ended Questions

Latisha is a 30-year-old female client who is struggling to understand a court order; time spent with her stepdaughters will be every other weekend, five hours at a time. The judge handling the divorce case has ordered her and her ex-husband Frank to attend counseling sessions as part of the divorce decree.

Latisha: I really don't understand why the judge has required us to be here. We are divorced, and she has made it very clear that I can't see the girls as often as I would like. I never expected that I would be a mom to a five- and eight-year-old, and now they are being taken away from me.

Social Worker: That sounds like devastating news. (Reflection of feeling)

Latisha: It was. How do I go from seeing them every day to twice a month?

Social Worker: Hmmmm, that is a really good question. Clearly, their place in your life has been very meaningful. (Pause) How do you see your role as Tuwana's and Deneca's stepmother? (Paraphrase and open-ended question)

Latisha: I really care about the girls. I have been their mom since they were babies. I am the one the girls come to, not so much their dad. Frank does love them but on his own terms. I feel like they are being ripped from me because we are divorced. Tell me, does that seem fair?

Social Worker: I can tell that this is extremely hard and you don't understand how the judge could make such a decision. Since you meet with the judge next Tuesday, what are some things that you want to make sure you have a chance to say? (Paraphrase and open-ended question)

In the example in Box 5.9, the social worker combines paraphrasing and reflection of feelings while asking open-ended questions that focus the interview. The social worker is trying to gain a fuller understanding of how Latisha feels and offers a suggestion to plan out what she wants to say to the judge on Tuwana's and Deneca's behalf.

If the client responds to an open-ended question with a "yes" or a "no," the social worker can try rephrasing the question. If, after several attempts, the client still does not fully respond, the topic of conversation should be changed (e.g., "I can tell that you don't want to talk about Andre. Maybe we can talk about him next time. So let's spend some time discussing your housing situation. I know the landlord has decided to renovate the building. How does this affect you?"). Always ask yourself, "Do I press forward or back off? Which approach will help our relationship grow more trusting?"

Watch as Diane asks Mrs. Kita to tell her more about her job and how she is managing. What open-ended questions would you use to gather more information about her situation?

As with all social work interviewing skills, remember that asking questions in some cultures can be seen as intrusive and rude. One way to address this issue is to ask the question, "Can you tell me about . . . ?" This question allows for client self-determination about sensitive or difficult issues as clients consider whether they would like to discuss this aspect of the problem. Try your hand at writing some open-ended questions using the case example in Box 5.C.

Box 5.C Now You Try It . . . Open-Ended Questions

A 30-year-old male talking to the social worker about his reactions to a car accident six months ago:

"Since my car accident, I'm really afraid to drive again. I get into the car and I feel my heart start to pound and my hands get really sweaty. I don't want to end up behind the wheel and start to panic, but that is what is happening right now. I panic. I've tried to make myself do it, but . . . I can't. I have flashbacks from the accident; the car turned upside down and I'm trapped inside."

A. Additional information needed from the client:

1. ______________________________

2. ______________________________

B. Your reflection of feeling and open ended question:

1. ______________________________

Closed-Ended Questions

A closed-ended question (e.g., "How many times has your daughter run away?") enables the social worker to check details of the client's narrative for accuracy. They also can help gather small but useful pieces of information, such as date of birth, number of siblings, and number of previous arrests (Cormier et al., 2011). Guiding the interview through a series of questions helps the social worker focus on important issues. Closed-ended questions can also be used to scale the severity, intensity, and/or frequency of a problem. For example, asking your client to rate her level of marital satisfaction (or level of depression, motivation, etc.) on a scale of 1 to 10 is a good way to quickly assess the situation from the client's point of view. Listen as the instructor walks you through how closed-ended questions can provide important details that can enhance and deepen your understanding of the client's situation.

▶ Closed-Ended Questions

Closed-ended questions can also bring into focus a particular issue, and, depending on the answer, the social worker can follow up with related questions. It is helpful to ask questions that relate primarily to the client's present situation. It can be easier to ask a series of questions that require the client to think about a current situation than to reflect on past concerns (Hepworth et al., 2013). Exploring past issues, patterns, and behaviors, especially if brought up prematurely, can be seen as a pitfall or a common error. Box 5.10 demonstrates the social worker asking a series of closed-ended questions.

In the example in Box 5.10, Kyle is initially reluctant to talk. Because the social worker has conveyed her understanding of his situation, he starts communicating. By answering the simple closed-ended question, the client has given the social worker an opening to pursue a deeper understanding of his conflicts with his parents.

Box 5.10 Kyle—Closed-Ended Questions

Kyle is a 14-year-old male student who has been referred to the social worker due to severe conflicts at home. His parents are threatening to send him to his aunt's home in another city.

Social Worker: Tell me about things at home between you and your parents. (Open-ended question)

Kyle: It's okay. I don't really want to talk about this with you.

Social Worker: I know; it's hard to talk to a stranger about your family. (Paraphrasing)

Kyle: It's not me; it's my parents. They order me around all the time. I can't stand all the yelling.

Social Worker: How often do you get yelled at? (Closed-ended question)

Kyle: Probably 15 times a day.

Social Worker: That is a lot. From your point of view, what seems to start the fights? (Lead-in response/open-ended question)

Beginning social workers can overuse closed-ended questions. Be careful not to rely heavily on this skill because the interview can feel more like an interrogation, which may cause the client to feel frustrated with the interview process. The interview can become focused on the social worker, as you are doing all the work and trying to come up with questions and simultaneously the client can sit back and simply answer "yes" or "no." While closed-ended questions are very useful in pinpointing the details of a situation, asking too many in close succession can make for a superficial interview (or cross-examination) that fails to get at underlying issues (Hepworth et al., 2013).

Engagement

Behavior: Use empathy, reflection, and interpersonal skills to effectively engage diverse clients and constituencies.

Critical Thinking Question: Explain how a social worker may use open- and closed-ended questions to move the interview forward in the helping process.

Watch this clip as Louis asks Kim the closed-ended question, "Was it enough to cover your expenses?"

When working with nontalkative clients, asking a series of closed-ended "yes" or "no" questions can get the interview moving. Pay attention to the client's nonverbal communication, and if you see some form of interest develop, switch to an open-ended question as a follow-up. You may have sparked enough interest to get the client talking more expressively. You can practice forming closed-ended questions using the example provided in Box 5.D.

Box 5.D Now You Try It . . . Closed-Ended Questions

A 65-year-old female talking to the caseworker at the senior citizens center:

"We've been together for a long time, going on five years. You would think by now my children would accept our marriage. They pretend like my husband doesn't exist. I want them to get along. Is that too much to ask? Sometimes I feel like they treat me as a child. They think he is going to take all my money. Is that crazy or what?"

A. Specific information needed from the client:

1. ______________________________

2. ______________________________

B. Your paraphrase and closed ended question:

1. ______________________________

Clarification

Clarification is a skill that allows the social worker to identify more fully what a client is thinking, feeling, and experiencing. When the client's messages are too abstract or hazy, the social worker may ask for the client to be more specific about the meaning of words or the frequency and duration of problems. Clients may assume that the social worker understands their messages and therefore may not fully explain their meaning unless the social worker asks for clarification. Watch the segments below as the instructor defines a clarification. How is it used to clear up any vague or confusing messages between the social worker and the client?

Clarification

Now watch this video as Anthony states that he hangs out with his boys. James, the social worker, clarifies who the boys are, and Anthony discloses that his boys are his associates in his gang.

Be sure to clarify what a client means when referring to "they," "them," "us," "my friends," and so on. It is important to know all the important players. A client may use qualifiers such as "always," "sometimes," or "kinda." The astute social worker will want to determine exactly what these qualifiers mean (Cormier et al., 2011). To further clarify, the social worker can check the client's understanding of what was just said; for example, "You are saying that nothing is going well in your life right now. Am I hearing you correctly?" This gives the client an opportunity to confirm, disagree, or clear up any misunderstanding the social worker might have.

Engagement

Behavior: Use empathy, reflection, and interpersonal skills to effectively engage diverse clients and constituencies

Critical Thinking Question: Using the example in Box 5.10, how would you intervene with Kyle using at least three of the skills presented in the chapter?

In addition, many clients have a "pop culture" understanding of psychological jargon and circumstances. Watching TV and reading self-help books and magazines have exposed clients to a wide range of issues, many of which may be misunderstood by the client. For example, your client states, "I was watching TV last week, and this doctor talked about this thing called anorexia nervosa. I think that is what my wife has; she diets constantly and is so skinny, it seems like she could break in half." Given this information, it is the social worker's responsibility to make clear or decode what the client has learned from the "TV expert" and help to educate or clarify further.

Clarification should be used when a client is discussing a situation that the social worker does not fully understand. It can be used as a tool to help the client comprehend or explain the details of the situation. For example, Brent is a 68-year-old client seeking the services of an in-home counseling program. The social worker may have a series of questions related to his needs, his expectations with respect to the agency, others living in the home, and his present health status. All of these questions help to clarify for both of them the issues surrounding Brent's self-referral and the services he may be eligible for through the program.

In turn, the social worker must make responses as clear as possible so that the client understands the true meaning of the social worker's words. Clarification thus becomes a reciprocal process between the social worker and the client (Hepworth et al., 2013). The social worker may misinterpret the client's messages and develop incorrect perceptions or assumptions about the client's situation. Therefore, it is essential that the social worker clarify when she or he is uncertain about the client's message, asking, for example, "Is this what you mean?" or "Is this what you're saying?" Additionally, the social worker may want the client to elaborate on a particular topic or to give specific examples regarding the situation, behavior, or feeling (Cormier et al., 2011). Box 5.11 provides an example of the social worker using clarification to better understand the client's point of view.

In the example in Box 5.11, the social worker attempts to gain an understanding of Brittany's point of view on her troubles at school. The social worker wants to be certain that they are "speaking the same language" (i.e., "What does that mean, exactly?"). If Brittany is given the opportunity to present and clarify her position without feeling blamed or accused, she is likely to contribute more to the session. Practice using the clarification skill in the example in Box 5.E.

? Assess your understanding of interviewing skills by taking this brief quiz.

Box 5.11 Brittany—Clarification

Brittany is a 16-year-old female attending sessions with a social worker because of her repeated fighting with other students. She has a history of behavioral disruptions at school and is in danger of being expelled.

Brittany: It's not fair. The teachers are always busting me for fighting. They have it in for me.

Social Worker: You think that's the reason you're here, because of all the fighting? (Lead-in response/clarification)

Brittany: Yeah; I was sent to your office because the teachers are definitely out to get me.

Social Worker: When you say the teachers are out to get you, what does that mean, exactly? (Clarification)

Box 5.E Now You Try It . . . Clarification

A 13-year-old male talking to his foster care caseworker:

"I've never liked living with this foster family. They just seem to "put up" with me. My foster brother, Jimmy, is picking on me all the time, and he makes fun of me, especially at school. Could you please find me a new family? I don't think I can take it anymore."

A. What information needs to be clearer from the client?

1. ______________________________

2. ______________________________

B. Your clarifying response:

1. ______________________________

VIDEO ASSESSMENT

Watch these videos and identify the attending behavior or interviewing skill that is demonstrated.

SUMMARY

- In this chapter, you were introduced to the use of attending behaviors in the social work interview and were provided with examples of the appropriate use of attending behaviors and opportunities to practice applying attending behaviors in written case studies and in video instruction.
- You have learned how to use the attending behaviors, including body positioning and spatial considerations, maintaining eye contact, the appropriate use of touch, using tone of voice to convey understanding, offering silence when necessary, mirroring the client's facial expressions, and the use of furthering responses.
- You have learned how to responds to a client using several basic interviewing skills, such as paraphrasing, reflection of feelings, open- and closed-ended questions, and clarification.
- Attending behaviors supplement the basic interviewing skills in the therapeutic interview. In this chapter, students have read about, seen demonstrations of, and been given opportunities to appropriately apply the basic interviewing skills.

APPLY IT

1. Watch all sessions of Interactive Case Study #2, Anthony and social worker James. In each session, identify two examples of the basic interviewing skills: (1) closed-ended questions, (2) clarification, and (3) paraphrasing. Then watch all three sessions again without the sound. Identify three different attending behaviors displayed by the social worker and then by the client.
2. Watch all three sessions of Interactive Case Study #1, Anna and social worker Marie. In each session, identify two examples of basic interviewing skills: (1) open-ended questions, (2) paraphrasing, and (3) reflection of feelings.

Assess Your Competence

Use the scale below to rate your current level of achievement on the following concepts or skills associated with each competency presented in the chapter:

1	2	3
I can accurately describe the concept or skill	I can consistently identify the concept or skill when observing and analyzing practice activities	I can competently implement the concept or skill in my own practice

_______ Can identify, describe (note), and demonstrate all major attending behaviors.

_______ Understands the correct usage of lead-in responses and can demonstrate the three main lead-in, response-sensory categories.

_______ Understands the concept of furthering responses and correct usage of both verbal and nonverbal types of furthering responses.

_______ Can identify, describe, and demonstrate all basic interviewing skills.

_______ Resist the urge to fill every silence with a question or response.

6

Advanced Social Work Skills for Direct Practice

LEARNING OUTCOMES

- Demonstrate how to focus an interview using advanced level skills
- Practice advanced-level interviewing

CHAPTER OUTLINE

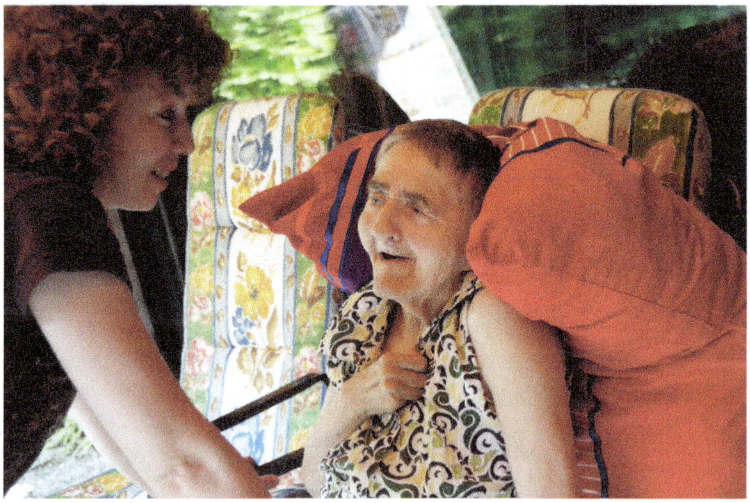

SILVIA JANSEN / E+ / GETTY IMAGES

The basic interviewing skills and attending behaviors discussed thus far in this book provide a foundation for direct practice. To fully develop a successful helping relationship, more advanced skills are needed. This chapter will explore ways to focus the interview, and provide an overview of the advanced interviewing skills, summarization, information giving, confrontation and interpretation.

FOCUSING THE INTERVIEW

A common concern among "newly minted" social work professionals is how to conduct an interview that has both breadth and depth. This chapter will introduce you to more advanced interviewing skills, with a focus on how and when to use them. When conducting an interview with a client, there will be some prescriptive questions, meaning a required part of the interview that must be covered. Although there is no way to predict the direction of the interview, having a tentative agenda for the meeting can be helpful. To prepare for an interview, think about what you already may know about the client and his or her situation. For example, a client recently discharged from a psychiatric facility may want to discuss the circumstances that led to his hospitalization, the hospitalization itself, the kinds of interventions he received while in treatment, his plans to remain stable, and supports needed to stay in his group home. A client who recently miscarried would likely be experiencing concerns such as her health, whether she will ever be able to get pregnant again and carry a child to full term, sadness and loss, how to tell people about the miscarriage, and where to find support while going through the grieving process and possibly concerns about her faith.

ADVANCED SKILLS

The attending behaviors and basic interviewing skills covered earlier in this text provide a foundation for direct practice. The skills presented in this chapter will enhance the student's basic skills, allowing them to delve deeper into nature of the client situation. The advanced skills of summarizing, offering information, and using the techniques of confrontation and interpretation are discussed and demonstrated below. Knowing how and when to use each of the skills takes time and practice. However, as students become more comfortable with all of the skills, the interview process will flow as a conversation between two people.

Summarization

When using **summarization**, the social worker pulls together relevant pieces of information from the interview into a composite response. Unlike a paraphrase or a reflection of feeling statement, both the feeling(s) and the content of the client's message are incorporated into the social worker's summary. Summarization is used throughout the interview to focus the discussion on relevant issues as well as to make transitions from one topic to another. Generally, a social worker will summarize what has been said when it appears that all of the relevant information has been shared regarding a particular topic. Summarizations are generally delivered as a statement, not a question. A good way to begin a session is to summarize what was discussed in the last session(s). This technique ensures continuity across sessions.

Summarization can also be useful at the end of a session to highlight relevant topics from the session and to set the agenda for the next visit (Hepworth, Rooney, & Larsen, 2013). This skill is also useful as a tool to curb clients who have a tendency toward long-winded storytelling. The social worker can recap what was said and then attempt to refocus the interview to more relevant parts of the problem. For some clients, this sprawling explanation is a good way to divert and deflect the interview process by focusing on tangential issues (Hepworth et al., 2013). Assisting the client to get back on track by focusing on the problem rather than a "story" is an appropriate use of this skill (Boyle, Hull, Mather, Smith, & Farley, 2011).

In the following clips, the instructor describes how and when to use summarization.

Summarization

Now watch this clip as Louis the social worker summarizes Kim's current situation, the death of her mother, estrangement from her sister Natalie, and lack of support from friends. Did Louis capture the highlights of Kim's situation? If not, what did he miss?

Knowing when to interrupt a client without appearing rude is a technique that can be learned. As you are attempting to get the client to refocus, be clear about the direction of the conversation and the reason for further discussion—for example, saying, "You have been talking a lot about your son Barry and his issues with your ex-husband. I can tell this is important to you; however, I would like to find out more about your relationship with your son. Maybe we can gain some insight into your frustrations if we spend some time talking about how you experience your son's behaviors toward you." Box 6.1 provides some general guidelines for using summarization.

Summarizations are also used to review progress over time. It allows the social worker to reflect back on past sessions and to bring to the fore themes and patterns that have emerged throughout the relationship. This is a good technique to use when the social worker is trying to organize thoughts and concerns about the issue under discussion. Clients can also work toward organization of content as they too attempt to review what was said either in the session or across sessions. Box 6.2 demonstrates the skill of summarization being utilized by the social worker.

In the example in Box 6.2, Kate talks about several important issues: 1) her relationship with her foster parents, 2) graduating from high school and going to college, 3) disappointment with her mother yet understanding her mother's situation, and 4) wanting to do things differently in her own life. The social worker pulls together several issues presented by Kate and develops a concise statement reviewing the important points.

Engagement

Behaviors: Use empathy, reflection and interpersonal skills to effectively engage diverse client and constituencies.

Critical Thinking Question: What benefits does using the skill of summarization provide to both the client and the social worker?

Box 6.1 Guidelines for Using Summarization

1. Identify key aspects of the client's messages over time, that is, within the session or over the course of several sessions.
2. Use summarization as a way to focus the interview. The social worker takes the lead in setting the agenda (of course, with the client's input).
3. Use summarization to tie messages together and make a coherent whole.
4. Verify with the client that you are on the right track, for example, "There are a few things you said that I want to be sure I have understood. You are thinking about leaving your husband and will make the final decision after you complete your degree. Is that the gist of what you said?"
5. Use summarization to begin a session, switch directions, or wrap up a session.
6. Recap what was said, sometimes using the client's own words, for example, "You just said 'I want the abuse to stop.' That is the first time I have heard you utter those words. Good for you."

Source: Hepworth et al. (2013).

Box 6.2 Kate—Summarization

Kate is an 18-year-old female who has been living with a foster family since age eight. She is discussing recent events in her life with her social worker, focusing particularly on her relationship with her biological mother.

Kate: Dennis and Julia [foster parents] have taken good care of me. I know that they're proud of my accomplishments, especially me getting accepted at the university.

Social Worker: You've done so well and proven that you can make it. (Paraphrasing)

Kate: Yeah! I want to make something of myself. I want to do better than my mom did for me. You know, she didn't even show up for my graduation.

Social Worker: You sound disappointed and saddened that she didn't come and celebrate your special day. (Lead-in response/reflection of feeling)

Kate: I know I should have prepared myself—she's not going to show, but I always hope she will.

Social Worker: I sense that you are hurt and frustrated with her. (Lead-in response/reflection of feeling) Can you tell me more about your relationship with your Mom? (Open-ended question)

Kate: I wish that she wanted to be a part of my life. Sometimes I think she's jealous of Dennis and Julia. Maybe she feels bad about everything that has happened, especially the stuff with her husband. He never wanted me around, and maybe that's part of why she stays away too.

Social Worker: Although you love Dennis and Julia, you wish things had turned out differently with your mom. You understand her circumstances, but it doesn't change the fact that you feel let down by her time after time. Does that capture how you feel? (Summarization and clarification)

Summarization provides focus throughout the interview, highlights important points, and helps identify themes, patterns, and insights. A summarization is not merely a "list"; rather, it is a composite of the most significant parts of the interview. It can be beneficial to ask the client to summarize at various points throughout the interview. It gives both the social worker and the client an appreciation for the client's point of view and can serve as a way to confirm the accuracy and the understanding of the message by both parties. The social worker can also clarify or ask an open-ended question to be certain a full understanding of the situation has been achieved. It is always a good idea to ask the client to confirm the accuracy of your understanding, for example, "You are still feeling hopeful, even after all these disappointments, that you will be able to reunite with your mom. Do I understand what you just said?" Finally, when providing a summarization, be sure to recap what the client said, not your opinions, values, and judgments. Practice your summarization skill by completing the exercise in Box 6.A.

Information Giving

The social worker uses **information giving** when the client is in need of useful knowledge. Information may include knowledge about available resources in the community, such as a local food pantry or a homeless shelter (Murphy & Dillon, 2011), or it might be information relevant to the client's presenting problem (e.g., informing a client with a substance abuse problem about the progressive nature of an addiction). Information is power. If your client is equipped with knowledge about resources, data, and facts, he or she is more likely to make changes. You can use this skill to convey details and an

Box 6.A Now You Try It . . . Summarization

A 75-year-old African American female, Mrs. Eleanor, is living in a nursing home. She wants to go back home, but her children feel strongly that this is her only option.

Social Worker: Mrs. Eleanor, you've been here for the past two months. I know at times you've been very unhappy. How have you been doing recently?

Eleanor: I want to go home. My roommate, Emma, cries all the time. There's not a moment's peace. I get hungry, and I can't eat until they come get us. My kids haven't been here. And I'm really lonely.

Social Worker: As time wears on, it's even harder for you to find a way to feel comfortable being here?

Eleanor: Yes, it is just getting worse. It's really depressing. I had the fall and broke my hip and, next thing you know, here I am. I have my wits about me. I know who I am, and I feel like I can take care of myself.

Social Worker: It's been very difficult for you. From talking with your son and daughter, they feel it's not possible for you to go home.

Eleanor: They don't give me enough credit—I can take care of myself and that I don't need somebody with me 24 hours a day. I don't know why they think that.

Social Worker: They don't see your strength—that you are capable of managing with some assistance?

Eleanor: When I first broke my hip, I was in bad shape and was not able to do for myself. But I'm better, and I'm getting around with my walker. And there are many things I can do now.

A. Most important aspects of the client's statement:

1. ______________________________

2. ______________________________

3. ______________________________

B. Your summarization response:

1. ______________________________

explanation about the helping process, the role of the social worker, and interventions to be used. Sharing specifics about developmental norms, life transitions, and consequences of behaviors is important, as this information can help the social worker and client sort out what is a fact, a falsehood, or a myth (Gambrill, 1997). For example, it is appropriate to help a client realize that physical abuse is not something every woman experiences or, after talking with a client about "sexting" and cyberbullying, to help her realize that she has an unrealistic understanding of the multiple risks associated with such behaviors (see Box 6.3 for guidelines for using information giving).

In the following clips, the instructor explains how and when to use information giving.

▶ Information Giving

Information should always be presented in a way that is sensitive to the client's culture. For example, in talking to an African American client about mental illness, it is important to understand that within this minority group, sources (or the cause) of mental illnesses are often thought of as organic or inherited. Talking about

Box 6.3 Guidelines for Information Giving

1. Identify the kind of information that is useful to the client.
2. Identify reliable sources of information, such as the library, telephone book, websites, social service agencies, schools, and universities.
3. Determine readiness for information and whether the client can find it on his or her own.
4. Identify sequencing of information, presenting the most important information first.
5. Present information in a way the client can hear it but be sure to include facts if they are relevant.
6. Don't overload the client with too much information; sometimes a small dose of information is all the client can handle.
7. Discuss the client's reaction to the information.
8. Ascertain how well the client understands the information by asking him or her to repeat it.
9. Write down information (or provide a brochure).

Source: Hepworth et al. (2012); Sheafor and Horejsi (2015).

Policy to Practice Temporary Assistance to Needy Families (1999)

As a social worker, it is imperative that you understand the policies and procedure that dictate services to clients. Communicating some of the complexities of eligibility requirements and what documentation is necessary for services can be confusing. Some governmental programs are complex and difficult to understand, and a social worker is needed to help the client navigate the system. In 1996, a welfare reform law, the Personal Responsibility and Work Opportunity Reconciliation Act, established the Temporary Assistance for Needy Families (TANF) program. TANF is a block grant program designed to make dramatic reforms to the nation's welfare system by moving recipients to work and turning welfare into a program of temporary assistance. TANF replaced the national welfare program known as Aid to Families with Dependent Children (AFDC) and the related programs known as the Job Opportunities and Basic Skills Training (JOBS) program and the Emergency Assistance (EA) program. Because Mrs. Anderson has legal custody of Maria, she is eligible for a "child-only" grant. With this benefit, Mrs. Anderson can receive up to $111.00 per month and a medical card to cover any of Maria's health-related needs. Mrs. Anderson may also want to pursue applying for the Supplemental Nutrition Assistance Program (SNAP). However, in order to qualify for the SNAP card, she is required to provide proof of her gross income, as eligibility is income based. Because Mrs. Anderson is retired and receives a small pension, she may want to explore the SNAP benefit.

Mrs. Anderson: I love Maria, but I'm feeling old. I raised Crystal and her sister. I didn't think I'd be raising any more kids. I don't have as much energy as I used to.

Social Worker: I am sure it is exhausting.

Mrs. Anderson: Plus, I want to be a grandma. I love to spoil her, but money's tight. You know, they do give me that little bit of money. And that helps, but I really don't want to take money to take care of my granddaughter, but I gotta feed her.

Social Worker: So on top of everything else, you're worried about making ends meet. You'd want to be the "grandma," but right now you *have* to be the mom. There are some resources right here in the county that we can talk about. There is the Temporary Assistance for Needy Families. It is a program that can provide some financial help with Maria's care, plus she can get free medical care too. You may also get some assistance with paying for food. I'll bring you some information at our next visit.

Mrs. Anderson: Maybe that would help.

medication as the first treatment choice may convey that the social worker does not want to work with the client (Paniagua, 1998). Some clients assume that social workers can't be trusted because they are members of the dominant group. In this case, understand the trepidation clients might experience when asking for more traditional social services. It is your responsibility to convey understanding and interest and provide services that are relevant to your client's needs.

Policy Practice

Behaviors: Identify social policy at the local, state and federal level that impacts wellbeing, service delivery and access to social services.

Critical Thinking Question: Consider that Mrs. Anderson is your client. Nicole has provided her with information about various state and federal programs that might assist her. Write your response to Mrs. Anderson, after she says, "Maybe that would help."

In terms of potential language barriers, if you have clients who do not understand English, having written materials available in their native language is important. Providing the client with concrete recommendations or services early on in the helping process is also beneficial (Paniagua, 1998). If you don't speak Spanish, for example, a translator may be required to assist with the interview. Be aware that a translator, whether a family member or a professional, can be seen as intrusive. Certainly, training bilingual social workers to provide services to members of their ethnic or racial group can be an effective way to convey consideration and sensitivity. It is essential that as a helper, you understand that external sociopolitical forces have influence and shape the worldview of our clients.

In the example in Box 6.4, Mandy is expressing concern about her health status, her possible pregnancy, and her lack of judgment in having unprotected sex. The social worker provides relevant information to Mandy and then refocuses the interview on her emotional state. In addition, the social worker empowers Mandy by suggesting that she decide what she wants to discuss first. Also note that the social worker does not interject an opinion here. The worker is referring to the facts only. No judgment is attached to the information given.

Box 6.4 Mandy—Information Giving

Mandy is a 19-year-old female who discloses in the middle of a session that she is very frightened. She attended a party where she had unprotected sex with a man she knows only casually. She is concerned about sexually transmitted infections and being pregnant.

Mandy: I can't believe I did this. I mean, it was really stupid.

Social Worker: Having unprotected sex could have serious consequences, one of which is getting infected with a sexually transmitted infection (Information giving) and, of course, pregnancy.

Mandy: I get the pregnant part, but do you mean like AIDS?

Social Worker: Possibly. (Information giving)

Mandy: But I feel okay. I don't think I have a disease, and I sure hope that I'm not pregnant.

Social Worker: The only way you'll know whether you're infected will be to get an HIV antibody test in three to six months. (Information giving) You sound scared about all this. (Reflection of feeling)

Mandy: My parents are going to kill me. We are Catholic.

Social Worker: So to make a difficult situation worse, you are scared and anxious about your parents' reaction. (Reflection of feeling)

Mandy: Yep. If I'm pregnant, an abortion is out of the question. In my family, it would be better to die from AIDS than to be a single mom or have an abortion.

Social Worker: You feel like there are no good choices, but let's talk about one thing at a time. There is no reason right now to panic about the what-ifs. Where do you want to start? (Information giving and open-ended question)

Watch this clip to see how Diane uses the skill information giving. Put yourself in Mrs. Kita's position. How is she likely reacting to the information that Diane is sharing?

Social workers present information to educate clients about options and help them to make changes, not to dictate choices in a judgmental way. We provide information as a way to teach or instruct. We can fill in the gaps, as a client may have partial information about a resource, topic, issue, or circumstance. For example, showing a client how to use the public bus system or develop a budget are examples of information giving. Keeping within the social work ethic of self-determination, information should always be presented in a way that allows the client to accept or reject the information being offered. Specifically, it is important to distinguish between advice and information. Giving "advice" is telling clients what you believe to be in their best interest, while providing information allows clients to make choices based on all the available alternatives (Sheafor & Horejsi, 2015).

Diversity and Difference in Practice

Behaviors: Present themselves as learners and engage clients and constituencies as experts of their own experiences.

Apply self-awareness and self-regulation to manage the influence of personal biases and values in working with diverse clients and constituencies.

Critical Thinking Question: When working with a client who has an "invisible disability" or an "unseen disability" such as deafness, mental illness or epilepsy etc. what information is important for you to know (or ask) when working with a person with such a disability?

If the social worker doesn't have the necessary information, he or she should be honest and amenable to gathering the information for the next session or follow-up contact. It is important to remember that social workers don't know all the answers and that reaching out to others for resources, information, and referrals on behalf of our clients is a necessary part of our work. Providing a reading list, a brochure, or a pamphlet about a service or agency can be very empowering to the client. Be sure your information is up to date. It is a good idea to review and critique any articles, brochures, or informational sheets before giving them to a client. Always consider the reading level of your client. Sometimes you may need to present or adapt the information in a way that addresses the client's cognitive level or limitations.

Developing Cultural Competence Working with a Client Who is Deaf

The American Disability Act was signed into law on July 26, 1990. This act guarantees that people with disabilities have the same opportunities as everyone else to fully participate in all aspects of life, employment, housing, transportation, health care, schooling etc.

Your client Rebecca has a BSW degree from a small private school. She has completed her internship and is now looking for a job. This is your first session and you have no experience with a person who is deaf and are unsure how to interact with her.

Below are some suggestions regarding how to communicate with Rebecca:

- Ask which combination of techniques work best for her, signing, lip/speech reading.
- Ask if she would like an interpreter? If she does, make sure that you speak directly to Rebecca and not the interpreter.
- You may need to repeat what you have said to be sure that Rebecca hasn't missed anything.
- Look directly at Rebecca when speaking, use gestures, maintain eye contact, use facial expressions.
- Speak slowly and clearly, but don't yell.
- Have Rebecca chose the seating arrangement that works best for her and be sure the environment is quiet.
- Use visual aids, offer materials to her in writing, texting, pen and paper can be helpful in communicating with her.

Box 6.B Now You Try It . . . Information Giving

Raven, a 10-year-old girl is talking with the school social worker:

"Last week my parents told us they're getting a divorce. It's been coming for a long time, but I really want them to stay together. My sister says there is no chance of them staying married, but I don't believe that. Please give me some ideas about how I can stop this from happening."

A. Most important pieces of information in the client's message:

1. ______________________________

2. ______________________________

B. Your information-giving response:

1. ______________________________

Before giving information, determine what the client already knows. For example, you wouldn't want to repeat the steps involved in applying for medical assistance if the client had already completed an application. Check back with clients to ascertain if they understand all the information. This way, you can clear up any misunderstandings or gaps in the information shared. Pay attention to the client's verbal and nonverbal reaction to the information and use either a paraphrase, reflection of feeling, or clarification to make sure you understand his or her point of view ("You look surprised that there are so many steps to enroll your child in school. It does require lots of paperwork"). Try using the skill of information giving using the case scenario in Box 6.B.

A word of caution about giving information: be careful not to use information as a way of sounding like the expert. Overwhelming your client with the breadth and depth of your knowledge may impress you but at the same time may intimidate the client. The timing of information, in small, understandable, and relevant doses, works best for both you and the client.

Confrontation

Confrontation is a skill that a social worker uses to address a discrepancy in the client's message (Hepworth et al., 2013). This discrepancy can take two forms: 1) the client's behavior in contradiction to his or her statement or 2) the client's statements in contradiction to one another. An example of the first type of discrepancy, when the client states one thing yet behaves differently, would be the following scenario: A client says, "I want Claudia back—the agency is keeping her from me. You want to give her to that foster family." The social worker responds by saying, "I know you want Claudia to be with you, but as we have talked about before, if you continue to miss visits with her, it will delay her coming home." It is important to note that the social worker may be confused by this apparent disconnect between the client's verbal and nonverbal messages and may need to explore this further. An example of the second type of discrepancy, when two or more of the client's messages or statements contradict each other, would be a client denying that she is experiencing stress in her relationship with her husband while also reporting in the same session that she hates talking to him. The social worker points out this discrepancy in hopes of providing some insight that could possibly lead to client change. It is best to offer a series of recent examples rather than a distant event the client might not remember as a way of reinforcing the message (Hill & O'Brien, 2014). A confrontation should be offered in a nonjudgmental and nonthreatening and nonadversarial way. Regardless of the way a confrontation is delivered, it may be difficult for the client to accept or acknowledge identified discrepancies. There may be a tendency to save face.

In these clips, the instructor explains how and when to use a confrontation.

Confrontation

Hill and O'Brien(2014) suggest that the social worker use the following two-part format when confronting clients:

- On one hand you . . . but on the other hand . . .
- You say . . . but you also say . . .
- You say . . . but nonverbally you seem . . .
- I am hearing . . . but I am also hearing . . .

Box 6.5 provides some guidelines for using confrontation in a caring and effective manner with clients.

For confrontation to be used effectively in the helping relationship, the social worker must first establish a trusting and safe environment with the client. This will lower the client's defensiveness and reduce the client's anxiety and feelings of being "attacked." Confrontation is a skill that should be used sparingly and with a great deal of support from the social worker. This skill helps clients address issues that they may have been avoiding. A confrontation is also helpful in identifying the reality of a situation versus the client's perception (Hepworth et al., 2013).

Box 6.5 Guidelines for Using Confrontation

1. Use confrontation sparingly and when a relationship has been firmly established.
2. Offer a confrontation because you care, for example, "It is because you are a good person with a lot of potential that I am bringing this up right now."
3. Do not confront a client if he or she is extremely emotional. Use empathy skills, such as a reflection of feeling as a way of diffusing the situation or to moderate the client's feelings.
4. Change takes time; be realistic and understanding, not combative. Long-standing patterns, issues, and feelings are hard to change. Think of this skill as shining a light on a blind spot.
5. Give examples of inconsistencies within the context of care and concern, for example, "I really want to see you succeed, but last week and yesterday you showed up to school smelling of alcohol. You said that you don't want to be suspended, but, honestly, I don't know how many more chances you will get. If you want to finish your senior year, you have to take the necessary steps. I can help you find a program in the area that works with teenagers and families. Your thoughts?"
6. Depending on the client's reaction to the confrontation, you may need to acknowledge that you misspoke. It doesn't mean that your concerns aren't valid; it just may be too soon for the client to talk about. You may want to revisit the issues when the client seems more receptive.
7. Consider an obstacle to change as a challenge for the client and one the social worker handles with grace and dignity.

Source: Hepworth et al. (2013); Miley, O'Melia, and DuBois (2013); Sheafor & Horejsi (2015).

Engagement

Behavior: Use empathy, reflection, and interpersonal skills to effectively engage diverse clients and constituencies.

Critical Thinking Question: Why is it important to identify the possible discrepancies between what the client says he or she wants and the realities of what the client is actually doing?

As the social worker, always remember that your life experiences can affect your reaction to clients and their circumstances (Hill & O'Brien, 2014). Be sure to keep your values, personal standards, and beliefs out of the helping relationship. Monitor your reactions to clients. If you find yourself getting angry (or abrasive) with the client, it is important to process this response—and what it might mean—with your supervisor.

Small confrontations over a period of time may work best with some clients. These individuals may need more time to absorb the reality of what the confrontation may mean in the long term. Think of these lesser confrontations as chipping away at the client's protective shell, bit by bit. Often, a client may be scared or ambivalent about confronting issues that have contributed to long-standing patterns or ways of doing something. Understanding a client's reluctance to immediately change and to do or think about something in a different way is unrealistic. Change takes time and occurs over a period of time. For many clients, this is the decision point: "Do I use these new insights to make changes or remain stuck with the status quo?"

Watch as James, the social worker, confronts Anthony very firmly by commenting on his "yes, but" approach to life. He challenges Anthony to consider his attitude about the future. Through this confrontation, Anthony may be more willing to confront himself and make better choices regarding his gang-related activities.

In the example in Box 6.6, the social worker confronts Gardenia about the treatment of her father. She points out the problems related to leaving him locked in his room. She also conveys understanding of the frustrations associated with caring for an elderly disoriented parent. Because Gardenia feels understood, she is more likely to acknowledge the dangers involved in her choice. The next step in the helping process will involve discussions between the social worker and Gardenia on how to improve her father's care and maintain a balance in her life.

Confrontation should be used with professional discretion and always with the best interest of the client in mind. Consider asking for the client's reaction to the confrontation. Remember to attend to the client's reactions (both verbal and nonverbal) to the confrontation by offering a paraphrasing, reflection of feeling, or summarization response.

Leave enough time after offering a confrontation for the client to talk about it and learn from it. When clients come to a new insight, awareness, or realization, using the skill of interpretation (see next section) may be helpful in beginning to explore the rationale behind the action, thought, behavior, or belief (Hill & O'Brien, 2014).

In the example in Box 6.7, the social worker is helpful in moving Melvin toward a possible reconciliation with his children. She points out some of the conflicts he is experiencing. By attending to his feeling of despair and sadness, she slowly moves toward assisting him in possibly reaching out to his children.

Box 6.6 Gardenia—Confrontation

Gardenia is a 45-year-old married female who is the mother of three teenage sons. Recently, her 75-year-old father, who has been diagnosed with Alzheimer's disease, has come to live with the family following his wife's death.

Gardenia: Dad can be so demanding of my time and energy. I know this is related to the Alzheimer's, but. . .

Social Worker: You can end up feeling very overwhelmed. (Reflection of feeling)

Gardenia: Yeah, especially when I get so little help from my husband and kids. They all head off to their activities, leaving me alone with Dad. I can't just let him wander off, so I lock him in his room.

Social Worker: I hear the frustration you're experiencing. (Reflection of feeling) However, locking your father in his room is could be very dangerous. (Confrontation)

Gardenia: I know you're right, but I don't know any other way to keep him safe.

Social Worker: I understand the dilemma—caring for your dad, your husband, and your children leaves you feeling exhausted and depleted. (Summarization)

Box 6.7 Melvin—Confrontation

Melvin is a 50-year-old male. He has been married three times. He has two daughters from his first marriage but has very little contact with them.

Social Worker: You have talked about how much you love your girls. I can see in your face and hear in your voice your pride in them. (Reflection of feeling)

Melvin: I do love them, but it is too late to try and get things back on track. Too much time has passed. They are teenagers now and don't need me for anything but money.

Social Worker: You seem to be disappointed and hurt by the way things have worked out. (Lead-in/closed-ended question/reflection of feeling/paraphrasing)

Melvin: My ex-wife wants me to call the kids, send cards, you know, that kind of stuff, but after so many years of not really seeing them, it feels forced.

Social Worker: Do you want to continue to let things go as they are or maybe try a new way of approaching them? (Closed-ended question)

Melvin: I don't think I can handle their rejection—what if they really want nothing to do with me?

Social Worker: Melvin, they may want nothing to do with you. You make it seem as if it's *their* responsibility to make things better. If you don't take some responsibility for contacting them and keeping in touch, it is possible that too much distance will develop between you and the girls. If that happens, you may find yourself cut out of their lives completely. (Summarization/confrontation/information giving)

Melvin: How do I do it? It is so hard to admit that I have screwed up.

Social Worker: This is a very difficult for you. I can see the sadness in your face. Let's talk about how you see yourself as their father and what you want to do to make things better. (Reflection of feeling/open-ended question)

Always consider the individuality of your client. Although not specifically related to the skill of confrontation, be cautious with clients who have a long history of disorderly conduct and aggressive behavior. These clients may need to be confronted in a more careful way, sometimes direct and forceful, other times providing reassurance and speaking in a gentle and soothing manner. Demonstrate empathy and understanding of their frustration and anger. Be sure to pay attention to the client's nonverbal behaviors and

Box 6.C Now you try it . . . Confrontation

A 25-year-old male who is schizophrenic refuses to take his antipsychotic medication because the side effects include headaches and nausea. He states that in the past, he has experienced long periods of feeling fine and has no need to take the medication. The staff at his current day treatment program have informed you that he must continue taking his medication, or he will be terminated from the program.

A. What issue(s) would you address?

1. ______________________________

2. ______________________________

B. Your confrontational response:

1. ______________________________

reactions as well. Intervening with a potentially violent or aggressive client will require that the social worker be alert to indicators of escalating behaviors, such as the presence of firearms, the influence of alcohol, or membership in a violent peer group. In a dangerous situation, your safety comes first. Trust your gut feeling. Be aware of escape routes and office procedures that outline emergency responses to volatile situations. When making home visits, always inform your agency of your whereabouts (Sheafor & Horejsi, 2015). See Appendix C for more information about deescalation strategies.

To begin to understand how to use this skill of confrontation, provide a confrontational response to the client in Box 6.C who denies the need for his psychotropic medication.

Interpretation

Interpretation is a skill that the social worker employs to go beyond the client's stated problem to find deeper meaning. This is a process of getting to underlying issues associated with the problem (Cormier, Nurius, & Osborn, 2011). By definition, this skill can call on both the social worker and the client to be introspective. Given the level of discomfort or vulnerability a client might experience as you begin to "peel away the layers of the onion," be sure there is a well-established relationship of trust and goodwill. Otherwise, the client may become defensive or annoyed. Remember that not all clients have the capacity to (or interest in) interpret their behaviors, actions, and intentions. Some clients are more interested in behavioral changes, where the results are more immediate. However, it is often the case that behavioral change is dependent on the client developing a deeper understanding of the situation.

Ethical and Professional Behavior

Behaviors: Use reflection and self-regulation to manage personal values and maintain professionalism in practice situations.

Critical Thinking Question: Explain a situation in your life where the light went on for you. What did you learn about yourself through the process?

Interpretations can point out the causal connection between repeated behaviors, feelings, and thoughts. In this case, the light goes on, and the client may see his or her way clear to change long-standing patterns. These insights can be motivating as the client reevaluates his or her goals toward considering major life changes. Focusing on the client's strengths and potential is also an important part of using this skill. For example, what does the client see as personal and professional assets? How can those characteristics be used to make changes?

Watch the instructor discuss how the skill of interpretation can be used to help the client understand possible underlying issues that may be difficult to address in the helping relationship.

Interpretation

Frequently, clients are emotionally attached to a problem, and their judgment is clouded. Consequently, they have difficulty seeing a way out of the situation. Interpretation allows clients to see the problem in a new light, which can give them hope that change is indeed possible; however, clients may need time to absorb new ways of looking at the issue or situation. Timing is critical—always consider whether the client is ready for a deeper understanding. If not, the client will most likely reject the interpretation. When offering an interpretation, it should relate closely to the client's experiences and reality. For example, your client has a long history of being passive and submissive in her marital relationship. She reports that her husband wants a divorce. She states that she will need to talk to her teenage children about this, as she doesn't want to make any decisions on her own. You see the connection between her passiveness as a spouse and her role as a parent. Given the current crisis, consider whether the timing is right to identify this pattern and process its meaning and impact on her life or to wait until the crisis has been resolved and then explore these issues in retrospect. As with any social work interviewing skill, consider the impact of using a particular skill both in the moment and over the long term. Box 6.8 provides you with a series of suggestions regarding when to use the skill interpretation.

Box 6.8 Guidelines for Using Interpretation

1. Consider whether the client shows readiness to explore or examine deeper issues.
2. Is your interpretation based on client's actual message rather than on your biases and values?
3. Relate past issues, themes, or patterns to what is currently happening in the client's life. For example, "You have talked a lot about your mom's drinking and the tirades that occurred when she was drunk. Sometimes you felt powerless to say anything and took her verbal insults to heart. I wonder if her behaviors relate in any way to you how you feel about your boss, who yells without cause and belittles you?"
4. Word your interpretation as a tentative statement—" I wonder whether . . ." or "Is it possible that . . ."
5. Allow enough time to explore the client's reaction. Digging deeper into the client's world may open up old wounds or trauma. Be prepared to help the client manage the pain by using reassurance, empathy skills, and attending behaviors. Give the client ample time to explore these issues before moving on or ending the session.
6. Depending on the client's reaction to the interpretation, you may need to acknowledge "probable error." Tuck the information away, however, as you may have touched on something very significant. You may want to revisit the issues when the client seems more receptive.
7. Sometimes a "molehill is just a molehill," meaning that what the client is experiencing may have no deeper meaning. Do not assume that your insights are correct, valid, or relevant.

Source: Hepworth et al. (2013).

Box 6.9 Pamela—Interpretation

Pamela is a 30-year-old female who is experiencing multiple problems. Today, she is discussing her boss. This is her third session with the Employee Assistance Program social worker.

Pamela: I hate this guy. He's always looking over my shoulder on the assembly line. So I show up late; I take a few minutes more for lunch. That really gets to him. (Said with a smile)

Social Worker: So, you do things that you know will irritate your boss. (Paraphrasing)

Pamela: Yeah, I mean he never has a kind word to say; I've never gotten a raise; he finds fault with everything I do.

Social Worker: You seem to have figured out how to make things uncomfortable for yourself at work. (Paraphrasing)

Pamela: Yeah, but it's kinda fun to piss him off. Once he's mad, he loses his train of thought and gets all red in the face.

Social Worker: I wonder what causes you to find ways to make people mad at you. For example, you said that you and your husband fight a lot too. Could it be that you find it hard to be close to people? Given the way your dad treated you, being criticized and yelled at is what you are used to. Setting up a conflict between you and others in your life is something you know how to do very well. (Lead-in response/interpretation—said very softly and carefully)

Pamela: Yeah, I hadn't really thought about it that way before. I have been getting into fights with people my whole life. That is pretty much how I am with everyone. Pretty messed up, huh?

Good interpretations are based on data. A lofty interpretation may make the social worker sound like an intelligent and gifted professional, but at the same time the interpretation may make the client feel "psychoanalyzed". Be sure to offer an interpretation that is fairly short so as to not lecture the client (Hepworth et al., 2013). Box 6.9 demonstrates the social worker interpreting the probable underlying message of a client.

Watch this clip as Karen offers an interpretation to Mike about his drinking. As you reflect on how the interpretation is delivered, identify two ways that she could have done it differently. If you feel as though her response was appropriate, identify two reasons why you agree.

Offering an interpretation is a delicate process. The social worker offers a tentative statement and then gauges the client's reaction to find out whether the interpretation was helpful, for example, "I wonder if it could be . . ." or "Could it possibly relate to . . . ?" (Hackney & Cormier, 2012). It is important to note that the client may accept or reject the social worker's interpretation. Also, by responding to the actual client message, the social worker is less likely to impose a personal bias. The client may offer his or her own interpretation if the one offered by the social worker doesn't fit. Success in using this skill is very dependent on the length, timing, and quality of the social worker–client relationship. Interpretation is most beneficial when the social worker and the client have a good rapport and the client appears ready to explore underlying issues related to the problem (Kadushin & Kadushin, 2013). Asking the client for his or her interpretation of "why they do what they do" may be a good way to assist the client in coming to his or her own conclusions. This approach also is consistent with empowerment and self-efficacy. Conversely, the client may want your interpretation and ask, "Why do I do what I do?" How would you respond to the client in Box 6.D?

Box 6.D Now You Try It . . . Interpretation

A 30-year-old woman reports that her best friend has no time for her anymore now that she has a boyfriend. Although she would like to be in a relationship, she doesn't want to get hurt. Her pattern of behavior includes excessive jealousy, saying one thing yet doing something else and "testing" the other person. She states that it is hard for her to trust people, especially men. She's afraid they'll leave her too, "just like my dad did."

A. What underlying issues in the client's statement would you address?

1. ______________________________

2. ______________________________

B. Your interpretation response:

1. ______________________________

Box 6.10 Possible Social Worker Responses Following an Interpretation

I can tell that you are uncomfortable with what I just asked. . . .

It makes sense that you had a strong reaction to what I just said; let's talk about that. . . .

You seem to understand the consequences of the situation. Your tears say it all. Let's focus on your sadness. . . .

What caused you to respond so strongly to that?

Your feelings are very understandable; it is hard to face this alone. . . .

There is a lot of stress and pressure on you right now; I can see the tension in your face; what is your reaction. . . .?

As the social worker offers an interpretation, he or she should be alert to the client's verbal and nonverbal responses. Interpretation can stimulate a variety of feelings in the client. If the social worker feels that the client needs additional support to deal with the new insight, then interpretation should be paired with paraphrase, reflection of feeling, or summarization (Hepworth et al., 2013). Box 6.10 provides some examples of possible social worker responses to a client's reaction of an interpretation.

Assess your understanding of interviewing skills by taking this brief quiz.

Does this interpretation help the client to begin to see things in a different light? Is the social worker able to help move Anna beyond what is stated and to delve deeper into the meaning behind the message? Now watch this clip as the social worker Marie offers an interpretation to Anna.

INTEGRATING SOCIAL WORK SKILLS AND ATTENDING BEHAVIOR SKILLS

Interviewing skills work best when used in combination with one another, leading to social work interviews that are richer and deeper in meaning. The following two examples illustrate the use of several skills used together.

In the case example in Box 6.11, the social worker and client come to some understanding of the depth of Dakesah's sadness and guilt. Through attending to the client's verbal and nonverbal messages, the social worker is able to provide Dakesah with a safe place to cry and mourn the loss of her daughter.

Box 6.12 shows the dialogue between the client and social worker in Interactive Case Study #5. In their final session, Mrs. Kita and social worker Diane terminate their professional relationship, recognizing that their work together has ended. Throughout the interview, the social worker continues to encourage and affirm Mrs. Kita. Diane, utilizes many basic and advanced skills during the session. You can see how the social worker weaves in open- and closed-ended questions, paraphrasing, reflection of feeling, information giving, summarization, interpretation, and clarification.

? Assess your understanding of cultural awareness by taking this brief quiz.

Box 6.11 Dakesah—Integrating Social Work Skills

Dakesah is a 40-year-old female. Her teenage daughter Laila ran away several months ago. There has been no word from Laila since she left.

Social Worker: You said the days just drag on and on as you wait for a phone call about your daughter Laila. (Paraphrasing) How do you manage to get through the day? (Open-ended question)

Dakesah: I try to keep myself busy. Since she ran away, I haven't been able to sleep much. I wake up because I have terrible nightmares. My husband acts as if none of this is happening.

Social Worker: That must make it even more painful for you, like you're in this alone. (Reflection of feeling; the social worker leans toward the client, pauses, and maintains eye contact) What is your relationship with him like right now? (Open-ended question)

Dakesah: Very distant. I can't talk to him; he says it is all me. I can't stop thinking about her. He is no support at all. I wish he had left, not Laila.

Social Worker: You are very concerned about Laila and at the same time you feel regret. (Summarization)

Dakesah: Laila left home because of all the yelling and screaming. She was into drugs, getting high and skipping school. She refused to listen to me; her dad just tuned us both out. He was not home much, but when he was, it did get ugly.

Social Worker: What do you mean by ugly? (Clarification)

Dakesah: He yelled all the time. He came home drunk almost every night. He is in no position to judge her behavior.

Social Worker: You sound really angry at him. I am wondering, do you blame him for Laila leaving? (Reflection of feeling and interpretation)

Dakesah: I mostly blame myself. I saw this coming. I didn't want to leave him, but now I think I should have. Here I am without my daughter, not knowing if she is dead or alive. (Client is crying)

Social Worker: (The social worker remains silent for approximately one minute) This is so painful for you. (More silence, leaning in, handing the client a tissue)

Dakesah: (The client is still crying) I haven't cried about this in a long time.

Social Worker: I am here; it's okay. (Direct eye contact, offering assurance and information giving, and more silence)

Box 6.12 Final Client–Social Worker Session between Mrs. Kita and Diane

In their final session. Mrs. Kita and the social worker, Diane, are reviewing all of the progress Mrs. Kita has made and are saying good-bye. The termination process is bittersweet, as they have developed a bond and genuinely care about each other. Note the attending behaviors of the social worker and Mrs. Kita. You can see the care with which they say good-bye. Leaving the door open for Mrs. Kita to contact her again is helpful, as there are a few more pieces of business to complete. As in any helping relationship, planning for the ending is as important as planning for the beginning.

Social Worker: Hi, Akira, it's so good to see you again. (Opening statement)

Mrs. Kita: You too. I can't believe this is our last session.

Social Worker: Me either. (Long pause) How have you been? (Open-ended question)

Mrs. Kita: Fine, Nori is doing really well and he loves school. He is so happy.

Social Worker: That is fantastic. How is Maiko? (Closed-ended question)

Mrs. Kita: She is good too.

Social Worker: And I see your mom is fine. (Says this with a smile.)

Mrs. Kita: Yes. (She smiles) Since most of my financial problems are pretty much resolved, I feel like I can breathe again.

Social Worker: I am so glad. A huge weight has been lifted. (Pause) Have you heard anything from Social Security? (Paraphrasing and closed-ended question)

Mrs. Kita: No, just the standard letter saying they are reviewing my file.

Social Worker: It will probably be a few more months until you get a decision. If they deny you benefits, there is an appeal process. (Information giving)

Mrs. Kita: (Nodding head) I wish now I had started this a long time ago, like you said.

Social Worker: But you have taken the steps. (Pause) What about the assistance you got from Community Action? (Paraphrasing and closed-ended question)

Mrs. Kita: I am still getting help with utilities.

Social Worker: Good. So between the loan, working again, your part-time job, the rental subsidy, and Community Action, you are doing okay. (Summarization)

Mrs. Kita: Yes, things are easier. Mrs. Jerry has been understanding too. Right now, as long as nothing bad happens with Nori's health, I am fine.

Social Worker: Great. Is there anything else that you would like to talk about today? (Closed-ended question)

Mrs. Kita: Actually, Jirou called yesterday, and I am still upset about our conversation.

Social Worker: In what way? (Clarification)

Mrs. Kita: He wants me to visit this weekend, and I don't want to go; at least that is how I am feeling right now.

VIDEO ASSESSMENT

Watch these videos and identify the attending behavior or interview skill that is demonstrated.

SUMMARY

In this chapter, students were introduced to advanced practice skills, summarization, information giving, confrontation and interpretation. Using social work skills effectively requires more than just knowing the skill; the social worker must determine when it is appropriate to use the skill by gauging the client's likely response. This level of expertise takes considerable effort to develop, but it can be learned.

- Establishing and maintaining a helping relationship is critical to planned change. It involves putting your client's needs and interests at the forefront. It means fully listening, comprehending, and incorporating his or her life situation and experiences into your frame of reference. It means not being preoccupied by your own biases, values, internal voice, or distractions. This "tuning in" (Shulman, 2012) is an essential ingredient to the helping relationship. Without this level of commitment, focus, and concentration, the helping relationship cannot evolve and move forward.
- Remember that when social work skills are first used by the beginning social worker, they can seem mechanical. With time and practice, they will become almost second nature. Keep in mind, though, that even the most experienced social workers benefit from an ongoing commitment to improving their interviewing skills.
- Through contact with other social workers, membership in professional organizations such as the NASW, and, most important, the development of the habit of self-evaluation, you will be well on your way to becoming a skilled professional.

APPLY IT

1. Watch all 5 sessions of **Interactive Case Study # 6**, Kim and the social worker Louis (and the shelter director, Yesenia). In each session, identify at least one information giving and one summarization response. Additionally comment on the relationship between Kim and Louis as it develops over time. Now put yourself in Kim's place. Identify 5 examples in which Louis showed care and concern for her wellbeing. The meeting between Louis and Yesenia provides a good example of how to communicate with other professionals who are involved in the case. Put yourself into their shoes, what do you believe each can do to help Kim through this difficult time?

Assess Your Competence

Use the scale below to rate your current level of achievement on the following concepts or skills associated with each competency presented in the chapter:

1	2	3
I can accurately describe the concept or skill	I can consistently identify the concept or skill when observing and analyzing practice activities	I can competently implement the concept or skill in my own practice

_______ Understands how to conduct a constructive interview and can explain the importance of a tentative interview agenda.

_______ Can identify and describe how to utilize the technique of summarization.

_______ Understands and can describe correct use of confrontation.

_______ Understands interpretation, including when and how to employ this technique.

7

Common Errors in Direct Practice (Pitfalls)

LISA F. YOUNG / SHUTTERSTOCK

LEARNING OUTCOMES

- Identify common errors (pitfalls) in the helping process.
- Analyze how common errors (pitfalls) can divert the helping process.

CHAPTER OUTLINE

OVERCOMING COMMON BARRIERS IN DIRECT PRACTICE

Knowing how and when to correctly use social work interviewing skills provides the foundation for the helping relationship. Social workers strive to ask the "perfect" open-ended question or deliver the "perfect" paraphrase, but even the most skilled professionals make mistakes. The goal of this chapter is to provide an explanation of common mistakes, or pitfalls, made by beginning social workers and the negative consequences that may result, to provide examples of these pitfalls in video clips, and give you an opportunity to practice offering more appropriate responses. Being aware of the pitfalls, or "what not to do," can help the social worker avoid potential problems that could damage or abruptly end the helping relationship. When a client reacts (verbally or nonverbally) with embarrassment, anger, or silence, the social worker may have fallen into one of the common interviewing pitfalls.

If you find yourself making a mistake by inadvertently stumbling into a pitfall, you can recover and continue with the interview.

For example, if you ask an inappropriate question and realize that you have done so, refocus the interview by posing a question that relates more to the topic at hand. You may want to acknowledge that the question was "off base" before trying again. Should you respond judgmentally, you will probably be able to tell by the client's verbal and nonverbal reaction. In that case, use an empathy statement, such as, "I can tell from your reaction that I have said something that has caused you to feel judged—that was not my intent, and I am sorry. What I meant to say was . . ."

THE PITFALLS

In this section, you will learn about and watch examples of 10 pitfalls that social workers sometimes make during interactions with clients. In the Now You Try It boxes, you will be prompted to correct the pitfalls by thinking of more appropriate social worker responses.

Advice Giving

Social workers should not tell the client what to do to solve the problem. It is vital to the helping process that the client be an active participant in the therapeutic relationship. The ethic of self-determination is critical because the purpose of the social work relationship is to empower the client to make decisions that will improve his or her own life (Kadushin & Kadushin, 2013). The client will ultimately live with the consequences of decisions, weighing the costs and benefits of each decision that is made. If a social worker does offer advice, it should focus on the means or ways toward problem resolution. Social workers should not give advice regarding the ends or major life decisions that clients have to make for themselves. Once a client has made a decision that involves the end point or goal, **giving advice** about how to reach the goal can be very helpful and instructive.

Watch this video in which the instructor talks about the pitfall of advice giving.

Now watch this clip as Nicole offers advice to Mrs. Anderson. How would you correct her response?

Box 7.1 illustrates this distinction regarding **advice giving** and information giving.

In the pitfall example in Box 7.1, the social worker is telling the client what she thinks he should do, which is counter to client self-determination. Should the client decide to retire, the social worker can then provide information about retirement options. This type of advice can help to broaden Mr. Randall's life choices, many of which he may not even know exist.

If the social worker is too quick to give advice, the client may never learn the art of problem solving, self-responsibility, and making well-informed decisions. Developing

Box 7.1 Pitfall Example: Advice Giving

Mr. Tim Randall is a 63-year-old high school English teacher. He is considering retiring within the next few years. One of his concerns is a sense of being a "has-been." He worries that he will have too much idle time on his hands and will miss interacting with students and fellow teachers.

Mr. Randall: I have taught for over 30 years—same subject, basically the same students, year after year. I guess that I am bored with teaching.

Social Worker: What do you see yourself doing if you do retire? (Open-ended question)

Mr. Randall: I don't know what I want to do with my life; I just know that teaching is not interesting or challenging to me anymore. I have a hard time getting myself to work every day. My best teaching years are behind me.

Social Worker Pitfall: I would retire. You've put in a lot of good years. Use your pension money to travel. (Advice giving)

Correct Social Worker Response: What does seem to interest you? (Open-ended question)

Mr. Randall: I like to travel, but I am alone.

Social Worker: As you see it, retiring means lots of quiet and unoccupied time, but it doesn't have to be that way. If you decide to retire, there are ways to fill some of the voids. (Paraphrasing and information giving)

a sense of independence and autonomy is very important because the social worker's involvement is time limited. The lifelong skill of problem solving will always serve clients well.

It is the social worker's role to help clients discover options for probable solutions and together agree on a realistic direction. The social worker helps clients evaluate past decisions and how they have affected their life circumstances in positive or negative ways. The focus is on helping the client examine the current situation from a clear perspective. The social worker can usurp this right by jumping in and advising because of self-imposed pressure to fix the problem (Hill & O'Brien, 2014). Social workers who are new to the field may have an inclination to give the client advice within the helping relationship, with the potential of establishing an unhealthy client dependence on the social worker (Hepworth, Rooney, Rooney, Strom-Gottfried, & Larsen, 2012). A "quick fix" to a problem that may stem from deep-rooted patterns of dysfunctional behavior will eventually reemerge if the origins of these behaviors are not thoroughly explored and resolved. For example, a gay client continues to meet men via the Internet. The social worker's advice to him might be, "Stop using the Internet to meet men; people search the Web looking to prey on vulnerable people." The underlying concern for this client may be lack of self-esteem, feeling unattractive and unlovable, as well as a lack of opportunity to meet gay men. He may see Internet dating as a safe, accessible, and less threatening way to meet people. By quickly dispensing advice, the social worker may have cut off any discussion about issues related to his choice and the meaning he attaches to it. In addition, the social worker may be conveying a possible judgment about his sexual orientation.

In another example, Alicia is a divorced female who has been involved in a string of unhealthy relationships. She asks the social worker about her current relationship and what she should do to remedy the problem. Rather than offering advice, the social worker could explore the nature and dynamics of the relationship. Once Alicia has developed some insight into her repeated pattern of unhealthy relationships, with the assistance of the social worker, she may be willing to commit energy into developing strategies to assess and determine what she wants and needs to move forward.

Box 7.2 Pitfall Example: Advice Giving

Amanda is a 25-year-old female who recently gave birth to twins. She also recently learned that her mother has cancer. She is talking to the social worker about her current stresses.

Amanda: I have six-month-old twins: a boy and a girl. They are wonderful, but I am tired all the time. I try to take good care of them, take care of the house and my husband. I am scheduled to go back to work full-time next month. I really enjoy my job, but I don't know how I am going to manage. My mom, who had originally agreed to take care of them one or two days a week, was just diagnosed with cancer. So I have that to worry about too.

Social Worker: What about waiting to go back to work until the twins are older and your mom is better? (Advice giving)

Amanda: I can't do that; we need the money.

Social Worker Pitfall: But can you really take care of the twins and work full-time? You have managed on one income for six months; why not continue doing what you have been already doing? (Advice giving)

Correct Social Worker Response: Amanda, it sounds like you are trying to take care of everything and everybody. Right now there is a lot to handle. What part of your situation do you want to talk about first? (Paraphrase and open-ended question)

In the pitfall example in Box 7.2, the social worker is advising the client rather than helping her to explore options regarding her life stressors. The social worker is exhibiting the pitfall of advice giving. Telling the client what she should do takes away any opportunity for the client to tap into her internal and external resources.

Another example of the pitfall of advice giving is demonstrated in Box 7.A. See if you can provide more appropriate responses to clients in the Now You Try It Boxes following each Box 7.A- 7.K, in the spaces provided.

Inappropriate Use of Humor

When a social worker uses **inappropriate humor**, the client can feel belittled, targeted, intimidated, criticized, or mocked. Humor should never be used at the client's expense, as the client may believe that you are minimizing the problem and not taking him or her seriously (Kadushin & Kadushin, 2013). Sarcasm may be misunderstood as rudeness or insensitivity by the client, creating a climate of mistrust in the social worker–client relationship. Humor, if appropriately used, can buffer a "blow," reduce the impact of a stressful situation, or minimize emotional pain. For example, Daryl, an Iraq War veteran, shared that "Jack" was his closest friend. The social worker asked what made that relationship so important. Daryl, with a straight face, stated, "Daniels." They both laughed as the social worker said, "Oh, that Jack Daniels," and it set the stage for a more open

Box 7.A Now You Try It . . . Correcting Advice Giving

Client: I'm back at home, but my dad barely talks to me anymore. I really want to make things better, but it seems impossible.

Social Worker: How about trying to say something nice to him tonight? Try to talk to him without a negative tone in your voice.

What is a more appropriate response?

1. ______________________________

____

conversation. The social worker did not dwell on the alcohol reference, she just acknowledged it, as they laughed together. The social worker may find humor in the client's situation, but the client may not have the same subjective perspective.

> Watch this video in which the instructor talks about how using inappropriate humor can be detrimental to the helping relationship.

Inappropriate humor can convey that the social worker is not empathic or sensitive to the client's point of view (Kadushin & Kadushin, 2013). For example, Maurice is a 45-year-old client who is frustrated because he has been unable to find a job. Cracking a joke about becoming homeless or begging on the streets is ill timed and insensitive. Maurice will assume that you are not taking his unemployment situation seriously and will feel foolish for coming to you in the first place.

The client may use humor to mask a problem by minimizing it or distancing themselves from pain. The social worker should be aware of this possibility and search for deeper meaning in the client's message (Hepworth et al., 2012). Certainly, humor has its place in any human relationship, and it can lighten the tension. Sometimes, the best thing to do in a crisis is to diffuse some of the seriousness with lightness, to allow the sadness to be lifted with hope (Brems, 2001). Laughing and humor can also help the client see a situation in a different light by literally "lightening" up or reducing the tension of a situation. In a counseling relationship, there may be humorous moments; however, humor should never detract from the professional helping process. It is very common that the general gravity of what clients discuss in social service settings is quite serious and emotionally charged. Thus, humor should be used with great discretion and never at the expense of the client. It is also important to recognize that laughing and smiling carry different meanings across cultures. In Video Case #5, Mrs. Kita, born in Japan, appears to cover up her embarrassment regarding her husband's incarceration with a slight smile. (Kadushin & Kadushin, 2013). Light banter or humor that puts the client at ease, reduces tension, or offers a creative outlet to pain and suffering can help desensitize the client's pain. In essence, the social worker is using humor to provide hope.

> As you watch this video clip, describe how Diane tries to find some humor in Mrs. Kita's situation.

> Watch this clip of Louis as he makes light of Kim's statement that she came home without physical injuries. How does his "joke" about having all of her body parts come across?

Box 7.3 illustrates the social worker using the pitfall of inappropriate humor.

In the pitfall example in Box 7.3, the social worker makes fun of and belittles her client when she makes light of the client's disappointment by joking about her own safety. In the corrected response, the social worker appropriately acknowledges Nick's disappointment and then asks a closed-ended question: is the scholarship his only option? Similarly, the social worker diminishes the client's problem with her inappropriate

Box 7.3 Pitfall Example: Inappropriate Humor

Nick is a 19-year-old male discussing his disappointment in not getting a music scholarship. He has spent years of his life devoted to music and has great expectations for a musical career. Nick just learned that he did not get the scholarship he was counting on.

Nick: I am so upset about the way things turned out. Everyone kept reassuring me that I would get the scholarship. I have always wanted to be a musician; even before I could walk, I was banging on pots and pans in the kitchen. Drumming is my passion, my life. I am obsessed with percussion. Now what do I do?

Social Worker Pitfall: Well, don't hit me on the head with those drum sticks! (Inappropriate humor)

Correct Social Worker Response: What a huge letdown! You were really counting on the scholarship to the university. (Reflection of feeling)

Nick: Yeah, I was. I'm sick of working for minimum wage at the bookstore. This is not how I see my life turning out.

Correct Social Worker Response continued: Is the scholarship to the university the only way that you can afford to attend? (Closed-ended question)

Box 7.B Now You Try It . . . Correcting Inappropriate Humor

Client: My daughter has been getting in trouble at school. She is a very expressive child. She loves to do artwork and would spend every hour of the day drawing. The school keeps contacting me about Liza's lack of interest in her other classes. I think it is important to pay attention in class, but her artwork will take her places a math class can't.

Social Worker: So, today it's Walt Whitman High School, tomorrow it's the Sistine Chapel.

What is a more appropriate response?

1. ______________________________

____

attempt at humor in Box 7.B. Provide an alternative response to the client that would be more supportive and understanding.

Interrupting the Client and Abrupt Transitions

In the course of an interview, social workers ask many questions. The social worker who is attuned to the client is an active listener and aware of the verbal and nonverbal cues signifying when the client has finished speaking. Too many **interruptions** may cause the client to lose his or her train of thought or to feel that the social worker does not care about the problem. As a consequence, the focus of the interview tends to be more on the social worker than on the client's concerns. Inappropriate interruptions can be annoying and disruptive to the client and may divert the client from exploring important areas and feelings (Hepworth et al., 2013). For example, Jamie is a 25-year-old drug addict. She begins to give the social worker details related to her drug history and usage. Before she is able to complete her statement, the social worker interrupts Jamie with a question about where she slept last night. In this case, the focus shifts from the client to the social worker. Jamie is likely to feel cut off and frustrated. It's possible that Jamie might have revealed important information about her situation, but the opportunity has been lost.

Watch this clip as the instructor talks about the pitfall of interrupting the client.

A well-paced interview includes taking turns speaking (Cormier & Hackney, 2011). Both the client and the social worker may need sufficient time to put together what it is they want to say or ask and how to respond. There may be some silences. Unfilled space is preferred to cutting the client off. Sitting quietly allows the social worker to make nonverbal observations of the client.

Abrupt transitions or moving to a new topic very suddenly can leave the client feeling annoyed and cut off. Sometimes, the social worker may be uncomfortable with topics such as sex, death, religion, ethnicity, and politics or disinterested with the subject matter and therefore steers the interview to another (possibly safer) topic. In this case, the worker has full control over the direction of the interview, and may ignore a serious topic that needs further exploration. If the social worker disagrees with the client's views or opinions, rather than get involved in an uncomfortable exchange, the social worker might change the topic to something more compatible with his or her views. It is imperative that the social worker reflect on why he or she is moving away from these areas and to identify ways to increase his or her comfort level with such issues. For example, a client is discussing the recent death of his child. Because the social worker is uncertain how to proceed with such a difficult issue, he moves the client away from feelings about the child's death to how other family members are reacting. The topic is still relevant, but the focus has changed significantly. In this case, the abrupt transition is social worker driven, not client driven. Box 7.4 illustrates the social worker using the pitfalls of interruption and abrupt transition.

In the pitfall example in Box 7.4, the client has come to the social worker for specific reasons: child care and financial resources. The social worker is not listening to the client and frequently interrupts as she abruptly shifts direction away from the child care issue to her daughter's developmental disability. This fits the social worker's agenda but clearly avoids what the client has in mind. In the corrected response, the social worker acknowledges Lucy's concerns.

Box 7.4 Pitfalls Example: Interrupting the Client and Abrupt Transitions

Lucy is a 35-year-old female talking about her desire to start a job training program at the community college. She is seeking the social worker's help in locating possible child care options (and funding) so that she can further her education and eventually secure a job.

Lucy: My case manager told me to come and talk to you.

Social Worker Pitfall: About what? (Interrupting the client)

Lucy: Well . . . I want to start a job training program, but I need child . . .

Social Worker Pitfall: How many children do you have? (Interrupting the client)

Lucy: Child care for my daughter, who is developmentally disabled . . .

Social Worker Pitfall: Yes, I see on this intake form you indicated that your daughter is developmentally disabled. (Interrupting the client)

Lucy: Yes, she is.

Social Worker Pitfall: Oh . . . well, let's talk about what it's like to be her parent, before we discuss child care. (Abrupt transition)

Correct Social Worker Response: So you need to think about a program that provides appropriate services for her and education for you too. (Paraphrasing)

Box 7.C Now You Try It . . . Correcting Interrupting/Abrupt Transitions

Client: The days just keep getting longer. I hate when it gets dark at 4:30. I need sunlight; otherwise, I could just sleep all day. I feel like hibernating and would if I could.

Social Worker: Let me check my watch . . . the sun sets at 5:15 now.

What is a more appropriate response?

1. ______________________________

____

In this clip, Diane the social worker abruptly changes the topic without regard for Mrs. Kita's reference to her mother. How would you feel if you were Mrs. Kita and Diane totally misses the significance of her mother's help? She moves on to how she will pay her rent. Now using a summarization, what would you say differently?

Inappropriate and Irrelevant Questions

Typically, questions that are asked by the social worker are not neutral; rather, they convey the worker's biases, values, attitudes, preferences, and beliefs. As social workers, we are curious about our clients' lives and their "back stories." However, asking too many or **inappropriate questions** may make the interview seem more like an interrogation than a helping session (Egan, 2014). Use questions to get only needed information, as the social worker doesn't have the inherent right to all information about the client, only that which is essential to the helping process. Being a curiosity seeker is to misrepresent and misuse the client–social worker relationship. A worker's interest in "entertainment" or voyeuristic needs may supersede the privacy rights of the client. Asking questions unrelated to the problem can also cause a lack of focus in the session, leading the client to feel distracted and misunderstood.

Watch the instructor discuss the pitfall of asking inappropriate questions.

Brems (2001) identifies several types of problematic questions:

- Leading/Suggestive—gives hidden (or not-so-hidden) advice disguised as a question. Can be used to coerce the client, predetermine what is important information, or exert unnecessary pressure through controlling the line of questions.

  Client: I want to be more independent and not count on men to rescue me.

  Social Worker: Given your interest in becoming more self-sufficient, have you ever been to the home shows at the convention center?

In reality, the social worker is expecting the client to go to home shows in order to meet men.

- Assuming—gives the impression that the social worker is expecting a particular answer.

  Client: I work day and night; I never have enough time with my family. And, if I am with them, I fall asleep.
  Social Worker: You really don't mean that you fall asleep, do you?

In reality, the social worker is telling the client how she thinks he should respond. This may cause the client to pretend to agree.

- Controlling or Intrusive Questions—ignores the client's agenda and needs and instead focuses on the social worker's interests (or need to avoid), as the worker determines the agenda and usually for some personal reason. The social worker may also be exerting pressure on the client to defend a particular stance or to define the scope of the problem.

  Client: My company is going down the tubes. I have no money set aside. My wife is so angry at me for losing the business. She is starting to pull away too.
  Social Worker: I don't want to focus on your marital finances right now; please tell me about your sexual practices.

In reality, the social worker is meeting her own needs: her curiosity about the client's sex life versus the financial difficulties within the marriage. Or, conversely, the social worker may be comfortable talking about finances and steers clear of more intimate material.

- Tangential—stems from a lack of empathy; questions are off the mark and fail to get to the heart of the issue and keep the client from delving deeply into the problem situation.

  Client: I wish everyone would leave me alone; I am tired of all this crap. I can't wait to get out of here. Life is miserable.
  Social Worker: And where do you plan to go?

In reality, the social worker misses the most relevant issue: the client's feelings of frustration and hopelessness. Instead, she focuses on tangential information that may be important at some point but not at this time.

- Pseudoquestions—disguised commands or directives when there is no choice.

  Social Worker: Do you want to begin now?

In reality, the social worker is not asking the client his or her preference but is directing the client to begin.

- Judgmental—"why" questions may suggest disapproval and lead to the client feeling defensive.

  Client: Yesterday the checkout lady at the drugstore yelled at me again—this time in front of everyone in the line. She thought I was shoplifting or something. I go there all the time, and this is probably the twentieth time she has done this to me. I was so embarrassed.
  Social Worker: Why do you shop there then?

In reality, the social worker is judging the client's choices and excusing the clerk's inappropriate behavior. The client likely feels as if she needs to explain or defend her reasons for shopping at the drugstore. This type of question will not move the therapeutic relationship along.

- Attacking—these questions are demeaning and embarrassing, as these "challenges" can shame the client. Asking the client a question such as "Where is the evidence to support your actions?" can lead to increased distrust, as though you are trying to "catch" the client.

Client: I left the party last night feeling really mad about the whole thing. My boyfriend wants me to get high with him. I just don't want to. I think he's gonna break up with me if I don't start doing what he wants.
Social Worker: Really, do you want to be a "doormat" for the rest of your life?

In reality, the social worker is degrading the client and causing her to feel ashamed. The social worker may be on to an issue that is important to address but not in this mean-spirited way.

- Stacking—asking several questions at one time, leading the client to be confused about which question to respond to first. Stacking questions also convey uncertainty about the direction of the interview.

Client: I want to go back to college next semester, but my grades are so bad I doubt I will be readmitted. I really blew it, and I am paying a high price. Everyone is giving me a hard time, but no one is harder on me than I am on myself.
Social Worker: What happened that caused you to flunk out of school? And what have you been doing this past semester? What are you doing to get your life together?

In reality, these questions are suitable, given the situation, but the social worker's questions are confusing to the client. Stacked questions can also diffuse the significance of each question, as the client is considering one question, only to be distracted by another (Hepworth et al., 2013).

- Shotgun—a long series of closed-ended questions that cover nothing in depth or breadth, leaving the client feeling bombarded.

Client: I stopped taking my medication about a month or so ago. It wasn't helping any more.
Social Worker: Do you think that was such a good idea?
Client: Well, I am not sure, but since I wasn't feeling too bad, I didn't see any reason to keep taking it. Plus, it is very expensive, and my insurance only covers about 50 percent of the cost.
Social Worker: When exactly did you stop taking it?
Client: My prescription ran out May 15. I feel fine.
Social Worker: Do you know how serious the side effects can be when you abruptly stop taking your medicine?
Client: But I feel fine, better than I did when I was taking my medication.
Social Worker: What insurance do you have?
Client: The state program.
Social Worker: How long had you been on the medication before you stopped taking it?
Client: I think eight months or so.

Box 7.5 Pitfall Example: Irrelevant and Inappropriate Questions

Mrs. Frieda Goldberg is an elderly widow talking about her living situation. She discloses to the social worker that she has some fears about living alone now that her husband has recently died.

Mrs. Goldberg: I am living alone now. My husband died two months ago. I like my apartment, but I don't care for my neighbors. They are very loud and have lots of late-night parties. In fact, I told the landlord about all the noise, and she has talked to them a few times. I hate to cause problems, but I don't feel safe anymore.

Social Worker Pitfall: How old are your neighbors? (Irrelevant question)

Mrs. Goldberg: I don't know; they look pretty young.

Social Worker Pitfall: How old are you? (Irrelevant question)

Mrs. Goldberg: Eighty-three, but what does that matter?

Correct Social Worker Response: I am sorry to hear about your husband's death. (Long pause) Now that you are living alone, you don't feel as safe as you did before. (Lead-in response/paraphrasing)

Mrs. Goldberg: No I don't. The landlord keeps telling me to calm down, that the noise isn't all that loud.

Correct Social Worker Response continued: But that doesn't help when you are trying to sleep or get some rest. Being alone now is hard enough; it is even more difficult because you don't feel as if the landlord is listening to your concerns. (Lead-in response/reflection of feeling)

In reality, the social worker is overwhelming the client with questions, none of which produce very helpful information. This exchange is an interrogation and accusatory in nature.

In the pitfall example in Box 7.5, the social worker misses some very important pieces of information by focusing on irrelevant questions. The client's loneliness, vulnerability, and fears are ignored. He is too busy asking questions that don't produce new information or attend to the client's concerns.

Box 7.D provides another example of a social worker engaging in a pitfall. Take a moment and provide a more thoughtful and appropriate response to the client.

Judgmental Response

The client is coming to the social worker for help, not to be judged. Part of the social worker's role is to understand the client's problems. With that understanding, the social worker helps the client to find solution(s) to the problem. If the client perceives that he or she is being labeled or judged, a defensive response may occur that can delay or impede the development of trust between the client and the social worker. This could create further difficulties in the helping relationship because the client will not feel comfortable discussing personal information and may view the relationship as an adversarial one (Hepworth et al., 2013).

Box 7.D Now You Try It . . . Correcting Irrelevant/Inappropriate Questions

Client: All I have ever wanted to do was to be a social worker. I love helping people and feel really good about the classes I am taking this semester. My instructors are great, and I have finally made a few friends.

Social Worker: Who is your favorite instructor?

What is a more appropriate response?

1. ______________________________

____

Watch this clip and listen as the instructor points out some of the possible consequences to responding from a position of judgment rather than acceptance.

Ethical and Professional Behavior

Behaviors: Use reflection and self-regulation to manage personal values and maintain professionalism in practice situations.

Critical Thinking Question: In your opinion, what are the most significant barriers in developing a helping relationship?

As a social worker, it is sometimes difficult to separate our personal feelings, values, and beliefs from our professional values and obligations. Part of a social worker's professional development includes accepting clients who may have very different values, perspectives, and lifestyles. Respecting differences and not expecting clients to see the world in the same way as the social worker is a core social work value (National Association of Social Workers [NASW], 2008). For example, Alexis is a 30-year-old female who recently came out to friends and family about her relationship with her partner, Melody. Today, Alexis discloses that she is exploring the possibility of becoming pregnant through artificial insemination. The social worker responds judgmentally to her plan, stating, "It's one thing to be a lesbian, it's another to bring a child into this. Have you thought about how your child will be affected by your decision?" Alexis will likely react with disbelief, in part because up to this point the social worker has appeared supportive of her lifestyle. Now that the social worker's true feelings (judgments) have surfaced, Alexis is likely to respond defensively and with anger and therefore withdraw from the helping relationship.

Judgmental responses made by the social worker clearly violate the social work ethic of a nonjudgmental attitude and acceptance (Hepworth et al., 2013; NASW, 2008). Judgmental responses carry with them the social worker's ethical, moral, personal, or political standards. The client may take into account the social worker's judgmental remarks when thinking of his or her own self-concept. Such remarks are detrimental to the entire helping process. Our job is to help our clients learn how to make and use good judgments about their life choices, not to make judgments about the client.

Watch this video in which Nicole responds judgmentally as she challenges Mrs. Anderson. How would you respond differently?

In the pitfall example in Box 7.6, the social worker is conveying criticism and frustration with the client and her circumstances. The client will be reluctant to share any other information with the social worker given her condescending attitude. The appropriate social worker response invites the client to elaborate on her life and the struggles she is experiencing. Review the example of a judgmental response provided in Box 7.E and suggest a more appropriate response from the social worker.

Inappropriate Social Worker Self-Disclosure

Although the social worker and client may have much in common, the focus of the session should be on the client's concerns. When the social worker shares too much personal

Box 7.6 Pitfall Example: Judgmental Response

Marta is a 22-year-old single mother talking with a child welfare worker. She is struggling to manage the care of her three children, all under the age of five.

Marta: I have three kids, ages two, four, and five. They are good kids, but sometimes I just lose it with them. My sister says I am a bad mom, but I think she is in my business. She is the one that called you. I told her to keep away, that I am okay, the kids are okay, but she thinks she is all high and mighty.

Social Worker: What do you see as the problems? (Open-ended question)

Marta: Well, I am tired a lot. I have three kids running around all day. I try to calm my nerves, but I can't sometimes. Everybody is in my business. If she thinks I am such a bad mom, why doesn't she come and help me out?

Social Worker: Have you asked her for help? (Closed-ended question)

Marta: No way; if I ask for help, she will have all the reasons she needs to keep in my business.

Social Worker Pitfall: So, someone is offering help, and you are too stubborn to accept it. Just because of your pride. What about the kids? I thought you people are supposed to care about helping each other. (Judgmental response)

Correct Social Worker Response: I get the impression that it is hard for you to accept help and that you are worried she will be more involved in your life than you want her to be. Can you tell me what it is like here with your kids all day? (Lead-in response/reflection of feeling/open-ended question)

Box 7.E Now You Try It . . . Correcting Judgmental Response

Client: My boss told me not to come to work next week. He thinks I "need" a nonpaid week of vacation. Can you believe that? All I did was talk to the girl in the station next to me, and then she goes and tells him that I was bothering her.

Social Worker: What did you say to her exactly?

Client: Something about how pretty she is. I don't really remember what I said.

Social Worker: Well, you must have said and done something that caused such a harsh penalty. Sexual harassment is a surefire way to lose a job.

What is a more appropriate response?

1. ____

____

information, or **inappropriate self-disclosure**, the client may assume that the social worker is a friend, not a professional (Murphy & Dillon, 2015). It is safe to say the client will be curious about you—what you think and believe. It is common for clients to ask personal questions (in part to relieve their own anxiety) in an effort to get to know the social worker better. This is a common response, as the client is sharing very personal information with the social worker. Should the situation arise, ask what motivates his or her interest and then decide if the information requested is something you want to share. When sharing personal information, be sure to gauge the client's verbal and nonverbal reactions.

Watch this clip and listen to the instructor as she addresses the pitfall of inappropriate self-disclosure.

Using self-disclosure appropriately takes time to learn, in part because there are some instances where self-disclosure is necessary and helpful. For example, sharing with a client that you too are a recovering alcoholic may help move the relationship

Box 7.7 Appropriate Information to Disclose

Education and Work (Specialized Training)-Related Credentials

Examples

1. ***Social Worker Response:*** I am an undergraduate student at the university. I am doing my internship at the Office on Aging. I have been here a few months and really like what I am doing.
2. ***Social Worker Response:*** I have an undergraduate degree in social work from the university and three years of work experience with the state child welfare agency. Most of my clients are kids who are living in foster care right now.
3. ***Social Worker Response:*** I am an intern in the social work program at the university. I don't have a lot of experience yet, but I am here to help and also learn from you. Do you have any questions for me?

Disclosure of Feelings about a Particular Issue in an Effort to Model Feelings for Clients

Examples

1. ***Social Worker Response:*** I feel passionate about kids and what happens to them. I take my responsibilities very seriously. I am not here to judge you; I am here to try and help make things better for everyone involved.
2. ***Social Worker Response:*** I am married, and I have two children. I can relate to how hard it is to find the balance between taking care of them and their needs and trying to find time for my marriage too. I would like to know more about your family and the issues that are of most concern for you.

Disclosure of Feelings in an Effort to Normalize the Clients' Experiences

Examples

1. ***Social Worker Response:*** Many people struggle with depression and sadness, particularly after experiencing a traumatic event. What you are feeling is normal.
2. ***Social Worker Response:*** In my life, there have been times when it has been difficult for me to go with the flow too. But I think it is unrealistic to expect everyone around you to pick up the pieces, especially after such an unexpected event. It makes sense that people are being cautious and careful.

Source: Hill and O'Brien (2014).

forward as rapport is established. That sense of camaraderie, intimacy, trust, and shared understanding can be therapeutic. It is a good idea to tell the client up front that there may be some times when you feel it is appropriate to share something about yourself, but do so only if it is useful to the client and not to meet your own needs (Egan, 2014). Double-check your intentions by asking yourself, "Why am I sharing this information?," "What do I hope to accomplish by disclosing this about myself?," and "How will this help the client?" But too much disclosure on the social worker's part can be seen as an annoying or unnecessary diversion from the client's problems. Box 7.7 offers some examples of appropriate kinds of information to disclose and modeled social worker responses.

A more subtle example of self-disclosure is the use of religious or cultural symbols, whether as office decor or the clothing and jewelry worn. If you are working in a faith-based agency, religious artifacts may be appropriate. However, in conveying openness to all who come through the doors, minimizing such symbols is preferred so as to indicate that everyone is welcome.

As you share information about yourself, you are modeling what is appropriate to talk about and ways to do it (Egan, 2014). The client has the opportunity to learn by your example. This type of self-disclosure communicates commonalities and shared perspectives. If you do share something personal about yourself, be sure that your disclosure is short and to the point and that you immediately return the focus to the client. For example, Daniel is a 50-year-old Jewish scholar who has been in counseling for one month. His presenting problems focus on his relationship with his wife, Marian. In an effort to convey commonalities, the social worker discloses that she converted from Judaism to Catholicism in order to marry her husband. This self-disclosure has the potential to harm the helping relationship. Given Daniel's strong faith and religious background, he may have a difficult time separating his feelings related to her conversion. He now has information that may change his view of the social worker, causing him to be distracted from the problems related to his marriage. Too much self-disclosure may cause the client to feel uncomfortable and put on the spot to respond to the social worker's message (Kadushin & Kadushin, 2013). However, providing general information can help to establish and maintain a relationship (e.g., saying, "I have children, too. They can be a handful," instead of, "Let me tell you about my daughter, Susan. She is such a handful. Last night . . ."). Box 7.8 offers a few points to consider as you think about the benefits and risks associated with social worker self-disclosure.

Social worker self-disclosure must be relevant to the client's problem (Kadushin & Kadushin, 2013). Never reveal any information that might be detrimental to the helping process (e.g., "I sometimes drive drunk, but I have been lucky so far"). Additionally, be careful not to disclose feelings of disapproval or shock, such as "I'm horrified by what you just told me, how you could hurt your wife!" The client may interpret this as judgment or disbelief.

Watch this clip as Nicole shares personal information. How would you expect Mrs. Anderson to respond to Nicole's disclosure about her family?

Watch this clip as Louis offers to Kim his willingness to serve as her Alcoholic Anonymous sponsor. Put yourself in her shoes, and describe how you would react.

In the example in Box 7.9, the client and social worker have some things in common. However, in this case, the social worker moves too far toward inappropriate self-disclosure. The focus has shifted from the client to the social worker as she reminisces about her losses. The corrected social worker response stays focused on Laura's problems and offers support and information. How might the social worker respond to the client that keeps the focus on the client and avoids inappropriate social worker self-disclosure?

Box 7.8 Cautions about Self-Disclosure

With too much or inappropriate self-disclosure from the social worker, the client may do the following:

- Perceive the social worker as a friend and expect mutuality in the relationship.
- Feel compelled to "help" the social worker.
- Feel as if the social worker can't help because the social worker's own life issues are so distracting.
- Use the information shared by the social worker in a self-serving or manipulative way.
- React negatively and feel cheated out of his or her opportunity to disclose.

Box 7.9 Pitfall Example: Inappropriate Social Worker Self-Disclosure

Laura is a 19-year-old female talking about the possible changes in her life. She is in jeopardy of being evicted from her apartment. She has a long history of conflicts with her parents. Laura is trying to maintain her independence and distance herself from her parents.

Laura: My life is a mess. I'm just about to get evicted from my apartment, and my probation officer told me if I don't find another place, I may end up having to move back with my parents. That would be a disaster. I have worked really hard to get away from them. They are nuts. You know what I mean; you've met them.

Social Worker Pitfall: Your parents seem nice. They are concerned about you. My parents haven't spoken to me in years, so in my eyes, you are lucky to have them. (Inappropriate social worker self-disclosure)

Correct Social Worker Response: Laura, you have managed to get through some very difficult times with your parents. If necessary, there is a shelter on Main Street where you can stay, plus we can also start looking at other places for you to live. I am really glad that you came to see me before making any decisions. (Summarization/information giving/self-disclosure)

Box 7.F Now You Try It . . . Correcting Inappropriate Self-Disclosure

Client: My favorite television show is *Criminal Intent*. It is on late-night reruns. There are times when I stay up all night watching the show. I channel surf, and when I find an episode of *CI*, I watch it, even if I come in the middle.

Social Worker: I stay up late too, but I watch the Home Shopping Network. My problem is that I end up spending money on things that I really don't need. My husband is frustrated with me.

What is a more appropriate response?

1. ____

____

Box 7.F provides you with an opportunity to offer a more appropriate self-disclosure. Try it and then compare yours with the modeled social worker response.

Premature Confrontation

The social worker must always approach the client with respect and concern. **Premature confrontation** can cause the client to feel defensive. Challenging the client too early in the relationship can hinder the development of trust and confidence (Kadushin & Kadushin, 2013). Pace the confrontation according to the development and nature of the relationship. A confrontation must be planful and purposeful. Before confronting a client about inconsistencies between stated goals and behavior, the social worker should be able to answer "yes" to the following question: Have I demonstrated my ability to help the client along the way by demonstrating care and concern? Sometimes, the manner in which a confrontation is delivered is more important than the actual substance of the confrontation. For example, in Video Case #6, Louis uses a nonthreatening tone of voice while confronting Kim about her drinking and disruptive behavior in the shelter.

Sometimes, a social worker may be incorrect in his or her perceptions about a client's situation because of the social worker's own issues or because there is not enough information about the client. Make sure that the confrontation is not to meet your own needs, such as to appear insightful, to retaliate, or to elevate yourself in relation to the client (Hill & O'Brien, 2014).

Watch this clip to learn about the pitfall of premature confrontation.

The skill of confrontation should be used sparingly and not be a style of interviewing. It is not about forcing the client—"Oh, see I caught you!" or "Do this or else"—but about helping the client develop new insights and awareness. A confrontation is a therapeutic intervention, not a social interaction (such as with a family member or friend) (Brems, 2001). A client may not be ready to do the work necessary to change a behavior, thought, or feeling, but forcing the issue may leave the client feeling powerless and with few options but to retreat further.

For example, Jacob is a 30-year-old single parent. His wife abandoned the family five months earlier, leaving him to care for their sons, ages eight and four. Jacob is currently unemployed and reports that he is looking for a job but has been unsuccessful. The social worker believes that Jacob has a drinking problem and that he was fired because of his sporadic attendance and poor job performance. The social worker confronts him with suspicions, stating, "I think that you have a problem with alcohol, and that's why your wife left and you are out of a job." Jacob feels attacked by the social worker and refuses to continue in treatment, stating, "How dare you accuse me of having an alcohol problem? Which I don't."

As you watch this clip, think about ways that you could have responded to Mrs. Kita that would be more appropriate. What might the social worker have said instead?

Box 7.10 is an example of the social worker using the pitfall of premature confrontation.

Box 7.10 Pitfall Example: Premature Confrontation

Max is a 25-year-old male. He recently graduated from college and started working part-time as a computer programmer. He is talking to a social worker about his mother.

Max: My Mom has a gambling problem. She used my two credit cards and maxed them out at $5,000 each. I am trying not to let this bother me.

Social Worker Pitfall: What do you mean, this doesn't bother you? If you don't stop her, *your* credit will suffer. I realize that she's your mother, but come on. . . . (Premature confrontation)

Max: I can't say anything. My dad would kill her if he knew what was going on.

Social Worker Pitfall: If you don't stop her, she'll end up ruining both your credit and your life? (Advice giving and premature confrontation)

Max: Well, what am I supposed to do? She can't help herself; I'm the only person she can count on. I know it's not the answer, but she is my mom.

Social Worker Pitfall: You have a problem . . . it is not your responsibility to keep her out of trouble. What do you think is going to happen down the road? (Judgmental response and premature confrontation)

Correct Social Worker Response: You are feeling responsible for your mom and determined to take care of her and her gambling problem. Max, what do you think about this situation you are in now? (Lead-in response/reflection of feeling/open-ended question)

Box 7.G Now You Try It . . . Correcting Premature Confrontation

Client: I want to study abroad next year. I have looked into at least five different programs, and the one that sounds the best is through another university. I have sent a letter of inquiry to find out more about their admissions requirement.

Social Worker: What leads you to believe that you have the grades to be accepted? From what I can tell, you are barely passing any of your classes.

Client: Well I am trying to get my grades up, it's not that easy.

What is a more appropriate response?

1. ____

____

As Box 7.G illustrates, the social worker may have some good points to share; however, the timing and tone are too confrontational. There is no relationship established, and the social worker is being critical of the client's choices. This confrontation feels hurtful and will likely push the client away. The corrected response illustrates the social worker challenging the client but in a thoughtful and nonthreatening manner. Now you try it.

Overwhelming the Client with Too Much or Irrelevant Information

Giving the client **too much information** makes it difficult to identify what is the most important part of the social worker's message. Excessive information can overwhelm the client and confuse critical issues that the client must take time to consider (Egan, 2014). Presenting information in small doses, from most to least significant, can assist the client in taking necessary action (e.g., "Let's talk about finding a safe place for you tonight. Tomorrow you can contact the state's attorney about an Order of Protection against your husband").

Watch this clip and listen to the instructor address the pitfall of offering too much information at one time.

Elyse is a 40-year-old stay-at-home mother with three children, ages 12, seven, and five. She has expressed an interest in going back to school and getting an undergraduate degree in education. She has some concerns regarding admission procedures, financial aid requirements, and her ability to do college-level course work. The social worker states, "There are so many details to getting into the university. First, you have to get a copy of your high school transcript to send in with the application. Then you will fill out the application and send a $50 check to cover the cost of processing your application. Financial aid and loans are available too, especially because you are a returning student." Because Elyse has been given too much information at once, it is difficult for her to sort out her priorities. She is left feeling confused and overwhelmed with details. It is possible that she may not act on her plan because it feels so daunting.

Ethical and Professional Behavior

Behaviors: Use reflection and self-regulation to manage personal values and maintain professionalism in practice situations.

Critical Thinking Question: How do you respond when a person in your life is judgmental or condescending toward you?

Providing too much information may undermine the client's self-efficacy. Be careful not to sound like the expert and know-it-all. You may be impressed with the vast amount of information you have, but it can come across as condescending. Provide information sparingly, as it should not be your primary mode of interacting. Information should be up to date, accurate, understandable, and relevant to this situation or problem. Also, remember that if you share your opinion with a client, it is important to identify it as opinion, not fact. Far from empowering the client with new knowledge, giving too much information may also cause the client to become confused about all of the options, thus leading to inaction. The timing of information is critical. Ask yourself, "Is the client ready to hear what I'm sharing?" Preparing the client for emotionally charged information is best done in small doses (Egan, 2014).

As you watch this clip, what information does Diane provide? Is it too much at one time? How would you do it differently?

The illustration in Box 7.11 points out the problem with overwhelming the client with too much information. In this case, the client is trying to keep up but falls behind. The social worker sounds like the expert who can't wait to share all her knowledge and expertise. In the appropriate social worker response, she offers written information that the client can take with him as well as concern for Tim and his family.

In Box 7.H, the client touches a nerve. The social worker's response could easily overwhelm the client and escalate the situation. What would be a more appropriate response that would address the client's concern and reassure her?

Box 7.11 Pitfall Example: Overwhelming the Client with Too Much Information

Tim is a 48-year-old male talking about his recent job loss with a caseworker.

Tim: I just lost my job. I want to find out if I qualify for any financial help.

Social Worker Pitfall: Depending on your circumstances, you may be eligible for unemployment. The office hours are from 9 to 5, Monday to Friday. They tend to be very busy in the morning, so I'd suggest going at around 3:30. The person you want to speak to is Raven—she's the most helpful. I'd call before going down there, just to be on the safe side. The phone number is . . . (Overwhelming the client with too much information)

Tim: Do you think I will qualify for benefits? I don't want to go all the way over there if they are just gonna say "too bad."

Social Worker Pitfall: You will never know until you get yourself down there. The eligibility requirements vary depending on how long you have been employed and the circumstances surrounding your job loss. It is very important that you look for a job at the same time you are collecting benefits because you have to document that you have completed so many job-finding tasks per week. (Overwhelming the client with too much information)

Tim: What do I do first?

Correct Social Worker Response: The Employment Security Administration is a good place to start. Here is some information about who qualifies for unemployment benefits, regulations, office hours, and the address. (Hand the materials to him) Before you head over there, how are you and your family managing? (Information giving and open-ended question)

Tim: Okay, I guess, this came out of the blue . . .

Box 7.H Now You Try It . . . Correcting Overwhelming the Client with Too Much Information

Client: I am sick of you coming to my house and telling me what I am doing wrong. I think I am fine. Look at how well Danika is doing. She hardly cries at all, and I have been feeding her baby food, just like the nurse told me to do.

Social Worker: Well, my job is to come here and check on you. I am the person responsible to the court; it is my job to let the judge know how you are doing. I am the person assigned to look after you and Danika. If you want to file a formal complaint, I have the number here.

Client: I don't want to file anything. I am sick of you pointing out all of the troubles Danika is having. She seems fine to me.

What is a more appropriate response?

1. ____

____

Premature Problem Solving

Social workers are skilled at problem solving; however, this does not mean that the social worker is there to solve the problem for the client. A full understanding of the problem is necessary in order to help the client choose the next step in problem resolution (Hepworth et al., 2013). If the social worker prematurely problem solves, important information may be overlooked. It is also a missed opportunity for the client to be involved in the process. In order for problem solving to be effective, the client has to be invested in moving and reaching toward his or her goals. If problem solving occurs too early in the process, the opportunity to capitalize on the client's strengths is lost (Kottler, 2011).

Watch this clip and listen to the instructor talk about what is lost when a novice social worker jumps in too quickly to solve the problem for the client.

Clients explore problems and develop an understanding of their problems at varying speeds. What may be the apparent problem may be a symptom of another layer of difficulty or the result of associated patterns of behavior. If the social worker moves too quickly to problem solving, the methodical process of problem exploration, assessment, and intervention is circumvented, thus leading to a limited understanding of the risks and benefits associated with the goal. The client and social worker need time to explore all facets of the problem. By moving too rapidly toward problem resolution, the social worker's agenda may be met (e.g., "I have three home visits to make this afternoon" or "I get this situation; I have heard it 100 times before"), but the pacing needs of the client are ignored (Kottler, 2011). For example, David is a 40-year-old homeless veteran. He has been living in shelters off and on for the past four years. He is eligible but is not receiving Veterans Administration or Social Security benefits. David has come to the shelter for the night. He informs the social worker that he is a veteran and hasn't received a check for one year. He appears somewhat disheveled and disoriented during the intake interview. The social worker says, "The first thing we have to do is get your benefits reinstated." The social worker completely overlooks his current situation and begins to focus on financial resources. Although this is a viable avenue to explore with David, his immediate need of food and shelter was completely ignored.

As you watch this video with Mrs. Kita and Diane, what would you do differently?

Premature problem solving is a common pitfall, one that many social workers unintentionally use. Remember that what the client presents as the problem may not be the real problem. Therefore, if the social worker jumps to problem solving, she may miss essential information that could help resolve the problem. Change occurs both internally and externally, and we develop goals with our clients to address both facets. Meaningful and lasting change takes time and commitment and can't be done in a hurried or directive fashion.

Finally, there are some situations that require very quick information gathering, assessment, and planning. For example, a client who will be without shelter by sundown or a client who will not have enough medication to get through the next day will require immediate intervention. These types of crises require the social worker to take on a more active role in order to ensure client safety (Egan, 2014).

In Box 7.12, the social worker rapidly jumps to problem solving with Gina. She misses some very important messages the client was attempting to share, such as her fear, the impact of bullying, and the personal circumstances that may have caused her to be so vulnerable. By rushing to solving the "outfitting problem," she ignored more relevant issues. How does the social worker's response in Box 7.I represent premature problem solving? What might be a better response from the social worker?

Box 7.12 Pitfall Example: Premature Problem Solving

Gina is a 10-year-old student talking to the school social worker about being bullied. She is scared to provide any details about the bullying incidents for fear of retaliation.

Gina: The kids pick on me at school. I don't tell the teachers because if I do, it will make things worse.

Social Worker Pitfall: Who are these kids? (Irrelevant question)

Gina: I am not giving names; you know what will happen to me if I do.

Social Worker: Okay, so then what seems to cause the problems at school? (Open-ended question)

Gina: They pick on me because of the way I look and my clothes.

Social Worker Pitfall: Oh. That's easy to take care of. Let's find some fashionable outfits for you to wear. (Premature problem solving)

Correct Social Worker Response: Gina, from what you are sharing with me, it sounds like other kids are bullying you. This is a serious problem. Let's talk about what we can do so that you feel better protected. (Paraphrasing and information giving)

Box 7.I Now You Try It . . . Correcting Premature Problem Solving

Client: My mother was diagnosed with Alzheimer's, and she is steadily getting worse. I can see it almost every day that I visit her. She doesn't seem to recognize me, but I think she knows that she is supposed to know me. I just don't know if I should go along with her to try to make her understand that it is me, Margaret, her oldest daughter.

Social Worker: Well, there are a lot of tests that we can run to see if her symptoms are getting worse or is there something else going on. Sometimes, a urinary tract infection can cause a person to seem more disoriented. Let me talk to the nurse, and I will get right back to you.

What is a more appropriate response?

1. ______________________________

____

Offering False Assurance/Minimizing the Problem

Although a social worker should always look for strength and hope in a client's situation, being realistic and honest is an imperative (Hepworth et al., 2013). When the social worker provides **false assurance**, the client's problem is minimized. False assurance can lead the client to feel discouraged and resentful toward the social worker when things don't work out as hoped (Hepworth et al., 2013). False assurances can also cause the client to overlook possible roadblocks, thereby making a problem worse. Clients must come to terms with their difficulties and possible consequences of the situation. These realizations help prepare the client to take action. Additionally, meaningless clichés, such as "That's the way it goes" or "Things will be better in the morning," gloss over a client's pain. These responses are hollow and have no therapeutic value. For example, Rose is a 70-year-old resident of a nursing home. She has been there for two weeks and is eagerly waiting to be discharged into her daughter's care. Today, her daughter Eve called, stating, "Mom can't move in with us. My husband refuses to let her stay here, even for a few weeks." The social worker says, "Really, your mom is doing much better, and I'm certain she would not get in his way at all." The social worker ignores Eve's concerns and jumps directly into offering assurances. Clearly, the social worker wants to gloss over the problems and focus on *her* task—discharge planning. This approach serves the needs of the social worker, not the client. Eve isn't heard or understood, causing her to feel even more confused and guilty.

Watch this clip and listen to the instructor address the importance of offering realistic outcomes to a problem rather than glossing over them.

Louis is trying to reassure Kim that taking the bus will be an adventure. He glosses over her uncertainty. How do you think Kim is feeling?

False assurances may overlook the client's feelings of discomfort, hopelessness, or despair. However, it is also important for the social worker not to be *overly* sympathetic toward the client's situation. The social worker should strive to convey understanding, not pity (Hepworth et al., 2013).

If the client senses an implicit message of "it's no big deal, why are you bothering me?" from the social worker, the client is likely to withdraw from the relationship. The client may also feel that he or she is overreacting based on the social worker's minimal reaction. Remember that the client may also attempt to minimize the impact of the problem situation. The social worker uses problem identification and assessment skills to analyze underlying issues (perhaps unexpressed or downplayed by the client) that determine the severity of the problem.

Ethical and Professional Behavior

Behaviors: Make ethical decisions by applying the standards of the NASW Code of Ethics, relevant laws and regulations, models for ethical decision making, ethical conduct of research, and additional codes of ethics as appropriate to context. Use reflection and self-regulation to manage personal values and maintain professionalism in practice situations.

Critical Thinking Question: Identify ways in which you can "recover" from a pitfall. What are some of the ethical issues to consider when inadvertently using a pitfall?

For the client to feel understood, the social worker must be able to communicate a full understanding of the significance of the situation (Cormier & Hackney, 2011). The client may be feeling overwhelmed by circumstances. To offer support, the social worker should use words that capture the intensity of the problem. If the social worker misses the intensity (e.g., Client: "I am so angry I could just strangle him." Social Worker: "You sound sort of upset right now"), the client may wonder whether the social worker is truly listening.

Coming across to a client as being artificial, insincere, or rude can cause the client to become suspicious of the social worker's intentions. A straightforward and honest manner communicates authenticity (Kadushin & Kadushin, 2013; Sheafor & Horejsi, 2015). Clients can detect a social worker pretending to care. Simply going through the motions, responding with little interest or concern, detracts from the helping relationship. For example, Irving is an 80-year-old male, currently a patient in a rehabilitation hospital. He suffered from a stroke one month ago, and his recovery process has been slow and painful. He wants to regain all of his capacities, and he is currently expressing frustration with himself and others. Having heard this at every session, the social worker uses a very harsh and angry tone of voice to say, "Irving, you will get better; just be patient." Although the words are reassuring, the tone of the social worker's voice conveys a lack of care or concern. Irving is likely to feel even more frustrated and isolated by his circumstances and withdraw from the relationship. In Box 7.13, the social worker uses the pitfall of false assurance.

In the pitfall example in Box 7.13, the social worker quickly realizes that Mrs. Kern is having more difficulty than she had initially understood. In the social worker's effort to provide a sense of hope, she inadvertently minimized Mrs. Kern's feelings and

Box 7.13 Pitfall Example: False Assurance

Mrs. Betsy Kern is a 75-year-old female. She was in a car accident several months ago. She suffers from intermittent pain as a result of the accident. She was driving at the time, and her good friend Hazel was injured too.

Social Worker: You look tired today, Mrs. Kern. (Social worker is attending to her nonverbal cues)

Mrs. Kern: I can't sleep. I keep having flashbacks from the accident. I don't think I will ever be able to drive again.

Social Worker Pitfall: Oh! I am sure once your injuries have healed, you will be ready to get out there and drive again. (False assurance)

Mrs. Kern: Just the thought of getting behind the wheel makes me sick. I get so nervous even riding in a car now. I worry that I won't ever feel like myself again. (Said with tears in her eyes)

Social Worker Recovery Response: Mrs. Kern, I didn't mean to suggest that it would be easy for you, just to say that maybe things will feel better for you eventually. I am sorry if I made it sound like no big deal. (Paraphrase and appropriate self disclosure)

Mrs. Kern: It has been so hard for me. I am in a lot of pain too. I can't ever get comfortable, and if I see anything moving fast towards me, I get panicky. In fact the other day . . .

Box 7.J Now You Try It . . . Correcting False Assurance

Client: My business was destroyed in the last tornado. There is nothing left of the building, just piles of rubble. The insurance company guy came to talk to me last week about rebuilding and getting the business going again. I just don't see how I can start all over. I am old, and I don't have the energy.

Social Worker Pitfall: So many people count on you for jobs around here. I have no doubt that folks will help in every way they can. This community pulls together, you know that. I am sure it will work out. (False assurance)

What is a more appropriate response?

1. ______________________________________

____

Box 7.14 Pitfall Example: Minimizing the Problem

Theresa is a 16-year-old tenth grader. Her parents recently informed her that because of her mother's job change, they will be moving to a new community. Theresa doesn't want to leave her friends and her school. She is afraid of moving, in part because it has always been difficult for her to make friends. She is shy and introverted.

Theresa: I don't want to move; I am so scared and nervous that I can't eat or sleep.

Social Worker Pitfall: Moving can be fun and exciting, and you'll be able to start off with a clean slate. (Minimizing the problem)

Theresa: It's hard to meet people, especially when everyone already has their friends.

Social Worker Pitfall: But you'll be the new kid; people will be curious about you. (Minimizing the problem)

Theresa: Yeah, right. I'm ugly, and I don't like meeting new people.

Social Worker Pitfall: You are not ugly; you are a lovely young lady! (Minimizing the problem)

Correct Social Worker Response: Moving can be scary. There is no way to make this easy, but talking to your parents and keeping in touch with your friends here at school might help a little bit. (Paraphrasing and information giving)

Theresa: I can't talk to my parents. They are already packing boxes.

Correct Social Worker Response continued: They don't get how hard this is for you because right now they are so involved in their own excitement. (Paraphrasing)

Theresa: Yeah, they figure since they are happy, I should be happy. But I am *not* happy.

Correct Social Worker Response continued: I can tell that you are very upset about this. Let's talk about some ways you can get ready for the move. (Reflection of feeling and open-ended question)

experiences related to the accident. Once she attends to Mrs. Kern's response, she corrects the mistake and continues with the interview. Review the social worker's response in Box 7.J. How would you revise the response to provide support to the client while avoiding false assurance?

In Box 7.14, the social worker wants to help Theresa manage her fears and anxiety about the upcoming move, but does so in a way that communicates that her feelings aren't valid.

Box 7.K Now You Try It . . . Correcting Minimizing the Problem

Client: My son and his family lost everything during the hurricane. Even after all these years, they are still not completely back on their feet. We send them money every month to help out as much as we can, but it is taking a financial toll on us.

Social Worker: That is too bad, but from everything I hear on the news, the city and county governments are working together now. Just do what you can. But, there is no quick fix and I am sure they know that too.

What is a more appropriate response?

1. ____

____

In Box 7.14, the social worker attempts to help the client feel better by offering a series of statements that reduces the client's concerns to almost nothing. The social worker believes that she understands Theresa's concerns when in reality she is missing the point entirely, as the social worker attempts to reduce the complexity of the issue to a few statements. Theresa is likely to feel unheard, causing her to retreat even further. In the corrected version, the social worker acknowledges Theresa's feelings of despair and begins to focus on how she might manage this upcoming change in her life. Practice providing appropriate responses to clients facing problems by correcting the social worker response of minimizing the problem in Box 7.K.

LEARNING FROM MISTAKES

? Assess your understanding of pitfalls by taking this brief quiz.

When mistakes are made during an interview, the social worker's goal should be to learn from the experience so that when presented with a similar situation, he or she can respond with a new level of professionalism. Sometimes, social workers fail to recognize pitfalls. However, clients often react in ways that highlight mistakes (e.g., saying, "That's not what I said," or using nonverbal cues, such as avoiding eye contact or not showing up/canceling the next appointment) when the social worker has said something that has hurt, angered, or offended them.

For example, a social worker who has just responded to a client in a judgmental manner should apologize and start over (e.g., "I can tell my comment has made you very upset. I'm sorry; that was not my intent. Let me rephrase what I was trying to say"). This is a face-saving measure for both the social worker and the client. Hopefully, the relationship has not been permanently damaged, and the client and the social worker can move on in the problem-solving process. Being able to admit a mistake also models another important life skill: acknowledging an error and attempting to repair the damage.

Box 7.15 Social Worker Recovery Statements (Fill in the Blanks)

- I can tell my comment about ______ upset you; that was not my intent.
- You look upset by what I just said about your ______; let me try to say it in another way.
- Sorry, that came out wrong about your ______; what I meant to say was . . .
- That was rude; I can tell I hurt your feelings when I said ______. What I should have said was . . .
- That came out all wrong. I sometimes put my foot in my mouth. I will try again.
- Oops, that was out of line.
- You are right to be confused by what I said.
- I will rephrase that.
- It doesn't sound the way I had intended; I apologize.
- I regret the way that sounded. You are right to feel ______.

In the field of social work, the word "practice" is used in many contexts and is almost synonymous with every aspect of our work. Practice means just that. It is important as a student to remember there is a certain amount of responsibility attached to practice. You will not always get it correct because you are human. Even the most experienced social workers make mistakes. But you can acknowledge where you were wrong without going overboard (see Box 7.15 for some helpful recovery statements). This means being clear about the line between inadvertently hurting or offending another person and being overly apologetic.

In the example in Box 7.16, the social worker does eventually convey to Molly that she is trying to understand her frustration with her parents' overprotectiveness. It does take several attempts, but finally the social worker slows the pace of the interview down and really listens to what Molly is saying without prematurely trying to fix the problem, minimizing it, or unnecessarily confronting her.

? Assess your understanding of learning from mistakes by taking this brief quiz.

Through practicing social work skills and maintaining an awareness of common pitfalls, social workers can achieve a positive, helping relationship with clients. Remember that even as seasoned professionals, we all make mistakes. There is no such thing as a perfect response or question. It is up to you to learn from your mistakes and to reflect on ways you can improve. Take time to learn and challenge yourself when you do make a mistake.

Box 7.16 Examples of Pitfalls and Social Worker Recovery Statements

Molly is a 21-year-old female who was recently discharged from the inpatient mental health unit and is speaking to the caseworker in the outpatient unit. Molly had attempted suicide and suffers from a long history of depression.

Molly: I think I am doing okay. I have been taking my medication, but my parents don't believe me.

Social Worker Pitfall: What makes them doubt that you are taking your medicine? Is it something you are doing? (Premature confrontation and stacked questions)

Molly: I don't think so; I am following the directions on the bottle. My doctor said that I should be responsible for taking my pills, not my parents. I am 21, you know.

Box 7.16 Examples of Pitfalls and Social Worker Recovery Statements *(Continued)*

Social Worker Pitfall: I know that you're old enough, but in the past you haven't followed through with taking your medication. I am sure that's why your parents are so concerned. (Premature confrontation and false assurance)

Molly: Yeah, but I haven't given them any reason to doubt me this time.

Social Worker Pitfall: Have you tried to talk to your parents? (Premature problem solving)

Molly: I have, but they treat me like a child, just like you are.

Social Worker Recovery Statement: You are right. I *am* sounding like your parent too. Sorry about that; let's get back on track. You were saying that you take your medication independently and have been doing this for the past two weeks.

Molly: My parents do care about me, I know that, but I feel like a five-year-old, needing a parent's hand to cross the street.

Social Worker Recovery Statement continued: There is a part of you that is really scared. You have been through a lot in the past few years. You want to be more independent and take charge of your own life. Right now, that seems like a faraway dream. Is that how you feel? (Summarization and clarification)

Molly: I do feel that way. My parents always step in and bail me out. I want to get better on my own. I just need them to have faith in me.

Social Worker Recovery Statement continued: Well, let's talk about some things you can do to convince them that this time you want to do things differently. Any ideas? (Open-ended question)

SUMMARY

- All of us make mistakes during the social work interview that can inadvertently cause a small ripple to a rupture in the helping relationship. Knowing how to spot a pitfall and attempt to repair possible damage is as important as knowing how and when to use all of the skills.
- You have learned how to identify common errors in the helping process and how these errors can divert the process. However, do not to get discouraged. The goal for any social worker is to learn from mistakes, using what you have learned to integrate it into the whole of the relationship. In this chapter, you have learned ways to provide a corrective response that is appropriate to the situation/context.
- Focus not on a pitfall or common error that may have occurred but rather on the relationship in its entirety.

APPLY IT

1. Watch session 1 of **Interactive Case Study #4** of Maria, Mrs. Anderson, and social worker Nicole. At one point, Nicole inappropriately discloses information about her family. What would you have said differently?
2. Watch session 4 of **Interactive Case Study #5** of Mrs. Kita and social worker Diane. In this session, Diane states, "Was that hair cut expensive? You are trying to save money." Although this is a very true statement, how could she have addressed this concern more tactfully?

Assess Your Competence

Use the scale below to rate your current level of achievement on the following concepts or skills associated with each competency presented in the chapter:

1	2	3
I can accurately describe the concept or skill	I can consistently identify the concept or skill when observing and analyzing practice activities	I can competently implement the concept or skill in my own practice

_______ Can identify and explain major pitfalls social workers may fall into when conducting an interview.

_______ Can provide an example of each type of pitfall.

_______ Understands and can demonstrate how to recover after falling into a pitfall.

_______ Can identify types of problematic questions.

8

Intake and Engagement

ANDY DEAN / FOTOLIA

During the early phases of the helping process, the social worker seeks to build a connection with the client. Through the intake and engagement process, the social worker strives to develop a rapport with that client that will help to facilitate the client's commitment to work together on problem resolution. This chapter explores the many dimensions, dynamics, and necessary skills for successfully completing the intake and engagement processes.

LEARNING OUTCOMES

- Identify essential information to be included as part of the intake process.
- Illustrate ways to manage all aspects of the first client contact, from intake through signs of successful engagement with the client.

CHAPTER OUTLINE

THE INTAKE PROCESS

The **intake process** is the initial step in developing a relationship with a client. First impressions are made as you venture forward. During those awkward first few minutes, both the client and social worker are taking stock. Introduce yourself, share information about your experiences, and provide a short description of your role and function within the agency setting. Of importance is sharing with the client information about confidentiality, the helping process, the type of treatment or services offered, and what he or she can expect as a result of entering services. If there is a need to get a release of information signed or a referral (see example in the Appendix C) to be made, you can do so during the intake portion of the interview.

Watch as Diane walks Mrs. Kita through the intake process.

When discussing the release-of-information form, be sure to include why it is needed, who will have access to the information obtained through the release, and how long the release will be valid. You may need a third party to witness all required signatures, including the social worker's. In addition, let the client know that your intention is to be helpful, that favorable outcomes are possible (with a commitment on the part of the client as well), and that the his or her needs will be addressed.

It is important to view this step as an opportunity to learn about what has brought the client into care. The process of an intake interview can be done in person, on the telephone, or even over the Internet. Always ask clients how they would like you to address them. Also, be sure to let the client know how you would prefer to be addressed.

The kind of information gathered during the intake process is then used as the foundation for the next phase of the helping process: the assessment. Part of the intake process requires understanding what event(s) motivated the client to seek help (including whether the client was mandated to see a social worker) and some general history of the problem and previous circumstances. Specific information, such as address, date of birth, number of children, race, identified disabilities, medical conditions, employment and school history, languages spoken in the home, marital status, and criminal background, are standard questions on most intake forms. Typically, there are questions related to what steps the client has taken to resolve the presenting issues and identification of informal and formal support networks. The goal of an intake interview is to develop a foundation or composite of the client's worldview (Carpetto, 2008).

It is essential to discuss your role and that of the agency in addressing the needs of the client. The social worker in Video Case #5, identifies her role and ways in which she hopes to be of assistance. She refers to the intake form, which Mrs. Kita had filled out a few weeks earlier, as a good starting point. In the first session, Diane states, "Although we talked on the phone last week, I wanted to reintroduce myself and tell you a little bit about why I am here. I have been with the housing program for three years. Our program offers a lot of services that I think will be helpful to you. The goal is to provide families with financial resources, specialized trainings, and encouragement. If you need help with child care or finances that is something I can assist you with." Diane is clearly stating the parameters of the relationship and ways the agency and she can be helpful.

The intake interview is primarily a question-and-answer session. Typically, intake questions are considered rudimentary and simple (Carpetto, 2008). Agencies use the intake interview as a screening tool to determine whether services offered fit the needs of the client. It is possible that an intake worker will complete the form and then pass along the information to the appropriate person, such as a caseworker, a therapist, or an in-home counselor. Depending on the intake process, the client may have already completed the forms independently, and therefore you can review the paperwork and move right into the assessment itself. When working with a client who may have a cognitive disability, a language barrier because English is not his or her first language, or limited reading skill, you can offer to complete the intake form, read the form, or paraphrase the questions. If this is offered, try to approach this as though it is common practice so as not to make the client feel inadequate. It is good practice to have forms available in a variety of languages, as it makes this process less cumbersome.

Intake forms typically have questions that relate to the client's culture, religion, and ethnicity. Understanding how the client makes decisions and where the client is situated relative to his or her culture can give the worker a beginning knowledge of the systems involved and insights into systems that may need to be involved to fully address the client's needs and circumstances.

Never underestimate the toll that oppression or prejudice can take on a person. A general lack of trust for "mainstream workers" or institutions is understandable given past negative and unjust experiences that clients may have experienced directly or indirectly with various societal institutions and systems. Such experiences can cause clients to feel as though they are entering a hostile environment when they seek assistance (voluntarily or by court mandate) from a social service agency. In this case, there is all the more reason to be respectful, thoughtful, and genuine. If you and your client speak different languages, find out whether your agency provides translators (or an interpreter in the case of a person who is deaf). If not, this may be an important service that you can advocate for on behalf of diverse clients that the agency serves.

No matter who completes the intake form, it will be used as the entry point into the problem-solving process. There are probably as many different types of intake forms as there are service providers. It is most important to familiarize yourself with the form used in your agency. The more familiar you are with the questions, the less likely you are to read them one by one, making the intake process feel more like an interrogation than a safe welcoming into the helping process. The best intake interviews are those conducted as a conversation. Tryon's (2003) research concludes that the more positive and collaborative the relationship, the more likely the client will return for a second session. Following this line of thinking, if the client feels heard, valued, and a part of the process, his or her commitment is greater, with a higher likelihood of success. The intake phase is a time to be accepting and respectful. Realize that asking personal questions can cause a client to feel embarrassed, nervous, or anxious. Posing thoughtful, mindful, and tactful questions without appearing to be over solicitous is an essential interviewing skill. The initial interview sets the stage for further or future contact and the development of the helping relationship. Putting the client at ease and explaining the intake process and what the client can expect can be very helpful in ensuring the client's return. It invites clients to be open and encourages him or her to trust and to engage with the social worker. Asking questions that cause the client to really think about the issue at hand can lead to deepening of the relationship and set the stage for all future contacts. (See Appendix C for examples of intake forms.)

Sometimes the situation that brings a client into your care is an immediate crisis, and there is no time to complete a formal intake. In the case of a suicidal client calling a hotline, just getting the person's first name may be all you can ascertain. As you develop a rapport with the client, you may be able to negotiate getting more descriptive information, including support networks, other professionals involved with the caller, contact information, and history of suicidal thoughts and attempts. It is important to be able to switch gears quickly should the client reveal information that is unexpected. For example, during an intake interview in which a client reveals that he is having an affair with a coworker, it is imperative not to appear shocked or disapproving. By assuring the client that you are listening without judging him, he will be more likely to continue with his story and continue to engage the helping process.

The intake process provides information in a way that is presented in an organized and straightforward fashion, and typically the questions are already prepared for the intake worker to ask. The type of agency and field of practice, such as gerontology, will predetermine the types of questions that are most helpful in the collection of information. When conducting an intake interview, it is best to ask a series of questions that allows the client to give a complete history of the problem and of all the systems involved. For example, you are a social worker in a nursing home. The intake interview may involve family members, friends, and the soon-to-be resident. Questions that would be covered in this early data collection process could relate to referral source, financial status, insurance coverage, medical conditions, independent living skills, orientation to time and place, physical status, chronic health concerns or an acute distress, cognitive functioning, safety issues, supports, and others involved in the care. Additionally, the type of care the client (or family) is requesting and whether the request fits with the services provided by the agency can be explored. Previous involvement with other health providers and social service providers can also be discussed.

After the social worker has completed the intake interview, the client is informed about the next step in the helping process. It is the social worker's ethical responsibility to keep clients fully informed. Having this information can put clients at ease and help to ensure their return for a second session. For example, there may be a waiting list for services, and therefore some time may pass before getting a social worker assigned. If this is the case, help the client identify some ways to cope, people to reach out to, or a support group or, if necessary, explore the possibility of a referral to another agency. During times of economic recession, it becomes more challenging to respond to client needs immediately because of the increase in the number of people seeking assistance and the need of social service agencies to stretch resources. Under these economic conditions, providing immediate assistance to clients may be difficult. Waiting lists for services and resources are fairly common. Unless the presenting client situation is determined to be a crisis that requires immediate intervention, there may be some delay in providing services. Sharing information about after-school programs, recreational centers, food pantries, and short-term shelter can be very reassuring and convey to the client that you can assist in very practical and immediate ways. Because each agency operates differently, it is hard to gauge how long it may take to confirm or deny services. It is good practice to "walk" the client through the process. Transparency is important; you want clients to know where their application is in the system and how things are progressing. There are circumstances when the immediate needs of the client are such that waiting for services through your agency is not an option. Given the nature of the problem, a referral to a crisis center or another agency may be your best response.

Should your agency be unable to provide services in a timely manner or if the referral is not appropriate, it is important to have other referrals and options ready (the role of a broker is essential in this situation). Explaining the process and how the denial-to-provide-services decision was made can be helpful to the client. Providing this information conveys a sense of integrity and honesty on the part of the agency and

Box 8.A Now You Try It . . . Ethical Communication regarding Service Provision

You work with a job training program through the local community college. Mr. Oliver is in your office. You have completed the intake form with him and indicated that the decision to provide services is made by a committee.

You, the social worker, say, "It will be three days before I have an answer for you. I think you should go home and try to talk to family members about ways they can help you. Your income looks too high, and I am not optimistic that our program can help you. We normally work with really poor people."

Your corrected social worker response:

____

____

____

A modeled social worker response: "It may be a few days before I have an answer for you. But in the meantime, here is a list of some other training programs in our area that may be an option for you."

Box 8.B Now You Try It . . . Intake Forms

The intake interview can be documented electronically on a computer system or handwritten. This is determined by the agency's standard operating practices. When doing handwritten documentation, be sure to write legibly, as this information becomes part of the permanent record and other workers may depend on the information if someone other than the intake worker is assigned the case. Know the process for completing the intake form and be sure that every question is answered. This is the entry point into your agency, and the quality of this report sets the stage for all future interactions. (For documentation, see Appendix A.)

Now try your hand at completing an intake interview with a classmate. Use either version of the intake form found in Appendix C and then answer the following questions:

1. What did you find the most difficult about completing the intake form?

   ____

2. Where did you falter?

   ____

3. Where did you feel most confident?

   ____

social worker. The reasons for the denial of service may be as straightforward as the county where the client resides, income guidelines, or a very long waiting list. As an intake worker, the social worker becomes the advocate and broker of services for the client. It is through your report that an agency (or members of a review panel) decides whether to provide services to the client. If you believe your client is an appropriate candidate for the services offered by your agency, advocate for him or her. Use your voice to speak on your client's behalf.

Taking into consideration ethical communication in practice, provide a corrected response to the example in Box 8. A. Try your hand at completing an intake interview and answer the questions in Box 8.B.

Engagement and the Professional Relationship

When people experience difficulties in their lives, they can select from a wide variety of strategies to overcome them. Some turn to family and friends; others look within and draw on internal resources. When they choose to see a professional social worker, they are seeking specific knowledge and skills that are usually not available to them through informal helping relationships. Most likely, they have been unsuccessful in resolving

Assessment

Behaviors: Collect and organize data, and apply critical thinking to interpret information from clients and constituencies.

Critical Thinking Question: What are some of the most important aspects to consider when completing an intake interview with an 80-year-old male recently placed in your long-term care facility? He has come to your facility by way of a discharge from a local hospital.

their problems through informal means and now seek the assistance of a well-trained and experienced professional who can assist them in dealing with their life problems. The purpose and goals of a professional relationship between a client and a social worker "are conscious and deliberate and come within the overall purpose and value system of the profession" (Compton, Galaway, & Cournoyer, 2005). Implicit in this definition is the belief that clients will experience some type of improvement in their lives and will be empowered to make changes as a direct result of working with the social worker. As discussed earlier, the relationship between the social worker and client is a purposeful one that includes the systematic process of beginning, middle, and ending phases.

The relationship between the client and the social worker is unique. Both come into the relationship with a distinctive set of circumstances and life experiences. As social workers, we consider ourselves to be trained helpers and problem solvers. Social workers operate from an established knowledge base and a set of professional values, skills, and techniques. To affect a client's life, we draw on this professional knowledge and use it as the keystone for building the professional relationship between the client and ourselves. During the **engagement** phase, the social worker should focus on building a mutual commitment to the helping process and developing a cohesive relationship. Clients who view themselves and their social workers as engaged are more likely to achieve positive outcomes (Orlinsky, Ronnestad, & Willuzki, 2004).

Clients who participate in the helping relationship may be uncertain about what to expect and what is required of them. It is likely that many of our clients have never interacted with a social worker. At most, they may have seen a news report or an episode on TV depicting a social worker taking children from their home or "losing" children within the state's foster care system. As you know, this characterization is rarely accurate and at best limits the role of the social worker to the child protective worker role. In reality, social workers work across the continuum of human needs with clients of all ages, cultures, and walks of life who often are seeing them for the first time. Sometimes, clients have had previous interaction with a social worker as a result of being court mandated into treatment and, as such, are involuntary clients. Under this set of circumstances, our job of engaging a client in the helping process can be a very challenging one.

What does it mean to engage a client in the therapeutic helping process? It is important to understand the circumstances under which a client is coming to you for help. Many clients are scared about being "shrunk," that the social worker will qualitatively "change them". Although as professional social workers we are sometimes sanctioned to intervene in our clients' lives, we must do so with the utmost respect and care. A challenge that we face, however, is helping our clients to understand the true nature of who we are as professionals and what we do.

Box 8.1 presents a series of reflective questions that can assist in increasing your understanding of the reciprocal nature of the helping relationship.

Now write your responses to the questions in Box 8.C. Pay special attention to those areas of your personal and professional characteristics that are in need of the most attention (and possibly modifying).

Box 8.1 The Reciprocal Nature of a Relationship

The nature of the helping relationship is reciprocal, meaning both parties seek to influence the other. As you develop a greater sense of yourself as a professional, consider the following:

How do you convey to the client that you are competent?

- What is your level of skill, education, specialized trainings, certificates, licenses, and experience and the type of setting where you practice?
- How do you convey being an expert (which means not that you have all of the answers but that if you are unsure how to proceed, you will seek assistance)?
- How do you convey a sense of confidence, even when you may not feel that way?
- How do you convey an appreciation for the influences of your own culture and that of others?
- How do you convey a respect for the diversity of values?
- Are you sensitive to the unique differences arising out of social class, race, gender, and so on?
- How do you manage conflicting feelings and situations?
- Do you derive meaning from work, and is this a passion for you?

What makes you an approachable person?

- Are you friendly and welcoming?
- Are you an honest and sincere person?
- Can you find humor where it is appropriate?
- Do you appear interested in what the client is saying?
- Are you the type of person who seems to be easy going but not a "pushover"?
- Are you willing to share some information about yourself while always being mindful of professional boundaries?
- Do you look for some similarities between you and the client (sports team, hobby, neighborhood where you live)?
- Do you respond to your client in ways that encourage nonverbal behaviors, such as eye contact, body posture, smiling, and head nodding?

How does a client sense that you are trustworthy?

- Do you have a reputation for honesty?
- Are you a person who is not motivated for personal gain?
- Can you maintain confidentiality?
- Is your word your honor? Does your "promise" mean something?
- Do you convey to your client, "I believe what you tell me"?
- Can you understand the client's point of view and suspend judgment?
- Do you convey a sense of "knowing" that the client may be on the threshold of change and it is scary?
- Are you consistent in your verbal and nonverbal messages?

How does the social worker pass the "can I trust you" test? From the client's point of view, consider the following questions.

- Can I tell you a secret?
- Are you a person with whom I can be honest and vulnerable?
- Will you truly listen to me?
- Can I ask a favor of you and you will assist me, if my request is within reason?
- Can you handle what I am telling you without being shocked, judgmental, or embarrassed?
- If I am requesting information from you or some other type of resource from you, will you follow through?

What characteristics do you have in common with a client? How do these enhance or detract from the relationship?

- Do you believe that each person brings to the helping relationship a history of struggles, challenges, and successes?
- Do you believe that some clients may be more susceptible to the workers' influence based on race, gender, age, beliefs, culture, religion, or disability?
- Do you believe that clients come to the helping relationship with a set of perceptions about the process?
- Do you believe that change is possible?
- Are you open to change?
- Do you and your client share a similar vision for what is possible?

Box 8.C Now You Try It . . . Self-Assessment

Using the categories presented in Box 8.1, provide answers to each of the questions presented below.

1. How do you convey to the client that you are competent and know what you are doing?
2. What makes you an approachable person?
3. How does a client sense that you are trustworthy?
4. What characteristics do you have in common with a client? How do these enhance or detract from the relationship?

The setting of a social worker's practice will, in part, determine the types of clients and the range of problems that will be addressed. A client may be referred to your agency by a teacher, a probation officer, an outreach worker, a physician, a public health official, a judge, or a public housing employee. You may also have clients who seek out services from your agency because they recognize their need for help.

One important aspect of engaging the client is establishing **rapport**. Rapport is the entry point to the relationship (Cormier & Cormier, 2011). It is the intangible goal of connecting at a central or core level with your client. It is more than comfort, receptiveness, and respect. It is a commitment to stay with the client—to display warmth, interest, and care in a way that encourages trust and confidence. When a client feels understood, honored, and valued, he or she is more likely to open up. It is through this relationship that the client's anxiety over time diminishes as his or her self-esteem and self-worth are enhanced (Hill & O'Brien, 2014).

Rapport connotes a relationship of mutual understanding and trust between two people and requires the ability to put oneself in the position of another. **Empathy** is an important skill in developing rapport with a client. It is trying to understand your client's life experiences without having to experience them yourself. Small talk, such as a few comments about the weather, traffic, or how the children are feeling, is one aspect of rapport, but building rapport is a much more complex and methodical skill. Small talk is never a substitute for genuine rapport.

As a social worker, you may find yourself in situations that are far outside your comfort zone or beyond anything you can imagine. Although some of these situations may be scary or uncomfortable, it is your responsibility to put your discomfort aside. However, don't ignore clear warning signs of real danger. In cases of imminent harm to yourself, either leave immediately and/or contact the police. Social workers can also use these experiences to understand and empathize with clients regarding how frightened or overwhelmed they may feel when entering into unknown or foreign territory. It is always wise to expand your life experiences (without taking unnecessary risks) by reading, asking questions, and educating yourself about other cultures, practices, and lifestyles that you are unfamiliar with or that challenge your value system. We can all relate to experiences of being disappointed, rejected, happy, or sad. So, as you are trying to relate to your client's situation, remember that even if you haven't experienced something similar, emotions are universal. For example, you are an undergraduate student completing your internship at a nursing home. A 78-year-old resident is on your caseload. You knock on his door and ask if you can come in and talk for a few minutes. He angrily states, "You're just a child, what can you possibly do to help me! I'm stuck here, no one ever visits me. You can do anything you want. I have to wait in my room for my food, my mail, being helped to the bathroom. And no, I don't want your help!" Putting yourself in his place, what feelings come to you as you attempt to absorb the meaning of his message? Probably, you too have felt lonely and frustrated. You know what it feels like to have little control over your life; you may even have experienced a situation where you have lost your own autonomy and independence. Even though you are not a resident of a nursing home (nor are you in your late seventies), you can relate to his feelings of loss, isolation, and powerlessness. This is the first step in developing empathy and engaging the client.

Watch as Marie and Anna begin to develop a relationship, even this early in the process.

Marie's care and concern puts Anna at ease. As Anna feels understood, she is more open to talking about her fears and anxiety.

Actively seeking to understand clients' values, needs, and purpose and seeing them as unique human beings doesn't mean we always agree with them. Empathy is entering into the feelings and experiences of another without losing oneself in the process: "feeling not as the client, but as if the client" (Compton et al., 2005). It is important to give up stereotypes when working with a diverse client population. Gaining full understanding of a client's life experiences can only be approached but not achieved. Social workers do, however, provide a safe place to assist clients in exploring thoughts and feelings and come to new understandings of the issues. It is through this process that clients try out new behaviors and make life-enhancing changes.

Skovholt (2007) offers an interesting framework, the Cycle of Caring, as a way to understand the process of attaching to our clients. The Cycle of Caring is a model that describes a continual series of professional attachments and separations within a one-way helping relationship, such as that of a social worker and client. Being able to repeatedly enter into the Cycle of Caring can be exhilarating as well as exhausting.

The Cycle of Caring is not a static technique. It is rather a dynamic model that takes into account scores of these helping connections. It is the ability to make positive attachments, to provide a relational process between the social worker and the client, and to do it over and over again (Garber, 2004). This cycle has three distinct phases: empathic attachment, active engagement, and felt separation. The first two stages will be introduced here, and the third phase will be addressed more fully in later chapters.

Phase 1 of the Cycle of Caring, empathic attachment, means finding the balance between caring too much and caring too little. Excessive caring on the part of the social worker can lead to burnout and consequently a demonstrated lack of concern. Another consequence of overcaring is secondary trauma to the social worker as a result of emotional depletion and fatigue from the amount, intensity, and duration of effort invested in the relationship. Listening to clients' pain and distress without appropriate caring boundaries can cause emotional injury to the social worker (Skovholt, 2007). To truly attach to our client, we must feel what the client feels but not take on the responsibility for the client's pain or healing. Newly minted social workers may have difficulty maintaining **professional boundaries** while also staying connected to the person and his or her circumstances. To do this well, the social worker needs to attach with his or her caring side to individuals who often are struggling with emotional, intellectual, or physical needs. The most effective way to stay connected without being overloaded is through expressed limits or boundaries within the professional relationship and a clear understanding of who is responsible—the social worker or client—for different work in the relationship (Skovholt & Jennings, 2007).

Phase 2 of the Cycle of Caring, active involvement, focuses on the most intensive part of the relationship. The central idea of this phase is to share a vision together of a future state of the client's life and work toward that vision (Skovholt, 2007). A shared vision may include the client's lifelong goal of getting a college education or committing to marrying a high school sweetheart. Whatever the shared vision, having a caring social worker to appreciate and share the trials and tribulations of these important markers in the client's life is an essential part of the helping process. This phase demands the continuous attachment of the social worker to the client. The support–challenge balance is a critical dimension. These two components, support and challenge (or a gentle confrontation), are keys to the development of a relationship. Support means active encouragement and enthusiasm for the other, whereas challenge means the pushing and demanding of performance or readiness to change within the client's capabilities (Sullivan, Skovholt, & Jennings, 2007).

Phase 3 of the Cycle of Caring, felt separation, explores how both the social worker and the client move toward an ending and the impending loss of the relationship experienced by both parties. The level of attachment, intensity of the work, and time spent working together will affect how each person feels during and following the final phase of the relationship.

Engagement

Behaviors: Use empathy, reflection, and interpersonal skills to effectively engage diverse clients and constituencies.

Critical Thinking Question: What are the ways to demonstrate empathy and authentic understanding toward your clients? Identify and explain at least five specific ways to show genuine care and concern.

Understanding Empathy and Rapport Building

Rapport building and empathy go hand in hand. You may establish rapport with your client in a relatively short period of time, but it is the conveying of empathy, through the repeated application of basic interviewing skills such as paraphrasing, reflection of feeling, furthering responses, and attending behaviors, on which you ultimately build the helping relationship over time.

According to Ragg (2011), the elements of empathic response are the following:

- Client disclosure—The social worker listens, hears, and observes a client disclosure by their questions or reactions about some event, person, or situation. (What did the client say?)

Policy to Practice Education for Homeless Children and Youth

Public Law 100-77, the McKinney-Vento Homeless Improvements Assistance Act, was passed into law in 1986. Prior to its final passage, there were various forms of policies and procedures impacting children who did not have fixed, regular, or adequate nighttime residences. These children were considered homeless. Because of this, each state must now have an educational agency that ensures that a child of a homeless individual, and each homeless youth, has equal access to the same free appropriate public education, including a public preschool education, such as Head Start, as provided to other children and youth. The act stipulates that homelessness alone is not reason enough to separate children from their home school. Efforts must be made to provide services such as transportation, school meals, and special education and gifted student services. School personnel must assist families with gaining access to the child's school records, birth certificate, immunization records, and so on, and while this documentation is being obtained, the student will be in full attendance. Social workers typically serve in the role of the liaison, the person who assists families in finding resources that can lead to housing stability. As a social worker working with a student who is homeless, how might you begin a conversation with him or her? Looking long term, what are some of your concerns regarding this student?

Example: As a court service social worker, you are meeting with Yvonne, a 22-year-old female client who was recently released from prison after a 24-month sentence. Prior to her incarceration, Yvonne was selling drugs and working as a prostitute. The social worker will need to consider the obstacles the client may face, such as living arrangements, job opportunities (or lack thereof), and relationships with family members and other people inside and outside of prison. Ask questions about training and opportunities provided while she was incarcerated and how she coped and managed to live day to day (assessing her strengths throughout the session). In addition, it is important to understand where the client is at the moment and what issues are relevant to her. Pay attention to her nonverbal body language, for example, how she is sitting (erect, slumped, not facing you), her verbal tone, and her choice of words.

- Identification of action element—The social worker listens to the client's statements and identifies what contributes to the disclosing feeling. (What are people saying and doing?)

  Example continued: Yvonne discloses that she has become very religious while incarcerated. She attends prayer meeting daily (including Alcoholics Anonymous meetings) and feels a strong pull toward her faith. Yvonne will disclose more about her religious experiences and what is important to her if the social worker attends to the significance of her new discovery and the strength it provides to her on the outside. She shares with the social worker that her family and friends never attended church and have been making very negative comments about her newfound religion. Yvonne has maintained close telephone contact with the prison chaplain since her release.

- Identification of processing elements—While listening and observing, the social worker reflects on the client's statements and mentally labels the important thinking and feeling themes. (What are the beliefs, thoughts, and feelings that seem to be important?)

  Example continued: As you listen to Yvonne talking about her faith, you begin to realize that she is worried about her family's negative reactions. She begins to distance herself from her family by stating, "They don't get me anymore, and I can't count on them. I knew this was going to be a problem; they are a bunch of heathens. But God will take care of them and me. If they don't start going to church and praying, they will pay the price." Yvonne also had indicated that she wants to start over and maybe get her GED.

- Core concerns—From the action and processing elements of the client statement, the social worker identifies what appears to be most important to the client. (What are the critical concerns?)

  Example continued: As the social worker, you understand that Yvonne's family has been a very important part of her life. Her experiences in prison have changed her in significant ways. Yvonne is determined to make a new life for herself, even if it means no longer maintaining as close a relationship with her family. You also want to attend to Yvonne's goal of getting her GED. A high school education will open up more job and training possibilities for her.

- Validation and exploration—When the worker has tuned into the concerns and questions that might be evident for the client, the challenge is to get the concern out in the open and address it. (How can I validate this concern? Where do I take this to explore the experience of the client?)

  Example continued: You can explore with Yvonne ways that she can still maintain a relationship with her family. As a social worker, you understand the need and value of support, be it financial or emotional. You can confirm and acknowledge her choices and beliefs but also validate the value of her family. Be careful not to judge her past experiences and troubles. At the same time, provide a sense of hope and certainty that she can use those strengths and skills to turn her life around while also maintaining a belief in her family. The struggles to stay clean and off the streets may be a challenge for Yvonne. Help her to anticipate some of the obstacles and barriers she may face.

Watch this clip as James and Anthony begin the early steps of the helping process. James puts Anthony as ease as he shares his role and desire to help.

By the time clients come to seek the services of a social worker, often they have exhausted other sources of help and have experienced considerable emotional pain (Kottler, 2010). As the social worker listens to the client's story, typically it becomes apparent that the client has given quite a bit of consideration to the problem prior to your first session with him or her. It is important to listen to his or her story as relevant pieces of information come to light. You can ask questions that relate to your understanding of the situation, gaining insight into the client's perceptions. As the social worker begins this helping process, it is imperative to understand the client from his or her unique vantage point, taking into account his or her personal and family background, culture, education, developmental stage, environmental factors, and health status. Egan (2014) suggests understanding clients in three ways: 1) understand clients from their point of view, including feelings surrounding this point of view; 2) understand them through the context of their lives; and 3) make a commitment to understand the dissonance between clients' points of view and objective reality.

Social workers are equipped to deal with many different challenges on the client's journey toward self-determination, but a road map can be helpful. This map consists of the profession's knowledge, information, and skills (Egan, 2014). We are called on to assist our clients in problem solving, resource acquisition and management, and advocacy. The social worker's ability to use basic interviewing and assessment skills is an important aspect of conveying competency. As the helping relationship evolves, the responsibility is clearly more shared, and the collaborative nature of the relationship becomes an essential building block.

Box 8.D asks three questions regarding a time in your life when you asked for help. Think about what it felt like to be the receiver rather than the giver of assistance.

Countertransference

Social workers can feel very strongly about a situation, client, or circumstance. We may find ourselves experiencing a personal or emotional reaction to a situation. This is referred

Box 8.D Now You Try It . . . Self-Reflection

Identify a time in your life when you asked someone for help. What convinced you the person was really listening and cared?

How did you feel, knowing that you were understood and being cared for?

____

to as **countertransference**. Countertransference is an emotional reaction to clients where the social worker is overly involved in the client's life, seeing the client as a sexual object, a friend, an adversary, or even an extension of themselves (Shebib, 2010). It is important to respond to our clients in a nondefensive manner, meaning being able to respond to the client without feeling a need to guard or justify your decisions, positions, actions, feelings, or perceptions. Box 8.2 has some warning signs that countertransference is occurring (Miley, O'Melia, & DuBois, 2010; Timberlake, Farber, & Sabatino, 2002).

As a social worker, you will be exposed to many details and facets of your client's life. You are sanctioned as a professional to provide services to clients via your position within an agency or mandated by law. Because of this power differential between the client and the social worker, we must always be mindful of the power we hold—not only sanctioned power through the positions we hold within our society, such as reporting a suspected case of child abuse or determining services and benefits, but also the power within the relationship. Clients will look to the social worker as the expert and may feel intimated by their perceptions or beliefs of who you are. These perceptions can be based on the reality of the relationship as well as subjectively viewed by the client, commonly known as transference.

Clients may respond differently, depending on the social worker's age, gender, socioeconomic status, marital status, position within the agency, experience, gender, physical appearance, intelligence, social demeanor and attitude, ethnicity, race, or religion (Shebib, 2010). Some clients will wait for the social worker to assume leadership or power within the relationship based on their perceptions of the worker and the worker's role. For example, clients may be used to having others do things for them or may see themselves as victims with no power to change anything in their lives. In this instance, the social worker must "start where the client is" and should focus on the client's needs by imparting information and knowledge to assist in confidence and self-esteem building.

Box 8.2 Signs of Countertransference

- Having intense feelings (e.g., irritation, anger, boredom, sexual attraction)
- Feeling of attraction or repulsion
- Being reluctant to confront or tending to avoid sensitive issues or feelings
- Continually running over time with certain clients and wishing that other clients would not show up for appointments
- Acting with rescuing behaviors, such as lending money, adopting abused children, or protecting clients
- Being reminded by clients of other people you know
- Dealing with clients who have similar histories or problems as yours
- Employing unnecessary or excessive self-disclosure
- Feeling reluctant to end the helping relationship

Source: Shebib (2010), p. 87.

Box 8.3 Danielle

Danielle is a 21-year-old female social work intern. She has been in her internship placement for five weeks. She has completed all the required orientation and training. Danielle and her 15-year-old female client Chaney have met three times before. (See information later in this chapter regarding home visits.) Today, Danielle meets Chaney at the group home and suggests that they go out for ice cream. Danielle asks Chaney what has been happening in the group home since the last time they met. Chaney discloses that she and Jimmy, who is also a group home resident, have started eating together every day at school. She then whispers to Danielle that they have had sex while in the group home (this is a violation of the rules) and that she doesn't like it. Danielle responds by saying, "You shouldn't be having sex with Jimmy; it is wrong, and you will get kicked out of the group home. Don't tell me anymore about this. Let's forget you said anything at all."

Analysis 1: In this case, Danielle in uncomfortable talking about sex, the violation of group home rules, and the possible consequences of Chaney's decisions. Because of Danielle's discomfort about the situation, she puts her own needs and feelings ahead of Chaney's. She uses her position as the intern to communicate disapproval as well as demonstrating "breaking the rules and trying to cover it up" as her problem-solving strategy. Danielle also communicates that she can't handle the reality of Chaney's situation. She cuts off communication because of her own nervousness and anxiety. This intervention is not helpful to Chaney in any way.

Box 8.4 Danielle, Part 2

Danielle responds by saying, "Oh, do I know what you mean! My boyfriend, Seth, wants to have sex all the time. I wish he would back off sometimes, but I love him and don't want our relationship to end."

Analysis 2: In this case, Danielle is inappropriately self-disclosing information that reflects a friendship rather than a professional relationship. She also takes the focus off Chaney and her situation as she begins to share her own story. Chaney is likely to misinterpret the role of the intern, as she feels obligated to respond to Danielle's struggles with her sexual relationship as well as her own.

Once the client believes that he or she is capable of making positive changes, a sense of worth and a belief in his or her own ability can serve as the guide and motivator throughout the helping relationship and the person's life.

Box 8.3 illustrates how a social work intern, Danielle, allows her own personal views and discomfort interfere with the helping relationship. She abdicates her professional (intern) role to the client.

In Box 8.4, Danielle responds to Chaney as a good friend might. She has difficulty remaining professional as her interest is piqued.

In Box 8.5, Danielle responds more appropriately to Chaney by remaining professional and using her role as an intern to educate and support her client.

Distinguishing between a Friendship and a Professional Relationship

Finding the balance (or maintaining the boundaries) between a **friendship** and a **professional relationship** can be challenging in part because so many of the qualities we find in a good friend are similar to those needed in the helping relationship. For example, trust, care, honesty, and genuineness are essential characteristics of both a friendship and a professional relationship. Box 8.6 provides a list of some similarities and differences between these two types of relationships.

Box 8.5 Danielle, Part 3

Danielle responds by appearing calm and asks Chaney to further describe her relationship with Jimmy. She listens quietly as Chaney discloses that they are not using any kind of birth control and that she feels pressured to have sex with him. She talks with Chaney about breaking the house rules and ways that she can communicate with Jimmy about her fears and concerns. Danielle offers that unprotected sex can lead to pregnancy and sexually transmitted infections. She also empowers her with information about how to assertively communicate to Jimmy that she doesn't want to have sex with him right now. Simultaneously, Danielle also affirms Chaney's decision to be honest.

Analysis 3: In this revised example, Danielle realizes this information is very important to share with her internship supervisor and the group home staff, but she is unsure how to proceed, as she also takes into account the bounds of confidentiality. Danielle wants to be helpful to Chaney but also realizes the potential consequences to her behavior. Rather than condemning Chaney and shutting her down, Danielle explored more about the circumstances surrounding her relationship with Jimmy without being judgmental. She provided useful information about birth control, sexually transmitted infections, and saying "no" to his sexual advances. Chaney also encouraged her to tell the group home supervisor about what is happening. Danielle puts her client's well-being above her own discomfort. She responded appropriately within her role as an intern.

Box 8.6 Friendship versus Professional Relationships

Friendship	Professional Relationship
Caring and concern	Caring and concern
Warmth and genuineness	Warmth and genuineness
Supportive and safe	Supportive and safe
Investment of self	Purposeful investment of self
Trust	Trust/confidentiality as defined by the NASW *Code of Ethics*
Shared interests	Similar or different interests
Comparable levels of disclosure	Unequaled levels of disclosure
Similar or compatible values	Social work values guide the relationship
Physical intimacy/space	Physical proximity and touching is regulated by the NASW *Code of Ethics*
Friendship has no "fee" attached	Client or other entity pays for services
Roles are fluid	Roles are constant; that is, the client is always the client
Natural progression of the friendship	Beginning, middle, and ending phase of the relationship/time limited/termination
No set agenda or purpose to meeting	Each session has an agenda/plan for work toward problem resolution and is purposeful
Feedback/advice is open and unsolicited	Feedback is specific to the problem area
Offering opinions	Offering options
Reciprocal (two-way communication and disclosure/focus is on both parties)	Nonreciprocal (focus is on the client)
Power differential is determined by parties	Power differential is determined by authority of the position
No formal education or training required	Degreed professional, ongoing training and education; seeks consultation

Source: Based on Brill and Levine (2012); Egan (2014); Shebib (2010).

Several social work educators and authors (Compton et al., 2005; Cormier & Cormier, 2011; Egan, 2014; Kottler, 2000) offer building blocks for creating a strong foundation for your professional therapeutic relationships with your clients:

- Be warm, authentic, genuine, down to earth, and engaging—Be approachable and friendly (smile). Be spontaneous. Let your humanness come through. Explore the client's expectations of the process and determine if it is realistic. Avoid social worker defensiveness and stay open and responsive to your client.
- Strength and confidence—Appear to be knowledgeable and capable even if you don't always feel that way. Clients want to believe that there is hope. It is through the safety of the relationship that the client is most likely to take risks. Always be mindful of the power differential in the relationship. Serve as a partner and collaborator. Form a working alliance with your client. Making an appropriate referral to a more experienced professional and/or consultation with your supervisor may be necessary if you are in too deep or over your head.
- Be consistent and dependable—Trust is built over time and is easy to break. For example, if you say you will check into housing options for your client, do it. Otherwise, trust is broken, and the relationship will suffer. Be on time, respect confidentiality, and follow through with promises and commitments.
- Model honesty, frankness, and integrity—Through your own actions, clients can see and learn to respond similarly. The helping relationship can serve as a guide throughout the client's life; be frank, respectful, consistent, and considerate. Always follow the NASW *Code of Ethics* (available on the NASW website) in all professional interactions.
- Stay with client needs, not your own—Deal with your own issues so they do not cloud or color the relationship or your judgment. It is important to focus and attend to the needs of the client, putting your own issues and struggles aside during the session. Convey a nonjudgmental attitude and actively seek to understand your client from his or her point of view. Stay objective so that you can give the client a new way of looking at an old problem. Keep your eye on the long view of the problem, remembering that change takes time. Consider which feelings are yours and which feelings are the client's. Go beyond yourself to help a client. Know your agency's policies and procedures on, for example, how and what can be done to assist a client.
- Focus on the client's nonverbal messages and the immediacy of the interview (what is happening within the session)—Be aware of your own attending behaviors. Are you fully present? Are you maintaining a relaxed demeanor and intermittent eye contact and mirroring the client's emotional reactions?
- Go with the flow—Be willing to shift gears from one strategy or intervention to another, mid-session if necessary. Consider what is and what isn't working between you and the client and adjust accordingly. Remember that relationships do change over time—both through this interaction and during the helping process itself. Be tolerant of ambiguity. View new situations as a challenge rather than a threat. Expect to be surprised and believe that you have the confidence to figure out whatever may come your way.

- Stay flexible—As you get to know your client and what makes him or her tick, be careful not to pigeonhole the client based on information about his or her culture, religion, family background, spirituality, socioeconomic status, and so on. Avoid stereotypes. Be open-minded. This allows you to work with a wide variety or range of clients. Clients often feel that "if the social worker accepts me, then I must be okay."
- Respond therapeutically—There are many ways to respond, but pick one that is helpful and does no harm to the client. With enough goodwill between the client and the social worker, regrouping and moving ahead is possible. Put aside your own concerns to fully engage with the client; however, connectedness and shared understanding are critical aspects of the helping relationship. Learn from your mistakes and respond accordingly.
- Show care and concern—Use all the social work interviewing skills as a way of communicating that you value your client as a human being. Communicate this concern through the relationship. The best predictor of outcome of the helping process is the relationship between the social worker and the client (Hill & O'Brien, 2014).
- Offer ongoing support and encouragement—Offering a supportive word may be exactly what is needed. For example, a client may be unsure how to approach a situation that is new to him or her. A word of encouragement, such as "good job," "keep up the good work," or "you did the right thing," is extremely helpful. Encouragement that is grounded in a job well done is different from false assurance.

Three questions are posed in Box 8.E regarding how you differentiate between a professional relationship and a personal relationship.

Self-Awareness

It is important to elaborate on the necessity of knowing yourself as a person and as a professional. Brill and Levine (2012) describe the process of becoming knowledgeable and disciplined in relationships and the importance of developing a personal objectivity based on qualities such as **self-awareness**. Below is a series of questions to help you begin the self-reflection process:

1. Awareness of self and personal needs, weaknesses, and strengths
   - What factors contributed to your decision to become a social worker?
   - What makes you tick and contributes to who you are?
   - How do you communicate to others regarding your needs, wants, and interests?

Box 8.E Now You Try It . . . Professional Relationships versus Friendship

Define what friendship means to you.

Define what a professional relationship means to you.

How do you differentiate between the two?

- What is your understanding of how your family and life experiences contributed to who you are today?
- What strengths do you possess? Are others aware of these strengths?
- How do you protect your feelings and your self-esteem?
- What are some of your anxieties and fears?
- What would others who know you well say are your strengths? Weaknesses?

2. Awareness of and ability to deal with our own personality patterns and with the "stuff" that tends to cloud our perceptions
    - What are some of the patterns or ways that you conduct your life that work well for you?
    - What are the barriers that get in your way?
    - What does your "inner voice" say to you? (Negative or positive self-talk?)
    - How do you view "power" within a relationship?
    - What is your view on stereotypic roles within the family?
    - What is your view on childrearing and discipline?
    - How do you handle conflict? Change?
    - What relational issues (between you and close family and friends) seem to come up time and time again?
3. Openness and freedom to perceive with clarity and relate with honesty regardless of differences and similarities
    - What are your religious and political beliefs and values?
    - How are these beliefs and values reflected in your daily life?
    - How do you convey these beliefs and values?
    - What personal needs do you have that might interfere with the helping relationship?
    - What personal values guide your decisions?
    - How do you conduct yourself when disagreeing about religion or politics and values?
4. Ability to perceive and evaluate values, attitudes, and patterns of behavior of the group which the client considers himself or herself a part
    - How open are you to people who are different from you?
    - In what ways do you feel (or have felt) vulnerable, disempowered, or oppressed?
    - How do you feel about interacting with people from other cultures?
    - What group(s) of people do you think are most like you?
    - Are there any groups of people you feel as though you could not interact with?
    - If you dig deep, what are your stereotypes and prejudices?
5. Ability to differ and stand alone
    - How do you handle differences of opinion?
    - What issues in your life do you feel most passionately about?

Box 8.F Now You Try It . . . Self-Awareness

Using the five categories presented above, answer the questions presented in each grouping.

1. Awareness of self and personal needs, weaknesses, and strengths.
2. Awareness of and ability to deal with your own personality patterns and with the "stuff" that tends to cloud your perceptions.
3. Openness and freedom to perceive with clarity and relate with honesty regardless of differences and similarities.
4. Ability to perceive and evaluate values, attitudes, and patterns of behavior of the group of which the client considers himself or herself a part.
5. Ability to differ and stand alone.

- If you had the opportunity to stand up for one social issue or social value, what would that be?
- What is your greatest fear about going out on a limb for a cause?
- What would you hope to gain or lose by advocating for an unpopular position?
- How do you receive feedback from others, and what do you do with it once you get it?
- What are your views on power and authority?

Using the preceding questions, answer those posed to you in Box 8.F.

Cormier et al. (2011) address the importance of social workers knowing their own needs (i.e., need for control, need for approval, etc.), motivations for helping others, awareness of personal feelings, strengths, limitations, triggers, and coping skills. This kind of self-awareness is important for several reasons. First, objectivity in dealing with a client is a crucial component in avoiding blind spots or perceptions, behaviors, or ways of being that the social worker is unaware of but that may detract from building a professional relationship with clients. For example, if the social worker has unresolved issues around being abused as a child, the worker will see every client's life experience through this lens. Consequently, the social worker can project onto the client his or her own issues, perceptions, and experiences rather than dealing with the client's concerns. The relationship becomes focused on the social worker's needs instead of the client's needs. The social worker may be unaware of these perceptions; indeed, this can contribute to the client not feeling understood and the social worker remaining "stuck." Unresolved personal issues can also lead a social worker to feel angry and defensive because he or she feels attacked. In this situation, the focus is on self rather than the needs of the client.

When a social worker inadvertently uses pitfalls, such as advice giving or being judgmental, the client can become disengaged from the helping process. The frustration a client may experience when the social worker is not listening or is generally not attending to the client's needs can cause extreme frustration and disillusionment. Repairing the "damage" of unintentionally using a pitfall is discussed earlier in this text.

A client named Curtis is presented in Box 8.I. Using the Rogerian approach to practice, follow how the social worker joins with him, through positive regard and empathy. It is the nature of their relationship that brings about constructive change in Curtis's life.

Developing Cultural Competence In the Shoes of Children Who are Homeless

The culture of homelessness is one that many of us can't imagine. There are many situations that can lead to a child becoming homeless. Consider a parent fleeing an abusive home with her children in tow, a youth who has runaway, or been kicked out of his or her home, who has been abused, or a child with serious mental health and substance abuse issues. For this example, think of yourself as a 10 years old, not having a space to put you head at night and wondering where your next meal will come from. What does it feel like to move from place to place or live in a temporary shelter that you know is only for a week or so? What about living in a car, crashing on a couch, or sleeping on a bench? Put yourself in the position of a child who has to go to school, gets a free lunch every day, wears clothing that is too big, has no sustainable friendships within his or her school and has survived through months of not knowing what tomorrow might bring. Imagine the student's locker becoming the only place that is his or hers. Imagine falling behind in math and reading because you have switched schools three times in the past year. Having imagined yourself as a 10-year-old, what words best describe the culture of homelessness for school children? How might this inform your approach to children who are homeless? What are your perceptions about children who are homeless? As the social worker in a school setting, how would you address this child in relationship to his or her homelessness? Do you ask direct questions? What information would you share with the teachers? How might you support and encourage this student to stay in school?

Box 8.1 Theory into Practice—Rogerian (Client-Centered) Therapy: Case Study

Rogerian therapy is drawn from humanistic theory and the work of psychologist Carl Rogers, its founding father. Rogerian therapy is grounded in a fundamental belief in the human capacity for change. Through the use of active and accurate listening, empathic reflection, and clarification, the social worker facilitates client growth toward self-actualization. The essential attitudinal conditions for effective Rogerian therapy are empathy, unconditional positive regard, and congruence or genuineness. Congruence is defined as a good match between a person's affect, cognition, and behavior that results in high levels of authenticity and sincerity (Carpetto, 2008; Rogers, 1957). Consider the following case:

Curtis, a court-ordered client, age 18, and the social worker, Randall, are meeting for the first time. Curtis has been mandated to see a social worker after being charged with shoplifting. During the intake interview, Curtis answers all of the questions with short responses, such as "I don't know" or "Yes" or "No."

Randall tries to engage Curtis in the conversation, veering away from the standard questions on the intake form. Curtis continues to respond in an uninterested and nonchalant way. Randall states, "You seem really bored as though I am wasting your time. I would like for us to talk to each other. But it seems like I am talking to myself, or to a brick wall. Is there anything at all that I can do to help you feel more comfortable and be more willing to give me a chance?" Looking at Randall, Curtis said, "No." The session ended. As Curtis left, Randall said, "I hope to see you next week," and Curtis mumbled something unrecognizable.

Session 2: Curtis is 20 minutes late for his appointment. Randall did not mention it at all; he just started the session with a welcoming smile. Curtis again sits down in his chair and shows no interest in a conversation. Finally, Randall asks Curtis if he knows how to play chess. Curtis states that he does not and that it is a game for smart people. Ignoring this remark, Randall pulls out the board and places the pieces in their correct spots. Curtis seems only slightly interested but is listening as Randall describes the role of each piece. Randall gives him a book on the game of chess, and he takes it unenthusiastically.

Session 3: Curtis is on time and brought back the chess book. After some small talk about the weather and the latest sports event on TV, Curtis states, "I read the book, and I would like to learn how to play." A connection has been made. Randall introduces the strategies of the game. By the end of the session, Curtis is smiling and thanking Randall for the chess lesson.

Session 4: Curtis is on time and brings his own chessboard. Randall is surprised and very pleased. Curtis explains that the chessboard was his dad's and that when he was little, they used to play together. Randall listens as Curtis tells him that his father was killed by a drunk driver five years ago. Curtis is now living with his mom, who is very depressed and hardly ever leaves the house. Randall listens with

Box 8.I Theory into Practice—Rogerian (Client-Centered) Therapy: Case Study (*Continued*)

understanding and compassion. He offers Curtis a gentle tap on the shoulder as Curtis's eyes fill up with tears.

Session 5: Curtis is on time and smiles as he walks into Randall's office. He has done the homework assignment that Randall had given him the week before. He has written a short story about his dad. It is filled with funny tales about a boy named "Curtis" and a dad named "Joe." While playing chess, Randall demonstrates unconditional positive regard, support, and encouragement. Curtis is starting to trust Randall. He tells him more about his mother and how he worries about her. He feels it is his responsibility to try to make her happy. Randall affirms the burden he must feel and listens to him, letting the next part of the story unfold. At the end of the session, Curtis said, "I never thought I would end up liking you, but you are an okay guy. Thanks."

Over the course of five sessions, Curtis and Randall's work together deepens. Randall is accepting of who Curtis is and does not push change on him. In this case, the social worker is patient and understanding. It is because Curtis feels heard and accepted that he eventually begins to open up. It is through Randall's show of genuine empathy and positive regard that Curtis begins to respond. Although Curtis is a mandated client, he is no longer an involuntary client. He now comes to sessions ready to talk about his mom and the challenges that they are facing together. If Randall had pushed Curtis into opening up and disclosing the sadness in his life, Curtis may never have returned (even facing jail time as an alternative). Randall very gently offered him an opening, and Curtis eventually followed through. He knows Randall is on his side.

Developing Your Personal Style

As you become more confident using interviewing skills, you have the opportunity to develop your personal interviewing style. Some social workers are more verbal throughout the interview; others are more reflective and less talkative. Neither approach is correct or better. Watch other workers and mentally note what you liked about their interviewing style. The more opportunities you have to observe others in action, the wider your interviewing options will be. Convincing yourself that you can do this and that you are confident and feel in control is one way to overcome the anxiety you may feel. In some ways, the adage "fake it till you make it" holds true. Hold your head up high. You want the client to see you as a capable social worker even though you may not feel that way at all. Keep it a secret, and before you know it, using the skills will be second nature. As indicated throughout this text, it will take time to develop your personal interviewing style. By understanding your strengths and developing comfort in who you are as a person, interviewing will soon be fun and a source of professional confidence, fulfillment, and pride.

In Box 8.G, you are asked to reflect on your personal style. How would people whom know you well and in a variety of roles and situations describe your style?

? Assess your understanding of the intake process by taking this brief quiz.

Box 8.G Now You Try It . . . Personal Style

What is your personal style?

How would your best friends describe your personal style?

How would your coworkers describe your personal style?

How would your classmates describe your personal style?

How would your family members describe your personal style?

____

Assessment

Behaviors: Develop mutually agreed-on intervention goals and objectives based on the critical assessment of strengths, needs, and challenges within clients and constituencies.

Critical Thinking Question: As a new social worker, you are concerned about how to start your first session with a client. The intake process has been completed, and you are meeting the client tomorrow. You know that the client is 18, pregnant, and living with her mother. She is a senior in high school and works part-time at a local grocery store. The intake form indicates that she is undecided about adoption or raising the child on her own. Plan out your introductory statement and develop a list of items you would like to address in the meeting (of course always understanding that the best laid plans can easily change).

MEETING THE CLIENT

As you reflect on your readiness to work with clients face-to-face, eventually the time comes to step out of your comfort zone into the world of your clients. All the practicing and role playing you have done in your classes will finally pay off as you put on your professional hat and forge ahead. You are ready and eagerly waiting for the client to arrive at your office or to make that first **home visit**. You can never undo a first impression, so make it count. Be polite, respectful, and genuine.

Preparing for the First Meeting

Probably one of the scariest things a novice social worker faces is how to prepare for the first visit with a client. As mentioned above, the client is already preparing to meet you, thinking about what to say, and how to present himself or herself. As you plan for the first visit, whether a home visit or an **office visit**, be sure to have reviewed any material about the client that may be available. For example, the client may have completed an intake form, or perhaps information was collected over the telephone about the client's needs. You may have received a formal referral letter from another social worker, a teacher, a physician, or some other helping professional. Generally, some basic data accompany the client as an introduction. Through this introductory information, you may learn how the client came into contact with the agency's services. An important piece of information to know is whether the client is voluntary or involuntary.

Additionally, if you have some background information, such as a completed intake form, it can be helpful to do some preliminary informal and formal research about that particular topic, issue, or circumstance. In keeping with the social worker's obligation to develop multicultural competence, if your client is a member of a group that you have little familiarity with, this is a great opportunity to learn more.

Conversely, you may be working on a 24-hour hotline, and the nature of the call is unknown. You have very little time to prepare for the interview other than to introduce yourself and ask the client how you may be of assistance. What you do know, however, is that the person is experiencing some type of distress. Mastery of basic interviewing skills and knowledge of resources may be the most beneficial preparation for engaging a client in this situation.

Favorable environmental conditions include a private office or space with comfortable seating. Keep light in your office that is not too glaring or bright. Chairs facing each other, placed within a comfortable distance for you and the client, is preferred. Obviously, few agencies have budgets for office decorating, but think about what you can include in the space to convey who you are as a helper. You can also express a sense of who you are and how you perform as a social worker based on the appearance of your office. A neat and well-ordered office can communicate to the client that you are organized, systematic, prepared, and focused. A messy, cluttered office can send the message that the worker is unprepared, incompetent, scattered, and unfocused. As you set up your office space, consider what types of artwork, pictures, plants, certificates/diplomas, and furnishings can help the client to see you as human and approachable. Displaying artwork and having magazines that represent the client populations you work with can be an effective way of communicating interest and acceptance. Beware that small objects can be used as a weapon against you. For more details regarding your safety, see Box 8.7.

Box 8.7 Safety Principles and Precautions Inside and Outside of the Agency Setting

Sometimes a client may become agitated or hostile. It is important that workers and supervisors discuss how to handle such situations early on so that the social worker is informed of agency policy and a recommended course of action should such an event occur.

1. In an office setting, know how to activate the agency's alarm system or who to contact for help. Keep your desk relatively clutter free.
2. It is common for social workers in a variety of social service settings to conduct interviews in a client's home. Such visits do expose you to risks. Home visits should be made with the full knowledge of your supervisor, including the client's address and phone number, your cell phone number, time of departure, time of return, other activities while on the trip, and so on.
3. Workers should not conduct home visits when they feel uncomfortable or threatened in the situation. You should return to the agency and report the situation to your supervisor. Beware of dogs or other household pets that might be a threat. Ask the client to secure any pets if you feel threatened. You should not continue a home visit when alcohol and/or drugs are detected. As a general rule, if possible, go with a coworker. In addition to safety issues, it is helpful to have a second pair of eyes to keep track of the visit, interact with children, and take notes. Finally, a visit with a coworker can provide the opportunity to process what happened during the visit, high points, low points, impressions, and recommendations for future visits.
4. Know who to call (or page) regarding what steps to take if a vehicle breaks down. Using AAA (American Automobile Association), your agency's roadside emergency card, or On Star, for example, can keep you safe and get you back on the road quickly. When traveling by car to an agency or a home visit, it is important to know how to reach your destination. Consult a map, use GPS, and/or request directions from a reliable source before driving to unfamiliar areas. If you must stop and ask for directions, a convenience store or gas station is your best option. In general, remember to be alert and to lock doors and close windows.
5. Mental health and correctional institutions serve client populations whose behavior may be unpredictable. It is important to learn strategies for handling clients whose behavior becomes threatening. Whenever you feel uncomfortable with clients, inform your supervisor. Another staff person may accompany the social worker when serving such clients.
6. Some social service settings have activities that occur beyond normal office hours. Be aware of the location of these activities, such as the neighborhood, street lighting, open spaces, parking lots, shrubs, and other growth. It is appropriate for workers to ask someone to accompany them to their cars after dark. Do not take risks.
7. When working with clients, it is important to remember that the treatment process often makes people feel vulnerable and may challenge their usual coping mechanisms. With some clients, this can contribute to problems with impulse control and can raise issues of safety for the client, the social worker, and others.
8. At times, a social worker will work with clients who have difficulty with being present and lucid, dealing with overwhelming emotions, and controlling their anger. Some of them may be prone to violence and may possess weapons. Other clients may be intoxicated, high on drugs, or in withdrawal or may have other medical or neurological disorders. It is very important that you consult with your supervisor regarding preparation for and handling of specific situations that are potentially difficult or threatening. Never keep information about potentially dangerous clients to yourself, even if you believe you have good relationships with your clients.

(Continued)

Box 8.7 Safety Principles and Precautions inside and outside of the Agency Setting *(Continued)*

9. When traveling by foot or public transportation, it is advisable to carry as few valuables as possible. Money, license, keys, and other essentials might be carried in a pocket. If a handbag carried under the arm is grabbed, it is best to let go of it. It is advisable to dress in comfortable clothes that are loose fitting and sturdy, flat walking shoes. Be alert to the surroundings and walk with purpose and a clear destination. Be aware of people in the immediate area, without staring or maintaining eye contact.
10. Prior to an in-office meeting with a client with whom the social worker does not feel safe, the social worker should discuss the situation with the supervisor. When considering the location of the meeting, think about what is in the room, whether there is more than one exit, and where each person might sit. Think about whether to include someone else in the meeting. When discussing the time of the appointment, consider whether people are around at the time. Discuss the plan for backup and assistance in the event that the client becomes agitated. Do not meet a potentially dangerous client alone.
11. Prior to meeting with clients in their homes, determine whether there is a question of safety and plan accordingly with your supervisor. Meeting at a neutral place or going with another worker may be the most appropriate plan. Again, always make sure that someone at the agency is aware of itineraries.
12. Follow agency procedures during a fire alarm, power outage, and national disaster.
13. The following safety precautions are strongly advised:
    - Take a cellular phone or pager to the meeting.
    - Lock personal items (e.g., jewelry and purse) in the vehicle's trunk prior to departing for the client's home.
    - Be aware that items such as a necktie, earrings, a necklace, or a scarf can be used in a harmful way.
    - Use all five senses when approaching the neighborhood, leaving the car, and when entering and departing the premises.
    - Keep car keys handy/accessible while in the client's home.
    - Park vehicles so that it is possible to make a safe and quick departure in an emergency.
    - After entering a client's home, stay near the door if possible. Observe all exits in the home.
    - Ask for permission to write/take notes.
    - Listen to clients and allow them to ventilate.
    - Should clients seem threatened by your presence in their home, do not force the issue. Politely excuse yourself and leave immediately.
    - If an incident occurs in which you are personally threatened or hurt, immediately contact 911 and inform your supervisor. (see Appendix D for ways to deescalate potentially volatile situation)

In preparation for the first meeting, the social worker (or designated office personnel) may call or text to confirm the appointment a few days prior to the scheduled appointment. This can serve as a reminder as well as convey that you are looking forward to meeting the client. Of course, some clients cannot be reached by phone. In that case, you may want to send a short note or an e-mail reminder of the appointment. It is a good idea to leave a number where you can be reached as well as the exact location of your office to facilitate the client in making the appointment on time. It is also important to schedule visits, when possible, during a time of day that is convenient for the client. A person working a 3 P.M.–11 P.M. shift may be sleeping during your normal office hours. Asking a client how he or she will be getting to your office can also be helpful in planning a time to meet. A client may be relying on a neighbor for a ride, a taxi, or public transportation.

Assessment

Behaviors: Collect and organize data, and apply critical thinking to interpret information from clients and constituencies.

Critical Thinking Question: As you plan for a first home visit in a neighborhood about 35 minutes from your office in what is considered a "rough" part of the city, what are some important steps and pieces of information you will need?

Keep in mind that you will not click with every client you meet. Clearly, the social work adage *goodness of fit* applies here. It is sometimes difficult to admit when the fit between the client and social worker is not good, and the time may come when you have to refer the client to another person, in part because your interactions may cause the client frustration at best and harm at worst. For example, you may have very strong feelings against abortion, and your 23-year-old client is considering this intervention for resolving her unwanted pregnancy. You realize that you cannot be objective in your work with her because your personal beliefs are in conflict with her right to self-determination. Rather than convey a sense of disapproval or disgust either consciously or unconsciously, refer her to an agency or worker who can provide this service in a more accepting way. To do otherwise would be in violation of the NASW *Code of Ethics*, specifically the ethical principle that social workers respect the inherent dignity and worth of the person and their right to self-determination.

Regardless of how unprepared you may feel, your clients have a set of expectations that you may be unaware of. It is up to you to come across as a caring person who is interested in learning about the client and helping him or her. The responsibility for this initially rests with you. To accomplish a favorable outcome, you as the social worker must know what you are doing, communicate with the client that you are prepared to help, and plant the seed for change and hope (Kottler, 2010). Clients who seek help want to be assured that the worker is credible, knowledgeable, and committed to helping them through the long haul.

Although most social workers with a bachelor's degree are trained in the generalist practice mode, you may have developed a specialization along the way. For example, you may be a child welfare worker, and your area of practice is within the foster care arena. The expectation would be that you have a unique perspective, expertise, experience, and understanding of the issues facing the children, biological parents, and the foster parents. Additionally, a first-year master's degree in social work education focuses on generalist versus specialization of practice. Regardless of your level or area of practice, social work skills must be applied within the values and ethics of the profession in your first meeting with the client and throughout the helping relationship. First meetings set the climate and tone within which the relationship will develop.

The First Face-to-Face Office Meeting with the Client

Social workers should do an occasional visual survey of their office reception area. Is it welcoming, does it have a quiet area for clients to fill out paperwork, and is there a play area for children with age-appropriate toys? Are the restrooms clean and the hallways and stairways well lit? Are there pieces of artwork and magazines that represent the clients who access services? Does the agency appear welcoming? As a client, would you want to sit in a dirty or uncomfortable chair waiting to be greeted by a social worker? As a social worker in your agency, advocate for some of these very inexpensive modifications. There are easy ways to let the clients know that the agency and, by association, the social worker are invested in them.

Watch this video clip with the volume off and Just look at the physical space of the shelter: the waiting room and office. Does this shelter provide a warm and welcoming environment? What suggestions might you make for improvement?

Assuming that you have some basic information about the client and the presenting problem (what the client described as the reason he or she is there) via the intake form or interview, you may already have some knowledge about his or her particular issues or concerns. Smiling at clients and welcoming them with a caring tone of voice and a handshake are ways to help put clients at ease (review session 1 of each of the six case studies for examples of these attending behaviors). Ask the client how he or she or would like to be addressed, as this begins the process of self-determination (Ragg, 2011). If the client is in a waiting area, you may have to walk a long hall together or ride up in an elevator. Small talk about traffic or the weather may help you both feel more at ease. Once in the office, motioning or asking the client where he or she would like to sit is a good way to get started. As much as possible, given the many configurations of offices, be sure that your space is private as possible.

You may share your role with your client and how you became involved in the case. This is also a good place for client introduction. The social worker's opening statements should affirm the client's experience as they relate to the helping situation. The social worker also needs to normalize the client's feelings by acknowledging that this can be a difficult and uncomfortable process. Finally, it is important for clients to feel a sense of hope that change is possible through the helping relationship. Once you have covered the introductory topics, it is helpful to ask if the client has any questions (Ragg, 2011). Discussing the parameters of client confidentiality and informed consent should also be included in the introductory segment of the session.

An open-ended question, such as "Can you tell me what brought you in?," "I have read the reports, can you tell me how you see the situation?," or "What do you see as the problem?," can help begin the first session. These open-ended questions invite the client to tell you his or her story. Of course, not all clients are willing to (or interested in) jump right into the problem, so be patient. You may need to ask a series of related questions, trying each one out until one finally hits a note for the client. But be careful not to come across as an interrogator, as the client will likely feel defensive and frustrated. During this early stage of the relationship, building trust and developing an atmosphere of care and concern is essential if the helping relationship is to move forward. Sometimes a statement as simple as "How can I help you today?" can give the client hope that help is here and prompt him or her to tell the story.

The First Home Visit and Beyond

Social workers have been making home visits since the days of "friendly visitors." Given our commitment to the person-in-environment perspective, a social worker can best understand a client's life situation by viewing, participating, and joining in it. Many helping professionals see clients only in their office and never have the opportunity to witness what day-to-day life is like for their clients. The benefits of a home visit often outweigh the limitations. For example, one of the authors experienced visiting a teenage client's home, taking note that there was not a single picture of the client anywhere. The client's sense of lack of place and belonging was confirmed by this glaring omission in her home and life. There were no markers of her presence in the house. Although the client had talked about her feelings of isolation and being unwanted, observing how the family interacted with her and one another spoke volumes about her day-to-day life. This home visit gave the author/social worker a new appreciation for her client's sadness and sense of desperation to leave home.

Clients come from a wide range of socioeconomic backgrounds. For example, you may make a home visit to a very wealthy family with poor parenting skills or a family in which drugs and alcohol are pervasive and the home situation is chaotic. Given that social workers are committed to working with the vulnerable populations, you will visit families living in housing projects, trailer parks, rooming houses, group homes, and so on. In fact, you can never fully anticipate what you will see on the other side of the door. It is important to understand that many of your clients may live in ways or circumstances that do not meet your standards of hygiene. Be careful not to communicate your displeasure or discomfort. This is your client's home.

With time and commitment, you may eventually be able to assist in helping your client to develop better housekeeping skills, but unless the situation is deemed a public health hazard, try to relax. Take time to observe the surroundings and learn about how your client lives. Always seek information on acceptable behaviors, courtesies, customs, and expectations that are unique to the clients of specific cultures, religions, and ethnic groups (Goode, 1999). Always think to yourself, what are some of the societal obstacles and barriers that contribute to this client's life difficulties?

In reality, most clients you will see on a home visit are not dangerous and are often glad to see a social worker. For example, the client Mrs. Anderson is relieved to see Nicole. Because Mrs. Anderson has multiple sclerosis, her mobility is limited. Having a social worker come to her home is more convenient for the client, and Nicole also has the opportunity to see how Mrs. Anderson is managing. Mrs. Anderson also refers to case aides who visit as well as a homemaker who assists her with some of her more physically challenging chores. Because several people a week are visiting Mrs. Anderson, she feels supported (and maybe a bit intruded on), but the workers are able to keep a pulse on how she is managing given her medical condition. Any changes or limitations in her ability to manage independently because of her multiple sclerosis, age, energy level, ability to get up and down stairs, driving, and caring for Maria's daily needs can be assessed during the visits.

If you have a concern about your safety, talk with your supervisor, take advantage of self-defense classes, and always pay attention to environmental cues, such as poor street lighting, large groups of people congregating, high bushes and shrubbery, loose animals, or an individual carrying a weapon. Wear a name tag and carry a business card or another form of identification as a way of assuring the client that you are a worker from a social service agency. Generally speaking, don't enter a client's home if you suspect drugs or alcohol are in use. (Of course, if you are a child protection worker, you may have to enter potentially dangerous situations. It is a good idea to ask for a police escort if you anticipate the threat of violence.) Once in a client's home, remember you are a guest. Attend to the family customs, religious beliefs and folk beliefs, and cultural courtesies, such as acknowledging first the oldest member of the household when visiting an Asian American family. In some cultures, such as African American, small talk may be perceived as unprofessional. Don't appear hurried during the visit. You want to convey your full and undivided attention. Ask where to sit; if offered food or drink, it is polite to accept.

Watch this segment with Mrs. Anderson and Nicole. How does meeting Mrs. Anderson in her home help to further the relationship? Are there any environmental/safety concerns that Nicole may have as she is walking in to her home?

It may be helpful to suggest a quiet private space to talk if there are a lot of people around. Sometimes the client puts up barriers, such as loud music, the TV blaring, or a dog barking, as a way to communicate that "I don't want to be meeting with you." It is important to acknowledge that you are not necessarily a welcomed guest. By acknowledging this reality, you may help to reduce the obstacles and work toward collaboration.

Although home visits can be scary, there is no better way to learn about your clients. Visits also give you insight into environmental barriers of the neighborhood, such as lack of public transportation, grocery stores, wheelchair accessibility, and safe parks. For some clients, just the day-to-day task of getting up and facing the world can be truly overwhelming. Being nonjudgmental and supportive can provide the client with hope.

In the example in Box 8.8, Julie, the outreach social worker, expects to discuss LaTonya's disease with Mrs. Moore. What she had not anticipated is the issue of Mrs. Moore's pregnancy and its impact on her life. She shifted gears and began to assess the additional family stress rather than focusing strictly on LaTonya's physical health. Julie presents herself as caring and nonjudgmental, and therefore Mrs. Moore. appears to be willing to engage in the helping relationship. She sees Julie as a partner and feels hopeful that LaTonya's situation (and her family's situation) may improve.

Box 8.8 LaTonya's Home Visit

LaTonya Moore. is a 12-year-old female. She is currently living with her mother and father. She has a younger brother, Dion, age eight. LaTonya has sickle cell anemia disease, an inherited blood disorder that causes anemia (shortage of blood cells) and periodic pain due to sickle-shaped blood cells. LaTonya is more vulnerable to infections and has a hard time fighting them off once they start. Because of this disease, she is considered to have delayed growth and is very slightly built for her age. Both her parents are employed by a local grocery store: her father is the 11 P.M.–7 A.M. manager, and her mother is the head cashier.

The school's outreach social worker, Julie, was notified by the seventh-grade teacher that LaTonya was tired, lacked energy, and appeared to be in pain much of the time. Julie contacted the family and identified herself as the outreach social worker, explained the reason for her call, and asked about coming out to meet them. Mrs. Moore agreed to meet her in their home the following day. In preparation for the visit, Julie read the school file. There was little information except that LaTonya was diagnosed with sickle cell disease when she was a baby. Julie read some information about the disease (she downloaded information from the sickle cell disease website at www.sicklecelldisease.org). Julie talked to LaTonya's teacher, Mrs. Berry, in order to get a better understanding of how LaTonya is managing in her classes both academically and socially. Finally, Julie consulted with the school nurse, who has been involved in LaTonya's medical care since she came to the middle school. The nurse indicated that LaTonya has frequent bouts or flare-ups related to her disease. LaTonya has missed 10 or more days of school over the past semester. There was no social history or any other information regarding the family in the school records.

Julie is relatively new to her position. She doesn't know the neighborhood well and asked Mrs. Moore. for directions. Julie arrived on time. Knowing that Mr. Moore. was sleeping, she knocked on the door. Latoya's younger brother, Dion, answered the door. Julie introduced herself and gave Mrs. Moore her business card.

Social Worker: Hi, Mrs. Moore, I spoke to you on the phone yesterday. My name is Julie.

Box 8.8 LaTonya Home Visit *(Continued)*

Mrs. Moore: Hello, did you have any trouble finding us?

Social Worker: No not at all, you gave me great directions.

Mrs. Moore: Come on in; do you want something to drink?

Social Worker: A glass of water sounds good. (She is aware of the offer and doesn't want to offend Mrs. Moore by saying, "No, thank you.") I am a social work intern at University College. Thanks for meeting with me today.

Mrs. Moore: So why are you here?

Social Worker: As I mentioned on the phone, LaTonya's teacher, Mrs. Berry, is concerned about her and her health and asked if I would come out to talk with you and Mr. Moore

Mrs. Moore: LaTonya is fine; she is fine.

Social Worker: Mrs. Berry did mention that LaTonya has missed 10 days of school since the beginning of January. Sometimes when LaTonya is in class, she is tired and has trouble staying awake.

Mrs. Moore: Well, she goes to bed on time, and I make sure that she gets plenty of rest when she is home. This is the first time the school has contacted me about LaTonya.

Social Worker: Sorry if my visit is catching you off guard.

Mrs. Moore: Well, yes it is, but tell me more about what is going on at school.

Social Worker: I know that LaTonya has sickle cell anemia disease, and the teacher was wondering if LaTonya was having any flare-ups, which might be the reason she is so tired at school. Mrs. Berry also mentioned that LaTonya is having trouble concentrating during her classes.

Mrs. Moore: Maybe it is the sickle cell causing her these problems, but she hasn't had any flare-ups or infections recently. She has been eating okay, and I take her to see the doctor when she is sick. I know she has been missing some school, but I make sure that we catch up on all her work.

Social Worker: Okay, if it isn't the sickle cell anemia causing her tiredness in school, what do you think it could be?

Mrs. Moore: I don't know; I try to keep up with all her appointments, but sometimes it does get so busy around here that I have to cancel or reschedule appointments. I don't do it very often, but . . . things just get so busy here. I have to find a sitter for Dion, and my work schedule is busy too. My husband sleeps during the day, so he doesn't help much.

Social Worker: So most of LaTonya's health care falls on you.

Mrs. Moore: Yeah, it does, and normally I can handle everything, but I am four months pregnant, and I have been feeling kinda run down myself.

Social Worker: You have a lot going on. You are very concerned about her and do what you can to keep her healthy. Let's talk about what is going on here.

Mrs. Moore: Well, I have the kids, I work all day, and my husband works all night. I don't get any breaks, and if I have to go somewhere, there is no one to help me out. I know that LaTonya wants to play with other girls and have friends, but I am not here, so I say "No." She does watch Dion sometimes but not that often. One thing for sure, we love her. I really want to protect her, I thought I had.

Social Worker: Well, there are some ways that the school can help you and LaTonya. There is a Girl Scout troop that meets once a week after school. One of the teacher assistants, Mrs. Chin, is the troop leader. She is really nice, and the girls do all kinds of fun things.

Mrs. Moore: I can't pick her up after Girls Scouts because I have to be here when the bus drops Dion off.

Social Worker: I don't know if this is possible, but there is a late bus that takes kids home once all the activities have ended. She may be able to ride that bus. I can check into that for you.

Mrs. Moore: Oh, I think she would like that. Do they have a tutor for her after school too? Maybe she could get some help with her homework. I just want her to do well in school; she has so many other things to get her down.

Social Worker: When you say "get her down," what do you mean?

Mrs. Moore: You know, it is hard for her to feel like everyone else. We try to keep up with everything. Now I am pregnant again. Dion is fine, but . . .

Social Worker: Are you worried that this baby will have sickle cell too?

Mrs. Moore: They tell me it's 50-50. I want them to tell me everything will be fine.

(Continued)

Box 8.8 LaTonya Home Visit *(Continued)*

Social Worker: (Silence)

Mrs. Moore: There is nothing I can do but wait.

Social Worker: Well, the school nurse was telling me about a group for parents who have kids with sickle cell. I know you have a lot going on, but maybe we could find someone to stay with LaTonya and Dion. It might be helpful to talk to other parents.

Mrs. Moore: The other social worker had mentioned that a few years ago. We did go once, Mr. M. and me, but I was not comfortable talking. That's what my sister and my church are for.

Social Worker: I would be happy to get you some information.

Mrs. Moore: Well, that might be okay, but I don't think a support group is for me.

Social Worker: One positive about talking with other parents is they know about resources and specialists.

Mrs. Moore: Okay, I will think about it and talk to Mr. M. I want to meet with LaTonya's teachers too. I will call Dr. Good tomorrow and see if she can see her this week.

Social Worker: I would be happy to drive LaTonya to Dr. Good's office, if that would help you out.

Mrs. Moore: That would be great; her office is on the other side of town. I will call her office, and can I get back to you about the appointment time?

Social Worker: Sure. I will check into the Girl Scouts and tutoring and let you know what I find out the next time we meet.

Mrs. Moore: Okay.

Signs of Successful Client Engagement

You have worked hard to join with your client, and there is now a connectedness and commitment on your client's part to move forward and make some changes. You have covered all the basics, and now it is time to get down to work. It can be very difficult to maintain a sense of direction and focus, and without a goal to work toward, clients will lose motivation and interest.

Frame the client's concerns or problems for work in terms that are meaningful to the client. Ask the client about what changes he or she wants to make. Social worker–driven goals provide no incentive for the client to change, but a goal that is truly meaningful to the client may spark action. Mutually agreeing on goals and objectives is the keystone to effective partnering.

Ragg (2011) identifies a four-step approach to reframing the problem in an effort to move forward. This four-step approach is summarized in Box 8.9.

Referring back to the case of LaTonya, her parents, and the outreach social worker, Julie, there is an agreement now about how to move forward in defining goals and interventions. Mrs. Moore has successfully engaged in the helping process, as indicated by her willingness to meet with Julie again and to contact LaTonya's physician about her medical condition. Julie has agreed to locate child care services for the family and a tutor for LaTonya and to explore options related to age-appropriate activities (and fun ones), such as Girl Scouts. Providing specific services, such as providing LaTonya with a ride to the doctor's office, is essential if LaTonya is to receive the medical care and the emotional care she needs. As in this case, once the client (who really is Mrs. Moore as well) has begun to reframe the problems into more workable solutions, you can join together, developing a plan of action that feels manageable, and provide realistic ways to move forward. Small and incremental steps work best. Start with the big picture, the long-term goals, and work backward, taking one step at a time.

Box 8.9 Reframing the Problem

1. Listen to the client and understand the client's definition of the problem—How does the client explain his or her situation? How does the client experience it? Does the client feel challenged or thwarted by it?
2. Identify the elements of the client's current understanding of the problem that may interfere with solving the problem—Often, the client's perspective is clouded by conflicting factors. Clients may experience multiple, and shifting feelings about the situation. It is also important to understand how feelings contribute to behavioral actions. Who else is involved in the problem? What are the dynamics of those relationships? Does the client feel hopeful?
3. Identify the important themes, constructs, and language that the client identifies with the problem—Themes of loss, powerlessness, and hopelessness can keep the client from seeing any possible solution. The duration of these feelings and ongoing and repeated patterns and experiences can contribute to the client feeling overwhelmed.
4. Create an alternative definition—Clients can see that change is possible if given the opportunity. Asking questions such as "How would you like things to be for you six months from now?," "If you could make the current situation different (or better), what would it look like?," or "You wake up tomorrow and things are better; what has happened while you were sleeping?" can provide a new way of looking at an old problem, meaning that it is fixable, even if only in small but often compelling ways.

In Case Study #4 of Maria and Mrs. Anderson, the long-term goal may be Maria's reunification with her mother, Crystal. However, the reality of Crystal's life circumstances may very well preclude Maria's return home. In this case, it may be more realistic to work on goals to help Maria adjust to life with her grandmother. Concurrently, as Maria's situation becomes more stable, Nicole, can also work with Crystal in an effort to find employment, drug and alcohol treatment, safe housing, and other supports that she will need in order to become an effective parent to Maria. Taking each one of these goals and breaking them into small and manageable pieces will help Crystal feel successful and help maintain her motivation to regain custody of Maria. Nicole can also help Mrs. Anderson identify ways to make this transition more manageable. What kinds of resources might be beneficial to her during this stressful time? "Success" is a relative term. What is success to you may be quite different from the client's definition. A good way to evaluate success is to continually assess the client's level of motivation and commitment to goal setting and problem solving. As social workers, we play the roles of collaborator, advocate, teacher, broker, and so on, but the client must do the work. The social worker can encourage and assist in this process, but ultimately it is the client's self-determination that will shape the outcome of the helping relationship.

As you develop an ongoing relationship with your client, you will witness mood shifts, interest levels varying, and motivation waxing and waning. A relationship that spans many sessions (or months) will be different from a short-term crises-oriented one. Regardless of the time commitment, continuing to convey interest and concern is the key to the helping process. Knowing the parameters of the relationship can help you work more effectively and efficiently. For example, in the case of Mrs. Kita, the social worker, Diane, has been meeting with her for over four months. The nature of the relationship has changed from formality to more openness and ease. As always, Diane has to be mindful of cultural differences and never presume to be a part of Mrs. Kita's "family or inner circle." You can see how the nature of the relationship is changing as they work toward Mrs. Kita's goals together.

A challenge of maintaining an ongoing relationship with a client is staying engaged and connected. As hard as it may be to hear the client tell the same story over and over again, the social worker demonstrates patience by listening with openness. Sometimes the smallest detail or change in status can lead to an entirely different direction in the helping process. Be aware of opportunities to assist the client from point A to point B. Don't be discouraged if the relationship does not progress. Sometimes the change is slow, or there is no notable change at all. Remember the old expression that you can lead a horse to water, but you can't make it drink. Using the systems theory approach, any interaction causes a reaction, even if the change is not readily noted.

? Assess your understanding of meeting the client by taking this brief quiz.

SUMMARY

- The overall goal of the helping relationship is to assist in improving the well-being of clients. How each individual social worker meets this lofty goal may vary greatly in style and creativity; however, varying approaches should be grounded in the same knowledge base, skills, and social work values and ethics. Remember to be yourself. Always be open to learning from your clients. Follow the NASW *Code of Ethics*; seek help, guidance, and information when needed; and use your supervisor's expertise and experience to guide you along the way. As you progress through the remaining stages of the helping process, keep in mind that the initial stages of intake and engagement are the building blocks to the relationship.
- In this chapter, you have learned how to initiate the intake process and the importance of developing rapport. Engaging with the client is critical if the relationship is to continue.
- You have learned the importance of understanding and reflecting on self as an essential tool in helping others.
- You have learned how to conduct a visit with a client, whether in an office or in a home and ways to minimize potential risk to yourself or others.

APPLY IT

1. Review session 1 of **Interactive Case #3** of Mike and social worker Karen. What did Karen do or not do to establish a helping relationship with Mike? Consider at least two ways that Karen could have improved in this area.
2. Review sessions 1 and 2 of **Interactive Case #4** of Maria, Mrs. Anderson, and social worker Nicole. Consider what Nicole did and said to convey care and concern regarding Maria and her relationships with her mother and grandmother. What would you say and do to communicate to Mrs. Anderson that you understand her situation? Identify at least two ways Nicole was able to maintain balance between understanding Mrs. Anderson's health concerns and being the care provider to Maria and also encouraging her to explore the nature of the mother–daughter relationship.

Assess Your Competence

Use the scale below to rate your current level of achievement on the following concepts or skills associated with each competency presented in the chapter:

1	2	3
I can accurately describe the concept or skill	I can consistently identify the concept or skill when observing and analyzing practice activities	I can competently implement the concept or skill in my own practice

_______ Can differentiate between rapport and empathy and describe the importance of each.

_______ Understands and can describe countertransference.

_______ Understands and can articulate the importance of social workers knowing their own needs and how lack of self-awareness can impact professional relationships with clients.

_______ Can identify and describe safety and engagement guidelines for home visits.

9

The Assessment Process

LEARNING OUTCOMES

- Demonstrate how to conduct a multidimensional assessment.
- Recognize how to use interviewing skills to assess a client's strengths.
- Apply interviewing skills to assess a client in his or her environment.
- Demonstrate how to use interviewing skills to assess a client's physical functioning and his or her overall well-being.
- Plan how to use interviewing skills to assess a clients' cognitive functioning.
- Demonstrate how to use interviewing skills to assess a client's spiritual and religious functioning.
- Explain how to use interviewing skills to assess a client's emotional functioning.
- Practice how to use interviewing skills to assess a client's behavioral functioning.
- Demonstrate how to use interviewing skills to assess a client's family and social support functioning.
- Demonstrate how to use interviewing skills to assess a client regarding suicide assessment.
- Synthesize material collected through the assessment process.

CHAPTER OUTLINE

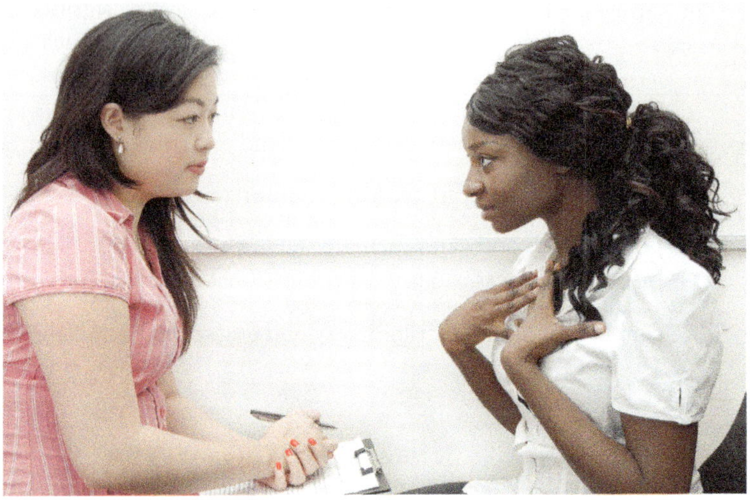

PAULA CONNELLY/E+/GETTY IMAGES

OVERVIEW OF ASSESSMENT

Assessment involves gathering information and synthesizing the information to develop a comprehensive picture of the client and his or her circumstances. It is the assessment process that sets the stage for all future work, including planning, contracting, interventions, evaluation, and termination. This chapter will explore the nature of the helping process through the lens of multidimensional assessment. Each agency, school, medical center, correctional facility, and so on has an assessment format that relates specifically to the population that it serves. An assessment completed at a medical center will focus primarily on discharge planning and what resources are needed for the patient on leaving. An assessment used to determine if a child has been physically and sexually abused would look quite different, with the social worker using dolls, puppets, or drawings to assist with the assessment. When assessing a client who is involved with the court system, there are some prescriptive areas to explore, such as history of criminal behaviors, precipitating events, support systems, and decision-making abilities. There are also areas of the client's life that are specific to that individual, for example, family of origin issues, the effects of poverty and marginalization, level of education and substance abuse/usage. From the initial intake meeting forward, the social worker is in a constant state of evaluating and examining the client's situation from different perspectives at any given time. It is helpful for the social worker to prepare for meeting with clients by becoming informed about the prevalent issues, demographics, and dynamics of the population of concern. For example, when working with a child who has been physically and sexually abused, understanding the secrecy surrounding the child, reviewing the literature for effective intervention methods, and consulting with a supervisor will help the social worker set a tentative agenda for the next meeting or the early stages of the helping process.

Assessment is a joint venture (Boyle, Hull, Mather, Smith, & Farley, 2011) between the client and the social worker that becomes the basis for developing the road map to planned change. The purpose of an assessment is to reach an understanding of the presenting problem, client, and situation so that the social worker, in collaboration with the client, can construct a plan of action to alleviate or at least mitigate the problem. Ultimately, the purpose of an assessment is to gather information that will contribute to the understanding necessary for appropriate planning (Compton, Galaway, & Cournoyer, 2005). In order to fully understand what the client is experiencing, it helps to look at the problem through a variety of lenses. Understanding the client's life from social, familial, biological, spiritual, emotional, cultural, behavioral, cognitive, and environmental perspectives lays the foundation for comprehensive social work practice. Keep in mind that an assessment is an ongoing process and a product. It is seeking information for the purpose of action (Compton et al., 2005). The process includes the social worker's knowledge about human behavior, theories that inform practice, an active thinking process, data collection, and an ability to synthesize information and develop insights. The assessment process also includes the client's understanding and insights during every phase of the helping process (Boyle et al., 2011). The product is the written report that documents all aspects of the client's situation, including a preliminary plan for change.

There are many different ways to collect assessment-related data. In this chapter, a multidimensional assessment process is presented that includes eight separate sections. Use these sections as a way to organize your report; however, it is important to note, these categories are overlapping and intersect in many places. As you read this chapter, keep in mind that these categories are artificial in some ways because as the social worker, your focus is on the "whole of the person," not one aspect of the client's life taking priority over another. Starting with the **strengths-based assessment**, each section will cover many different aspects of the client's circumstance. As a social worker, you will explore areas surrounding the client's physical and mental health, examining how spirituality and religion fit into the client's worldview and how thoughts, behaviors, and emotions can affect the client's situation. Consider ways in which family, social supports, and environmental factors can have a profound impact on the person's day-to-day life. This multidimensional assessment approach is comprehensive, far reaching, and thorough. Hepworth, Rooney, Rooney, Strom-Gottfried, and Larsen (2012) look at assessment from four vantage points: 1) the source of the material, such as client self-reporting and self-monitoring; 2) collateral contacts, such as a family member, a teacher, a physician, or a neighbor (with a signed release of information); 3) tools and measurement instruments, such as the Beck's Depression Inventory (Beck, 1996), the Index of Self-Esteem (Hudson, 2000), or the Substance Abuse Audit (World Health Organization, 2001); and 4) the professional experiences of social workers, including their practice wisdom and knowledge accumulated over time. It is through the assessment process that the definition and formation of the problems for work become more systematic and eventually narrowed down into manageable pieces.

? Gauge your understanding of assessments by taking this brief quiz.

THE MULTIDIMENSIONAL ASSESSMENT

Once the intake process and documentation have been completed, the social worker moves into the next phase of the helping process, assessment, and begins to gather information that will culminate in a multidimensional assessment. The social worker stays abreast of what is currently happening in the client's life by asking pertinent questions; following up with deeper, more probing questions; and ultimately weaving that information into an integrative whole. No matter what the situation or presenting problem, things are always changing in the client's life. Being flexible in your approach and open to new ways of seeing the client and his or her situation is a critical aspect of the helping process. Box 9.1 provides some examples of "opening" questions, used as a way to start an interview. Consider asking any of these questions throughout the helping process as a way to collect information about a client.

The goal of any assessment is to define the problem in such a way as to make the solution seem manageable. Initially, it is helpful to ask the client to describe the problem(s) in general terms. How does the client see the problem affecting him or her and other people in the client's life? What led the client to seek services at this particular time? What are the issues that are most pressing or concerning? Asking the client to discuss what brings him or her in today can give the social worker insight into what may be the presenting problem. It is always best to start with the client's definition of the problem. The social work value of "starting where the client is" is most important at this early phase of the relationship. The social worker may have some hunches that point in different directions, however, using rapport-building skills, asking probing questions, and linking patterns together while providing respect, support, and encouragement is usually the best approach.

As already mentioned, the areas to explore will depend on the reason for referral or the client's presenting problems.

Box 9.1 Opening Questions

Opening questions can include the following:

How are you today?

What are some of your specific concerns?

How can I help you figure out some of these concerns?

When you are most upset about these concerns, how do you manage?

What are some ways that you have solve problems in the past?

Who are the people in your life that you are most concerned about?

What are their concerns about you?

Watch as Mike presents himself as an occasional drinker who is a good employee with an almost flawless attendance record.

Mike's boss has referred him to Karen, the social worker, because he believes that Mike has a significant drinking problem. He believes the referral is unwarranted. What other information could Karen have collected as she begins to understand the problem from Mike's perspective?

Over the course of the first interview, Mike begins to see how his drinking may have a negative impact on his work and on his relationship with his wife. He agrees to complete an alcohol assessment and, eventually, to inpatient treatment. Through Karen's assessment of his drinking and the impact it has on all areas of his life, Mike finally takes his first steps toward recovery.

Anna is referred to Marie, the social worker, because of a medical crisis. Marie takes the necessary time to explore Anna's immediate needs and expectations. They discuss what can be done to assist Anna with resources, support, and care for her children. In the second interview, Anna is discussing how she is preparing for her upcoming hospitalization. Marie continues to assess the needs of the family by asking questions related to her life, coping skills, social and familial support, child care, finances, and the process of preparing for a long hospital stay. In session 3 several months later, Anna is home and now must deal with the reality of the cancer returning. Marie will continue to assess the needs of Anna and her family as she starts the next chapter of her life. It is clear the social worker is becoming more emotionally invested as she continues to assess Anna's needs. A deeper understanding of Anna's struggles, hopes, resources, strengths, and a plan of action comes into view.

Watch these three sessions and observe Anna and Marie moving toward a deeper relationship as time goes on. As you reflect on Anna's life circumstances, how can Marie be of further help to her?

Understanding all aspects of the client's life is central to completing a thorough assessment. Everything that you talk about with the client must have some basis in the reality of his or her life. For example, Jeanne is a 24-year-old single mother. Her three-year-old son, Shawn, was recently diagnosed with autism. The reason for the referral is fairly clear: learning more about autism, gaining support from the social worker, determining what Jeanne needs, and linking her to other service providers. As her social worker, ask questions that relate primarily to her son's diagnosis, her support systems, how she is managing, financial issues, and schooling. Assessing her coping skills, problem-solving skills, how she is adjusting to the diagnosis, her perceived level of responsibility for her son's diagnosis, her range of emotions, her support systems in place, and her internal strengths (hope, resiliency, and creativity) to carry on would be important aspects of the case to explore.

Assessment

Behaviors: Collect and organize data, and apply critical thinking to interpret information from clients and constituencies.

Critical Thinking Question: When completing a multidimensional assessment, how will you introduce the process to the client? Using the skill of information giving, practice specifically what you may say.

Evaluate your understanding of multidimensional assessments by taking this brief quiz.

Strengths-Based Assessment

There are as many ways to conduct a multidimensional assessment as there are articles and social work textbooks. One such approach is to shift to viewing possibilities and strengths rather than focusing on labels, pathology, and deficits. The strengths-based perspective is seen as a way to engage clients from a position of what is going well in their lives. It is the starting point to understand the client's natural talents, supports, and skills. One aspect any assessment must include is, "What are the strengths of the client" Acknowledging what is going well or right in a client's life can serve as the foundation for future work together. From this vantage point, the social worker communicates a shared vision of what can be accomplished together (Skovholt, 2005). By building on strengths, the client and social worker work toward increased understanding, motivation, self-esteem, resiliency, hope, and confidence in the future.

Saleebey (2012) presents the principles of the strengths perspective in social work practice. They are as follows:

1. Every individual, group, family, and community has strengths. Social workers must be respectful and interested in the narratives of these systems and in their collective history.
2. Trauma, abuse, illness, and struggle may be injurious, but they may also be a source of challenge and opportunity. Social workers must believe that through tragedy, clients can learn skills, acquire traits and capabilities, and develop personal attributes that are life affirming.
3. Assume that you do not know the upper limits of the capacity to grow and change. Always consider the individual, group, and community aspirations. Social workers must hold high expectations and share in the client's hopes, aspirations, and dreams.
4. We best serve our clients by collaborating with them. Social workers must consult with the client, understanding that our education, tools, and knowledge make up only half of the equation.
5. Every environment is full of resources. Social workers must believe that communities are full of possibilities. Each community has something to give, knows what is best for itself, forms partnerships, and develops strategies to get things done.
6. Caring, caretaking, and context. Social workers must adhere to the belief that all people need care and to be cared for. We must care for each other as a form of civic participation.

As indicated throughout this text, clients come to a social worker for many reasons. Some are required to interact with a social worker; others are seeking assistance for a specific problem. Rarely does a client come to a social worker out of curiosity or to gain self-enlightenment. The reasons are typically profound and affect many aspects of the client's day-to-day life.

Box 9.A introduces you to Henry, a college freshman. Put yourself in Henry's shoes and answer the following questions.

Box 9.A Now you try it . . . Strengths-Based Assessment: Case Study

Thinking from a strengths perspective, consider Henry, a freshman in college. Henry is feeling isolated from his friends and family and spends up to eight hours a day playing video games and watching sporting events on TV. He is not going to classes and rarely leaves his room. You have been called in by the resident assistant to talk with him. As the social work intern, you may have some strong negative feelings about Henry's choices, but if you want a relationship with Henry, you must validate his choices and see him as a person with skills and talents (such as his eye–hand coordination and the ability to stay focused on an activity). Henry is the expert on his life and is the best source of information and insight. You are in a short-term partnership. Assuming he is not in danger of harming himself, the best approach is to find a few strengths and work from there. Henry is more likely to commit to a plan that he creates, using his own skills and creativity, than one imposed on him. However, Henry is a challenging student who appears to be quite content.

From Henry's perspective, answer the following questions:

1. How does Henry view his life?
2. What does he do day to day?
3. Does he see himself as capable of making some changes in his daily routine?
4. What would his perfect day look like?
5. What motivates him?
6. What feels good to him, even for just a little while?
7. How might you get through to Henry?

Box 9.I introduces you to Lou Ann, as 23-year-old single parent. Using the strengths based perspective to understand her circumstances, answer the questions presented.

Box 9.I Theory into Practice—Strengths Based Perspective and Attachment Theory: Case Study

Attachment theory emphasizes the importance of the emotional bonds in relationships. These emotional ties are enduring to a special person, characterized by a tendency to seek and maintain closeness, especially during times of stress. Attachment is a lifelong, distinct behavioral system whose goal is proximity to the special person. Healthy attachment brings love, security, and joy; unhealthy attachment brings anxiety, grief, and depression (Bowlby, 1988).

As you read the case below, assess Lou Ann's situation from a strengths perspective. While considering her case, assess her attachments to other people in her life.

Lou Ann is a 23-year-old single mother. Mia, age two, was removed from her care 10 months ago after multiple "founded" reports of neglect. Since then, Mia has been living with Lou Ann's brother Mark in a relative foster care placement. Mark lives two hours away with his fiancée, Petra. Mia is doing well and is flourishing in their care. Lou Ann, on the other hand, is struggling to fulfill the conditions of her treatment plan. She is not going to counseling, and she dropped out of her support group. She is drinking again and refuses to leave urine drops at the outpatient treatment center. Lou Ann was attending a job force integration program but has not been there for several weeks. She told the social worker there is no reason to attend, as "the economy sucks, and no one is hiring anyway."

Lou Ann shared that her mother committed suicide four years ago from a prescription drug overdose. Her parents got a divorce when she was a junior in high school. At that time, she and Mark went to live with their grandparents, a loving couple living in a small rural community. Lou Ann's grandmother died a year ago after a long illness. Grandma Lilly did meet Mia, which was very important to Lou Ann. Lou Ann's father has a long history of depression and anxiety. He is on medication for both, but Lou Ann reports that she doesn't see any change in his "mean-spirited behaviors." She reports that her dad did bail her out of jail, and she is thankful she did not have to "rot" in there. While she was in jail on drug possession charges, she became increasingly more anxious and could not stop shaking. She reported that her mental state was at its worst and that at times she could not catch her breath. After her release, she disappeared for five weeks, losing all contact with family members.

(Continued)

Box 9.1 Theory into Practice—Strengths Based Perspective and Attachment Theory: *(Continued)*

Lou Ann contacted the social worker two weeks ago. She indicated that she was tired of running and wanted to make some changes in her life. In assessing her current situation, the social worker decided to meet her at the local library, as Lou Ann did not want to come to the office and she is living temporarily with a friend. On seeing Lou Ann, the social worker immediately notices that she is extremely thin and appeared tired. She was wearing a long-sleeved jacket on an 80-degree day, which caused the social worker to wonder about drug abuse or violence. The social worker smiles at Lou Ann, who starts to cry. She hangs her head down and softly says, "I need help."

Questions for session 1:

How might the social worker demonstrate care and concern?

What are Lou Ann's strengths?

What issues must the social worker address that are of immediate concern?

How can the social worker engage Lou Ann in the helping process?

Questions for session 2:

What are some issues that may be impeding Lou Ann from taking the necessary steps to get Mia back?

What needs to be in place for Mia's return?

Questions for session 3:

What issues could the social worker focus on while addressing Lou Ann's attachments or lack of attachments to significant people in her life?

How may her mother's suicide and grandmother's death affect Lou Ann and her ability to attach to Mia?

Using the strengths-based perspective, consider the following questions: What strategies may work to help Lou Ann start thinking about possibilities rather than barriers? What are her sources of support, and what are her options? What possibilities do you see for Lou Ann? When is she at her best, and under what circumstances? What about solutions? What would Lou Ann's miracle be?

Box 9.2 contains a wide range of questions that focus on client strengths. As you begin to familiarize yourself with the strengths-based approach, there are many ways to ask questions as part of a natural conversation. Choose questions and topics based on the nature of the client situation.

Analyze your understanding of strengths-based assessments by taking this brief quiz.

Box 9.2 Tips for Doing a Strengths-Based Assessment

What to include in a strengths-based assessment:

1. Believe in the client and his or her understanding of the facts (Hepworth et al., 2013).
2. Offer support and a shared vision of what is possible.
3. Look for personal and environmental strengths, such as where the problems occur and how they are managed.
4. Acknowledge the client's ability in facing problems, venting, and seeking help.
5. Understand that there are barriers to change that are outside of the client's control.
6. Appreciate the client's willingness to be open and share information with a stranger.
7. Focus on the client's perseverance in times of stress and showing resilience.
8. Appreciate the client for being resourceful and creative, such as managing on a very limited budget.
9. Acknowledge that the client is seeking skills, education, and knowledge.

Box 9.2 Tips for Doing a Strengths-Based Assessment *(Continued)*

10. Express care and understanding about family and friends, such as the role of each person in the family and where they fit into the unit.
11. Encourage the assertion of one's rights versus being satisfied with the status quo.
12. Acknowledge the client's responsibilities in work and meeting financial obligations.
13. Encourage the client's capacity for introspection and weighing alternatives.
14. Acknowledge when the client shows self-control, even when pushed to the brink.
15. Understand the pressure from the external world pushing on the client, and yet the client gets up every day and starts the routine all over again.
16. What is the client's ability to adapt to change?
17. Appreciate the client's ability to consider a variety of ways to get to the same result and his or her flexibility in thinking.
18. Celebrate the client's natural talents, acquired skills, and uniqueness.
19. Embrace the client's cultural ethnicity, social network, and religion as strengths.
20. Strive to understand the client's personal history and what the client needs, wants, and hopes for.
21. Understand what motivates the client. Is it to get his or her children back? get off drugs? pass a class?
22. Assess and develop the environment and community resources.
23. Acknowledge that self-esteem is based on accomplishments and a sense of personal power (Miley, O'Melia, & DuBois, 2013).
24. Understand that the client has successful relationships in other arenas.
25. Understand the value and meaning of immigration status and the political relationship with the client's country of origin. For example, if the client is from Iraq, what are some issues the client may feel being in the United States at this point in time?
26. Look for strengths. (What do you want your world to look like? What is going right? Who are the people [system] you know you can count on no matter what? Where/when do you feel most like the person you want to be? Describe how you make decisions. When are you most proud of yourself? How does a person very close to you describe the best parts of who you are?)

Sources: Hepworth et al. (2013); Miley et al. (2013); Rothman (2008); Saleebey (2012); Skovholt (2005).

Watch this clip as James attempts to affirm some of Anthony's strengths. Identify at least two additional strengths that you see in this client.

Person-In-Their-Environment Assessment

Looking at a client's functioning within their environment calls attention to difficulties as well as strengths. It focuses on function and dysfunction or balance and imbalance between persons and their environment. Social functioning is identified and described in terms of social role performance. Social role performance is understood as one's ability to fulfill role expectations across the multiple roles of a client's life, for example, how a client fulfills his or her role of employee in terms of company policies, such as showing up to work on time and absenteeism, or in relation to meeting the job expectations for which the person was hired. Clients are also assessed on the roles in their personal lives, such as parent and spouse (Karls & Wandrei, 1994).

Conducting a **person-in-their environment assessment** provides a way to analyze the complexities of clients' lives, including the biological, psychological, physical, and social aspects. It is best described as a method for understanding the whole problem focusing on all aspect of the client's life.

When assessing the client's environment and physical surroundings, remember that some people live in institutional settings. These clients have fewer personal options or choices, as their self-determination may be significantly impacted. The client's living environment may be regulated in a setting such as a rehabilitation hospital, a group home, a residential treatment facility, a juvenile detention center, or a nursing home. Assist clients with personalizing their living space as much as possible. Pictures from home, comfortable and sturdy furniture, and clean bedrooms, bathrooms, and common spaces are essential. If the minimum standards of sanitation and care are not met, it is your responsibility as a social worker to advocate on the client's behalf.

Box 9.3 introduces you to a variety of ways to assess the client's environment.

In Box 9.II, looks at Charlene (the individual) through an environmental lens.

Diversity and Difference in Practice

Behaviors: Apply self-awareness and self-regulation to manage the influence of personal biases and values in working with diverse clients and constituencies. Apply and communicate understanding of the importance of diversity and difference in shaping life experiences in practice at the micro, mezzo, and macro levels

Critical Thinking Question: Where did you grow up? What did your home look like? What did your neighborhood look like? Was there a park nearby? Could you walk to school? Did you feel safe in your home? Did you interact with people in your community? Were resources accessible to you? Have you ever visited a person living in a residential facility? What was that experience like for you?

Box 9.3 Tips for Doing a Person-in-Their-Environment Assessment

What to look for when assessing a client's environment:

1. Is there a goodness of fit between the client and the environment?
2. What are the client's unique needs in relationship to what the environment can offer (Hepworth et al., 2013)?
3. Where does the client live, and with whom?
4. Is it a stable living arrangement?
5. Determine the affordability of housing. For example, is the housing safe, clean, and rodent free? Is the plumbing adequate? Is there hazardous clutter? Is there loose carpeting or unstable flooring?
6. Is the neighborhood safe? Do police survey the area?
7. Describe the interior and exterior of the client's home. (If you are a social worker within a licensing unit, these questions will be much more specific.)
8. Is there accessible and affordable public transportation?
9. Where does the client live in relation to schools, the community center, social service providers, work, parks, legal services, grocery stores, fire station, emergency medical response units, and day care?
10. Consider the role of social services in the client's life. How involved is the formal social service community?
11. Does the client receive monetary or in-kind benefits from the local social service community? What is the availability of resources?
12. Does the client have a place of worship? Is the client affiliated with a particular religion or culture?
13. Is there an adequate level of financial or donated resources to help sustain the family?
14. What are the formal and informal support systems or networks, such as a place of worship?
15. What skills can the client develop to help him or her navigate more effectively within his or her environment?
16. How does poverty impact the client's life?
17. Does the client have enough money to meet basic needs?
18. Look for strengths. (How does the client manage on a limited budget? What are some strategies the client uses to make the environment safe? How does the client navigate from point A to point B? Who provides support in the client's life? How does your client define resiliency?)

Box 9.II Theory into Practice—Person in their Environment Assessment: Case Study

When assessing a client's functioning within his or her environment, it is helpful to examine the client's function/dysfunction or balance/imbalance. Assessing a client's social functioning helps to determine the client's ability to fulfill multiple role expectations in his or her life (Karls & Wandrei, 1994).

As you consider this case, you are a social worker in a rehabilitation center working with Charlene.

Dennis, aged 35, and Charlene, aged 33, have lived together for the past 12 years. They met when they were in college and have been in a committed relationship since. Two months ago, Charlene was in a serious car accident that left her paralyzed from the waist down. Currently, she is in an excellent rehabilitation program approximately three hours away from home. She is slowly making progress, but at times she is so depressed and despondent that she is unable to get out of bed. To make matters worse, her private medical insurance is running out, and she will be transferred to a long-term nursing facility closer to home. Charlene desperately wants to be home with Dennis. However, Dennis has shared with you that he does not believe that he can care for Charlene. Although he visits her on the weekends, he does not want to take on the day-to-day responsibility of her care. His professional life is very busy, and he travels three or four times per month. You have encouraged Dennis to talk to Charlene about his fears and anxiety about being her primary caregiver. Yesterday, Charlene's medical team met to discuss her discharge plan. Dennis was not present at the meeting, nor did he call to say that he would not be there. He has not returned either Charlene's calls or your calls. Charlene is convinced that he no longer loves her and that he is leaving her for good. She feels so overwhelmed with grief and worry that she is unable to complete thoughts or sentences. The nurse in charge of her care is so concerned about her emotional state that she has called in the crisis response team.

As you think about this case, what environmental factors do you need to consider when working with Charlene? When working in the rehabilitation center? What if she goes home with Dennis? What are some of your concerns regarding the relationship between Charlene and Dennis?

How would you like this situation to be resolved? Consider both short-term and long-term goals.

Watch this clip as Kim talks about her mother's death, her sister's disengagement with her, and her lack of a support network. As you watch it, think about her time in the military and how she describes her friends and life in Afghanistan. What are some areas of concern that you would want to address with her as you get to know her better?

Analyze your understanding of person-in-their-environment assessment by taking this brief quiz.

Physical Functioning and Well-Being Assessment

Assessments can also focus on clients' **physical functioning and well-being**. Physical functioning can impact clients' ability to care for themselves and make sound decisions. Factors of physical functioning encompass physical characteristics, health, genetic history, and drug and alcohol usage. In determining a client's health status, there are standard questions that are routinely asked, such as the date of the client's last health exam, medications currently taken, and a history of medical issues. When conducting an assessment, it is always important to consider that many health-related problems can be linked to multiple factors. For example, when assessing someone with a behavioral disorder, it will be important to consider a wide range of health factors that may contribute to the presenting problem, such as attention deficit disorder, lead poisoning, hormonal imbalance, diabetes, and dementia (Hepworth et al., 2013). Risky behaviors, such as unprotected sex or

Assessment

Behaviors: Collect and organize data, and apply critical thinking to interpret information from clients and constituencies.

Apply knowledge of human behavior and the social environment, person-in-environment, and other multidisciplinary theoretical frameworks in the analysis of assessment data from clients and constituencies.

Critical Thinking Question: You are a social worker in a domestic violence shelter. A client came to the door with several bags filled with clothing and covered in bruises. You welcome her in and get her settled. After she has been in the shelter two full days, you two sit down to complete an assessment. What aspect of the assessment will you focus on first, second, third, and fourth? Explain why you have chosen to ask questions and to explore the related issues in that order.

sharing of needles, may have negative health-related consequences. Always consider the possible medical or health-related roots to the problem before looking for other possible explanations.

The client's religious beliefs can have a significant relationship to the problem. For example, religious beliefs may dictate food choices, customs on death and birth, use of modern conveniences, organ donation, use of blood products, or tattoos (Hepworth et al., 2013). In fully understanding a client, consider how religious and cultural practices can support or deter him or her from services. Does the client seek the consultation of a rabbi or priest, a faith healer, a tarot card reader, prayer circles, a shaman, or an indigenous healer from within his or her community? How has the family coped with present and past illnesses? Regardless of your personal beliefs about health care, always be respectful of the client's beliefs and practices.

The client's physical functioning and well-being is an area that will be reassessed over the course of the relationship. For example, consider Nori, the chronically ill child in case #5. If we focus on the physical aspects of an assessment, the social worker would gather information about the diagnosis, treatment options, and financial and insurance coverage; support from family, school, and the medical community; medical needs being met; and possible developmental or physical delays related to his illness. We know from the interview that Nori has been hospitalized many times throughout his life and that the toll this is taking on his family is getting progressively more difficult. He will have two more surgeries during the time the social worker is involved with the Kita family. Over time, as Nori's health improves, the social worker and Mrs. Kita begin working on her finances, her relationship with her husband Jirou, and planning for the future.

Watch this clip as Mrs. Kita talks about all of Nori's health problems. As the social worker, what are some of the possible barriers to health care and support for Mrs. Kita as she tries to provide for him, his sister, and her mother?

Mrs. Anderson is a person with multiple sclerosis who has occasional flare-ups, especially during times of stress. The assessment in her case would focus on the management of her symptoms, ongoing medical care, ability to complete all of her independent activities of daily living skills, ability to care for her granddaughter, medications, self-reporting on how she is managing her chronic illness, sources of support, and other health-related issues she may want to discuss.

Watch this clip. Look for environmental clues to Mrs. Anderson's ability to navigate independently? As she has more difficulty managing her MS symptoms, how might a social worker intervene to assist her?

Box 9.4 introduces you to a list of questions and points regarding how to assess a client's physical health and well-being. The list includes several items that look beyond the individual and to the systems in place to either assist the client or serve as a barrier to health care.

Box 9.B asks a series of questions related to Inez, a 14-year-old female. These questions focus primarily on her health, home, school life, and ways that she interfaces with the wider community.

? Evaluate your understanding of physical functioning and well-being assessments by taking this brief quiz.

Box 9.4 Tips for Doing a Physical Functioning and Well-Being Assessment

What to look for when considering the client's physical health and well-being functioning:

1. Determine the age and life stage of the client.
2. Describe the client's general health, including any known illnesses, diseases, substance abuse issues, physical abuse, and prescription and over-the-counter medications.
3. What is the cost of medication, and can the client pay?
4. What is the client's history of hospitalizations, including medical and psychiatric? What is the date of the last physical exam?
5. Does the client have access to medical care? For example, is there a health clinic in the community, or is the emergency room the only after-hours option for care?
6. What is the family medical history? Is there a family history of heart problems, diabetes, stroke, or genetic disorder?
7. How does the client cope with illness?
8. Describe how the client presents himself or herself: Dress? Baseball cap covering eyes? Tattoos?
9. What is the client's perception of self? How does the client describe himself or herself?
10. Is the client well rested and dressed appropriately for the weather?
11. Assess the client's level of comfort in the present surroundings.
12. Are the client's nutritional needs being met?
13. What is the client's activity level and degree of physical mobility?
14. What are the client's sleeping patterns?
15. How does the client's describe his or her body image?
16. Assess for substance abuse
17. Identify the client's history of mental illness, both chronic and acute.
18. What are the client's independent activities of daily living skills, such as independence in dressing, getting to work on time, and housekeeping skills?
19. Does the client have unmet dental and eye care needs?
20. Look for the nonverbal clues as to general health, such as tremors, using an assistive device, stuttering, or paralysis.
21. What are the critical health issues, developmental delays, and milestones?
22. Assess the client's mental health status. What are the symptoms? Is the client intoxicated? Is the client oriented to time, place, and day?
23. What is the client's relevant sexual history, such as physical or sexual abuse?
24. What are the client's physical talents and skills?
25. Where and what are the stressors, both internal and external, in the client's life?
26. Look for strengths.

Box 9.B Now You Try It . . . Physical Functioning and Wellbeing Assessment: Case Study

Inez is a 14-year-old female, neatly dressed and looking very sad. She is currently living with her mother, a part-time city bus driver. She was referred to you, the school outreach worker, after repeatedly being bullied by other eighth graders. From reading the intake report, you know that Inez lives in a community with a high poverty rate. You know that her neighborhood does not have a full-service grocery store, a medical clinic, or a safe park. Because of her mother's limited

(Continued)

Box 9.B Now You Try It . . . Physical Functioning and Wellbeing Assessment: *(Continued)*

income, Inez receives free lunches through the National School Lunch Program. Inez is a young person who is morbidly obese, weighing 200 pounds. As Inez sits down, she can barely fit into your office chair. This is an embarrassing moment for both of you. Not wanting to address her weight directly, you ask her about school, her life at home, friends, and hobbies. She opens up about how much she hates school. She indicates that students call her offensive names and tease her. One student recently came up from behind her, pinched her arms, and then took off laughing. She tells you there is no one at school that she can go to for protection, including her teachers. Inez reports she recently heard a teacher referring to her as lazy. Her mother insists that she go to school, but even getting on the bus is difficult and embarrassing for her. You are very concerned about her weight, as you know many of the health complications that come from obesity. You are also concerned about her emotional health, as she appears depressed and angry. You want to rule out any medical issues, such as hormone problems, diabetes, an underactive thyroid, and other conditions, including some that are genetically based.

1. Referring back to Box 9.4, identify at least three health-related issues that factor into the well-being of Inez.
2. Identify four environmental concerns that you have regarding Inez's school, home, and community. (See Box 9.3.)
3. Identify five strengths of Inez. (See Box 9.2.)

Developing Cultural Competence Working with a Student Who Has Health Related Issues

Using Inez and her mother for this exercise, consider how the environment, including her home, school, and neighborhood, impact on who she is today. What steps must you take to assure them both that you are culturally competent? What are some of your assumptions about Inez and her mother? Put yourself in Inez's place, being labeled a "free-lunch" kid. How would you feel, knowing that you are "that student"? She is overweight and extremely self-conscious. As a social worker, how would you help her through the challenges of everyday life while at school?

Policy to Practice National School Lunch Program

The National School Lunch Program is a federally assisted meal program operating in over 100,000 public and nonprofit private schools and residential child care institutions. It provides nutritionally balanced, low-cost or free lunches to more than 31 million children each school day. Children from families with incomes at or below 130 percent of the poverty level are eligible for free meals. What type of assumptions do you hold regarding Federal programs such as this one?

Source: U.S. Department of Agriculture Food and Nutrition Service.

Cognitive Functioning

Many personal problems, troubling moods, and feelings are caused by faulty, irrational, and rigid thinking about the way things should be. Generally, people behave in ways that are consistent with their beliefs, values, and moral standards. How the client understands, thinks about, interacts with, and makes sense of the world is referred to as **cognitive functioning** (Sheafor & Horejsi, 2015). Our thought patterns are influenced by intellectual functioning, such as academic, social, street smarts, and common sense. Judgment, reality testing, coherence, cognitive flexibility, values, beliefs, self-concept, cultural belief systems, and the interaction among cognition, emotions, and behaviors influence social functioning (Hepworth et al., 2013). There are many reasons to explore the thought processes of a client. For example, can the client grasp simple directions, express himself or herself more abstractly, and find common connections between events and circumstances?

Watch this clip as Nicole and Maria talk about her hopes and wishes. Put yourself in Maria's place, what do you want Nicole to understand about your situation?

Consider how your client makes a decision: Are the alternatives weighed, does the client learn from past mistakes, and are others consulted? A person who makes impulsive decisions will often be in trouble with the law, with a family member, or with personal and professional finances. The social worker's role is to provide a counterbalance to these decisions by providing another way of thinking about the situation or circumstance. For example, Kylee is a 28-year-old graduate student. She is currently receiving a small stipend from the university to cover her monthly expenses. A credit card company offered her a "once in a life time offer," and she now owes $4,298. She took out a small Payday loan to cover a portion of her debt. When talking with Kylee about her financial situation, she discloses that she has never learned how to manage her money and that this is the second time she has declared bankruptcy. She doesn't want to talk to her parents, as they told her their help the first time was a "one-time-only offer." She has been mandated through the court to seek the services of a credit counselor (you), and she is sitting in your office crying uncontrollably. Through her tears, Kylee states, "I have no idea how I get myself into these messes, I am a total screw-up. I keep thinking this mess will just go away. I am the worst person in the whole world, and things will never get better." From the social worker's perspective, there were many choices along the way that could have changed the course of Kylee's financial ruin. The social worker and client begin to map out a realistic spending and saving plan, identify ways to find a balance between the cost/benefits of making a purchase, find ways to develop other forms of recreation and entertainment, and think through her short- and long-term goals. Understanding how Kylee thinks about money and makes decisions is the first step in helping her to move toward financial solvency. She does take full responsibility for getting herself into this situation, which is clearly one of her strengths.

When developing goals with a client, be sure to develop goals that are realistic and attainable. Always take into consideration the client's cognitive ability. Setting goals the client can meet will provide incentive to keep working. Using language the client understands will keep him or her engaged in the helping process. Box 9.5 provides a list of questions to consider when assessing a client's cognitive and intellectual functioning.

Box 9.6 introduces you to Dorothy, a client living in a memory support care facility. After familiarizing yourself with the case, answer the questions in Box 9.C.

Assess your understanding of cognitive functioning by taking this brief quiz.

Box 9.5 Tips for Doing a Cognitive Assessment

What to look for when considering the client's cognitive (and intellectual) functioning:

A. What is the client's thinking and understanding of the world?
1. What is the client's level of schooling? Is the client meeting the grade-level expectations?
2. What is the client's employment performance and history?
3. Does the client have the necessary skills and abilities to meet the expectations of an employer?
4. Does the client experience a sense of self-worth and confidence?
5. Is the client able to make decisions that emphasize self-efficacy, a belief in one's abilities?
6. What is the client's ability to follow a conversation?
7. Can the client express a sequence of events in a logical manner? For example, can the client recount what he or she did to get ready for the meeting today?
8. How does the client communicate with others?
9. What is the client's proficiency in his or her native language? Level of English proficiency?
10. Is the client able to think about possible solutions and ways to resolve issues?
11. Can the client ask for help?
12. Does the client show an aptitude for creativity?
13. Is the client optimistic and hopeful about the future?
14. Is the client able to articulate why and how the problem occurs?
15. Does the client blame circumstances rather than taking some personal responsibility?
16. Does the client understand the basics of work-related resources, such as medical insurance, employee assistance plans, and 401(k) benefits?
17. What does the client understand about the helping process (roles, confidentiality, and so on)?
18. Can the client read, write, and follow basic instructions? For example, is the client able to complete a simple math test?
19. Does the client understand how to access services within the community, such as legal services, medical care, and the library?

B. Does the client demonstrate distorted thinking?
20. Does the client have the ability to tell the difference between reality and fantasy? For example, does the client insist that there are people out to get him or her? Does the client ramble or have tangential thoughts that do not fit with the circumstances?
21. Explore the values and ideas the client holds. For example, a client might stay in a physically abusive marriage because she believes it is her husband's right to exercise control over her, even to the point of physical harm.
22. Check the client's mental status, such as orientation to time and place.
23. Determine whether the client understands time lines, such as current events and/or distant past.
    a) immediate—ability to recall things within seconds (can the client repeat a list of words?)
    b) short term—last 25 minutes (what did we talk about when I first came into your room?)
    c) recent memory—current events, situation within last few weeks (how long have you worked for your current employer?)
    d) remote—(where were you born, who was the president of the United States when your first child was born?) (Sheafor & Horejsi, 2015)
24. Assess the client's intellectual functioning; determine if there is a cognitive deficit, such as mental retardation/intellectual disability.
25. Does the client show insights into the problem? For example, can the client accept some responsibility for what happened? Does the client understand the concept of cause and effect?
26. Does the client demonstrate an ability to learn from past mistakes?
27. Does the client appear open to modifying misconceptions? For example, when presented with contrary evidence, can the client modify his or her idea about all teenagers being drug users or that social workers snatch children from their homes?
28. Can the client demonstrate flexibility in thinking? For example, is the client open to new ideas and ways to do things? Or does the client think in all-or-nothing terms? For example, do things appear black or white, good or bad, yes or no?

Box 9.5 Tips for Doing a Cognitive Assessment *(Continued)*

29. Does the client demonstrate faulty and inconsistent thought patterns? Does the client have distorted thinking, such as "All people who wear glasses are possessed by the devil" or "Everything is bad and will never get better"? Does the client always discount the positive? Overgeneralize? Use wishful thinking?
30. How does the client make decisions? For example, is the client impulsive (e.g., buys everything in sight or quits a job without prospects of finding another)? Can the client differentiate between necessity and want?
31. Can the client distinguish between rational and irrational beliefs?
32. Where are the stressors, both internal and external, in the client's life?
33. Look for strengths. (Identify examples of the client's past efforts at problem solving. What are some examples of good decisions?)

Source: For a full description of mental disorders, see Corcoran and Walsh (2014).

Box 9.6 Cognitive Assessment: Case Study

Dorothy resides at a memory support care facility in a small rural community. She is a person with a dual diagnosis of dementia and anxiety. Dorothy and her husband, Paul, recently celebrated their 55th wedding anniversary with a huge family gathering. A few weeks after the party, Dorothy's husband was diagnosed with cancer. On learning that he had cancer and needed chemotherapy treatments, he informed the nursing staff at the support care facility that he would not be able to visit Dorothy every day, as was his custom. Because of Dorothy's confusion and anxiety, he decided to not tell her about his treatments. To protect Dorothy from undue worry, on chemotherapy days he called Dorothy in the afternoon and told her he was at home sick with flu. Dorothy seemed to understand that Paul was sick and unable to visit her.

Unfortunately, Paul's health quickly deteriorated, and he died three months after his diagnosis. Dorothy and Paul's two grown daughters attended the funeral and spent time visiting their mother. When they told Dorothy that Paul had passed away, she had a blank expression on her face. Within 30 minutes of hearing the news, she asked her daughter if she could call Paul about dinner arrangements for that night. The nursing staff gently reminded Dorothy that her husband had passed away. A little while later, she once again asked if she could call him.

Dorothy's daughters and the memory support staff had discussed whether Dorothy should attend Paul's funeral. The primary concern about Dorothy attending the funeral was that she could become overwhelmed, disruptive, and confused. The staff advocated that Dorothy attend her husband's funeral. Her daughters, however, believed that the stress related to the visitation and funeral could cause her too much distress. Therefore, Dorothy did not attend the funeral.

Dorothy asks every day if Paul is coming to visit her. Because of her dementia, she has to be reminded that he has died, and every time she hears the news, she cries and cries all over again.

Box 9.C Now You Try It . . . Cognitive Assessment: Case Study

Dorothy is a person with Alzheimer's disease. She is experiencing extreme distress.

1. What information is most relevant in understanding Dorothy?
2. What are some important issues to consider when talking with her daughters?
3. Prepare an opening statement.
4. What are some of the challenges that you may encounter when talking to a person with Alzheimer's disease?
5. What can you do to connect with Dorothy, given her situation?

Spirituality and Religious Functioning

Spirituality involves experiencing a deep-seated sense of meaning and purpose in life, a sense of belonging, a sense of connection to "the deeply personal with the universal," and an acceptance, integration, and sense of wholeness (McDonald, 2006). Spirituality emphasizes the healing of the person. It views life as a journey where good and bad experiences can help you to learn, develop, and mature. Spirituality is not tied to any particular religious belief or tradition. Although culture and beliefs can play a part in spirituality, every person has his or her own unique experience of spirituality—it can be a personal experience for anyone, with or without a religious belief. Spirituality also highlights how connected we are to the world and other people (McDonald, 2006).

Within the social work literature, **spirituality and religious functioning** is often incorporated into practice by way of assessment because of the linkage between the client's cultural worldview and spirituality. Spirituality can provide meaning and understanding of difficult life events for clients. Religion and spirituality can be connected to coping resources and a person's resiliency (Coates, Graham, Swartzentruber, & Ouellette, 2007) Inquiries about spirituality should be performed in a competent manner by demonstrating spiritual sensitivity. In addition to an initial intake, clients should be permitted to express their spirituality and religious beliefs, if they wish to, in a respectful and supportive environment. Spirituality often becomes more important for clients during times of distress, emotional stress, and physical and mental illness.

If your client brings up the topic of religion or makes comments about God, Allah, Buddha, a higher power, or some other deities, use that opening to discuss spirituality. For example, John, your client, may tell you that he is HIV positive and believes that God is punishing him. You can explore his beliefs further to better understand his faith and where these beliefs come from. Within the context of the interview, it is important to convey understanding and not to dispute his beliefs. As the social worker, your role is to listen and offer alternative ways of looking at a situation, not to talk a person into or out of his or her beliefs.

Suggested responses to John:

1. John, there are many reasons that people get sick. You describe your God as merciful and loving. I wonder how the God that you love could not show compassion toward you. (Information giving and confrontation)
2. You believe that your God is loving and compassionate, yet you say that God is punishing you. I wonder how you reconcile these different perspectives. (Summarization and confrontation)
3. I am not sure what I believe about God or a higher power, but my faith teaches that God is forgiving and loving and does not want people to suffer. Please tell me more about your views on God. (Appropriate self-disclosure and open-ended question)
4. In times of severe disabling illness, such as yours, hope can come through rituals, meditation, music, prayer, traditional sacred narratives, or other inspirational readings. (Information giving)

Box 9.7 Tips for Doing a Spiritual-Religion–Focused Assessment

By asking these questions, you may determine your client's main spiritual concerns and practices:

1. Would you say you are spiritual or religious in any way?
2. What is your faith or belief?
3. Do you practice a religion currently?
4. Do you believe in God Allah, Buddha, or a higher power?
5. What sustains you and how?
6. What keeps you going in difficult times?
7. Do you feel there is a spiritual aspect to your current problem?
8. Would it help to involve someone from your faith community?
9. What do I need to understand about your religious background?
10. Are you worried about death and dying or about the possibility of an afterlife?
11. What are your main fears about the future?
12. Please tell me, do you feel the need for forgiveness about anything?
13. What, if anything, gives you hope?
14. What things do you believe in that give meaning to your life?
15. What influence does faith or spirituality have on how you take care of yourself?
16. How have your beliefs influenced your behavior during stressful times?
17. Are you part of a spiritual or religious community? Is this of support to you? If so, how?
18. Is there a person or group of people you love and who are really important to you?
19. How would you like your religious and spiritual beliefs to affect your care?
20. How important are these beliefs to you?
21. What religion did your family practice when you were growing up? How religious were your parents/caregivers?
22. Can you ask for forgiveness for hurting someone?
23. What have been your important experiences and thoughts about God/Allah/Buddha/higher power?
24. How would you describe God/Allah/Buddha/higher power?
25. Do you follow any spiritual path or practice (e.g., meditation, yoga, chanting)?
26. What significant spiritual experiences have you had (e.g., mystical experience, near-death experience, 12-step spirituality, drug-induced dreams, tarot readings, etc.)?
27. Do you pray? When? In what way(s)?
28. How has prayer worked in your life?
29. Have your prayers been answered?
30. What are your thoughts about end-of-life decisions? Do you support a person's right to die as they wish?

Box 9.7 offers a series of questions that a social worker may ask when completing the spirituality and religiosity sections of an assessment.

Lynn has been severely affected by a tornado that ripped through her home and community. Answer the questions regarding Lynn's crisis of faith presented in Box 9.8.

? Gauge your understanding of spiritual and religious assessments by taking this brief quiz.

Box 9.8 Spiritual Assessment: Case Study

Lynn lives in central Illinois, commonly known as tornado alley. Last spring, a major tornado ripped through her community, leaving devastation behind. No lives were lost, and the Red Cross and other emergency response teams quickly came to help people begin the recovery process. Lynn is a self-described Christian, and she found her religious community a great comfort following the tornado. Now she is struggling to put the pieces of her life back together. She lost her home and is living with her daughter and son-in-law. Her feelings of helplessness and lack of control are

(Continued)

Box 9.8 Spiritual Assessment: Case Study *(Continued)*

causing her to not go to work or look for a permanent home. Lynn no longer goes to church and doesn't feel as though God is there for her anymore. She has stopped praying and feels as though her life has lost all meaning. As the social worker, you have a very strong Christian faith and feel a personal connection to God. You were raised to believe that all things happen for a reason, some of which you will never understand. As you are talking with Lynn, you find yourself becoming frustrated with her defeatist attitude. Using the questions in Box 9.7, how might you address her crisis of faith? What questions relate specifically to her feelings of abandonment by God?

Emotional Functioning

Many clients have not learned how to express their feelings in a healthy way. It is the client's subjective way of responding to a situation that causes an emotional reaction. **Emotional functioning** represents the workings of our inner world and are what motivate us to action. Consider that emotions tend to guide the client's motivational pull toward seeking help. It is essential that for behaviors to change, an understanding of the feeling attached to the situation must occur. For example, fear of a beloved pet dying may cause the client to seek out the services of a veterinarian. The joy of seeing your baby being born causes awe and wonder. The client's intuitive response to protect the baby leads to caretaking behaviors, such as feeding or holding the baby close. Emotions are the type of communication that signals our state of mind and intentions toward others, and they can overpower the client's capacity to think (Sheafor & Horejsi, 2015). It is important to remember that even if the client cannot change his or her emotional reactions to a situation, it is still possible to make conscious choices about how to act and behave.

The client's understanding and interpretations of his or her own feelings are partly based on previous experiences that may have little basis in the reality of today. For example, a fairly routine situation occurred between two coworkers. There was a disagreement about an office policy. Client B was only trying to make a point, but client A responded with tears and hurt. This is an example of client A's subjective response to a situation that may have been triggered by previous events or life circumstances. Bottom line: emotions influence behavior. Sheafor and Horejsi (2015) identify sequential steps to understanding the interplay between feelings and behaviors:

1. An event or situation occurs.
2. We notice, interpret, and think about the event.
3. Depending on our interpretation, we have a particular emotional response.
4. The emotional response may elicit a certain behavior.

Always keep in mind the importance of cultural factors in the life of a client. For example, is your client from a large Italian family that spends hours sitting around the dining room table affectionately "yelling at each other"? Could the sadness in the room come from a person who has survived the Holocaust or a Latino man who can't find a way to keep his wife from being deported? Demonstrate empathy and understanding regardless of the client's situation. Box 9.9 presents a wide variety of ways to understand the inner workings of a client's life. The internal (emotional) world of a client dictates how that client will navigate through the highs and lows of everyday life.

Box 9.9 Tips for Doing an Emotional Assessment

What to look for when considering the client's emotional functioning:

1. Does the client's nonverbal response match his or her verbal response? Pay attention to the client's bodily reactions.
2. Does the client experience some relief once he or she has shared his or her emotional reactions?
3. Does the client seem embarrassed about the "presenting problem"?
4. Is this a problem the client can discuss without shame or fear of being judged?
5. How does the client identify his or her feeling?
6. Can the client discern other people's emotions and share intimate moments?
7. Can the client relate to past situations with appropriate affect (e.g., expressing sadness at the loss of a loved one)?
8. Assess whether the client is experiencing any suicidal ideation (see Box 9.12).
9. Consider the client's ability to control emotions. Is this a person with a "short fuse" who is overly responsive to a situation that appears out of proportion to the actual event? (e.g., How does the client respond after being fired from a job?)
10. How does the client manage his or her feelings? For example, do the client's feelings related to the situation become overwhelming? distorted?
11. How does the client experience feelings of fear? hurt? loss and love? For example, a client loses a home in a fire—how does the client manage his or her feelings once the initial shock has worn off?
12. Always consider the precipitating factors that have led to the situation and the client's feelings.
13. How does the client demonstrate an openness or readiness to expressing feelings?
14. Understand the client's range of emotion. Is the client able to feel both positive and negative feelings and distinguish between them? If the client expresses verbally a sense of accomplishment and pride, is he or she able to experience these feelings internally?
15. Can the client express a wide variety of feeling based on the circumstances? For example, in times of great joy, is the client able to express some aspect of happiness, pride, excitement, wonderment, and so on? Is the client able to differentiate between feelings of joy and despair? Look for signs of apathy or emotional bluntness.
16. Consider whether the client's emotional reaction is appropriate for the situation.
17. Understand that some clients are so traumatized by their experiences and feelings that assisting them in "unblocking" those feelings can be a slow process. The client may be able to manage only small portions of information and "enlightenment" at a time.
18. Assess the level of depression a client is experiencing. See Box 9.12 regarding how to assess the client's level of suicidology.
19. What are the meaningful rituals in the client's life?
20. Look for strengths. (When does the client best manage his or her feelings? What are a few examples of when the client was proud of himself or herself? When does the client feel at most peace? How does the client describe when he or she is feeling great? When was the last time the client felt as if things were turning around and there was a "light at the end of the tunnel"? In what relationship is the client most at ease? Under what circumstances does the client feel control over his or her emotions so as to not be overwhelmed by them?)

Source: Hepworth et al. (2013).

Box 9.D presents Stuart, a 45-year-old male who has been struggling with mental illness throughout most of his adult life. Using the assessment questions posed in Box 9.9, assess Stuart's emotional functioning.

Assess your understanding of emotional functioning by taking this brief quiz.

Watch this clip as Karen attempts to assess Mike's emotional functioning. How is Mike feeling as he talks about having left the unit the night before? Does Karen adequately capture the depth of his feelings?

Box 9.D Now You Try It . . . Emotional Assessment: Case Study

Stuart is a 45-year-old male who is currently attending a day treatment program for individuals with chronic mental illness. He lives in a group home with four other adults. Stuart stated that he had a fairly happy childhood. At age 20, while attending a junior college, he began to experience dissatisfaction in all parts of his life. He became easily agitated and aggressive. He became physically threatening to his parents and refused any attempts to get help. Ten years ago, after a physical altercation with a police officer, he was placed in the county jail for three days. During that time, he became more and more agitated, yelling and screaming and banging his head against the cell wall, and was eventually transferred to the local hospital's psychiatric unit. It was during his hospitalization that he was diagnosed as a person with schizophrenia. Over the course of his life, he drifted from low-paying job to low-paying job. Although he had maintained a cordial relationship with his parents over the years, there is very little contact now. Stuart sporadically takes his medication. When taking Risperdal, an antipsychotic medication, there is evidence that his functioning improves. He showers regularly, eats healthy foods, attends his day treatment program, sleeps better, and is more talkative and social. When not on his medication, Stuart is very easily upset, hears voices (auditory hallucinations), and believes that his caretakers are stealing his money and food. At this time, he is not taking his medication and is at risk of being hospitalized. Today, you noted that he seems less agitated and more open to talking. During a brief meeting at the group home, he stated, "I want to talk to my mom, and I miss her." It is the first time in several months that he has mentioned his mom, and you want to explore this further.

Using the items presented in Box 9.9, what questions do you want to ask in order to explore and further understand his emotional functioning? Answer the following:

1. Do you acknowledge his interest in contacting his mother?
2. How can you support him in his effort to reach out to his mother?
3. What does Stuart hope to have come from their conversation?
4. What was their relationship like previously?
5. Why does he want to reach out to her now?

Behavioral Functioning

Behavior patterns are a series of movements that recur under a particular set of circumstances with little variation over time. To look for patterns, the social worker sifts through many stimuli to identify the central elements of the interaction (Middleman & Wood, 1990). How the client feels is less important than the client's actions, as actions become the target for change. Ask the client about the absence or presence of specific behaviors that are related to the problem (Cormier & Cormier, 1998). For example, does the client check the lock on the back door multiple times before leaving for work, or does the client yell at coworkers when frustrated? According to Cormier and Cormier (1998), clients often describe problem behaviors in nonbehavioral ways, saying, for example, "I am not getting along very well with my math teacher," without specifying exactly what behaviors are demonstrated toward the teacher. Not getting along very well could mean, "I hit my teacher yesterday and I am now expelled from school," "I spoke without raising my hand and she looked at me funny," or "I failed the math test, it is her fault, she is a bad teacher." Asking for specific behavioral cues can help the social worker understand client situations better. Box 9.10 offers a series of questions that a social worker may consider when completing the **behavioral functioning** segment of an assessment.

Box 9.10 Tips for Doing a Behavioral Assessment

What to look for when assessing a client's behavioral functioning:

1. Does the client's behavior match his or her emotional response? For example, consider a client who is angry about a recent breakup with his girlfriend. Does the client react by threatening to hurt her? Does he follow her by sitting outside the apartment waiting for her to come home? Does he follow her to work and leave insulting messages on her voice mail? Are the client's actions liable to get him arrested for stalking?
2. What is the client's cultural and religious background? How a client behaves can be directly related to his or her upbringing and family norms.
3. Are there any learned behaviors that could also be unlearned?
4. What are the client's personal habits, such as cleanliness, dress, personal traits, and communication patterns (Hepworth et al., 2013)?
5. Does the client appear motivated to bring about change in his or her life?
6. The ABCs of problematic behavior: A = *A*ntecedent, what leads up to the problematic behavior; B = the problematic *B*ehavior itself; and C = *C*onsequence of behavior (O'Leary & Wilson, 1987).
7. Collect baseline data before an intervention is introduced and assess and document the frequency and duration of target behaviors.
8. What are the client's interests and hobbies?
9. Does the client have a criminal history?
10. What are the specific triggers to the behaviors (e.g., time of day or yearly event)?
11. How does the client behave when under pressure? For example, does the client react to a new situation by panicking and losing objectivity or by taking a step back, taking a deep breath, and considering possible options?
12. Are there any major life changes that are occurring, such as a new baby, a divorce, or a new job?
13. What are the client's established long-standing behavioral patterns? Does the client have a default way of behaving? For example, when presented with difficult test questions on a final exam, does the client attempt to figure them out or leave the testing site in a state of frustration and anger?
14. What are the discipline practices within the home? For example, who does/did the disciplining, and how does the client perceive authority figures?
15. Are some of the client's behaviors self-destructive? For example, does the client forget to take his or her medication and therefore end up experiencing mania, which leads to shoplifting, which leads to an arrest? Is this pattern repeated over and over again?
16. Is there a pattern to the client's behaviors, such as ritualistic, compulsiveness, avoidance, phobic, and controlling others?
17. Where are the stressors, both internal and external, in the client's life?
18. Look for strengths. (How does the client manage his or her temper? What is going right? What does the "calm before the storm" feel like? How can the client focus more on the calm versus the turmoil? What talents and skills does the client have? How can these talents and skills be used to problem solve? How does the client adapt to change?)

Source: For a review of functional versus dysfunctional patterns of behavior, see Hepworth et al. (2013).

To fully appreciate a client's behavioral functioning, consider observing and interacting with him or her during a home visit, at the school, with a sales clerk in a department store, with a child's teacher, or during an interaction with a peer. These real-life situations can be very helpful in pointing out to the client what the social worker observed and for the client practicing alternative ways of behaving.

Watch as the social worker, Diane, asks the client, Mrs. Kita, to role play how she may approach her landlord about owing late rent. In this clip, behavioral feedback and rehearsal prepared Mrs. Kita to assert her position and ask for what she wanted.

Assess your understanding of behavioral functioning by taking this brief quiz.

Box 9.E introduces you to Felicia. Using Sheafor and Horejsi's (2015) four sequential steps in assessing her emotional and behavioral functioning, answer the questions presented.

FAMILY AND SOCIAL SUPPORT FUNCTIONING

As social workers, it is our responsibility to understand how one's **family and social support** can have a significant impact on the client, as these connections provide the glue between people. McGoldrick, Giordano, and Pearce (2005) define families to include extended kin, the community, and cultural groups. Families come together through marriage, commitment, birth or adoption, informal arrangements, family of creation or choice, and extended family ties. Social supports refer to the assistance and caring provided by others in day-to-day living. There are many types of social supports, such as help with organizing bills, grocery shopping services, mentoring an adolescent in the neighborhood, providing child care to a family member, offering advice or emotional support, conducting a youth choir, working in an after-school program that provides help with homework, volunteering at a senior center, and caring for a coworker in your faith community.

Box 9.E Now You Try It . . . Behavioral Assessment: Case Study

Felicia is a 30-year-old married female with one daughter, Jessica, age seven. She was recently promoted to the position of vice president in a large corporation. Felicia is a person who describes herself as hardworking, motivated, and dedicated to everything that she does. Recently, she reports difficulty sleeping and on several occasions has been awakened by night terrors. What precipitated the social worker's involvement was her being rushed to the hospital during what she thought was a heart attack. Following a series of tests, the medical team determined that she had a panic attack.

On exploring Felicia's patterns of behavior, she disclosed that she graduated from an Ivy League school with high honors. Both her parents are college professors and have always held very high expectations for her. Her younger brother, Bernard, disappeared five years ago. He has not been in contact with any family members, and she assumes that he is dead. Their relationship was not very close, as they fought and bickered "all the time." She stated that she feels guilty and wonders if it is her fault that he left home. Exploring further, Felicia tells you that Jessica is very nervous and anxious and that she has been diagnosed as a student with school phobia. Currently, she is being homeschooled. Felicia does not anticipate that she will go back to school for the remainder of the year. They have a full-time teacher who works with Jessica.

Today during the session, Felicia shares with you that her husband has been offered a job in another state. She is concerned that he will accept the position but tells you that she has not expressed her feelings and concerns to him about this possible move. When the social worker asks her the reasons for not talking to him, she stated, "I can't lose him too." She reports that she is not sleeping and eats energy bars to keep herself going. Her boss noticed that she seems more irritable than usual and expressed concern. She was extremely angry that he said such a thing to her, as her moods are none of his business.

Apply Sheafor and Horejsi's (2015) four sequential steps to understand Felicia's emotions and behaviors by answering the following questions:

1. What event or situation occurred?
2. What does Felicia notice, interpret, and think about the event?
3. What are her interpretations of the particular emotional response?
4. How do her emotional responses elicit certain behaviors?

When completing an assessment, look for ways the family interacts. Do they love watching sport events on TV, cooking together, planting a garden, or singing in a choir together? These types of activities can help solidify relationships, even when there are many stressors to manage. For example, 14-year-old Roberta and her mother Clara are experiencing "typical" family conflicts that resulted in a recent physical altercation. Following the incident, Clara contacted the social worker regarding ways to improve her relationship with Roberta. After one session with Clara, it became clear that spending time together doing something both she and Roberta enjoyed was a great way to improve communication. They both love the television show *Dancing with the Stars*, and no matter the tension between them, they call a cease-fire during the show. They like rating the contestants and have found one hour a week when they can laugh together. This simple intervention has served to reduce the tension between them.

Assessing the family's connectedness is helpful in understanding how and where the client fits in. Is the client the peacemaker in the family? How is the client affected by the yelling and screaming that goes on within his or her home? How are decisions made? Who holds the power, and how is the power used? (See Box 9.11.)

Box 9.F introduces you to Ben and Charles, identical twins. Following the case description, there is a series of questions. Give each question full consideration before moving on to the next one.

Assessment

Behaviors: Collect and organize data, and apply critical thinking to interpret information from clients and constituencies.

Apply knowledge of human behavior and the social environment, person-in-environment, and other multidisciplinary theoretical frameworks in the analysis of assessment data from clients and constituencies

Select appropriate intervention strategies based on the assessment, research knowledge, and values and preferences of clients and constituencies.

Critical Thinking Question: You are working with a female client, Jenna, age 16. You have been working with her for three months. Like any teenager, she is occasionally moody and quiet during sessions. In your session today, you notice that she is less engaged and more distant than usual. Her journal entries this week are very dark and death oriented. She is currently living with her uncle in foster care, while her mother is in a drug rehabilitation program. She does not get along with her cousins and says that she feels trapped with no place to go. Are these changes the result of typical adolescent behavior, or should a suicide assessment be done with this client? Explain your answer.

Box 9.11 Tips for Doing a Family and Social Support Assessment

Consider the following when assessing the client's blending of family and social support functioning:

1. What is the client's affiliation and role with family, friends, employer, school, teammates, religious community, and so on? Always consider the client's place within the cultural context of his or her world.
2. Is the client able to demonstrate empathy toward others?
3. Does the client have a sense of belonging? Is there intimacy between family members? between members of the client's social circle?
4. Assess the boundaries within the family. Are they open, enmeshed, or fluid? How do family members communicate with each other?
5. What are the family rules and roles? For example, no one talks about Mom's drinking or Dad's infidelity. In this case, the client's role is to be the mediator between family and the outside world.
6. How do family members demonstrate they care for each other? How does the client find nurturance?
7. Do family members participate in after-school programs, faith-based activities, cultural events, or community-wide activities?
8. Who are the key people in the client's life? For example, a client may feel most attached to his foster parent even though there is regular contact between the client and his biological parents. In this case, he looks to his foster family for guidance.
9. Who does the client turn to for help and support? How frequent is the contact, and what is the depth of the relationship? Describe the stability of the relationship.

(Continued)

Box 9.11 Tips for Doing a Family and Social Support Assessment *(Continued)*

10. What roles do the extended family or support network play in the client's life?
11. How are decisions made? What is considered a fair agreement or compromise?
12. How does the client perceive himself or herself and his or her place within the wider system? Who shares similar values?
13. Does the client seem at ease with others in his or her world?
14. Explore the client's familial history. For example, ask about physical abuse, family violence, substance abuse, and mental illness. Are there health-related concerns or beliefs that affect the client's life? Is there a family history of mental illness? Does the family access traditional medical services or the services of a shaman or faith healer?
15. Assess how conflict is resolved within the family unit and wider community. How is a crisis managed? What is the impact on the family?
16. Explore the client's job history/school history. Are there long periods of unemployment? Did the client complete high school? What are his or her life aspirations?
17. Is the client able to cover living expenses? nonessential expenditures?
18. How does the client find privacy, solace, or respite from outside forces?
19. Who provides emotional and physical care to the client?
20. What is the client's immigration history? level of acculturation? language spoken in the home?
21. Does the client appear motivated to make needed changes?
22. How does the client define himself or herself from a social and legal identity standpoint?
23. Look for strengths. (What does the client want the world to look like a few months from now? a few years from now? Who can the client count on for help? What personal history and stories convey what has come before? What skills did the client use to get through some of the difficult times? What is going right? Describe what a successful relationship looks like to you.)

Box 9.F Now You Try It . . . Family and Social Support Assessment: Case Study

Charles and Ben are identical 17-year-old twin brothers. Ben was referred to the school social worker after getting into a physical fight with his brother on school property. The altercation was severe enough that a teacher had to pull them apart.

Charles and Ben come from a lower-middle-class background, growing up in a midsize rural/farming community. As the school social worker, you live in the same community and know just about everyone in town. There have been times when your roles as the high school social worker and community member have been difficult to separate. You have a child who attends the high school as well.

Both boys are set to go to the same junior college next year. Ben reports they have always been close and up until recently did almost everything together. A few weeks ago, Charles began dating Janice, a classmate at school. Since that time, Ben has been very upset with his brother. He has expressed to the social worker that he hates Janice and thinks she is "using Charles." He reports feeling shut out of Will's life and can't understand what he sees in her.

He tells you about an incident that happened a few weeks ago. They were at an out-of-town party with "drugs and alcohol being passed around like candy." The police showed up at the party, and because no adult was present, they panicked and let the police in to search the house. Everyone fled the scene except Ben and a few others who "were so stoned we could not move." They were arrested and taken to the county jail.

His parents were called, and they came to the police station and bailed him out. He must pay back the bail money and is grounded from the car, the computer, and any after-school activities. Charles, on the other hand, is off the hook completely, as the twins' parents have no idea that he was at the party. Ben is angry with his parents for being so "stupid and blind." He feels targeted and hurt that Charles has not owned up to his part in the Friday night raid. On further questioning about their relationship, Ben acknowledges that he is the quieter and more introverted of the two. He has relied on Charles for things such as assistance with homework, entry into social situations, and access to pickup sports and to smooth the way with his parents.

1. As the social worker, what are your concerns regarding the family dynamics?
2. How might you assist this family?
3. Are you obligated to tell the school personnel of the police raid?
4. What community supports are available to help the family?

In this clip, watch as Nicole begins to explore with Mrs. Anderson some of her struggles regarding parenting Maria. Identify at least four issues that Nicole addressed with her to better understand the functioning of her family. How does Crystal, Maria's mother, factor into this case?

Crisis Intervention and Suicide Assessment

Assess your understanding of family and social support functioning by taking this brief quiz.

Crisis intervention techniques are widely used to assist people in adjusting successfully following stressful events or crises that temporarily overwhelm their capacity to cope. A crisis is when the client's usual and customary coping skills are no longer adequate to address a perceived stressful situation (Kanel, 2015). Often, such situations are novel and unexpected. A crisis occurs when unusual stress, brought on by unexpected and disruptive events, renders the client physically and emotionally vulnerable. It is because the client's coping mechanisms and past behavioral strategies prove ineffective that he or she is now at a crisis point (Kanel, 2015). A crisis overrides an individual's normal psychological and biological coping mechanisms—moving the individual toward maladaptive behaviors. A crisis limits one's ability to utilize more cognitively sophisticated problem-solving and conflict resolution skills. Crises are, by definition, time limited. However, every crisis is a high-risk situation; for example, the crisis of an unexpected loss of a parent can put an adolescent son or daughter at risk for suicide. If the social worker has reason to believe that a client may be at risk for suicide, it is imperative that a **suicide assessment** be completed. (see Box 9.12).

Box 9.12 Tips for Doing a Suicide Assessment

What are the triggers that might cause the client to feel suicidal? Possible triggers include the loss of a job or a loved one, a psychiatric disorder, a newly diagnosed health problem or a worsening condition, or a childhood trauma. Has there been a severe conflict with a loved one?

1. Is the client threatening to hurt or kill himself or herself?
2. Is there a specific plan? Is the client looking for ways to kill himself or herself, such as seeking access to pills, weapons, or other means? Is the plan realistic, and can it be implemented?
3. Is the client displaying impulsivity, poor self-control, or poor decision making?
4. Is the client talking or writing about death, dying, or suicide?
5. Is the client feeling hopeless, as if there is no reason for living or no sense of purpose in life?
6. Is the client feeling rage or anger or wanting to seek revenge?
7. Is the client acting reckless or engaging in risky activities, seemingly without thinking?
8. Is the client feeling trapped or constrained, as if there is no way out?
9. Is the client increasing alcohol or drug usage?
10. Is the client withdrawing from friends, family, or community?
11. Is the client experiencing heightened anxiety, agitation, sleeplessness, or excessive sleeping?
12. Is the client experiencing dramatic changes in mood?
13. Has the client attempted suicide in the past?
14. Is there a family history of suicide attempts and completion?
15. What is the age, gender, and race of the client? (e.g., a newly widowed elderly person is at high risk)
16. What is the client's sexual orientation? Is the client LBGTQ? (Lesbian, Gay, Bisexual, Transgender, Transsexual, Queer and Questioning.)

(Continued)

Box 9.12 Tips for Doing a Suicide Assessment *(Continued)*

Protective factors include the following:

1. Positive social support (see Boxes 9.2 and 9.11)
2. Spirituality (see Box 9.7)
3. Sense of responsibility to family, children in the home, beloved animals (see Boxes 9.2 and 9.11)
4. Life satisfaction (see Boxes 9.2, 9.4, and 9.7)
5. Reality testing ability: if this happens, then what? (see Box 9.5)
6. Positive therapeutic relationship
7. What stopped the client from committing suicide? (see Box 9.2)

Sources: American Psychiatric Association (2014). Compiled from (2015) and Sheafor and Horejsi (2015).

Watch as Louis and Yesenia are assessing Kim's level of suicidal risk. Based on her answers, are you concerned that she may suicidal? If you believed that she is, how might you have responded differently?

Assessment

Behaviors: Collect and organize data, and apply critical thinking to interpret information from clients and constituencies.

Apply knowledge of human behavior and the social environment, person-in-environment, and other multidisciplinary theoretical frameworks in the analysis of assessment data from clients and constituencies

Develop mutually agreed-on intervention goals and objectives based on the critical assessment of strengths, needs, and challenges within clients and constituencies

Select appropriate intervention strategies based on the assessment, research knowledge, and values and preferences of clients and constituencies.

Critical Thinking Question: You are a member of a mobile crisis team in your community. You are often called out in the middle of the night to respond to suicidal clients. Tonight, a call came in from the supervisor in a group home for people with mental illness. You know that people with mental illness are at higher risk for suicide. Identify what else you know about mental illness. How will you start the meeting? How will you determine if he or she needs to be hospitalized?

If you suspect that a client is in danger of hurting himself or herself or others, as a professional you must breach confidentiality and take the necessary steps, which may include contacting a family member, a crisis center, or the police (Cooper & Lasser, 2011). This can be difficult because you may feel conflicted about taking this course of action, especially if it is against the client's wishes. If ever in doubt, take the most cautious route possible, which may mean involuntary hospitalization. If the client does not seem to be at high risk for suicide, consider developing a safety plan with the client and his or her support system. If a plan is in place, surrounding the client with care and concern, the risks go down. If you are working with a client who indicates there are no support people in his or her life, then, as the social worker, you can be that person. Ensure that your client has access to you or a designated person throughout the crisis situation. It may be that the quality of the relationship and his or her commitment to you is keeping your client alive. Having leverage with the client during the crisis can help to stabilize the situation. Once the immediate crisis has dissipated (it is hoped within a few weeks), close contact with the client should be lessened as other supports are put in place. After the immediate crisis has passed, the client may be more open to an ongoing therapeutic relationship, as an alliance has been formed. As part of the assessment, consider whether you believe the client could benefit from additional sessions or whether other social supports can be put into place.

Box 9.G introduces you to Alicia, a young woman who is feeling depressed and hopeless. Using the checklist, determine what your course of action will be while working with her.

Evaluate your understanding of crisis intervention and suicide assessment by taking this brief quiz.

Box 9.III Theory into Practice—Systems Theory and Crisis Intervention: Case Study

Crisis Intervention: The goal of crisis intervention is to provide support and direction to clients in identifying and performing tasks or behaviors that are essential to regaining a level of functioning equal to or higher than the precrisis level and to restore the client to a state of feeling in control in a safe, secure, and stable environment. A crisis is typically time limited, being oriented to the here and now and requiring a high level of activity by the social worker. Assisting the client in activating his or her resources and providing concrete suggestions is an approach that can be especially helpful during a crisis situation.

Frank is a veteran who recently returned from the war zone in the Middle East. In a debriefing session with the social worker, he reports that he was involved in some low-risk military operations. He did not see any combat but always felt a sense of foreboding. He is married with two children: Brooke, age 14, and Brandon, age 12. His wife Marcia has been functioning as the single parent for the past 18 months. Now that Frank is home, there are many changes within the system. For example, Marcia now works full-time as a medical technician. Prior to Frank's deployment, she worked from home. In order to get her children back and forth to school, Marcia joined a car pool. Brooke and Brandon have been staying at home alone after school until Marcia gets home from work. All members of the family pitch in and help with cooking, cleanup, and chores around the house, something Marcia was primarily responsible for doing. On Saturdays, both children are involved in soccer, and games take up most of the day. Sundays include a trip to visit Marcia's parents, who live about an hour away. There is a rhythm to their life now—the family has pulled together, and they are managing well.

Now that Frank is home, there are some rough spots. He is on an 18-month rotation and will be heading back to Afghanistan. He describes himself as depressed, moody, and irritable. He is not sleeping very well, feels jumpy, and misses the camaraderie of his fellow soldiers. Frank is trying to get back into the routine of life but is finding it very difficult. He feels as if his family has moved on and there is no place for him. He reports a sense of alienation and not feeling like himself. Today in a follow-up session, Frank reports that he is requesting another rotation back to Afghanistan, as he feels more connected to the army than his family. Using the crisis intervention model with Frank, the social worker quickly assesses whether he is serious about the rotation back in or whether this is a cry for help. He is feeling disengaged from Marcia and his children and thinks everyone would be happier if he were redeployed. In assessing the situation, it is important to determine his level of depression.

Questions the social worker may ask to determine if he is at risk of self-harm may include the following: Are you feeling overwhelmed by guilt? Are you behaving in impulsive ways? Are you thinking of hurting yourself? or someone else? Can you contain your behaviors? Are you suffering inside? To determine whether Frank is suffering from posttraumatic stress disorder, ask about flashbacks, nightmares, avoidance behaviors, phobias, hyperarousal, sleep problems, irritability, poor concentration, blackouts, poor memory, and startle reaction.

In this case, the social worker has moved beyond understanding the dynamics of Frank's family and the interdependent systems to assessing him for potential suicide or possible posttraumatic stress disorder. Her work now is to provide safety net. She now focuses on his support systems, his hopes and dreams for the future, ways to take better care of himself, and assessing whether he has a plan to hurt himself (or someone else) and whether he has the means. The social worker is now in crisis intervention response, knowing that her role could eventually lead to Frank being hospitalized.

Source: Kanel, Kristi (2014). Cengage Learning, A Guide to Crisis Intervention, 5th edition.

Box 9.G Now You Try It . . . Suicidal Assessment and Crisis Intervention: Case Study

Alicia, a 25-year-old, is currently living with her parents in a small two-bedroom apartment in an urban setting. She has completed high school and dental technician training and had been working as a dental assistant for the past three years. Last month, she was fired from her job after repeatedly arriving to work late or not reporting to work at all. Her employer had given her four written warnings before she was terminated. Because this was a termination for cause, she is not able to collect unemployment benefits. Her finances were tight prior to losing her job, as she is paying for a new car and contributing to rent and food expenses, but living with her parents has allowed her to save some money. Now she is extremely anxious about finding a job and paying her share of the monthly expenses. She has been job hunting without much success. It is a very tight economy, and no dental offices are hiring. She has gone to a temporary employment agency

(Continued)

Box 9.G Now You Try It . . . Suicidal Assessment and Crisis Intervention: Case Study *(Continued)*

but has not had any offers to work even a few hours a week. She does not have a good job reference from her previous employer, which is also hindering her job search.

Yesterday, you responded to a crisis call at her parent's apartment. Her mother is very concerned about her, specifically her anxiety and expressed feelings of hopelessness. She found a note on her bed stating, "I feel like I am a burden to you and Dad. I will never find another job. I am 25 for god's sake and a complete and utter failure. I am sorry that I have let you both down."

When you arrive at the apartment, you see a very frail and disheveled individual. With her mother in the room, you start to explore the circumstances that led her to feel this way. Using the checklist below, assess Alicia for suicidal risk:

0 = cannot determine	2 = moderate
1 = low risk	3 = high risk

What are the triggers that might cause the client to feel suicidal?

____ Is Alicia threatening to hurt or kill herself?

____ Is there a specific plan? Is Alicia looking for ways to kill herself, such as seeking access to pills, weapons, or other means?

____ Is Alicia's plan realistic, and can it be implemented?

____ Is Alicia displaying impulsivity, poor self-control, or poor decision making?

____ Is Alicia talking or writing about death, dying, or suicide?

____ Is Alicia feeling hopeless, with no reason for living or sense of purpose in life?

____ Is Alicia feeling rage and anger and seeking revenge?

____ Is Alicia acting reckless or engaging in risky activities, seemingly without thinking?

____ Is Alicia feeling trapped or constrained, as if there is no way out?

____ Is Alicia increasing her alcohol or drug usage?

____ Is Alicia withdrawing from her friends, family, or community?

____ Is Alicia experiencing heightened anxiety or agitation?

____ Is Alicia unable to sleep or sleeping all the time?

____ Is Alicia experiencing dramatic changes in her mood?

____ Has Alicia attempted suicide in the past?

____ Is there a family history of suicide attempts and completion?

____ How old is Alicia?

1. Now that you have completed the suicide assessment, what areas are you most concerned about?
2. What are the protective factors in place for Alicia right now?
3. Do you think she should be hospitalized?
4. What would you want to include in a contract with her regarding keeping herself safe from self-harm?

SUMMARY

A multidimensional assessment provides the social worker with a nearly 360-degree view of the client's life. It is through this process that the social worker and client begin to define the problems for work and to set the stage for change.

In this chapter, students were introduced to how using interviewing skills to collect data can provide multidimensional information regarding the client's life situation.

- You have learned how to collect data through the use of interviewing skills to analyze and assess information regarding the client's strengths and the environment in which they live, play and work.
- You have learned how to collect data regarding the client's physical functioning and wellbeing and to assess cognitive and behavioral functioning.

- Combined with other types of assessments, you have learned how to understand the ways in which emotions, spirituality and religiosity impact a client's life.
- You have learned how to assess a client's family and informal network system, including how to complete a suicide assessment.

APPLY IT

1. Review all three sessions of **Interactive Case Study #1** as Anna and the social worker Marie develop rapport over time. Putting yourself in the role of the social worker, how would you begin the interview with Sally, Anna's eight-year-old daughter? What activities would you include to help Sally feel comfortable with you? How would you adjust your communication style to relate on her level? How do you anticipate Sally will respond to you? What will Sally's reaction most likely be as you try to address her mother's illness and its effect on her?

Assess Your Competence

Use the scale below to rate your current level of achievement on the following concepts or skills associated with each competency presented in the chapter:

1	2	3
I can accurately describe the concept or skill	I can consistently identify the concept or skill when observing and analyzing practice activities	I can competently implement the concept or skill in my own practice

_______ Understands and can identify and describe the major assessment categories.

_______ Can describe the uses of understanding a person in relationship to their environments.

_______ Can articulate the correct lines of questioning for all types of assessments.

10

Problem Identification, Planning, and Contracting

LEARNING OUTCOMES

- Identify the presenting problem from the client and social worker's perspectives.
- Develop a plan of action with the client, taking into account the multidimensional assessment and problem identification processes.
- Develop an understanding of how to contract with your client.

CHAPTER OUTLINE

MONKEY BUSINESS / FOTOLIA

Working with people who are facing challenges in their lives is perhaps one of the most complicated and unpredictable endeavors but also one that is most rewarding. The stages of the helping process give the social worker a guide to helping people navigate the obstacles in their lives, and while we present it as a linear model, in practice you will find it to be an overlapping and flexible process with much moving back and forth between stages. For example, when faced with new challenges, a client may begin to disengage from the helping process; then you, the social worker, must take a step forward and reengage the client. Similarly, new challenges may also require you to revisit the assessment to include new developments in the client's life. When the client is fully engaged and the assessment is complete, it's time to move toward problem identification and prioritization and the making of a plan for addressing the challenges confronting the client. Once the social worker and the client have agreed on a plan of action, a formal or informal contract for your work together is acknowledged and agreed on. The contract becomes the basis of your work together and provides direction for the rest of the helping process.

PROBLEM IDENTIFICATION

Problems are a part of everyday life and can get very complicated and confusing for clients. They may find themselves in need of help to see the possible paths out of their problems and to muster the internal and external resources needed to move forward in their lives. The task of **problem identification** is critical to helping the client see where the challenges lie and to charting a new direction in collaboration with the social worker.

Probably one of the first therapeutic events in the helping process is giving the client the space and time to tell his or her story. Listen to not only how the client views and defines the problems he or she faces but also how the client feels, sees, and experiences the problem. Listen to the story without judging or predetermining what needs to be done. Many times, clients carry the answers to their problems within themselves. As the social worker, you can help them to discover their internal wisdom about their lives and what they need. In this process of listening to the clients' stories, delving into their lives, and helping them to find the confidence to move forward, you will discover some common ground to begin your work together.

You have completed the intake process and have gotten started on completing the multidimensional assessment. You have assessed the situation—you and the client now agree on the problems for work. You are always assessing the client and the client's situation, as things can change very quickly and unexpectedly. **Planning** for change and following through can be equally as challenging. What the social worker and client agreed to do today could be different tomorrow, depending on the circumstances. For example, while talking to the social worker in an outpatient rehabilitation program, Herb is describing his process of recovering from heart surgery. He is feeling physically better and is ready to go back to work. He is worried about paying all of the medical expenses and getting the okay from his physician to return to work. He tells the social worker that he doesn't feel like himself and is experiencing moments of self-doubt regarding his capacity to do his job. He doesn't want the physician to know about his extreme tiredness and lack of focus. Although reluctant, Herb has agreed to get his release-to-work physical completed by the end of the next week so he can be cleared to report back to work. Because Herb feels understood and validated by the social worker, he agrees to meet again the following week. When you next see Herb, you learn that his daughter Tiffany was suspended from school for bullying other students. His focus is now less on getting his physical exam completed and more on managing what has happened to Tiffany. Suddenly, Tiffany's behavior in school and the consequences of her behavior take on a higher priority. Herb's finances and his health are still important, and he needs to get back to work in order to pay his bills. Tiffany's situation has now placed these concerns in a different light. It is now a matter of balancing his own priorities with those of his daughter. As a social worker, the focus of your work will shift to helping Herb manage both concerns simultaneously: his health, work, and financial concerns and the pressing issue of Tiffany. He will need to address the most immediate need of his daughter's behavior and her suspension from school before he can talk about getting back to work. Flexibility and fluidity are very important personal characteristics that will serve the social worker well in direct social work practice.

Now that you and the client have made a commitment to work together, it is time to figure out the major concerns and decide how to address them, either one at a time or simultaneously. Suitable levels of change will depend on factors such as the presenting problem, the desire to change the behaviors, the seriousness of unaddressed consequences, and the domino effect that often accompanies unresolved life problems. The client's internal and external resources are also important factors to consider when creating an action plan with the client. Internal resources may include the client's level of motivation, resilience, self-esteem, hope, and a belief in his or her ability to change. Community services, a support group, family networks, access to public transportation, and financial resources are some examples of external resources. Is the client ready, and to what degree are the conditions suitable for change? What fears does the client bring to the helping process that may create resistance to change? What factors external to the client may be contributing to his or her problems?

Sometimes the client and the social worker may have different views on what the problem really is. Building trust over time and getting to the underlying issues can bring new insights to the client and open him or her up to even more possibilities. Following Lisa's case in Box 10.1, there are recurring issues that impact her daily functioning, such as her anxiety and self-questioning. In developing longer-term goals, the social worker will

Box 10.1 Problem Identification: Case Study

Lisa, age 38, and her husband of 10 years have been trying to conceive a child for the past four years without success. Lisa has become very depressed and anxious because she cannot get pregnant. She describes herself as jumpy and restless and fears that something bad is about to happen. She states, "I sometimes think I am going crazy, I worry about everything." As the social worker, you are aware of treatment issues regarding her anxiety, but you also must be careful to addressing these issues in a time-sensitive way. At this point, you help Lisa by listening to her story and offering understanding and support.

While the first things to come to your mind may be to help Lisa in locating a fertility clinic or discussing ways to financially cover the cost of infertility treatments, you know that this would be bad timing. To do so at this point would lead you into the practice error of premature problem solving. In this case, you would now be trying to figure out ways to fix the problem without discussing issues that are salient to Lisa's anxiety and infertility. If you jump in too soon, the underlying concerns may be overlooked, and the real problems, such as health, perfectionism, and anxiety-related issues, may fail to be addressed. Through a shared vision of what is possible, Lisa may find ways to live a fulfilled life without focusing entirely on getting pregnant. Over the course of the relationship, Lisa and you begin to identify ways that help her focus on a more balanced life rather than giving all of her attention to conceiving.

Several months later, Lisa meets with you again. She is pregnant and is extremely anxious. She is certain something bad will happen, such as a miscarriage. She can't sleep, and she finds herself constantly worrying about the success of her pregnancy. She is unable to focus on her job as a teacher. You can assist Lisa by helping her to reframe her anxiety into action. Using strengths-based problem solving, you can affirm her concerns and continue to talk things out. It may be helpful to assist Lisa in recognizing some patterns in her behavior and problem-solving skills. For example, she has a tendency to worry and prepare herself for the worst-case scenario. Helping her to manage her anxiety and develop ways to address self-doubt will be extremely helpful in her role as a mother. As in any assessment, identify Lisa's coping strategies, her supports, her capacity to manage many things at once, and her commitment to do exactly what she can to ensure a healthy baby.

In the short term, help Lisa identify ways that she can relax, stay healthy, and maintain a level of success as her pregnancy continues. As part of the planning phase, offer her suggestions such as meditation, deep breathing, physical movement, journaling, touch, eating healthy foods, guided imagery (at the beach on a warm sunny day listening to the waves crashing on the shore), laughing, taking a relaxing bath, listening to music, reading a book, turning off the television, enjoying nature, and hugging her partner (and pet).

assess her patterns of self-defeating behaviors and explore her need to do everything perfectly. Look at when and under what circumstances this coping style developed and how Lisa sees herself in the world. Offer her an alternate perspective, such as developing strategies to manage her everyday struggles without being immobilized. Understand what contributes to her struggles, and therefore anticipating, planning, and managing them better is a step forward in developing confidence in her role as a parent and a spouse.

Generally, starting where the client is and then developing a plan of action toward problem resolution is the best approach. The social worker must be patient and supportive while always remembering the client has the final say and is the only expert on his or her life. The client's presenting problem can also help to focus the assessment. Is the client acknowledging problems voluntarily and taking responsibility? Or is the client considered involuntary (referred to as a *potential client* by Compton, Galaway, & Cournoyer 2005) because of a mandate from another source, such as a family member, a probation officer, or a teacher? As indicated throughout the text, an involuntary client is not necessarily an unmotivated or unwilling person. The social worker's goal is to engage the client in the helping process so that he or she will begin to see value in making changes.

There are fairly straightforward ways of asking a client to describe the problem. An open-ended question such as "What brought you in?," "What is your understanding regarding why you are here?," "Can you tell me the reasons for seeking help at this time?," or "How did you come to the decision to talk with me today?" can open the dialogue. Offer brief comments to encourage the client to continue talking and to convey active listening. All these questions can provide you with some ideas about what is most troubling.

Watch this clip as Mike says to Karen, "I'll just tell you up front what happened. I work as an accountant, and I was caught with alcohol on my breath. My boss sent me to the employee assistance program. They interviewed me, and they told me that I had to initiate a 28-day inpatient program. Otherwise, I won't be able to continue working." How is Karen able to help Mike explore the relationship between alcohol and the primary systems in his life?

A client may describe all the things that are not going well, such as problems at work, an unfulfilling marriage, money concerns, no shelter, and depression. All of these problems are significant, and the two of you will discuss, negotiate, and then decide how to prioritize them. Regardless of how the client describes the problem, it is imperative to listen with care and concern. Entering into the relationship is tenuous as you try to build rapport and engage the client. Understanding the reasons for seeking help at this point in time without disputing the client's reasoning is important. Sometimes a client needs to speak about his or her problems first in order to relieve some of the emotional pressure behind the situation. Voicing feelings of misery, sadness, and despair and being validated by the social worker can be an important step before moving on and dealing with problems. You may have a few hunches about the client's circumstances, but until you have a commitment to work together, keep those ideas and thoughts to yourself. According to the strengths-based approach to problem identification, the client is the final authority on defining the problem. By listening to the client's story, the social worker gains insight and understanding that will be helpful in determining which areas of the multidimensional assessment to explore. By understanding the client's perception of the problem, you will also ascertain who else may be part of the problem system, such as a spouse, a friend, or an employer.

The way the client identifies the problem gives the social worker insight into where the problem may be emanating from. Maybe the problem relates to lack of affordable housing for a mother of three or a soldier just returning from the war zone. The situation could be related to differing expectations of a friendship or a recent diagnosis of cancer. As discussed earlier in this text, the environmental context in which the problem occurs is extremely important because you cannot divorce the person from his or her surroundings. When developing an understanding of the problem, consider who the players are.

Box 10.A introduces you to Jonah, a high school student. As the case unfolds, it becomes evident that Jonah is facing many challenges.

It is not uncommon for a problem to occur only during a specific time of the day or in a specific place. Maybe the client is fine at school but once at home is unable to maintain his or her composure. It is important to understand what may be contributing to the change in behavior. Looking at this from a strengths perspective, consider when things are going well for the client instead of only when the problematic behaviors occur. While working with a client, ask about specific situations or circumstances. Use the client's understanding and insights to help you figure out how to help him or her. For example, a child may have nightmares only when spending the night with a relative. When trying to understand the client's perception of the problem, ask about how frequently the problems occur. Is it daily that Mary Ann is depressed and has trouble getting out of bed? How often is Jim late for work? Is there constant yelling between

Box 10.A Now You Try It . . . Problem Identification: Case Study

Recently, Jonah stopped turning in his homework, began coming to class unprepared, and is now flunking a few of his classes. He has a sports scholarship to a local community college when he finishes high school if he maintains a certain GPA. Because Jonah is flunking history, he will be kicked off the football team, which means losing the scholarship. His mother, Mrs. Bert, is convinced that Ms. Spencer, his teacher, is out to get him and has brought her complaints to the principal. The principal, Dr. Reardon, followed up with Ms. Spencer regarding the allegations. Both Jonah and Ms. Spencer met with the principal during lunch. On further exploration, Jonah shares with them that he will likely fail all of his classes. Immediately following football practice, he goes directly to work as a nighttime stocker at a hardware store. His family received an eviction notice, and they are trying to find a way to keep the apartment. His mother lost her job three months ago, and his dad works periodically as a truck driver. Because he is 17 and the eldest in a family of five, he feels an obligation to do what he can to help his family during this time of crisis. Jonah is very concerned about his grades but admits that he is so far behind in his classes that he is likely to fail, leaving him unsure about his future. He wants to finish high school but believes that without his financial contribution, his family will be out on the street within a month. He also shared that his girlfriend, Faith, may be pregnant. As the outreach social worker, you are asked by Dr. Reardon to assist with this case.

Consider the following:

1. How does Jonah define the problem?
2. How does the outreach social worker define the problem?
3. What external systems are involved in this problem?
4. What factors precipitated this problem?
5. How would you like to see this situation be resolved?

Kate's parents? Using the skill of clarification can help you determine the frequency and duration of the problem. "Constant yelling" may mean every day or twice a week to the client. Understanding how often and for how long the client feels distressed is an important consideration in assessing the situation.

Knowing the history or development of the problem is helpful. When did the problem begin, and how long has the problem occurred? Were things going well for your client until a beloved pet died? Look for patterns in the client's behaviors. For example, Meg is currently enrolled in a job training program through the local community college. This is her third attempt at going back to school. Last week, she quit the program again, stating, "This is too hard for me. My daughter is three and I have no transportation or child care. I have been on a list for five months, and there is no aid to help me. I have to stay home even if it means I have to wait until Darlene is in school to complete the program."

Hepworth, Rooney, Rooney, Strom-Gottfried, and Larsen (2013) identify three primary reasons that clients seek help:

1. People gain relief simply by expressing troubling emotions related to their problems. Such reactions include worry, concern, resentment, hurt, fear, helplessness, feeling overwhelmed, and hopelessness. The nature of the relationship provides a secure place to vent feelings and a safety valve. Sharing the burden can be freeing and provide the client with insights into feelings they may not have previously acknowledged.
2. Emotions influence behavior. It is the behaviors, such as impulsivity and aggressiveness, that tend to cause problems in the client's day-to-day life. Sometimes the situation becomes worse because of the heatedness of the situation.
3. Intense emotional reactions can become the primary problem, sometimes becoming the reason for the intervention itself. As the social worker, respond to the emotional reactions as well as what may be the precipitating event.

Looking at the client's strengths can be very helpful in determining where the problem lies. How the client has coped in the past can give the social worker insight into how he or she utilized these skills and strategies before. What is different this time, as it appears the client's coping mechanisms are less effective now?

Ask the client to rank order the problems as he or she defines them; for example, the client should identify what needs to be addressed immediately. This approach follows the strengths-based perspective as the client articulates the nature of the problems and identifies probable solutions. The best approach is to work together to identify a reasonable number of problems to focus one at a time. Overwhelming the client with too many problems to address can lead to frustration and consequently the client losing motivation for change. The bottom line is that goal setting is much more than the client simply saying he or she wants something to happen—it is a planned and purposeful process.

Assess your understanding of problem identification by taking this brief quiz.

PLANNING

Effective planning must involve the commitment and collaborative efforts of both the social worker and the client. Research consistently finds a correlation between goal consensus and mutual collaboration and positive client outcomes (Tryon, 2002). Is there a goodness of fit between the parties and the planning process? Does the social worker believe in the client, and does he or she have the capacity to help the client move forward? Does the social worker understand how other systems, such as family, community, or school, are involved with the problem? These considerations are central to planning.

During the intake, assessment, and problem identification stages, the amount of information collected can be exhaustive. There can be so much data that it becomes difficult to sift through and organize it all. It is the planning stage that helps the social worker and client begin to develop strategies for change that are realistic and solution focused. In developing ways to address what the client hopes to accomplish, it is important to have a shared vision of what is possible. Without planning, there is no direction for where to go and how to get there. All planning efforts should be done in collaboration with the client even if he or she appears apathetic and disinterested.

Social workers do not offer a one-size-fits-all approach to planning. It is through listening, asking questions, and synthesizing all of the information that the client will be able to choose a path. The path may take many turns and twists, but the goal is to help the client accomplish the objectives set out in collaboration with the social worker.

If a client chooses a path that you believe is detrimental or unattainable, be honest and gentle in your feedback. Do not shy away from difficult conversation when the information is in the best interest of the client. Consider Chester, a 55-year-old male who is currently homeless. He is living at the shelter. One of the shelter's requirements is that he must be involved in daytime activities, such as looking for a job or attending a training program. He has told the social worker, Joe, that he is shoplifting from grocery stores and gas stations in order to eat. The social worker does understand Chester's level of desperation and his need to eat, but his behaviors could eventually lead to an arrest. The social worker talks with Chester about the consequences of his choices and offers some suggestions. Options include volunteering at a local food pantry and attending a training program (which also offers a lunchtime meal).

In considering Chester's current situation, Joe becomes aware of how the "out of the shelter during the day" policy is causing his client to resort to stealing food. After talking with his supervisor about the shelter's policy, Joe contacts the agency administrator for further clarification. Now in his role as a class advocate, he speaks for all of the residents of the shelter who are affected by this policy, resulting in possible change on the macro level.

Mike finally admits that he is an alcoholic. What steps does he need to take and plan for in order to stay sober? Watch this clip as Mike and Karen have an emotionally charged conversation. How convincingly does Mike communicate to Karen his desire to remain sober? In your opinion, how likely is he to remain sober after leaving treatment?

When planning for change, make sure the client's goals relate to what the client will commit to doing. Use the client's own words whenever possible. This demonstrates that the social worker is listening and may serve as a verbal reminder that this is the client's plan. Sometimes planning for change means there are competing goals. For example, "I want out of this hellhole; this apartment is not fit for human life. But I can't leave my pets here, so where do I go?" In this case, the client expresses conflicting statements; she wants to find a new apartment, but finding another one that allows pets may not be an option. How does she prioritize if she is not able to find a new place to live? It is possible to still work on both by asking where there may be some agreement or commonality? You can rank order goals by starting with goal A and eventually coming back to goal B.

As social workers, the goal is not to always remove the underlying issues and experience but to find a solution to the problems. Sometimes forces such as family, friends, or the community can contribute to the problems by not wanting change to occur. For example, a client in a violent relationship may feel pressure from her family to stay because there are cultural norms that prohibit leaving one's husband. The probability of her success in leaving the relationship will rest on where the problem lies. In this case, her problem may be exacerbated because there is no safe place (family members will not support a violation of cultural norms by providing housing and support), and therefore she feels trapped with no escape route.

Focus on instituting or beginning something new rather than what cannot be changed. By offering different ways to think about experiences and problems, the social worker is offering an alternative set of beliefs about the client.

Sheafor and Horejsi (2015) identify ways to help the client and social worker set priorities in the planning process:

1. The client determines what are the problems or concerns needing attention. (What specifically do you want to do?)
2. The social worker offers insights and recommendation.
3. The problems are reviewed together and grouped into categories, such as problems at work, problems within a marriage, and problems with the neighbor.
4. Collaboration between the client and social worker takes place to determine which problems hold the highest priority. Which ones have the greatest likelihood of positively affecting the client immediately, midrange, and long term? Which goals are not realistic at this time? Consider how the client's life will be different once these goals are accomplished. (i.e., What does success look like?)

The Rule of Three, or pick your top three choices, proposes that no more than three goals be worked on at a time. This particular approach forces the client to choose wisely. It also helps the client and social worker focus on the end, not the means. One of the best ways to get results is to stay flexible in your approach while keeping one's eye on the prize. Rather than get overwhelmed by tasks, take on three things that can be accomplished. This puts the client in control.

The more clearly the goals are stated, the more manageable and attainable the solutions tend to be. Ultimately, what the client wants will determine the course of action to be followed. Basics such as shelter, food, and clothing may be the client's Rule of Three, or top three choices, until life improves enough to focus on the next three problems, such as a job, a school placement for his or her children, and follow-up medical care. Goals must be clear and well defined. Vague or generalized goals are unhelpful because they don't provide sufficient direction. Goals show the client the way. Make goal setting as easy as possible to help the client get to where he or she wants to go by defining precisely the end point.

Intervention

Behaviors: Critically choose and implement interventions to achieve practice goals and enhance capacities of clients and constituencies.
Facilitate effective transitions and endings that advance mutually agreed-on goals.

Critical Thinking Question: As a social worker, you will encounter many clients who are not invested in problem solving and seeking resolution. They may be mandated to receive services via a probation officer or parent. How will you work toward involving them in the process, even when the client seems resistant to your help?

When a client sets goals, it is important to assess if these goals are important and what the value is in achieving them. If the client has little interest in the outcome or sees the goals as irrelevant given the larger picture, then the chances of a client putting in the work to make them happen are slim. Motivation is the key to achieving goals. Set goals that relate to the client's highest priorities. Goal achievement requires commitment. To maximize the likelihood of success, the client must feel a sense of urgency and have an "I must do this" attitude. Otherwise, the client is risking putting off what needs to be done. This in turn can leave the client feeling disappointed and frustrated in an "I can't do anything" frame of mind.

Help your client understand why the goals are important and valuable. Ask the client, "If you were to share these goals with others, what would you tell people to convince them it was a worthwhile goal?" This motivating value statement is helpful especially if the client begins to doubt his or her ability to make the goals actually happen. Goals are power; they give direction and focus to every aspect of the client's life. Goals that matter to the client must be based in his or her beliefs and value systems; otherwise, there is no commitment or follow-through.

Nicole talks about contacting the school social worker and getting the case aide more involved. Mrs. Anderson is relieved to hear that there are some supports available to help her cope with the adjustment of Maria now living full-time with her. Watch this clip as Nicole and Mrs. Anderson begin to narrow down some ways that Nicole can be of assistance to her.

In working with a client to identify goals, it is also beneficial to determine if you and your agency are the best option available for the client or if there is an alternative resource that can better serve the client's needs. It is hoped that this decision will be made during the intake process. However, depending on the information gathered at the point of entry (or any point along the way), the problem to be worked on may be different from the presenting problem at intake. This may be the point at which you refer the client to another professional or seek out specialized supervision and consultation. For example, Lana is a 37-year-old female who is currently receiving dialysis treatments three times a week at the local clinic. She generally comes in for treatment in a good mood, full of funny stories and tales of her children's escapades. Today, Lana came to the clinic extremely agitated and could not be calmed. The social worker immediately noticed the change in her demeanor. After a few minutes of sitting with her, Lana shared that her 12-year-old daughter was sexually assaulted by a neighbor. The Child Protection Agency had been called and an investigation has begun. At this point, the social worker realizes the need for a referral to a person who can help Lana manage the entire trauma associated with the assault. Although the social worker at the clinic will continue to provide supportive services, a person with more specialized training and expertise would be an appropriate referral. The presenting problem is kidney failure; the problem for work has changed to the crisis with her daughter.

Box 10.2 Guidelines for Writing Goal Statements and Contracts

What to include:

1. Goals to be accomplished and the client's expectations for completing the goals (goals ranked by priority, sequential order, and time frames).
2. Divide the goals into smaller and more manageable pieces that are measurable.
3. Phrase goals in simple terms and clear language, using the client's word choices.
4. Be specific about what goals and objectives will be included in the contract.
5. Emphasize the commitment of both parties and clarify the roles of client and social worker in an effort to eliminate discrepancies and possible misunderstandings.
6. Clarify under what circumstances the contract will be renegotiated, such as when new details emerge or significant progress is made.
7. Both parties can request changes to be made in the contract.

When working with a client to reach a desired goal, it is important to determine if the goal is realistic and achievable. The goal must be defined in operational terms so that both parties know what is to be accomplished, how, by whom, and by when. The more specific the goals, the greater the likelihood of the client staying motivated. Hepworth et al. (2013) encourage social workers to consider what is lacking in the client's life, such as housing, a job, or an intimate relationship, and to translate those deficits into possibilities.

It is beneficial to explain the rationale for goal setting, as it gives the client a sense of direction and purpose. When a goal is defined, the roles of each person are established, and a plan of action is in place, the real work of problem solving begins. See Box 10.2 for guidelines regarding how to write goals and develop a contract with your client.

To understand how social learning theory can be applied to practice, see Box 10.I.

? Assess your understanding of planning by taking this brief quiz.

Box 10.I Theory into Practice—Social Learning Theory and Social Skills Training: Case Study

Social learning theory emphasizes the importance of observing and modeling the behaviors, attitudes, and emotional reactions of others. Thus, it focuses on learning by observation and modeling. Social learning theory addresses how both environmental and cognitive factors interact to influence human learning and behavior. It focuses on the learning that occurs within a social context. It considers that people learn from one another, including such concepts as observational learning, imitation, and modeling (Bandura, 1986).

Carlos is a 22-year-old male living in a group home for adults who are intellectually challenged. He completed high school and a vocational training program and is currently working part-time as a dishwasher and occasional short-order cook at a local restaurant. He functions at the high moderate range of mental retardation, can read simple books, and has moderately good personal hygiene skills, attentional capacity, and conversational skills. He has no biological family but occasionally visits the Ruiz family, with whom he lived from age 5 to 12. On reaching adolescence, there were concerns regarding his "inappropriate behaviors" directed toward one of their daughters. Although never substantiated, he was removed from their care and placed in a residential program. The transition was very challenging for him, but keeping in touch with the Ruiz family served as a reminder of their care and concern for him. Carlos made great progress in the residential program and by age 16 was moved to the group home where he currently lives.

Last week, Carlos shared with you that he met a young woman, Lily, at a social event and has "fallen in love." As the social worker, you understand that Carlos is a person with the

(Continued)

Box 10.1 Theory into Practice—Social Learning Theory and Social Skills Training: *(Continued)*

same interests and desires as other people. You appreciate Carlos for the sensitive person he is. He has talked with you on several occasions about love, finding a girlfriend, and getting married. You support his interest in having a girlfriend, especially if the relationship is mutual and both are consenting adults. Your role is to help Carlos develop appropriate dating behaviors such as taking turns in a conversation, touching, and intimacy.

As you begin to think about ways to help Carlos, you read articles that focus on helping intellectually challenged individuals develop social skills. What you propose is to teach him how to interact with members of the opposite sex, using role plays and modeling. You practice with Carlos how to ask a girl out on a date, offer a compliment, and ways to compromise such as who decides the activity. You role-play ways to nonverbally communicate by focusing on smiling, showing warmth, and practicing appropriate interpersonal distance. You make up scenarios about dating and praise him when he demonstrates the targeted behavior. You help him to relax and take better care of his appearance and personal hygiene. You also develop a social skills group with other young adults so they too can learn and practice these behaviors. You model and practice these skills with Carlos over several months, as you know repetition is the best intervention approach. Finally, he asks Lily out on a date and reports back to you that he "likes her a lot."

As the social worker, you know that more sensitive topics, such as practicing safe sex, using contraceptives, and the mechanics of sexual intercourse, may be topics that will be addressed as Carlos and Lily's relationship continues. Through repeated conversations and role plays, Carlos is able to recite word for word the guidelines for "good touch" and "bad touch." He can point to his and her "private parts" using a doll and picture cards, and he can tell you about hugging and kissing. As the social worker, you will continually assess his readiness to explore more intimate aspects of his relationship with Lily. As his interest in Lily continues to develop, be sure to consult with your supervisor or an expert in the field regarding the best ways to teach clients about sex education and the "mechanics" of safe sex.

Cultural Competence Working with a Client from Iran

Shohreh is a 45-year-old woman who is married with two children. Her family emigrated to the United States from Iran when she was fifteen. Approximately five years ago, Farzin, her husband, was critically injured in a car accident.

Although Farzin has recovered and is back to work at the university, there have been significant cracks in their relationship. While Farzin seems to have moved on from the accident, Shohreh, who was with him in the car, continues to have flashbacks and relives the details of the event as though it were yesterday. She has sought you out as a social worker in her community, as there are no helping professionals who have a similar cultural background as she and her family. You are a fairly new practitioner, working in a small agency near campus. You are a bit anxious about meeting her. Your concerns are as follows: Will she be open to you, a Caucasian female from Minnesota? How do you address her? Where does she position herself in relationship to her marriage? How do you view yourself in relationship to her culture? How does her faith and spirituality fit with her presenting problem? What is her role within the family unit? How do you prepare for the meeting? Put yourself in the social worker's place and begin to think about how to proceed in this helping relationship. What do you know about her faith, her spiritual practices, and the way she sees herself within the community where they live. Are there appropriate referrals, such as a traditional healer? How do you learn about her upbringing in Iran and the United States, and her concerns about Western counseling approaches.

CONTRACTING

Contracting by its very nature is a partnership. It is a way to facilitate change as a process rather than dictating "I know what is best for you." A core value of social work is client self-determination, and, as such, the client is the primary partner. Without his or her commitment to the process, the worker can develop a perfect contract that will never be implemented because there is no shared vision and collaboration. Contracts specify the goals to be accomplished and the means to accomplish them, clarify the roles of the participants, and establish the conditions under which assistance is provided. As a social worker, it is important to understand the agency's policies regarding how contracts are to be written and documented and, ultimately, how they are to be used to facilitate the helping process.

Box 10.3 introduces you to Tony. After reading the case study, consider whether you believe this contract reflects Tony's goals. If not, what would you do differently?

In developing a contract with a client, consider that long-term goals are typically focused on the future (a year or more) and can remain quite similar over the long term. It is the action plan that can change significantly. A long-term goal is "Get a master's degree within the next five years." Short-term goals generally can start immediately and may continue for up to one year. For example, a short-term goal that can help the client stay focused on the long-term goal may be "Study for the GRE," "Find a career path that will help me determine where my strengths and interests lie," or "Develop a network of people in my field who can mentor me through the graduate school process." Once you have developed a long-term goal and short-term goals, it is

Assessment

Behaviors: Develop mutually agreed-on intervention goals and objectives based on the critical assessment of strengths, needs, and challenges within clients and constituencies.

Select appropriate intervention strategies based on the assessment, research knowledge, and values and preferences of clients and constituencies.

Critical Thinking Question: Your client Jason is a 45 year old man recently diagnosed with cardiovascular disease, following a heart attack. Jason shares with you the need to change his life style. Jason is morbidly obese, his father died at age 55 from a heart attack and he is a smoker. You and Jason have completed the intake form; you have assessed his situation and now you are ready assist him, as he begins the process of "getting healthy." Identify one long term goal and three short term goals. Provide an explanation of why these goals were selected.

Box 10.3 Contracting: Case Study

Tony is 21 years old. He is currently living at home with his parents, but their relationship has worsened over the past several weeks. He was working as a mechanic in a body shop, making enough money to live at home, make car payments, pay for food and a small portion of the rent. One month ago, Tony was nearly fired. He had been caught sleeping at work and "disappearing for long stretches of time." He talked his boss into giving him another chance, which he did. Tony's work performance improved, and he was hopeful about retaining his job. Last week, he came to work late, was heard yelling at a customer, and left his work station without letting anyone know. His supervisor told Tony to clean out his locker and leave the key with the secretary. Tony left the body shop feeling remorseful and saddened. Several of his good friends work there, and it was a great place to socialize. He has to tell his parents but is concerned about their reaction, especially because they know he was given a second chance.

Tony is now looking for a job but admits he is not overly motivated. His parents are providing him with food and housing. Since he was fired, the tension has increased at home with daily yelling and accusations being launched. He does understand his parent's frustrations but doesn't think he deserves to be treated with such disregard. He states, "My dad had the nerve to call me an asshole and threatened to call the police. He accused me of breaking into my own house and stealing money from them. I would love to get out of there, but I have nothing right now but my car. What am I supposed to do?" As the social worker, you are concerned that Tony is not taking responsibility for his work-related troubles and is minimizing his father's accusations. However, in talking with him, he does not appear ready to accept his role in either the termination or the problems at home. But you two do agree on the following goals:

Step 1: What are Tony's long- and short-term goals? (the Rule of Three/top three choices, in rank order)

1. To find a job (up to one year)
2. To find a place to live (up to one year)
3. To get along better with my family (up to six months)

Step 1 helps the client and social worker to identify what the "big" issues are. These long- and short-term goals are the ones that provide direction and are the driving force in the relationship. Dreaming and wishing for something to happen

(Continued)

Box 10.3 Contracting: Case Study *(Continued)*

is not goal setting. Goals are plans put into action. They involve hard work and sticking to it, even when the client may lose focus and motivation. In Tony's case, his goals are interrelated. For example, in order to pay for an apartment, he needs a job. In order for his relationship with his parents to improve, he must find a job, move out, and acknowledge the circumstances that led to his father accusing him of stealing money.

Step 2: What skills and resources does Tony have to reach his goals?

1. A high school degree
2. A friend with an apartment for rent
3. Transportation to a job
4. Work skills/a trade
5. A small savings account
6. A network of supportive friends
7. A desire to be independent
8. Decision-making capacity
9. Motivated to improve communication with family members
10. A community that is rich in resources
11. Hopeful about his future work prospects
12. Motivated to find a job
13. Insight into the circumstances that led to his termination
14. Good verbal communication skills
15. Good health (currently covered under his parent's medical insurance plan)

Step 2 involves identifying what skills and resources Tony has. Many of his resources are internal to the person, such as his desire to be independent or his insight into what led to his termination. Other resources are more tangible such as a car, health insurance, and a small savings account.

Step 3: Turning skills, resources, and obstacles into action

1. Determine if the goal is reasonable and realistic.
2. Determine how important the goal is to Tony.
3. In what ways is it worthwhile to pursue this goal?
4. Determine the time frame for accomplishing the goal.
5. Is the goal challenging enough to keep Tony motivated?
6. To what extent does Tony want to reach his goal or not reach his goal?
7. Does Tony really want to be independent?
8. Who cares if Tony accomplishes this goal?
9. How will other people in Tony's life be affected if he finds a job or not?
10. Look at the benefits and consequences of achieving the goal.
11. How will Tony's life be different if he achieves this goal or not?
12. How will you and Tony determine if the goal was accomplished?
13. If Tony attains this goal, will it lead to the resolution of other issues, such as his relationship with his parents?
14. Who is involved in assisting Tony in reaching his goal?

Step 3 provides the opportunity to go beyond identifying skills and resources but also to identify issues, people, or circumstances that may be detrimental to goal achievement. Help the client think about ways to accomplish the goals in a more concrete way. How can Tony take his internal strength of "good decision-making capacity" and turn it into a workable goal? What does that actually mean? For example, how has he made decisions in the past that have proven successful? He completed high school and developed a trade. He can save money and is a good friend to others. Break it down and figure out how he can use those strengths to help him through his current situation.

Step 4: Brainstorm/plan of action ideas and tasks—to be accomplished within six months (in consultation with the social worker)

1. Where does Tony start looking for a job?
2. What kind of work interests him?
3. Contact temporary placement agencies.
4. Complete applications.
5. Practice interviewing skills.
6. Purchase an interview outfit.
7. Network with others in the auto body business.
8. Locate a union for auto body workers.
9. Look for an apprenticeship.
10. Check out want ads.
11. Find a mentor to consult with regarding job opportunities.
12. Document examples of Tony's work.
13. Develop a script regarding what led to Tony being fired, what he learned, and what he will do differently.

Box 10.3 Contracting: Case Study *(Continued)*

Step 4 is the brainstorming and preparation for the action stage. This is the stage when social worker and client get creative and throw out any ideas that are even remotely possible. Given all that the social worker knows about the client (and, it is hoped, the client is learning about himself), what is next? What are the time lines to accomplishing the goals? How does the social worker assist Tony from point A to point B? What will success look like, and how will he know that he is making progress?

Step 5: Contract—Break it down by what is to be accomplished, how, by whom, and by when (top three choices by category)

To be done first:

1. Get examples of work, photos, and client testimonies by _______ (date). (#12)
2. Develop a script by _________ (date). (#13)
3. Contact temporary placements agencies for short-term (interim) employment by _______. (#3)

Step 5: Continued: Break it down again (top three choices)

To be done second:

1. Network with others and find mentor by _______ (date). (#7 and #8)
2. Look for apprenticeship by ______ (date). (#9 and #11)
3. Locate a union for auto body workers by _______ (date). (#8)

Step 5: Continued: Break it down again (top three choices)

To be done next:

1. Check out want ads, contact at least three temporary placement agencies, and complete four applications a week by ______ (date). (#1, #3, and #10)
2. Practice interviewing skills by _______ (date). (#5)
3. Purchase an interview outfit by _______ (date). (#6)

Step 5 is the actual writing of the document itself. This document can take many forms (see Appendix C). As you and the client are hammering out the details of the contract, remember this agreement belongs to the client. No matter how beautifully written a contract may be, if the client isn't in full accord, this could be one more failed attempt. Be positive and encouraging. Be realistic and pragmatic. Your competence as a social worker is not dependent on the client's successful completion of the contract. Sometimes the client chooses not to complete the terms of the contract yet may revisit it in years to come.

time to think about specific tasks to keep the client on track. Five years is a long time, but buying the GRE study guide is something the client can do today or within a short amount of time. Short-term goals serve as the stepping-stones to the long-term overarching goal. Frame your goal statements positively and use solution-focused vocabulary such as the following:

Achieve	Appreciate	Collaborate	Complete
Create	Empower	Expand	Facilitate
Generate	Honor	Initiate	Institute
Organize	Produce	Respect	Start

Include precise steps to be taken in order to determine if the goal has been accomplished. If the goal is defined as "to get along better with my parents," how will the client and social worker know when success has been achieved? A better way to determine if the goal is accomplished is to state it in measurable terms. For example, "When with my parents, I will show respect and be courteous to them for up to one hour at a time." Without a way to measure success, the client can miss out on the celebration that comes with knowing he or she actually achieved something. A client who sets a goal with no hope of achieving it can be demoralized, leading to lack of confidence. Accomplishing a goal that is too easy can be anticlimactic. By setting realistic yet challenging goals, the client finds balance. Goals that require the client to raise the bar bring the greatest personal satisfaction.

When planning for the client's care, focus on completing the following:

1. Identify which interventions or techniques will be used, such as relaxation training, role playing, conflict resolution, cognitive and behavioral modification, guided imagery, and psychotherapy.
2. There are many routes to any goal; therefore, explore the most effective and cost efficient.
3. When identifying interventions, consider the skills of the social worker and his or her areas of expertise. If the intervention is focused on marital strife, does the social worker have the specialty skills to be most helpful? The social worker's skills and knowledge must be continually reassessed to determine that his or her skill set meets the client's needs. If you believe that you are not the best person to provide treatment, discuss this with your supervisor. Depending on the community (or resources available), you may be able to refer the client to another service provider. There are times, however, when the social worker may need to quickly educate himself or herself on a specific area of practice or intervention so as to provide services to the client. If this is the case, always do so in close consultation with an expert in the field.

Intervention becomes the stage in the relationship where the majority of the work is carried out by the client. It is the "the rubber hits the road" part of the helping process.

Watch this segment of the video as and Yesenia are talking to Kim about her thoughts regarding suicide. She clearly states that she is not thinking about taking her own life, but regardless Louis and Yesenia get her to verbally agree to reach out to a staff person or call the VA Hotline if she feels suicidal. She reluctantly agrees.

Time Frames and Logistics for the Client's Care

The following elements should be discussed with the client and be part of the planning included in the client contract:

1. Tentative start and end dates for the contract (no social worker has unlimited time to spend with a client; be realistic and follow through).
2. What are the limits to the helping process (not promising more than what can be offered)?
3. How often will the concerned parties be meeting (include the length of each session)?
4. Where will meetings take place (in the office, client's home, foster family's home)?
5. Who will be involved (foster parents, case aide, nursing home administrator)?
6. A social worker can never commit to a contract that is unethical or detrimental to a client or that puts another party in danger.

7. Under what circumstances may a meeting be terminated (e.g., client smells of alcohol, pets present a safety hazard, no quiet place to meet, or social worker is sick)?
8. What is the cancellation policy of the agency?
9. How are changes in scheduled meetings addressed?
10. Is there a fee for services? How will the fee be paid?
11. Structural constraints of the agency, such as resources, and policies that determine service delivery, such as long- or short-term treatment.

This part of the process is extremely important because the more precise the contract, the less the likelihood of misunderstanding and miscommunication. Holding each other accountable for meeting the conditions of the contract is an important part of the process. Regardless of who agrees to do what, there is a joint commitment, a shared vision for what life may hold as the client gets closer to his or her goal.

Progress over Time

Equally as important as time frames for interventions is the understanding of how the treatment will be assessed and when success has been attained. Discuss with the client the measures that you will use to determine when the problem is effectively responding to the intervention. Also involve the client in the monitoring and assessment of the treatment when appropriate, such as keeping a journal of behaviors and feelings. Finally, set points in the helping process when you and the client will review the data and progress over time. When planning and contracting for evaluation, consider the following:

1. How progress will be evaluated will depend on the nature of the problem.
2. Collect baseline data using assessment tools such as Beck's Depression Inventory and compare it with current data.
3. Ask the client how he or she has progressed over time (self-reporting).
4. Collateral contacts, such as a teacher, foster parent, or spouse, can provide insight into whether change has occurred.

How does the client report changes that have occurred in his or her life? Is the change noticeable to the teacher, the foster parent, and the client? Being able to tick off each task as it is accomplished is a great motivator. Help the client to celebrate, even though there may be more work to be done. Box 10.B provides you with an opportunity to consider all the components that go into a service plan/treatment plan and contract.

Written Contract

When developing a **written contract** with a client, consider that he or she may view a written contract as a "legal document" that must be followed, or consequences will occur. As this may be the case, many agencies do require the written contract be signed and dated, and it becomes a part of the client's permanent record. If the contract is in writing, explain where the document will be housed, who will have access, and how it will be used to monitor the helping process. It is the social worker's responsibility to help the client understand the nature of a written contract. It is critical that a client not feel coerced into signing a contract. Explaining the participatory nature of the contract and

Box 10.B Now You Try It . . . Planning, Goal Setting, and Contracting: Case Study

Sonia is a 56-year-old female who was recently diagnosed with breast cancer. After working for 35 years as a social worker, she retired looking forward to her life as a grandmother and a free spirit. Her husband Ron is also retired and works part-time as a freelance photographer. They have two daughters, Lori, age 25, and Terri, age 29, and a son Micah, age 19. Sonia was caught completely by surprise, as she sees herself as a balanced person who exercises daily and eats a healthy diet. There is no family history of breast cancer, which also contributed to her shock.

Sonia has come to the cancer center following a mastectomy and is extremely depressed. She is a chemotherapy patient and will also have several rounds of radiation. Her husband has been very supportive but is unsure how to help her. Sonia reports that she has a hard time concentrating, feels tired and weak, and can barely put one foot in front of the other. During one of her chemotherapy sessions, you approach her. Sonia begins to cry as she tells you about her interrupted life plan. She had hoped to volunteer at the local domestic violence shelter and promised her daughter Terri that she would provide child care to her newborn son Adam. Now she is sick and can barely make it through a few hours without collapsing from exhaustion. She tells you that her mother Eva has dementia and is also ill with kidney failure and in need of dialysis. She wants to help her mother but doesn't have the patience or energy at this time. Her son Micah is joining the Marines, which is also causing her distress. Sonia has always been the "go to" person in the family, and now she is unsure of her place. Throughout the interview, the social worker offers support and a listening ear.

The following week, Sonia has come back for another round of treatment. The social worker asks her how she is managing. Sonia is still feeling sick and extremely tired. Her sister, Helen, has come to "help" but is of no assistance. They have been arguing about their mother's care, specifically the need to place her in a long-term care facility. Sonia reports that she believes it is time to place her in a nursing home and that the day-to-day care is more than she can manage. Helen's perspective is different. She is concerned that once their mother is placed in a long-term care facility, it is the equivalent of signing her death certificate. Sonia asks you to help her sort things out, as she is unsure of her thinking process and her decision-making skills.

1. Identify one long-term goal and three short-term goals that relate to Sonia's situation. Include some smaller tasks that she can do, to help her reach her goals.
2. What factors did you consider in determining what the long-term and short-term goals would be?
3. How might the changes in Sonia's circumstances effect renegotiating the contract?

the possible consequences of not following it are important steps in developing trust. The more transparent the process, the greater likelihood the client will be a full participant. Clients may feel as if they have no choice in the nature and the conditions of the contract. The relationship that has been built over time may help to relieve some of these concerns. The bottom line, however, is that if a client agrees to the contents of the contract and does not meet the goals by a specified date, there could be significant consequences, such as a child being removed from a parent's home. Not all contracts have this level of identified consequences attached to the outcome. Many contracts focus on internal changes, such as developing more patience or longer periods of sobriety, rather than external forces pushing on the client. Give the client a copy of the fully executed contract. Suggest that he or she post the contract in a visible place, such as a wall, desk, computer monitor, bathroom mirror, or refrigerator, or carry it in a pocket as a constant reminder. Encourage the client to check off goals as they are accomplished, as this can be very motivating. Conversely, not making much progress can be discouraging.

Verbal Contract

A client may view a **verbal contract** as "my word is my bond," meaning that nothing is of higher importance than the client's word. When entering into a verbal contract, be sure to inform the client that a general description of the contract will be documented in the record. It is the responsibility of the social worker to enter into the case file the gist, as some type of documentation is needed to verify services. A verbal contract does not lock the client into specific time frames and goals, as there tends to be more flexibility regarding the nature of the work together. Understanding the social worker's role and influence is as important as the nature of the relationship. Trust is built over time and will be an essential factor in the two-person commitment. The nature of the client's problems may remain fairly constant throughout the course of the relationship, but understanding ways in which the client may approach and avoid a task concurrently can be helpful in this stage of the relationship.

Example of a verbal contract:

Social Worker: What one or two issues do you want to focus on for next week?
Client: I want to figure out if I am going to accept the graduate assistantship and go to grad school.
Social Worker: Is it reasonable to make a decision within the next week?
Client: I want to. I just don't know where to start.
Social Worker: How about a Pros and Cons list? What are the benefits to going to grad school and what are the benefits to working for a year or two?
Client: I can do that.
Social Worker: Consider this a homework assignment. (Said with a smile)
Client: Okay, I will come up with a list and try to make a final decision soon.
Social Worker: Great, I look forward to hearing what you decide.

In Box 10.C, meet Marla, a new client, and try developing a contract with her that will for the basis of your work together.

Box 10.C Now You Try It . . . Developing a Contract: Case Study

Marla is a senior at a large urban university. She grew up in a small town surrounded by good public schools, plentiful recreational activities, and close to her extended family. Throughout her junior and senior high school years, she was very involved in her church, specifically the youth group. Marla's home life has been a source of stress and angst. Evelyn, her mother, is an alcoholic. She has been in and out of treatment over the past 10 years but has not been able to stay sober. Her father George is also a heavy drinker, but according to Marla, he can handle the alcohol better and is able to "function pretty well."

During Marla's senior year of high school, she got pregnant. Ken, her boyfriend, broke up with her days after she told him that she was pregnant. He refused to talk to her, and within a few weeks of the breakup he was dating another girl. Given Marla's strong religious faith and her belief that abortion is a sin, she spent most of her senior year trying to decide what to do. Her parents and close friends were supportive of her and provided her with a safe place to talk about and think about the future.

After many hours of considering what to do, Marla decided to explore an open adoption through a local agency. This would allow her to have some contact with the family and baby. Once Timothy was born, Marla experienced regret and extreme sadness. She clearly questioned her decision and did not find any comfort in her faith.

Marla went off to college and has spent the last four years trying to figure out where things went so wrong. She is now graduating with at least a $60,000 debt and no job prospects. She doesn't want to move back home yet has nowhere to live after mid-May. Clark, Marla's boyfriend, is not very helpful or supportive; he is currently unemployed and has plans to move to Denver. She is very concerned about him and their future together. In talking to her friend Jenny, she states, "I am always taking care of other people; when will someone notice that I am barely hanging on?" Jenny encourages Marla to seek out the services of the university counseling center, where she meets you for the first time.

During the session, you ask her general questions about how she is doing, what brought her in today, and how she is managing. You quickly discover that she is barely able to talk about what is going on right now. She appears numb and is looking out over your shoulder. You attempt

Box 10.C Now You Try It . . . Developing a Contract: Case Study *(Continued)*

to engage her in conversation. Finally, you say, "I can tell whatever is going on right now you are in a great deal of pain; I am here to listen and help. There is no pressure at all; I will follow your lead." Slowly, Marla recaps all that has happened in her life, focusing specifically on losing Timmy. Over the next several sessions, Marla is becoming more comfortable talking to you and has agreed to develop some short- and long-term goals to help her figure out what are the next steps.

Step 1 Long-term goals for Marla (in rank order). What does she hope to accomplish over the next few years?

Step 2 What skills and resources does Marla have to reach her goals?

Step 3 Turning skills, resources, and obstacles into action?

Step 4 Brainstorm/plan of action ideas and tasks (in consultation with the social worker).

Step 5 Contract (time frames and accountability).

There are many ways that a contract (or treatment plan) can be written. Of importance is that the social worker follows the documentation requirements of the agency. Each program or agency will provide the social worker with a general outline or, in some cases, a very detailed outline that must be completed as directed. It is recommended that the social worker initially have a supervisor review the contract to be sure that everything is appropriately written and documented. The agency's quality assurance review team will continue to monitor all record keeping and documentation as part of their accreditation standards. However, the close scrutiny of a supervisor will lessen as the social worker gains experience in developing contracts with clients.

Barriers to Progress

As social workers, we take pride in our clients' accomplishments. However, there are times when we may want a client to succeed more than he or she does. This can be frustrating as we find ourselves working harder than the client. For example, if the social worker is transporting a client to collect job applications and then is filling them out for the client and returning them to the potential employer, you are working harder than the client. If the social worker is looking for housing for the client while the client is staying at the homeless shelter, the social worker is working harder than the client. Finally, if the social worker is there for every supervised visit with the children yet the client is not, the social worker is working harder than the client.

There are many factors that contribute to **barriers to progress**, such as the client not following through or appearing not to care about services. The mandated client, or who Compton et al. (2005) refer to as the "potential client," there are some considerations to take into account. This person may be required to meet with the social worker against his or her will. Be understanding and supportive of the situation, acknowledging this is a difficult situation for both of you. It is important to have the facts straight regarding the reason for the referral and the limits to confidentiality. Let the client decide if he or she wants to continue with services while explaining the consequences of not following through with the order. Be honest and open about your role and what the client can expect from you. Encourage the client to be honest too, as there is no benefit to lying, even if it seems like the most expeditious approach. Use your best active listening skills and offer choices to the client where appropriate. (See Appendix D for more information on deescalating potentially volatile situations.)

All social workers will interact with clients who appear to be manipulative. Sometimes it can be difficult to identify the client as manipulative because he or she can be so agreeable and charming. Being very clear about professional and personal boundaries is an important aspect of working with him or her. A client who attempts to manipulate those around him or her is typically looking for ways to control the situation. As the social worker, it will be essential to hold firm on the agency policies, guidelines, expectations, and roles as the client may try to bend them or ask for a favor. Be on the lookout for deception and always consult with others if you feel as though the client is using you for his or her own gain. Pay attention to the client's nonverbal facial expressions, as these can sometimes provide a window into the client's inner world. A person telling the truth does not have to think about what to say because it is the truth. A person who is a skilled liar may still need to remind himself or herself of the lie by taking an extra second or so to respond.

Ethical and Professional Behavior

Behaviors: Use reflection and self-regulation to manage personal values and maintain professionalism in practice situations.

Critical Thinking Question: Think about possible barriers to goals that have gotten in *your* way. If you could go back and do things differently, what specifically would you address to ensure a greater likelihood of success?

A disinterested client may become a potential client, a motivated, and, over time, an invested client. Find something that gets the client interested in the process. Look to the client for ideas about what really matters. Find areas of agreement, even if initially there is not much effort on the client's part to engage. By being genuine and authentic in your relationship with the client, almost any situation can turn into a win-win.

? Assess your understanding of contracting by taking this brief quiz.

From session 1 to session 3, you see Mike begin to take responsibility for his drinking. He is able to acknowledge there are some underlying issues that he needs to address, such as his relationship with Susie, how he manages stress, honesty, work ethic, and how to anticipate his drinking triggers. Mike's work is not done. Through admission to discharge, Karen served as a support person. She was deliberate in her work with him, as she pushed him to confront his drinking and begin to make different life choices. Now watch as Mike and Karen as they work their way through the helping relationship.

SUMMARY

Understanding that clients come to the helping process from a variety of life perspectives and experiences can be very instrumental in setting the stage for planned change. Whether you enter into a lengthy or a short-term relationship will depend on the agency setting, client expectations, and the goodness of fit between the two of you. However, when working together, you both commit to finding solutions that are reasonable and attainable and that provide motivation throughout the course of treatment and beyond. As a social worker, it is your responsibility to guide the client through the process by assisting him or her toward a successful and timely termination.

- You have learned how to frame the problem so there is a workable solution
- You have learned how to start the process of contracting with a client to help facilitate his or her progress.

- You have learned how important time frames are and how to manage the logistics for the client's care.
- You have begun to assess how progress over time is evaluated and the importance of developing realistic goals with the client.
- You have learned about different types of agreements that a client may enter into. Both written and verbal contracts have value, and it is up to the social worker to decide which approach is better, depending on the client and the situation.
- You have learned about barriers to progress that can slow a client down or completely derail the process. It is important to learn from your clients, as they are the experts on their life.

APPLY IT

1. Review **Interactive Case Study #2,** sessions 1 and 2, with Anthony and social worker James. Then develop a treatment plan/service plan for Anthony. Include two long-term goals and three short-term goals for each long-term goal. Identify three tasks for Anthony to complete under each short-term goal. How did you prioritize which goals would be most immediate?
2. Watch **Interactive Case Study #5,** sessions 1, 2, and 3, with Mrs. Kita and social worker Diane. Then develop a treatment plan/service plan for Mrs. Kita. Include two long-term goals and three short-term goals for each long-term goal. Identify three tasks for Mrs. Kita to complete under each short-term goal. How did you prioritize which goals would be most immediate?

Assess Your Competence

Use the scale below to rate your current level of achievement on the following concepts or skills associated with each competency presented in the chapter:

1	2	3
I can accurately describe the concept or skill	I can consistently identify the concept or skill when observing and analyzing practice activities	I can competently implement the concept or skill in my own practice

_______ Understands and can describe the process of problem identification as well as methods for helping the client discover causes of problems.

_______ Understands and can articulate the importance of developing achievable goals, and methods of planning.

_______ Can describe the importance of contracting with a client, and how to determine and develop short- and long-term goals.

_______ Can articulate methods to draw up written and verbal contracts and can identify major barriers to client progress.

11

Treatment and Intervention

LISA F. YOUNG/FOTOLIA

Preparing for client treatment is an important step in the helping process that ensures the best alignment of interventions with client needs and desired outcomes. The work social workers do with their clients from the first meeting forward influences treatment selection and how well the client engages the treatment phase of the helping process. Engaging a client helps to make the client feel valued and worthy of your time and expertise and builds client confidence in the belief that change is possible and life can be better. All these elements impact how well the client will engage the treatment and intervention phase and remain motivated throughout the helping process. The thoroughness of your assessment and your ability to collaborate with the client in the planning of treatment will naturally lead the client into accepting her or his role in the partnership the social worker will form with the client when working to achieve client goals.

SELECTING TREATMENT OPTIONS

The selection of intervention and treatment modalities should be in alignment with the goals and time frames set out in the contract

LEARNING OUTCOMES

- Articulate the steps in determining treatment options for a client.
- Describe the cultural and agency contexts of treatment.
- Distinguish the central concepts of motivational interviewing.
- Appraise the value of building client capacities and coping skill in meeting client treatment goals.
- Link specific practice theories to specific brief therapies prominent in social work practice.

CHAPTER OUTLINE

with the client. Monitoring client responses to treatment interventions will also determine the length of treatment, and helps to determine quickly if the treatment mode selected is having the desired effect. It may be necessary to change interventions if a client is not making progress toward his or her goals.

Steps in determining treatment approach:

1. Review the treatment options that are appropriate to the problem identified and the goals set out in the contract.
2. Assess the extent to which treatment interventions are supported by evidence of their effectiveness (evidence-based practice).
3. Identify the interventions and techniques that best fit the client's need.
4. Do an honest self-assessment of your practice skill set and determine whether you are qualified to institute the intervention, whether you will need to implement the treatment under the supervision of a more experienced and competent practitioner, or whether the client should be referred to another social worker more qualified to provide the selected treatment.

? Assess your understanding of selecting treatment options by taking this brief quiz.

THE CONTEXT OF TREATMENT AND INTERVENTION

Treatment applications should vary from client to client and take into consideration the context of the problem being addressed and the treatment application. **Contextual factors** can include the emotional and psychological states of the client, the client's intellectual/cognitive abilities, cultural beliefs and practices (as well as cultural taboos), agency rules and practice orientation, treatment setting (agency, client's home, school, or community setting), family context, and social support networks.

Cultural Context

As a social worker treating diverse client groups, it is vital to be aware of the visible and nonvisible cultural aspects of your clients' lives. While gender and ethnicity may be the more apparent cultural features when first meeting a client, other values and cultural aspects of a client's life are equally important to your work together and in building culturally appropriate and competent methods of intervention. For example, sexual orientation, spiritual or religious practices, political persuasions, and general philosophy of life are cultural elements you may need to discover about your client and incorporate into your treatment and intervention methods. Likewise, to the extent that your client's personal culture is an extension of his or her family and community culture, the use of these resources and networks in the treatment and intervention phase should be thoughtfully selected and instituted.

Comprehensive cultural knowledge of your client is necessary when selecting and applying appropriate intervention methods. For example, a client experiencing problems with intimacy in his or her life may benefit from an exercise that requires the client to make prolonged eye contact with the social worker with the intent of "seeing" the other's essence or inner goodness and bonding with the social worker. While this technique would be appropriate for problems of intimacy, it would not be appropriate in cultures where eye contact is considered bold, confronting, or disrespectful, as in the Japanese culture.

Watch the video case study of Mrs. Kita. Notice how she often averts her eyes when talking with her social worker, Diane.

Internal Culture—Psychological, Emotional, Cognitive, and Intellectual Capabilities/Limitations of the Client

The completion of multidimensional assessment gives the social worker insight into the **internal culture** of the client. This knowledge will help the social worker select a treatment intervention that is well matched with the client's capabilities while building on client strengths and minimizing their challenges. For example, an unemployed client presenting with irrational thoughts, cognitive distortions, and rigid thought patterns may need an intervention that gently challenges these cognitive limitations (cognitive restructuring) and that consequently opens up opportunities for the client to engage in employment interviews in a manner that exposes his or her talents, skills, and qualifications for the jobs rather than in ways that reflect his or her unrealistic and fearful thoughts. This then may lead to accomplishing a short-term contract goal, such as "complete three successful job interviews by the end of three weeks," or a long-term goal, such as "find appropriate employment that utilizes client strengths within six months." Cognitive interventions concentrate on helping the client achieve rational linkages between external events in the client's life and the thoughts and behaviors that the external events generate (Walsh, 2013).

Emotional health is closely tied to cognitive health. Emotions are a reaction to our thoughts and interpretations of events (Sheafor & Horejsi, 2012; Walsh, 2013). To the extent that these fall within the realm of rational thinking, emotions follow suit, as do behaviors, because emotions influence and direct our behavior. Just as we have thought patterns, so too we have emotional patterns. Emotional responses to events should be appropriate to the event; laughter in response to a happy event should be consistent and predictable and within the range of feeling responses. Smiling and giving a light chuckle to a baby blowing bubbles would seem appropriate, while bursting into tears and having to leave the room might suggest some emotional health issues. For example, the sight of a joyful baby to someone who has recently suffered a loss of a child or grandchild could open fresh wounds and cause a tearful reaction.

When selecting a treatment intervention for a client, be cognizant of the client's emotional functioning around the problem being addressed and the meaning and emotions attached to the problem. For example, a client who presents with great shame around a sexual assault she experienced may not be a good candidate for a survivor of a rape/sexual assault support group at the outset of your work together. This may be a long-term treatment goal that you work toward after the client has had a response to a treatment method that provides her the freedom to express her rage about the event and to begin to see herself not as the cause of the rape but, rather, as the person who was injured as a result of the aggressive act.

Finally, when working with clients who are developmentally and intellectually challenged, it is important to use interventions that match their physical, cognitive, and emotional developmental levels. When in doubt, refer back to your assessment in these areas and work with a supervisor to guide you in this area of practice.

Agency Context

Agencies have cultures that are driven by their philosophy of service delivery, their mission statement, and the vision of their role in the community. The community setting may also influence the culture of an agency and the people who work there. As social workers, we bring our own cultures and life experiences to the agency, thus adding another layer to the **agency culture**. Some agencies are more flexible in their cultural development, changing or expanding over time in response to community and client needs. Alternatively, clients and workers may experience some agencies as more rigid and static in their culture, holding onto original values, beliefs, and practices on which the organization was founded. Some agencies may be perceived as more open and inviting, while others may be more closed and private. Both types of cultures may be appropriate, depending on the client base that the agency serves. For example, an agency that provides protection and temporary housing and counseling services to victims of domestic violence will best serve its clients by securing a location that is not publicly known and that is physically and emotionally secure. Providing treatment interventions within this agency culture will dictate that treatments selected be in line with the psychological and emotional needs of the client and be delivered within the context of the agency. A new client recently released from the hospital and recovering from severe traumatic injuries incurred from a domestic battery will need the safety of the domestic shelter and the calm of a quiet, safe space while healing.

In contrast to a closed agency, an open and easily accessible agency may be experienced as more inviting by clients and community members. For example, an agency serving academically at risk children and their families would do well to have an open and inviting environment that provides a play area for children, an information center on other resources available in the community, and even a communal kitchen where snacks are served to children attending after-school programs.

Finally, some agencies have a preferred theoretical approach to treating their client base. For example, some agencies may be invested in cognitive restructuring treatments for addressing the anxiety issues of their clients, while another may prefer the use of psychoanalytical approaches, such as brief psychodynamic therapy. The treatment preferences and practices of your agency may limit your selection of options or at best make it difficult to institute interventions not commonly used in your agency setting. The extent to which your agency is open and flexible to new ideas and treatments will determine the ease with which you will be able to expand the repertoire of treatment options within your agency and provide a wider range of interventions for your clients.

Engagement

Behavior: Apply knowledge of human behavior and the social environment, person-in-environment, and other multidisciplinary theoretical frameworks to engage with clients and constituencies.

Critical Thinking Question: Take a moment and assess your agency for cultural elements. How would you define your agency's culture in terms of openness/closedness? How well does your agency's culture align with the client groups it serves? The mission of the agency?

Assess your understanding of the context of treatment and intervention by taking this brief quiz.

CLIENT MOTIVATION IN TREATMENT

What motivates clients to actively engage in treatment? Whose responsibility is it to make sure the client becomes invested and remains engaged in treatment? The transactional understanding of motivation sees it as coming from the client's inner world and also from the experiences in his or her outer world as he or she interacts with the social worker and others in the service delivery system. To the extent that these interactions are uplifting and empowering, the client is provided with hope and reasons to be motivated. This conception of transactional motivation has support from prominent theories used in social work practice, such as systems theory, cognitive-behavioral theories, and symbolic interactionism (Ellis, 1991; Ritzer, 2013). Further responsibility of keeping the client motivated and engaged is shared by the client, the social worker, and the system of care (Miley, O'Melia, & DuBois, 2013). **Client motivation** is important not only because it keeps the client engaged in treatment but also because we know from intervention research that when client and social worker motivations are focused in the same direction and in agreement with treatment methods and time lines, client outcomes improve (Del Rea, Flückigerc, Horvathd, Symondse, & Wampoldf, 2012; Hogue, Dauber, Cecero, Stambaugh, & Liddle, 2006; Meissner, 2007). This social worker–client alignment is referred to as therapeutic alliance.

Client Resistance in Treatment

Resistance to change is a common human response, even when the client has a desire for change. Unfamiliar territory can raise anxiety and fears in clients. Understanding those fears and the meaning they have for clients can help the social worker lead the client into the treatment phase. Setting a comfortable pace for the progression of treatment can also help ease client fears and resistance until the client has become accustomed to the first signs of change. When resistance occurs, look to see where you and the client are not in alignment and where adjustments need to be made. This may be in relation to the time line of the intervention, the direction of the intervention, or some new issue you have yet to learn about from the client, as in the case of Mrs. Kita in Interactive Case Study #5.

> Mrs. Kita is resistant to asking the Japanese community and elders for help. Her hesitancies may be a cultural norm or an expectation she holds that is not attached to the reality of her situation.

Change can also have a rippling effect. While making progress toward one client goal, this change may impact other areas of the client's life that neither you nor the client had anticipated. See the case study of George in Box 11.1 for an example.

Understanding George's surface resistance demonstrated in Box 11.1 as something that has most likely occurred between your last and present sessions will help the social worker to interpret it as a sign that George needs extra support in understanding and giving meaning to this new development in his life. It is important not to take client resistance personally and become defensive. Rather, you might begin by inquiring, through a series of open ended questions about how George's life with his family, friends, community, and work has been going since you last talked. Building on your established relationship with

Box 11.1 George: A Case of Client Resistance

In working with George in a substance abuse program, you had found him to be highly motivated and committed to being involved in treatment and to achieving his goal of sobriety. Achieving this goal has many rewards, such as keeping his job, repairing his relationships with his wife and children, and feeling more in control of his life and health. As George made progress in all of these areas of his life, he began to feel strong and empowered. However, when he returned to work and declined the usual Friday after-work drinking crowd, he experienced ridicule and rejection from his male coworkers, and his commitment to sobriety began to falter. When he returned to outpatient treatment the following Monday, he appeared less enthusiastic and began to define his alcohol consumption as "normal male behavior." The risk of losing his male friends in the workplace had undermined his motivation and had surfaced as resistance in the treatment phase. How would you manage the client's resistance? How might you use this resistance to move the helping relationship forward, to reengage George in his treatment, and to restore his commitment to his goals?

the client and being consistent in your use of empathy and genuineness may help George to relax and open up. Seeing client resistance as a source of information that, when uncovered, can help to move the treatment forward, reflects the transactional nature of motivation, and the power of environmental resistance to undermine the client's commitment to treatment goals. George's friends were resistant to his decision to change and live a sober, stable, and balanced life. This negative interaction with his coworkers served to weaken his commitment to treatment and sobriety (Miley et al., 2013). Resistance is a normal and expected element of the treatment phase. Expect it and learn to use it to promote client growth and the achievement of client goals (Cooper & Lesser, 2015).

Motivational Interviewing

What we have consistently observed and learned about clients over time is that how the social worker interacts with clients has a direct and significant impact on client motivation and levels of resistance to change (Miller & Rollnick, 2013; Wahab, 2005). **Motivational interviewing** builds on this wisdom and through the use of empathy accepts resistance as a normal dynamic in the helping process. Motivational interviewing is a specific brief therapeutic approach used to help clients resolve resistance or ambivalence toward change, recognizing that clients come to the helping process with different levels of readiness to change. When using motivational interviewing, a major function of the social worker is to help the client work through his or her ambivalence by raising awareness of the implications of changing versus not changing. Collaboration between the social worker and the client is a foundational element of motivational interviewing. Through this collaboration, clients grow in self-efficacy and thus self-confidence in their ability to change (Lundahl, Kunz, Brownell, Tollefson, & Burke, 2010; Walsh, 2013).

Social work practitioners trained in using motivational interviewing work from four tenets of practice:

1. Expressing empathy to clients—this deepens the rapport with clients and reduces resistance to change.
2. Developing discrepancies—the client is allowed to argue against change while the social worker raises awareness of the client's current problem. Ultimately,

the client sees the discrepancies between his or her stated position/beliefs/values and the problems he or she is currently experiencing.

3. Rolling with resistance—there is acceptance of the client's resistance; the social worker understands it as a normal part of the helping process.
4. Supporting client's self-efficacy—here the social worker acknowledges the client's ability to change (Lundahl et al., 2010).

While motivational interviewing emerged out of the substance abuse field of practice, it has proven to be particularly effective with clients who are reluctant to acknowledge and actively address problems (Lundahl et al., 2010; Walsh, 2013). Motivational interviewing incorporates many theories used in social work practice, but the most notable are Rogerian theory, cognitive theory, and the transtheoretical model of change. Because of its emphasis on acceptance, empathy, a nonjudgmental approach, and belief in client autonomy and self-determination, motivational interviewing has a good fit with the profession and values of social work. The 'theory into practice' example below presents a case study and social worker–client dialogue that demonstrate the application of motivational interviewing and its usefulness in engaging clients. In this case study, the social worker helps the client, Tania, consider discrepancies in her beliefs, values, and perspectives.

? Assess your understanding of client motivation in treatment by taking this brief quiz.

Policy to Practice Motivational Interviewing: Case Study

This case example of motivational interviewing takes place within a domestic violence shelter and is conducted by a social worker trained in motivational interviewing. Notice the nonjudgmental acceptance of the client, the use of empathy, and the intentional use of skills to help develop discrepancy and to help reduce the client's resistance to change.

Tania is a 28-year-old woman, originally from Guatemala. Currently she resides in Denver, Colorado with her husband Marc, and their two children, Felipe, age 8 and Sarai age 5. Following the domestic violence incident, the children were sent to live with Tania's parents who had immigrated to Southern California 3 years before. Tania entered a domestic violence shelter to continue recovering from the emotional and physical injuries she suffered from her husband's attack, and to be assured of a safe place to stay. Marc's violence against Tania had increased in frequency and severity over the past year and she now feared for her life. The most recent episode had been the worst. He had left her for dead after severely beating her with a heavy wrench. Her survival was attributed to the mail carrier who saw her unconscious body on the floor of the living room through the porch screen door and called 911. Marc had already fled the scene. Tania was transported to the hospital by ambulance where she remained for 5 days before being released to the domestic violence shelter. She agreed to go, but needed encouragement from the hospital social worker. When the shelter social worker reviewed the notes from Tania's intake interview, she became aware that she had been badly beaten by her husband on many occasions. She had been seen by the emergency room staff for domestic violence related injuries 5 times in the two years that Tania and her family had resided in Denver. On two occasions, Tania left her husband for 6 weeks and stayed with her parents in California. She found comfort and safety in her parents' home. But after each absence from her husband she returned to Denver with her children, believing that her husband was sincere in his claim that he was deeply sorry and would never hurt her again. Tania had never pressed charged against her husband. She feared deportation and did not want to return to live in Guatemala. She also feared permanent separation from her children if she was deported.

Social Worker: I'm pleased that you are staying here right now. It is a safe place for you. May I begin by learning more about your current circumstances? (Ask client permission; and await her response) What episode helped you to decide to come to the shelter? (Appreciation. Open-ended question)

Tania: I disobeyed my husband and he got so angry that he hit me. I messed up his plans to go out with his friends because I did not have dinner ready on time like I usually do. I was helping my friend next door with her children and lost track of

(Continued)

Policy to Practice Motivational Interviewing: Case Study *(Continued)*

time. Before I knew it, it was 5:15 P.M. and I had not started dinner yet. I rushed home, hoping he was not there yet, but when I saw him standing in the doorway I could see he was very angry at having to wait for me.

Social Worker: You were anxious about not having dinner ready. Then what happened? (Reflection of feelings. Open-ended question).

Tania: He just went kind of crazy and was screaming at me and hitting me. I pleaded with him to please stop, but he did not. He continued beating me as I slumped to the ground. Then he was mad that I would not stand up and he dragged me across the room and began kicking me when I did not get up. The more I pleaded, the more I cowered, the angrier he got and the more he beat me. So I stopped moving and crying or making any sound as best I could. I also did not want anyone to hear and call the police. I was afraid they would arrest him and throw him in jail. Then I don't know what happened, because the next thing I remember was waking up in the hospital (Tania is crying)

Social Worker: He was beating you but still you were afraid of what would happen to him if the police came. You were worried about his well-being. (Reflection of feelings)

Tania: I hate it when he gets like this, but I do love him and don't want the police involved. They do not much care for people like us and I am afraid for my family.

Social Worker: You believed that the circumstances could become much worse if the police came. (Paraphrase)

Tania: Yes I am glad that he was able to get away before the police came, otherwise, things would be much worse right now. I don't know what to do. But pretty soon he will calm down again. Right now I have time to think things through. I will get my family back together when I am ready. For now I am safe and my children are fine with my parents

Notice that the social worker did not react to Tania's remark about reuniting her family; rather, she remained focused on exploring Tania's history of battering from her husband; and attempts to discover the resources and supports she has used in the past to get through many domestic violence incidents. Notice how the social worker mirrors Tania's language. She does not call what has happened to her 'abuse.' Therefore, neither does the social worker. The social worker continues to delve into Tania's feelings about her husband and her thoughts about what to do next.

Social Worker: Your husband has beaten you many times but you still love him and care about him. (Summarize. Reflection of feelings)

Tania: He really is a wonderful man. It may not always seem that way, but he is my best friend and I know that he loves me. He is a good father to our children. We have been together for a very long time.

Social Worker: You have a past together that is full of twist and turns, and even though he beats you, you still admire many aspects of who he is. (Pause) You remarked that you will reunite your family and return to him after you have healed and he has calmed down. Tell me a bit about the benefits of returning to your husband. (Reflection of feelings. Paraphrase. Begin to unravel the ambivalence)

Tania: Well, I know that when I return, he will be relieved to see us. He will be sorry for what he has done and because of that he will be very good to all of us for a while. That is the way it always goes at first. And, I will have the money I need to care for myself and the children. Without Marc, I have no way of making money. I have my friends nearby that care for me and my children. We help each other raise our children together. Without Marc, I may have to stay with my parents in California, but they can't support me and my children for very long. I may have to return to Guatemala if I can't find a job to support my children. And because I am not legal I am afraid to look for a job....afraid I will be reported to the authorities and be deported.

Social Worker: So you will have the honeymoon phase to look forward to when you return home, and there is financial security, seeing your friends and being able to stay in the U.S. Anything else? (Paraphrase followed by an open-ended question)

Tania: I can't think of anything else. Those are the most important things to me.

Social Worker: You have named many benefits to returning to Marc. What are some of the thing that worry you about returning? (Explore ambivalence. Clarification)

Tania: That my best friend, Jennifer won't talk to me if I go back. She gets very upset and worries that he will kill me. She told me that if he hits me again and I stay we are finished being friends.. It is only a matter of time before I do something wrong and piss him off again. Each time we go through this, it gets worse. It scares me to think about it. He could easily kill me when he is in a rage.

Social Worker: So, you see some significant risks to returning. . . . your safety and your very life may be at stake. (Amplified reflection.) You have voiced many reasons to return to your husband and significant reasons not to go back. (Summarization)

Policy to Practice Motivational Interviewing: Case Study *(Continued)*

Tania: When I think about it, I think the pros outnumber the cons. I know that might sound kind of crazy, but it seems right to me.

Social Worker: I can see that from your point of view that money, friends and deportation are things that you do not need to worry about if you go back. But, I also hear you say that your husband may kill you the next time if you go back. (Paraphrase) Risking your life seems reasonable to you right now because of all of the positive things you can count on if you go back. (Develop discrepancy through a gentle confrontation)

Social Worker: Where does this leave you now? (Support self-determination. Develop discrepancy. Elicit self-motivational statements)

Tania: I'm not sure . . . it gets confusing and scary when I think about it. I need some time to think this through.

The social worker does not pressure Tania to come to a decision in the moment, nor does she imply that Tania should not return to her husband. Rather, she supports and respects Tania's statement of need for time to think things through. The social worker allows Tania the time to consider both the positive and the negative prospects of returning to her husband.

Social Worker: This is a tough time. There is much for you to consider. You are concerned about Marc's well being and possible trouble for him. You love him. You have experienced the advantages and disadvantages to going back in the past. Right now, you want time to think and heal. Then you will feel better prepared to make your decision about what to do next. This is your choice. I am confident you will make the best choice for you and your children, as you know Marc and the circumstances better than anyone. You are the expert on your life. I am here to support you in your healing and decision process. (Express empathy. Summarize. Support self-determination and choice. Express confidence and support)

In the session, the social worker helped Tania explore what she wants for herself and her family. The social worker guides Tania in understanding her situation and advantages and disadvantages of future decisions regarding her husband; however she never gives Tania advice on what to do. Rather, she uses her many social work interviewing skills such as reflective feeling, clarification and summarizing as a mirror for Tania. The social worker using motivational interviewing understands that it is only if and when Tania feels safe, accepted, and supported for who she is can she consider doing something different.

Source: Based on Wahab, S. (2005). Motivational interviewing and social work practice. *Journal of Social Work, 5*(1), 45–60.

Now in Box 11.A, try to use some motivational interviewing techniques in your response to client George in the scenario below.

Box 11.A Now You Try It . . . Motivational Interviewing

Recall our client George (Box 11.1), who was losing motivation for achieving and maintaining his treatment goal of sobriety. He experienced ridicule and rejection from his after-work drinking buddies when he declined to participate in their end-of-the-work week drinking ritual. His loss of motivation and his subsequent resistance to treatment was observed by the social worker when he returned to outpatient treatment the following Monday. George now defined his alcohol consumption as "normal male behavior."

As George's social worker, how would you respond to George using motivational interviewing techniques that reflected empathy, acceptance, and nonjudgmental positive regard?

Social Worker's response:

____

How could you begin to lead George into the exploration of discrepancy?

Social Worker's response:

____

BUILDING CLIENT CAPACITIES AND COPING SKILLS

Intervention

Behavior: Critically choose and implement interventions to achieve practice goals and enhance capacities of clients and constituencies.

Critical Thinking Question: Consider the encounter that you had with your last client in your field placement or in your work setting or as a volunteer at a local agency. On reflection, what components of motivational interviewing did you intuitively use in your interaction with the client?

Often, when clients come to see the social worker, their **coping skills** and capacities are compromised because external environmental forces have taken their toll. Clients who in another time in their lives were gainfully employed, healthy, socially engaged, and leading a balanced life may appear for treatment revealing little of their former self. Take, for example, Gayle in the case study presented in Box 11.2.

Building client capacities and coping skills is essential for helping clients in creating a functional, self-sustaining life, but it is also important for helping them restore their sense of self-efficacy and to improve self-esteem (Schwellnus, King, & Thompson, 2015; Smith, 1999). In this section we will review just a few approaches to helping clients build their capacities and coping skills. Social workers will need to tailor capacity building and coping skill enhancement interventions to fit client needs and aptitudes.

Coping-Skills Training

Coping-skills training (CST) has been a staple in the treatment of alcohol and drug addictions for several decades, but in recent years its successful application to other problem areas in clients' lives has been documented (Porter et al., 2011; Smith, 1999). With CST, the social worker attempts to provide interventions that strengthen clients' existing skills and teach new strategies to effectively cope with situations that place clients at greater risk of engaging in behaviors that impede their abilities (Monti & Rohsenow,

Box 11.2 Case Study: Gayle

One year ago, Gayle was happily married to Trey, a successful developer and business owner. Gayle worked as a part-time accountant for a large firm and was a success in her own right and maintained a high sense of self-efficacy in all areas of her life. She was very involved with her children, Brittany, age five, and Terrance, age three. She also volunteered at her children's schools once a week. She loved spending time in her home art studio, and gardening. Her extended family lived nearby, and they gathered frequently for celebrations and checked on each other regularly. Life was very good. Then, unexpectedly, Trey asked for a divorce. He had been involved with another woman for some time and wanted to end the marriage. The shock of the news and the realization at how well her husband had hid this secret sent Gayle into a tailspin. She stopped going to work, lost all interest in food, and considered herself an utter failure. She felt responsible for not being able to sustain a successful marriage and felt like a fool for trusting Trey. Six months after Trey moved out, Gayle had lost 50 pounds, was losing her hair, had ended all of her volunteer activities, and was able to care for her children only with the help of her mother and sister. While financially able to get by on savings, Gayle was unable to see a future for herself or to find any sense of internal worth or value. When Alex, the social worker, first encountered Gayle, she was very depressed and barely engaged with him. The social worker realized that in order to rebuild her life, Gayle would need to restore her sense of self as a competent but now single woman and to reactivate her capacities as a wage earner, mother, and community member. The social worker also recognized that as Gayle restored her self-confidence and became reengaged in life, her depression would begin to lift.

1999; Porter et al., 2011). For example, the application of CST when treating alcoholics is geared toward helping the client develop skills to successfully negotiate situations, people, or settings that have historically been associated with drinking. For clients with other problems, such as pain management, skill development could provide strategies to meet the client's specific needs such as pain reduction, and improve the quality of their life. (Porter, et. Al, 2011). In another example, the social worker may assist a client with diabetes to develop skills to control her intake of sugar and carbohydrates when in social situations where food is served. Part of this skill development might include a class on nutrition and learning to use the food exchange list for diabetic meal planning. Based on social learning theory and classic conditioning, CST helps clients learn new and healthier behaviors that support a life of physical, emotional, financial, and psychological well-being. For example, a person newly diagnosed with diabetes failing to maintain a diet low in sugar may compromise the client in each of these areas: she may feel guilty for not maintaining a diet that supports a normal blood sugar and the guilt may trigger comfort eating high in sugar; she may become ill and lose days at work, thus compromising her income and job security; and she may develop health complications such as heart disease or poor eyesight as a result of poor diet compliance. Finding ways to help the diabetic client develop skills for dealing successfully with her new diabetic illness has long-term implication for all areas of her life.

The interventions you design with your clients should be specific to certain high-risk situations that can threaten their well-being, but may also involve general social skills that can be of help with many types of clients. For example, alcoholics who have improved social skills feel less social pressure when in groups and are less likely to drink (Monti & Rohsenow, 1999). Similarly, clients who suffer from anxiety may also find some relief from enhanced social and communication skills. CST can also include such interventions as cognitive-behavioral mood management, anger management, relaxation techniques, job training, self-defense training, assertiveness training, stress management, and decision-making skills. Work with your clients to identify their specific CST needs and then look for the resources in your community. If none exists, this may be a good opportunity to work with other professional providers in your area to create new resources. Chances are that if your client is in need, so are others.

? Assess your understanding of building client capacities by taking this brief quiz.

BRIEF TREATMENT STRATEGIES AND TECHNIQUES: EXAMPLES FROM PSYCHODYNAMIC, COGNITIVE-BEHAVIORAL, AND POSTMODERN THEORETICAL PERSPECTIVES

Brief treatment with clients has become the norm in recent years, as constraints of third-party insurance payments have limited the number of therapeutic sessions. In addition, new forms of therapies that bear quick results have proven effective in relieving client symptoms, making brief therapies the treatment of choice in many cases. Practice theories support distinct therapies in social work practice. In this section, **brief therapies** are selected from categories of theory to demonstrate the types of interventions commonly used in social work practice and to link the specific practice theories to practice interventions.

In social work practice, it is usual to have a blending of theories that direct treatment with clients while having one theoretical perspective dominate the treatment phase. For example, many psychodynamic therapists also incorporate cognitive-behavioral techniques into their treatment with clients. Elements of humanistic client-centered interventions are universal in their use with other therapeutic approaches and are observable across most clinical interventions. Regardless of theoretical and practice approach, it is universally recognized that clients respond better to treatment when they feel heard, accepted, and received with nonjudgmental, unconditional regard.

Brief Psychodynamic Therapy

Brief psychodynamic therapy finds its origins in Freudian thought and is the oldest of the contemporary approaches to client issues and "dysfunctions." As its origin suggests, it is concerned with unconscious processes and how they influence present behavior. The hope of the practitioner is to bring the client to self-awareness about how the unconscious elements of one's past influence present behaviors (Scott, 2015).

Box 11.3 provides an example of the linkages between a client's presenting problem of panic disorder, psychodynamic theory, and treatment strategies that the social worker might pursue. On a conscious level, the client sees no connection between his current panic attacks and past or current events. The attacks occur out of the blue and do not seem to be associated with any triggers. Theoretically, the practitioner working from a psychodynamic perspective will understand the client's symptoms as a manifestation of unresolved conflicts. The focus of the treatment interaction will be to explore with the client the symbolic emotional meaning of the panic attacks and link them to past unresolved conflicts. When the client becomes conscious of these connections, the symptoms will recede (see the case example in Box 11.3).

Box 11.3 Brief Psychodynamic Therapy: Case Study

Martha is a 19-year-old bisexual college student with a diagnosis of panic disorder. Martha often has severe panic attacks when stress at school runs high. To manage her panic attacks Martha began seeing a social worker at the student counseling center. Within just a few visits Martha was seeing improvements as a result of engaging in panic-focused psychodynamic psychotherapy, a form of brief psychodynamic therapy. The social worker observed that Martha, while pleasant and cooperative stayed distant and aloof, and during times of high academic stress was often late for her session or missed them altogether. When her social worker shared her observation, Martha admitted that she felt somewhat conflicted about being in treatment stating that coming to sessions made her feel dependent and somewhat childlike. At her final session, the social worker noted that Martha appeared sad and more emotional than she usually allowed herself to experience in her sessions. The social worker observed that Martha had a history of avoiding feelings of love and attachment, especially with important people in her life including her family, close friends, lovers, and now her social worker. The social worker raised these observations with Martha during the termination phase of the helping relationship, highlighting Martha's conflicts about intimacy and how some aspects of her panic attacks may be associated with feelings of guilt about exceeding her father in her academic achievements. This connection between Martha's panic attacks and her academic work can be seen in excerpts from the follow session with her social worker:

Social Worker: It's almost like you would go to great lengths to avoid feeling emotions, attachment, and love. (Interpretation)

Martha: Sometimes when I'm with my dad I feel like my heart will burst, especially when I say good-bye to him after a

Box 11.3 Brief Psychodynamic Therapy: Case Study *(Continued)*

week-end visit. It is so odd because we don't really talk much about anything. There is not an easy exchange between us. Our relationship is so weird . . . all this not talking but when I think about him not being there to not talk to, I feel sad. . . . And not seeing him makes me feel so lonely. . . . I wonder why I miss him so much, because we don't really talk. Does that make any sense at all? . . . It's like what I have done here . . . spent a lot of time not talking about him. . . . like he has spent so many years just showing up but not talking to me about anything . . . when I really do want to talk about him. . . . and talk to him.

Social Worker: What are the things that you have avoided saying wish you could say? (Open ended question)

Martha: I would like to say to him that I wish he were happier. . . . that I wish he had been more successful. But maybe being more successful wouldn't make him happier. . . . I don't know. It's like when I won that writing contest . . . most people would have jumped for joy, but it made me feel really uneasy on the inside . . . kind of queasy, you know. It's almost like I'm not allowed to be successful and happy too. Like it's not OK . . . maybe because he never won a writing prize. I'm beginning to see the connection now between my dad, my success, and my panic attacks. . . . like you have been pointing out to me for a while now . . . I get it now . . . I can see it.

Source: Based on Milrod, B., Busch, F., Shapiro, T., Leon, A. C., & Aronson, A. (2005). *Adolescent Psychiatry, 29,* 289–314.

Brief psychodynamic therapy (BPT) grew out of traditional psychoanalysis. Because it uses free association that allows the client to address many unconscious issues and make connections among them, psychoanalysis is a long-term treatment. The primary difference in BPT is a shift in focus to one major issue. Practitioners of BPT focus change on one problem rather than many, and by doing so the client is able to experience focused change in a brief period of time. Within the first or second session, the client and the social worker will agree on a central problem to work on and a goal to attain in treatment. For example, in the case study presented in Box 11.3, the client and social worker were focused on one agreed-on problem, panic attacks, with the goal of alleviating the attacks. The narrowed focus of their work together provides the client with insight and relief in a short period of time (Haggerty, 2006; Milrod, Busch, Shapiro, Leon, & Aronson, 2005). Two qualities of practitioner behavior considered essential in BPT are 1) the attention of the worker to the client's identified focus or issue, and 2) the quality of the social worker's delivery of treatment. The social worker's level of competence in the use of BPT and ability to be present to the client's needs and respond in a supportive and appropriate manner are central features of successful intervention (Butler & Strupp, 1986; Curtis & Silberschatz, 1986; Messer, Tishby, & Spillman, 1992; Scott, 2015).

Cognitive-Behavioral Therapy

The merger of behavioral and cognitive techniques into a well-formulated **cognitive-behavioral therapy** (CBT) emerged in the 1980's and has been growing in its application to a broad range of issues ever since. This is due primarily to its documented effectiveness in clinical studies and the quick responsiveness of clients to CBT techniques. Meta-analyses by Butler, Chapman, Forman, and Beck (2006)and Windsor, Jemal, and Alessi (2015) reported the effectiveness of CBT in the treatment of depression, anxiety and panic disorders, phobias, posttraumatic stress disorder, substance use, marital distress, anger, childhood somatic disorders, and chronic pain. They also found CBT to be effective in the treatment of adult depression, obsessive-compulsive disorder, bulimia nervosa, and schizophrenia. The strength of the empirical evidence of the usefulness in treating such a wide range of disorders underlies its expansive use in social work over the past 30 years.

CBT focuses on the relationship between how a client thinks (cognitions) and the resulting problematic feelings and behaviors. CBT is grounded in the belief and evidence that how we think and interpret our world has a direct impact on how we experience our internal and external worlds. This direct connection between thinking, feeling, and behavior dictates that if we can change the way we think about things, examine faulty beliefs and assumptions, and restore them to healthy perspectives, then we will feel better about ourselves and our relationship to the world, and our behaviors will be more in line with our life desires and aspirations (Beck, 1970; Ellis & MacLaren, 1998). Destructive ways of thinking include things such as cognitive distortions, conflicts in belief systems, dysfunctional assumptions, negative thoughts about self and others, and misconceptions that contribute to problematic behaviors and symptoms in the client.

In the case study in Box 11.4, Mr. Mahoney lived his life under the assumption that "if people know I am gay, I will be shunned." As a guiding principle in how he conducted his

Box 11.4 Cognitive-Behavioral Therapy: Case Study

Mr. Mahoney is a 68-year-old gay male with a 15 year history of being HIV positive. He sought treatment for depression, and reports feeling overcome with a sense of helplessness in managing his illness and life. He reports frequently feeling exhausted, hopeless and wanting to give up. At the time of intervention, Mr. Mahoney had been treated for bladder cancer, involving two surgeries and a round of chemotherapy. His doctors reported that he had a 50/50 chance of the cancer returning. Mr. Mahoney's cancer treatments required an adjustment to his HIV medications, resulting in multiple GI upsets. Mr. Mahoney presented with additional symptoms of insomnia, weight loss, feelings of guilt and worthlessness, and passive suicidal ideation.

Mr. Mahoney's CBT Interventions

Mr. Mahoney engaged in CBT for about a year beginning with individual weekly sessions that tapered off over time but culminated in a total of 30 sessions. For the first three months he met weekly with his social worker, and thereafter sessions became less frequent. He was asked to keep a daily journal where he recorded his mood, sleep and energy levels that he rated on individual rating scales. With the permission of Mr. Mahoney, the social worker tape recorded all sessions. He then took home each recorded session, with the instruction to listen to each sessions and identify patterns of behavior and thoughts.

One of the benefits of reviewing the sessions for Mr. Mahoney was his ability to identify automatic thoughts about himself and current conditions. His assignment was then to rewrite those unhelpful automatic thoughts into more positive and helpful responses. This exercise taught Mr. Mahoney the basic cognitive skill of reframing (such as seeing 'problem' as an opportunity), cognitive restructuring, semantic analysis (What do I mean when I refer to myself as a 'loser?' What is a loser? How do I define a 'winner?') and identifying his biases. Some of Mr. Mahoney's frequent automatic thoughts included "I have made a mess of my life," "I am gay, and therefore I am bad," and " AIDS is my penance for living a gay lifestyle." Outwardly, he expressed an attitude of acceptance and fulfillment in being gay; however, his implicit homophobic biases, as reflected in his automatic thoughts, seemed to be prominent during periods of depression and vulnerability. In this regard, he suffered in two ways—initially from his negative thoughts about himself and his life; and subsequently, from the disgrace and self-loathing he felt at having had those thoughts. Over time, Mr. Mahoney came to terms with his homosexuality, and began to experience changes in his automatic thoughts which brought him relief. For clarity on his journey, Mr. Mahoney was also inspired to develop a list of conditional assumptions and core beliefs he held about himself—which while consciously he knew were not true, nonetheless he identified as his "bedrock of self-hate." Having some understanding of his faulty thinking, he began "chipping away at my bedrock of self-hate" by incorporating affirmative statements and appraisals of his sexuality and age. Outcomes from these exercises were used to construct mantras that he substituted for automatic homophobic and ageism thoughts. Mantras were used as a tool to pivot his thoughts to more constructive thoughts about himself. Over time he developed a sense of himself, which chipped away at his self defeating beliefs.

Source: Based on Excerpts taken from Satterfield, J. M., & Crabb, R. (2010). Cognitive-behavioral therapy for depression in an older gay man: A clinical case study. *Cognitive and Behavioral Practices*, *17*, 45–55.

life, he believed himself to be unlovable and consequently found himself alone and depressed at age 68. The social worker utilizing CBT worked with Mr. Mahoney in revising his faulty beliefs to a more accurate one, such as "I am a person of value and worth, deserving of love and connection." A shift in such a fundamental belief will contribute to how Mr. Mahoney relates to himself and others and may ultimately open up possibilities for connection and relationships in his life. The social worker sought to help the client restore his thought patterns to accurate, healthy, and self-supporting thoughts that would lead the client back to healthy behavior patterns and an enhanced quality of life. In Box 11.5, Walsh (2013) offers some common cognitive distortions.

Because CBT requires the active involvement of the client in changing thought patterns, client "homework" between sessions is a central part of this therapeutic approach (Martin, 2011). Through restructuring how a client thinks about himself or herself and his or her world, symptoms can be reduced or eliminated and quality of life restored. The social worker guides the client in these cognitive changes through the use of specific interventions during the helping process. Box 11.6 provides a brief overview of some commonly used CBT intervention techniques for working with clients.

Assessment

Behavior: Apply knowledge of human behavior and the social environment, person-in-environment, and other multidisciplinary theoretical frameworks in the analysis of assessment data from clients and constituencies.

Critical Thinking Question: As you review the faulty beliefs of Mr. Mahoney in the case study presented in Box 11.4, how would you match his beliefs with the cognitive distortions outlined in Box 11.5?

Box 11.5 Cognitive Distortions

Irrational Beliefs	Examples
Arbitrary inference: Drawing a conclusion about an event without evidence, little evidence, or even contradictory evidence.	"I'm not going to do well in this course. I have a bad feeling about it." "The staff at this agency seems to have a different practice approach than mine. They aren't going to respect my work."
Selective abstraction: Judging a situation on the basis of one or a few details taken out of a broader context.	"Did you see how our supervisor yawned when I was describing my assessment of the client? He must think my work is superficial."
Magnification of minimization: Concluding that an event is far more significant or far less significant than the evidence seems to indicate.	"I got a 'B' on the first assignment: There is a good chance I will fail this course." "I don't really need to get to work on time every day. My clients don't seem to mind waiting, and the administrative meeting isn't relevant to my work."
Overgeneralization: Concluding that all instances of a certain kind of situation or event will turn out a particular way because one or two such situations did.	"My supervisor thinks that my depressed client dropped out because I was too confrontational. I don't have enough empathy to be a decent social worker."
Personalization: Attributing the cause to or accepting responsibility for an external event without evidence of a connection.	"The instructor didn't say this, but our group presentation got a mediocre evaluation because of my poor delivery."
Dichotomous thinking: Categorizing experiences as one of two extremes: complete success or utter failure (usually the latter).	"I didn't get an A on my final exam. I blew it! I'm not competent to move on to the next course."

Source: Walsh, J. (2013). *Theories for direct social work practice* (2nd ed.). Pacific Grove, CA: Brooks/Cole, p. 154. Used with Permission.

Box 11.6 Cognitive-Behavioral Therapy Techniques

Capturing automatic negative thoughts—underlying negative core beliefs about ourselves that we may not be fully conscious of because of their constant presence. The social worker can help the client capture these thoughts through the use of homework activities, such as keeping a diary or record of recurring thoughts. In doing so, negative core beliefs about the client that need to be restructured will begin to emerge.

Cognitive restructuring—replacing clients' self-defeating thoughts and cognitive distortions with more accurate and life-enhancing thoughts using a number of techniques, such as challenging client beliefs with evidence, teaching clients to assess beliefs with evidence, having clients substitute positive self-talk, and deconstructing beliefs in discussions with the social worker.

Decentering—replace the client's faulty belief that he or she is the center of attention of others who know what he or she is thinking and feeling. Through discussions and use of evidence, the social worker helps the client decenter, and the client is thus relieved of the anxiety he or she experiences when he or she feels he or she is being watched and judged by others.

Redefining—replace clients' negative interpretation of an event with a more positive interpretation. For example, in response to failing a driving test, an adolescent concludes, "I'm a terrible driver." A more positive and useful redefining of this event might be "I need more practice at driving with an experienced driver."

Semantic analysis—teasing out the meaning in automatic negative thoughts that can then be challenged with evidence and redefined using more accurate language, such as "What does it mean when I say I'm a terrible student?," "What makes me a terrible student?," "What is the basis of this conclusion?," "In what areas do I do well as a student?," or "In what areas do I need support?" Following this line of analysis, the student may come to the conclusion that he or she needs practice at taking time-limited tests. This is a helpful insight for improving one's grades.

Sources: Boyle, Grafton, Mather, Smith, and Farley (2009); Satterfield and Crabb (2010); Walsh (2013).

Solution-Focused Brief Therapy: A Postmodern Approach

Solution-focused brief therapy (SFBT) is a fairly recent intervention that focuses on solutions rather than problems and concentrates on future desired states rather than current problems. This approach works from the assumption that clients have within them the strengths and resources to create a solution. The social worker acts more in the role of a coach, urging the client to explore and discover his or her own problem-solving strategies. In doing so, the client grows in competence and self-efficacy. Clients will more eagerly make changes that have emerged from within themselves, and the changes will likely endure longer than change suggestions that originated with the social worker (deShazer, 1985; deShazer & Berg,1997; Walsh, 2013). Early in the exploration of client strengths, the client is asked to look for exceptions in his or her life where the problem does not occur and is invited to envision his or her life without the problem through the use of the "miracle questions" (see Box 11.7). There is an inherent trust in the client to master his or her own life and create it to his or her liking.

Developed in the 1980's by deShazer and Berg (1997), SFBT operates from a set of straightforward assumptions:

1. It is not necessary (usually) to understand the origins of a problem in order to solve it.
2. Not all client problems need to be addressed; address only the pressing problem.
3. The focus is on change rather than cure.

Box 11.7 Solution-Focused Brief Therapy—The Language of Solutions: Sample Interview Questions

1. **The miracle question:**

   "Imagine a miracle occurring tonight that would (sufficiently) solve the problem which brought you here, but you were unaware of this as you were asleep. In the morning, how would you notice that this miracle had taken place? What would be different? What would you be doing differently? Who would be the next person to notice that the miracle has happened? How would this person notice? How would he or she react?"

2. **Scaling questions:**

   On a scale of 1 to 10, with 10 meaning you have every confidence that this problem can be solved and 1 meaning no confidence at all, where would you put yourself today?

   On the same scale, how hopeful are you that this problem can be solved?

   What would be different in your life when you move up just one step?

3. **A focus on solutions rather than the problem:**

   How are things better?

4. **Exploring exceptions:**

   How will you know when our work together has helped?

   How would you say you are different when you are a little bit less depressed?

   What would it take to move up one notch on the scale? When you force yourself to get out of bed and walk the kids to school, what do you suppose your children will notice that's different about you?

   Tell me what is different for you on those days when you don't drink?

Sources: Bannink (2007); Pennsylvania Child Welfare Training Program (n.d.); Walsh (2013).

4. Client and social worker collaborate in their work together, with the client leading the processes of defining the problem, goal setting, and intervention.
5. The client is an expert on his or her own life.
6. Solutions are grounded in client strengths.
7. If something works, keep using it; if something doesn't work, discard it (Bannink, 2007; deShazer, 1985, 1997; Walsh, 2013).

In their work together developing SFBT, deShazer and Berg (1997) discovered that when SFBT social workers engaged in three specific types of practice behaviors, clients were significantly more likely to discuss change, solutions, and resources. These behaviors included the use of the following:

Eliciting questions—What would you like instead of the problem? What is better?

Questions about details—What exactly did you do differently?

Verbal rewards—Giving compliments and asking competency-based questions, such as "How did you manage to do that?" and "Where did you get that good idea?" (Bannink, 2007, p. 88)

The social worker can help monitor client progress and encourage work by asking the client at the end of every session to rate the progress toward achieving his or her treatment goal using a scaling question, such as "On a scale of 0 to 10, with 10 being complete achievement and 0 being no progress, where do you see yourself in relation to your goal?" The social worker uses opportunities to amplify the client's competence when progress

Practice Contexts

Critical Thinking Question: Tim is a client referred to you as part of a court-mandated sentence to complete an anger management course. Tim has been consistently losing his temper at work and yelling at coworkers and once screamed at his boss. He is at risk of losing his job if he does not successfully complete the course and learn to manage his anger. What mode of treatment would you recommend for Tim and why? What specific techniques might you employ to help Tim gain control of his anger and his life?

is made. For example, if the client moved from 1 to 4 on the scale from the first session to the second session, the social worker might respond by noting the progress and the significant size of the progress and then follow up with a question that allows the client to recite and review the skills he or she used to make the progress; for example, "How did you move from 1 to 4 in just two sessions?" (Bannink, 2007). Box 11.7 provides some examples of solution-focused questions commonly used in SFBT. The case study in Box 11.8 demonstrates how solution-focused questions can be applied with clients.

? Assess your understanding of brief treatment strategies and techniques by taking this brief quiz.

Box 11.8 Solution-Focused Brief Therapy: Case Study

Mr. Richardson is a 55 year old married man. He is a secondary school teacher presenting with symptoms of palpitations, panic attacks, crying fits (sometime occurring in the classroom), and high blood pressure. His symptoms began interfering with his ability to teach his classes and Dr. Potter, the school principal requested that he take sick leave to get help with his condition. He has been on leave for eight weeks, and has consulted his family doctor, but his symptoms persist. The idea of returning to the classroom elicits visceral reactions, of nausea, cold sweats, and hyperventilation. In spite of being home and away from the pressures of work, his physical and emotional symptoms have worsened. Mr. Richardson links the onset of his symptoms to the suicide of a colleague, Janna Smith, during the previous year. He has felt alone, confused, and angry about her death. He acknowledges that he has been unable to successfully deal with the aftermath of her suicide. His reactions to Janna's suicide were compounded by his father becoming ill and moving in with him and his wife. Prior to taking sick leave, Mr. Richardson's responsibilities at work had increased as a result of a fellow teacher, Pat Herman also experiencing psychological problems and missing work. Mr. Richardson now finds himself worrying that Pat may also be contemplating suicide. The events at work have contributed to the deterioration in morale and comradery among school faculty, which Mr. Richardson has counted on over the years as a source of support.

***Goal formulation*: At the end of the treatment, what should be achieved in order to say that the intervention has been useful?**

Mr. Richardson's goal is to teach again and to rebuild supportive bonds with his colleagues. He envisions himself returning to his former classroom teaching style, one that is relaxed and light. He wants to be able to make jokes with his students again.

The therapeutic relationship is considered to be a *customer relationship*, as the client is motivated to change his or her behavior. The social worker *compliments* the client for seeking help and for his or her ability to clearly formulate what he or she would like to achieve during treatment. The client's power in the helping relationship is acknowledged by asking if he or she would like to return and if so when.

During the second session with Mr. Richardson, the social worker asks a scaling question about his current conditions, such as "How are you feeling today?" He is asked to rate his well-being on a scale of 1 – 10 using the following interpretation: 10 = feeling completely well again and his goal has been achieved; 0 = the moment when he felt worst and there was little hope.

Mr. Richardson replies that he rates himself at a 4, whereas during the first meeting he scored a 1. He clarifies by saying that he feels more cheerful, has been more active during the past week, even attending a concert; he is sleeping better and is more at ease among people. He has noticed a reduction in the number of panic attacks he has experienced over the past 2 weeks. When the social worker asks Mr.Richardson how his wife would rate his well-being, he responds that she would probably give him a 4 as well. The social worker then asks him, "How did you manage to advance from a 1 to a 4 so quickly?" He responds by saying that the first session helped him to focus on what he wanted to achieve. That prompted him to think about what he could do to get there and he was able to identify some activities that he enjoyed and found the confidence to try them. He acknowledged feeling better but is not ready to return to school or to engage colleagues. The social worker compliments Mr. Richardson on the initiative he has taken and the progress he has made in such a short period of time. She then asks him, "What would a 5 look like?"

Mr. Richardson responded that at a 5, he would expect to have fewer physical symptoms, and that he would begin to have some contact with his colleagues. The social worker suggests some activities for Mr. Richardson to engage in between

Box 11.8 Solution-Focused Brief Therapy: Case Study *(Continued)*

sessions. She asks him to think about what might help him to reach a 5; and to also ask others (such as his wife) what they would imagine his behavior would look like at a 5. Finally, the social worker suggested that he look for moments where he is already feeling like a 5, and to reflect on what he is doing at that moment to move him closer to his goal of a 5.

During this third session with Mr. Richardson the social worker begins by asking, "What is better?" He begins by describing how his physical symptoms have continued to abate, and with a hint of pride reports that he sent a colleague an e-mail apologizing for an angry outburst. He was happy to receive a forgiving and positive response back. He also contacted his principal and requested to return to work at half-time initially with hopes of gradually increasing to full time. The social worker asked Mr. Richardson how confident he felt that his goal will be reached, on a scale of 1 – 10. He responded a 7 to 8. He based his expectations on the fact that he feels better rested and is experiencing friendly reactions from family, friends and colleagues. He reports that he is feeling happy and hopeful. To protect himself from setbacks he has decided to distance himself from Pat, his colleague who is experiencing psychological problems.

The social worker genuinely compliments Mr. Richardson on his progress, pointing out all that he has achieved and terminates their sessions. Three months later Mr. Richardson contacts the social worker requesting a follow-up session. The social worker begins the session with the question: "What is better?" Smiling, he talks about how happy his is to be back at school and enjoying his students and colleagues again. He was touched by the sincere welcome he received from his students. Physically his is active and feeling healthy with few symptoms remaining. He is focused on his well-being at work and at home, has taken up jogging, and has lost his obsession with Janna's suicide. He rates himself at a 9; but report his wife and colleagues would probably rate him at an 8. Everyone acknowledges that he has returned to his relaxed and jovial self. The social worker then asks, "What would you have to do in order to revert to a 4 or even a 1" (relapse prevention)? Mr. Richardson recognized that he would most likely increase his stress level by working overtime which would influence his relationships with his colleagues (quarreling) and students (putting too much pressure on them) and also putting too many demands on himself. Working too much would also curtail his outside activities such as jogging that add balance to his life. While reclining in his chair and in a jovial manner, he says that he does not see that happening again.

The social worker offers genuine congratulations and compliments on how well he has managed to refocus his life and bring it back into a happy balance. The social worker asks, "How are you going to celebrate this happy fact?" Mr. Richardson pauses for a moment and declares that he will celebrate his positive life changes by taking his wife out to a candle-lit dinner.

Source: Based on Bannink, F. P. (2007). Solution-focused brief therapy. *Journal of Contemporary Psychotherapy, 37,* 87–94.

SUMMARY

- Preparing for client treatment ensures the best alignment of interventions with client needs and desired outcomes.
- The selection of treatment modalities should be in alignment with the goals and time frames set out in the contract with the client.
- Contextual factors of treatment can include the emotional and psychological states of the client, the client's intellectual/cognitive abilities, cultural beliefs and practices, agency rules and practice orientation, treatment setting, family context, and social support networks.
- Client motivation keeps the client engaged in treatment and improves client outcomes.
- Resistance to change is a common human response.
- Motivational interviewing can help clients resolve resistance or ambivalence toward change.

- Building client capacities and coping skills is essential for helping clients in creating a functional, self-sustaining life as well as helping to restore a sense of self-efficacy and improved self-esteem.
- Brief treatment with clients has become the norm in recent years. Three commonly used therapies in social work practice are 1) brief psychodynamic therapy, 2) cognitive-behavioral therapy, and 3) solution-focused brief therapy.

APPLY IT

1. Watch all three sessions of **Interactive Case Study #3** of Mike and social worker Karen. Consider the behaviors Mike displayed that might be an expression of resistance to treatment. How did Karen use Mike's resistance to further the therapeutic relationship and enhance Mike's motivation? Using motivational interviewing techniques, create your own responses to Mike's resistance to treatment.
2. Review all sessions of **Interactive Case Study #5** of Mrs. Kita and social worker Diane. How did Diane show her understanding of the cultural context of her practice with Mrs. Kita? Are there other cultural aspects or opportunities that Diane misses in the relationship that she could have responded to in a more culturally appropriate way? If yes, identify where those opportunities were and how Diane could have taken advantage of them.

Assess Your Competence

Use the scale below to rate your current level of achievement on the following concepts or skills associated with each competency presented in the chapter:

1	2	3
I can accurately describe the concept or skill	I can consistently identify the concept or skill when observing and analyzing practice activities	I can competently implement the concept or skill in my own practice

_______ Understands and can describe the importance of the many aspects of the cultural context of therapy.

_______ Understands and can articulate the impacts of client motivation and client resistance on therapy outcomes.

_______ Understands and can articulate the three types of common brief treatment therapies.

12

Practice Evaluation

INTHESKIES/FOTOLIA

An important aspect of direct social work practice involves monitoring and evaluating how the client is doing in response to interventions. Social workers have an ethical obligation to the client, the profession, and society at large to provide evidence that the treatment that they are providing is helping the client or, at the very least, is causing no harm. Having tools and techniques in place to assess client progress and the impact of interventions helps to keep the therapeutic relationship focused on client goals and can also help in keeping the client motivated to continue treatment. Seeing week-to-week improvement can also bolster clients' sense of self-efficacy. Treatment evaluations can also be of help to social service agencies. When monitoring and evaluation processes are used and data are available to document the success of practice interventions, the credibility of the agency increases, and funders are more likely

LEARNING OBJECTIVES

- Describe three methods for evaluating client progress in social work practice.
- Outline two uses for baseline data in practice evaluation.
- Apply an individual rating scale to evaluating client outcomes.
- Explain how a Goal Attainment Scale is used to monitor and assess client progress in treatment.
- Interpret two single-subject designs and their application to practice.

CHAPTER OUTLINE

to continue supporting services that work. Today, many funders, as well as third-party payers require evidence of treatment effectiveness.

EVALUATING DIRECT PRACTICE

As the social worker and the client work together to develop treatment goals and design a treatment/service plan identifying specific desired client outcomes, the social worker has already begun the evaluation process. Key to monitoring and evaluating client progress and the impact of the intervention on the client's well-being is setting concrete and measurable goals. It is usually helpful to break down the goals into small manageable steps that can be measured from session to session or at predetermined time intervals. This also makes the work required of the client less overwhelming, as he or she is able to focus on one step at a time in moving toward his or her goals. Monitoring and evaluating client progress not only helps in documenting the movement toward goals but also helps the social worker to determine when a specific intervention is not working and when an alternative approach may be warranted.

There are many methods available to social workers to help evaluate his or her practice with clients. Some are formal, analytical, and quantitative, such as standardized assessment tools and software applications that provide statistical outputs. Others are more qualitative and rely on client statements, the clinical experience of the social worker, **supervision**, and feedback from fellow social workers (Corey, Haynes, & Moulton, 2010; Patton, 2015). Both forms of information can play a vital part in evaluating direct social work practice. **Quantitative data** can objectively demonstrate client progress or lack of progress using valid and reliable assessment tools that provide invaluable data on client mental health status, such as depression and anxiety scores, and other areas of client functioning. **Qualitative data** can provide rich information on how the client experienced the helping relationship. Knowing what the client found most or least helpful during the helping process also informs the way social workers conduct their practice with clients. Building periodic qualitative questions into the evaluation process provides insightful information to the social worker and opportunities for the client to participate in guiding the helping process.

Supervision has long been a valued tool in social work practice for building skills and practice wisdom and is also a valid tool for evaluating practice (Corey et al., 2010; Miley, O'Melia, & DuBois, 2013). In developing practice skills, it is imperative that new social workers seek out clinical supervision as you enter the practice field. Get in the habit of seeking out support from seasoned social workers, and you will find supervision to be a valuable resource throughout your career. The National Association of Social Workers (NASW) *Code of Ethics* also refers to social workers' ethical obligation to stay abreast of new treatments and interventions as they move to the forefront of practice, and to gather evidence of the effectiveness of new interventions. Other methods for growing in practice wisdom, best practice, and evaluation techniques include reviewing new studies and best practices in professional journals, attending professional conferences and workshops, and staying up to date with your agency's practice standards, new programming, and evaluation requirements. All of these professional activities reflect a lifelong commitment to your clients' well-being and your own professional development.

Three methods commonly used to monitor and evaluate treatment interventions with clients are briefly introduced and demonstrated in this chapter are 1) individualized rating scales, 2) goal attainment scaling, and, 3) single-subject design, a more research-oriented evaluation method used in professional social work practice. Single-subject design is an evaluation method introduced to students in their research courses and is applied to practice cases in this chapter. Standardized psychometric scales are common for assessing client emotional and mental well-being (such as depression, anxiety, and self-esteem) and are frequently used in social work practice. They are excellent tools for collecting valid and reliable data that help in understanding the client and in monitoring client progress. Follow-up measures help determine the degree to which the client is finding relief from symptoms and if the treatment interventions are having the desired effect. Some common **standardized instruments** used in clinical practice include the Beck Depression Scale, the Rosenberg Self-Esteem Scale, and the Clinical Anxiety Scale. Social workers who use these tools are trained in the application of the instrument and the interpretation of the scores they generate.

? Assess your understanding of evaluating direct practice by taking this brief quiz.

BASELINE DATA

It is always helpful to have baseline data at the outset of the helping relationship so that progress can be measured and tracked over time. **Baseline data** are simply concrete measures of client symptoms or presenting client problems before intervention begins. Baseline data can be collected in several ways, and the method that best matches the client's presenting problem should be the method of choice. Baseline data can be assessed during the intake assessment when the social worker is making observation of the client, by using archival data on available client records, or retrospectively, based on questionnaires completed by the client or by significant others in the client's life. Baseline data tell the social worker in a very quantifiable way the severity, frequency, or duration of the problem (Di Noia & Tripodi, 2008). For example, a client referred for anxiety may describe how his anxiety feels and how it affects his behavior. However, to quantify the anxiety and thus establish baseline data, the social worker could administer a standardized instrument that measures "anxiety," such as the Clinical Anxiety Scale (CAS). The client's score on the CAS would provide baseline data and a measure of the severity of the client's anxiety before an intervention is begun. Having baseline data makes it easier to document the client response to treatment. If scores on the CAS go down after the intervention has been introduced, this suggests that the intervention is working.

> **Research-informed Practice**
>
> **Behavior:** Apply critical thinking to engage in analysis of quantitative and qualitative research methods and research findings.
>
> **Critical Thinking Question:** When a student client presents with a problem of academic failure, what might be one source of baseline data that the social worker could use in evaluating future progress?

While it is always desirable to have baseline data to work from, there are circumstances when taking the time to collect such data would be inappropriate. For example, when clients are in crisis and in need of immediate attention, such as a suicide risk, taking the time to collect baseline data would put the client at greater risk of harm. In most cases, however, social workers have the time to prepare for and collect information about the client's symptoms, presenting problems and challenges before intervention is begun. The type of data the social worker will need to collect is determined by the nature of the problem the client is experiencing. When seeing a child with the problem of bedwetting, an appropriate measure might be the number of times a week the child wets the bed. For an adolescent who is truant from school, the average number of days absent from school each month would be helpful in setting a baseline. In cases of clients experiencing mental health problems, standardized measures can be used for establishing baseline data. For example, a new client, Marci, was referred from the local OB/GYN doctor because of postpartum depression. On the first visit with Marci, the social worker observed that she was a bit listless and difficult to engage. In addition, she appeared tired and complained of wanting to sleep all the time. Marci is six months postpartum, and the baby seems to have adjusted well and is sleeping through the night and eating on an every-four-hour schedule. Marci expresses little interest in returning to her activities that she enjoyed prior to motherhood, such as weekly lunches with a group of friends, amateur photography, her part-time job as activity director at the local community center, and working in her greenhouse growing orchids. To assess her level of depression in a measurable way, the social worker administered the Beck Depression Inventory (BDI), a short 21-question standardized survey. Marci's score of 28 indicated that she was suffering from a moderate level of depression and is in need of treatment. Having a baseline measure of Marci's depression will make it possible to gauge Marci's progress once treatment has begun. By administering the BDI at regular intervals during the treatment phase, the social worker can monitor Marci's response to treatment. It is common to construct a graph to visually track client progress (see Figure 12.1). This helps the social worker and the client see concrete evidence of improvement or, conversely, when a treatment is not working and the intervention needs to be changed. When a client sees movement in the direction of a desired goal, it can act as a motivating force to keep the client engaged in treatment.

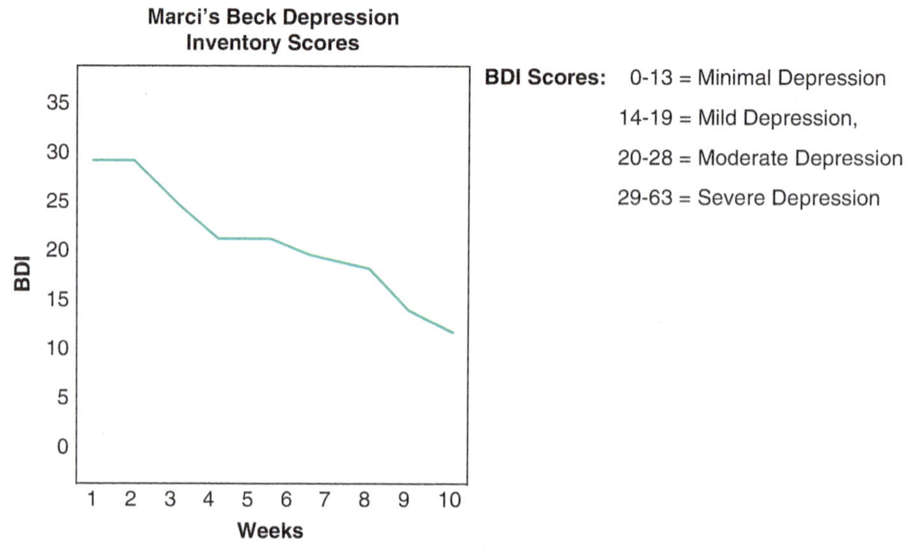

Figure 12.1
Depression score over the course of 10 weeks of client treatment

When designing an evaluation process for a client, social workers will need to consider the sources of information available to them and who might be the best source given the client's problem and circumstances. Social workers gather some information from the client, but there are times when others can also help to fill in the picture of how the client is doing in various settings. It is important to get the client's permission and to have him or her sign a release of information before talking with collateral contacts.

Watch the video clip of the social worker Diane gaining written consent from her client, Mrs. Kita, to talk to collateral contact.

Research-informed Practice

Behavior: Use practice experience and theory to inform scientific inquiry and research.

Critical Thinking Question: Identify three sources of information that may help the school social worker evaluate a student with a behavioral disorder to determine his progress in reducing inappropriate behaviors across multiple settings.

When treating a child, parents are helpful in understanding a child's behavior at home, while teachers, school social workers, and guidance counselors will have better knowledge of the child's behavior in the school setting. The after-school child care provider may be another source of information. Therefore, when evaluating a client's progress over time, integrate and synthesize all of the information into a cohesive whole.

Assess your understanding of baseline data by taking this brief quiz.

INDIVIDUAL RATING SCALES

The first steps in the evaluation process are to decide what behaviors or symptoms need to be quantified and measured, how they will be measured, and with what frequency. Identifying a desired end is necessary in order to assess movement toward or away from a goal and to determine when the goal has been achieved. Creating **individualized rating scales** is one method of monitoring client progress. These types of rating scales are tailored to specific client needs, are easy to use, and require little time for the client to complete. For example, one short-term goal was to "develop consistent parenting skills and patterns." The social worker could talk with Mrs. Anderson during each visit and ask her how confident she felt in her parenting. She may ask her to rate her confidence level on a scale of 1 to 10. She could also work with Mrs. Anderson to develop a checklist or individualized rating scale of parenting behaviors that she would like to work on attaining. Then on each visit, the social worker would ask Mrs. Anderson to rate herself on each behavior.

Watch Interactive Case Study #4, in which the client Mrs. Anderson and social worker Nicole work together to develop a treatment plan and decide on some specific goals for Mrs. Anderson to work toward. Following the video clip, see the parenting checklist the social worker developed to help monitor Mrs. Andersons parenting skills for raising her granddaughter, Maria (see Box 12.1).

As a new primary caregiver to her granddaughter, Mrs. Anderson has many concerns about how to manage her new role and her time, daily routines, and resources in order to take good care of her granddaughter, Maria. In the social worker's first

Box 12.1 Mrs. Anderson's Parenting Skills Checklist

Skill	How I Am Doing: Not at All	Once in a While	Some of the Time	Most of the Time	Comments about Successes/ Difficulties
I make sure that Maria knows the rules of the house.			X		I try to remind Maria of the rules when I think of them.
I am successful at getting Maria to follow the rules of the house.		X			Maria is used to being on her own and doesn't listen to me.
I provide Maria with healthy well-balanced meals and snacks throughout the day.			X		Sometimes I forget to go to the store or we run out of things.
I am able to encourage Maria to eat the healthy food provided for her.		X			When we eat together, I try to get her to eat healthy foods, but sometimes it just sounds like nagging.
I make sure that Maria is in bed by 9:00 on school nights.		X			Maria stays up late in her room.
I provide Maria with the structure and space to complete her homework.			X		Right now she is using the kitchen table. I want to get her a desk for her room.
I am available to help Maria with her homework.		X			When Maria asks, I try to help as much as I can.
Maria completes her homework.		X			Her teacher called yesterday to tell me that Maria isn't doing her homework.
I am aware of where Maria is when she is not at home.		X			I try to get her to understand how important it is that I know where she is, but she is not used to "reporting in."
I check on Maria's whereabouts when she is not at home.		X			I don't even know where to look when she is not at home. She is used to having free reign when she was with her mother.

interview with Mrs. Anderson, she mentions that she wants to make sure that Maria follows the house rules, eats healthy foods, gets to bed by 9:00 on school nights, and attends to her homework, and also wants to know where Maria is at all times. Based on this information, Nicole the social worker and Mrs. Anderson construct an individualized rating scale to help assess how Mrs. Anderson is managing in these areas from week to week (see Box 12.1). On the next follow-up visit, the social worker supports Mrs. Anderson in completing the rating scale, encouraging her to be as honest as possible, and stressing that there is no "wrong" answer. It takes Mrs. Anderson less than 10 minutes to complete the scale. In just a few minutes, Nicole has much more information about where Mrs. Anderson's strengths and challenges are in parenting Maria. In addition, she has some baseline data to help gauge Mrs. Anderson's improvements over time. The social worker can also use this new information to select new interventions that will help Mrs. Anderson attain her goal of developing good parenting skills. Now take a moment and review the treatment plan for Interactive Case Study #2, client Anthony in Box 12.2.

Box 12.2 Anthony's Treatment/service Plan

TREATMENT/SERVICE PLAN

Client: Anthony Davis

AGENCY: Outreach Service Agency

Date: October 10, 20--

	Responsible Party	Date to Begin and End	Means for Monitoring Progress	Outcome: Completed; Incomplete; or In Progress
A. Long-term goal:				
Anthony will develop skills that will enable him to lead a productive life.				
B. Short-term goals:				
1. Anthony will complete high school.				
Objectives/Tasks				
• Pass 10th grade/all classes				
• Attend every class, every day				
• Get involved in school-related activities				
• Attend after-school study sessions				
• Complete all homework assignments				
• Prepare for all exams (at least one hour per subject area)				
• Ask for help when needed				
2. Anthony will get a job.				
Objectives/Tasks				
• Identify employment options				
• Complete application process				
• Practice interviewing skills				
• Enroll in the job readiness class at school				
• Explore the work-study course option offered through school				
• Talk with career/vocational counselor at school				
• Talk to music teacher for job-related leads				
• Explore transportation needs				

Box 12.A Now You Try It . . . Preparing for an Individualized Rating Scale

In Interactive Case Study #2, James the social worker has developed a treatment plan (Box 12.2) with Anthony, who is experiencing difficulties in school, at home, and in the community. Use the treatment plan that James and Anthony have developed together. Review all the details of the first short-term treatment goal: "Anthony will complete high school." Then determine the elements that you will need in order to construct an individualized rating scale:

What you will measure?

____

____

How you will measure it? Provide an example.

____

____

How frequently will you measure it?

____

____

Assess your understanding of individual rating scales by taking this brief quiz.

Using stated goals in the treatment plan, develop an individualized rating scale to assess Anthony's progress. Use Box 12.A to guide you in this exercise.

View Case Study #2, session #1, with Anthony and his social worker James. See if you can identify in the their initial session what led to James adding each element to Anthony's treatment plan.

GOAL ATTAINMENT SCALING

Similar to individualized rating scales, **goal attainment scaling** uses an evaluation scale customized to the client's desired outcomes. As in other methods of evaluating client outcomes, target goals are set with the client, and specific behavior changes are concretely defined. A good source of client goals is the treatment plan developed by the social worker and client. For example, see the specific treatment goals outlined in Box 12.2 for Anthony, the client in Interactive Case Study #2. Each of these goals can be assessed using goal attainment scaling by using the standard five-point scale. The goal attainment scaling five-point scale ranges from +2 (most favorable outcome) to −2 (least favorable outcome):

- Most unfavorable (−2)
- Less than expected success (−1)
- Expected level of success (0)
- More than expected success (+1)
- Most favorable outcome or much more than expected success (+2)

On the continuum of −2 to +2, the middle measure of 0 is the expected client outcome, or the client goal that the social worker and client have set. Adding additional levels of attainment beyond the expected goal leaves open the possibility for greater success for the client. The social worker periodically rates the degree to which the client has moved toward or away from treatment goals. Each value is given a definition

Box 12.3 Goal Attainment Scaling: Case Example

Mrs. Khan is a 77-year-old woman admitted to a rehabilitative care unit following a bilateral knee replacement surgery. The social worker developed a goal attainment scale that was used to gauge Mrs. Khan's progress during the first three weeks of recovery.

Goal Attainment Levels	Patient Mobility Level	Activities of Daily Living (ADL)	Care at Discharge
−2 (much less than expected)	Needs caretaker assistance to chair and bathroom	Dependent in ADLs, including dressing	In rehabilitative care unit
−1 (somewhat less than expected)	Ambulates with a walker for less that 25 steps	Dependent in ADLs except for dressing,	Discharged to nursing home
0 (expected level; program goal)	Ambulates independently indoors with cane for 75 feet	Independent in ADLs, needs help with meal preparation, housework, and transportation	Discharged home with home support
+1 (somewhat better than expected)	Meets goal in 2 weeks, or walks 100-200 feet with walker or cane.	Independent in ADL except outside activities	Discharged home with support for transportation only
+2 (much better than expected)	Fully mobile inside house with cane; uses walker outside	Independent in ADLs	Discharged home without supports

Based on Stolee, P., Zaza, C., Pedlar, A., & Myers, A. M. (1999). Clinical experience with goal attainment scaling in geriatric care. *Journal of Aging and Health*, *11*, 96–124. Used with permission.

that specifically fits the client's situation in order to assist the social worker in evaluating client progress. Goal attainment scaling has been found to be an effective evaluation process and feasible with a wide range of clients, including the elderly and chronically ill (Toto, Skidmore, Terhorst, Rosen, & Weinerc, 2015). For an example of a completed client goal attainment scale, see Box 12.3. Here the client, Mrs. Khan, is recovering from a knee replacement in a rehabilitation facility. The social worker has created a goal attainment scale that is specific to Mrs. Khan's needs and that corresponds to her level of functioning prior to her knee replacement surgery. As the social worker monitors Mrs. Khan's progress over the expected two- to three-week recovery period, she will gain insight into Mrs. Khan's probable discharge planning and home support needs.

Evaluating client progress is a fundamental part of direct social work practice. It begins at the initial meeting with the client when problems are being defined and continues throughout the helping process. Evaluation is an ongoing process that keeps the social worker and the client focused on the treatment goals and helps the social worker to know when treatment is working and when it needs to be enhanced or changed. When goals are achieved and the client is ready to move toward termination, evaluation can play an important part in helping the client in this transition. Reviewing with the client how far he or she has come, what skills the client has acquired, and his or her ability to commit to goals and achieve them is an empowering springboard for launching the client into their next phase of life. Take a moment to try to apply goal attainment scaling

Box 12.B Now You Try It . . . Creating a Goal Attainment Scale

Revisit the treatment plan for our interactive client Anthony in Box 12.2. The second treatment goal for Anthony is to get a job. Review the objectives/tasks outlined below the goal that will move Anthony toward finding a job. Select one of these tasks and create a goal attainment scale item that defines the possible levels of attainment for −2 to +2.

−2 (Most unfavorable behavior/lowest expectation):

−1 (Less than expected behavior/below goal expectation):

0 (Task goal):

+1 (Somewhat more than expected behavior):

+2 (Much more than expected behavior):

- Most unfavorable (−2)
- Less than expected success (−1)
- Expected level of success (0)
- More than expected success (+1)
- Most favorable outcome or more than expected success (+2)

View Case Study #2, session #2, with Anthony and his social worker James to help you in creating specific task for each measure on the goal attainment scale for the second treatment goal.

to the client, Anthony, in Interactive Case Study #2. You have familiarized yourself with Anthony's treatment goals located in his treatment plan Box 12.2 and developed an individualized rating scale. Building on this client knowledge and using Box 12.B to guide you, develop a goal attainment scale to evaluation Anthony's progress toward his goals of finding employment and completing high school.

Ultimately, social workers attempt to use evaluation tools such as goal attainment scaling not only to measure client progress but also to motivate and empower clients in achieving their life goals. Empowerment theory goes hand in hand with monitoring client progress. Box 12.I provides a case study of Leah, who discovered her own power in creating her life the way she wanted it. The social worker helped Leah appreciate her own strengths and skills by evaluating her progress each week. By doing so, the social worker led Leah into a place of self-empowerment.

Box 12.I Theory into Practice—Empowerment Model and Client-Centered Practice: Leah

The *empowerment model* of social work practice focuses on accentuating client potentials and resiliencies and minimizing client vulnerabilities. It builds on client strengths and promotes client connections with their internal power (resources) and seeks to increase client mastery in shaping their environments in desirable ways, thus enhancing client feelings of competency. Carl Rogers's *client-centered approach* recognizes that the client is an expert on his or her own life and has the internal resources to discover his or her own answers in the context of a nurturing and accepting helping relationship.

Leah Smith, age 33, came to the ABC Center for Help. She and John, age 35, have been married for seven years and have two children: Alex, age four, and Dora, age two. Leah is currently living in the family home but stated that she is "fed up and ready to move out."

Leah is a self-referred client and indicates that she suffers from severe mood swings that she is unable to control. She worries about the future and stated, "I can't imagine staying with John, but I have nowhere else to go." Leah is currently working part-time as a secretary at State University and likes her job. She sees her coworkers as very supportive and helpful, especially concerning issues in her private life. Leah sees her problems as "living an unfulfilled life" and her mood swings, which leave her feeling exhausted.

Leah appears to lack confidence in her presentation of self. She either looked down/away or expressed anger. She stated that she is unhappy in her marriage. The client reported that she cannot have a "civil" conversation with John. When the worker asked her to elaborate, she stated, "He has this nasty habit of spitting when he gets mad, and I end up walking away; it is disgusting."

Box 12.1 Theory into Practice—Empowerment Model and Client-Centered Practice: Leah *(Continued)*

Her frustration came through as she became louder and pounded her fists on the arm of the chair. Leah's range of emotion appears to be limited to either expressing irritation or annoyance. She stated that she has few friends and feels isolated from everyone except her coworkers. Leah is "stressed out" all the time. She does not have any emotional outlets, such as supportive network of family or friends. She identifies herself as very moody and easily upset.

Leah stated that her children should be a source of pride and love, but she can't find it within herself to express anything other than frustration. When the worker asked her to further describe her relationship with her children, she indicated that she is a "terrible mom," always yelling and being impatient with them. Leah expresses regret in her inability to parent the way she believes she should. She would like to stop being so negative and enjoy her time with Alex and Dora rather than resenting them. Leah is oriented to time and place and appears to be self-reflective. She is very hard on herself, criticizing many of her past and present choices, especially her marriage to John. See Appendix C for a full multidimensional assessment on Leah.

In working with Leah, the social worker has explored her concerns, specifically related to mood swings, feeling trapped in her marriage, and feeling ineffectual as a parent. Using the empowerment and client-centered approaches, the client and social worker join together to form a partnership. One strategy that has been very beneficial to Leah is assisting her in developing a plan of action. For example, the social worker has helped her to interact more positively with her children and husband. Now Leah is using "I" statements. Through practice and encouragement, she is now able to say to John, "When you said that to me, I felt hurt by the sharpness in your tone of voice." She is no longer blaming John and her children for her own feelings of annoyance and irritation. Additionally, the social worker has helped her to develop a wish list. The list includes her dreams and hopes for the future, such as interacting more with her children. She reported to the social worker that having one-on-one time with Alex and Dora has helped her feel closer to them and that she is enjoying their special time together. Leah has also met with a psychiatrist to discuss her mood swings. She is now taking medication for bipolar disorder and reports that she is feeling less reactive and more patient. She joined the State University Recreation Club and has completed a nutritional assessment. She is also enrolled in a yoga class.

How did Leah make all this progress in a matter of eight sessions? Each week, Leah and the social worker reviewed her progress using a goal attainment scale, standardized instruments, and individualized rating scales. Over time, Leah was able to see her progress in concrete ways by viewing the quantitative data produced by the evaluation tools the social worker used in her treatment of Leah. In addition, the social worker provided Leah with a framework in which she could make decisions. No matter the circumstances, Leah had to think about ways to empower herself and her life. It was through the encouragement and support of the social worker that Leah was able to move forward and make decisions that were congruent with what she wanted for herself and her family. Leah now believes she is entitled to feel better and enjoys spending time with her children in a more positive way. She agreed to be evaluated by a psychiatrist for medication and is starting to focus on her physical well-being. Leah is developing decision-making skills, such as ways to be thoughtful and mindful of what she says and how she says it. She has not made a final decision about leaving John but reports that "there is less tension between us." By tuning in to Leah's needs (client centered) and empowering her to make choices that feel good, the social worker has helped her to rethink her priorities. She is feeling more self-assured and comfortable. If Leah decides to divorce her husband, the decision will be made with a plan in place so that it will be the

Assess your understanding of goal attainment scaling by taking this brief quiz.

least disruptive for all members of the family. The use of an evaluation tool throughout the helping process can support the client and the social worker in moving toward client goals.

SINGLE-SUBJECT DESIGN

As noted earlier in this chapter, social workers are ethically obliged to provide treatment and interventions to clients that have been shown to be effective. This means that social workers are required to know that the interventions they select for clients have been tested scientifically and shown to improve client outcomes. When social workers engage in practice following this standard, we say they are engaged in **evidence-based practice** (EBP). The NASW defines evidence-based practice as "interventions for which scientific evidence consistently shows that they improve client outcomes" and consisting of three elements: 1) the best research evidence/support for the intervention, 2) the best clinical experience for the client, and 3) interventions that are consistent with client values. While elements 2 and 3 above can be met with individualized rating scales and goal attainment scaling discussed earlier, for monitoring and evaluating practice interventions, they do not meet the standards for generating scientific evidence. To meet this standard in evaluating individual client outcomes, we turn to a more sophisticated method of practice evaluation: **single-subject design** (SSD). To meet the scientific standard, clinicians statistically test the differences in client presenting problems between the baseline measures assessing the level of a particular client problem, and the level of the problem during and after the intervention. This analysis helps to determine if the changes in client outcomes are statistically significant from before and after the intervention. Data analysis is discussed later in this section on SSD.

Preparing for Use of SSD

There are many SSD practice evaluation designs to select from when preparing to evaluate practice with a client. The nature of the client's problem, the type of client intervention chosen, and the methods and type of data collected to assess treatment effectiveness will influence the type of design most appropriate for the case. While there are multiple SSD options that range from the simple to the complex, as an introduction to SSD, two basic designs are described here, and case studies are used to demonstrate their application to practice. These are the AB design and the ABAB design. The ABC and multiple baseline designs are discussed briefly in the 'additional designs' section below.

In preparing for practice evaluation, the social worker needs to consider many factors before selecting the appropriate SSD and will need to make some practice decisions. Clients often present with multiple problems. In the development of the treatment plan, the social worker and client agree on problems to be addressed during the helping process and prioritize the problems. In agreement with the patient, the social worker selects the problem to be treated and evaluated. In preparation for the evaluation process using SSD, the social worker will need to make a series of decisions before implementing the SSD evaluation process. These decisions include:

- The client problem of treatment and evaluation focus
- Behaviors/cognitions or other selected variable(s) to be measured
- How the variable will be measured

- How often the variable will be measured
- The nature of the intervention
- The length of baseline data to be collected
- The frequency with which client data will be measured and collected (Di Noia & Tripodi, 2008).

AB Design

Typically, SSDs are labeled by phases of the evaluation, from phase 1, or phase A, to the final phase of the evaluation, which may be as limited as one phase or may include many phases, depending on the design selected. In the AB design, the first phase (A) is designated as the baseline, which measures the level of the client's problem at entry into the helping process when no intervention is in place. At this stage, the social worker will measure the selected variable that represents the frequency, severity, or duration of the problem multiple times and at equally spaced time intervals, such as once a day or once a week. The time interval will depend on the nature of the problem. For example, if the client presents with the problem of school truancy, then it may be appropriate to use weekly intervals or even monthly intervals for collecting baseline data. As a school social worker engaging the student in treatment, access to student records on absenteeism may be available to the social worker. Thus, the data for measuring the problem would be the number of days per month the student has been absent from school in recent months. In this case, the social worker would have the option of using archival data to establish a retrospective baseline. Baseline data points can be as few as three to as many as needed to establish some level of horizontal stability (Di Noia & Tripodi, 2008). In the case of the truant student, the social worker could access school data on the number of absent days per month for as far back as needed to assess trends in absenteeism and some level of consistency in number of days absent per month. The baseline establishes a benchmark against which the client's behavior can be compared at a later date after intervention have been set in place (Byiers, Reichle, & Symonsa, 2012). The baseline data are placed on a graph that displays trends in client behavior (see Figure 12.2).

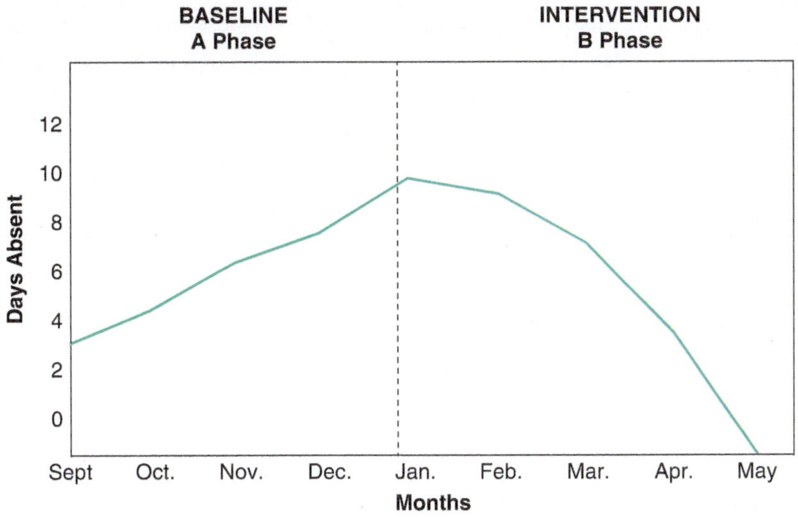

Figure 12.2
AB Design—Case Example

Phase 2, or phase B, of the AB design represents the intervention phase. During this phase, the social worker introduces the preplanned intervention while continuing to take repeated measurements of the client's behavior at the same interval that was established during the baseline. Like the baseline data, the data collected during the intervention phase are placed on the graph. The baseline, or "A" phase, and the intervention, or "B" phase, are separated by a line on the graph and labeled appropriately. If the intervention is helping the client, then client behaviors should improve and will be reflected on the graph (see Figure 12.2).

As a case example, let's pick up on the truant student introduced above. We will call the student William and present the client evaluation AB design, graphing the baseline data collected by the school social worker from school records and the intervention data collected during the intervention phase. Let's imagine that after doing intake with the student and reviewing his records, the social worker discovered that William was from a low-income single-parent family and that he attributed his absenteeism to his need to work in order to help support the family of four: himself, his mother, and his two siblings As the oldest child and being male, the cultural values of the family looked to him to help support the family while also completing high school. Living within his family and cultural values, William took a night job at a local 24-hour grocery store where he worked four nights a week, getting off duty at 6 A.M. This gave him enough time to sleep for an hour and then get ready for school, which started each day at 8:45 A.M. He often failed to wake up and make it to school on time. Consequently, his absenteeism and tardiness escalated over the previous three months since school had started in September, and he now faced suspension from school. Such a threat motivated William to follow his principal's advice and seek help from the school social worker. Recognizing William's need to work and contribute to the family income while still attending school, the social worker enrolled William in an antitruancy community–school partnership program especially geared at helping low-income students (Rodríguez & Conchas, 2009). The program provided William with 20 hours per week of community employment with local businesses that sought to match student career interests with local businesses that aligned with student interests. William had a strong interest in music and had once taken drum lessons. He was placed as a salesperson in a local music shop where he worked from 3 P.M. to 8 P.M. three nights a week and from 9 A.M. to 2 P.M. on Saturday. Because the community–school partnership program was partially funded by a U.S. Department of Education grant and partially funded by a U.S. Department of Juvenile Justice grant, the program was able to pay students at a rate above minimum wage. This constituted a pay raise for William, making it possible to quit his night job and enter the program without a loss in pay. The new arrangement provided William with time for his studies and time for adequate rest. The intention was to see if these changes in William life would increase his attendance at school. The social worker began tracking William attendance while continuing to meet with William once a week during school hours to see how he was adjusting to the program and to address any issues that might arise. On examination of the baseline and intervention data displayed in Figure 12.2, what can you conclude about the success or failure of the intervention in addressing William's problem of school truancy?

During weekly meetings with William and by following monthly data on William's school attendance, the school social worker came to learn that William's problem was largely his inability to integrate and meet family expectations that were culturally driven—to stay in school while working and contributing to the family income. Given the right structure and support through the community–school partnership antitruancy program, William was able to attain both goals. His exhaustion abated, and his school attendance improved. The alignment of William's interest (music) with his job placement (working in a music shop) reignited William's interest in music, and he was able to restart drum lessons free of charge as an employee benefit. William remained in the antitruancy program until the end of the school year and was given a full-time job at the music shop during his summer break. The intervention was successful in reducing days absent from school from a high of 10 days in January to zero days in May and removing the threat of school suspension. Added benefits included fostering William's love of music and securing a full-time job for the summer months.

ABAB Design

The ABAB design provides two periods of baseline data and two periods of intervention data using the same intervention. This design, also referred to as a reversal design, can prove to be effective in reversing client behaviors that may return after an intervention has been completed or withdrawn. This type of reversal design can strengthen the validity of the data and client outcomes if the same intervention can be shown to be effective with the same client more than once. We know with greater certainty that changes in the client's behavior were attributed to the intervention and not something else. The ABAB design can also help in determining how long a treatment is needed in order to extinguish a client behavior and thus reduce its chance of returning.. Figure 12.3 displays

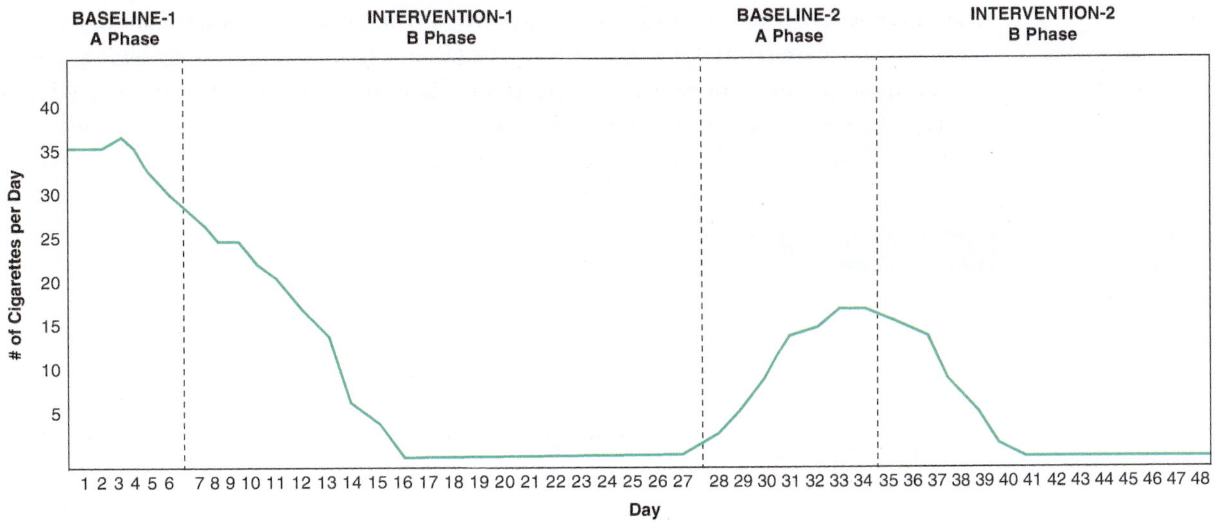

Figure 12.3
ABAB Design – Case Example

the data collected using an ABAB design discussed in the case example below. Notice how the client behavior returns after the first intervention is removed. The return of the undesirable client behavior is noted at the beginning of the baseline-2. Also notice how the client behavior begins to abate much faster after the intervention is introduced a second time.

As a case example, a hospital social worker is employed in the Employee Assistant Program (EAP), which has a primary focus of improving healthy living habits of employees in an effort to reduce employee insurance costs, reduce sick days used, and improve the overall health and productivity of employees. Joe, a respiratory therapist, was referred to the EAP social worker because of recurring health issues and frequent sick day usage. Ironically, Joe has chronic bronchitis that has keep him out of work for three to five days a month over the past three months. On initial assessment, the social worker learns that one way that Joe manages the stress of his job is through smoking, a habit that exacerbates his chronic bronchitis. The hospital sponsors a three-week "quit smoking" clinic repeatedly throughout the year. The clinic uses hypnosis as its primary intervention but also provide support groups and individual stress management sessions to assist employees in developing and maintaining healthy stress management behaviors. Joe has already been issued a warning from his supervisor because of his high absenteeism and is in danger of losing his job if he does not find ways to improve his health. Joe enters the "quit smoking" clinic, and the social worker monitors Joe's smoking behavior by asking him to honestly report the number of cigarettes he smokes a day. For the six days before the "quit smoking" clinic begins, Joe reports the number of cigarettes he smokes. After intervention begins, the cigarette smoking data are collected by the social worker running the clinic and is sent to the EAP social worker to record and graph. Initially, Joe had difficulties giving up his cigarettes, but after two hypnosis sessions and attending two support group sessions, his usage began to decline rather quickly. By the end of the three-week clinic, Joe had been off cigarettes for two weeks, had substituted exercise for managing his stress, and had not missed a day of work due to illness since entering the program. Two weeks following the completion of the clinic, Joe received word that his father had died suddenly. Joe took a grievance leave from work to attend to his father's burial and to do his own grieving. During this process, Joe began smoking an occasional cigarette at the initial offer of a cigarette by a sibling and fellow smoker. Joe returned to work and immediately made an appointment to see his EAP social worker for grief counseling and also to get help to reverse his smoking behavior. Joe began weekly session in a grief group and with the encouragement of his social worker reentered another three-week "quit smoking" clinic. Through retrospection, the social worker was able to reconstruct Joe's smoking behavior from the time he took his first cigarette from his sibling until he returned to the EAP and his second "quit smoking" clinic intervention. Figure 12.3 displays the data for Joe during both baselines and both intervention periods. What can you conclude from a visual analysis of the data?

Joe's return to an intervention that had already proven effective in the past extinguished his smoking quickly. Notice also that although Joe did relapse in his smoking behavior, he did not return to the level of smoking that he had before his first intervention.

Research-informed Practice

Behavior: Use and translate research evidence to inform and improve practice, policy, and service delivery.

Critical Thinking Questions: Examine the data in Figure 12.3. Provide an interpretation of the data in terms of client cigarette smoking behavior. How do you account for the periods of increased cigarette smoking? The periods of decreased cigarette smoking? What would your conclude from these data? How might this influence your future practice with clients seeking to quit smoking?

The use of supports in the "quit smoking" clinic intervention and the additional grief support group provided Joe with the help he needed to return to a healthy lifestyle.

Additional Designs

The AB and the ABAB designs provide an introduction to using SSD in evaluating treatment interventions and client outcomes. There are many more designs, and some you will be introduced to in your research class. Two commonly used designs are the ABC design, where C represents a second but different intervention. This design is often used when the first intervention (B) does not produce the desired effects with the client and the social worker decides to replace it with a different intervention in hopes of better client outcomes. In this scenario, the graph would have three phases: A, B, and C. See Figure 12.4 for an example.

Another commonly used design is the multiple baseline design. This design is useful when clients present with multiple related problems and/or when the social worker is collecting data on more than one variable. In the case study of Joe above, a multiple baseline design could have been instituted to measure the number of cigarettes Joe smoked per day. In addition, using a second graph, the social worker could have monitored the number of days Joe missed from work per month. This would act as a second indicator of how effective the intervention was at reducing both smoking and absenteeism: two related problems. In this same case, the social worker could have also created three or four additional graphs to monitor Joe's participation in the various services offered in the "quit smoking" clinic, such as how often he attended the "quit smoking" support group, participated in hypnosis, and attended the stress management classes. When using multiple baseline design, the social worker will need to create a graph for each variable being measured.

Data Analysis

The initial analysis of the data from SSD is based on visual comparison between two or more conditions. Typically, these conditions include baseline data and intervention

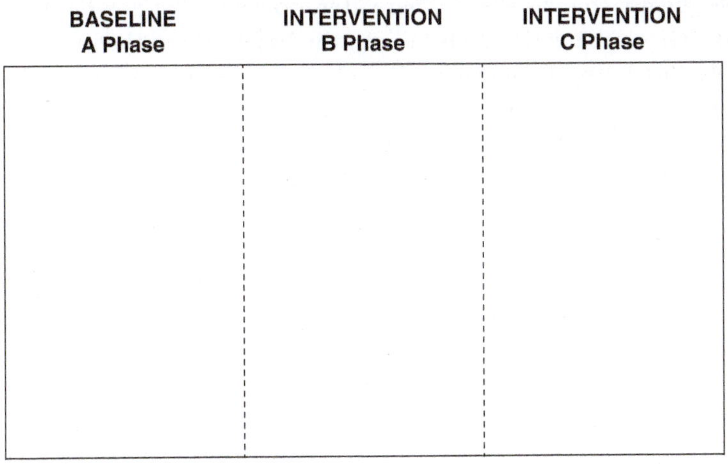

Figure 12.4
ABC Design

data. The baseline phase establishes a benchmark, and the social worker wants to determine if client behaviors changed during the intervention and to what extent treatment goals were achieved. The data for comparison across two phases require certain qualities. First, we look for horizontal stability in the baseline data. As mentioned earlier, baseline data are collected until consistency is present in the data, meaning that they display limited variability. In addition, there is a desire to have a lack of a trend toward improvement in the baseline data. This suggests that the client is getting better without the interventions. In such cases, then, it would be difficult to determine if the client improved because of the intervention or if he or she would have improved anyway without the intervention. Once the data have been graphed, the social worker examines them for changes in level, trend (slope), and/or variability. Level refers to the average rate of performance during a phase. For example, in the case example of William above, his average monthly rate of truancy during the baseline phase was 5.25 days (September [3] + October [5] + November [6] + December [7] = 21/4 months = 5.25). The social worker then compares this to the average performance during the intervention phase. For William, his average number of days absent from school during intervention was 6 (30 days/5 months). By this standard, William did not improve his truancy behavior. However, if we examine the parameter, trend, or slope of his month-to-month performance in baseline compared to intervention, we gain a different perspective on William's performance. During the baseline phase, the trend was upward, or an incline in the slope representing more days missed from school with each passing month. When compared to the intervention phase, we see an opposite trend, or downward slope. William's absenteeism declined with each passing month from a high of 10 days in January to a low of zero days in May.

Finally, we look for variability in the data or unpredictable change in the data from month to month. For our client William, there is a stable upward trend in the baseline data. In the intervention phase there is a stable downward trend. These trends begin to look predictable from month to month, thus presenting low variability. Furthermore, the higher truancy average during the intervention can be explained by the initial high rate of absenteeism in the first month, when treatment had not yet begun to take effect. Thereafter, however, the downward trend begins and persist. Given the data trends in both the baseline and the intervention phases and the low variability, the social worker can conclude from visual analysis that William benefited from the intervention and was able to meet the treatment goal of no truancy in the month of May (Byiers et al., 2012).

Visual analysis can be supplemented with statistical analysis using software developed specifically for SSD, such as Singwin or R. This supplemental analysis is desirable when the visual analysis does not show dramatic changes and could benefit from a statistical analysis to establish significant change in client behavior. Statistical outputs can tell the practitioner if the changes in client behavior were statistically significant (adding scientific rigor) and how much of the change in client behavior was due to the intervention, also known as effect size. Supplemental statistical analysis adds certainty to the conclusions drawn by the social worker regarding the effectiveness of the intervention and increases the credibility of the SSD findings within the scientific community (Bloom, Fischer, & Orme, 2009; Bulté & Onghena, 2013; Byiers et al., 2012; Moeyaert et al., 2014).

? Assess your understanding of single subject design by taking this brief quiz.

SUMMARY

- Three methods commonly used to monitor and evaluate treatment interventions with clients are 1) individualized rating scales, 2) goal attainment scaling, and 3) single-subject design (SSD), a more research-oriented evaluation method used in professional social work practice.
- Baseline data are simply concrete measures of client symptoms or presenting client problems before intervention begins and can be gathered during the intake assessment by the social worker or by using archival data on available client records or retrospectively based on questionnaires completed by the client.
- Creating individualized rating scales is one method of monitoring client progress. These types of rating scales are tailored to specific client needs, are easy to use, and require little time for the client to complete.
- Goal attainment scaling uses an evaluation scale customized to the client's desired outcomes. Target goals are set with the client, and specific behavior changes are concretely defined.
- To meet the standard evidence-based-practice in evaluating individual client outcomes, we turn to a more sophisticated method of practice evaluation: SSD. Common designs are the AB, ABAB, ABC, and multiple baseline designs.

APPLY IT

1. Review all sessions of **Interactive Case Study #6** of Kim and social worker Louis. Identify indicators of Kim's progress in the helping process. What goals was she able to attain? What type of evaluation method would have been most useful for monitoring Kim's progress over time? Why?

Assess Your Competence

Use the scale below to rate your current level of achievement on the following concepts or skills associated with each competency presented in the chapter:

1	2	3
I can accurately describe the concept or skill	I can consistently identify the concept or skill when observing and analyzing practice activities	I can competently implement the concept or skill in my own practice

_______ Understands and can articulate evaluation-related ethical issues.

_______ Can identify and describe evaluation approaches and models for individuals.

_______ Can identify two common standardized instruments for assessing client progress in treatment.

13

Termination

LEARNING OUTCOMES

- Identify ways in which termination, the last phase of the helping process, is implemented over the course of the relationship.
- Demonstrate an understanding of how themes of separation and loss effect both the client and the social worker.

CHAPTER OUTLINE

STANCIUC/FOTOLIA

TERMINATION: ENDING THE HELPING RELATIONSHIP

Termination is the final phase of the helping process, and how the social worker concludes the relationship will influence the extent to which clients may be able to maintain the progress achieved. Ending the client–social worker relationship in a planned and sensitive manner can empower clients to continue to grow long after leaving the services of the agency. A major goal of the helping process is to assist clients toward independence and empowerment. Being clear about your role and the time-limited nature of the relationship from the outset can assist the client in managing possible hardships associated with termination. It is good practice to discuss the process of ending as you begin the helping relationship. Letting the client know from the intake process and beyond the parameters of the relationship can be affirming. A client will less likely interpret the ending of the relationship as something personal, such as you don't want to meet any more, you no longer like him or her, or you are frustrated with the client's lack of progress.

Separation and Loss

When the helping relationship has ended successfully for the client, it represents a culmination of a committed partnership between the client and the social worker. It is only natural that ending the helping relationship will evoke mixed feelings in the client. Client reactions to termination can vary in intensity and are influenced by the nature of the relationship that has been established, the length of time working together, the client's previous experiences with **separation** and **loss** from important people in his or her life, and how well the client has been prepared for the ending of the relationship. When clients are prepared for the ending, they are able to accomplish the goal of termination and leave the relationship with a sense of pride and hope for the future. Although this type of termination is ideal, all helping relationships do not end in this way.

Both clients and social workers can sometimes experience a sense of loss during the termination phase. It is appropriate for the social worker to express his or her feelings to the client within the context of maintaining professional boundaries. It is imperative that the social worker not take the ending of the professional relationship personally. It is easy to attribute a client's decision to terminate the relationship prematurely to something the social worker did or did not do. This is an easy trap to fall into, as the decision to end the relationship may be as straightforward as a family crisis that must take priority. By sharing your feelings about ending the relationship, it affirms the client's contribution to the relationship and his or her value to the social worker.

Clients may unilaterally terminate the relationship in obvious ways, such as not showing up for appointments or returning calls and text messages. In less obvious ways, they may "forget" about an appointment, come late, "forget" to complete a homework assignment, or show little or no interest in being present. It is the social worker's responsibility to ascertain where the client is in regard to the continuation of services. Reasons may include being court ordered, ordered by an employer (e.g., Mike, the client who is dealing with alcohol related issues), or mandated by a parent. If the client is not coming prepared or appears hostile, disinterested, and disengaged in the process, having a conversation about possible outcomes of staying or going is warranted. Laying out what might happen (children going into foster care, probation being revoked, termination of employment) is essential in providing information that may have a significant impact on clients' decisions about the helping relationship and their future lives. But following the social work value of self-determination, allowing the client to decide his or her course of action is ultimately the best approach. If the client decides to terminate the relationship and you believe it is not in his or her best interest, be honest and straightforward. The social worker should always leave the door open for the client to return should he or she change his or her mind about leaving the helping relationship.

When the client is giving signs of disengagement, the social worker should clarify his or her intent to withdraw. In this clarifying process, the social worker may come to realize that the client has attained a level of success with which he or she is satisfied even though it may fall short of the goals set throughout the helping process. It is in the looking back that clients often gain a greater appreciation for how far they have come in the healing and growing process. Still, some clients will chose to terminate

Intervention

Behaviors: Facilitate effective transitions and endings that advance mutually agreed-on goals.

Critical Thinking Question: What steps must a social worker consider when planning for termination with a client who has experienced repeated losses? Identify 3 possible strategies for helping your client through this transition.

before all of the treatment goals have been attained. Clients who have developed a high self-esteem may experience the separation as a "sweet sorrow," recognizing that it is time to move forward in their lives but also acknowledging the loss of a valued relationship. For other clients who have experienced repeated loss and separation in their lives, ending the helping relationship may be more painful and difficult. Understanding how your client's previous relationships ended can assist you in managing the current termination. Termination handled with care and sensitivity can set the stage for all future relationships, but especially if the need for further treatment arises. The client may reach out for help again if his or her last experience with a helping professional was constructive and ended with a positive sense of closure.

The Process of Termination

Client–social worker relationships are terminated for many reasons. For example, clients may move out of the service area, social workers may take new jobs, clients may terminate prematurely because they believe they no longer need services, a social work intern providing services to clients graduates, and so on. In the best-case scenario, we envision clients leaving because treatment goals have been achieved and no longer in need of services. As clients resolve their problems and acquire new coping and problem-solving skills and knowledge of resources available to them, the social worker and client acknowledge the progress made and begin to discuss the timing of the termination phase. Coming to a mutual decision about terminating is by far the best approach to this final stage of the relationship.

Revisiting the idea of termination from time to time, especially as the client achieves more and more successes, helps to prepare the client for the ending and provides opportunities to discuss gains and to resolve emotions that may be evoked with the thought of termination. These are also times to review the client's growth in terms of skills, resources, and decision making that can bolster his or her self-confidence and further prepare him or her for future termination. Involving the client in the process of termination helps to avoid a sense of abandonment that a client may feel when a relationship is ended abruptly or without adequate preparation Termination can also be viewed as a period of new beginnings for the client. This moves the client beyond grief or loss and into embracing the future armed with the new skills he or she has acquired.

As the termination phase of the relationship draws nearer, revisit the key points of the helping process. Reviewing the progress the client has made over time, builds confidence in his or her ability to trust in the future. The social worker can discuss with clients how the new skills and resources they have gained can be used to resolve future problems or concerns or how they can be used to pursue new goals in their lives (Boyle, Grafton, Mather, Smith, & Farley, 2009). It is helpful to review with your client who they will turn to for support, as these people may serve as natural helpers. Natural helpers can include friends, family members, a teacher, a clergyperson, a peer, or individuals who are part of the client's life but not in the role of a professional helper. Boxes 13.1 and 13.2 present ways in which social workers and clients may react to the termination process. As you are reviewing these lists, identify other emotions and situations that you could envision in your role as the social worker or client.

During austere times, when services are not as readily available, resources are diminishing, and staff are being let go, it is important to serve in the role of a broker. Your agency may have a policy regarding the length of services offered (e.g., up to 12 sessions), but the client clearly is in need of additional support. Knowing how and to whom to refer a client is important so as to ensure their momentum is not slowed down or sidetracked. Unfortunately, social worker caseloads are ever increasing,

Box 13.1 Examples of Social Worker Reactions to Termination

There are many ways that a professional may react to the ending of the helping relationship. Below are both positive and negative ways that endings might occur.

Positive responses to termination

- Sense of accomplishment and pride in what the client has achieved
- Excitement regarding what the future holds
- Confidence in self and clinical judgment
- Competence
- Ability to plan for an ending
- Understanding the nature of a time-limited relationship
- Supports client's efforts for independence and self-determination

Negative responses to termination

- Sense of sadness and loss
- Guilt for not helping enough
- Frustration and wondering how things could have turned out differently
- Wanting to hold on to the relationship
- Offering more sessions so as to keep in contact with the client
- Difficulty with endings
- Curiosity about the client that is beyond what would be expected
- Looking to the client to fill a space for the worker, meeting own needs

Box 13.2 Examples of Client Reactions to Termination

There are many ways that a client may react to the ending of the helping relationship. Below are both positive and negative ways that endings might occur.

Positive responses to termination

- Sense of pride and accomplishment
- Increase confidence in navigating through hardships
- Stronger attachments to others
- Relief as the situation has improved
- Understanding and insight into what contributed to problems
- Understanding the nature of a "helping relationship"

Negative responses to termination

- Sense of disappointment
- Extreme loss or sense of abandonment
- Denial or recurrence of problems
- Request to be friends with the social worker
- Anger or hostile feelings
- Testing limits of the relationship
- Missing appointments
- Abruptly dropping out

and helping the client understand this reality can help him or her work even harder to reach the goals, as time becomes a motivator to change.

What happens if the social worker and client have not been able to establish a solid relationship and one or both choose to terminate? Ideally, it is best to identify what the barriers are, such as recognizing a significant age difference between social worker and client which can be an impediment to the relationship. Or the social worker and client have very different cultural backgrounds that cause difficulty in relating to each other. It is helpful to have an honest conversation about the barriers and mutually determine if they are surmountable and, if not, what are the next steps. It might be a referral to another professional, a different agency, or another type of resource, such as a self-help group. Offer to assist in the referral process, as this is the stopping point for the relationship. The social worker can also offer to hold a joint session with all parties, including the client and the new worker. State this as an option (if it really is one) but it is the clients' decision. If the client chooses to hold a meeting, you are setting the stage for a more seamless transition, by assisting the client to get from point A to point B.

Reviewing what has or has not been accomplished and what each party learned from the other can be helpful to ensure the relationship ends on a high note rather than on one of discontent. The more notice the social worker can give the client regarding the upcoming ending, the better. Never assume the client won't care, even if you have not developed a close working relationship; it is your responsibility to prepare your client, and it is his or her right to know when the relationship will end. Box 13.3 provides you with the opportunity to think "as Kim" as she is transitioning toward termination.

Depending on the nature of your relationship with the client, choosing to reduce the frequency of visits over time is a good way to help the client prepare for termination. It is in some ways weaning the client off the relationship by encouraging more independence and checking in rather than remaining in such close contact. Consider meeting weekly, shift to monthly sessions, then to every other month. It is important to consider the type of setting and situation too; as the social worker may meet with the client for only a few minutes and refer him or her on. Or the worker may assist a client through a crisis situation

Assessment

Behaviors: Develop mutually agreed-on intervention goals and objectives based on the critical assessment of strengths, needs, and challenges within clients and constituencies.

Critical Thinking Question: In Box 13.3, Kim and Louis are talking about all of the progress she has made since they met several months ago. In assessing her progress from the social worker's perspective, what do you see as her greatest accomplishments?

Box 13.3 Termination through the Eyes of Kim

Watch the final session with Kim and Louis. Put yourself in Kim's position as she is wrapping up her conversation with Louis.

1. How is she feeling about herself?
2. What are some of her ongoing concerns regarding the progress she has made?
3. How can she assure herself and Louis that she is on track moving forward?
4. How does she feel about her sister's involvement, specifically in regard to her inheritance?
5. What can she do to maintain sobriety?
6. What can she do to locate a job and an apartment?
7. What is Claudia, the social worker's role in helping Kim to transition to independent living?
8. How does Kim envision her life now that she is sober? What are the most significant gains she has made?

that is resolved within an hour, such as finding shelter for the night. But the **continuum of care**, that is, finding and linking the client to resources beyond your services, is an important part of termination. For example, a patient leaving an inpatient psychiatric hospital is referred to a community mental health agency, a psychiatrist, and a day treatment program. As the social worker, you will serve as the broker, connecting the client with these services. Ultimately, you have provided services along the continuum of care, from inpatient hospitalization to linkages of resources in the client's community.

Box 13.A demonstrates a variety of ways that a social worker–client relationship might end. Presented are four different scenarios. Read each one and answer the following questions.

Box 13.A Now You Try It . . . Termination Scenarios

Long-Term Relationship and the Ending (Planned)

You are a social worker who has been working with Cynthia for almost two years. You visit her once a month to check in on her and her children, ages three and four. You have recently accepted another position in a community about an hour away. Following your supervisor's request, you have a month to close out all your cases. Taking a two-pronged approach, how do you help prepare Cynthia with your leaving and convince your supervisor of her continued need for services? In your professional opinion, although you have seen much progress, you believe she will still benefit from services. Your supervisor is not willing to assign another worker to her without a strong case from you.

1. Identify three concerns you have regarding Cynthia and her need for continued services?
2. Identify how you will assist Cynthia in terminating with you, as you two have grown close over the years.

Short-Term Relationship and the Ending (Unplanned)

You are a seasoned social worker in a domestic violence shelter, and you have seen many women and children come and go. Monica and her two children, ages seven and five, came to the shelter two days ago. After helping them to get settled and providing a safe place, she decides to return home. You have the opportunity to talk with her before she leaves, as her mother is picking them up in an hour. You want to support her right to self-determination and at the same time point out some potential consequences.

1. Identify ways that you can continue to support her after she leaves.
2. What might you say to her regarding her decision?

Short-Term Relationship and the Ending (Planned)

You are a social worker in a medical facility. Harry is a patient who had a heart attack and was admitted to the hospital three days ago. Following surgery to place a stent in his heart, he is going home. He lives with his wife, Patsy, and their beloved dog, Coop. You have talked with Patsy twice over the course of Harry's stay, and she seems somewhat hesitant to have him come home. You have developed a particular liking to Patsy, as you too have a beloved dog and a husband with health problems. As the social worker on the unit, it is your responsibility to work on his discharge planning.

1. Given Harry is leaving tomorrow morning, identify how you would go about planning for his discharge.
2. What are the resources you plan to suggest as they prepare to return home?

Long-Term Relationship and the Ending (Planned based on the ending of an internship)

You are an undergraduate social work student interning at the Human Service Center. Your clients are individuals with mental illness, ranging in age from 18 to 82 years. You have loved your internship and feel sad about leaving. As a yearlong intern, you had a winter and spring break, and now you are officially ending. One of your clients, Desiree, refuses to believe that you are leaving. She points out that you left before but came back, and she is sure this will happen again. You have been telling her since September that you are a student and will be graduating in May.

1. What steps can you take to help her understand the reality of your leaving?
2. You realize that you need to talk with your field instructor about this situation. What are the questions you will ask her as you prepare to leave your placement?

Watch this clip as Karen and Mike review his progress over the past three weeks. Karen offers up some information regarding ways to manage his stress once he is home again. What would you say to Mike as part of the final good-bye? Be specific.

In a more long-standing helping relationship, offering some type of ritual helps celebrate accomplishments and brings closure to the relationship (Miley, O'Melia, & DuBois, 2011). (It is important to talk with your supervisor about the agency's policies regarding gift giving and receiving.) However, in recognition of the ending of a positive relationship with the client provide him or her time and space to express sadness and grief as well as pride.

In this clip, watch Diane and Mrs. Kita review all of the progress she has made over the course of their relationship. At the end of this clip, watch as they exchange gifts and hug one another, as this marks the ending of their relationship. In the case of Mrs. Kita, the exchange of gifts fits well with her Japanese culture and is an appropriate way to end the helping relationship.

Now watch as Anthony and James terminate their relationship. James reviews all that Anthony has accomplished as he wishes him well. Put yourself in James's shoes and assess the work you have done over the course of the relationship. What are your greatest accomplishments as you think about the work done with Anthony? Where did you fall short?

Finally, it is important to end the helping relationship on a positive and hopeful note. This leaves the door open for reengagement of services in the future should the need arise. Let the client know who will be their contact person and how to reaccess services by saying, "Just call the office and let the person know you would like to come back for services," "My social worker is no longer working there, but he told me to contact Jane," or "I am not eligible for services at your agency anymore, but I need help finding a program." Offering up ways to reestablish a relationship can be helpful to the client, knowing that if a situation arises, there will be help again.

It is helpful to the social worker and the agency to take the opportunity to ask clients to evaluate the services they received. What was most helpful to them? Were there services that would have been helpful but were not offered? Was there anything that they found uncomfortable or uninviting? Asking clients to provide honest answers to these types of questions can provide social workers and agencies with opportunities to improve services and practices that may help future clients. Offering feedback to the agency can also afford the client an opportunity to be heard, knowing that their feedback matters. If there are particular issues (e.g., the worker rarely returned phone calls, or the worker always came prepared for a meeting), this information may be considered when a supervisor is completing an employee review. Asking for specific examples of the way the client's life has improved (or not) can give you good information about how they evaluate themselves. Letting the client know there will be some type of formal

Ethical and Professional Behavior

Behaviors: Make ethical decisions by applying the standards of the NASW Code of Ethics, relevant laws and regulations, models for ethical decision-making, ethical conduct of research, and additional codes of ethics as appropriate to context.

Critical Thinking Question: A client gives you a $50 gift certificate to a local restaurant. It is her way of thanking you for helping her make some important life decisions. She insists that you accept her gift. What do you do?

Box 13.4 Termination Checklist for Social Work Students

One to Two Months before Ending:

- Determine your last day.
- What tasks do you need to complete before ending (e.g., transferring cases, writing termination notes, finishing projects)?
- Who needs to know that you are ending (i.e., clients, coworkers, community partners)?
- Process your feelings about leaving with your supervisor.

Final Weeks before Ending:

- Begin to say good-bye to clients, groups, and community.
- Discuss what will be different if you stay on as an employee/volunteer.

Last Day:

- Turn in keys, identification tag, and parking pass.
- Complete any last-minute paperwork.
- Say good-bye and thank you.
- Celebrate your growth and learning.

follow-up, maybe a survey by phone or a questionnaire, can be helpful to them, as they will be prepared when such a survey arrives.

Endings are as important as beginnings, as they set the stage for future work relationships and other professional opportunities. Most endings carry with them some excitement and some trepidation. The more carefully planned the ending is, the better prepared all parties are when the ending finally does arrive. Box 13.4 has a suggested list of tasks to complete as you are moving toward the next phase of your career and life.

Ethical and Professional Behavior

Behaviors: Use reflection and self-regulation to manage personal values and maintain professionalism in practice situations.

Critical Thinking Question: As a social worker new to the field, how might you react to a client who just stops showing up for appointments or is not home when you have repeatedly arranged a convenient time to meet with him or her?

As you move forward

Throughout this text, you have been presented with information that is relevant and essential in your development as a competent social work professional. You have been exposed to the meaning and breadth of social work, the roles we fulfill in an effort to provide the best service possible, and the ethics, values, and theories that guide our practice. You have also had the opportunity to learn about developing cultural competence in your practice with clients. All of these components of knowledge come together as a complete practice ensemble when you fully engage your clients in the helping process.

The accompanying workbook will give you the opportunity to practice the essential interviewing skills and attending behaviors that are the foundation to practice. You have been exposed to common pitfalls in practice, providing you with techniques for recovery when errors are made in the interviewing process. Individual and small-group exercises are designed to increase your self-awareness and cultural competency in practice. Be patient (and positive) as you continue to review the interviewing and attending skills. As you watch the case examples, put yourself in the social worker's place, in other words, how might you respond, given all you have learned. What might you do differently from the social workers in the interactive case studies? Continue to assess your skill development as you move through this learning process.

Assess your understanding of termination by taking this brief quiz.

Finally, we learn in incremental steps (as do our clients). It takes time and practice to achieve a level of comfort and competence as a professional. Even the most skilled and seasoned social workers are learning and fine-tuning their skill sets. It is a lifelong journey and well worth the time and effort.

SUMMARY

You have learned how the helping process can assist clients to overcome challenges. Once the client has made sufficient progress, understanding when and how to terminate the relationship is the final phase of the relationship.

- You have learned about loss and separation from both the social worker and the client perspective.
- You have learned the steps involved in termination, including both when planned and unplanned.
- You have learned the importance of helping the client to identify ways to maintain the progress made over time, including follow-up sessions if needed.
- As a new social worker, you have learned how to put into practice the skills necessary to provide direct services to clients.

Assess Your Competence

Use the scale below to rate your current level of achievement on the following concepts or skills associated with each competency presented in the chapter:

1	2	3
I can accurately describe the concept or skill	I can consistently identify the concept or skill when observing and analyzing practice activities	I can competently implement the concept or skill in my own practice

_______ Can describe the process and tasks of termination.

_______ Can describe common reactions to termination from the client and social worker's perspective.

_______ Can appreciate professional growth and development overtime.

Appendix A

PROFESSIONAL WRITING AND DOCUMENTATION GUIDELINES

Agencies will generally provide the social worker with the forms and standards of documentation practice used by their particular organization. However, here are some general guidelines that have application across practice settings.

The Importance of Strong Writing Skills

1. Service documentation—*if it's not written down, it didn't happen.* Fill out every line and space; even if it is not applicable, simply write "NA." By doing so, you have communicated something important.
2. Accreditation and accountability—poorly written records may impede accreditation or funding reimbursement for your agency and therefore can be a direct disservice to the clients you serve.
3. Best practice—professional standards are not optional or subjective but are instead prescriptive and based on empirical evidence. Agency auditors will conduct periodic quality assurance reviews to make sure that all documentation is done correctly.
4. Credibility—people may forget what you say, but your written word will live on for as long as the file remains. This can be beneficial to you and the client when seeking clarity around any issue in dispute and provide concrete evidence in court cases where your records may be subpoenaed.
5. Adherence to professional ethics and standards—your writing is a reflection on your school, your supervisor, your agency, and your profession. Know your agency's procedures and guidelines regarding documentation.
6. Faulty memory—it is impossible to remember all elements from all your cases. For example, multiply 40 cases times an average of four family members times weekly visits.
7. Insurance against future problems—good records verify that you have provided a standard level of care and have fulfilled your professional responsibilities and can be used to defend you in case of a lawsuit or dispute. The file is a legal and permanent document for adoptions, verification for disability benefits, TANF, and so on. Use extreme caution if keeping "personal notes" separate from the "official record." Even a social worker's personal notes can be subpoenaed in a court hearing. Whatever is written down can end up in court under scrutiny from the judge and multiple attorneys.
8. Documents build on each other chronologically—one poorly written report can create ripple effects on future documentation and case activities. Documentation should be done in logical progression.

9. Financial—reports and service documentation, such as for Medicaid, translate into revenue for your agency. Poorly written documents may be rejected and/or not reimbursed.
10. Writing is an investment in the case for you and the client. A sloppy or poorly written report, letter, or assessment can imply a lack of care or mismanagement of the case.
11. Written documentation serves to facilitate the coordinating of services between professionals and agencies. These reports are used as a way to ensure continuity of care.
12. Professional versus conversational—professional writing and e-mailing or texting are very different. Your writing sets a tone. Make sure the tone is appropriate for the right occasion. A casual e-mail to a work colleague is different from an e-mail to the administrator of an agency.
13. Employability—writing skills are extremely important to successful job performance in any social work specialty.

Consider Your Audience and the Purpose of Each Written Document

1. Documentation provides the who, what, where, when, how, and why.
2. Who is your audience, and what do they need to know about your case? Be mindful of HIPAA and confidentiality restrictions (see Appendix B). It's important that the right people have the right information. For example, Johnny's school social worker does not need to know that his mother is an adult sexual abuse survivor, but he or she will need to know that the family is being evicted at the end of the week and that the bus needs to pick him up at the shelter.
3. Each document has to "stand alone," as some readers will have limited or no prior knowledge of case issues and information. Workers often make the mistake of assuming their audience has more background knowledge than they actually do. For example, the judge may have presided over a case several times during the past year; however, he or she may hear an average of six cases per day.
4. Know when to be brief and summarize and when every detail, including quotes, is critical. Too much detail is cumbersome, and readers won't take the time to sort through it all, but too little implies lack of case knowledge and/or services on the worker's part.
5. Remember that clients can access their records.

Writing Suggestions

1. Keeping your writing clear and simple and to the point.
2. Planning—you will need to file documents prior to actual events, such as court and administrative case reviews.
3. Staying caught up on paperwork—if you get behind, you will rush through, and the end product may suffer. The goal will become just completion of the writing, and the *quality* of the writing can cease to be a consideration. Do a little writing every day rather than waiting until the end of the week when it's already piled up. Up-to-date records also let others know exactly where things are in regard to the case.

4. Interviewing—asking the right questions to elicit the right information.
5. Note taking—without thorough notes, the finished product is compromised. (If you are taking notes, be sure to ask the client's permission and/or explain the reason for your note taking.)
6. Accuracy—a document can be beautifully written, but if the facts it contains are wrong, it is useless or, in the worst-case scenario, can be harmful to your client.
7. Be sure to use the correct word choice for words such as "there," "their," and "they're." All three words sound the same but have very different meanings.
8. Proofread your work. Don't rely on spell check and grammar check. Consider reading what you write out loud, as hearing the written word can also be helpful in making sure the report flows together.
9. When writing case/progress notes, always keep a supply of necessary forms with you in the field. Some agencies have moved exclusively to electronic documentation and record keeping.
10. Using quotes can be very powerful. What sounds better: saying the client is cooperative (what does that really mean?) or saying the client stated, "I will do anything to get my children back"?
11. Be specific and objective—if a client has attended eight out of 10 treatment sessions, say he or she has attended eight out of 10 sessions, or 80 percent, but don't say the client attended "most" of them or "several." Ambiguities erode your credibility—the audience will assume you don't know what really happened.

Common Writing Errors

1. Well-documented strengths and weaknesses give a total picture that will speak for itself. If a client is doing well in treatment but had a relapse, say so.
2. Do not omit the worker's observations. Outside of the interview, many significant things occur during a visit. For example, physical appearance of all parties, interaction between parent and child, home conditions, and nonverbal communication are all important observations to record.
3. Never record an impression as fact. Report only what you see, hear, touch, and observe.
4. If you use an acronym or abbreviation, spell it out the first time you write it and thereafter use the acronym. For example, "Individual Educational Plan (IEP)."
5. Avoid using professional and agency jargon.
6. If you are documenting an omission or error in the record, be sure to document it as a late entry and reference where the information should have been placed.
7. Refer to yourself in the body of the report as "this worker" instead of "I" or by your name. Depending on the agency, a less formal approach to documentation may be appropriate. Be sure to talk with your supervisor and review other workers' documentation styles.
8. Record your name and the date after every entry.

Writing a Case/Progress Note

A case note or progress note is a common method of recording contacts with clients and his or her collateral contacts. Typically, these entries are in chronological order. Be sure to include all of the steps taken in an effort to assist your client. All case/progress notes should be dated and include the type of contact and where the contact took place.

Include who was involved in the contact and detail any new or significant information obtained. Finally, state what occurred during the session, what was accomplished, plans for follow-up, homework assigned, and obstacles to treatment goals. Note any out-of-the-ordinary occurrences during your contact with a client.

Outline for Sample Case Note/Progress Note:

This is an example of an outline for writing a case note. There are many formats, but all case notes have requirements such as the name of the client, reason for the contact and signatures.

Name of client:

Date:

Reason for contact:

Type of contact (face-to-face, telephone contact, or collateral contact):

Major facts noted during the contact:

Other pertinent information:

Current status, including appearance, cognition, emotional state, orientation to time and place:

Progress toward achieving goals:

Summary / conclusion / future plans:

Social Worker's Signature:

Outline for SMART Goals

When writing goals with clients, consider using the template for S.M.A.R.T. Goals. This format for writing goals is a shorthanded way of documenting the work to be done by the client. This outline is easy to follow. Again, each agency will have their own way of documenting the client's progress in attaining his or her goals.

S. = Specific—simply written and clearly defined. Be specific about what is to be accomplished.

M. = Measurable—how will you determine if the goal is reached? What is the tangible evidence that the client has accomplished the goal?

A. = Attainable—is this goal achievable and reasonable, and can it be accomplished. It is important to determine the client's skills and knowledge or abilities to reach the goal.

R. = Realistic—is the goal relevant, and does the client see it as worthy of attention?

T. = Timing—what is the time frame for reaching the goal? What are the deadlines to reach the goal?

Source: Compiled from Kagel and Koppels (2008), Reamer (2013), and Sheafor et al. (2011).

Appendix B

HIPAA AND CONFIDENTIALITY ISSUES

HIPAA (Health Insurance Portability and Accountability Act)

The HIPAA privacy rule provides federal protection for a person's physical and mental health information held by covered entities (physicians, hospitals, mental health clinics, nursing homes, etc.) and gives patients an array of rights with respect to that information. This federal law gives the client the right to determine who can have access to the information, whether electronic, written, or oral. It also ensures that the client can have access to his or her record and add or delete data if the file is incorrect. For more information on HIPAA law and for a complete summary of HIPAA regulations and guidelines, visit The U.S. Department of Health and Human Services.

HIPAA Guidelines for Exceptions to Confidentiality

There are a number of circumstances under which the privacy regulations ***permit*** use and disclosure of protected health information without the client's consent or authorization:

- public health activities as required by state and federal law for such purposes as vital statistics collection and disease reporting;
- reporting of abuse, neglect, or domestic violence to the extent required by law;
- oversight of the health care system;
- law enforcement;
- judicial and administrative proceedings;
- serious, imminent threat to health or safety;
- research purposes;
- specialized government functions;
- worker's compensation—to comply with laws relating to workers' compensation or other similar programs;
- uses and disclosures about decedents (generally to enable coroners, medical examiners, and funeral directors to carry out functions of their job as applicable or authorized by law).

The authorization can be revoked (in writing) except to the extent that the covered entity has already acted in relation to the consent (United States Department of Health and Human Services, Office of Civil Rights, May, 2003). For a complete summary of the HIPPA regulations and guidelines, go to the U.S. Department of Health and Human Services website.

Guidelines for Authorization to Release-of-Information Form

An *authorization* is required in most cases for use and disclosure of client-protected health information for purposes other than treatment, payment, and health care operations. An authorization must:

- be written in plain language.
- include a description of the protected health information that is to be disclosed.
- identify the person(s) authorized to make the requested use or disclosure.
- identify the person(s) to whom the covered entity can disclose protected health information.
- state the client's right to revoke, in writing, the authorization and any exceptions to this right.
- note that the client's health information may be re-disclosed by the recipient and at that time would no longer be protected by these regulations.
- include an expiration date or event.
- include the client's signature and date.
- provide the client with a copy of the signed authorization (United States Department of Health and Human Services, Office of Civil Rights, May, 2003). For a complete summary of HIPAA regulations and guidelines the US Department of Health and Human Service website.

Guidelines for an Informed Consent Form: 1.03 (NASW Code of Ethics)

(a) Social workers should provide services to clients only in the context of a professional relationship based, when appropriate, on valid informed consent. Social workers should use clear and understandable language to inform clients of the purpose of the services, risks related to the services, limits to services because of the requirements of a third party payer, relevant costs, reasonable alternatives, clients' right to refuse or withdraw consent, and the time frame covered by the consent. Social workers should provide clients with an opportunity to ask questions.

(b) In instances when clients are not literate or have difficulty understanding the primary language used in the practice setting, social workers should take steps to ensure clients' comprehension. This may include providing clients with a detailed verbal explanation or arranging for a qualified interpreter or translator whenever possible.

(c) In instances when clients lack the capacity to provide informed consent, social workers should protect clients' interests by seeking permission from an appropriate third party, informing clients consistent with the clients' level of understanding. In such instances social workers should seek to ensure that the third party acts in a manner consistent with clients' wishes and interests. Social workers should take reasonable steps to enhance such clients' ability to give informed consent.

(d) In instances when clients are receiving services involuntarily, social workers should provide information about the nature and extent of services and about the extent of clients' right to refuse service.
(e) Social workers who provide services via electronic media (such as computer, telephone, radio, and television) should inform recipients of the limitations and risks associated with such services.
(f) Social workers should obtain clients' informed consent before audiotaping or videotaping clients or permitting observation of services to clients by a third party (NASW, 2011, section 1.03).

An exception does allow providers to disclose clients' protected health information prior to obtaining consent for "emergency treatment situations." As noted in the July 2001 HHS guidance, health care providers need to exercise their professional judgment in making this determination. The provider is expected to obtain consent as soon as is reasonable and practical after the provision of services.

A provider can refuse to treat a patient who is unwilling to provide consent for disclosure of protected health information for treatment, payment, and health care operations.

A provider only needs to obtain the client's written consent one time (NASW, 2011).

Privacy and Confidentiality: 1.07 (NASW Code of Ethics)

(a) Social workers should respect clients' right to privacy. Social workers should not solicit private information from clients unless it is essential to providing services or conducting social work evaluation or research. Once private information is shared, standards of confidentiality apply.
(b) Social workers may disclose confidential information when appropriate with valid consent from a client or a person legally authorized to consent on behalf of a client.
(c) Social workers should protect the confidentiality of all information obtained in the course of professional service, except for compelling professional reasons. The general expectation that social workers will keep information confidential does not apply when disclosure is necessary to prevent serious, foreseeable, and imminent harm to a client or other identifiable person. In all instances, social workers should disclose the least amount of confidential information necessary to achieve the desired purpose; only information that is directly relevant to the purpose for which the disclosure is made should be revealed.
(d) Social workers should inform clients, to the extent possible, about the disclosure of confidential information and the potential consequences, when feasible before the disclosure is made. This applies whether social workers disclose confidential information on the basis of a legal requirement or client consent.
(e) Social workers should discuss with clients and other interested parties the nature of confidentiality and limitations of clients' right to confidentiality. Social workers should review with clients circumstances where confidential information may be requested and where disclosure of confidential information may be legally required. This discussion should occur as soon as possible in the social worker client relationship and as needed throughout the course of the relationship.
(f) When social workers provide counseling services to families, couples, or groups, social workers should seek agreement among the parties involved concerning each

individual's right to confidentiality and obligation to preserve the confidentiality of information shared by others. Social workers should inform participants in family, couples, or group counseling that social workers cannot guarantee that all participants will honor such agreements.

(g) Social workers should inform clients involved in family, couples, marital, or group counseling of the social worker's, employer's, and agency's policy concerning the social worker's disclosure of confidential information among the parties involved in the counseling.

(h) Social workers should not disclose confidential information to third party payers unless clients have authorized such disclosure.

(i) Social workers should not discuss confidential information in any setting unless privacy can be ensured. Social workers should not discuss confidential information in public or semi public area such as hallways, waiting rooms, elevators, and restaurants.

(j) Social workers should protect the confidentiality of clients during legal proceedings to the extent permitted by law. When a court of law or other legally authorized body orders social workers to disclose confidential or privileged information without a client's consent and such disclosure could cause harm to the client, social workers should request that the court withdraw the order or limit the order as narrowly as possible or maintain the records under seal, unavailable for public inspection.

(k) Social workers should protect the confidentiality of clients when responding to requests from members of the media.

(l) Social workers should protect the confidentiality of clients' written and electronic records and other sensitive information. Social workers should take reasonable steps to ensure that clients' records are stored in a secure location and that clients' records are not available to others who are not authorized to have access.

(m) Social workers should take precautions to ensure and maintain the confidentiality of information transmitted to other parties through the use of computers, electronic mail, facsimile machines, telephones and telephone answering machines, and other electronic or computer technology. Disclosure of identifying information should be avoided whenever possible.

(n) Social workers should transfer or dispose of clients' records in a manner that protects clients' confidentiality and is consistent with state statutes governing records and social work licensure.

(o) Social workers should take reasonable precautions to protect client confidentiality in the event of the social worker's termination of practice, incapacitation, or death.

(p) Social workers should not disclose identifying information when discussing clients for teaching or training purposes unless the client has consented to disclosure of confidential information.

(q) Social workers should not disclose identifying information when discussing clients with consultants unless the client has consented to disclosure of confidential information or there is a compelling need for such disclosure.

(r) Social workers should protect the confidentiality of deceased clients consistent with the preceding standards.

Guidelines for Access to Records: 1.08 (NASW Code of Ethics)

(a) Social workers should provide clients with reasonable access to records concerning the clients. Social workers who are concerned that clients' access to their records could cause serious misunderstanding or harm to the client should provide assistance in interpreting the records and consultation with the client regarding the records. Social workers should limit clients' access to their records, or portions of their records, only in exceptional circumstances when there is compelling evidence that such access would cause serious harm to the client. Both clients' requests and the rationale for withholding some or all of the record should be documented in clients' files.

(b) When providing clients with access to their records, social workers should take steps to protect the confidentiality of other individuals identified or discussed in such records (National Association of Social Workers [NASW], 2011, section 1.08).

Client Records: 3.04 (NASW Code of Ethics)

(a) Social workers should take reasonable steps to ensure that documentation in records is accurate and reflects the services provided.

(b) Social workers should include sufficient and timely documentation in records to facilitate the delivery of services and to ensure continuity of services provided to clients in the future.

(c) Social workers' documentation should protect clients' privacy to the extent that is possible and appropriate and should include only information that is directly relevant to the delivery of services.

(d) Social workers should store records following the termination of services to ensure reasonable future access. Records should be maintained for the number of years required by state statutes or relevant contracts (NASW, 2011, section 3.04).

Appendix C

PRACTICE TOOLS—EXAMPLES

Consent for Treatment/Services (Adult)
ABC Center for Help

Name ______________________ Date of Birth ______________________

I understand that I am eligible to receive a range of services at the ABC Center for Help. The type and extent of services that I will receive will be determined following an initial intake and assessment. The goal of this process is to determine the best course of treatment for me. Typically, treatment is provided over the course of several weeks to several months.

I understand that all information shared with the social worker at the ABC Center for Help is confidential and no information will be released without my consent. During the course of treatment it may be necessary for social workers to communicate with providers. In all circumstances, consent to release information is given through written authorization. Verbal consent for limited release of information may be necessary in special circumstances. I further understand that there are specific and limited exceptions to this confidentiality, which include the following:

A. When there is risk of imminent danger to myself or to another person, the social worker is ethically bound to take necessary steps to prevent such danger.
B. When there is suspicion that a child or elder is being sexually or physically abused or is at risk of such abuse, the social worker is legally required to take steps to protect the child, and to inform the proper authorities.
C. When a valid court order is issued for medical records, the social worker and the agency are bound by law to comply with such requests.

If I have any questions regarding this consent form or about the services offered at the ABC Center for Help, I may discuss them with my social worker. I understand that I have the right to ask questions about treatment decisions and to appeal those decisions. I have read and understand the above. I consent to participate in treatment offered to me by the ABC Center for Help. I understand that I may stop treatment at any time.

______________________ ______________ ______________________
Signature: Date: Witness:

Release of Information
ABC Center for Help

I, (Client or Guardian) ________________________, hereby authorize and give consent for (Name of social worker) ________________ to release / receive / exchange information.

To ____ / from _________________________________ / with

____

(address, city, state, zip)

Type of Information:

1. Medical (specify)

____

2. Psychiatric / Psychological (specify)

____

3. Educational (specify)

____

4. Social History / Assessment (specify)

____

5. Financial (specify)

____

6. Other (specify)

____

The purpose of requesting this information: ____

Planning ____

Provision ____

Other ____

This consent is valid until _____ / _____ /_____

I understand that I have the right to inspect and copy the information to be disclosed, and that I may revoke this consent at any time.

The consequences for refusing to sign this release are ____________________________________

____ _____ /_____ /_____

Client (Minor 12–17 years old) Date

____ _____ /_____ /_____

Parent / Guardian Date

____ _____ /_____ /_____

Witness Date

Notice to Receiving Agency/Person: Under the provisions of the Mental Health and Developmental Disabilities Confidentiality Act, you may not re-disclose any of this information unless the person who consented to this disclosure specifically consents to such a re-disclosure.

Intake Form (Filled out by the CLIENT)
ABC Center for Help

Client Information

Please fill out this information form as carefully and as thoroughly as possible. This information is confidential.

Client Name ______________________________

Date of Birth (*day/month/year*) ______________________________

Address ______________________________

City ______________________________ ZIP Code ______________________________

Please include only phone numbers where you can be contacted

Home/Cell phone ______________________________ Work phone ______________________________

Email ______________________________

Current occupation/place of employment ______________________________

Education completed ______________________________

Current Marital Status

Single ○ Engaged ○ Married ○ Separated ○ Common-Law ○ Divorced ○ Widowed ○

Years married/common-law ______________________________

Name of spouse/partner ______________________________ Age ______________________________

Occupation of spouse/partner ______________________________

How would you describe your current relationship?

____

____

Have you been previously married? Yes ______________ No ______________ How long? ______________

Family Information

Name of child ______________________________ Gender __________ Age __________ Living with you? __________

Name of child ______________________________ Gender __________ Age __________ Living with you? __________

Name of child ______________________________ Gender __________ Age __________ Living with you? __________

Name of child ______________________________ Gender __________ Age __________ Living with you? __________

Are your parents or primary caretaker still living? Mother ______________ Father ______________

Did either parent or primary caretaker ever have problems with alcohol/drugs/other forms of addiction? mental illness concerns? If yes, please describe.?

____

____

How would you describe your life in the last six months?

____

____

Medical Information

List any present health problems, major surgeries, injuries (with dates).

____

____

____

Date of last medical checkup __________ Reason ______________________________

____

Physician and contact information ______________________________

Are you taking medication now? __________________ Name(s) of your medication ______________

____

____

Reason for taking medication ______________________________

____

____

Emotional Information

List any significant crises, losses, or stressors.

____

____

____

Have you ever received counseling or other treatment for personal and/or relationship problems?

Yes ______ No ______ Dates ______

Please describe what issues were addressed.

____

____

Identify at least three aspects of your life that are going well.

1. ____
2. ____
3. ____

Supplementary Questions

My greatest fear is ______________________________

____

My greatest hope is ______________________________

____

Please describe the problems for which you are seeking help.

____

____

____

Who is aware of your problem(s)?

____

____

What would you like to see happen as a result of coming for help?

____

____

____

Religious/Spiritual Information (*optional*)

Religion ____

Denomination (*if applicable*) ___________________________________

Do you attend a place of worship? Yes ____________________ No ____________________

How does your faith/spiritual life affect your present situation?

____

____

____

Do you have any requests for including elements of your faith in your counseling session?

____

____

Additional Comments

Please use this space if there is anything you wish to add.

____

____

____

____

Signature: ____________________

Date: ____________________

Intake Form (Filled out with CLIENT PRESENT)
ABC Center for Help

Date: ____________________

Name: ____ Date of Birth: ________________________

Address (where you can be contacted):

Phone (where you can be contacted):

Referral source: ________________________

Received past services—when and where:

____

____

Reasons for being here today: ____

____

Is this a situation you are seeking help to resolve?

____

____

Relationship status: ____

____

Parental/caretaker status: ____

____

Medical status, including medications: ____________________________________

____

Educational status: ____

____

Work/occupational status: ____

____

Cultural and religious status: ____

____

Stressors (current, six weeks, six months, past year): _______________________

____

Supports (family, work, friends, treatment group): ___________________________

____

Strengths: ____

____

–1–

Current social services status (TANF, WIC, housing, SSI disability, VA benefits):

____

____

What are you hoping will happen after the meeting today?

____

____

Important people and contact information (physician, family member, school, probation officer, case aid):

____

____

____

Other information: ____

____

____

Release of information signed ____________________

Consent signed ____________________

HIPAA signed ____________________

Next appointment: ____________________

Worker's name and signature: ____________________

Sample Case/Progress Note
ABC Center for Help

Name: Shirley Anderson Case # _____ Date:_____
March 2, 201 _____ (3:00–4:00 PM)

Contact with: Mrs. Shirley Anderson

Reason for contact: To verify a report regarding Crystal's unauthorized overnight visit.

Type of contact (face-to-face, telephone contact, or collateral contact): Face-to-face

Major facts noted during the contact:
Mrs. Anderson was very forthcoming with information regarding Crystal's unauthorized overnight visit. She asked for a meeting between Crystal, Mrs. Anderson, and this worker.

Current status:
Caring for Maria seems to be taking a toll on Mrs. Anderson. She reports being pulled between her roles as a parent to Crystal and as the guardian of Maria.

Appearance:
Mrs. Anderson appeared very tired and worn out today, as her hair was not combed and her clothing looked wrinkled. This worker didn't have much chance to observe her mobility today; we sat in the living room rather than the kitchen (which requires her to walk further).

Cognitive state:
Mrs. Anderson initially was hesitant to acknowledge Crystal's overnight stay. She understands the potential risks associated with these visits and that Maria's placement with her could be in jeopardy.

Feeling state:
Mrs. Anderson appeared very concerned and upset about the entire incident. She acknowledged that Crystal's drinking does effect Maria. She asked six times during the session if this worker was going to take Maria away.

Memory state/orientation:
Oriented to time, place, and person

Progress toward achieving goals:
Mrs. Anderson has provided Maria with a clean, safe, and loving home. She reports the struggles of being caught between Maria and Crystal and the Child Welfare Agency. She reports feeling very tired and wants the conflicts to be resolved so they can move forward. She seems to have accepted that Maria may be living with her for an extended period of time. She also reported that she wants to be available to Crystal but has a hard time setting limits with her daughter.

Summary/conclusion/future plans:
This worker will arrange for a face-to-face meeting between the three parties. Mrs. Anderson appeared to be very upset about the possibility that Maria could be moved if the rules aren't followed. She stated, "I understand how serious this is now. I won't let it happen again."

Social Worker's Signature:_________________________

Multidimensional Assessment—Case Example
ABC Center for Help

Name: ______________________ Case #: ______________ Date: __________

Reason for Referral and Presenting Problem

Leah Smith, age 33, came to the **ABC Center for Help** after being "hit hard" by her husband. Leah reports that she and John, age 35, have been married for seven years and have two children, Alex, age four, and Dora, age two. Leah is currently living at home but stated that she is "fed up and ready to move out."

Leah is a self-referred client and reports that she has been thinking about seeking services from this agency for two years. She indicates that she suffers from severe mood swings that she is unable to control. She worries about the future and stated, "I can't imagine staying with John, but I have nowhere else to go." Leah is currently working full time as an office assistant at State University and likes her job. She sees her coworkers as very supportive and helpful, especially around issues in her private life. Leah states her problems as "living an unfulfilled life" and her mood swings, which leave her feeling exhausted.

Physical Functioning (e.g., general appearance, health concerns, substance abuse)

Leah reports that she is in good physical condition. She last saw her physician, Dr. Lamont, on October 15, 201______, for a routine checkup. She is currently taking birth control pills and a multivitamin. She reports that her hair has been falling out, and she is concerned about her hormonal levels. Leah stated that she doesn't sleep well and paces for up to an hour each night. Eventually she does fall asleep but indicated that she wakes up many mornings feeling very tired and not well rested. Leah reported that she drinks a few glasses of wine on the weekends but generally not during her workweek. She does not believe there is a relationship between her drinking and her nighttime restlessness.

Three years ago, Leah had a medical issue that resulted in her being hospitalized for several days. When this worker inquired into the medical issue, she stated, "It was no big deal; I can't even remember any of the details other than I am fine and they never figured out what was wrong with me." On further questioning by this worker, she stated, "There is nothing more to say."

Cognitive Perceptual Functioning (e.g., work/school history, judgment, decision making, reality testing)

She has a full-time job and reports her work evaluations are "stellar." Leah is oriented to time and place and appears to be self-reflective. She is very hard on herself, criticizing many of her past and present choices, especially her marriage to John. She indicated that she is most proud of her work-related accomplishments, as work is where she feels appreciated and understood.

Emotional Functioning (e.g., range of emotion, appropriateness of affect, depression, mental illness)

Leah appears to lack confidence in her presentation of self. She either looked down/away or expressed anger. She stated that she is unhappy in her marriage. The client reported that she cannot have a "civil" conversation with John. When this worker asked her to elaborate, she stated, "He has this nasty habit of spitting when he gets mad, and I end up moving away as fast as I can; it is disgusting." Her frustration came through as she became louder and pounded her fists on the arm of the chair. Leah's range of emotion appears to be limited to expressing either irritation or annoyance. She stated that she has few friends and feels isolated from everyone except her -coworkers. Leah is "stressed out" all the time. She does not have any emotional outlets, such as a supportive network of family or friends. There is no reported family history of mental illness.

She identifies herself as very moody and easily upset. Leah stated that her children should be a source of pride and love but that she can't find it within herself to express anything other than frustration and meanness. When this worker asked her to further describe her relationship with her children, she indicated that she is a "terrible mom," always yelling and being impatient with them. Leah expresses regret in her inability to parent the way she believes she should. She would like to stop being so negative and enjoy her time with Alex and Dora rather than resenting them.

Social and Family Functioning (e.g., composition, extended family roles, power, birth order, patterns of communication, wider community)
Leah comes from a two-parent home, having grown up in a small farming town of approximately 1,600 people. Her father was a car mechanic, and her mother did not work outside of the home. She has a younger brother, Richard, who is a Peace Corps volunteer living in Ecuador. She speaks very proudly of Richard, but they have not seen each other in almost two years. Leah stated that she missed him but she doesn't "want him involved with anything regarding her failing marriage." Her parents are both still living, and she reports they never see each other. She did indicate that her father is a controlling person and that she sometimes feels badly that her mom has nowhere to go either.

Leah stated that John grew up in a foster care placement and that her parents "warned her about him." "He was a nice kid, and we got serious during high school. I don't think I was ever madly in love with him, which is a good thing given how much I can't stand him now."

Her patterns of communication with John and her children seem to be limited to short responses and angry outbursts. She reports that no one at work could picture how "dysfunctional we are at home." When this worker asked her to elaborate, she said, "I am pleasant at work, very polite and a great listener."

Leah has access to many amenities through her employment at State University. She plans to go back to school and finish her degree.

Behavioral Functioning (e.g., problematic issues, power and control, personal habits, criminal history)
Leah has expressed some concerns regarding her decision-making and coping skills. She reports that last week she was so frustrated and angry with her husband and children that she left them at the mall and walked home in the rain. She did not speak to any family member for over a 36-hour period. When her children sought her out, she slammed the door and told them to leave her alone. She has bouts of yelling and screaming that she reports she is not able to control. Her coping skills include eating too much and "vegging out in front of the TV." Leah reports that when John hits her, the bruises are always in places that people can't see. She did show this worker a large black and blue mark on the inner side of her upper arm. When this worker asked her to describe some of the circumstances that led up to John hitting her, she stated, "It really depends on our moods. I know that I can egg him on and get him going. He just falls right into his old patterns by trying to keep me from leaving and he thinks that hitting me is the way to do that."

Motivation (e.g., for services, employment)
Leah is a self-referred client and states that she really wants to figure out why she is so unhappy in her life and marriage. She appears to be a very talkative person, with good social skills.

Spiritual/Religious Affiliation (e.g., belief system, church/synagogue/mosque)
Leah reports that she is not a very spiritual or religious person. She grew up in the Catholic Church and was involved in a youth group during her high school years. She and John were married by a priest in order to "calm my mother down." Leah does not socialize with anyone from her church and hasn't attended a service

in over four years. She reports no interest in pursuing this aspect of her life. She stated, "God is not there for me and my kids. Why should I go and be a hypocrite?"

Environmental Systems (e.g., neighborhood, social service community)
Leah lives in a three-bedroom town house in a small midwestern community. There are many services available to her family, including public transportation, medical clinics, and safe parks. She reports the neighborhood where she grew up was "working class" and that all of the women were "stay-at-home-mothers." Her parents did use social service agencies when she lived with them but could not recall which ones. She stated that her parents could not have made ends meet without the help of social service agencies and the church. On graduating from high school, she moved to _________ to attend college. She did not complete her degree but hopes to one day, as the university offers employees free tuition.

Leah works full-time at State University and has health and dental insurance, good wages, and retirement benefits. John is a carpenter. The economic downturn has caused some financial concerns for them because his work is sporadic and he has no benefits. Leah is not concerned about her finances at this time. They have two cars, and public transportation is available. Both children attend a day care center on the State University campus, which is subsidized by the university.

Leah's community has a domestic violence program that provides 24-hour shelter and support. She has not contacted the hotline and indicates that she would go to a hotel before going to a shelter.

Cultural Factors (e.g., background, ethnicity, impact of culture)
Leah describes herself as "being whiter than white bread." She grew up in a farming community where her parents were members of the Catholic Church. Being from a rural community, "there were limited things for kids to do, except drink out in the fields." She was active in her church youth group and did well academically. She does not know about her parents' background other than "they are white too." It wasn't until she came to State University that she interacted with people other than those from her home community. She stated, "It was a shock at first; I didn't even know what a Jewish person looked like or believed in. That kind of stuff was always interesting to me. My roommate was Jewish, and she was a very nice person; of course, that is not the way my Catholic Church described Jewish people." Leah believes that she is open-minded and enjoys interacting with people, regardless of their background, religion, ethnicity, or color.

Strengths (e.g., interests, hobbies, support system)
Leah is a hardworking employee and has a secure job. Her employer provides her and her family with good benefits and services. She came to the **ACB Center for Help** voluntarily and continues to meet with this worker weekly. Her community offers many recreational and social outlets. She reports that she is in good health and drinks moderately. She is a very articulate person with three years of higher education completed. A goal identified by Leah is to finish her degree within the next few years. Although she is unhappy in her marriage, it appears as if she is moderately involved in the care of her children. This worker has no reason to be concerned about their immediate health and safety needs.

Barriers to Service (e.g., personal, societal, family)
Leah stated that she is uncertain if she wants to stay married, although she indicated that John is not often violent, reporting, "five to six times a year he hauls off and hits me." She does not see the shelter or their services as a resource to her at this time. She has no contact with her parents and reports no friends other than coworkers.

–3–

Worker's Impressions of the Client (e.g., hunches, issues for further exploration)
How Leah manages her feelings and behaviors can be a potential problem for her. Although she reports interest in getting help, she could not identify anything that she could do differently. She stated several times that she feels stuck and has no option but to stay in her marriage. This worker will explore further what may be leading her to feel so disempowered and dissatisfied in her life. Is there a history of violence in her life? This worker will continue to support her in her decision-making process. This worker will follow up on her hospitalization several years ago. Why are her parents so disengaged from Leah? Where do friends fit in her life?

Submitted by: ________________

Date: ________________

Service Plan/Treatment Plan and Contract
ABC Center for Help

Client Maria Rodriguez

Date April 4, 20--

	Responsible Party	Date to Begin and End	Means for Monitoring Progress	Outcome: Completed; Incomplete; or In-progress
A. Long-term goal:				
Long-term goal: Maria will develop an understanding of her life circumstances, both past and present. *	Maria, Mrs. Anderson and/or Nicole	6-12 months	Observation and self reports	
B. Short-term goals:				
1) Adjust to current living environment Objectives/Tasks • Follow house rules established by Mrs. Anderson and Child Welfare Agency • Address feeling about the current situation with Jennifer (case aide) or Nicole (social worker) • Develop skills in managing feelings, especially related to Crystal, Brian, Ramon, and Grandma • Improve self-esteem and self-confidence • Develop conflict resolution skills • Begin to accept situation regarding mother • Continue to assess level of depression • Practice role playing with Nicole (focusing on developing problem solving and coping skills)				

	Responsible Party	Date to Begin and End	Means for Monitoring Progress	Outcome: Completed; Incomplete; or In-progress
2) Develop age appropriate activities and interests Objectives/Tasks • Develop friendships with peers and classmates • Join a school related activity (i.e. student council) • Join the Girl Scouts, 4-H club etc. • Participate in the After School Sports Program • Participate in a church related and youth focused activity				
3) Develop a Latino cultural identity Objectives/Tasks • Learn simple Spanish words and phrases • Watch TV/movies that have Latino/Mexican focus • Attend culture fests/celebrations • Read about Mexican culture • Subscribe to appropriate teen magazines • Seek out information about extended family				
4) Maintain current academic performance level at school Objectives/Tasks • Participate in class when called on by teacher (Mrs. Learner) • Complete all homework assignments • Study for tests • Ask for help from teacher or teacher aid (Ms. Sharer) when needed				

Contract

I, Maria Rodriguez agree to complete all the goals, and tasks Nicole (social Worker) and I talked about. I also understand that if I don't do my share of the work, Nicole and Grandma will have the final say in what happens next. I understand we can talk about this agreement every week and decide how well I am doing in meeting my goals. Nicole Good will stay in weekly touch with me and my grandmother, Mrs. Anderson.

Date: ____________ Client Signature: ____________________ Social Worker's signature: ____________________

Service Plan/Treatment Plan and Contract (BLANK)

Client: ____________________ **Agency:** ____________________

Case # ____________________ **Date:** ____________________

A. Long-term goal #1:	Responsible Party	Date to Begin and End	Means for Monitoring Progress	Outcome: Completed/ Incomplete/or In Progress
1. Short-term goal: *Tasks:* *1.* *2.* *3.*				
2. Short-term goal: *Tasks:* *1.* *2.* *3.*				
3. Short-term goal: *Tasks:* *1.* *2.* *3.*				

Contract

I, ____________________, agree to complete all the goals and tasks as outlined in this contract by the designated dates. I also understand that if I fail to comply with the terms of the contract (what will happen) ______________________. I further understand this contract may be renegotiated should my/our life circumstances change significantly. I understand that my progress will be monitored by ______________________ (social worker) (frequency) ___________________.

____________________	______________________________	______________________________
Date:	Client's signature-(Guardian signature)	Social Worker's signature

Appendix D

DEESCALATION TECHNIQUES

Below is a list of suggestions, in no specific order, to consider when working with potentially aggressive, violent or unpredictable clients.

1. Have frequent contact as a way to break down barriers between you and the client. (A client who is unwilling to cooperate with the social worker may need frequent reminders that you care and will be there for him or her. A card, phone call, tokens for public transportation, or a small gift basket of food are possible ways to engage a client.)
2. Offer that you do not intend to harm the client; you are there to help.
3. Create some physical space between you and the client. Avoid sudden movements, as they may be seen as provoking.
4. Assure the client that he or she will be heard and listened to.
5. Ask the client what he or she needs to make the situation better.
6. Ask short questions that can be answered in a short response. Ask about facts, not just feelings.
7. Understand the signs of aggressiveness, such as a red face, a rapid and high-pitched voice, muscles tensing, clenched fists, "standing tall," pacing, rapid breathing, and exaggerated gestures. Recognize subtle changes in behavior.
8. Understand the reasons for aggressiveness, such as frustration, humiliation, learned behaviors, mental illness, unfairness, reputation, decoy, and immaturity.
9. Understand the client has a choice regarding his or her aggressiveness, such as behaviors that have led to the client getting what he or she wants, getting people's attention, gaining control of the situation, and providing an escape for what he or she does not want to do.
10. Emphasize the client's strengths (e.g., what is going well right now, people who count on the client, the progress he or she has made, a family that supports him or her).
11. Be clear about your role and authority (you work for the state, and as a social worker you are there to assist the client).
12. Assume and acknowledge there are negative feelings about the process (communicate to the client that you understand this is not something he or she wants to do; you support his or her frustration regarding being required to meet with you and being court mandated and about losing control over a situation all of which can be devastating).

13. Use the "If What-Then" approach (What are the natural consequences? Help the client think things through; e.g., if she hurts you, what will be the consequences? If she attempts to hurt herself, who will be left behind?).
14. Offer some self-disclosure. (e.g., you know how it feels to be backed into a corner, you want to help, no one likes to be told what to do. The client's options are limited, and you can assist where possible.)
15. Sometimes silence can be a time for the client to self-reflect and determine if this is how he or she wants things to go.
16. Understand the client's need for control. (e.g., in situations when a client feels threatened, it is possible his or her reactions are because he or she feels misunderstood, vulnerable, or hurt in some way.)
17. Convey a sense of calm; have your hands visible, maintain an open posture, and avoid an audience if at all possible.
18. Reduce eye contact, as it may be interpreted as staring the client down.
19. Be sure that you sound confident and self-assured even if you aren't.
20. Show a willingness to let the client have some control; for example, deciding whom to call or what to wear can be helpful in deescalating the situation. Offer choices whenever possible.
21. If appropriate, apologize; the social worker can say he or she is sorry for what is happening without taking blame.
22. A history of violence can be an important indicator of future violence. (To prepare, read the client's file before the meeting. If you know there is potential danger, contact the police for an escort. Never go into a room where you see firearms.)
23. You have a duty to warn: you are required by law to warn a potential victim if the threat to harm that person is believable.
24. Let the client know that you are a mandated reporter and will contact the police. For many clients, the threat of contacting the police is enough to help them calm down.
25. Consider an involuntary or voluntary hospitalization, as violent impulses can be controlled through medication or other forms of therapy.
26. Never threaten or give an ultimatum. Once you do, you have lost all leverage.
27. If you feel threatened in any way, leave immediately and contact your supervisor and the police.
28. Debrief with a trusted person. Be open to offers of help and assistance. This kind of situation can leave a social worker feeling depleted and immobilized.
29. Recognize the signs of posttraumatic stress both in yourself and in your client.
30. Listen to your internal voice; trust your judgment. If it feels dangerous, it is.

Appendix E

CASE STUDIES

Case Study 1: Anna and Marie

Summary:

Anna is a 35-year-old female. She has been married for 10 years and is the mother of three children. Two years ago, Anna was diagnosed with cancer. After months of treatment, she thought that she had made a full recovery. During her checkup two weeks ago, an X-ray indicated that the cancer had returned. Anna is facing another hospitalization and an uncertain future. Marie, the social worker, provides Anna with support as she goes through this health crisis. After a month of being hospitalized, Anna is finally home and trying to adjust to her life as her health continues to decline.

Concept Map for Anna

Video Case of Anna and Marie

Case Notes for Anna

Sample Treatment Plan for Anna

Case Study 2: Anthony and James

Summary:

Anthony is a 15-year-old African American male, a very streetwise adolescent, and a member of a gang. However, his involvement in the gang is marginal at this time. Anthony is attending school but has little interest in academics. School provides him the opportunity to socialize with his friends. James, the social worker, provides Anthony with a positive role model and "sounding board." James is able to help Anthony develop a better relationship with his mother and to begin thinking about the future.

Concept Map for Anthony

Video Case of Anthony and James

Case Notes for Anthony

Sample Treatment Plan for Anthony

Case Study 3: Mike and Susan

Summary:

Mike is a 40-year-old male. He is currently employed as an accountant. Recently, he was caught at work with alcohol on his breath. His employer is requiring that Mike have a substance abuse assessment before he can return to work. After the initial assessment, it was recommended that Mike needed inpatient treatment. Susan, the social worker, helps Mike recognize that he is an alcoholic. Over time, you see their relationship develop as he moves toward the first stages of his recovery. These interviews take place after Mike has started an inpatient treatment program.

Concept Map for Mike

Video Case of Mike and Susan

Case Notes for Mike
Sample Treatment Plan for Mike

Case Study 4: Maria, Mrs. Anderson and Nicole

Summary:

Mrs. Anderson, Maria's grandmother, is currently providing her with kinship care. Mrs. Anderson struggles with multiple sclerosis, which is a chronic disease, and the severity of her symptoms vary almost daily. Nicole, the social worker, and Mrs. Anderson, work together to help Maria adjust to her new living situation. Nicole also provides Mrs. Anderson with emotional support and resources to help her manage day to day. Nicole also helps Maria process her thoughts and feelings toward her mother, Crystal, and what life is like now that she is living with her grandmother.

Concept Map for Mrs. Anderson
Video Case of Mrs. Anderson and Nicole
Video Case of Maria and Nicole
Case Notes for Mrs. Anderson
Sample Treatment Plan for Mrs. Anderson
Sample Treatment Plan for Maria

Case Study 5: Mrs. Kita and Diane

Summary:

Mrs. Kita is the parent of two children. Nori, her oldest, has major medical issues that complicate their lives. Her husband Jirou is in prison. Mrs. Kita is raising her children with her mother's assistance, but finances are tight, and she is in jeopardy of losing her home. With all the stress of Nori's illness and managing day to day, Diane, the social worker, helps her get back on her feet by providing support, encouragement, and resources.

Concept Map for Mrs. Kita
Video Case of Mrs. Kita and Diane
Case Notes for Mrs. Kita
Sample Treatment Plan for Mrs. Kita

Case Study 6: Kim and Louis

Summary:

Kim is an Army veteran who returned home from Afghanistan two years ago. Since then, her mother has died, she is drinking heavily, and she is now homeless. After being removed from her home (a shed on her deceased mother's property) by the police, she is now at a temporary shelter for people who are homeless. Louis, the social worker, and Kim work together to help her manage the struggles she is experiencing related to family conflict, substance abuse, depression, and possible posttraumatic stress disorder. Over time, Kim becomes more willing to accept services and eventually moves into a program specifically developed for vets who are homeless.

Concept Map for Kim
Case Video of Kim and Louis
Case Notes for Kim
Sample Treatment Plan for Kim

Glossary

Advice giving telling the client what you believe is in their best interest.

Agency culture reflects the values and beliefs of the organization, the philosophy of service delivery and mission statement, and the vision of the agency's role in the community.

Assessment the comprehensive gathering of information about the presenting problem and the client, from the client and others in their environment, with the consent of the client; client needs and strengths are identified during the assessment phase.

Attending behaviors a variety of ways the social worker conveys interest and concern through nonverbal interactions.

Barriers to progress what the client believes (and possibly the social worker too) as being a roadblock to change; it could be something as simple as getting a bus pass to ensure that the client can get to his or her job or as complicated as being in a violent relationship and believing there is no safe place to go.

Baseline data a concrete and quantitative measure of client symptoms before an intervention begins.

Behavioral functioning looking at what may sustain a particular pattern of behavior; why a client does what he or she does.

Body positioning is the way clients and social workers physically situate themselves in relation to each other. Leaning in, sitting comfortably during an interview, considering the physical space between participants.

Brief psychodynamic therapy a therapeutic approach concerned with unconscious processes and how they influence present behavior.

Brief therapies therapeutic approaches that bear quick results and that have proven effective in relieving client symptoms.

Brief treatments A range of therapeutic interventions that quickly relieve client symptoms.

Clarification attempting to verify that the social worker and client have the same understanding of the same situation; vagueness of language is addressed.

Client motivation positive interactions that are uplifting and empowering, providing clients with hope, which comes from the client's inner world and also from the experiences in his or her outer world, such as in his or her interacts with the social worker.

Closed-ended question asking for details that are specific to the situation and can be answered with one to two words.

Code of ethics a set of professional standards put forth by the National Association of Social Workers for conducting social work practice across settings and areas of practice, that uphold the profession's mission and values and provide guidance for ethical and competent social work practice.

Code switching a minority cultural members' technique for living in two or more cultural realities by changing behaviors, language, and appearances, depending on the context within which they find themselves; often understood as a survival skill, such as African Americans switching from Standard English to African American vernacular, depending on the setting in which they find themselves.

Cognitive functioning the client's ability to process thoughts, recall memories, learn new skills and acquire new information. It involves executive functions such as sequencing, reasoning, problem solving and integrating information so it can be understood.

Cognitive-behavioral theories focus on present conditions in a client's life and identify cognitive distortions, conflicts in belief systems, and misconceptions that may contribute to problematic behaviors and symptoms in the client.

Cognitive-behavioral therapy focuses on the relationship between how a client thinks (cognitions) and the resulting problematic feelings and behaviors; grounded in the belief that how we think and interpret our world has a direct impact on how we experience our internal and external worlds.

Competence demonstrates knowledge and skill to engage in social work practice in assigned or chosen areas; graduating from an accredited school of social work and passing your state licensure exams are beginning levels of competence.

Confidentiality the safeguarding of the information that passes between the social worker and the client that facilitates the evolution of a trusting relationship; trusting that what transpires during the interview session will remain private.

Confrontation points out message discrepancies to the client; should be undertaken when the social worker and the client have a therapeutic relationship and trust has been established; identifying consequences of actions, thoughts, and feelings is done with the client's best interests in mind.

Contextual factors these may include the emotional and psychological states of the client, the client's intellectual/cognitive abilities, cultural beliefs and practices (as well as cultural taboos), agency rules and practice orientation, treatment setting (agency or client's home, school, or community setting), family context, and social support networks.

Continuum of care an integrated way of providing services to clients by assessing their level of need; the type of services required to meet the intensity of the need of a client is the guiding principle.

Contracting is the process in which the client and social worker come to an agreement regarding goals for work. The contract typically includes what was agreed upon, who is responsible for which part of the agreement, and time frames to meet the goals.

Coping skills Capacities that help clients and others navigate life's challenges.

Coping-skills training therapeutic approaches that help clients build capacities and develop skills that will enhance client functioning.

Countertransference becoming too involved in the client's life, where the social worker loses objectivity; bound by the NASW *Code of Ethics.*

Crisis intervention immediate and short-term response aimed at helping the client to minimize distress and return to pre-crisis functioning.

Cultural awareness the state of knowing one's own values and biases; requires an ongoing self-exploration of one's own cultural background and the values and attitudes that go with it.

Cultural competence embodies a set of values, behaviors, and practices that enables individuals and organizations to work effectively across cultures; reflects a valuing, honoring, and respect for diverse beliefs, language, and interpersonal styles represented across clients and client groups.

Cultural desire a component of caring where social workers really want to build their cultural knowledge, skill, and awareness in order to better serve their cross-cultural clients.

Cultural diversity refers to human differences as generated by membership in various identifiable human groups.

Cultural empathy the ability to empathize and internalize the feelings, thoughts, and behaviors of members from different cultural groups.

Cultural encounter the willingness to seek out face-to-face experiences with diverse individuals, groups, and communities in order to increase one's cultural knowledge and sensitivity and to better engage and serve cross-cultural clients.

Cultural imposition the tendency to impose one's individual beliefs, values, and assumptions on another culture or individual different from oneself.

Cultural sensitivity an attitude of acceptance, respect, and appreciation for each client's cultural uniqueness and a willingness to learn about each client's uniqueness.

Culturally aware to approach the client relationship with the intent and ability to adjust the interview to best meet the client's needs.

Culturally responsive when social workers demonstrate the ability to use client-perspective-centered practice skills as a method to achieve true multicultural competence with each client they serve.

Culture broadly stated, a quality of all communities of people identified by geographic location, common characteristics, or similar interests. This includes values, norms, beliefs, language, and traditions.

Cycle of caring the repeated supporting of clients, one at a time, through the helping process that entails empathic attachment, active involvement, and felt separation of the social worker.

Developmental Model of Intercultural Sensitivity (DMIS) a progression of cross-cultural awareness along a continuum, moving from an ethnocentric worldview to an ethnorelative perspective.

Dignity and worth of the person respect for every human being's innate greatness; regarding clients/individuals as having worth and treating them with esteem regardless of their outward appearances and behaviors.

Disability Experiencing physical, emotional or intellectural challenges.

Ecological perspective the person-in-environment perspective provides more concrete ways for understanding the person in environment through family and human systems; the notion of "goodness of fit" between a person and the environment provides a lens through which to assess the extent to which a person's adaptive behaviors promote growth and health (a good fit) or support a decline of physical, social, or psychological functioning (bad fit).

Emotional functioning ability to communicate and demonstrate how a client feels, such as anxious, depressed, or happy.

Empathy understanding the client's situation from his or her perspective; putting yourself in the client's life circumstances.

Empowerment through knowledge, support, and skillful guidance, clients are able to move themselves toward their life goals through making informed choices about their lives; when clients are able and willing to take these steps, they have empowered themselves.

Empowerment-based practice emerged from work with women and people of color and built on the belief that members in groups with limited social and political power suffer personal loss of power and opportunities across systems in mainstream society.

Engagement with client joining with the client by demonstrating a desire to learn more about them; mutuality in the relationship.

Engagement the initial contact with the client where the social worker begins to establish the framework for the helping relationship and gathers information that is used as the foundation for the next phase of the helping process: assessment.

Ethic of care a comprehensive theoretical framework that offers insight into how people can best live together in a more just society; focuses on the life span and our interdependence as members of society.

Ethical dilemmas "Ethical dilemmas occur when social workers must choose among conflicting professional values, duties, and rights that arise sometimes due to their competing obligations to clients, employers, colleagues, the social work profession, and society at large" (Reamer, 2008, p. 144).

Ethnocentric worldview occurs when individuals' culture dominates their thinking to the exclusion of other cultural perspectives.

Ethnorelative worldview occurs when individuals experience their culture in the context of, or relative to, other cultures; consequently, they gain a greater awareness of and appreciation for other cultures.

Evaluation an assessment that occurs after the completion of the intervention to determine how successful the intervention has been at addressing the client problem(s).

Evidence-based practice (EBP) the use of social work practice approaches supported by scientific evidence that demonstrate the effectiveness of specific interventions and predicts specific outcomes.

Facial expressions mirroring back to the client by using facial animation to communicate the social worker's understanding of their situation.

False assurance/minimize the problem offering platitudes, overlooking the severity of the problem, or diminishing the client's concerns.

Family and social support the ingredients that lead to a client feeling cared for and supported.

Friendship a relationship of a personal nature that holds both parties on equal footing.

Furthering responses one- or two-word utterances used to encourage the client to continue expressing with his or her thoughts and or feelings.

Goal attainment scaling uses an evaluation scale customized to the client's desired outcomes; consists of a standard five-point scale of goal attainment ranging from +2 (most favorable) to −2 (least favorable) with a value of zero representing the client's goal.

Helping process the systematic care of social work clients through the stages of intake and engagement, assessment, problem identification, planning and contracting, treatment/intervention, evaluation, and termination.

Home visits Home visits are the primary way for a social worker to meet face to face with a client in his or her residence. It is through a home visit that services such as a well-baby check, a health screening or supportive services such as counseling can be offered. When making a home visit, remember that you are a guest in the client's home. Pay attention to the internal and external environment for data regarding your client's life.

Humanistic theories posit that people have within them everything that they need to achieve their full potential.

Importance of human relationships an understanding that relationships between and among people are the core mechanism through which change occurs.

Inappropriate humor using sarcasm, making light of a client situation, or mocking or making fun.

Inappropriate questions too many or tangential questions that don't warrant or merit further exploration or offer new insights.

Inappropriate self-disclosure sharing information with a client that is personal to the social worker and that could lead the client to presume that a friendship is evolving.

Individualization the process of knowing people for themselves, instead of "knowing" people through the distortions of our own biases (Zastrow, 2013).

Individualized rating scales a rating scale tailored to specific client needs; these are easy to use and require little time for the client to complete (e.g., asking the client to rate his or her pain on a scale of 1 to 10 from week to week to monitor progress or the recession of pain).

Information giving providing useful, relevant, up-to-date information to the client, such as a reference to a health care provider or information that generalizes or universalizes the client's experience, such as "Almost every adolescent will try to test the boundaries; that is just what teenagers do."

Intake process first step in learning about the client's problem: collecting data to understand the problem from the client's perspective.

Integrity emanating trustworthiness in all areas of social work practice and personal arenas.

Internal culture the psychological, emotional, cognitive, and intellectual capabilities and/or limitations that clients bring to the helping process.

Interpretation to go beyond the stated problem and begin to delve more deeply; interpretation can provide the client with an alternative way of viewing the problem.

Interruptions/abrupt transitions a sudden break in the continuity or flow of a client's thoughts, which diverts him or her from the issue at hand.

Intersectionality a relatively new theory of diversity that presents an understanding of the complexity of culture and the many facets of life that position individuals in places of privilege and power or in places of discrimination, exploitation, and marginalization.

Interviewing skills set of interrelated verbal responses and questions that convey understanding and empathy to the client.

Judgmental response condescending, labeling a client, blaming rather than empowering.

Lead-in responses used as a sentence stem to solicit an understanding and to encourage the continuation of the interview; used as a way to tie pieces of the interview together.

Life model a practice method that implements the concepts of the ecological perspective that focus on client strengths.

Loss an emotion of sadness and sorrow, typically, a client who has bonded well with a social worker will feel a sense of mourning the relationship.

Macro-level social work practice involves work with communities, states, and federal agencies and may require the social worker to fill the roles of activist, broker, community advocate, community educator, community facilitator, community planner, and coordinator.

Meta-frameworks overarching and general theories of social work practice, such as systems theory, the ecological perspective, and the strengths perspective.

Mezzo-level social work practice involves working with groups and organizations and may require the social worker to fulfill the roles of agency administrator, agency staff trainer, broker, class advocate, mediator, organizational facilitator, program planner, and researcher/program evaluator.

Micro-level social work practice involves work with individuals and families and often requires social workers to fill the roles of case advocate, case manager, client educator, clinician/counselor, enabler, group facilitator, and outreach worker.

Motivational interviewing a therapeutic approach that builds on empathy and that accepts resistance as a normal dynamic in the helping process; used to help clients resolve resistance or ambivalence toward change; grounded in empathy and collaboration that supports the building of client self-efficacy.

National Association of Social Workers the oldest and most prestigious professional organization for social workers that sets practice standards and provides credentialing for specialization in social work practice.

Office visit when the client comes to the social worker's setting; the client should feel welcomed by friendliness and openness.

Open-ended questions invitation to expand on a particular topic.

Paraphrase restatement of the content of the client's thoughts/situation using the social worker's own words.

Person in their environment looking at the client as an individual and the intersectionality of their political, economic, social, global, and environmental structures that serve as resources or barriers.

Personal style how the social worker blends who he or she is in relationship to maintain professional boundaries.

Physical disability a person experiencing long term physical impairments in daily functioning as a result of chronic illness, injury, or congenital defects.

Physical functioning and well-being combining health and physical characteristics, genetic history, and drug and alcohol usage in the creation of an assessment of the client's overall well-being and physical functioning.

Planning Planning is a stage in the helping process in which the client and social worker set goals, explore strategies and find solutions to problems. It is a systematic and collaborative effort to work out the details regarding actions to be taken.

Postmodern theories are grounded in the belief that reality is subjective in nature and therefore open to multiple interpretations, which themselves are influenced by personal experiences and values and the social and political norms and language in a given historical context.

Practice theory a body of knowledge that has been empirically tested and shown to be effective.

Premature confrontation challenging the client too early in the relationship can cause the client to feel defensive or retreat.

Premature problem solving too early in the relationship to start the planning process, as many clients will not disclose the "real problem" or problem for work initially; further exploration is needed to fully understand the situation or context.

Problem identification a phase of the helping process which is done in collaboration with the client and social worker. Once there is agreement on the problem(s) for work, efforts are made to address the issues and resolutions sought.

Professional boundaries ways that a social worker communicates caring without taking the client's problem(s) to heart.

Psychodynamic theories attempt to link current problems to past traumas, usually occurring during childhood; common psychodynamic theories include psychoanalysis, ego psychology, object relations theory, psychodynamic therapy, and self-psychology.

Qualitative data provide rich narrative data on how the client experienced the helping relationship.

Quantitative data objectively demonstrate client progress or lack of progress using valid and reliable assessment tools and numerical data that provide invaluable information on client mental health status, such as depression and anxiety scores, and other areas of client functioning.

Rapport building showing genuine concern and interest in the client's situation.

Reflection of feelings restatement of the emotional state of the client's situation using the social workers own words.

Resistance client opposition to treatment; a common and normal human response to change reflective of fear and anxiety of entering unfamiliar territory.

Self-awareness knowing yourself and what you value and hold to be most important.

Self-determination the act of giving clients the freedom to make choices in their lives and to move toward established goals in a manner that they see as most fitting for themselves as long as clients' choices don't infringe on the rights of others (Zastrow, 2013); grounded in self-determination theory, which posits that client changes are more apt to be long lasting and more effective if they are autonomously motivated to change (Deci & Ryan, 2012).

Separation the moving away from a relationship, in this case the client–social worker dyad.

Service supported by the ethical principle of helping people with their social problems, service, as a value, is expressed in how services are structured, accessible, and relevant to the needs of those being served.

Silence a quiet moment in the client/social worker exchange that allows the client and/or the social worker time to consider how to respond.

Single-subject design (SSD) a scientific approach to practice evaluation that includes a range of designs from the simple to the complex; designs usually include both baseline data and intervention data that are collected at consistent intervals and graphed on an SSD table; practitioners complete a visual and statistical analysis using software developed specifically for SSD.

Social justice comes through social change that promotes equality of opportunity for all (NASW, 2008a).

Social work ethics practice guidelines established by the National Association of Social Workers (NASW), which reflect the values of the profession, and translates the abstract values of the profession into concrete action statements for ethical ways of being in the practice setting.

Social work mission to advance the quality of life for all people through the enhancement of mutually beneficial interactions between individuals and society (Minahan, 1981); social work stands for the social welfare of all people and is committed to social justice through social change at the individual, family, community, agency, and structural levels.

Social work role expected professional behaviors and functions accepted by the social work profession and frequently employed in social work practice.

Social work values an idealistic and difficult-to-sustain value set that guides the profession toward the fulfillment of its mission. The six core values are 1) service, 2) social justice, 3) dignity and worth of the person, 4) importance of human relationships, 5) integrity, and 6) competence.

Social work the art and science of helping others and whose professional mission is to enhance human well-being and help meet the basic human needs of all people, with particular attention to the needs and empowerment of people who are vulnerable, oppressed, and living in poverty.

Solution-focused brief therapy a therapeutic approach that focuses on solutions and concentrates on future desired states rather than current problems; works from the assumption that clients have within them the strengths and resources to create a solution.

Special populations unique client groups that require specialized knowledge for effective engagement and treatment. Some examples of special populations include children and adolescents, mentally ill, disabled, and elderly populations.

Spiritual and religious functioning a holistic view of connecting with something bigger than oneself; a system of faith and belief.

Standardized instruments measurement tools that have established validity and reliability.

Strengths perspective social worker–client interactions focus on client strengths become the resources for change that move them forward to growth, mastery, and self-actualization.

Strengths-based assessment looking at the client's capacity and assets, including family and social supports.

Suicide assessment looking at what factors may be contributing to a client feeling hopeless or that life is not worth living.

Summarization enables the social worker to pull together key ideas and themes regarding the most important aspects of the client's problems and also provides focus and continuity to the interview; both the content and the feeling of the client's message are incorporated into the social worker's response.

Supervision a valued process and tool in social work practice for building skills and practice wisdom through seeking guidance from clinical supervisors and seasoned social workers.

Systems theory a framework for understanding people's problems in the context of individual, family, community, and larger systems and how they impact clients lives but also serve as resources; systems theory also provides direction for social workers when intervening in the lives of their clients.

Termination the ending of a relationship at a mutually agreeable time; the worker and client identify progress made and develop ways to maintain progress; endings can be mutual or unilateral, planned or unplanned.

Termination the final stage of the helping process where the client and social worker mutually decide how and when the relationship will end; often accompanied by a sense of loss for the client and the social worker.

Tone of voice communicates through the volume and pace of responses the social worker's ability to convey understanding.

Too much information prioritizing materials and resources in ways that the client cannot manage all the details.

Touch a way to communicate care by reaching out via hand gestures, arm tapping, or a slight hug.

Treatment/intervention implementation of the agreed-on plan of action developed by the client and social worker.

Verbal contract an agreement that is agreed on by the client and social worker's words; a verbal contract can be seen as more fluid and less intimidating; regardless, the terms of a verbal contract should be placed in the client's file/record.

Written contract a more formal agreement, designed to hold the client accountable; a written agreement tends to be viewed a "legal document" by the client and therefore carries more weight to what has been agreed on; giving the client a copy of the contract can be helpful in assisting them in meeting their goals and time lines.

References

Chapter 1

Arnow, B. A., Steidtmann, D., Blasey, C., Manber, R., Constantino, M. J., Klein, D. N., & Kocsis, J. H. (2013). The relationship between the therapeutic alliance and treatment outcome in two distinct psychotherapies for chronic depression. *Journal of Consulting and Clinical Psychology, 81*(4), 627.

Bedics, J. D., Atkins, D. C., Harned, M. S., & Linehan, M. M. (2015). The therapeutic alliance as a predictor of outcome in dialectical behavior therapy versus nonbehavioral psychotherapy by experts for borderline personality disorder. *Psychotherapy, 52*(1), 67–77.

Bureau of Labor Statistics. (2014). *Occupational outlook handbook* (2010–2011 ed.). Washington, DC: Author. Retrieved from http://workforce.socialworkers.org/studies/fullStudy0806.pdf

CMS.gov: Centers for Medicare and Medicaid Services (2015). *History*. Retrieved from https://www.cms.gov/About-CMS/Agency-Information/History/index.html?redirect=/History/

Cummins, L. K., Byers, K. V., & Pedrick, L. (2011). *Policy practice for social workers: New strategies for a new era* (Updated ed.). Boston: Allyn & Bacon.

Dinerman, M. (1984). The 1959 curriculum study: Contributions of Werner W. Boehm. In M. Dinerman & L. L. Geismar (Eds.), *A quarter-century of social work education*. Washington, DC: National Association of Social Workers, ABC-CLIO, Counsel on Social Work Education.

Drisko, J. (2013). The common factors model: Its place in clinical practice and research. *Smith College Studies in Social Work, 83*(4), 398–413, DOI: 10.1080/00377317.2013.833435

Ehrenreich, J. H. (1985). *The altruistic imagination*. Ithaca, NY: Cornell University Press.

Germain, C., & Gitterman, A. (2008). *The life model of social work practice: Advances in theory and practice* (3rd ed.). New York: Columbia University Press.

Hepworth, D., Rooney, R., Rooney, G. D., Strom-Gottfried, K., & Larsen, J. (2012). *Direct social work practice: Theory and skills* (9th ed.). Pacific Grove, CA: Brooks/Cole.

Johnson, L. D., & Yanca, S. J. (2011). *Social work practice: A generalist approach* (10th ed.). Boston: Allyn & Bacon.

Julkunen, I. (2011). Critical elements in evaluating and developing practice in social work: An exploratory overview. *Social Work and Social Sciences Review, 15*(1), 74–91.

Mark, C., & Keenan, E. K. (2010). The common factors model: Implications for transtheoretical clinical social work practice. *Social Work, 55*(1), 73–73.

Miley, K. K., O'Melia, M., & DuBois, B. (2013). *Generalist social work practice: An empowering approach* (7th ed.). Boston: Allyn & Bacon.

National Association of Social Workers. (2008). *Code of ethics*. Retrieved from http://www.socialworkers.org/pubs/code/code.asp

National Association of Social Workers. (2015a). *NASW credentials and specialty certifications*.Retrieved from http://www.socialworkers.org/credentials/default.asp

National Association of Social Workers. (2015b). *Practice*. Retrieved from http://www.naswdc.org/practice/default.asp

Richmond, M. E. (1930). *The long view: Papers and essays by Mary E. Richmond*. New York: Russell Sage Foundation.

Sheafor, B. W., & Horejsi, C. R. (2015). *Techniques and guidelines for social work practice* (10th ed.). New York: Pearson.

Skovholt, T. M. (2005). The cycle of caring: A model of expertise in the helping professions. *Journal of Mental Health Counseling, 27*(1), 82–93.

Stern, M. & Axinn, J. (2012). *Social welfare: A history of the American response to need* (8th Ed.). New York: Pearson.

Trattner, W. I. (1999). *From poor law to welfare state: A history of social welfare in America* (6th ed.). New York: Free Press.

Tryon, G. S. (1986). Client and counselor characteristics and engagement in therapy. *Journal of Counseling Psychology, 33*, 471–474.

Tryon, G. S. (1989). Study of variables related to client engagement using practicum trainees and experienced clinicians. *Psychotherapy, 26*, 54–61.

Tryon, G. S. (2003). A therapist's use of verbal response categories in engagement and nonengagement interviews. *Counselling Psychology Quarterly, 16*(1), 29–36.

Tryon, G. S., & Winograd, G. (2011). Goal consensus and collaboration. In J. C. Norcross (Ed.), *Psychotherapy relationships that work* (2nd ed.). New York: Oxford University Press.

University of Albany (2006). *Licensed social workers in the United States, 2004*. Rensselaer, NY: Center for Health Workforce Studies, School of Public Health. Retrieved from http://workforce.socialworkers.org/studies/fullStudy0806.pdf

Wampold, B. (2001). *The great psychotherapy debate: Models, methods, findings*. Mahwah, NJ: Lawrence Erlbaum Associates.

Zastrow, C., & Kirst-Ashman, K. (2013). *Understanding human behavior in the social environment* (9th ed.). Pacific Grove, CA: Brooks/Cole.

Chapter 2

Barker, R. (2014). *The social work dictionary* (6th ed.). Washington, DC: National Association of Social Workers.

Boyle, S., Hull, G., Mather, J. H., Smith, L. L., & Farley, O. W. (2009). *Direct practice in social work* (2nd ed.). Boston: Allyn & Bacon.

Brill, C. K. (2001). Looking at the social work profession through the eye of the NASW Code of Ethics. *Research on Social Work Practice, 11*(2), 223–234.

Cummins, L. K., Byers, K., & Pedrick, L. (2011). *Introduction to policy practice: New strategies for a new era* (Updated ed.). Upper Saddle River, NJ: Pearson.

Deci, M., & Ryan, R. M. (2012). Motivation, personality, and development within embedded social contexts: An overview of self-determination theory. In R. M. Ryan, *The Oxford handbook of human motivation*. Oxford: Oxford University Press.

Dolgoff, R., Harrington, D., & Loewenberg, F. M. (2012). Empowerment series: *Ethical decisions for social work practice* (Ethics & legal issues) (9th ed.). Belmont, CA: Brooks/Cole.

Ehrenreich, J. H. (1985). *The altruistic imagination*. Ithaca, NY: Cornell University Press.

Fisher, B., & Tronto, J. (1990). Toward a feminist theory of caring. In E. K. Abel & M. K. Nelson (Eds.), *Circles of care: Work and identity in women's lives* (pp. 35–62). Albany: State University of New York Press.

Hackney, H. L., & Cormier, S. (2013). *The professional counselor: A process guide to helping* (7th ed.). Upper Saddle River, NJ: Pearson.

Holland, S. (2010). Looked after children and the ethic of care. *British Journal of Social Work 40*(6), 1664–1680.

Human Rights Campaign. (2015, May). *Marriage center*. Retrieved from http://www.hrc.org/campaigns/marriage-center

Levy, C. (1976). *Social work ethics*. New York: Human Sciences Press.

Loewenberg, F. M., Dolgoff, R., & Harrington, D. (2000). *Ethical decisions for social work practice*. Itasca, IL: F. E. Peacock.

Miley, K. K., O'Melia, M., & DuBois, B. (2013). *Generalist social work practice: An empowering approach* (7th ed.). Boston: Allyn & Bacon.

Minahan, A. (1981). Purpose and objectives of social work revisited. *Social Work, 26*(1), 5–6.

Mizrahi, T., & Davis, L. (2009). Legal issues: Confidentiality and privileged communication. In *Encyclopedia of social work* (20th ed.). Washington, DC: NASW Press and Oxford University Press.

National Association of Social Workers. (1998). *Current controversies in social work ethics: Case examples*. Washington, DC: NASW Press.

National Association of Social Workers. (2008a). *Code of ethics*. Washington, DC: Author. Retrieved from http://www.socialworkers.org/pubs/code/code.asp

National Association of Social Workers. (2008b). *Encyclopedia of social work* (20th ed.). Washington, DC: NASW Press.

National Association of Social Workers [NASW] General Counsel & NASW Legal Defense Fund. (2014). *Social workers and child abuse reporting: A review of state mandatory reporting requirements* (NASW law note). Washington, DC: Author.

Ng, J. Y. Y., Ntoumanis, N., Thøgersen-Ntoumani, C., Deci, E. L., Ryan, R. M., Duda, J. L., & Williams, G. C. (2012). Self-determination theory applied to health contexts: A meta-analysis. *Psychological Science, 7*(4), 325–340.

Perlman, H. H. (1976). Believing and doing: Values in social work education. *Social Casework, 7*(6), 381–390.

Polowy, S. M., Bailey, W. D., & Gorengerg, C. (2008). Confidentiality and privileged communication. In *Encyclopedia of social work* (20th ed.). Washington, DC: NASW. DOI: 10.1093/acrefore/9780199975839.013.7

Reamer, F. G. (2008). Ethics and values. In *Encyclopedia of social work* (20th ed., pp. 143–151). Washington, DC: NASW Press.

Reamer, F. G. (2014). *Social work values and ethics* (4th ed.). New York: Columbia University Press.

U.S. Department of Health and Human Services. (2014, May). *About the law*. Retrieved from http://www.hhs.gov/healthcare/rights/index.html

Zastrow, C. (2013). *The practice of social work: A comprehensive worktext* (10th ed.).Pacific Grove, CA: Brooks/Cole.

Chapter 3

Addams, J. (1893). *Philanthropy and social progress: Seven essays*. Boston: Thomas Crowell.

Ashford, J., &Lecroy, C. (2013). *Human behavior in the social environment* (4th ed.).Belmont, CA: Brooks/Cole.

Beck, A. (1970). Cognitive therapy: Nature and relation to behavior therapy. *Behavior Therapy, 1*, 184–200.

Beckett, J. O., & Johnson, H. C. (1997). Human development. In *Encyclopedia of social work* (19th ed.). Washington, DC: NASW Press.

Boscarino, J. A., Figley, C. R., & Adams, R. E. (2004). Compassion fatigue following the September 11 terrorist attacks: A study of secondary trauma among New York City social workers. *International Journal of Emergency Mental Health, 6*(2), 57–66.

Boyle, S. W., Hull, G. H., Jr., Mather, J. H., Smith, L. L., & Farley, O. W. (2009). *Direct practice in social work* (2nd ed.). Boston: Allyn & Bacon.

Bronfenbrenner, U. (1977). Toward an experimental ecology of human development. *American Psychologist, 32*(7), 513–531.

Bronfenbrenner, U., & Ceci, S. J. (1994). Nature-nurture reconceptualized in developmental perspective: A bioecological model. *Psychological Review, 101*(4), 568–586.

Carpetto, G. (2008). *Interviewing and brief therapy strategies: An integrative approach*. Boston: Allyn & Bacon.

de Shazer, S. (1988). *Clues: Investigating solutions in brief therapy*. New York: Norton.

Dinerman, M. (1984). The 1959 curriculum study: Contributions of Werner W. Boehm. In M. Dinerman & L. L. Geismar (Eds.), *A quarter century of social work education*. Washington, DC: National Association of Social Workers, ABC-CLIO, Council on Social Work Education.

Ellis, A., & MacLaren, C. (1998). *Rational-emotive behavior therapy: A therapist's guide*. Atascadero, CA: Impact Publishers.

Germain, C. B. (1973). An ecological perspective in casework. *Social Casework, 54*, 323–330.

Germain, C. B. (1979). Introduction: Ecology and social work. In C. B. Germain (Ed.), *Social work practice: People and environments* (pp. 1–22). New York: Columbia University Press.

Germain, C. B., & Gitterman, A. (1997). *The life model of social work practice* (2nd ed.). New York: Columbia University Press.

Germain, C. B., & Gitterman, A. (2008). *The life model of social work practice: Advances in theory and practice* (3rd ed.). New York: Columbia University Press.

Germain, C. B., & Gitterman, A. (2011). Ecological perspective. In T. Mizrahi & L. E. Davis (Eds.), *Encyclopedia of social work* (20th ed.). Washington, DC: NASW Press.

Guhn, M., & Goelman, H. (2011). Bioecological theory, early child development and the validation of the population-level early development instrument. *Social Indicators Research, 103*(2), 193–217.

Gutiérrez, L. M., DeLois, K. A., & GlenMaye, L. (1995). Understanding empowerment practice: Building on practitioner-based knowledge. *Families in Society, 76*(9), 534–542.

Gutiérrez, L. M., & Ortega, R. (1991). Developing methods to empower Latinos: The importance of groups. *Social Work with Groups, 14*(2), 23–43.

Lindemann, E. (1944). Symptomology and management of acute grief. *American Journal of Psychiatry, 101,* 141–148.

Lock, A., Epston, D., & Maisel, R. (2004). Countering that which is called anorexia. *Narrative Inquiry, 14* (2), 275–302.

Miley, K. K., O'Melia, M., & DuBois, B. (2013). *Generalist social work practice: An empowering approach* (7th ed.).New York: Pearson.

Miller, J. G. (1978). *Living systems.* New York: McGraw-Hill.

Minahan, A. (1981). Purpose and objectives of social work revisited. *Social Work, 26,* 5–6.

Moss, D. (2015). The roots and genealogy or humanistic psychology. In K. J. Schneider, J. F. Pierson, & J. F. T. Bugental (Eds.), *The handbook of humanistic psychology: Theory, research, and practice* (2nd ed.). *Los Angeles: Sage.*

National Association of Social Workers. (1997). *Encyclopedia of social work* (19th ed.). Washington, DC: NASW Press.

Paquette, D., & Ryan, J. (2001). *Bronfenbrenner's ecological systems theory.* Retrieved from http://pt3.nl.edu/paquetteryanwebquest.pdf

Richmond, M. E. (1917). *Social diagnosis.* New York: Russell Sage Foundation.

Rogers, C. R. (1957). The necessary and sufficient conditions of therapeutic personality change. *Journal of Consulting Psychology, 21*(2), 95–103.

Saleebey, D. (1992). Conclusions: Possibilities of problems with the strengths perspective. In D. Saleebey (Ed.), *The strengths perspective in social work practice* (pp. 169–179). New York: Longman Press.

Saleebey, D. (1996). The strengths perspective in social work practice: Extensions and cautions. *Social Work, 41*(3), 296–305.

Saleebey, D. (2001). Practicing the strengths perspective: Everyday tools and resources. *Families in Society, 82*(3), 221–222.

Saleebey, D. (2013). *The strengths perspective in social work practice* (6th ed.). New York: Pearson.

Sheafor, B. W., & Horejsi, C. R. (2015). *Techniques and guidelines for social work practice* (9th ed.). Boston: Allyn & Bacon.

Singer, J. B. (Host) (2009, June 21). Theories for clinical social work practice: Interview with Joseph Walsh, Ph.D. [Episode 52]. *Social Work Podcast.* Podcast retrieved March 12, 2011, from http://socialworkpodcast.com/2009/08/theories-for-clinical-social-work.html

Sommers-Flanagan, J., & Sommers-Flanagan, R. (2004). *Counseling and psychotherapy theories in context and practice: Skills, strategies, and techniques.* San Francisco: Wiley.

Trattner, W. (1999). *From poor law to welfare state* (6th ed.). New York: Free Press.

Turner, F. J. (Ed.). (2011). *Social work treatment: Interlocking theoretical approaches* (5th ed.). New York: Oxford University Press.

Turner, S. G., & Maschi, T. M. (2015). Feminist and empowerment theory and social work practice. *Journal of Social Work Practice: Psychotherapeutic Approaches in Health, Welfare and the Community, 29*(2), 151–162, DOI: 10.1080/02650533.2014.941282

Walsh, J. (2013). *Theories for direct social work practice* (3rd ed.). Stamford, CT: Cengage Learning.

Wedding, D., & Corcini, R. J. (2014). *Current psychotherapies* (10th ed.). Belmont, CA: Brooks/Cole.

Worden, J. W. (2009). *Grief counseling and grief therapy: A handbook for the mental health practitioner* (4th ed.). New York: Springer Publishing Company.

U.S. Department of Veterans Affairs (2014). *Homeless veterans.* Retrieved from http://www.va.gov/homeless/hud-vash.asp

Zastrow, C. (2013). *The practice of social work.* Stamford, CT: Cengage Learning.

Chapter 4

Anderson, J., Anderson, A., & Gear, A. (2015). Family literacy programs as intersubjective spaces: Insights from three decades of working in culturally, linguistically and socially diverse communities. *Language and Literacy: A Canadian Educational E-Journal 17*(2), 41–58.

Awad, G., Cokley, K., & Ravitch, M. (2005). Attitudes toward affirmative action: A comparison of color-blind versus modern racist attitudes. *Journal of Applied Social Psychology, 35,* 1384–1399.

Bennett, M. J. (1986). A developmental approach to training for intercultural sensitivity. *International Journal of Intercultural Relations 10*(2), 179–195.

Bennett, M. J. (1993). Towards ethnorelativism: A developmental model of intercultural sensitivity. In M. Paige (Ed.), *Education for the intercultural experience.* Yarmouth, ME: Intercultural Press.

Bennett, M. J. (2004). Becoming interculturally competent. In J. Wurzel (Ed.), *Toward multiculturalism: A reader in multicultural education* (2nd ed., pp. 62–77). Newton, MA: Intercultural Resource Corporation.

Bennett, M. J., & Hammer, M. (1998). *The developmental model of intercultural sensitivity.* Retrieved from http://www.intercultural.org/pdf/dmis.pdf

Borman, K., Mueninghoff, E., & Piazza, S. (1988). Urban Appalachian girls and young women: Bowing to no one. In L. Weis (Ed.), *Class, race, and gender in American education* (pp. 230–248). Albany: State University of New York Press.

Brah, A., & Phoenix, A. (2004). Ain't I a woman? Revisiting intersectionality. *Journal of International Women's Studies, 5*(3), 75–86.

Bronfenbrenner, U. (1979). *The ecology of human development: Experiments by nature and design.* Cambridge, MA: Harvard University Press.

Campinha-Bacote, J. (2002). The process of cultural competence in the delivery of healthcare services: A model of care. *Journal of Transcultural Nursing, 13*(3), 181–184.

Carr, D. (2011). Racial differences in end-of-life planning: Why don't Blacks and Latinos prepare for the inevitable? *Omega: Journal of Death & Dying, 63*(1), 1–20.

Chaiken, S. (1980). Heuristic versus systematic information processing and the use of source versus message cues in persuasion. *Journal of Personality and Social Psychology, 39,* 752–766.

Cohen, A. B., Hall, D. E., Koenig, H. G., & Meador, K. G. (2005). Social versus individual motivation: Implications for normative definitions of religious orientation. *Personality and Social Psychology Review 9*(1), 48–61.

Colby, S. L., & Ortman, J. M. (2015). *Projections of the size and composition of the U.S. Population: 2014 to 2060.* Washington, DC: U.S. Census Bureau.

Collins, P. H. (2000). Gender, Black feminism, and Black political economy. *Annals of the American Academy of Political and Social Science, 568,* 41–53.

Cooper, C. R., Cooper, R. G., Azmitia, M., Chavira, G., & Gullatt, Y. (2002). Bridging multiple worlds: How African-American and Latino youth in academic outreach programs navigate math pathways to college. *Applied Developmental Science, 6,* 73–87.

Crenshaw, K. W. (1991). Mapping the margins: Intersectionality, identity politics, and violence against women of color. *Stanford Law Review, 43*(6), 1241–1299.

Cummins, L. K., & Gray, S. (2008). *A culture of one: A model for teaching diversity in the classroom.* Paper presented at the Council on Social Work Education's 54th Annual Program Meeting, Philadelphia, November 1.

Fong, R., & Furuto, S. (2001). *Culturally competent practice: Skills, interventions, and evaluations.* Boston: Allyn & Bacon.

Frame, M. W., & Williams, B. C. (2011). Counseling African Americans: Integrating spirituality in therapy. *Counseling and Values, 41*(1), 16–28.

Frankenberg, R. (Ed.). (1997). *Displacing whiteness: Essays in social and cultural criticism.* Durham, NC: Duke University Press.

Greenwald, A. G., & Banaji, M. R. (1995). Implicit social cognition: Attitudes, self-esteem, and stereotypes. *Psychological Review, 102*(1), 4–27.

Guss, C. D. (2002). Decision making in individualistic and collectivistic cultures. In W. J. Lonner, D. L. Dinnel, S. A. Hayes, & D. N. Sattlet (Eds.), *Online readings in psychology and culture.* Retrieved from http://www.wwu.edu/~culture

Harding, S., & Norberg, K. (2005). New feminists approaches to social science methodologies: An introduction. *Signs, 30*(4), 2009–2019.

Hodge, D., & McGrew, C. C. (2006). Spirituality, religion, and the interrelationship: A nationally representative study. *Journal of Social Work Education, 42*(3), 637–654.

Kagitchibasi, C. (1996). *Family and human development across cultures.* Mahwah, NJ: Lawrence Erlbaum Associates.

Lakoff, G., & Johnson, M. (2003). *Metaphors we live by* (2nd ed.). Chicago: University of Chicago Press.

Leininger, M. (1978). *Transcultural nursing: Concepts, theories and practices.* New York: Wiley.

Leininger, M., & McFarland, M. J. (2002). *Transcultural nursing: Theories, research, and practice* (3rd ed.). New York: McGraw-Hill.

Lum, D. (2010). *Culturally competent practice: A framework for understanding diverse groups and justice issues* (3rd ed.). Belmont, CA: Thompson.

Malveaux, J. (2002). Intersectionality—Big word for small lives. *Journal of Black Issues in Higher Education, 19*(12), 27–28.

McCall, L. (2005). The complexity of intersectionality. *Signs, 30*(3). 1771–1801.

McCarthy, M. K., & Peteet, J. R. (2003). Teaching residents about religion and spirituality. *Harvard Review of Psychiatry, 11*(4), 225–228.

Miley, K. K., O'Melia, M., & DuBois, B. (2013). *Generalist social work practice: An empowering approach* (7th ed.). Boston and New York: Allyn & Bacon and Pearson.

Miller, J., & Garran, A. M. (2008). *Racism in the United States: Implications for the helping professions.* Belmont, CA: Thomson Brooks/Cole.

National Association of Social Workers. (2001). *NASW standards for cultural competence in social work practice.* Washington, DC: Author. Retrieved from http://www.naswdc.org/practice/standards/NASWCulturalStandards.pdf

National Association of Social Workers. (2008). *Code of ethics.* Retrieved from http://www.socialworkers.org/pubs/code/code.asp

National Center for Cultural Competence. (n.d.). *Conceptual frameworks/models, guiding values and principles.* Washington, DC: Georgetown University. Retrieved from http://nccc.georgetown.edu/foundations/frameworks.html#ccdefinition

National Institute of Mental Health. (2013). *Any mental illness (AMI) among adults.* Retrieved from http://www.nimh.nih.gov/health/statistics/prevalence/any-mental-illness-ami-among-adults.shtml

Neville, H. A., Lilly, R. L., Duran, G., Lee, R. M., & Browne, L. (2000). Construction and initial validation of the color-blind racial attitudes scale (CoBRAS). *Journal of Counseling Psychology, 47,* 59–70.

Nurmi, J. E. (1987). Age, sex, social class, and quality of family interaction as determinants of adolescents' future orientation: A developmental task interpretation. *Adolescence, 22*(88), 977–991.

Oberhauser, A. M. (1995). Gender and household economic strategies in rural Appalachia. *Gender, Place and Culture: A Journal of Feminist Geography, 2*(1), 51–70. DOI:10.1080/09663699550022080

Oberhauser, A. M. (2014). *Global perspectives on gender and space: Engaging feminism and development.* New York: Routledge.

Ohbuchi, K. I., Fukushima, O., & Tedeschi, J. T. (1999). Cultural values in conflict management: Goal orientation, goal attainment, and tactical decision. *Journal of Cross-Cultural Psychology, 30,* 51–71.

Poehlman, T. A., Uhlmann, E., Greenwald, A. G., & Banaji, M. R. (2005). *Understanding and using the Implicit Association Test: III. Meta-analysis of predictive validity.* Retrieved from http://faculty.washington.edu/agg/pdf/IAT.Meta-analysis.15Nov04.pdf

Ponterotto, J. G., Gretchen, D., Utsey, S. O., Riger, B. P., & Austin, R. (2002). A revision of the multicultural counseling awareness scale. *Journal of Multicultural Counseling and Development, 30,* 152–183.

Saleebey, D. (Ed.). (2013). *The strengths perspective in social work practice* (6th ed.). New York: Pearson.

Schieman, S., Pudrovska, T., & Milkie, M. A. (2005). The sense of divine control and the self-concept: A study of race differences in late life. *Research on Aging, 27*(2), 165–196.

Scott, P., & Singleton, S. (2005). *Teaching diversity in the classroom: The application of intersectionality.* Presentation to faculty, School of Social Work, Barry University, Miami Shores, FL.

Summers, N. (2003). *Fundamentals for practice with high risk populations.* Florence, KY: Cengage Learning.

Thornton, A., & Young-DeMarco, L. (2001). Four decades of trends in attitudes toward family issues in the United States: The 1960s through the 1990s. *Journal of Marriage and Family, 63*(4), 1009–1037.

Transcultural C.A.R.E. Associates. (2015). *The process of cultural competence in the delivery of healthcare services.* Retrieved from http://transculturalcare.net/the-process-of-cultural-competence-in-the-delivery-of-healthcare-services

Turner, W. L., Wieling, E., & Allen, W. D. (2004). Developing culturally effective family-based research programs: Implications for family therapists. *Journal of Marital and Family Therapy, 30*(3), 257–270.

U.S. Census Bureau News. (2011, March 24). *Census 2010 shows America's diversity.* Retrieved from https://www.census.gov/2010census/news/releases/operations/cb11-cn125.html

Utsey, S. O., Ponterotto, J. G., & Porter, J. (2008). Prejudice and racism, year 2008—Still going strong: Research on reducing prejudice with recommended methodological advances. *Journal of Counseling and Development, 86,* 339–347.

Van der Zee, K. I., & Brinkmann, U. (2004). Construct validity evidence for the intercultural readiness check against the multicultural personality questionnaire. *International Journal of Selection and Assessment, 12*(3), 285–290.

Van der Zee, K. I., & Van Oudenhoven, J. P. (2000). The multicultural personality questionnaire: A multidimensional instrument of multicultural effectiveness. *European Journal of Personality, 14,* 291–309.

Chapter 5

Boyle, S., Hull, G., Mather, J., Smith, L., & Farley, O. W. (2011). *Direct practice in social work.* Boston: Allyn & Bacon.

Brems, C. (2001). *Basic skills in psychotherapy and counseling.* Pacific Grove, CA: Brooks/Cole.

Cormier, W., & Cormier, S. (2011). *Interviewing strategies for helpers* (4th ed.). Pacific Grove, CA: Brooks/Cole.

Cormier, L. S., & Hackney, H. L. (2011). *The professional counselor.* Boston: Allyn & Bacon.

Cormier, S., Nurius, P., & Osborn, C. (2011). *Interviewing and change strategies for helpers: Fundamental skills.* Florence, KY: Cengage Learning.

Hepworth, D., Rooney, R., & Larsen, J. (2013). *Direct social work practice: Theory and skills* (8th ed.). Pacific Grove, CA: Brooks/Cole.

Hill, C. E., & O'Brien, K. M. (2014). *Helping skills: Facilitating exploration, insight and action* (2nd ed.). Washington, DC: American Psychological Association.

Ivey, A. E., & Ivey, M. B. (2009). *Intentional interviewing and counseling.* Pacific Grove, CA: Brooks/Cole.

Kadushin, A., & Kadushin, G. (2013). *The social work interview* (4th ed.). New York: Columbia University Press.

Miley, K., O'Melia, M., & DuBois, B. (2011). *Generalist social work practice: An empowering approach* (7th ed.). Boston: Allyn & Bacon.

Sheafor, B. W., & Horejsi, C. R. (2015). *Techniques and guidelines for social work practice* (8th ed.). Boston: Allyn & Bacon.

Shebib, B. (2007). *Choices: Counseling skills for social workers and other professionals.* Boston: Allyn & Bacon.

Sue, S., & Sue, D. (2003). *Counseling the culturally different* (4th ed.). New York: Wiley.

Zangerle, K. (1996). *PATH Training Manual.* Bloomington, IL: Providing Access to Help (PATH), Inc.

Chapter 6

Boyle, S., Hull, G., Mather, J., Smith, L., & Farley, O. W. (2011). *Direct practice in social work.* Boston: Allyn & Bacon.

Cormier, S., Nurius, P., & Osborn, C. (2011). *Interviewing and change strategies for helpers: Fundamental skills.* Belmont, CA: Brooks/Cole.

Gambrill, E. (1997). *Social work practice: A critical thinker's guide.* New York: Oxford University Press.

Hackney, H. L., & Cormier, L. S. (2012). *The professional counselor.* Boston,: Allyn & Bacon.

Hepworth, D., Rooney, R., & Larsen, J. (2013). *Direct social work practice: Theory and skills* (9th ed.). Pacific Grove, CA: Brooks/Cole.

Hill, C. E., & O'Brien, K. M. (2014). *Helping skills: Facilitating exploration, insight and action* (2nd ed.). Washington, DC: American Psychological Association.

Kadushin, A., & Kadushin, G. (2013). *The social work interview* (4th ed.). New York: Columbia University Press.

Miley, K., O'Melia, M., & DuBois, B. (2013). *Generalist social work practice: An empowering approach* (7th ed.). Boston: Allyn & Bacon.

Murphy, B. C., & Dillon, C. (2011). *Interviewing in action: Process and practice.* Pacific Grove, CA: Brooks/Cole.

Paniagua, F. A. (1998). *Assessing and treating culturally diverse clients: A practical guide* (2nd ed.). Thousand Oaks, CA: Sage.

Sheafor, B. W., & Horejsi, C. R. (2015). *Techniques and guidelines for social work practice* (8th ed.). Boston: Allyn & Bacon.

Shulman, L. (2012). *The skills of helping individuals, families, groups and communities* (7th ed.). Belmont, CA: Brooks/Cole.

Chapter 7

Brems, C. (2001). *Basic skills in psychotherapy and counseling.* Pacific Grove, CA: Brooks/Cole.

Cormier, L. S., & Hackney, H. L. (2011). *The professional counselor.* Boston: Allyn & Bacon.

Egan, G. (2014). *The skilled helper* (8th ed.). Pacific Grove, CA: Brooks/Cole.

Hepworth, D., Rooney, R., Rooney, G. D., Strom-Gottfried, K., & Larsen, J. (2012). *Direct social work practice: Theory and skills* (8th ed.). Pacific Grove, CA: Brooks/Cole.

Hill, C. E., & O'Brien, K. M. (2014). *Helping skills: Facilitating exploration, insight and action* (2nd ed.). Washington, DC: American Psychological Association.

Kadushin, A., & Kadushin, G. (2013). *The social work interview* (4th ed.). New York: Columbia University Press.

Kottler, J. A. (2011). *Nuts and bolts of helping.* Boston: Allyn & Bacon.

Murphy, B. C., & Dillon, C. (2015). *Interviewing in action: Process and practice.* Pacific Grove, CA: Brooks/Cole.

National Association of Social Workers. (2008). *Code of ethics.* Retrieved from http://www.socialworkers.org/pubs/code/code.asp

Sheafor, B. W., & Horejsi, C. R. (2015). *Techniques and guidelines for social work practice* (8th ed.). Boston: Allyn & Bacon.

Chapter 8

Brill, N., & Levine, J. (2012). *Working with people: The helping process.* Boston: Allyn & Bacon.
Carpetto, G. (2008). *Interviewing and brief therapy strategies.* Boston: Allyn & Bacon.
Compton, B. R., Galaway, B., & Cournoyer, B. (2005). *Social work processes* (7th ed.). Pacific Grove, CA: Brooks/Cole.
Cormier, W., & Cormier, S. (2011). *Interviewing strategies for helpers* (4th ed.). Pacific Grove, CA: Brooks/Cole.
Egan, G. (2014). *The skilled helper* (8th ed.). Pacific Grove, CA: Brooks/Cole.
Garber, B. D. (2004). Therapist alienation: Foreseeing and forecasting third-party dynamics undermining psychotherapy with children of conflicted caregivers. *Professional Psychology: Research and Practice, 35,* 357–363.
Goode, T. (1999). *Promoting cultural competence and cultural diversity in early intervention and early childhood settings.* Washington, DC: Georgetown University Child Development Center.
Hill, C. E., & O'Brien, K. M. (2014). *Helping skills: Facilitating exploration, insight and action* (2nd ed.). Washington, DC: American Psychological Association.
Kottler, J. A. (2010). *Nuts and bolts of helping.* Boston: Allyn & Bacon.
Miley, K. K., O'Melia, M., & DuBois, B. (2013). *Generalist social work practice: An empowering approach* (7th ed.). Boston: Allyn & Bacon.
National Association of Social Workers. (2011). *Code of ethics.* Retrieved March 18, 2011, from http://www.naswdc.org
Orlinsky, D. R., Ronnestad, M. H., & Willuzki, U. (2004). *50 years of psychotherapy process-outcome research, continuity and change* (5th ed.). New York: Wiley.
Ragg, D. M. (2011). *Building effective helping skills: The foundation of generalist practice.* Boston: Allyn & Bacon.
Rogers, C. R. (1957). The necessary and sufficient conditions of therapeutic personality change. *Journal of Consulting Psychology, 21*(2), 95–103.
Shebib, B. (2010). *Choices: Counseling skills for social workers and other professionals.* Boston: Allyn & Bacon.
Skovholt, T. M. (2007). The cycle of caring: A model of expertise in the helping professions. *Journal of Mental Health Counseling, 27*(1), 82–93.
Skovholt, T., & Jennings, L. (2007). Mastery and expertise in counseling. *Journal of Mental Health Counseling, 27*(1), 13–18.
Sullivan, M. F., Skovholt, T. M., & Jennings, L. (2007). Master therapists' construction of the therapy relationship. *Journal of Mental Health Counseling, 27*(1), 48–70.
Timberlake, E. M., Farber, M. Z., & Sabatino, C. A. (2002). *The general method of social work practice: McMahon's generalist perspective* (4th ed.). Boston: Allyn & Bacon.
Tryon, G. S. (2003). A therapist's use of verbal response categories in engagement and nonengagement interviews. *Counselling Psychology Quarterly, 16*(1), 29–36.

Chapter 9

American Psychiatric Association. (2014). *Diagnostic and statistical manual of mental disorders* (5th ed.). Washington, DC: Author.
Beck, A. (1996). *Depression, causes, and treatment.* Philadelphia: University of Pennsylvania Press.
Bowlby, J. (1988). *Attachment and loss, Vol. 3: Loss, sadness and depression.* New York: Basic Books.
Boyle, S., Hull, G., Mather, J. H., Smith, L. L., & Farley, O. W. (2011). *Direct practice in social work* (3rd. ed.). Boston: Allyn & Bacon.
Coates, J., Graham, J., Swartzentruber, B. & Ouellette, B. (2007). *Spirituality and Social Work.* Toronto, Ontario: Canadian Scholars Press.
Compton, B. R., Galaway, B., & Cournoyer, B. (2005). *Social work processes* (7th ed.). Pacific Grove, CA: Brooks/Cole.
Cooper, G., & Lasser, J. (2011). *Clinical social work practice: An integrated approach* (3rd ed.). Boston: Allyn & Bacon.
Corcoran, J., & Walsh, J. (2012). *Mental health in social work: A casebook on diagnosis and strengths-based assessment.* Boston: Allyn & Bacon.
Cormier, W., & Cormier, S. (1998). *Interviewing strategies for helpers* (4th ed.). Pacific Grove, CA: Brooks/Cole.
Hepworth, D., Rooney, R., Rooney, G. D., Strom-Gottfried, K., & Larsen, J. (2013). *Direct social work practice: Theory and skills* (8th ed.). Pacific Grove CA: Brooks/Cole.
Hudson, W. W. (2000). Index of self-esteem. In J. Fischer & K. Corcoran (Eds.), *Measures for clinical practice and research* (Vol. 2, 4th ed., pp. 188–189). New York: Oxford UP.
Kanel, K. (2015). *The guide to crisis intervention* (5thed.). Florence, KY: Brooks/Cole.
Karls, J., & Wandrei, K. (1994). *Person-in-environment systems, the PIE classification system and social functioning problems.* Washington, DC: NASW Press.
McDonald, R. (2006). The spirituality of community life. New York: Hawthorn Press.
McGoldrick, M., Giordano, J., & Pearce, J. (2005). *Ethnicity and family therapy* (3rd ed.). New York: Guilford Press.
Middleman, R., & Wood, G. G. (1990). *Skills for direct practice in social work.* New York: Columbia UP.
Miley, K. K., O'Melia, M., & DuBois, B. (2013). *Generalist social work practice: An empowering approach* (7th ed.). Boston: Allyn & Bacon.
O'Leary K., & Wilson, T. (1987) *Behavior therapy: Application and outcome.* New Jersey: Prentice Hall
Rooney, R. H. (1992). *Strategies for work with involuntary clients.* New York: Columbia University Press.
Rothman, J. (2008). *Cultural competencies in process and practice: Building bridges,* Boston: Allyn & Bacon.
Saleebey, D. (2012). *The strength perspective in social work practice* (5th ed.). Boston: Allyn & Bacon.
Sheafor, B. W., & Horejsi, C. R. (2015). *Techniques and guidelines for social work practice* (9th ed.). Boston: Allyn & Bacon.
Skovholt, T. M. (2005). The cycle of caring: A model of expertise in the helping professions. *Journal of Mental Health Counseling, 27*(1), 82–93.
World Health Organization. (2001). *Substance abuse.* Retrieved July 8, 2011, from http://www.who.int/topics/substance_abuse/en/

Chapter 10

Bandura, A. (1986). *Social foundations of thought and action.* Englewood Cliffs, NJ: Prentice Hall.
Compton, B. R., Galaway, B., & Cournoyer, B. (2005). *Social work processes* (7th ed.). Pacific Grove, CA: Brooks/Cole.

Hepworth, D., Rooney, R., Rooney, G. D., Strom-Gottfried, K., & Larsen, J. (2013). *Direct social work practice: Theory and skills* (8th ed.). Pacific Grove, CA: Brooks/Cole.

Sheafor, B. W., & Horejsi, C. R. (2015). *Techniques and guidelines for social work practice* (9th ed.). Boston: Allyn & Bacon.

Tryon, G. S. (2002). Client and counselor characteristics and engagement in therapy. *Journal of Counseling Psychology, 33*, 471–474.

Chapter 11

Bannink, F. P. (2007). Solution-focused brief therapy. *Journal of Contemporary Psychotherapy, 37*, 87–94.

Beck, A. (1970). Cognitive therapy: Nature and relation to behavior therapy. *Behavior Therapy, 1*, 184–200.

Boyle, S. W., Grafton, H. H., Jr., Mather, J. H., Smith, L. L., & Farley, O. W. (2009). *Direct practice in social work* (2nd ed.). Boston: Allyn & Bacon.

Butler, A. C., Chapman, J. E., Forman, E. M., & Beck, A. T. (2006). The empirical status of cognitive-behavioral therapy: A review of meta-analyses. *Clinical Psychology Review, 26(1)*, 17–31.

Butler, S. F., & Strupp, H. H. (1986). Specific and nonspecific factors in psychotherapy: A problematic paradigm for psychotherapy research. *Psychotherapy, 23*, 30–40.

Cooper, M. G., & Lesser, J. G. (2015). *Clinical social work practice: An integrated approach* (5th ed.). New York: Pearson.

Curtis, J. T., & Silberschatz, G. (1986). Clinical implications of research on brief dynamic psychotherapy: Formulating the patient's problems and goals. *Psychoanalytic Psychology, 3*, 13–25.

Del Rea, A. C., Flückigerc, C., Horvathd, A. O., Symondse, D., & Wampoldf, B. E. (2012). Therapist effects in the therapeutic alliance–outcome relationship: A restricted-maximum likelihood meta-analysis. *Clinical Psychology Review, 32(7)*, 642–649.

deShazer, S. (1985). *Keys to solution in brief therapy*. New York: Norton.

deShazer, S., & Berg, I. K. (1997). "What works?" Remarks on research aspects of solution focused brief therapy. *Journal of Family Therapy, 19*, 121–124.

Ellis, A. (1991). The revised ABC's of rational-emotive therapy. *Journal of Rational-Emotive and Cognitive-Behavioral Therapy, 9*(3), 139–172.

Ellis, A., & MacLaren, C. (1998). *Rational-emotive behavior therapy: A therapist's guide*. Atascadero, CA: Impact Publishers.

Haggerty, J. (2006). *Psychodynamic therapy*. Retrieved from http://psychcentral.com/lib/2006/psychodynamic-therapy

Hogue, A., Dauber, S., Cecero, J. J., Stambaugh, L. F., & Liddle, H. A. (2007). Early therapeutic alliance and treatment outcome in individual and family therapy for adolescent behavior problems. *Journal of Counseling and Clinical Psychology, 74*(1), 121–129.

Milrod, B., Busch, F., Shapiro, T., Leon, A. C., & Aronson, A. (2005). A pilot study of psychodynamic psychotherapy in 18- to 21-year-old patients with panic disorder. *Adolescent Psychiatry, 29*, 289–314.

Lundahl, B. W., Kunz, C., Brownell, C., Tollefson, D., & Burke, B. L. (2010). A meta-analysis of motivational interviewing: Twenty-five years of empirical studies. *Research on Social Work Practice, 20*(2), 137–160.

Martin, B. (2011). *In-depth: Cognitive-behavioral therapy*. Retrieved from http://psychcentral.com/lib/2007/in-depth-cognitive-behavioral-therapy/2

Meissner, W. W. (2007). Therapeutic alliance: Theme and variations. *Psychoanalytic Psychology, 24*(2), 231–254.

Messer, S. B., Tishby, O., & Spillman, A. (1992). Taking context seriously in psychotherapy research: Relating therapist interventions to patient progress in brief psychodynamic therapy. *Journal of Consulting and Clinical Psychology, 60(5)*, 678–688.

Miley, K. K., O'Melia, M., & DuBois, B. (2013). *Generalist social work practice: An empowering approach* (7th ed.). Boston and New York: Allyn & Bacon and Pearson.

Miller, W. R., & Rollnick, S. (2013). *Motivational interviewing: Helping people change*. New York: Guilford Press.

Monti, P. M., & Rohsenow, D. J. (1999). Coping skills training and cue-exposure therapy in the treatment of alcoholism. *Alcohol Research and Health, 23*(2), 107–115.

Pennsylvania Child Welfare Training Program. (n.d.). *Module 11: Family service planning process/case transfer and closure handout #16*. Retrieved from http://www.pacwcbt.pitt.edu/curriculum/CTC/MOD11/Hndts/HO16_SltnFcsdQstns.pdf

Porter, L. S., Keefe, F. J. Garst, J. Baucom, D. H., McBride, C. M., McKee, D. C., et al. (2011). Caregiver-assisted coping skills training for lung cancer: Results of a randomized clinical trial. *Journal of Pain and Symptom Management, 41*(1), 1–13.

Ritzer, G. (2013). *Contemporary sociological theory and its classical roots: The Basics* (4th ed.). New York: McGraw-Hill.

Satterfield, J. M., & Crabb, R. (2010). Cognitive-behavioral therapy for depression in an older gay man: A clinical case study. *Cognitive and Behavioral Practices, 17*, 45–55.

Schwellnus, H., King, G., & Thompson, L (2015). Client-centred coaching in the paediatric health professions: A critical scoping review. *Disability and Rehabilitation, 37*(15), 1305–1315.

Scott, S. K. (2015). Psychodynamic theories: Approaches and applications. In D. Capuzzi & M. Stauffer (Eds.), *Foundations of couples, marriage, and family counseling*. Hoboken, NJ: Wiley.

Sheafor, B. W., & Horejsi, C. J. (2012). *Techniques and guidelines for social work practice* (9th ed.). Boston: Allyn & Bacon.

Smith, R. E. (1999). Generalization effects in coping skills training. *Journal of Sport and Exercise Psychology, 21*(3), 189–204.

Wahab, S. (2005). Motivational interviewing and social work practice. *Journal of Social Work, 5*(1), 45–60.

Walsh, J. (2013). *Theories for direct social work practice* (3rd ed.). Stamford, CT: Cengage Learning.

Windsor, L. C., Jemal, A., & Alessi, E. J. (2015). Cognitive behavioral therapy: A meta-analysis of race and substance use outcomes. *Cultural Diversity and Ethnic Minority Psychology, 21*(2), 300–313.

Chapter 12

Bloom, M. Fischer, J., & Orme, J. G. (2009). *Evaluating practice: Guidelines for the accountable professional* (6th ed.). New York: Pearson.

Boyle, S. W., Grafton, H. H., Jr., Mather, J. H., Smith, L. L., & Farley, O. W. (2009). *Direct practice in social work* (2nd ed.). Boston: Allyn & Bacon.

Brown, J. M., & Miller, W. R. (1993). Impact of motivational interviewing on residential alcoholism treatment. *Psychology of Addictive Behaviors, 7*(4), 211–218.

Bulté, I., & Onghena, P. (2013). Statistical software applications and review: The single-case data analysis package: Analysing single-case experiments with R software. *Journal of Modern Applied Statistical Methods, 12*(2), 450–478.

Byiers, B. J., Reichle, J., & Symonsa, F. J. (2012). Single-subject experimental design for evidence-based practice. *American Journal of Speech-Language Pathology, 21*(4), 397–414.

Corey, G., Haynes, R., & Moulton, P. (2010). *Clinical supervision in the helping professions: A practical guide* (2nd ed.). Alexandria, VA: American Counseling Association.

Di Noia, J., & Tripodi, T. (2008). *Single-case design for clinical social workers* (2nd ed.). Washington, DC: NASW Press.

Moeyaert, M., Ugille, M. Ferronm J. M., Onghena, P., Heyvaert, M., Beretvas, S. N., et al. (2014). Estimating intervention effects across different types of single-subject experimental designs: Empirical illustration. *School Psychology Quarterly, 30*(1), 50–63.

Miley, K. K., O'Melia, M., & DuBois, B. (2013). *Generalist social work practice: An empowering approach* (7th ed.). Boston and New York: Allyn & Bacon and Pearson.

Patton, M. Q. (2015). *Qualitative research and evaluation methods: Integrating theory and practice* (4th ed.). Los Angeles: Sage.

Rodríguez, L. F., and Conchas, G. Q. (2009). Preventing truancy and dropout among urban middle school youth: Understanding community-based action from the student's perspective. *Education and Urban Society, 41*(2), 216–247.

Sheafor, B. W., & Horejsi, C. J. (2012). *Techniques and guidelines for social work practice* (9th ed.). Boston: Allyn & Bacon.

Stolee, P., Zaza, C., Pedlar, A., & Myers, A. M. (1999). Clinical experience with goal attainment scaling in geriatric care. *Journal of Aging and Health, 11,* 96–124.

Totoa, P. E., Skidmorea, E. R., Terhorsta, L., Rosen, J., & Weinerc, D. K. (2015). Goal Attainment Scaling (GAS) in geriatric primary care: A feasibility study. *Archives of Gerontology and Geriatrics, 60*(1), 16–21.

Chapter 13

Boyle, S. W., Grafton, H. H., Jr., Mather, J. H., Smith, L. L., & Farley, O. W. (2009). *Direct practice in social work* (2nd ed.). Boston: Allyn & Bacon.

Miley, K. K., O'Melia, M., & DuBois, B. (2013). *Generalist social work practice: An empowering approach* (7th ed.). Boston and New York: Allyn & Bacon and Pearson.

Workbook Skills

This workbook is designed to teach social work interviewing skills and uses a two-pronged approach to do so: skill development and practice exercises. Under each skill, you will find two sections. Part I focuses on interviewing skill development. Part II provides relevant exercises that will enhance your overall development as a professional. Part II exercises are to be done primarily in small groups, referred to as "practice partner(s)." These exercises encourage the interaction and integration of theory and skill. Under each skill, there is also Cultural Competence Box. In your small groups, take the opportunity to think about, discuss, and apply different strategies and approaches when working with client who are culturally different from you. You will also have the chance to test yourself (Try It) following each section and to complete a quiz at the end of the workbook.

In order to assess how well you attend to another person's nonverbal communication, pick one of the 6 cases to review, viewing the first session only. Watch the video with your attention fully on the client. Determine how well the client was able to conveyed what he or she was feeling or experiencing by putting a check mark in the Client column as it relates to his or her attending behaviors. For instance, did Mrs. Kita clearly convey to Diane where she wanted her sit. Or did Kim's nonverbal messages match how she was feeling? Next watch the same session, now focusing your attention on the social worker. Did Karen's voice convey care and concern to Mike? In Nicole's interaction with Mrs. Anderson, did her tone of voice and leaning in help to further their conversation. In the Social Worker column, put a check mark in each box that reflects the attending behaviors of the worker.

Now compare the two columns to determine the overall interaction between the client and the worker. What are the patterns that you see emerge? Comment on what the social worker did well and ways that he or she could improve.

ATTENDING BEHAVIORS CHECKLIST FOR THE SOCIAL WORKER AND CLIENT	Session 1 Client	Session 1 Social Worker
Introduced self, discussed role, and greeting was welcoming		
Established rapport with client, put client at ease/relaxed demeanor		
Asked how to address the client and then used the client's name throughout the interview		
Addressed client's concerns about confidentiality		
Used good posture, leaned in to the client, faced client, appeared relaxed yet eager and ready to respond		
Use of head nodding, facial expressions matched the client's, hand gestures were purposeful (including touch)		
Tone of voice reflected the client's, appropriate and varied		
Nonverbal and verbal messages were congruent		
Maintained boundaries, such as physical distance and conveying professionalism, leaned in to client		
Limited verbal activity by mainly listening to the client, taking turns		
Used intermittent one-word vocalizations ("mmm," "hmm," "go on," "but," "and") to reinforce continuation of the interview		
Physical environment was neat, clutter free, and welcoming		
Conveyed authenticity, genuineness, care, and concern		
Spoke clearly and audibly, used "professional" language, each word was understood		
Used intermittent eye contact, looked at the client while talking and listening, observing the whole person		

(Continued)

ATTENDING BEHAVIORS CHECKLIST FOR THE SOCIAL WORKER AND CLIENT	Session 1 Client	Session 1 Social Worker
Facial expressions matched the client's, appropriately expressive while talking and listening to the client		
List nonverbal behaviors demonstrated that could have a negative impact on the relationship such as sitting too close, looking defiant, staring blankly, no facial expression, interrupting client, overly dramatic gestures, flat monotone voice, poor volume and clarity of voice, fidgeting, staring out the window, chewing gum, etc. (behavior of both client and social worker)		

Paraphrasing

Part I

Read the following items and

a. Identify the key points in the client's messages (at least two).
b. In your own words, restate what the client has said. Use different lead-in responses for each of your entries (refer to Box 5.3).

Example:

"I love to play hockey. I love coaching. My kids don't play anymore, but the other kids need me. My wife thinks I should spend more time at home. I don't agree with her. I'm home plenty."

a. Key points in the client's message:

i. hockey comes first

ii. disrupting marriage

iii. husband and wife have different expectations

b. Your paraphrasing response:

I hear you saying that hockey is a really important part of your life, but you and your wife see this issue differently, which is causing trouble at home.

1. **A 40-year-old African American male talking to the community mental health clinic caseworker.**

"I really need to talk to my doctor. It's been two weeks since I had my medication. I have to have it now. You don't understand; without the doctor's okay, I can't get my medicine. The pharmacy closes at five o'clock tonight. It's the only one in town that accepts my medical card. If I don't get my medicine soon, who knows what will happen to me—I need it for my nerves."

a. Key points in the client's message:

i. ______________________________

ii. ______________________________

iii. ______________________________

b. Your paraphrasing response:

____

____

2. **A Latina mother talking to the school social worker about her eight-year-old son.**

   "My son, Juanito, has a learning disability. He has a hard time in school. I know his teachers are frustrated with him, but I don't think they are doing enough to help him. We've been in this country for three years; there have been a lot of changes in his life.

   a. Key points in the client's message:

      i. ______

      ii. ______

      iii. ______

   b. Your paraphrasing response:

      ______

      ______

3. **A 47-year-old woman talking with her caseworker about her work situation.**

   "I am so miserable at work. My boss is a bully, and she is targeting me and my work group. We all got along fine before she came. I had a feeling about her. She seemed like a petty person, even during her interview. She commented on our work clothes and our hair. Seriously, who says those kinds of things during an interview? No one listened to my concerns, and look where we are now. I would quit today if I had another job."

   a. Key points in the client's message:

      i. ______

      ii. ______

      iii. ______

   b. Your paraphrasing response:

      ______

      ______

4. **A 22-year-old female talking to the intake worker at an outpatient treatment program.**

   "No, I'm not an alcoholic. Sure I drink, everyone I know drinks. It's part of being a college student. The DUI I got last month was no big deal; it was just a stupid mistake. I won't drive after drinking again, that's for sure. Everyone makes my drinking into a major catastrophe. I wish people would back off."

   a. Key points in the client's message:

      i. ______

      ii. ______

      iii. ______

   b. Your paraphrasing response:

      ______

      ______

5. **An 18-year-old male talking with an adoption specialist about his desire to locate his birth mother.**

   "My adoptive parents are great. I know that they love me a lot, and I love them too. But there is this feeling inside of me. I want to know who gave birth to me. I want her to tell me why she gave me up. Five years ago, the other social worker told me that I could look for her when I was older. Now I'm ready."

a. Key points in the client's message:

i. ______

ii. ______

iii. ______

b. Your paraphrasing response:

______

______

6. **A 35-year-old male talking about his relationships with friends.**

   "My friends seem to get bored and tired of me. They go out a lot without me. I find out later, like maybe they've gone to a movie. I call them. I hardly ever get calls back. It's weird. I always end up chasing people down."

   a. Key points in the client's message:

   i. ______

   ii. ______

   iii. ______

   b. Your paraphrasing response:

   ______

   ______

7. **A 14-year-old middle school student talking to the school social worker:**

   "I hate the way Mr. Jones, my social studies teacher talks to me. He thinks that I am stupid. He picks on me and the other kids have noticed it too. I don't trust him."

   a. Key points in the client's message:

   i. ______

   ii. ______

   iii. ______

   b. Your paraphrasing response:

   ______

   ______

8. **A 31-year-old male talking about the impact of prejudice on his life.**

   "I was born in the Dominican Republic and came to the United States when I was three. People sometimes look at me as if I have no right to be here. I'm an American citizen. I work hard to take care of my family. I'm a part of the community. Why do people have to question me all the time?"

   a. Key points in the client's message:

   i. ______

   ii. ______

   iii. ______

   b. Your paraphrasing response:

   ______

   ______

9. **A 15-year-old female talking with the school social worker.**

"My relationship with my stepdad has always been awkward. I have never felt comfortable around him. He definitely treats his own kids better than he treats me. I'm not saying I'm jealous or anything. In some ways it's easier when he treats me like an acquaintance. Just saying hello and good-bye and then going our separate ways. But sometimes I wish he'd be proud of me too."

a. Key points in the client's message:

i. ______

ii. ______

iii. ______

b. Your paraphrasing response:

______

______

10. **A 36-year-old female talking to the probation officer in charge of her husband's case.**

"I really do want to see Geo, but it is hard to pack up the three kids and spend hours on the bus. I don't know what to do; it takes all day to get there and back, to see him for only one hour."

a. Key points in the client's message:

i. ______

ii. ______

iii. ______

b. Your paraphrasing response:

______

______

Now apply what you've learned about paraphrasing in an online Try It exercise.

Part II

A. With your practice partners, complete the following role-play exercise. Three students are necessary to complete the exercise: 1) client, 2) social worker, and 3) observer.

Using the paraphrasing case #3 from above, in which your client is talking about her boss and the change in her work environment since her recent hire, role play this scenario for five minutes.

Client: Be sure to elaborate or enhance the situation so you can continue the role play for approximately five minutes.

Social Worker: Listen to the client and use the skill of paraphrasing when appropriate.

Observer: Identify the key components of the client's messages. What issues are most significant to the client? How did the social worker convey care, concern, and sensitivity to the client's life experiences? What other consideration should the social worker attend to?

After five minutes of role playing, discuss the observer's feedback within the practice group. What might the social worker have done differently? What were the strengths of the interview?

B. **Cultural Competence:**

Review case #10. Talk with your group about issues regarding the correctional system in the United States. What do you know about incarceration rates as it relates to people of color. What assumptions did you make about the client mentioned above?

Reflection of Feeling

Part I

After reading each item,

a. List four appropriate feeling words (see Box 5.7).
b. Write your reflection-of-feeling response using a different feeling word than the four listed.
c. Combine a reflection-of-feeling statement with a paraphrase. Be sure to use different lead-in responses for each of your entries.

Example:
"My dad and I always fight. He doesn't care about my feelings. He just keeps on accusing me falsely. No matter what I do, he refuses to listen. I just can't win. This shouldn't bother me, but it is so ridiculous, to not have him in my corner"

a. Feeling words:
- **i. hurt**
- **ii. angry**
- **iii. confused**
- **iv. frustrated**

b. Your feeling response:
You sound very hurt by your dad.

c. Combined response:
You want things to be better between the two of you. You sound hurt and disappointed.

1. **An 80-year-old male talking to the nursing home caseworker.**

   "This place is not working out. My family is too far away. The folks here are nice; they are just not family. My daughter and son were planning to come and visit me last month, but something came up. Who knows how long I'll last in here."

   a. Feeling words:
   - i. ______
   - ii. ______
   - iii. ______
   - iv. ______

   b. Your feeling response:

   ______

   ______

   c. Your combined response:

   ______

   ______

2. **A 17-year-old female talking to the school social worker.**

   "I really want to make the volleyball team. All my friends are varsity players. My grades are too low, even though I've tried really hard to bring them up. The coach wants me to talk to you. He thinks I'm not working hard enough. My parents have put a lot of pressure on me too. I feel really bad about myself. I can't seem to do anything right."

   a. Feeling words:

      i. ______________________________

      ii. ______________________________

      iii. ______________________________

      iv. ______________________________

   b. Your feeling response:

   ____

   ____

   c. Your combined response:

   ____

   ____

3. **A 12-year-old male talking to a hotline worker.**

   "My sister is five years older than me. Next year she is going to college. The thing is, she is very protective of me, especially when my mom and dad fight. I am worried about how I am going to be able to stay by myself once she leaves. She said when I am 18 I can come and live with her. That is six years from now."

   a. Feeling words:

      i. ______________________________

      ii. ______________________________

      iii. ______________________________

      iv. ______________________________

   b. Your feeling response:

   ____

   ____

   c. Your combined response:

   ____

   ____

4. **A 23-year-old male talking to his social worker.**

   "It's not enough that I went to college. I doubt I'll get a job when I graduate. Who would want to hire a person with cerebral palsy (CP)! People are uncomfortable around someone like me, stuck in a wheelchair. They don't understand that I'm a very capable worker."

   a. Feeling words:

      i. ______________________________

      ii. ______________________________

iii. ______________________________

iv. ______________________________

b. Your feeling response:

____

____

c. Your combined response:

____

____

5. **A 40-year-old male talking to a grief counselor.**

   "My youngest brother was killed in a plane crash. (Very angry tone) He was the greatest guy in the world. Where was God? How could God let this happen? My faith has been shaken. It's just not fair. I've gone to church to pray, but it doesn't help. Nothing does."

a. Feeling words:

i. ______________________________

ii. ______________________________

iii. ______________________________

iv. ______________________________

b. Your feeling response:

____

____

c. Your combined response:

____

____

6. **A 44-year-old lesbian female talking to a child protective services caseworker.**

   "You are absolutely wrong about me. I don't want to talk to you any more about this. You social workers are all the same. I can't believe you. You must have made a lot of enemies in this business. I would appreciate you leaving me alone. I can manage just fine. I always have, and I always will. Now, if you'd excuse me . . ."

a. Feeling words:

i. ______________________________

ii. ______________________________

iii. ______________________________

iv. ______________________________

b. Your feeling response:

____

____

c. Your combined response:

____

____

7. **A 76-year-old male talking to the senior citizen case manager.**

   "My kids are coming here from Alaska for the holidays, and this new relationship I'm in is the best ever. I'm so happy and thankful things have worked out. Five years ago, after my wife died, I was considering killing myself. I felt like a nobody, ignored and left behind. But today I feel great. You have no idea how helpful talking to you has been. Thank you."

   a. Feeling words:

      i. ______

      ii. ______

      iii. ______

      iv. ______

   b. Your feeling response:

   ______

   ______

   c. Your combined response:

   ______

   ______

8. **A 52-year-old female talking to a domestic violence shelter worker.**

   "I'm relieved to be out of that violent situation. I was scared for so many years. I hardly know how to act now. I still find myself looking over my shoulder, just waiting for him to find me. But mostly I'm thankful to still be alive."

   a. Feeling words:

      i. ______

      ii. ______

      iii. ______

      iv. ______

   b. Your feeling response:

   ______

   ______

   c. Your combined response:

   ______

   ______

9. **A 24-year-old college student talking to a sexual assault counselor about a sexual assault that occurred eight years ago.**

   "I was raped when I was in high school. I knew the guy, but we weren't friends. He pretended as if he liked me. I have never told anyone because I always felt like somehow I had encouraged him. It wasn't until recently that I've even started to think about what happened. I felt guilty then, but I blocked it out. Now I'm so angry. I feel so violated."

a. Feeling words:

i. ___

ii. ___

iii. ___

iv. ___

b. Your feeling response:

___

___

c. Your combined response:

___

___

10. **A 25-year-old female talking to an intake worker at an alcohol treatment center.**

"I want to get married to Tom. My parents hate him—because he drinks. I know that he drinks; he's never denied it. I grew up in an alcoholic family. It is second nature to me. I know how to handle him, and I know how to handle me."

a. Feeling words:

i. ___

ii. ___

iii. ___

iv. ___

b. Your feeling response:

___

___

c. Your combined response:

___

___

Now apply what you've learned about reflection of feeling in an online Try It exercise.

Part II

A. Discuss ways in which conveying understanding of a client's feelings can enhance the relationship. Under what circumstances might the discussion of emotions be problematic?

Think back to a time when you were very emotional (the type of emotion is not relevant for this exercise). Discuss how you felt and ways that you did or did not attempt to express your feelings. How did others respond to you at the time? Did they know you were experiencing extreme emotions? How well do you read other people's emotions, what signs do you look for?

Given the diversity of the clients we work with, what are some important issues to keep in mind regarding the expression of emotions?

Part II, Continued

With your practice partner(s), role play the reflection of feelings in case #5, a grief-stricken man who is mourning the loss of his brother.

Client: Do *not* convey any emotions, just speak the words. Continue this role play for five minutes. Discuss what the role-play experience was like for both the client and the social worker.

Now repeat the exercise again, using the same example, but this time, as the client, use your voice, gestures, and facial expressions to reinforce the emotional message.

Discuss how these two role plays were different.

B. **Cultural Competence**

Review case # 7. Talk with your group about issues regarding the aging of America. What does the "Graying of America" mean to you? What do you know about options available to families who have financial resources such as long term nursing care or in home care insurance? How do families with minimal financial resources manage, especially when 24 hour care is needed?

Open-Ended Questions

Part I

After reading each item, identify

a. At least two specific pieces of information that would further your understanding of the problem.

b. An open-ended question that would prompt the client to provide additional information.*

*In completing Part B, start by either reflecting the client's feelings or paraphrasing the content of the client's message and then ask the open-ended question.

Example:

***Client:* "I took my medication last night. I didn't want to, but I did. Now I am thinking about whether this is a good idea. I know I am depressed, but I should be able to get through this without drugs. It is time for me to be strong."**

a. Additional information needed:

i. How is the client managing on the medication?

ii. Type of medication

iii. Reservations about medication

b. Your open-ended question:

You are not sure about whether you want to continue taking the medication (paraphrase). What concerns do you have about taking the medication (open-ended question)?

1. **A 53-year-old fundamentalist Christian female talking with the social worker about her relationship with her daughter.**

   "My daughter is living with her boyfriend. We have talked about it a lot. She knows how I feel about her living situation. My religion means everything to me, and she knows that too. She is throwing all of her sins in my face. We've never been close, but this felt like the last straw. She is hurting me and hurting God."

a. Additional information needed:

i.

ii.

iii.

b. Paraphrase/reflection of feeling and your open-ended question:

2. **A 16-year-old male talking to the after-school social worker.**

I really like the people here, and it is a cool place to hang out. My mom thinks I should get a job. I know she is right, but I get my homework done here, and there is this great musical group I play with twice a week. You know how good we sound, right? I want to make money and help out, but if I don't come here after school, my grades will fall and I won't get to see all of you. Can you talk to my mom and tell her that I can't leave, please?"

a. Additional information needed:

i.

ii.

iii.

b. Paraphrase/reflection of feeling and your open-ended question:

3. **An 82-year-old female talking to the home interventionist.**

"Like I told the other social worker, my children mean the world to me. But I have to draw the line. I can't keep lending them the money; it would leave me with nothing. I thought once they were adults, I wouldn't have to take care of them. Don't they understand that? I can barely make ends meet. This is too much."

a. Additional information needed:

i.

ii.

iii.

b. Paraphrase/reflection of feeling and your open-ended question:

4. **A 33-year-old male discussing his relationship with his parents.**

"I told my parents that I am gay. They are very traditional, and it's hard talking to them about this. I know it would freak them out, but I want them to meet Michael. We've been together for two years. He is my life; we are free to get married now. We feel support from the Supreme Court but not my parents. Really?

a. Additional information needed:

i.

ii.

iii.

b. Paraphrase/reflection of feeling and your open-ended question:

____

____

5. **A 35-year-old female talking to the respite care worker about her five-month-old daughter.**

   "I have always wanted to be a parent. But how can I be a mom to a child who is mentally retarded? The doctors are of no help. This is not the way it's supposed to be. I feel like I'll never be able to love her the way that I should. Last week another social worker from the Children's Home came to interview me. She suggested that I meet with you. I can't do this alone."

   a. Additional information needed:

      i. ____

      ii. ____

      iii. ____

   b. Paraphrase/reflection of feeling and your open-ended question:

   ____

   ____

6. **A 17-year-old female talking to the case manager at the public assistance office.**

   "I'm really excited about having this baby. My boyfriend Dion is giving me a hard time though. He doesn't want the baby. Well . . . too bad, because I want this baby. I don't need him. We'll be just fine. I've got $400 saved up and a car to get us around. Plus I'm sure that you can help me too."

   a. Additional information needed:

      i. ____

      ii. ____

      iii. ____

   b. Paraphrase/reflection of feeling and your open-ended question:

   ____

   ____

7. **An 18-year-old female talking to the school social worker.**

   "I am the youngest of seven children. Sometimes I feel invisible. Sometimes I feel smothered. My oldest sister has always acted like she's my mom. Plus, mom shows up when she feels like it, and that makes me angry too. I want to have a normal family when I get married. But I look around, and everyone I know is pretty messed up.

   a. Additional information needed:

      i. ____

      ii. ____

      iii. ____

   b. Paraphrase/reflection of feeling and your open-ended question:

   ____

   ____

8. **A 50-year-old male discussing his home situation with the employee assistance program social worker.**

   "I love watching movies. It's the best way for me to relax. I can get away from the craziness of my day. My wife gets mad, though. She expects me to be more involved with the kids. I can't be with them when I feel so torn up inside. There's so much pressure. I'm supporting the family, helping out with my parents, and trying to keep my job."

   a. Additional information needed:

      i. ______________________________

      ii. ______________________________

      iii. ______________________________

   b. Paraphrase / reflection of feeling and your open-ended question:

   ____

   ____

9. **A 30-year-old female discussing her reactions to the sexual assault survivors group.**

   "This support group is not working for me. People in the group just come here to complain about their terrible lives. I want to move on with my life and not stay stuck in my misery. I feel like if I continue to come here, it will wear me down completely."

   a. Additional information needed:

      i. ______________________________

      ii. ______________________________

      iii. ______________________________

   b. Paraphrase / reflection of feeling and your open-ended question:

   ____

   ____

10. **A 15-year-old Native American female talking to an outreach worker.**

   "I've never had much to do with my mom, and now my grandmother is very sick. She is the most important person in my life. I couldn't bear it if something happened to her. I know I'm only 15, but I'd rather be on my own than have to stay with my mom. I doubt she'd want me to live with her anyway."

   a. Additional information needed:

      i. ______________________________

      ii. ______________________________

      iii. ______________________________

   b. Paraphrase / reflection of feeling and your open-ended question:

   ____

   ____

√ Now apply what you've learned about open ended questions in an online Try It exercise.

Part II

A. Refer to Box 8.8 in Chapter 8. Put yourself in the position of Julie, the social worker. You are going to a neighborhood that is considered "on the bad side of town." There are reports about gang violence, drug activity, and no police protection. You are required to make the visit but have some concerns. List 5 ways that you can prepare for this visit. What do you expect to see in LaToya's neighborhood? In her apartment?

B. **Cultural Competence**

In case #4, your client is gay and has been in a relationship for two years. He wants to come out to his parents but is worried about their reaction. What are your personal beliefs about homosexuality, and how might those impact the way you interact with this person? Do you agree with the US Supreme Court's decision to make same-sex marriages a right in every state? Why or why not?

Closed-Ended Questions

Part I

Read the items listed below and identify

a. At least two specific pieces of information that would further your understanding of the problem.
b. A closed-ended question that would prompt the client to provide additional information.

Example:

A 29-year-old male talking to the outreach caseworker. "I moved to this country from Argentina. I like it here, but I miss my family. Eventually I want them here too, but the US government isn't too friendly."

a. Specific information needed:

i. **How long has the client lived here?**

ii. Who is still in Argentina?

iii. **Who is here with the client?**

b. Closed-ended question:

How long have you been in the United States?

1. **A 14-year-old male talking to the school social worker about his suspension from school.**

*"I've never gotten into trouble at school. So what if I was using my cell phone, everyone does. I know I shouldn't have thrown the book at Mr. Walter, but seriously, he is an a**. Now my parents have to know; really this is ridiculous. You know what corporal punishment is?*

a. Specific information needed:

i. ______

ii. ______

iii. ______

b. Your closed-ended question:

____

____

2. **A 10-year-old female talking to her outreach worker.**

"My mom yells at me a lot. Sometimes she's nice, sometimes she's mean. I never know which way she's going to be. I try to do things right so she doesn't get mad at me. I hope she'll be nice to me after my meeting with you is over. She didn't like it when that social worker from child welfare came to our house."

a. Specific information needed:

i. ____

ii. ____

iii. ____

b. Your closed-ended question:

____

____

3. **A 16-year-old African American female talking to the group home social worker.**

"Everyone gets to go to the concert but me. The staff here at the group home are so strict. They never let me go out with my friends. They practically keep me locked up in my room. I hate being here; jail would be better."

a. Specific information needed:

i. ____

ii. ____

iii. ____

b. Your closed-ended question:

____

____

4. **A 75-year-old female talking to the caseworker at the senior citizens center.**

"I am having a harder time keeping track of things. Last week I got so confused that I ended up on the Interstate and couldn't figure out how to get back home. I did stop and ask for help, but I felt so stupid and afraid. I think my kids have noticed these change too."

a. Specific information needed:

i. ____

ii. ____

iii. ____

b. Your closed-ended question:

____

____

5. **A 36-year-old female talking to the community organization representative about her living situation.**

"My landlord has great plans for this building. Those plans include kicking us out so he can fix the place up and charge a higher rent. We would never be able to afford it. I don't have an extra dime at the end of the month. I've

always kept the place nice and paid my rent on time. I have nowhere else to go. It is so unfair. I hope that you will be able to help me."

a. Specific information needed:

i. ______________________________

ii. ______________________________

iii. ______________________________

b. Your closed-ended question:

____

____

6. **A 47-year-old female talking to the Red Cross crisis intervention counselor.**

"My house was destroyed by the last hurricane. I have spent five days here in the Red Cross shelter. You people have been nice, but now it is time for me to leave. I don't know where to start. The city is trying to get things up and running again, but all of this is just too much for me to bear.

a. Specific information needed:

i. ______________________________

ii. ______________________________

iii. ______________________________

b. Your closed-ended question:

____

____

7. **A 20-year-old African American male talking to his social worker.**

"I got a full scholarship for the next year. I worked so hard. I gave up everything in my life—my friends, my job—to win it. Now I feel let down—it's like nothing will ever satisfy me. I want to feel a sense of accomplishment. All I feel right now is a giant hole. Sometimes I feel selfish because my parents never had the opportunity to go to college."

a. Specific information needed:

i. ______________________________

ii. ______________________________

iii. ______________________________

b. Your closed-ended question:

____

____

8. **A 27-year-old female talking to the social worker in the eating disorder clinic.**

"Of course I eat properly. My parents and boyfriend are the ones who have a problem with my weight. They are completely obsessed with how I look and what I eat. It's really none of their business. I feel fine; I don't see any reason to talk about this with you or them."

a. Specific information needed:

i. ______________________________

ii. ______________________________

iii. ______________________________

b. Your closed-ended question:

9. **A 55-year-old HIV-positive male talking to a home interventionist social worker about his medical problems.**

"I take my antiretroviral medication on a regular basis. I just wish I didn't have HIV. The treatment is better than it used to be, but. . . . It's awful."

a. Specific information needed:

i.

ii.

iii.

b. Your closed-ended question:

10. **A 75-year-old Puerto Rican male talking about faith with the hospice social worker.**

"My religion has always been a comfort to me. No matter what, I've always turned to prayer during the hard times. You people might think I'm crazy, but I'm leaving my fate up to God. No more medicine, no more doctors. I have had it. It is my time to go. I have faith."

a. Specific information needed:

i.

ii.

iii.

b. Your closed-ended question:

Now apply what you've learned about closed-end questions in an online Try It exercise.

Part II

A. In video case #4, Maria's biological father is from Mexico. He moved to the United States when he was in his early twenties. He met Crystal, Maria's mother, while working at a meatpacking plant in Milwaukee, Wisconsin. Maria does not know her father and has not expressed any interest in meeting him. But as she gets older, she may want to know more about him or try to locate him. Put yourself five years into the future. How would you address her newfound interest in locating her biological father? How would you determine her readiness?

B. **Cultural Competence**

Using the closed-ended question case #10, a Puerto Rican male talking about his faith, list three different questions you want to ask.

Role play the example with your practice partner(s), integrating into the role play your questions. Continue the role play for five to seven minutes. Then answer the following:

Part II, Continued

1. How did the client respond to the questions?
2. Were the questions asked in a culturally sensitive way?
3. What issues are of importance when working with a client who is dying?
4. What issues are of importance when working with a client who has such a strong faith?

Clarification

Part I

Read the following items and identify

a. Information that needs to be made clearer (at least one).

b. A clarifying response.

Example:

"No matter how hard I try, they always yell at me."

a. What needs to be clearer:

i. Who are they?

ii. How often is "always"?

b. Clarifying response:

When you say "they," whom do you mean?

1. **A 40-year-old Peruvian female talking to an outreach caseworker.**

   "We're going to be evicted, I just know it. We have no money, and I don't know what to do next. My parents still live in Peru; I got no one here. I've got my kids to worry about too. I came here from Peru for a better life, but . . ."

   a. What information needs to be clearer?

   i. ______

   ii. ______

   b. Your clarifying response:

   ______

   ______

2. **A 34-year-old female talking to the home interventionist caseworker.**

   "I admit that the kids are fighting all the time. My husband wants me to settle it, but I don't see that as my job. I end up sticking up for them, which really pisses him off. I can't seem to win. I hate that I can't handle this on my own. Here I am in the middle again."

   a. What information needs to be clearer?

   i. ______

   ii. ______

b. Your clarifying response:

____

____

3. **A 17-year-old male talking to the caseworker from the child protection agency.**

   "So what if it's illegal! We got really high last night. It was a great time. I can forget all my worries. You ever been high? You social workers are all alike, trying to tell me what to do."

   a. What information needs to be clearer?

      i. ____

      ii. ____

   b. Your clarifying response:

   ____

   ____

4. **A 28-year-old female talking to the employee assistance program social worker about frustrations related to her job.**

   "I've been working at this job for five years, and the crap I have to put up with! My boss always singles me out and criticizes me in front of my coworkers. Can you believe that? Five years! Five long years!"

   a. What information needs to be clearer?

      i. ____

      ii. ____

   b. Your clarifying response:

   ____

   ____

5. **A 35-year-old male talking to his unemployment counselor about making the transition back to school.**

   "I'm trying hard to understand all the books I am supposed to read. I was never a very good student. Now here I am, 35 years old and back in college. All of my family is behind me, and I don't want to let them down."

   a. What information needs to be clearer?

      i. ____

      ii. ____

   b. Your clarifying response:

   ____

   ____

6. **A 38-year-old female talking to a sexual abuse counselor.**

   "My grandfather did awful and disgusting things to me when I was young. He made me promise not to tell my parents, which I never did. Now I'm a mom myself, and I can't stop thinking about him and what happened."

   a. What information needs to be clearer?

      i. ____

      ii. ____

b. Your clarifying response:

____

____

7. **A 15-year-old African American male talking to his foster care caseworker.**

"So last night my foster father came home drunk again. He picks on all of us when he's drinking, but I get it the worst. I want to go live with my dad. He drinks too, but I am his blood. I'm stuck here; this place sucks.

a. What information needs to be clearer?

i. ____

ii. ____

b. Your clarifying response:

____

____

8. **A 23-year-old male talking to a caseworker about his social relationships.**

"I have a lot of trouble saying no. People always ask me to do them favors I don't want to do, but I wind up doing them anyway. I've always been this way."

a. What information needs to be clearer?

i. ____

ii. ____

b. Your clarifying response:

____

____

9. **A 42-year-old male talking to a community-based social worker about his father.**

"I grew up in a troubled family. My dad has been in and out of mental institutions and prisons most of his life. I never really had a chance to get to know him. Now he's being released, and he'll be living in a halfway house. Someone is supposed to meet with me next week to help me figure out what other resources he'll need. I don't know what to do, and I don't know how I feel about all of this coming down on me."

a. What information needs to be clearer?

i. ____

ii. ____

b. Your clarifying response:

____

____

10. **A 35-year-old female talking to the shelter caseworker.**

"We've been living on the streets for a couple of months. My kids and I eat and sleep here at the shelter. Summer is almost over, which means that life gets even harder. I know they have to go to school too, and that worries me a lot."

a. What information needs to be clearer?

i. ____

ii. ____

b. Your clarifying response:

____

____

√ Now apply what you've learned about clarification response in an online Try It exercise.

Part II

A. You will need a minimum of four people for this exercise: one client and three social workers. Think back to the game you may have played as a child: 20 Questions. This exercise will follow the same format but will focus on a client situation that the social workers will need to tease out through asking 20 questions (or fewer!).

Client: Think of a situation but give out no information unless the *social worker* asks you a clarifying question.

Social Worker: Take turns asking only clarifying questions and wait for the client's response before proceeding to the next person. You, as a collective group, may ask no more than 20 questions. See if you can figure out the situation the client had in mind.

B. **Cultural Competence**

In your small group, discuss the following questions:

1. What kind of interactions have you had with people from other cultures and religions?
2. What were those experiences like for you?
3. What stereotypes do you hold regarding other cultural and religions groups?
4. What steps are you taking to increase your knowledge and comfort with people who are culturally and religiously different than you?

Summarization

Part I

Read the following vignettes and

a. Identify the two key aspects of the client's statement.
b. Provide a summarization response to the client's statement. Be sure to use appropriate lead-in responses.

Example:

A 40-year-old male talking with a caseworker at the domestic violence prevention center.

Social Worker: **So tell me more about your experience in the support group. I know you've been attending the sessions for the past 5 weeks.**

Client: **Well, it's okay. Most of the guys are a lot like me. We want our wives to stay home with the kids. Things would be better if my wife listened to me and stopped hassling me so much.**

Social Worker: **You want Leslie to back off and give you some breathing room.**

Client: **Definitely. She does things that aggravate me. Sometimes it feels as if she purposefully pisses me off. Like she's just waiting to see what I'll do next.**

Part I, Continued

Social Worker: What happens at those times?

Client: Sometimes I yell. Most of the time I leave. I know that if I stick around, I'm likely to do something that I'll regret, maybe hit her.

a. Most important aspects of the client's statement:

i. He attends a batterers support group.

ii. He feels as if his wife is purposefully testing him.

iii. He has seen some change in his behavior since attending the group.

b. Your summarization response based on the entire dialogue:

Now you are able to identify certain situations that could lead to hitting Leslie. Through the help of the support group, you're learning other ways of interacting with your wife.

1. **A 43-year-old overweight female talking with an intake social worker about her failures and loneliness.**

   Social Worker: Jeanne, let's talk for a minute about some of the things that are bothering you.

   Client: My weight. I guess it's all cyclical, I mean being overweight. Not a lot of people want to be your friend. I've felt rejected since I was little.

   Social Worker: It's hard for you to remember a time when you felt as though you belonged?

   Client: Yeah. I feel crappy about myself. Lonely. I don't make friends. I hurt the people who actually do love me. I let down my family all the time.

   Social Worker: Tell me about that. How do you let your family down?

   Client: Well, they always try to build me up. They support me. When I quit school, it hurt them. I work at a laundromat, I'm sure they want more for me than that. I was never motivated enough to learn trade. So I work in a laundromat, and I guess I do okay there. I don't know.

   a. Most important aspects of the client's statement:

   i. ____________________

   ii. ____________________

   b. Your summarization response:

   ____

   ____

2. **A 61-year-old female talking with the hospital social worker. She is considering suicide after recently learning that she has terminal cancer.**

   Client: The news is terminal cancer, so I am not going to live like this! I don't want to feel myself dying every day. I think I'm just going to take care of it on my own.

   Social Worker: What do you mean "take care of it"?

   Client: I think I'm just going to go off on my own, and whatever happens, happens. I don't want to live. I don't want to end up incapable of taking care of myself. I'm going to die anyway. I'll say my good-byes while I'm okay.

Social Worker: You feel hopeless about what the future holds, and you don't want to be a burden.

Client: I've always had a full life. Lots of friends. My family is the best. How can I put them through my slow and painful death? I don't want to inflict myself on the people I love. It would be so unfair.

a. Most important aspects of the client's statement:

i. ______________________________

ii. ______________________________

b. Your summarization response:

____

____

3. **A 76-year-old African American male who is living in on Alzheimer's unit.**

Social Worker: Mr. Holloway, how are you today?

Client: Oh, I am doing okay, just the usual. Mary hasn't come to see me today. I miss her so much.

Social Worker: I know that you miss her. Remember yesterday we talked about Mrs. Holloway and how she passed away last year?

Client: What happened to her again? Why doesn't she come anymore?

Social Worker: Mrs. Holloway was very sick, and she stayed here with you for as long as she could.

Client: Now where is she again? (He begins to cry)

Social Worker: She passed, and she doesn't live here with you anymore.

Client: How come no one told me? I think I should know this about my own wife.

Social Worker: You are right. Every day you tell me how much you miss her.

Client: Was she in pain when she passed? (Crying)

Social Worker: No, she passed in her sleep; you were right there beside her.

a. Most important aspects of the client's statement:

i. ______________________________

ii. ______________________________

b. Your summarization response:

____

____

4. **A 17-year-old male talking to the school social worker. He is considering dropping out of school.**

Social Worker: I know this is a really big decision for you, whether or not to stay in school.

Client: It's just those teachers, the homework, and the tests. I've pretty much come to a conclusion that school's got nothing to do with the real world. I'm sitting here learning about geography, snow glaciers, and what does this have to do with life, with the outside world? I think I've had enough. It's the conformity and the structure and all the rules. I'm thinking about quitting. A friend of mine quit. He's not employed right now, but he's doing okay. Not that I want to be a brain surgeon or anything. I just want to get a good job and pay my bills, and to live on my own.

Social Worker: What would you do if you quit school?

Client: I'd get a job. I don't know. Maybe just hang out for a while. I could use a breather.

Social Worker: A breather? (Pause) What else is going on in your life right now?

Client: The regular stuff; my parents yelling at me, my failing grades, you know, that kind of stuff.

a. Most important aspects of the client's statement:

i. ______________________________

ii. ______________________________

b. Your summarization response:

____

____

5. **A 44-year-old male talking to a hotline worker. He is a single parent with two teenage daughters and is feeling overwhelmed.**

Client: Being a single parent and having two teenage daughters isn't the easiest thing in the world, I tell you. They are rebellious. They are constantly on their cell phones. They're coming home later and later. I want to give them their space; they're individuals. But I'm worried about them too.

Social Worker: You sound like you're concerned about your girls and also realistic—knowing that part of being a teenager is having some freedom.

Client: Recently I gave them a curfew, and they are furious with me. They say, "Dad, you're not being fair. You're being too strict with us." Well, I don't want them out at all hours of the night. I want them to respect the rules of the house. They respect me, and I respect them.

Social Worker: That's very reasonable. You are the parent.

Client: It's not reasonable in their eyes, and we have been getting into fights. And it's just chaos. And I really wish my wife was still here because it's a lot for one parent. I guess dads and daughters are a struggle. It's a struggle. (Said with resignation in his voice.)

a. Most important aspects of the client's statement:

i. ______________________________

ii. ______________________________

b. Your summarization response:

____

____

6. **A 22-year-old female who won't be graduating with her class. Her mother is supporting her financially. She is talking to her college counselor.**

Social Worker: Kamaria, the last time we met, we spent time talking about your frustration because you are not graduating on time. We agreed that we would talk more about that today. Where do you want to start?

Client: Well, I'm still feeling like I'm letting my mom down and that I should be graduating this May. And that upsets me, and it makes me feel like I'm not doing what I should. My mom tells me, "Don't worry about it, everybody does things in their own time." I know that when she was in school, she finished . . . she went to a two-year college, and then came here. Plus, she had me. She graduated from here and she finished on time. I don't have any children, I don't have anything to set me back. It's just me. And it's gonna take me longer than it took her. I don't have those obstacles standing in my way, and I'm still not where I think I'm supposed to be. I feel bad about that.

Social Worker: Sounds like you feel guilty.

Client: I do. I don't have any of the complications that she did. The only responsibilities I have are credit card bills. So I work part-time. She says I haven't disappointed her, but I still feel like I have. She tells me that I don't have to live up to anybody's standards, but I feel like I'm letting myself down too.

a. Most important aspects of the client's statement:

i. ____

ii. ____

b. Your summarization response:

____

____

7. **A 23-year-old male who recently ended a relationship with his girlfriend. She has attempted suicide and he feels responsible.**

Client: I thought things were over. Then Lisa called me again on Monday.

Social Worker: Just two days ago?

Client: Right. Well, yeah. It's been over for me. I thought it was over for her too.

Social Worker: These last three months have been up and down, things change from minute to minute.

Client: Yeah.

Social Worker: David, what's your take on her suicide attempt?

Client: Well, a couple of days before the suicide attempt, we had a party at my house. I was running around trying to keep the house organized. And she kept yelling at me, "David, why don't you hang out with me?" Well, she got really upset with me and trashed my room. We got into an argument out in the parking lot. She grabbed me. I still have some marks on my arms from a fight two months ago. I said, "Stop, you're going crazy." She said, "I'll show you what crazy is." I walked away, and she got down on her knees and banged her head on the concrete.

Social Worker: That must have been very frightening for you.

Client: It was. I don't know, but I think she needs help, and I can't help her. I have too much going on in my life. I care for her, but I've done my part. I called the crisis hotline and her parents.

a. Most important aspects of the client's statement:

i. ____

ii. ____

b. Your summarization response:

____

____

Case 7: Continued with David—Session #2

Social Worker: David, we spent our last session talking about Lisa, your ex-girlfriend, who was very abusive to you. When we ended, we talked about exploring other relationships that you've been in and how you tend to get into relationships with females that are not necessarily good for you.

Client: Well, I think it started with my first girlfriend, my freshman year in high school. I was nice to her. When I broke up with her, she tried to kill herself. I felt like it was my fault. Then I dated a couple of people off and on. I had a really great relationship my senior year in high school. It lasted for a year or so. It was really good until we went away to college. And after that, I really haven't met any girls who have been very stable.

Social Worker: It seems as if you are questioning for yourself. . . . What is it that attracts these women to me or me to them? How can I make better choices in a relationship?

Client: Yeah! The thing I keep finding out about myself is that I'm too nice. I don't want people to be mad at me. I'll do anything for anyone.

Social Worker: What do you mean when you say "I'm too nice"?

Client: Just that I'll do whatever anybody wants me to. I want people, especially girls, to like me. Even if it means I get hurt. I know it sounds crazy.

a. Most important aspects of the client's statement:

i. ____________________

ii. ____________________

b. Your summarization response:

____

____

8. **A 33-year-old male talking to his caseworker at the day treatment program. He is chronically depressed and is not taking his medication.**

Social Worker: You know, Terry, we've been talking a lot about your medication, and you said that you would take your medication every day.

Client: Right. I know if I don't take my medication, I get depressed. And I've been depressed all week. I've been slipping, taking my medication.

Social Worker: When do you take your medication?

Client: Well, I'm supposed to take it three times a day: in the morning, at noon, and right after dinner. You know, if I'm out with my friends I get lazy. I understand it's important. I just need, I guess, to be more structured. I know that when I come in here, I always promise you that I am going to do everything on the treatment plan, and I screw up. I don't want to do that anymore. I was really, really depressed.

a. Most important aspects of the client's statement:

i. ____________________

ii. ____________________

b. Your summarization response:

____

____

9. **An 18-year-old female talking to a probation officer. She was recently arrested on drug charges. She denies that she's addicted to drugs but acknowledges that she's afraid of the legal consequences.**

Social Worker: What happened after you were arrested for possession of illegal drugs?

Client: Well, my mom and stepdad came and bailed me out of jail. I've got a public defender, and I go to court in a couple of months. I got caught with cocaine. It wasn't very much; it was less than a gram. But it seems that cocaine, any possession of any of it, is a felony offense. And my parents are really pissed off. They didn't really know that I was involved in drugs. They're real freaked out, and they want me to go into treatment. I don't think that's necessary because I don't have a drug problem.

Social Worker: You're not concerned about your drug usage, just the possible legal consequences.

Client: I suppose, yeah. I don't want to end up spending time in prison. I couldn't take that. Plus my parents are threatening me, too. It just seems like they're always surprised. Each time they find out about something new, something "bad," they're shocked. Which is weird considering I am 18 and been doing the same old things for a long time.

a. Most important aspects of the client's statement:

i. ______________________________

ii. ______________________________

b. Your summarization response:

____

____

10. **A 58-year-old female talking to a social worker about her struggles since her daughter was deployed by the military.**

Client: Things haven't been going very well since my daughter was deployed. She is in the military, and I worry constantly about her safety.

Social Worker: That is understandable. It must be hard to have her so far away and not see her to be sure that she is okay.

Client: It is. And to make matters worse, I have her two sons living with me right now. They miss her. They have bad nightmares. Both boys call out for her in the middle of the night. I don't know how to comfort them.

Social Worker: It must be very difficult to take care of them. How do you manage day to day?

Client: I am doing my best most of the time . . . just trying to get them off to school. The boys are involved in lots of activities, which is good, but it keeps me on the go too much. I am old now.

a. Most important aspects of the client's statement:

i. ______________________________

ii. ______________________________

b. Your summarization response:

____

____

√ Now apply what you've learned about summarization in an online Try It exercise.

Part II

A. Using the summarization in case #4, a student considering dropping out of school, list three aspects of the problem situation. Next, write down summary/transition statements, moving from one component to the next. Once you have completed the first two steps, role play the situation using the transitional statements you developed as a group.

Client: Put yourself in the client's place. Use your empathy skills to understand the client's perspective and experiences. Remember being in the client role is a very useful learning experience, as you have the opportunity to think and feel as the client might.

Social Worker: Use the written summary/transition statements in the role play that was developed by your group. Remember to use all the interviewing skills you have learned so far. Role play for 10 to 15 minutes.

____

Part II, Continued

B. **Cultural Competence**

Referring back to video case # 6, discuss some of the cultural aspects of Kim's life, including her time in Afghanistan. What do you know about culture of drinking or the culture of growing up in a single-parent household? What about the military culture? The culture of being a homeless person? How does her current living situation impact how she sees the world?

Information Giving

Part I

After reading each item, complete the following:

a. Identify the most important piece of information in the client's statement (at least one).

b. Provide an information-giving response. Use a paraphrase or reflection-of-feeling response either before or after giving the client information.

Example:

Client: **"I'm devastated. I want to have a family. My husband and I tried every medical procedure possible. We've spent all our savings; plus, it seems like we've talked to every specialist in the state. We have reached the end. We agreed if I wasn't pregnant by the time I turned 40, we would give up."**

a. Most important pieces of information:

i. They have spent all their savings in an effort to have a baby

ii. Time is also running out

iii. Feelings (disappointed, frustrated, anxious)

b. Your information-giving response:

Social Worker: **It's understandable that you feel frustrated, and disappointed, after so many unsuccessful attempts at getting pregnant. Maybe looking into some other options, such as adoption, might be a next step.**

1. **A 37-year-old male talking to a hotline worker about his marriage.**

"I think my wife is having an affair. She hasn't said it in so many words, but I can just tell. She's not home much, and when she is, she seems miles away. She is beautiful, and any guy would love to have her. I don't know how to ask her or even if I want to know. We've been married for seven years—sometimes have been better than others. This time I am sure that she is cheating on me."

a. Most important pieces of information:

i. ______________________________

ii. ______________________________

b. Your information-giving response:

____

____

2. **A 45-year-old female talking about her alcohol usage to an intake caseworker.**

"I drink a lot. I don't deny that, but an alcoholic, that's a joke. Alcoholics are bums on the street, drinking a bottle of whisky out of a brown paper bag. My father, now he was an alcoholic. He'd leave for days at a time, and he never held

down a job. He was a loser who never amounted to anything. I have a good job. I make decent money. There has never been a time that I haven't been able to control my drinking. Do I fit the alcohol profile?"

a. Most important pieces of information:

i. ______

ii. ______

b. Your information-giving response:

______

______

3. **A 13-year-old girl talking to the community outreach worker.**

*"So now I am in trouble at school because my 'best friend' decided to ditch me. We have been friends since the first grade. I can't believe she just went off with that b***ch! Does she expect me to just watch them laugh at me and walk away? I did what I had to do, to protect my honor and show her. I will not be bullied! Getting suspended is nothing to me, happens at least once a semester."*

a. Most important pieces of information:

i. ______

ii. ______

b. Your information-giving response:

______

______

4. **A 22-year-old female talking with another social work student about her guilt surrounding a cousin's sexual victimization.**

"I kind of knew my cousin was being molested by her father. She sort of hinted about it when we were younger, maybe 10 or so. Now I am in social work classes, and we are learning about sexual abuse. I should have done something then. I feel so guilty for doing nothing."

a. Most important pieces of information:

i. ______

ii. ______

b. Your information-giving response:

______

______

5. **A 21-year-old male talking with a crisis counselor on the hotline.**

"I'll never feel okay again. Losing my dad, having him die so unexpectedly, left me with no chance to say good-bye. He wouldn't want me to drop out of school, but I don't have the strength to keep up with my work or the motivation to study. I always counted on him, and now he's gone. I'm at such a loss. How do people get through this?"

a. Most important pieces of information:

i. ______

ii. ______

b. Your information-giving response:

______

______

6. **A 25-year-old female talking to the domestic violence shelter intake worker.**

   "Last night I was beaten up by my boyfriend. This is probably the fourth or fifth time. He treated me nicely when we first met, but now he gets so jealous. He refuses to let me see my friends or my mom, and I'm sure he followed me home from work last night. He's starting to really scare me. That's why I came to the shelter."

   a. Most important pieces of information:

      i. ______________________________

      ii. ______________________________

   b. Your information-giving response:

   ____

   ____

7. **A 17-year-old female talking with a child protection service social worker.**

   "I told that other social worker, the one at school, that I don't use drugs that often and frankly this is my body and my baby. I appreciate your concern, but it's none of your business. I'm 17 and old enough to make my own decisions. It pisses me off that now child protective services is involved. It's my life, my child, my choice."

   a. Most important pieces of information:

      i. ______________________________

      ii. ______________________________

   b. Your information-giving response:

   ____

   ____

8. **A 70-year-old man talking to the hospital social worker about his finances and future.**

   "My wife and I need help. Everyone says, 'Go talk to the social worker.' We're just about broke, and with my wife here in the hospital, we can't pay for all her medical bills or get help once she gets home. She had a stroke, so she'll need a lot of care, but . . . I don't want her going into a nursing home, no matter what. She wouldn't want that either."

   a. Most important pieces of information:

      i. ______________________________

      ii. ______________________________

   b. Your information-giving response:

   ____

   ____

9. **A 14-year-old girl talking with the school social worker.**

   My dad does the best that he can. I know that. He keeps telling us that he will get a job, but there are no jobs around here. I don't want to move, but I worry about how we are going to pay the bills. He is trying, I know that, but what can I do to help? I am in charge of my three brothers after school, and that is no fun!

   a. Most important pieces of information:

      i. ______________________________

      ii. ______________________________

   b. Your information-giving response:

   ____

   ____

10. **A mother talking to the school social worker about her 6-year-old daughter.**

"My daughter is having such a hard time making friends. She's so demanding and bossy to everyone. She's always been like this, but since her brother was born, it's gotten worse. At school Susie spends most of her time alone now—the other kids want nothing to do with her. I've tried everything I can think of. Her teacher suggested that I talk to you."

a. Most important pieces of information:

i. ______________________________

ii. ______________________________

b. Your information-giving response:

____

____

Now apply what you've learned about information giving in an online Try It exercise.

Part II

A. ***Social Worker:*** Role play the information given in case #10, a parent talking about her six-year-old child. Use the pitfalls of advice giving and overwhelming the client with too much information (and irrelevant information) in the interview.

Client: Respond genuinely to the social worker (and try not to laugh). Continue for five minutes. Now, role-play the scenario again. This time, offer information appropriately. Discuss the differences between the two role plays.

B. **Cultural Competence**

Write your own Code of Conduct regarding how to be a culturally competent social worker. For example, "When I am interacting with a client who comes from another culture, I will ask questions rather than assume I know the answer." Or "When interacting with a client who is much older than I am, I will be sure to call that person by their surname." Or "When interacting with a person with a disability, I will ask how I may help without jumping in to automatically assist."

Talk with your group about what aspects of diversity and inclusion are important to you. Discuss your as it relates to gender, race, education, ableism, ageism, etc.

Confrontation

Part I

Read the following items and identify:

a. Issues you would address related to the problem (at least two).

b. Your confrontational response. Be sure to include a paraphrase or reflection-of-feeling response either before or after delivering your confrontation.

Example:

A 26-year-old female has expressed an interest in working on improving her relationships with people in her life. The client has informed the social worker that she can only meet at 1:00 p.m. on Wednesday. For the past two weeks, she has come at 1:15 p.m., and today she did not attend at all.

a. What issue(s) would you address?

i. Her lateness

ii. Does she really want to be in counseling?

iii. What seems to be getting in the way of her attending the counseling sessions?

b. Confrontational response:

I'm concerned that you have either been late for our sessions or not coming at all. You asked to meet on Wednesdays, and you are not following through. I wonder if you are truly committed to this process.

1. *A 38-year-old male is fighting for greater visitation rights with his two children. He has shared with the social worker that he is having a sexual relationship with a coworker. The divorce decree states that he is not to have any overnight guests while the children are with him. He also reports that his ex-wife plans to take him back to court. She wants the judge to order only "supervised day time only visits" until the children are older (they are 6 and 10).*

   a. What issue(s) would you address?

      i. __________

      ii. __________

      iii. __________

   b. Statement of concern followed by your confrontational response:

   ____

   ____

2. *A 17-year-old female who is four months' pregnant comes to your agency, stating that she wants to keep the baby. She is excited about becoming a parent. During her session, she casually mentions that she is drinking alcohol and smoking marijuana. She reports that she feels good most of the time but has recently been experiencing low energy and a loss of appetite.*

   a. What issue(s) would you address?

      i. __________

      ii. __________

      iii. __________

   b. Statement of concern followed by your confrontational response:

   ____

   ____

3. *A 14-year-old male was caught breaking and entering into a local business. This is his second offense. He is on probation, and there is a good possibility of serving time in a juvenile facility. He appears to be fairly confident that nothing is going to happen.*

a. What issue(s) would you address?

i. ______

ii. ______

iii. ______

b. Statement of concern followed by your confrontational response:

______

______

4. *A 48-year-old male has experienced multiple sexual relationships. He states that he is careful in selecting partners and always asks if they have been exposed to any sexually transmitted infections. He uses protection periodically. He enjoys his freedom and sees nothing problematic about his behavior.*

a. What issue(s) would you address?

i. ______

ii. ______

iii. ______

b. Statement of concern followed by your confrontational response:

______

______

5. *A 37-year-old female has been married for five years to a controlling man. She recently lost 20 pounds because her husband told her she was too fat. Although she wants a child, she agreed not to get pregnant because she would no longer be physically attractive to him. She seems very timid and passive, looking away from you during the entire session. You wonder if she is being physically abused. She states that she loves her husband and can't imagine her life without him.*

a. What issue(s) would you address?

i. ______

ii. ______

iii. ______

b. Statement of concern followed by your confrontational response:

______

______

6. *A 22-year-old homeless veteran is living on the streets. You are an outreach worker assigned to find vets and encourage them to come to the center for services. He is agitated and upset that you have found him, as he is hiding from "everyone." You offer him a meal and a ride to the shelter, both of which he turns down.*

a. What issue(s) would you address?

i. ______

ii. ______

iii. ______

b. Statement of concern followed by your confrontational response:

______

______

7. *A 35-year-old woman admits to physically abusing her children, ages 8 and 11. She reports that she has taken parenting classes and has learned "time-out" procedures. During a family session, you observe the client raising her voice and threatening to hurt her eldest son.*
   a. What issue(s) would you address?
      i. ______________________________
      ii. ______________________________
      iii. ______________________________
   b. Statement of concern followed by your confrontational response:

   ____

   ____

   ____

8. *A 19-year-old college student who has a four-year scholarship is currently failing all of his classes. He reports that his instructors are hard on him and expect too much from freshmen. He did exceptionally well academically in high school and was the star of his football team. Recently, he stopped going to all of his classes, stating, "It's a lost cause." He reports that next year he will attend the community college at home and live with his parents. As he continues talking, he is becoming more and more agitated.*
   a. What issue(s) would you address?
      i. ______________________________
      ii. ______________________________
      iii. ______________________________
   b. Statement of concern followed by your confrontational response:

   ____

   ____

9. *A 21-year-old female college student admits to having weird dreams. She tells you that she wakes up scared and panicky. Last night she woke up afraid there was a stranger in her room. She thinks she is going crazy! Her roommate came with her for the intake appointment.*
   a. What issue(s) would you address?
      i. ______________________________
      ii. ______________________________
      iii. ______________________________
   b. Statement of concern followed by your confrontational response:

   ____

   ____

10. *A 14-year-old girl is currently living in a foster home. During a weekend visit with her mother, she ran away. Two days later, she was picked up by the police. She reports that she ran away from home because she didn't want to go back to the foster family. Her plan is to keep running until she can live permanently with her mom.*
    a. What issue(s) would you address?
       i. ______________________________
       ii. ______________________________
       iii. ______________________________

b. Statement of concern followed by your confrontational response:

____

____

√ Now apply what you've learned about confrontation in an online Try It exercise.

Part II

A. With your practice partner(s), discuss issues related to using the pitfall of premature confrontation. What are some issues regarding cultural differences and how confrontations might be interpreted?

Social Worker: Using the confrontation in case #5, a woman doing everything possible to please her husband, what issues are important to address? You suspect he might be physically abusive.

Given the nature of the client's relationship with her husband, what interviewing approach should you take? Continue this role play for 10 minutes. Discuss the client's strengths.

B. **Cultural Competence**

Mrs. Kita was born in Japan and emigrated to Portland, Oregon, as a high school student. What do you know about Japanese culture? What are the stereotypes identified with Japanese women and men? Describe ways in which Mrs. Kita fits with your assumptions and ways that she is different.

Interpretation

Part I

Read the following items and identify

a. At least two underlying issues that need to be addressed.
b. Your interpretive response. Be sure to use a paraphrase or reflection-of-feeling response before or after offering your interpretation.

Example:

A 28-year-old woman is currently in a violent relationship. She informs you that she doesn't mind a few punches now and then. "It's better than being alone. Look, I grew up in a violent home, I am used to it." She's been in two other relationships, both of which were violent.

a. What underlying issues should be addressed (at least two)?

i. pattern of abuse
ii. self-esteem
iii. fear of being alone

b. Interpretive response.

I get the sense that somehow you feel you deserve to be abused, that you're not worth being treated with respect.

1. *A 45-year-old man who is currently unemployed reports that he is looking for work, but no one is hiring a "middle-aged has-been." He also reports that there have been other times in his life when he has been unemployed for over six months. He was a mid-level manager at a welding company prior to his layoff. He is the sole financial support for his family.*
   a. What underlying issues could you address?
      i. ______
      ii. ______
      iii. ______
   b. What underlying issues could you address?
      ______
      ______

2. *A 56-year-old woman is currently the caretaker of her elderly parents. Her mother, age 80, is able to manage fairly well. Her father, age 85, has been diagnosed with Alzheimer's disease and is no longer able to recognize his family or do any self-care tasks. Your client refuses to place him in a nursing home, stating, "He'd never forgive me. Finally, after all these years, I'm able to repay him for all the trouble I caused. I never was the daughter he was proud of. My sister, the perfect one, is now nowhere to be found. I guess she's too busy." (Stated softly)*
   a. What underlying issues could you address?
      i. ______
      ii. ______
      iii. ______
   b. Statement of concern beginning or followed by your interpretive response.
      ______
      ______

3. *A 15-year-old girl who has always excelled in her academic classes recently has refused to answer questions during class and no longer completes homework assignments. She appears uninterested in any school activities and states, "I'm tired of sticking out. I hate people thinking that I'm the school brain."*
   a. What underlying issues could you address?
      i. ______
      ii. ______
      iii. ______
   b. Statement of concern beginning or followed by your interpretive response.
      ______
      ______

4. *A 37-year-old woman, a single parent, reports that her eight-year-old daughter, Karen, has refused to go to school for the past four weeks. Recently, the mother has decided "not to force the issue" because it's been nice having her company at home. She's now thinking about homeschooling.*
   a. What underlying issues could you address?
      i. ______
      ii. ______
      iii. ______

b. Statement of concern beginning or followed by your interpretive response.

____

____

5. *A 29-year-old man is considering leaving his job as a social worker and joining the priesthood. He has always felt a "calling" to help others and believes that he can best fulfill that need through his religion. Recently, he ended a five-year relationship with his college sweetheart, who is "pressuring me into getting married."*

   a. What underlying issues would you address?

      i. ____

      ii. ____

      iii. ____

   b. Statement of concern beginning or followed by your interpretive response.

   ____

   ____

6. *A 62-year-old divorced man has made the decision to retire after a successful career as an architect. He reports that he wants to sell his company but has yet to find the "right buyer." He acknowledges that he has always focused on his career and doesn't have many outside interests or hobbies. His daughter, recently widowed with two children, would like him to move to Chicago and "help her get back on her feet." His relationship with her has been strained since he divorced her mother 15 years ago.*

   a. What underlying issues would you address?

      i. ____

      ii. ____

      iii. ____

   b. Statement of concern beginning or followed by your interpretive response.

   ____

   ____

7. *A 30-year-old single woman reports that she loves children, wants to get married, and "have it all." She has been in several relationships during the past 10 years and has turned down two marriage proposals. The product of divorced parents, she feels it is essential to be "absolutely sure." She is waiting until the "perfect person" comes into her life. She also states that her younger brother is gay. She's sure it's because of all the conflicts between her parents while they were growing up that he is now a homosexual.*

   a. What underlying issues would you address?

      i. ____

      ii. ____

      iii. ____

   b. Statement of concern beginning or followed by your interpretive response.

   ____

   ____

8. *A 48-year-old man is currently attending an outpatient alcohol and drug treatment program. He reports having trouble staying sober. Recently, his wife was promoted, and she is now an executive at a major corporation. He is very proud of*

her accomplishments, but in a passing comment, he states, "I wish it was me. I've worked hard all my life, but she gets the job and the company car."

a. What underlying issues would you address?

   i. ______

   ii. ______

   iii. ______

b. Statement of concern beginning or followed by your interpretive response.

______

______

9. *A 30-year-old woman reports that her parents have moved to Florida following her mother's retirement from a position she held for over 35 years. She expresses how proud she is of her mother and how she wishes that she could have that same type of career path. Having worked with the client for six weeks, issues of self-confidence and self-esteem are themes that have been discussed throughout your sessions. You see a pattern of self-defeating behaviors, including excessive jealousy, saying one thing yet doing something else, and "testing" people. You want to talk more about her relationship with her mother; you sense there is something significant going on between them.*

   a. What underlying issues would you address?

      i. ______

      ii. ______

      iii. ______

   b. Statement of concern beginning or followed by your interpretive response.

   ______

   ______

10. *A 37-year-old man was recently diagnosed with cancer. He has started chemotherapy and is experiencing debilitating side effects. His physician reports that the prognosis for this client is very promising, but he must continue with the treatment. The client is unsure about whether he can handle all the struggles associated with his treatment. He states that he never imagined being so scared and wonders whether he'll ever feel like himself again. His wife is very supportive but tends not to assert herself in their relationship. He has always been the decision maker.*

   a. What underlying issues would you address?

      i. ______

      ii. ______

      iii. ______

   b. Statement of concern beginning or followed by your interpretive response.

   ______

   ______

√ Now apply what you've learned about interpretation in an online Try It exercise.

Part II

A. With your practice partner(s), talk about a time that you experienced some new insight into your behaviors, patterns, thought processes, and so on.

What was it like to have the "lightbulb" go on for you?
What led up to this acquisition of new insight?
How can you use this personal experience to relate to clients, especially those who may not trust you or who feel very threatened by your new way of looking at their situation?
If you choose to self-disclose to the client about a shared insight or experience, what might you say?

B. **Cultural Competence**

In video case # 2, both James and Anthony are African-American males. Use your imagination to visualize what James's home life was like growing up. Who were his supports? How did he navigate a system that may not have celebrated his strengths? Compare his life to Anthony's. Identify some possible similarities and differences in their life circumstances.

Pitfalls

In this section, you are presented with 14 scenarios. All of them have at least two problematic social worker responses. In completing these scenarios, review Chapter 7.

- Advice giving
- Inappropriate use of humor
- Interrupting the client / abrupt transitions
- Judgmental response
- Offering false assurance / minimizing the problem and insincerity
- Premature confrontation
- Inappropriate social worker self-disclosure
- Inappropriate / irrelevant questions
- Premature problem solving
- Overwhelming the client with too much or incorrect (inappropriate) information

At the end of this section, you will have the opportunity to watch clips as the social worker inadvertently uses a pitfall while interviewing a client. After watching each clip, provide your corrected response.

Read each case and complete the following:

a. In your own words, identify the mistakes that are made.
b. Explain why those problematic responses could lead to barriers in furthering the relationship.
c. Provide a correct social worker response.

Example:

The client is a 38-year-old female who has just miscarried for the third time.

Client: **This is awful. Three miscarriages, and my husband and I really want a baby. And I just feel, I don't know, if I'm paying for something that I have done before. This is terrible.**

Social Worker: **So, this is your third miscarriage. I know this great doctor who deals with problem pregnancies.**

Client: **Oh, yeah, tell me about him.**

Social Worker: **He's wonderful. He helped my sister with her pregnancy. You should go see him as soon as possible.**

Client: **What's his phone number?**

Social Worker: **Oh, I'll just set up your appointment right now because it's too stressful for you to worry about. You go home and rest.**

a. What mistakes were made?

i. Premature problem solving

ii. Inappropriate self-disclosure

iii. Minimizing the problem

b. How might that response lead to barriers in furthering the relationship?

Client feels discounted; the social worker didn't explore feelings, doing "for" versus "with" the client.

c. Corrected response: You've suffered a great loss.

1. *An 11-year-old female who is sharing for the first time that she has been sexually abused by her stepfather.*

Client: My stepfather. He touched me in places I know he is not supposed to touch. He told me that it was okay, but it doesn't feel okay.

Social Worker: I have to contact child protective services right away.

Client: No, please don't! He told me that he loves me. And we have done a couple of things that were a lot of fun together. He took me to a baseball game and bought me ice cream and took me to movies. He told me not to tell mommy about it.

Social Worker: Sharon, I'm really glad that you told me this secret. Lots of children are sexually abused. Sexual abuse is something that makes kids feel bad, like they've done something to deserve this. Now that I know, I have to contact the agency responsible for investigating sexual abuse.

Client: You know, maybe I do things to make him touch me in that way.

Social Worker: You are not responsible for an adult's behavior. It's his problem. He needs help. No matter what, you are not to blame. Abusers try to put the responsibility on the child. It's wrong for him to do that. Wait here while I make the call.

a. What mistakes were made?

i. ______________________________

ii. ______________________________

iii. ______________________________

b. How might that response lead to barriers in furthering the relationship?

____

____

c. Your corrected response:

____

____

2. *A 54-year-old male whose job performance is slipping; he has some concerns about his future with the company.*

Client: I've been this company's CEO for the past 25 years. I've been on top of the ladder for a long time, but I've seen a lot of things in the past year slipping. Dividends haven't been where they should be and, I don't know. People are starting to question me; I've started to question myself.

Social Worker: Are you saying that you are slacking off on the job?

Client: Well, I wouldn't call it slacking off. I just don't have the drive for success that I use to have.

Social Worker: It seems to me that maybe you don't care about your job. Maybe it's time for a change.

Client: I wouldn't say I don't care, but . . .

Social Worker: You just said you are not doing the same quality on the job. What do you plan to do to change your situation?

a. What mistakes were made?

i. ____

ii. ____

iii. ____

b. How might that response lead to barriers in furthering the relationship?

____

____

c. Your corrected response:

____

____

3. *A 22-year-old man who is in counseling at the insistence of his girlfriend and parents.*

Client: It's my fourth year in college, and my grades are not where they are supposed to be. My parents said they were going to cut me off financially if I didn't get my grades up. My girlfriend has been really getting on me, too, to do well in classes. Another thing, they think I have a drinking problem. I don't know if they are right or not.

Social Worker: You know it is really important for you to do well in your classes if you want to get a job someday.

Client: Yeah I know.

Social Worker: And you know it is wrong to drink because it causes problems with your girlfriend and with school, not to mention multiple health problems down the road.

Client: Well, I guess that's true.

Social Worker: How much do you drink each day?

Client: Maybe five or six beers a night, no more than my friends drink.

Social Worker: Wow! Sounds like you're on your way to becoming an alcoholic.

a. What mistakes were made?

i. ___

ii. ___

iii. ___

b. How might that response lead to barriers in furthering the relationship?

___

___

c. Your corrected response:

___

___

4. *A 33-year-old male who was severely injured in a recent accident.*

Client: Yeah. I had this accident two weeks ago, driving my truck. I went right through the window. I'm probably going to lose my right leg.

Social Worker: I'm sorry to hear that.

Client: Yeah. I'm sorry, too. Don't know if I can drive a truck without the use of both legs. The doctors say that with a prosthetic and rehabilitation, I'll be able to walk. I don't know how kindly I'll take to a fake leg.

Social Worker: When will you know about the surgery?

Client: I'll know in a couple of days.

Social Worker: If your leg is amputated, hopefully after a while, you'll get used to the idea. It takes time. Rehab can work wonders.

Client: If I lose my leg, I don't know if the firm will want me to keep driving. Maybe they have an office job for me, but I've never been real good at shuffling papers. Truck driving is basically all I've ever known.

Social Worker: It's too early to worry about the worst, especially when no decision has been made yet. Don't be so quick to jump to a bad conclusion.

Client: No, but there are bills to pay, you know. There's a whole family to support. This one truck accident, and everything falls apart.

Social Worker: But right now you don't know for sure how things will end up. Looking at all your strengths, I know you'll get through this. Plus, you'll be eligible for workmen's compensation since this is a job-related injury.

Client: Yeah, but these are pretty rough times, and there are hard days ahead of me. Truck driving is all I've really ever known.

Social Worker: Let's get more information from the doctors, then we can move on to plan B.

a. What mistakes were made?

i. ___

ii. ___

iii. ___

b. How might that response lead to barriers in furthering the relationship?

___

___

c. Your corrected response:

____

____

5. *A 14-year-old female who was caught shoplifting.*

Client: I got caught shoplifting yesterday. I went into the dressing room and put a shirt underneath my own shirt, and the security guard caught me. Now they say they're going to press charges. It's a new department store policy. I'm 14, so they can't try me as an adult, which is a good thing. But obviously my mother is very angry at me.

Social Worker: I know your mom is mad now, but she'll get over it.

Client: Yeah, I guess so.

Social Worker: Is this your first offense?

Client: Yeah.

Social Worker: Then don't worry. They never prosecute first offenders very harshly.

Client: Really?

Social Worker: Sure, this whole thing should be over pretty soon.

Client: Yeah, but my teachers know about it. They've been talking to me about it a lot. They make it seem like a bad situation.

Social Worker: It sounds like the teachers are trying to scare you. I'm not saying it's okay to shoplift, but it's your first offense.

a. What mistakes were made?

i. ____

ii. ____

iii. ____

b. How might that response lead to barriers in furthering the relationship?

____

____

c. Your corrected response:

____

____

6. *A 34-year-old woman who is frustrated with her neighbor.*

Client: You know my next-door neighbor, Betty? We've been friends for a long time. But she is starting to test my patience.

Social Worker: Go on.

Client: I've got these three kids, and I'm home all day. And, Betty, she just says to her daughter, "Why don't you go next door and play with Sue," my daughter. And her daughter comes over, which is fine. And the next thing I hear from Betty is that she's going out. She's gone, and I don't know where to find her. And her daughter is here with me for hours and hours at a time.

Social Worker: Well, does her daughter cause problems with your three kids?

Client: No, my kids like having her over.

Social Worker: Does she break things or roughhouse? Does she cry or complain about being at your place?

Client: No, she's really a good kid.

Social Worker: Then it seems to me that you don't have a problem. Be glad that your kids have a good friend.

Client: But, I want Betty to at least ask me rather than just sending Sue over.

Social Worker: You could say something.

a. What mistakes were made?

i. ______________________________

ii. ______________________________

iii. ______________________________

b. How might that response lead to barriers in furthering the relationship?

____

____

c. Your corrected response:

____

____

7. *A 15-year-old girl who hates school. She recently hit her teacher.*

Client: I hate these teachers. They're just pissing me off! Yesterday my English teacher wanted to keep me after school because I didn't do my homework. Screw her, you know? I got so mad I slapped her.

Social Worker: So, you think your teacher is a punching bag?

Client: Yep!

Social Worker: Well, when I was in school, we had this teacher we called Miss Latrine because she smelled really bad.

Client: That's hilarious. We call my English teacher Big Nose for obvious reasons.

Social Worker: Really, what other nicknames do you have?

a. What mistakes were made?

i. ______________________________

ii. ______________________________

iii. ______________________________

b. How might that response lead to barriers in furthering the relationship?

____

____

c. Your corrected response:

____

____

8. *A 36-year-old male who is frustrated with his parents' overinvolvement in his life.*

Client: It's my mother and father. They piss me off. They don't treat me like I'm 32; they treat me like I'm two. They want to know who my girlfriends are. They want to dictate where I work and where I live. They still want me to live at home. I want to live my own life.

Social Worker: So here you are, an adult, and your parents treat you as though you can't make any decisions for yourself? Or if you do, they're wrong?

Client: That's right. And sometimes I screw up just to spite them, just to get them angry. I think I got fired from my last job just so I could see the look on their faces after I told them I got fired from this really good job. I don't know what they expect from me. It's like I'm not their little baby boy anymore. I'm a man, I'm an adult. I need to make mistakes, and I need to do things on my own.

Social Worker: So, what was the job you got fired from?

Client: Oh, I worked at an insurance company as a consultant.

Social Worker: Did you find that to be a fulfilling job?

Client: Yeah, I guess. But weren't we talking about my relationship with my parents though?

Social Worker: Yes we were, but I need to know a little more about you. Do you currently have a girlfriend?

Client: No, not now.

a. What mistakes were made?

i. ______________________________

ii. ______________________________

iii. ______________________________

b. How might that response lead to barriers in furthering the relationship?

____

____

c. Your corrected response:

____

____

9. *A 17- year-old female who is experiencing trouble at home, particularly with her father.*

Social Worker: Juanita, you were talking about the difficulties you were having at home. The problems with your father and things were getting so bad that you decided to leave. Tell me what's been going on since the last time we met.

Client: I'm back at home, but my dad won't talk to me anymore. He's really upset that I ran away from home. My mother, I guess, didn't really deal with it well and was very upset. She cried all the time and couldn't eat. And he blames me for all that. He hates me more than he did before and won't even speak to me. So walking around our house is like, is like walking on eggshells. I hate being there. None of this is my fault.

Social Worker: Well, let's set some goals that you can work on in dealing with your father.

Client: Okay, what kind of goals?

Social Worker: Well, maybe you could try to start one conversation with him each day.

Client: I'm not sure I'm ready to do that.

Social Worker: If you want things to improve, this is what I'd suggest.

Client: Well, I don't know.

Social Worker: How about trying to say one nice thing to him between now and our next session? That will help open up communication.

a. What mistakes were made?

i. ______________________________

ii. ______________________________

iii. ______________________________

b. How might that response lead to barriers in furthering the relationship?

____

____

c. Your corrected response:

____

____

10. *A 22-year-old female who was recently released from jail.*

Social Worker: Hi, Andrea, how have you been recently?

Client: Well, I've been okay since . . .

Social Worker: So, that's nice. What is going on in your life now?

Client: I got out of jail about . . .

Social Worker: You were in jail?

Client: Yeah, I was in jail for hitting my supervisor.

Social Worker: That's terrible. Why did you hit your supervisor? You knew you'd get in trouble.

Client: She set me off. It's just so hard to be a black wo . . .

Social Worker: Keep going.

Client: To be a black woman in an all-white office.

Social Worker: But that's always a reality in your life—you can't just punch someone out because you don't like her attitude. Did you get fired?

Client: No, but I've been reassigned to another unit.

Social Worker: Good. It's best to keep your opinions and hands to yourself so this doesn't happen again. Next time you could lose your job for good.

a. What mistakes were made?

i. ______________________________

ii. ______________________________

iii. ______________________________

b. How might that response lead to barriers in furthering the relationship?

____

____

c. Your corrected response:

____

____

11. *A 26-year-old female whose boyfriend recently broke up with her.*

Social Worker: Hi, Tiffany. How are you today?

Client: Fine. How are you?

Social Worker: (Silence)

Client: So, how are you?

Social Worker: I'm okay. What brought you in today?

Client: Well, my boyfriend just broke up with me. It's been really hard to figure out if I want to date anyone else or just be single for a while. I'm getting older and starting to worry about my marriage prospects.

Social Worker: (Silence)

Client: And I don't know what to do.

Social Worker: (Silence)

Client: And I was wondering if you could help me.

Social Worker: Oh . . . ?

Client: See, I hate to be alone. I can't stand not having someone in my life.

Social Worker: Okay. What other problems do you have?

a. What mistakes were made?

i. ____

ii. ____

iii. ____

b. How might that response lead to barriers in furthering the relationship?

____

____

c. Your corrected response:

____

____

12. *A 16-year-old female who is pregnant and searching for guidance.*

Social Worker: So how have you been doing, Jennifer?

Client: Well, okay, okay I guess. Actually, I'm not okay.

Social Worker: What's been going on?

Client: I just found out yesterday that I'm pregnant, and I don't know what to do.

Social Worker: Are you positive that you are pregnant?

Client: Yes, I am.

Social Worker: Have you discussed it with your parents yet?

Client: No, I haven't. And I don't know if I should.

Social Worker: Why not? It's really important that your parents know.

Client: I know it is, but it's just too hard.

Social Worker: I realize that, but your parents can help you make decisions for you and the baby.

Client: I guess.

Social Worker: So, you could tell them right now and ask them to come over and meet with us.

Client: Well, if you think that's best, I will.

Social Worker: It is.

Client: What if they freak out?

Social Worker: I'm sure they'll be upset, but honesty is always the best policy. How long do you think you can hide the pregnancy from them?

a. What mistakes were made?

   i. ______________________________

   ii. ______________________________

   iii. ______________________________

b. How might that response lead to barriers in furthering the relationship?

____

____

c. Your corrected response:

____

____

13. *A 24-year-old male who is trying to get through college.*

Social Worker: The last time we met, you were talking about your birthday coming up and turning 25.

Client: Yeah. Well, I'm going to be 25 in December, and all my friends have graduated. And I'm not quite there yet. Everybody looks at me and they're saying, "Oh, he's still in college. He's never going to get out. He's wasting his life."

Social Worker: How do you see it?

Client: I feel badly about the whole thing. I transferred a lot, trying to find a decent major. And basically, I'm happy with social work. I'd like to get out sooner and start working so I can pay off all the loans that I have after the last six years of school.

Social Worker: I'm sure that even if you have to stay in school longer, you will get your loans paid off.

Client: I don't know. I owe a lot of money.

Social Worker: Most graduates owe a lot of money, but they make it.

Client: I guess most do, but I'm still worried about it.

Social Worker: It's scary to owe a lot of money. I know. I had college loans too. It took me 10 years to pay them off, but I did and now things are fine. I'm proud of myself; I accomplished a lot. Plus maybe by the time you graduate there will be student loan forgiveness.

a. What mistakes were made?

i. ______

ii. ______

iii. ______

b. How might that response lead to barriers in furthering the relationship?

______

______

c. Your corrected response:

______

______

14. *A 28-year-old female who is frustrated with the school's treatment of her six-year-old daughter.*

Client: You know, this is the fifth time this week that the teacher has called about my daughter, and I'm fed up. I don't see what the big deal is. So what if my daughter expresses herself through painting on the walls. I think she is creative and talented. And she is having fun. I stopped by the school the other day, and she had painted a bunny face on the mural, but it was cute and did not harm anyone. It seems to me that this is a creative expression. She's having fun.

Social Worker: I wonder whether Van Gogh's first-grade teacher complained to his mother.

Client: That's exactly how I feel about it. This could be creativity in the making. My kid, she just loves having fun at school. She's not a troublemaker. The teachers don't call to say she's hitting other kids or fighting or anything like that. It's always about expressing herself through art. I have this child, my prodigy, and the teacher is squashing her creativity.

Social Worker: So, today it's Walt Whitman Elementary School, tomorrow it's the Sistine Chapel.

Client: Well . . . I wouldn't say that.

Social Worker: I'd call the teacher, set up an appointment to meet, and tell her exactly how you feel.

Client: I don't want her to get mad at me.

Social Worker: Hey—this is your daughter here. You have to stand up for her, if you don't, who will?

a. What mistakes were made?

i. ______

ii. ______

iii. ______

b. How might that response lead to barriers in furthering the relationship?

______

______

c. Your corrected response:

______

______

Common pitfalls in interviewing include the following:

- Advice giving
- Inappropriate use of humor
- Abrupt transitions / interruptions
- Inappropriate / irrelevant questions
- Judgmental response
- Inappropriate social worker self-disclosure
- Premature confrontation
- Overwhelming the client with too much information
- Premature problem solving
- Minimizing the problem / offering false assurance

√ Watch these clips as the social worker uses the above pitfalls in his or her response. Provide an alternative response for each case.

Putting it all together

1. *A 18-year-old male is seeking help regarding a suspected health problem. He believes the illness may be serious.*

   Client: I've been fainting at different times. I don't know what's wrong. I don't know if it's something physical or if it's psychological or worse.

   Social Worker: Right now you are extremely unsure about what might be going on with you both physically and emotionally.

   Client: Yes, plus I'm afraid of what to tell my family. It might be something serious. I don't know if it is something, like, genetic. This could be a very bad thing and I don't know how my family would react.

   Social Worker: Part of your concern is not just for your own health, but you are scared to tell you parents; you are afraid of their reaction.

   Client: And I guess I'm also afraid of my reaction. I suppose I should go to the doctor. It sounds serious, these fainting spells. I've looked in medical books and online, but I can't figure out what it is. And I'm afraid that if I go to my doctor, she'll tell me it's serious. I don't know if I can take it.

   Social Worker: As you're trying to figure this out, you become more and more uncertain.

   Client: I feel scared. And I just feel in my gut that this is terribly serious.

   Your response: using a summarization:

   ___

   ___

2. *A 40-year-old female who has just had a third miscarriage. She is seeking help in coping with her loss.*

   Client: This is just awful. Three miscarriages, and my husband and I really want a baby. And I just feel, I don't know, as if I'm paying for something that I've done before.

   Social Worker: These miscarriages have left you feeling as though you have no control over your body.

   Client: And I thought that after the first one that . . . the doctor told me that it would be all right for the next time. And then it happened again. And now it happened again . . . I'm really depressed about it.

Social Worker: It's a tremendous loss.

Client: I know. And after the second one, I thought that it was just not worth going through this again. I feel like this cloud is over me. I don't know what to do now. I feel hurt and alone and scared.

Social Worker: Kelly, your feelings are very understandable. You suffered repeated loss. You wanted a baby, and now it feels as though it may never happen.

Client: Why? I mean, I ask why? Nobody deserves to suffer. I'm a healthy person. I just don't understand why God is punishing me like this.

Social Worker: You wonder, "I take good care of myself. I'm aware of my own body and the things I need to do. Now the bottom has fallen out, for the third time."

Client: I want a baby so badly; I just want to be a mom. I want to raise a child. And when I found out I was pregnant, it's like a roller coaster. Things were going so well, and we, we were going to build a nursery, and then this happened.

Your response: using a reflection of feeling and clarification:

____

____

3. *A 30-year-old Hispanic male who is considering going back to school to become a physician. His family obligations and self-doubt contribute to his dilemma.*

Client: Thirty years old. The big "3-0." When I was in my early twenties, I wanted to go to college, but I couldn't. I didn't have the money. My father was sick, and I had to work to pay the bills. Now I can afford to go to college, but I'm not 20 anymore. I want to be a doctor, but medical school at 30?

Social Worker: When you think about it, it's really exciting: the possibility of a new career, going back to school. But it's challenging. There's a lot of work involved. It is a huge decision.

Client: The thought of hitting those books, long hours studying—I don't know. It's tailor-made for the young. I always wanted to be a doctor. It's just now that I have the chance.

Social Worker: Now, the opportunity is there, but so is your sense of doubt.

Client: Right. Medical school is difficult. It is an uphill battle: lab work, classroom time, a lot of memorization. You know, now I'm married, I want time with my wife. I don't know what to do.

Social Worker: Part of what I'm hearing is that you really want to do this. But to take this on at 30 with a family, with other responsibilities, poses a real challenge.

Client: Yeah. Being a doctor has always been my life's ambition. But there's a lot of sacrifice, a lot of commitment to achieve this goal.

What issues would you want to discuss the next time you meet? (List three)

i. ____

ii. ____

iii. ____

Your response:

____

____

4. *A 30-year-old female who is fed up with her ex-husband. He continues to break his promises.*

Client: You know, we've talked about my ex. He's an absolute jerk. We have three kids. John said he wanted kids, marriage, the whole thing. Now he's dumped me, he's out of the picture. We never see him anymore, and I'm broke. He said he'd be involved in their lives, and now he's gone. And it really makes me mad that he made this promise to me about our kids. I don't care about me. It's our kids. And I can hardly afford to pay the rent, and now he's gone.

Social Worker: John has left you with all the responsibility, and you're furious with him.

Client: Yes. If he cared about our kids, like he said he did, he would come up with the child support. But you know what? I haven't heard from him in four months, not a dime. I just can't believe he's doing this to us.

Your response: using a reflection of feeling and open ended question:

____

____

5. *A 45-year old female who is currently in an emotionally abusive relationship.*

Client: You know, I really love Elaine a lot. But this crazy stuff has to stop.

Social Worker: Last week we were discussing the violence that has been going on between you two.

Client: Yeah. She got so mad at me. And no matter how much I try to make her understand, she just doesn't listen. And you know I tried talking to her, like you suggested, and you know what? It got me into bigger trouble.

Social Worker: What do you mean by bigger trouble?

Client: She told me that the social worker is feeding me a line of bullshit. She thinks that I should do what she says. She thinks that no matter what I want to do, it doesn't count. And you've been telling me that it's important to know how I feel and know what I want. And when I tell her what I want, she screams at me. This counseling thing is making matters worse between us.

Your response: using a confrontation and reflection of feeling:

____

____

6. *A 35-year-old male who is afraid of making a permanent commitment to his girlfriend. He wants things to remain "open" but is afraid of losing her.*

Social Worker: Antonio, the last time we met, you were talking about your girlfriend. You really love her, but recently you have been feeling pressure from her to get married.

Client: Right. We have been together for seven years now, which is a long time. The relationship has gotten very comfortable; it's almost like putting socks on, very natural. We both understand each other. We're very open with each other and know each other, pretty much inside and out. I guess the next step is to get married, and that is what she really wants. Her family is very traditional. And you know we live together and have been for four years now. I'm fine with just living with each other. I don't need a piece of paper. She wants it to be official.

Social Worker: You want to keep things as they are.

Client: Yes! Things are fine, you know? If it's not broken, don't fix it. I always thought that things were going fine. She is even thinking of having a child, which is okay with me. But she wants to go through the formalities. My parents are divorced, and everyone who's married seems to be very unhappy. And I don't know if I want that.

Your response: using an interpretation and paraphrase:

____

____

7. *A 28-year-old unemployed Native American who wants to remain on the reservation but has been unable to find a job.*

Client: The water company turned off the water. I think this is final, it's the last straw. I lost my job three months ago, and now I'm delinquent on all my bills. I don't know what to do about this.

Social Worker: That's a lot to handle right now. Did this just happen?

Client: Yeah. I've been out of a job for three months, laid off, you know. Working in an auto shop—I've been working there for 15 years, you know, living from paycheck to paycheck but still making it. What they give you on unemployment can't even pay for necessities like electricity. So they turned it off.

Social Worker: Now you're unsure where to turn, what to do.

Client: I mean, jobs are hard to find. I was born on the reservation; I grew up there. I don't want to leave. But it's looking like I'm going to have to. There's just no work. We were married five years ago. We didn't expect this situation. I guess nobody does. Her family lives nearby, too. She doesn't want to leave, but we're going to have to leave. Got to find work in the city.

Your response: using a reflection of feeling and open ended question:

____

____

8. *A 38-year-old female who is waiting for her mammogram results. She is certain that cancer was found.*

Client: They got the results of my tests. I went in for a mammogram. I knew it wasn't good news when the doctor called me and told me that he wanted to see me. Usually, they just send a piece of paper saying your test results came back and everything's fine. This time I got a call, and I have to go in. It sounds like they found a lump on my breast.

Social Worker: How are you feeling about this?

Client: Really scared. I've always kind of known that I was at high risk for breast cancer. My mom had breast cancer; her sister had breast cancer. Here I am, the third in the line. I'm sure it's cancer.

Social Worker: You are anticipating the worst.

Client: Yep. I hate having mammograms, which is why I have avoided them. I figure if I don't know, at least then I don't have to deal with it. I knew I had to go in for this mammogram. It's been about two years since I've been in, and that also scares me because if the cancer has been there for that long, who knows.

Your response: using a reflection of feeling and information giving:

____

____

9. *A 16-year-old girl who is discussing her unexpected pregnancy.*

Social Worker: The last time we met, you were trying to decide what to do about your pregnancy.

Client: Things are no better. My parents want me to have an abortion. I just don't feel I can do that. My boyfriend's parents want that, too. And Gary wants that. Everybody wants me to have an abortion, and I'm feeling a lot of pressure.

Social Worker: You keep hearing, "Have an abortion, get on with your life."

Client: Yeah, they just think that having a baby is going to ruin my life. And I realize that it's going to be difficult and it's going to be hard. But I just don't know if I can live with the fact that I killed my own baby.

Your response: using a paraphrase and closed ended question:

____

____

10. *A 50-year-old male struggling with job-related issues.*

Client: You know my job is really getting me down. I used to like going to work. I had lots of friends there, but now . . . I don't know.

Social Worker: When you say "I don't know," what does that mean?

Client: I was promoted last year because I did a good job on a project. I got lots of praise. After the job change, I never quite got used to all the things I need to do. Mostly, it's supervising people. I used to be their friend, now I'm kind of the boss.

Social Worker: Now you wonder if all this was worth the promotion.

Client: Definitely! I wish I could go back to being "one of the guys." I just don't like any part of what I'm doing now.

Your response: using a paraphrase and open-ended question:

____

____

11. *A 32-year-old male dying of brain cancer.*

Client: It is all so crazy . . . I want to find my brother, but I have no idea where to look. He literally disappeared five years ago. And not a word since. Now, I am dying of cancer, and I want to see him. I have always missed him, but now these feelings are even stronger.

Social Worker: For you, time is of the essence.

Client: Exactly. The last time I heard from him he had just gotten out of jail. He actually sounded pretty good. It is weird though, he kinda said good-bye.

Social Worker: What did he say?

Client: He told me that he was fine now and not to worry about him. That is a joke of course . . . I have worried about him since the day he was born. He never was quite right. Diagnosed with some kind of weird mental problem. . . . No one really talked about it though. He wanted to be like everyone else, but kids always made fun of him. I don't blame him for going off, leaving all of us behind. But now I gotta know what happened to him. Is he dead or alive? I think he wants to stay hidden, but now I am dying . . . I want to know.

Social Worker: Have you actually done any kind of search?

Client: No, I have no idea where to start, and it is expensive to hire a private detective. I seem to be the only person in my family even interested in this. Everyone else wants to pretend he never existed. I don't get it. But now I feel driven to find him. Is that crazy?

Social Worker: No, not at all. You want some kind of closure. He is your brother . . . you just can't cut that off.

Client: That is what I keep telling my family. They don't want me spending my last few months focused on him.

Your response: using a summarization:

____

____

12. *A 26-year-old female struggling with issues related to her ex-boyfriend. He recently got married, which has left her hurt and confused.*

Client: I just found out that Andy, the guy I dated for four years, got married.

Social Worker: That's a shock.

Client: It really was.

Social Worker: Did you have any idea?

Client: I knew that they had been together. But I didn't think they would get married.

Social Worker: How are you feeling about it all?

Client: I can't sleep. I can't eat. . . . And to top it off, he's having a wedding reception in my hometown and inviting all my friends.

Social Worker: It's like he's rubbing this in your face?

Client: Exactly. That's his main goal; get married and hurt me.

Social Worker: You really sound shaken by all of this. What led up to the breakup?

Client: I can't even explain what happened. We had broken up a hundred times before. He was evil; he was seriously an evil person. I just gave so much to him, and finally I felt like I couldn't give anymore. But I expected him to come back to me.

Social Worker: You put up with a lot from him, and then he leaves and marries someone else.

Client: Yeah, after knowing her for only six months.

Social Worker: Was your hope that eventually you two would get married?

Client: Honestly no. It was that he would want me back, and I'd be able to say "no." I've always been so weak with him. He would cheat on me and come back to me, and I'd take him back. This time, I wanted to hear, "Cheryl take me back," and I'd be able to say, "No way."

Social Worker: You wanted the satisfaction of saying to him, "I'm strong enough now. You're out of my life." And he didn't give you that opportunity?

Client: He had the nerve to bring her over to my house so we could meet. What kind of person is he? What kind of person am I to have put up with all of this crap?

Your response: using an interpretation and reflection of feeling:

____

____

12. *Continued:*

Social Worker: How were you able to end the relationship with him?

Client: It was kind of a fluke. It was New Year's Eve. We had been partying together. We met some people downtown. Next thing I know, Andy's with this girl. Later he came to my house. He wanted the money I owed him. I gave it to him and slammed the door. That was it.

Social Worker: That was it for you. You said that you felt unappreciated in the relationship and that you put up with years of abuse. Tell me more about that.

Client: Well, when I was in college, I was in counseling, trying to figure out my relationship with him, to do things that made me stronger. But every week I would go in there, my social worker wanted to strangle me. I'd come in there, "Oh we got back together" or "Oh we broke up." She never said I was stupid, but I was. I stopped counseling because I wasn't ready to end my relationship with Andy. And now I can't understand why he is so happy and I'm not. How dare he be happy?

Your response: using a summarization:

____

____

12. *Continued:*

Social Worker: You're asking, "What is it about me that I stayed in the relationship for so long?"

Client: "What's wrong with the way I look?" "Or am I not fun?" I gave him everything. I know I have low self-esteem—I can admit that. The four years that I was with him, I did nothing but be there for him. I took all kinds of abuse. There is nothing positive about me.

Social Worker: It's hard for you to see your strengths?

Client: Yep! It's always been that way.

Your response: using a reflection of feeling and open ended question:

____

____

12. *Continued:*

Social Worker: Cheryl, you have said that your family has always been a source of strength for you, that they rallied behind you after you told them about Andy's marriage. They knew you'd be devastated.

Client: My family is great. I mean, they definitely didn't like him. And they're glad it's not me he married. They stuck by me and helped me. Deep down I'm sure they are disappointed in me. That I stayed with him for so long.

Your response: using a clarification:

____

____

12. *Continued*

Social Worker: You said that you see yourself as a very caring and giving person. In some ways, that also may have caused the trouble with Andy. You were always giving and taking care of him.

Client: Oh yeah, definitely.

Social Worker: Because he expected it, too?

Client: I'm just like my mom.

Social Worker: You think you're just like your mom. What's she like?

Client: She's very caring. She would do anything for anybody, especially her children. She's a wonderful person. She and my dad have a great marriage. That's probably why they were so upset with me. They make it look so easy. Why can't it be that way for me too?

Your response: using information giving and interpretation:

____

____

Your response: using a closing summarization:

____

____

VIDEO ASSESSMENT

Watch these videos and answer questions to gauge your understanding of pitfalls attending behaviors and interview skills.